THE CENTER FOR CHINESE STUDIES

at the University of California, Berkeley, supported by the Ford Foundation, the Institute of International Studies (University of California, Berkeley), and the State of California, is the unifying organization for social science and interdisciplinary research on contemporary China.

PUBLICATIONS

Wakeman, Frederic, Jr. *Strangers at the Gate: Social Disorder in South China, 1839–1861* (1966).

Townsend, James. *Political Participation in Communist China* (1967).

Potter, J. M. *Capitalism and the Chinese Peasant: Social and Economic Change in a Hong Kong Village* (1968)

Schiffrin, Harold Z. *Sun Yat-sen and the Origins of the Chinese Revolution* (1968)

Schurmann, Franz. *Ideology and Organization in Communist China* (Second Edition, 1968)

Van Ness, Peter. *Revolution and Chinese Foreign Policy: Peking's Support for Wars of National Liberation* (1970)

Larkin, Bruce D. *China and Africa, 1949–1970: The Foreign Policy of the People's Republic of China* (1971)

Schneider, Laurence A. *Ku Chieh-kang and China's New History: Nationalism and the Quest for Alternative Traditions* (1971)

Moseley, George. *The Consolidation of the South China Frontier* (1972)

Mao's Way

———

THIS VOLUME IS SPONSORED BY THE
CENTER FOR CHINESE STUDIES
UNIVERSITY OF CALIFORNIA, BERKELEY

Mao's Way

Edward E. Rice

University of California Press

Berkeley Los Angeles London

UNIVERSITY OF CALIFORNIA PRESS
BERKELEY AND LOS ANGELES, CALIFORNIA
UNIVERSITY OF CALIFORNIA PRESS, LTD.
LONDON, ENGLAND
COPYRIGHT © 1972, BY
THE REGENTS OF THE UNIVERSITY OF CALIFORNIA
ISBN 0–520–02199–1
LIBRARY OF CONGRESS CATALOG CARD NUMBER: 70–186116
PRINTED IN THE UNITED STATES OF AMERICA
DESIGNED BY DAVE COMSTOCK

For Mary

Preface

AT the height of the Cultural Revolution, during which Mao Tse-tung demolished the organizational structure of the Chinese Communist party—of which he was, of course, the chairman—a bemused critic made some challenging observations which led me to undertake this work. In the review of a book about the Chinese, published in *The Atlantic,* he remarked that China remained an enigma to the west. No one outside Peking, he declared, had been able to predict or explain the developments of the preceding decade. The Hundred Flowers campaign to elicit public criticism of the party and the government, the Great Leap Forward in the economic sphere, and the Cultural Revolution, he asserted, each came as a surprise, and the reasons for each remained obscure.

At the time those remarks were published, I was the American Consul General at Hong Kong. The office I supervised had two sets of responsibilities. It was a post for handling the usual range of consular business in the busy colony of Hong Kong. And in the absence of any United States mission in Peking, it was responsible for reporting to the United States government on developments in Communist China. For this latter purpose, it had a staff of officers engaged in analytical and reporting work, served by a large unit which engaged in monitoring and translating the China mainland press.

The Cultural Revolution was a period during which the Maoists raked over the past for material with which to denigrate their opponents and allowed Red Guard organizations to publish it in their information sheets and newspapers. Many of these publications found their way to Hong Kong, where they were translated by our press monitoring unit and other organizations which make their output available to China watchers and interested scholars. During this same period, many eyewitness reports of developments in China also became available, both from foreign journalists and from travelers.

The period was one of great fascination, and as a long-time political reporting officer I could not content myself with merely supervising the reporting officers on my staff—with serving only as a watcher of my China watchers. In consequence, I became sufficiently engaged in the reporting work of my post to conclude that the Cultural Revolution was no inexplicable affair. It had roots, I felt sure, in the Great Leap, and perhaps in such earlier events as the campaign of the Hundred Flowers. Moreover, because all three had been initiated by Mao

Tse-tung, explaining such events would require a study of him and his political career. Finally, his career could be considered only in the context of the historical events which had helped shape him or in which he had played a role.

Hong Kong was my last field post, and my final year as a Foreign Service Officer, beginning early in 1968, was spent as a so-called diplomat-in-residence at the University of California in Berkeley, attached to its Center for Chinese Studies. There I had access to almost all the materials needed for this study. These included the press translations which had been done by my own Consulate General at Hong Kong, and such a wide range of other publications as to obviate any need for me to have recourse to classified information.

I came to the task with the advantage of some background knowledge of pre-Communist China. I had served there for a decade, first as a language student in Peking, and subsequently at several other diplomatic and consular posts. I had also spent two years as the second-ranking desk officer for China in the Department of State. But after that, and until my assignment to Hong Kong, my official contacts with Chinese affairs had been only those occasioned by tours of duty as a Far Eastern hand on the Policy Planning Council and as Deputy Assistant Secretary for Far Eastern Affairs. In consequence, I lacked acquaintance with much of what China scholars had published during the previous twenty years. The reading of a substantial portion of this material necessarily preceded any serious writing of my own, and it convinced me that the book reviewer of *The Atlantic* had underestimated the understanding to be derived from the existent body of scholarly works on Communist China. However, it also led me to conclude that there might be room for a book, based upon personal knowledge and on research into both the old and the newly available sources, written in seminarrative form and couched in language which would be intelligible to nonspecialists.

No presentation of events selected for their relevance to the career of one leader can represent a balanced history of his period, and this work is admittedly no exception. I have, for example, suggested that one of the main reasons for the Chinese Communist victory in the civil war was the superior military strategy of Mao Tse-tung. A balanced history of the period would also have to deal, as I do not, with the various other reasons for the Kuomintang's defeat. An element of distortion also results when the events which occur in one environment are recounted to the people of a different culture. For example, in China so-called dunce caps are sometimes placed on people in order to humiliate them, but the implication is that they are villains, rather than merely fools.

In addition, a nonspecialist, trying to follow an account in which the names of many Chinese are mentioned, is bound to have trouble remembering them. For this reason I have repeatedly cited the positions of persons being reintroduced into the narrative, and have appended a section which contains brief biographies of some of the persons whom I mention often. (I would advise the general reader to put a paper clip at the beginning of that section in order to make reference to it easy.)

I originally had hoped to complete my task during the one year of my official assignment to the University of California, but that year provided no more than a start. I consequently am more than doubly indebted to Chalmers Johnson, the chairman of the Center for Chinese Studies, and to Joyce Kallgren, its vice chairman. Professor Johnson not only encouraged me to undertake this manuscript and arranged for me to have the help of Miss Alexandra Close for several months, while she was serving as research assistant at the Center. He and Professor Kallgren also invited me to continue my association with the Center after my initial year had passed. The library and office staffs of the Center, as well as a number of the scholars using its facilities, were enormously helpful to me in many ways. My special thanks go to John S. Service, the Curator of the Library: he read each chapter, often in its successive forms, and made many helpful suggestions concerning matters of fact or style, but left the matter of content up to me. The notes appear at the back of the book, not as footnotes, at my particular request.

If a man is what he does, a portrait of Mao Tse-tung will emerge from these pages. It is a portrait which will please neither his wholehearted admirers nor his determined detractors: Mao Tse-tung, as he has himself asserted, is a man of dual character, and the role he has played reflects that duality.

E.E.R.

Contents

Mao's Way

————

THIS VOLUME IS SPONSORED BY THE
CENTER FOR CHINESE STUDIES
UNIVERSITY OF CALIFORNIA, BERKELEY

I

The Twig Bends, and the Tree Inclines

A GREAT chain of mountains, known as the Tsing Ling, reaches out from Tibet and across most of central China in the direction of the Yellow Sea. Acting as a barrier to the monsoon rains which sweep up from the South China Sea, it separates the dry, brown wheat country of the north from the humid, green ricelands of the south.[1] In the middle of this southern half of China lies the province of Hunan, and in the approximate center of the province there is a peasant village, composed of scattered clusters of houses, named Shaoshan. It is in a valley, amidst ricefields which stretch to surrounding hills and mountains, their slopes green with trees and bamboos.

Mao Tse-tung, the eldest of four children, was born in this village on the nineteenth day of the eleventh moon, during the nineteenth year of the reign of the Emperor Kuang Hsü, a date which corresponds to December 26, 1893.[2] The house in which he was born and passed his childhood still stands. It fronts on a pond which is supposed to have served as the young Mao's swimming pool, but which undoubtedly was used then, as now, as a convenient place for the people of the neighborhood to wash their clothes and cattle. The house was constructed only of mud bricks, but it is two-storied, somewhat more spacious than its neighbors, and roofed with tile. Connected to it are a cowshed, a pigsty, a storage place for grain, and a small mill.[3]

Mao Tse-tung's native province of Hunan is famous, among other things, for its soldiers and its brigands. Mao's own father had spent some years as a soldier, but at the time of Mao's birth he was in the process of rising from the status of poor peasant to that of rich peasant and grain dealer. Indeed, during Mao's childhood he had one or more hired hands, and while Mao was still a lad the father appears to have rented out some of his land. (After China came under Communist rule, of course, many men of similar status were executed as "enemies of the people," and their children were placed under the disadvantages inherent in having a wrong class background.) It appears from a family photograph that Mao's father was a man of spare build, with knifelike features set in a small face, the mouth bracketed by a thin mustache. His mother was, by contrast, plump. The young Mao Tse-tung was slender, but full of face, with a large mole somewhat left of the center of his chin. Only in later years would he attain a plumpness reminiscent of that of his mother.

The father, evidently a harsh and driving man, put Mao Tse-tung to work from the time he was five or six. Between the ages of eight and thirteen, Mao also studied in a local primary school, doing his chores in the early morning and at night. His teacher frequently beat the pupils, and when Mao Tse-tung was ten he rebelled against such treatment and ran away from school. No less afraid of getting a beating when he got home, he set out for the nearest city. Unable to find his way, he wandered around for three days, until members of his family finally found him. Mao has commented about this episode: "After my return to the family, however, to my surprise conditions somewhat improved. My father was slightly more considerate and the teacher was more inclined to moderation. The result of my act of protest impressed me very much." [4]

When Mao Tse-tung was thirteen, he had to leave school and begin working full-time, laboring in the fields by day and keeping the accounts of his father's business in the evening. About this same time he had a quarrel with his father and left the house, with his father pursuing and demanding that he return. When Mao Tse-tung came to the nearby pond he threatened to jump in, presumably to drown himself if his father came any nearer. "In this situation," Mao later recounted, "demands and counterdemands were presented for the cessation of civil war." His father insisted that he apologize and kowtow as a sign of submission—a seemingly appropriate demand in a society in which a chain of hierarchical relationships led from child to parents and upwards to the emperor, before whom all kowtowed. Mao offered to do a modified kowtow, getting down on one knee instead of both, if his father would promise not to beat him, and his offer was accepted. "Thus the war ended," according to Mao, "and from it I learned that when I defended my rights by open rebellion my father relented, but when I remained meek and submissive he only cursed and beat me the more." [5] Although he did not say so, he had also learned the value of threats.

As Mao explained the overall situation, there were two parties in the family, his father who was the ruling power, and the opposition made up of himself, his mother, a brother, and sometimes even a hired hand who worked for his father. The opposition constituted a united front, but within it there was a difference of opinion. His mother advocated a policy of indirect attacks. Overt display of emotion or open rebelliousness, she said, "was not the Chinese way." [6] In subsequent years Mao was to score great successes against ruling power types;

his greatest failures were to arise from the seemingly compliant Chinese people, following what his mother called "the Chinese way."

When he was fifteen Mao Tse-tung decided, despite his father's initial disapproval, to resume his schooling. The institution he chose, the Tungshan Higher Primary School, was in a town about fifteen miles from his home. Here most of Mao's schoolmates were the sons of landlords, well dressed and schooled in correct behavior. He was, by contrast, the ragged and uncouth son of a peasant, and already six years older than most of the others in his class. Being different exposed him to ridicule,[7] and this period may have marked the beginnings of his antagonism for the landlords as a class and of the ambivalence with which he came to regard China's so-called intellectuals, most of whom were drawn from the middle and upper classes.

A principal source of conflict between Mao Tse-tung and his father, both before Mao's resumption of his schooling and thereafter, was the lad's distaste for farm work. Like other peasants, the elder Mao conscientiously returned to the soil both human and animal manures, and when Mao Tse-tung was at home and had no other work to do, his father sent him out with carrying pole and basket to collect animal droppings. Mao Tse-tung would set out, only to find a place to hide and read the novels and historical tales to which he was addicted. In the father's eyes, this choice of reading materials compounded the offense: If Mao Tse-tung was to spend his time with books, his father wanted him to study the Confucian classics. The study of these classics was regarded as something practical; the examinations for entry into government service had been based upon them, and it was only through government service that men amassed great wealth.

Through his reading Mao became an admirer of Shih Huang-ti, the revolutionary emperor of the Ch'in dynasty, who unified China, and of Han Wu-ti who extended it and fought against the Huns.[8] Shih Huang-ti subjugated the feudal lords, and to make their loss of power permanent, he caused the families of the aristocracy to be taken from their hereditary lands and transported to border areas. He also broke the power and influence of the scholar-officials who had served the feudal lords, put military officers in their places, and ordered the burning of the histories of previous dynasties and the books of the Hundred Schools of philosophy on which the ideologies of the scholar-officials were based. It was Shih Huang-ti, too, who built the Great Wall—at the cost, according to tradition, of a million lives. Of his latter days it was said that "no man felt secure in his office; all were easily degraded."[9]

The protection of Shih Huang-ti's person, because he had many

enemies, was deemed to require that his whereabouts be known only
to his immediate entourage, and this requirement of his personal security proved destructive of the security of his regime. Because his life
was customarily shrouded in greatest secrecy, it was possible to conceal
the fact of his death. He died while on a journey, and his prime minister and chief eunuch kept his demise secret until they could arrange
the death of the crown prince, get back to the capital, and install an
heir of their choice. Inconveniently, the time was summer, the weather
was hot, and the emperor began to decompose. However, the prime
minister and the chief eunuch were a resourceful pair. They placed a
quantity of rancid fish on a cart which followed the imperial chariot.
In consequence, any attendants who might have become suspicious
were thrown off the scent. But the prime minister and the chief eunuch,
although equal to the tasks of grasping power, were unequal to those
of holding it. Within four years, the dynasty Shih Huang-ti had
founded was overthrown and replaced by another. Copies of the books
of the Confucian school were brought out of their hiding places and
became the ideological basis for the scholar-officials of succeeding generations. But the scholar-officials no longer served feudal lords; their
masters were the emperors of successive dynasties. Shih Huang-ti had
wrought too profound a change in the political and social structure of
China for the country ever to be the same again.[10]

Mao Tse-tung was fond also of tales about rebellions and banditry,
like *Shui Hu,* which Pearl Buck translated under the title *All Men Are
Brothers.* The brotherhood of this saga was a band whose members
had been driven into outlawry, one by one, in consequence of injus-
tices perpetrated by officials, and who avenged themselves upon the
military and civil officers of the government. However, not all members
of the band were discriminating about whose throats they cut. One of
the principal heroes, after entering an official's home and assassinating
him, killed everyone else he encountered in the house, including servants, women, and small children. Another member of the band kept an
inn, and when he ran low on meat and wayfarers fell in his power, he
would butcher them and use their carcasses to make the meat dump-
lings he sold to other guests.[11] It is clear that the young Mao drew
parallels between the officials of the saga and those of his own time.
He later told, at any rate, of having deeply resented the treatment
which officials of his own province had inflicted on some local people.
There had been a famine, and people who were hungry had gone to
the governor's office to ask for food. He had turned them away, and
they subsequently had attacked his headquarters, cut down the flagpole
that was the symbol of his authority, and driven him from his office.
Some of them were later beheaded, after which their heads were put up

on poles as a warning to future rebels. Some years later, while discussing with some fellow students the ways in which they might work
for their country's salvation, Mao rejected running for office—which
would require money and connections, and he rejected seeking to influence future generations through teaching—which would take too long.
The best way, he asserted, would be to take to the hills like the bandit
rebels of *Shui Hu*.

Mao Tse-tung's favorite story was probably *Romance of the Three
Kingdoms,* a long tale of the intricate warfare and intrigue through
which a China which had become divided into three kingdoms was
once again reunited. The two principal antagonists of the story are
Liu Pei, portrayed as a scion of the imperial house of Han and a model
Confucian ruler, and the ruthlessly ambitious Ts'ao Ts'ao, arch villain
in the eyes of successive generations of Chinese. It has been suggested
that Mao Tse-tung identified himself not with Liu Pei, whose chival-
rous behavior sometimes seems indistinguishable from stupidity, but
rather with the clever though treacherous Ts'ao Ts'ao. Whether or not
this surmise is correct, there is no question but what *Romance of the
Three Kingdoms* exerted a profound and lasting influence upon Mao
Tse-tung.[12]

According to one of his biographers, the young Mao Tse-tung
became enraged when fellow students insisted that this book was not
true history, but rather a romantic novel based on it. When the history
teacher confirmed their statements, Mao tried to start a movement
against the teacher. When the headmaster backed up the history
teacher, Mao even prepared a petition to the mayor asking that the
headmaster be replaced and urged the other students to sign it, but
this rebellion got nowhere.[13]

About this time Mao Tse-tung, who had not even known of the
existence of the United States, was stirred by an article about the
American revolution, with its tale of how Washington had fought a
protracted war, won final victory, and built his nation. In a book entitled *Great Heroes of the World,* he read about Napoleon, for whom
he evidently conceived an enduring admiration. In 1964 Mao was to
tell French visitors that Robespierre had been a great revolutionary,
but that he had been more impressed by Napoleon and had read everything about him that had been published.[14]

The young Mao Tse-tung already knew that China stood in need
of men of heroic mold. In the first half of the century in which he had
been born, China had pretended to be a universal empire, receiving no
foreign emissaries who did not come bearing tribute and willing to
kowtow before the Manchu emperors in recognition of Chinese suzerainty over the countries from which they had come. Now China ap-

peared to be in danger of being carved up and incorporated in the
empires of foreign powers. Even before he had gone away to school,
Mao had read a pamphlet telling about Japan's occupation of Formosa
and other territories in 1895, as well as of China's loss of suzerainty
over Korea, Indochina, and Burma. The writer of this pamphlet had
predicted that China would be subjugated, and Mao Tse-tung began
to realize that it would be the duty of all Chinese to help save their
country.

One of the key obstacles to saving China and its Manchu dynasty
had been a shrewd and strong-willed woman, the Empress Dowager
Tzu Hsi. She had been the *de facto* ruler of China since 1861, when
the Emperor Hsien Feng had died and she had become regent for her
son, the infant Emperor T'ung Chih. He in turn had died before
reaching the age of twenty, largely as a consequence of vicious debauch-
ery which she had encouraged, and she had then arranged to have
another infant, her nephew Kuang Hsü, chosen as successor. It was
only after Kuang Hsü had come of age that she had begun to relax
her control of affairs, retiring to the enjoyment of her Summer Palace
—a complex of buildings which owed much of their magnificence to
her diversion of funds ostensibly intended for the improvement of the
Chinese Navy. But in 1898, under the influence of a modern-minded
advisor from Kwangtung named K'ang Yu-wei, and of other like-
minded men, Kuang Hsü had issued a series of edicts which decreed
far-reaching reforms. Both Kuang Hsü and K'ang Yu-wei were aware
that the Empress Dowager would have little sympathy for these reforms, and that she might reassert her authority in order to negate
them. In the hope of forestalling her, K'ang Yu-wei persuaded the
young Emperor to attempt a coup aimed at making her a prisoner,
after which she was to have been confined to the buildings on a small
island situated in the middle of one of the lakes within the palace
grounds.[15]

The emperor entrusted the key role in this intended coup to a
senior official named Yüan Shih-k'ai, who had been charged in one of
the new decrees with the task of carrying out the reform of the army.
Unfortunately for Kuang Hsü, Yüan Shih-k'ai betrayed this plan to a
partisan of the Empress Dowager. Kuang Hsü was seized and placed
in confinement on the same small island on which he had intended
to imprison the Empress Dowager. She resumed the regency, and all
Kuang Hsü's reform decrees were revoked, except one which provided
for the establishment of a modern Peking University. Some time later
Kuang Hsü was allowed somewhat greater freedom within the palace
grounds. But from the day of his confinement until they died within
hours of each other in 1908, Kuang Hsü remained under the Empress

Dowager's control, kneeling in her presence and addressing the old lady—who had always wanted to be a man—as "dear papa." [16]

Mao Tse-tung did not learn that they had died, and that another infant was on the throne, until two years afterward. By then he had read about the intended reforms of 1898 and had become an enthusiastic admirer of K'ang Yu-wei. It seems unlikely, however, that he had also learned of the words which Tzu Hsi is reported to have uttered on her deathbed. "Never again," she is supposed to have warned, "allow any woman to hold the supreme power in the state." [17] At any rate, in later years Mao was to allow his own wife, herself an admirer of at least some aspects of the Empress Dowager's conduct of affairs, to exercise great power in her own right. This was to lead, among other things, to a great blowup between his wife and the acting chief of staff of his armed forces, in the course of which the chief of staff allegedly repeated an old saying, clothed in the language of signs and portents, to the effect that when an old hen crows at dawn, it means the empire is in danger.[18]

K'ang Yu-wei had tried to bring about reform, not start a revolution. But there were other Chinese who hoped to save China by overthrowing the Manchu dynasty and establishing a republic. Foremost among them was Sun Yat-sen. Like K'ang, he was a native of Kwangtung, a province which was, for the next eighteen years, to be the principal center of the Chinese revolution. The reasons why this was to be so were inherent in history and in the geographic position of Kwangtung as China's southernmost coastal province.

The Manchus had grown from a tribe into a powerful nation, in their homeland beyond the Great Wall, during the last century of China's Ming dynasty. In 1644 the forces of a rebel leader had occupied Peking, the Emperor had committed suicide, and the rebel leader had declared himself the emperor of a new dynasty. However, after taking Peking he had also taken the favorite concubine of a general whose troops guarded a strategic pass through the Great Wall and had refused to give her back. The general, in turn, refused to recognize the new dynasty, declared himself the avenger of the Ming emperor, and invited the Manchus to enter China as his allies. Their combined forces easily took Peking, where the Manchus settled in and proclaimed their own ruler the emperor of China. Since their occupation of north China caused little bloodshed or destruction, it also aroused relatively little resentment. But the conquest of the rest of China, to which some Ming loyalists had retreated, required almost two decades of bloody warfare and left in its wake a heritage of anti-Manchu bitterness.[19]

The Manchus began adopting Chinese civilization even before they had completed their conquest of the Chinese people. They ruled through a bureaucracy which was largely staffed by Chinese, which conducted its business in the Chinese language, and which applied a body of law that had been in effect under the previous dynasty. However, they never wholly ceased to be regarded as alien conquerors, and they did issue and enforce one new edict which reminded Chinese of their subordination to Manchu rule. This edict required all males, as a sign of loyalty to the dynasty, to follow the Manchu custom of wearing the queue.[20] This meant having most of the head shaved but leaving the hair long in one circular area, where it was braided and allowed to hang down the back. In enforcing this requirement, the Manchu government hired itinerant head-shavers. Their portable equipment included a miniature replica of the flagpoles which stood at the gates of official buildings, and a copy of the imperial edict, which was to be hung on the flagpole. The barber, coming upon a man without a queue, could compel him to kneel before the imperial edict, bow his head, and submit it to the razor.[21] Subsequently, cutting off one's queue came to be regarded as a symbolic declaration of rebellion.

China's Manchu rulers had been torn between a desire for the revenues brought by foreign trade and concern lest that trade—and the foreign barbarians who came to conduct it—might pose dangers to the status quo. Balancing one against the other, they had permitted such trade to be conducted for a season each year in the southern city of Canton. That city had the advantages of being as distant as possible from their capital of Peking and of being situated far enough upriver from the coast to facilitate Chinese control of access to it. The Ming predecessors of the Manchus had allowed the Portuguese to establish the small coastal settlement of Macao, downriver ninety miles from Canton, and some traders of other nationalities made Macao their off-season home.

This crack in China's closed door was enlarged by the British in 1841, when they forced the Chinese to cede to them the rocky island of Hong Kong, forty miles across the estuary of the Pearl River from Macao. Thereafter, with access to foreign shipping made easy, many natives of Kwangtung went abroad to work or to engage in trade. Those who went were predominantly men without women. When the men were financially able to do so, they either sent for their wives and children or returned to their native villages long enough to sire children, then left their wives and children behind with the extended families from which they came. And so a network of contacts grew up between Kwangtung and colonies of Chinese who sojourned or had settled abroad.

Sun Yat-sen was a product of this milieu, and he drew a large part of the financial support needed for his revolutionary activities from these colonies of overseas Chinese. He had been born in 1866 in a small coastal village near Macao, and he had received his early schooling there. He had been sent to Hawaii, when he was thirteen, at the suggestion and expense of a close relative who had emigrated there and prospered; in Honolulu he had been placed in Iolani College, a boys' boarding school run under the auspices of the Church of England. After three years, the family learned that Sun was becoming converted to Christianity, withdrew him from the school, and shipped him back to China. There he demonstrated his new beliefs by disfiguring an idol in the village temple, and for this he was banished from the village. Befriended by an American missionary doctor, he was soon able to resume his schooling, this time in Hong Kong, and in 1892 he received his medical diploma.

Sun Yat-sen proved to be less interested in private practice than in public reform, and before long he had abandoned his efforts in the latter direction in favor of the practice of revolution. He was later to explain that he had been depressed by the inability of the dynasty to defend China against foreign aggression (as demonstrated during Sino-French hostilities in 1884 and 1885), impressed by the relative efficiency of the British government of Hong Kong, and impelled by his Christian principles to work for change. China's defeat by Japan in the war of 1894–1895 further weakened the Manchu regime, making the task of overthrowing it appear less difficult than before and more urgent than ever. In 1895, Sun Yat-sen joined with some friends in an attempt to stage an armed revolt in the city of Canton. It was unsuccessful, and Sun Yat-sen fled to Japan with a price on his head. This marked the beginning of sixteen years of exile, years spent organizing a revolutionary party, soliciting funds in overseas Chinese communities, and making one abortive revolutionary effort after another.

China suffered further humiliations during Sun Yat-sen's years of exile, and Tokyo became a center for many Chinese political refugees, as well as for Chinese students bent on getting the modern educations which were available in Japanese colleges and universities. The number of such students swelled into the thousands in the wake of the Russo-Japanese war of 1904–1905. During that war the Japanese demonstrated that an Asian country could—through modernization—gain sufficient strength to defeat a European power. The spirit of revolutionary determination which characterized some of the students is illustrated by the case of the young Chiang Kai-shek, then not yet out of his teens. In 1906, anxious to prepare himself for a military career, he ensured that his family would not try to prevent his going abroad by cutting off his queue and sending it home. In Japan he studied at a military academy, graduated, and underwent training with a field artillery regiment of the Japanese Army. He also met Sun Yat-sen, and like many of the other Chinese students in Japan, he joined the *T'ung-meng-hui,* Sun Yat-sen's revolutionary organization.[22]

About the time Chiang Kai-shek was in training with the Japanese Army, during the winter of 1910–1911, Mao Tse-tung left primary school and walked the forty miles to Hunan's provincial capital of Changsha, in order that he might enroll in a middle school. In Changsha, in the spring or summer of 1911, Mao Tse-tung saw his first newspaper. It was, not surprisingly, a revolutionary journal, for a newspaper was itself a revolutionary thing in Manchu China. From this paper—which gave an account of an unsuccessful uprising which had been staged in Canton earlier in the year—Mao Tse-tung first learned about Sun Yat-sen, his *T'ung-meng-hui,* and its revolutionary program. He became excited and wrote and posted on the school wall an article advocating that Sun Yat-sen should be called back to China to become president of a new government.

That is what happened later in the year. But Sun Yat-sen was only indirectly responsible for the final uprising, which began among some troops in the central China city of Wuchang on October 10, 1911. The uprising had been scheduled for a later date, but the authorities had gotten wind of the plot, and it had become impossible to proceed as planned. Instead, some of the troops involved shot their commander, dragged a terrified colonel named Li Yüan-hung out of hiding, forced him to assume command, and went on from there to take over not only Wuchang, but also the adjacent cities of Hankow—which is a major transport center, and Hanyang—which contained an arsenal.

At this juncture, the Manchu authorities in Peking called upon Yüan Shih-k'ai to assume viceregal authority, and they gave him command of China's armed forces. He had built China's best army, its commanders owed their positions and hence their loyalty to him, and before the month was out they had occupied the cities of Hankow and Hanyang. Thereafter, having proven what he could do, Yüan Shih-k'ai held his forces aloof while revolutionaries in one Chinese province after another declared for the republic and slaughtered the Manchu garrisons. Yüan had undertaken the original operation only to ensure his own bargaining position, for he intended to abandon the Manchu dynasty to its fate much as he had betrayed the Emperor Kuang Hsü. At wit's end, the imperial regent resigned on December 6, and the next day the mother of the young emperor gave Yüan Shih-k'ai full powers to reach a settlement with the revolutionaries.

Sun Yat-sen learned about the Wuchang revolt from a newspaper while traveling by train between Denver and Kansas City. He of course immediately abandoned the fund-raising campaign which had brought him to the United States but traveled back to China via Europe, where he stopped over briefly in London and Paris. Finally, on December 25, 1911, he debarked at Shanghai, where he was accorded a hero's welcome. Four days later he was chosen for the presidency by a convention of provincial delegates which met in Nanking. On January 1, 1912, he proclaimed the establishment of the Republic of China and formally assumed office as its provisional president.

Meanwhile, however, the bargaining with Yüan Shih-k'ai was getting nowhere. During his London stopover, Sun Yat-sen had obtained a promise, from a four-power consortium which was making loans to the Chinese Government, that it would suspend the payment of further installments. He had not succeeded, however, in efforts to get a loan for his revolutionary *T'ung-meng-hui*. In consequence, neither side had the financial resources to undertake the military operations which might have enabled it to conquer the other. In order to break this impasse, Sun Yat-sen offered to resign his office, provided Yüan Shih-k'ai would declare his support for the republic and the Manchus would abdicate. Yüan Shih-k'ai was willing, and the Manchus had no choice. For them, history had come full circle: They had gained power after being invited in by one Chinese general, and they gave it up at the invitation of another. On January 30, 1912, Yüan Shih-k'ai succeeded Sun Yat-sen as provisional president.[23]

When the revolution broke out Mao Tse-tung cut off his queue, dropped out of school, and prepared to set out for Wuchang, where he intended to join the force of Li Yüan-hung. Before he could leave, fighting broke out in Changsha, which was soon occupied by revolutionary forces. Mao accordingly abandoned the idea of going to Wuchang. Instead he joined the local army and remained in it until early the following year. During this period he spent most of his pay on newspapers dealing with the revolution, and in the columns of one of them he read about socialism, which interested him very much. When it appeared that there would be no more fighting because of the agreement between Sun Yat-sen and Yüan Shih-k'ai, he left the army to resume his schooling.

The language of instruction in the school which Mao chose was English. He knew little more than the alphabet, so he soon dropped out and entered another school. Liking neither its curriculum nor its regulations, he left this school too, and spent some months reading Chinese translations of western works on political and social thought in the Hunan Provincial Library. Finally, in 1913, he succeeded in gaining entrance to the Hunan Provincial First Normal School. It was not actually a college-level institution, but it was a very good one. Entrance to it was by competitive examination; and once a student was admitted, his tuition, room, board, and uniform were free or supplied at very small cost. Mao Tse-tung was to remain here until his graduation five years later.[24]

In Peking, Yüan Shih-k'ai was beginning his presidency with a national treasury that was nearly empty. Among the strongest of ties, few take precedence over the strings of the purse. But Yüan Shih-k'ai gave the title of military governor to the army commanders of the respective provinces, and he left it up to them to cover their expenses by means of their own devising. In meeting the expenses of the central government, Yüan Shih-k'ai continued the practice of depending on loans advanced by what had been the four-power consortium, now grown to six through the inclusion of Japanese and Russian financial interests.

Early in 1915, Japan—taking advantage of the preoccupation of the European powers with World War I and seeking to obtain for itself a paramount position in China—secretly presented to Yüan Shih-k'ai a document which came to be known as the Twenty-One Demands. Yüan Shih-k'ai was unwilling to accept all the demands which the document contained, because this would have reduced China to the status of a dependency of Japan. Yet he did not dare reject them all, because the two wars Japan had fought in his lifetime—one against China and one against Russia but largely on Chinese soil—had taught him something of Japan's military power and readiness to use it. He therefore stalled until the Japanese offered to set some of the demands aside for future discussion, and then accepted the rest.

Meanwhile, the foreign loans which Yüan Shih-k'ai had negotiated had aroused the opposition of the new parliament, in which the party of Sun Yat-sen, now reorganized as the Kuomintang, had won the majority of seats. Yüan Shih-k'ai dealt with this opposition by declaring the Kuomintang illegal, dissolving parliament, and ruling by decree. Finally, in betrayal of his pledge to support republican government, he endeavored to have himself made emperor. To his chagrin, the country promptly responded with a rebellion which began in the southern province of Yunnan and quickly spread to other provinces. Yüan Shih-k'ai was not yet sixty, but to judge from his bust as it appears on a coin of the republican period, he was a man old for his years. It depicts a walrus-mustached man, head either shaved or bald, a roll of fat escaping from his military collar, wearing a coat which extends outward more than down as though it must cover an enormous paunch. At any rate, he fell ill, as though his physical health had been broken by the shattering of his hopes, and in 1916 he died.

The death of Yüan Shih-k'ai marked the beginning of a decade of warlord rule. Vice President Li Yüan-hung, the former colonel of the

Wuchang revolt, was Yüan Shih-k'ai's immediate successor. He proved unequal to the tasks of drawing the shattered country together and of controlling the military men who had been Yüan Shih-k'ai's political henchmen. A republican government with national pretensions continued to function in Peking, under a succession of leaders, but the territory under its full control remained limited. Real power there, and elsewhere in the country, was in the hands of military strongmen who made alliances of convenience with each other, fought civil wars, and changed sides with bewildering frequency.

The most colorful of these characters was perhaps Chang Tsung-ch'ang, a great, burly fighter who became known, perhaps because of his tastes in food, as the "dog-meat general." He came of a humble family; his mother was a practicing witch, reputedly skilled in exorcising evil spirits; his father was a head-shaver and trumpeter; and the young Chang Tsung-ch'ang sometimes accompanied him on the cymbals. All this, however, was not enough to protect them from periods of financial stringency. During one such period the elder Chang sold his wife to a grain merchant. A filial son, in later and better days Chang Tsung-ch'ang tried on his father's behalf to buy her back but found that she preferred the new connection. By then he had worked for awhile in a gambling den; switched to banditry; been given command of a military unit charged with suppressing bandits; and become the adjutant of the acting president of China. Later, as the military governor of Shantung, Chang Tsung-ch'ang reputedly never knew how much money, how many concubines, or how many troops he had. During that period his troops included a contingent of White Russian "soldiers of misfortune" and a unit, commanded by one of his sons, composed of small boys—whose average age was ten—for whom he had specially short rifles manufactured. Chang Tsung-ch'ang was described as having "the physique of an elephant, the brain of a pig, and the temperament of a tiger." This temperament eventually proved his undoing. In 1927, after suffering a military defeat, he relieved his feelings by executing some captives, one of whom had been a divisional commander. This created a blood debt which was to be paid off five years later, when that man's adopted son would slip in, with some visitors to Chang Tsung-ch'ang's private railway car, and assassinate him.[25]

Some of the warlords were men who, in another era, might have served their country well. Feng Yü-hsiang, for instance, perhaps deserved the appellation of the "Christian general," although the story that he baptized his troops with a fire hose may have been apocryphal. He was, at any rate, a man whose life style was marked by the frugal simplicity appropriate for a contender for leadership in a country where the common man lived a life of hard work and poverty. Nevertheless, at one juncture Feng Yü-hsiang formed an alliance with Chang Tso-lin, the warlord of Manchuria, whom the "dog-meat general" was then serving as a divisional commander.[26]

Although Mao Tse-tung's life was that of a student, during the years from 1913 to 1918, it necessarily was affected by what went on beyond the walls of the Hunan Provincial First Normal School. In this period, Hunan knew only one completely peaceful year, and each time Changsha was engulfed in fighting the school had to shut down until peace returned. To many Chinese, the character of successive Peking regimes, operating as they did behind a republican facade, tended to discredit the republican institutions which they had tried to transplant from the west, and the evils of warlordism lent urgency to the search for another way. For Mao Tse-tung, the search would proceed from the lessons he learned and the assumptions he accepted, during these school years, about the nature of man, of society, and of the world.

What Mao Tse-tung learned in this new school, and what he failed to learn there, were determined in part by his old attitude of rebelliousness, and his stiff insistence on following his own bent. Older and taller than most of his fellow students, self-confidence in his relations with them may have come easily. But he was no less bold in his dealings with his teachers, and experience undoubtedly taught him that aggressiveness often paid off. In an altercation with one teacher, he quickly won a satisfactory compromise by grabbing the man by the arm, intending to drag him to the principal's office. When a fellow student wanted to get out of an arranged marriage with the principal's niece, Mao took the fiance to see the principal and argued his case to a successful conclusion. He would have been expelled for opposition to the principal, on another occasion, had it not been for the intervention of several friendly teachers.

By Mao's own account, the normal school had many regulations, few of which he agreed with. There were required courses in the natural sciences, which he did not like, and which he accordingly refused to study. His reaction to some other courses, including mathematics, was much the same. His reading of works of the nineteenth century may have imbued him with that period's unbounded faith in the total conquest of nature by man, but his studies could hardly have taught him great respect for the limitations imposed by physical laws. Having dropped out of a previous school because the language of instruction was English, and taking little interest in it now, he accepted a limitation which may have led to his later rejecting opportunities to study abroad.[27]

The teacher who influenced Mao Tse-tung most strongly and enduringly was a scholar named Yang Ch'ang-chi, who taught courses in philosophy. Yang Ch'ang-chi was, among other things, a Confucian scholar, and he undoubtedly accepted the Confucian view that the fundamental nature of man was good. He laid great stress on the teachings of a seventeenth century Hunanese philosopher, who taught that human nature is highly malleable and readily adapts itself to environmental change. He imbued Mao Tse-tung with a conviction, based on the nineteenth-century European liberal tradition, that the energy needed to make a nation rich and powerful is hidden within each member of society, and that this energy can be released by stimulating the initiative of the individual.[28] These concepts—that man is basically good, that human nature can readily be changed, and that the world can be transformed through a release of hidden human energies—were to influence Mao Tse-tung, decades later, as he sought to guide China back to power and greatness and onward toward a communist society.

Yang Ch'ang-chi assigned as a textbook—and it was one which Mao studied assiduously—a Chinese translation of *System of Ethics* by the German philosopher Friedrich Paulsen, who placed great emphasis upon self-discipline and the power of the human will. To Mao Tse-tung, self-discipline evidently did not mean that he should cease to follow his own bent. In 1917 he still complained, perhaps not without justification: "In the educational system of our country, required courses are as thick as the hairs of a cow." [29] He also did not change his slovenly personal habits.[30] But he now subjected himself to cold baths, hard exercise, and exposure to the elements, in order to harden his body and strengthen his will. At that time he wrote, in language evocative of old tales of military valor: "Exercise should be savage and rude. To be able to leap on horseback and to shoot at the same time; to go from battle to battle; to shake the mountains by one's cries, and the colors of the sky by one's roars of anger; to have the strength to uproot mountains like Hsiang Yü and to pierce the mark like Yu Chi —all this is savage and rude and has nothing to do with delicacy." [31]

Yang Ch'ang-chi was an enthusiastic reader of the review *Hsin ch'ing-nien* (*New Youth*), edited first in Shanghai and later in Peking by Ch'en Tu-hsiu, dean of the College of Letters at Peking University from 1917 to 1919 and subsequently the first leader of the Chinese Communist party. Yang Ch'ang-chi introduced his students to the magazine, which put them in touch with the mainstream of China's intellectual life, and from 1915 onwards Mao Tse-tung was one of its regular readers. Ch'en Tu-hsiu, Mao later said, "influenced me perhaps more than anyone else." [32]

Ch'en Tu-hsiu believed, during his pre-Communist period, that China's salvation would be found through the adoption of democracy and the spread of scientific knowledge. At that time he wrote: "In order to support Mr. Democracy we are obliged to oppose Confucianism, the code of rituals, chastity, traditional ethics, old politics; and in order to support Mr. Science, we are compelled to oppose traditional arts, traditional religion." [33] Supporting democracy and science, he held, required opposing "the so-called national heritage," and the traditional literature through which that heritage was transmitted. Mao Tse-tung evidently agreed with him, for in one of his own early writings he declared that the science and democracy preached by Ch'en Tu-hsiu were exactly what China needed. And half a century later he evidently still was at least half persuaded of Ch'en's thesis that China's cultural heritage should be scrapped. That thesis seems, at any rate, to have been echoed in Mao's Cultural Revolution, launched as a movement to "destroy all the old ideas, old culture, old customs, and old habits of the exploiting classes," and to replace them with "the thought of Mao Tse-tung." [34]

In 1915, the year in which Mao Tse-tung first became a reader of *Hsin ch'ing-nien,* he began also to assume positions of leadership in the student organizations of Changsha. In 1917 he and a fellow student named Ts'ai Ho-sen founded and became leaders of a study group called the *Hsin-min hsüeh-hui.* The following year, during which Mao Tse-tung graduated from normal school, several developments combined to take him to Peking. One was the acceptance of a post at Peking University by his mentor, Yang Ch'ang-chi, who was in a position to help Mao Tse-tung get established there. At that same time, some members of the Kuomintang with European connections were recruiting Chinese students to go to France under a part-work, part-study program. Ts'ai Ho-sen went to Peking to investigate it on behalf of the members of the *Hsin-min hsüeh-hui,* and he wrote back urging their participation. In consequence, Mao helped organize the participation of students from Hunan, and he accompanied them to Peking where they were to study French prior to their departure.

In Peking, Professor Yang introduced Mao Tse-tung to Li Ta-chao, who was in charge of the library of Peking University, and Li gave Mao Tse-tung a job. It was a lowly one at which he earned only $8.00 a month—one dollar more than he had been paid as a common soldier before he had entered normal school. Moreover, Mao had come with no funds of his own, and he had borrowed the money to get to Peking. His living conditions were quite miserable, and he had to sleep in a small room with seven other men. With all eight packed on the *k'ang,* the platform which serves in many north China houses as a

bed, he had to warn the people on both sides when he wanted to turn over. At the library, one of his tasks was to register those who came to read, and among them he recognized the names of famous scholars, with whom he tried to strike up conversations on political and cultural subjects. He found, though, that these men, and one of the professors whose lectures he attended as auditor rather than regular student, had no time to listen to an assistant librarian speaking southern dialect. But in the parks and palace grounds of Peking, he enjoyed the beauties of the early spring, with the plum blossoms emerging in the sun while the ice still held on the lakes. And he met and fell in love with Yang K'ai-hui, the daughter of Professor Yang. He also studied anarchism, which had a great and perhaps not wholly transitory influence on him, and he found stimulus in a socialism study group of which Li Ta-chao was a sponsor and Ch'en Tu-hsiu a member.

In the spring of 1919, Mao Tse-tung left Peking for Shanghai, where the students who were to engage in the part-work, part-study program were to embark for France. He was not among those who had studied French while in Peking. According to his own account, he had felt that he did not know enough about his own country, and that his time could be spent more profitably in China. At any rate, he saw his friends off and then returned to Changsha. The most notable among the students who did go to France under this program was Chou En-lai —the handsome and poised son of a Mandarin family and the graduate of Tientsin's best schools. Chou En-lai had made a name for himself as a bright student, accomplished amateur performer of traditional Peking opera, student organizer, and political activist. Among Chou's fellow students in France were Li Li-san, Ch'en Yi, Li Fu-ch'un, Nieh Jung-chen, Teng Hsiao-p'ing, and others who were to play roles of importance in the Chinese Communist party. During this period in Europe, Chou En-lai helped organize a socialist youth league among his fellow students, and he visited Germany. There he convinced a Chinese general almost twice his age—Chu Teh, who had also gone abroad to study—that he should become a Communist.

At the time of Mao Tse-tung's return to Changsha, the Council of Foreign Ministers of the Allied Powers meeting in Versailles was discussing postwar territorial settlements. One of the territories involved was the Kiaochow bay area on the coast of Shantung Province, with the port of Tsingtao as its principal center. China had been forced in 1898 to lease the area to Germany for a period of ninety-nine years. Japan had declared war on Germany and seized the area in 1914. In 1915 Japan had extracted from Yüan Shih-k'ai, as one of the Twenty-One Demands, an undertaking—formalized by treaty—to accept any disposition of the territory which might be agreed upon between Ger-

many and Japan. Nevertheless, there were reasons to hope that the Kiaochow leased territory might be returned to China through the treaty being negotiated at Versailles. In 1917 China, too, had declared war on Germany, and this enabled China to send a delegation to Versailles. Moreover, when Germany had accepted the armistice of November 11, 1918, both sides agreed that the final peace should be concluded on the basis of President Wilson's "fourteen points," which envisaged territorial settlements based upon the interests of the inhabitants and the self-determination of peoples.[35]

However, Japan had taken the precaution, early in 1917, of obtaining secret assurances from Britain, Russia, and France that they would support its claim to succeed to the German rights in Shantung. At Versailles, Britain and France proved faithful to the specific assurances they had given to Japan, rather than to the spirit of President Wilson's "fourteen points," and the Council of Foreign Ministers decided in favor of Japan. Members of the Chinese delegation at Versailles had perhaps done their best, but the government in Peking was placed in an awkward position—because during 1918 it had been accepting one Japanese loan after another.

The China of 1919 was quite different from that of 1915, when Yüan Shih-k'ai had knuckled under to Japan. The stirring of the youth, to which men like Ch'en Tu-hsiu had contributed, had done its work. The students of Peking had already determined, before word of the decision at Versailles reached China, that they would hold mass demonstrations on May 7, the anniversary of acceptance of the Twenty-One Demands, which they had designated "National Humiliation Day." When news of the Versailles decision came, they decided not to wait. On May 4, thousands of students, drawn from thirteen colleges and universities, tried to march into Peking's legation quarter. Turned back by the legation quarter guards, they went to the home of one of the officials who had handled the negotiations of 1915 and burned it down. Next they caught the Chinese minister to Tokyo, who was pro-Japanese and who happened to be in Peking at the time, and beat him into unconsciousness.

Thus began the May Fourth Movement, during which students all over China organized demonstrations, strikes, business stoppages, and the boycott of Japanese goods. The authorities replied with numerous arrests, but participation was too widespread for suppression to be effective. In the end, some pro-Japanese officials were ousted and the Chinese government refused to sign the Versailles treaty. This of course left Japan in possession of the former German rights in Shantung, a situation which was not to be rectified until the Washington conference of 1922. But students and teachers had discovered the

power they could wield, and the May Fourth Movement continued, as one devoted to political change, long after the large-scale demonstrations of 1919 had subsided.[36] Mao Tse-tung was among those who participated in the May Fourth Movement, after it had spread to the provinces, and who were impressed by this early example of the power of mobilized student masses. Indeed, he was later to mention it, in connection with his decision to make similar use of China's students beginning in the spring of 1966.[37]

Soviet Russia was, of course, exempt from blame for the settlement at Versailles, because the government which had given Japan assurances of its support in 1917 had been overthrown soon afterward, and Soviet Russia had made a separate peace with Germany the following year. Chinese who had become disillusioned with the democracies of the west, and who sought basic changes, would henceforth be less likely to look to such models as that of the French revolution—with its concepts of liberty, equality, and fraternity—and more likely to look to the contemporary one provided by the Russian revolution of 1917.

On July 4, 1918, Soviet Foreign Affairs Commissar Chicherin had declared that Soviet Russia was reversing the Tsarist policy towards China by renouncing its special rights and interests there. A year later, in the wake of the May Fourth Movement, Deputy Commissar Karakhan made a direct approach, along somewhat similar lines, to both the government in Peking and to a military regime which had been set up in Canton under the nominal leadership of Sun Yat-sen but from which he had later withdrawn. Karakhan proposed to each of them that China and Soviet Russia establish friendly relations and enter into discussions looking toward the cancellation of the "unequal treaties" of Tsarist times, together with the special rights and interests Russia had derived from them. Neither the announcement of 1918 nor the message of 1919 evoked any reaction from either Chinese regime. Indeed, it was only after 1922 that Soviet Russia was able to initiate fruitful talks with the government in Peking. That year Russia sent an experienced diplomat named Adolph A. Joffe to the Far East, and his efforts eventuated in the formal establishment of diplomatic relations in 1924.[38] However, it did not take Soviet Russia that long to establish contacts of another sort, for in April of 1920 the Comintern sent three representatives to China.

Meanwhile, the political activities into which Mao Tse-tung had plunged after the outbreak of the May Fourth Movement had made it unsafe for him to remain in Hunan. In July of 1919 he had taken the editorship of a weekly magazine, put out under the auspices of the United Students' Association, called the *Hsiang River Weekly Review*.

He wrote most of it himself, often working into the small hours of the morning. (This practice, incidentally, became a lifelong habit—to the sorrow, in later decades, of officials in his government who liked to sleep at night.) The *Hsiang River Weekly Review* soon came to the unfavorable attention of the governor of Hunan, a member of the clique which was in power in Peking. When the governor banned the weekly after its fifth issue, Mao shifted to the editorship of another, but that one, too, was soon shut down. About this time the governor called a meeting of student representatives, abused them for meddling in politics, and screamed at them: "If you don't listen to me, I'll cut off your heads!" Evidently Mao Tse-tung did not listen to him, for in November he helped reorganize the United Students' Association, and in December he led a strike against the governor. By February 1920, things had become too hot for Mao Tse-tung in Changsha, and he made his second trip to Peking. There Mao again saw his beloved Yang K'ai-hui, and he had an opportunity to read Chinese translations of the first section of the *Communist Manifesto* and of several basic works on Marxism, which were just then beginning to appear in China. In April, perhaps wanting to discuss the works he had read with Ch'en Tu-hsiu, he left Peking for Shanghai.

In Peking, Ch'en Tu-hsiu had been jailed for some months in consequence of his involvement in the May Fourth Movement. After his release Ch'en had gone to Shanghai, which provided him a safer base. Shanghai had grown from the status of walled town to that of great metropolis as a result of its opening to foreign residence and trade under the terms of the same treaty of 1842 by which Hong Kong had been ceded to the British. This metropolitan area had come to consist of three parts, each under a different administration: Greater Shanghai, with upwards of 320 square miles, under Chinese jurisdiction; the International Settlement, with an area of about 9 square miles, governed by a Shanghai Municipal Council, made up then entirely of foreigners who were elected by the taxpayers; and a French Concession, which was about half as large.[39] With two of these three areas under foreign control and passage from one sector to another easy, Shanghai was a relatively safe place of residence for Chinese political refugees.

The three representatives of the Comintern, who had been sent to China in April 1920, had first gone to Peking to see Li Ta-chao. He gave them an introduction to Ch'en Tu-hsiu, and they had then traveled onward to Shanghai where they had several conversations with Ch'en Tu-hsiu. With their encouragement, Ch'en Tu-hsiu organized and became the leader of a seven-man Communist nucleus. It was the first such group to be established in China, and its members undertook the task of promoting the establishment of similar cells in other cities. Mao Tse-tung and the men from Moscow had gone to Shanghai to see Ch'en Tu-hsiu at about the same time, and it is clear that there was a substantial period during which all of them were in that city. Ch'en Tu-hsiu undoubtedly asked Mao Tse-tung to set up a cell in Hunan, and it would be interesting to know whether he introduced Mao to the representatives of the Comintern. It would also be interesting to know whether they offered to help him set up a cell in Changsha, as they did in some other provincial centers. If so, it would have been in character for Mao to refuse the offer, for the language he used in referring to Chinese who were subservient to foreigners was often contemptuous and sometimes scatological. He returned to Changsha prepared to help build a Communist apparatus there, but the evidence suggests that it was Ch'en Tu-hsiu to whom he looked for guidance.[40]

While Mao Tse-tung was in Shanghai, there was civil war in Hunan. His enemy the governor was overthrown, and in July it became safe for him to return to Changsha. He had obtained the money to go from Peking to Shanghai by selling a winter coat, and in Shanghai he had earned a precarious living by working as a laundryman. But upon his return to Changsha he was offered and accepted a position as principal of the elementary school attached to the Hunan First Normal School, a position which he held until the winter of 1922. This enabled him to marry Yang K'ai-hui, who subsequently bore him the first two of his several children. She was undoubtedly aware that there had been an arranged marriage between Mao Tse-tung and a village girl, when he had been thirteen or fourteen years of age. But according to Mao Tse-tung that earlier marriage had never been consummated, and he subsequently had repudiated it.

In August 1920 Mao Tse-tung and a number of friends in Changsha established a Russian affairs study group, which sponsored a work-study scheme for sending students to Soviet Russia; about the same time they formed a Marxist study group; in September some of them set up a Communist cell; and about the end of the year a socialist youth corps was established under Mao's direction. During this same period Li Ta-chao established a Communist cell in Peking, and similar groups were formed in other major cities of China, as well as among Chinese students in Tokyo and in Paris. Meanwhile, numbers of young Chinese were leaving for Russia, to begin periods of study and indoctrination.

In October 1920 the warlord Ch'en Chiung-ming—then a supporter of Sun Yat-sen—had occupied Canton, the capital and principal center of Kwangtung Province. Sun Yat-sen had returned there in November, hoping to use Canton as the base from which to launch a

northern expedition to unify China. He designated Ch'en Chiung-
ming governor of Kwangtung, and in December they invited Ch'en
Tu-hsiu to come to Canton to take charge of educational affairs. Ch'en
Tu-hsiu accepted, and this separated him from the rest of his cell and
from Shanghai—the center from which the building of the party had
been directed. In May 1921, according to a probably reliable account,
Ch'en Tu-hsiu and Li Ta-chao both came to Shanghai for a meeting
at which a "central Chinese Communist party" was established.[41] A
party center was clearly needed, and Shanghai was the logical location
in which to maintain it. However, the formal establishment of the
Chinese Communist party is generally considered to have been accomplished at a meeting which was convened in Shanghai sometime in
July. That meeting was attended by twelve representatives of seven
cells, as well as by Gregory Voitinsky and Henricus Sneevliet, alias
Maring, two of the three original Comintern representatives. The date
of July 1, 1921, was subsequently chosen as the anniversary of the
founding of the Chinese Communist party, and the meeting held sometime during that month has since been referred to as the First Party
Congress.

The twelve Chinese and two representatives of the Comintern first
gathered in the French Concession in a girls' school, then closed for
the summer holiday. However, the coming and going of so many men
aroused the suspicions of the police, who temporarily detained some
of the delegates for questioning. They therefore dispersed, and re-
gathered at a lake in nearby Chekiang Province—as though mere
friends on an outing—in order that they might carry on their deliberations undisturbed. The records of the meeting assertedly were later
lost, but it is believed that the delegates adopted a party constitution
and elected the first Central Committee of the Chinese Communist
party.

It seems improbable that many of those concerned saw this meeting of twelve men, representing a party of only fifty-seven members,
as a great historical watershed. Ch'en Tu-hsiu sent proposals, suggestions, and a member from a cell he had set up in Canton. Li Ta-chao
sent two men from his cell in Peking; one of them was Chang Kuo-t'ao,
who had studied at Peking University under Ch'en Tu-hsiu, and who
served as chairman of the meeting. But neither of the two principal
founders of the party came, and it was almost half a year before Ch'en
Tu-hsiu, who was elected to the top office of party secretary, gave up
his post in Canton and came to Shanghai to direct the affairs of the
party center.[42] It is also clear that Mao Tse-tung, who came as one of
the two delegates from Hunan, was as yet no commanding figure in
the party. Overshadowed in terms of education and experience by most

of the others, he was not among those elected to the first Central Committee, composed of three regular members and three alternates. The party held another congress the following year, but Mao was evidently not one of the participants.

Indeed, during the first two years after the founding of the party, Mao Tse-tung evidently held no post higher than that of secretary of its Hunan branch. His sphere of work, however, was not narrowly confined. His central task soon became that of labor organizer, and some of this work took him into the coalfields of the Anyüan Mining Company, in the neighboring province of Kiangsi. His collaborators in this work included his own two brothers, Mao Tse-t'an and Mao Tse-min, and two party workers who had participated in the work-study programs he had helped promote: Li Li-san from France, and Liu Shao-ch'i from Soviet Russia. This work in Kiangsi was to pay off for Mao Tse-tung in later years, but his activities in Hunan itself got him into trouble with its military governor. In April 1923, disturbed by the growing labor movement in his domain, the governor issued an order for Mao's arrest. Mao Tse-tung got out in good time and went to Shanghai, where he got in touch with the party center. He had come at an interesting time, for the Communist party was about to enter into a marriage of convenience with the Kuomintang of Sun Yat-sen.

2

United Front and Civil War

IN THE EARLY 1920S, Soviet Russia was a defeated country with the longest border to protect of any in the world. It had many neighbors, but no real friends, unless a regime which had been set up in Outer Mongolia—with the support of Soviet troops—should be counted an exception.[1] Because the most extended of the borders were those with China, Russia had a strong national interest in the establishment of satisfactory relations with Peking.

While it was the task of Moscow's diplomatic representatives to establish relations with the government in Peking, it was the function of the agents of the Comintern to promote a revolution which might bring about the overthrow of that government. It must have been apparent to them, in the latter part of 1921, that they could not soon achieve that purpose by depending solely on the infant and miniscule Communist party of China. This led the Comintern to take an interest also in the Kuomintang of Sun Yat-sen. Under one name or another, the Kuomintang had already been in existence—as a revolutionary organization to which modern nationalist elements had been drawn —for a quarter of a century. In addition, it had a territorial base in south China, where Sun Yat-sen had military supporters.

The agents of the Comintern may or may not have had an accurate appreciation of Sun Yat-sen's own shortcomings as a leader, but it is clear that they were aware of some of the principal reasons why success had so long eluded him. The Kuomintang was an amorphous body rather than an effectively functioning organization, and Sun Yat-sen, without a military force of his own, depended on alliances with military leaders whose first allegiance usually was to themselves. During a visit to Sun Yat-sen in south China, late in 1921, the Comintern representative, Maring, had proposed that the Kuomintang be reorganized, that a military academy be established at which a reliable corps of officers might be trained, and that the Kuomintang and the Chinese Communist party cooperate.[2]

At this point Sun Yat-sen had left his base at Canton. He was engaged in preparations for a military expedition against the warlords in power in central China and was not looking for advice. However, he had no sooner launched his campaign than the Kwangtung militarist, Ch'en Chiung-ming, with whom he had been allied, turned against him and occupied the city of Canton. Sun Yat-sen hurried back there but was unable to reassert his authority. Warned that he was in danger, Sun sent off a telegram to a young officer in whom he had learned to put confidence. He asked the officer to come quickly and then took refuge on a gunboat in the Pearl River. The young officer was Chiang Kai-shek, then at his family home in Chekiang, near Shanghai, observing the rituals imposed by filial piety in connection with the first anniversary of his mother's death. Chiang had remained true to the revolutionary resolve which had led him to cut off his queue, go to Japan for military training, and join Sun Yat-sen's *T'ung-meng hui;* but he had never liked serving in the south under Ch'en Chiung-ming.[3]

Chiang Kai-shek hurried to Canton, joined Sun Yat-sen on the gunboat, and stayed with him until they were able to get passage from Canton to Hong Kong aboard a British steamer. This demonstration of loyalty, and the closer acquaintance which came from spending several weeks together aboard a small craft, cemented their relationship and paved the way for Chiang's own subsequent rise to power. From Hong Kong the two men proceeded to Shanghai, and somewhat later in the year Sun Yat-sen sent Chiang Kai-shek back south to Fukien—the coastal province adjoining Kwangtung—to become the chief of staff of forces which had remained loyal to his cause. These forces were to succeed in reoccupying Canton early in 1923.[4]

When Sun Yat-sen got to Shanghai in August 1922, he was ready to take Maring's advice about reorganizing the Kuomintang and prepared to admit Chinese Communists into his own party, provided they would obey its discipline. The Communists, at their Second Party Congress held in Shanghai the previous month, had voted to join the Comintern. At Maring's urging, they had also agreed in principle to allying their party with the Kuomintang but had shelved the suggestion that they should join and work within it. When this became a live question, Maring found that Ch'en Tu-hsiu—the party secretary, and Chang Kuo-t'ao—the head of its Organization Bureau, were both opposed, and that their position had the support of a majority of the members of the Central Committee. But because the party had joined the Comintern, Maring was able to invoke its authority and make his will prevail.[5]

In August of 1922, Soviet diplomat Adolph A. Joffe—the third in a series of Russian government envoys—arrived in Peking. Like his predecessors, he was charged with the settlement of outstanding questions and the establishment of diplomatic relations between China and the Soviet Union. Joffe was an experienced negotiator, but he did not even succeed in getting negotiations started. In this situation, Russian national interests and the concerns of the Comintern appeared to converge. Both seemed to call for the overthrow of the Peking regime and its replacement by a government which might be expected to be friendly to the Soviet Union. Early in 1923, Joffe went to Shanghai, met with Sun Yat-sen, and laid the foundations for a program under which the Soviet Union was to assist the Kuomintang in unifying China.[6]

On January 26, 1923, the two men issued a joint statement in which Joffe purportedly agreed with Sun Yat-sen's contention that conditions in China were not ripe for the establishment of communism or the Soviet system; held that China's most important and urgent problems were national unification and the attainment of full independence; and promised that China could count on Soviet support. It was, of course, understood that this support was to go to the Kuomintang, and the details were subsequently worked out between Joffe and a trusted supporter of Sun Yat-sen—a San Francisco-born Chinese named Liao Chung-k'ai. Meanwhile Sun Yat-sen went off to reestablish his government in Canton, which was once again in friendly hands, and in April Chiang Kai-shek became the chief of staff in Sun Yat-sen's headquarters.[7]

Such, then, was the general situation in the spring of 1923, when Mao Tse-tung fled from Hunan to escape arrest and journeyed to Canton to attend his party's third congress. The Sun-Joffe agreements meant that the Kuomintang was to lead the struggle for national unification, and Maring insisted that the Chinese Communist party must accept subordination to the Kuomintang. Ch'en Tu-hsiu, despite his reservations, supported Maring's position. But Chang Kuo-t'ao and Li Li-san fought a bitter rearguard action, losing one issue by a single vote. According to Chang Kuo-t'ao, Mao Tse-tung supported him at first but then changed sides. Perhaps as a reward for this switch, Mao Tse-tung, for the first time, was elected a member of the Central Committee and of its Political Bureau.[8]

Ch'en Tu-hsiu had supported the basic position—that the Communist party must be subordinate to the Kuomintang—by advancing the thesis that the Chinese revolution would have to pass through two stages: the first, that of a bourgeois democratic revolution, during which the warlords were to be defeated and China reunified; the second, a Communist stage in which "the bourgeois republic could be overthrown and replaced by the dictatorship of the proletariat." The subsequently debated issue, which Chang Kuo-t'ao lost by one vote, is said to have been whether trade unions should be brought under the joint control of the two parties—as the majority decided, or kept out of the control of either party—as allegedly advocated by Chang Kuo-t'ao.[9]

Adopting and adhering to the rule that neither party should try to control the labor unions, and extending it to peasant associations as well, might have provided the key for maintaining Kuomintang-Communist collaboration until the reunification of China had been achieved. Joint control in principle was bound to mean Communist control in practice. This was true, first of all, because the Communist party, as the party of the proletariat, had a genuine interest in building and controlling unions, whereas most non-Communist members of the Kuomintang did not. It was also true because this was a field in which the Kuomintang could not compete on equal terms with the Communist party. The Kuomintang, like the Communist party, could appeal to the workers and the peasants on the basis of patriotism and the prospect of relief from the rapacities of warlord rule. It could also promise to improve the lot of the workers and peasants through social legislation and agrarian reform. But this was mild stuff compared with what the Communists were bound to promise—power to the worker and seizure of land for distribution among the peasants. The Communists and the Kuomintang could, in other words, maintain their collaboration so long as they confined themselves to the national revolution; once the Communists began unleashing the social revolution, the two would come to the parting of the ways.

Early in the autumn of 1923, a large body of Soviet advisors, headed by Michael Borodin, arrived at Canton. With his help the Kuomintang was rebuilt after the pattern of the Soviet Communist party. This meant that decision-making authority was highly concentrated at the top, and operational responsibility was dispersed among a set of bureaus, each organized to perform a particular set of related functions. This was a structure which had been tested under revolutionary conditions similar to those which faced the Kuomintang. It was also the one with which the Soviet advisors and the Chinese Communist members of the Kuomintang could work most readily. Because the Kuomintang now was so nearly like their own parties, there was no need for the Soviet advisors and Chinese Communists to lose time in familiarizing themselves with intricacies of structure and modes of operation. In January of 1924, the first Kuomintang Congress was held. At this congress three Communists were among the twenty-four members elected to the party's new Central Executive Committee, and six Communists were among the sixteen persons elected as reserve members. Li Ta-chao was one of the three Communists elected to full membership, and Mao Tse-tung was one of the six who became reserve members.[10]

In undertaking the reunification of China, the first task facing the
reorganized Kuomintang and its Soviet advisors was the creation of a
modern army. Two important aspects of this task were the building
of a new corps of officers and the training of the troops. Soviet advisors
helped with both, and the Soviet Union also shipped munitions to
Canton for the arming of the forces. In order to provide the needed
inflow of junior officers, a military academy was established at Whampoa, in the outskirts of Canton. Chiang Kai-shek became its com-
mandant, with a Soviet General Vassili Bluecher, alias Galen, as his
chief of staff; Liao Chung-k'ai, who had worked out the details of Sun
Yat-sen's agreement with Joffe, took charge of the party affairs at the
academy; and Chou En-lai became deputy head of its political department.

Chiang Kai-shek supervised the training of three classes—totaling
two thousand men—which were admitted between May 1924, and
January 1925. He also was in direct command when many of the cadets
first went into action in 1924. In that year it became necessary to use
the cadets in suppressing a local militia corps, which was maintained
by the merchants of Canton, and to throw back a final offensive
launched by Sun Yat-sen's former ally, the Kwangtung militarist Ch'en
Chiung-ming. In China, the teacher-student relationship served in theory, and to a substantial extent in practice, to create a lifetime bond
of mutual loyalty. Chiang Kai-shek was to be the chief beneficiary of
the personal relationships formed or strengthened at Whampoa. But
he was not the only one to profit from those relationships: At least
three of the political instructors who served there under Chou En-lai—
all three fellow-Communists who had been with him in France under
the work-study program—would serve under him in later years as vice
premiers: Ch'en Yi, Li Fu-ch'un, and Nieh Jung-chen.[11]

In 1923 Mao Tse-tung succeeded Chang Kuo-t'ao as head of the
Organization Department of the Chinese Communist party. During
most of 1924 Mao worked in Shanghai, both for his own party center
and in the executive bureau of the Kuomintang. This period in Shanghai, during which he was supposed to coordinate the activities of the
two parties, was hardly a happy one for Mao Tse-tung. Most of the
other leaders of the two parties were the graduates of well-known Chinese or foreign universities; his schooling had consisted of primary
school and five years at a provincial teacher-training institute. Many
of them had held responsible positions; his only experience had been
as a library clerk in Peking, as a laundryman in Shanghai, and as principal of a grade school in Changsha. He had not been elected a member of the Central Committee at the First Party Congress; presumably
disappointed, he had not attended the congress which had been held

the following year. Superficially, his position had been greatly improved through his election as member of the Central Committee of his own party, at its third congress in 1923, and as an alternate member of the comparable committee of the Kuomintang in January 1924; in actuality, his situation remained one from which he could derive scant satisfaction.

The two principal Kuomintang members of the bureau in which Mao Tse-tung worked were Wang Ching-wei and Hu Han-min. They had joined Sun Yat-sen's *T'ung-meng-hui* shortly after he had founded it in Japan, where they were students at Tokyo Law University. Thereafter, they had participated in one after another of Sun Yat-sen's attempts to overthrow the Manchus. Wang Ching-wei had been imprisoned in 1910 for attempting to assassinate the prince regent; with the fall of the Manchus, he had been released, a national hero. During the subsequent republican period, both men had been among Sun Yat-sen's closest associates. Mao Tse-tung could not work on a basis of equality with such men, and this placed him in an invidious position when it came to dealing with his fellow Communists, in his coordinating role. Li Li-san, who had been Mao Tse-tung's fellow student in Changsha—where they had never got along—and who had supported Chang Kuo-t'ao in his opposition to the subordination of the Communist party and its interests to the Kuomintang, mockingly referred to Mao as "Hu Han-min's secretary." [12] This shaft was double-barbed: Hu Han-min was a leader of the right wing of his party, and the phrase suggested both a criticism of Mao Tse-tung for entering too enthusiastically into cooperation with the Kuomintang and sardonic pleasure over Mao's position of *de facto* subordination.

Before the year 1924 had ended, Mao Tse-tung had evidently had about as much of this as he could take. Although there was to be a Fourth Party Congress in Shanghai in January, he pleaded illness, and returned to Hunan "to take a rest." [13] By leaving Shanghai at this time, Mao Tse-tung missed not only the 1925 party congress but also an event which came to be known as the May Thirtieth Incident. That day, some police of the Shanghai International Settlement, under the command of a British officer, fired on some "strikers" who were engaged in a demonstration and killed twelve of them. This event created a great upwelling of antiforeign feeling, and like the events of May 4, 1919, in Peking, it led to a protest movement of nationwide proportions. In the course of this movement there were numerous demonstrations against foreign interests, a widespread boycott of British goods, and a strike which paralyzed the port of Hong Kong. [14]

Borodin is supposed to have remarked: "We did not make May 30. It was made for us." This may have been true, insofar as the Kuomintang's Russian advisors were concerned, but the "strikers" involved in the May Thirtieth Incident can hardly have been trade unionists seeking higher wages or improved working conditions—all twelve of those killed were students. Moreover, the Chinese Communists, who dominated the Kuomintang's trade union activities, proved to be all set to exploit the incident. On the evening of May 30 there was a big meeting of labor unionists and students, as the prelude to a general strike which was to be called the next day. At this meeting, Li Li-san proposed that the participants, to coordinate their strike activities, should form a Shanghai General Labor Union. The proposal to set up this new body was accepted, and Li Li-san was elected its president. This helped give him—and such Communist colleagues as Liu Shao-ch'i and Ch'ü Ch'iu-pai—control of powerful unions in Shanghai and positions of increased prestige within the Chinese Communist party. The May Thirtieth Movement also gave the party itself an enormous boost: When the movement began, the party had about one thousand members; six months later it had approximately ten thousand members.[15]

The period of rest, for which Mao Tse-tung allegedly had returned to Hunan, did not prevent him from organizing peasant associations there. Once again his activities came to the attention of the governor, and once again he was forced to flee from his native province. This time, evidently unwilling to return to the party center in Shanghai, he made his way to Canton. In Canton, he served for some time as *de facto* head of the propaganda department of the Kuomintang, and as the director of its Peasant Movement Training Institute. Trainees of this institute, after completing their courses of study, were assigned to underground work in rural areas. There they organized peasant associations in anticipation of the forthcoming Northern Expedition, the military campaign through which China was to be reunified under the control of the Kuomintang. When the National Revolutionary Army reached the areas in which the party cadres worked, they were to mobilize the peasants to serve the army in supporting roles such as spies, guides, and porters.[16]

In 1924, the area under the control of the Kuomintang, centered in Kwangtung, had been expanded through an alliance with military leaders in the neighboring province of Kwangsi. Late that year Sun Yat-sen received an invitation, from the principal military leaders in north China, to visit Peking in order to discuss national problems, and he accepted the invitation in the evident hope of bringing about a peaceful unification of the country. However, Sun Yat-sen reached Peking sick with a cancer which proved inoperable, and on March 12, 1925, he died.

The fatal illness of Sun Yat-sen marked the beginning of a power struggle in which Hu Han-min, of the right wing of the Kuomintang, and Wang Ching-wei and Liao Chung-k'ai of its left wing, contended for the leadership of the party and its government. On August 20, 1925, Liao Chung-k'ai was assassinated; the finger of suspicion pointed at a close relative of Hu Han-min, and Hu Han-min resigned his posts and took a trip abroad. With his two colleagues removed from the running, Wang Ching-wei and the left wing found their power in the ascendant.[17] Moreover, the power of the left was confirmed, in January of 1926, when the Kuomintang held its Second Party Congress. Of the thirty-six members elected to the Central Executive Committee of the Kuomintang at this party congress, twenty were of the left wing; and of these twenty, seven were members of Chinese Communist party.[18]

Meanwhile, a complicated civil war had raged in north China. When it had died down, China remained divided in five parts, each under a different power group. This created conditions favorable to the early launching of the Northern Expedition.[19] However, by this time the interest of the Soviet Union in the Kuomintang had become diluted, and Soviet willingness to back an early Kuomintang effort to unify China was evaporating. In 1923, Sun Yat-sen's regime was willing to ally itself with Lenin's Russia, although the government in Peking was unwilling even to enter into diplomatic relations with it. By the latter part of 1925 both Sun Yat-sen and Lenin were dead, and the whole picture in north China—where Russian interests were centered —had been transformed.

On May 31, 1924, the Soviet Union had obtained from the Peking government agreements covering both the establishment of diplomatic relations and Soviet participation in the management of the Chinese Eastern Railway. The Russians had financed this railway, and it had been under their administration until the Chinese—taking advantage of Russian weakness during the preceding period of civil war—had taken it over. The new agreement was especially important to the Soviet Union for strategic reasons. The Chinese Eastern was a part of the Trans-Siberian Railway and provided the direct link between Manchuli and the port of Vladivostok.

The Chinese Eastern Railway crossed the Manchurian domain of the warlord Chang Tso-lin, and in dealing with him, too, Soviet diplomacy had been successful. He had refused to recognize the validity of the agreement reached in Peking, but on September 24 the Soviet Union had been able to get from him a treaty granting rights similar to those which had been accorded by the government in Peking.[20]

The northwestern provinces of China were under the control of Feng Yü-hsiang, whose geographic position had made him especially amenable to the approaches of Soviet representatives. His army of

275,000 was blocked off from access to the industrial areas to the east, with their arsenals, and from the seaports through which munitions might be imported. However, the territory he controlled was accessible to the USSR, and in April of 1925, Feng Yü-hsiang had accepted Russian instructors and Soviet military aid.[21]

In March 1926, Chiang Kai-shek was champing at the bit, wanting to begin the Northern Expedition to which Borodin had not yet consented. It may well be that Borodin believed the Kuomintang armies to be insufficiently prepared, but by then Chiang Kai-shek's suspicions of Soviet intentions had undoubtedly been aroused. That month he remarked to Wang Ching-wei: "The actual power of controlling the revolution must not fall into the hands of outsiders." [22] The Russians, with their interests in north China secured through agreements negotiated with the main power centers there, had evidently become loath to risk those interests by backing a military effort which was bound to upset the applecart. Stalin may have had this in mind, during the latter part of March, when he observed: "The Canton government should in the present period decisively reject the thought of military expeditions of an offensive character, and, in general, any such proceedings as may encourage the imperialists to embark on military action." [23]

When Chiang Kai-shek remarked that the power of controlling the revolution must not be allowed to fall into the hands of outsiders, he undoubtedly was referring to his Soviet advisors. But he may also have been thinking of the Chinese Communists, with whom Wang Ching-wei was so closely connected. Chiang Kai-shek undoubtedly knew that the Communist party had been growing mightily in size and surmised that its leaders intended to convert the Kuomintang into their own instrument.

On March 20, 1926, Chiang Kai-shek, facing several problems, staged a coup which was evidently designed to solve them all. Without consulting Wang Ching-wei, and to the accompaniment of vaguely-based allegations of a plot directed against his own position, he declared martial law, arrested a number of Chinese Communists, and put his Russian advisors under house arrest.[24] This public flouting of the authority of Wang Ching-wei had the effect of destroying that leader's position. Shortly afterwards, he resigned and departed on a trip to France, leaving Chiang Kai-shek as the top leader of the Kuomintang. With hostages under his control, Chiang Kai-shek was now in a position to demand, from Borodin and the Chinese Communists, the concessions which he wanted.

Borodin was up north in Urga conferring with Feng Yü-hsiang, when Chiang Kai-shek staged this coup, and he did not get back to

Canton until the end of April. Once there, he threatened to cut off Soviet aid if Chiang Kai-shek did not restore the *status quo ante*. Chiang Kai-shek played his own cards skillfully, agreeing to reinstate all the Soviet advisors except a few whom he particularly disliked, and carrying out a symbolic offensive against the right wing of the Kuomintang. In return, he got what he wanted. It was agreed that the number of Communists who could belong to the leading organs of the Kuomintang would be limited to one-third of the total number, and arranged that those Communists heading such important departments as organization, propaganda, and peasant affairs should be replaced by non-Communists. Moreover, the Russians withdrew their objections to Chiang Kai-shek's military plans. On July 9, 1926, Chiang Kai-shek assumed the position of supreme commander, or generalissimo, and launched the Northern Expedition.[25]

Mao Tse-tung's feelings about the March 20 coup and its consequences may have been mixed. As a Chinese nationalist with a strong dislike for foreign domination and a commitment to the reunification of his country, he undoubtedly was glad that Stalin had been forced to withdraw his objections to the Northern Expedition.[26] As a xenophobe, he must have enjoyed seeing a fellow Chinese get the best of Borodin, whom Mao had cursed behind his back as a "foreign devil." [27] As a Chinese Communist, he undoubtedly regretted the unfavorable consequences of the coup for his own party, even though his regret may well have been tempered by a feeling that he had himself been ill-used by the party's leaders. In the aftermath of the coup, he was relieved of his post as the Kuomintang's acting director of propaganda, though not of his position under its peasant department. With the Northern Expedition in the offing, and with a keen interest in the military uses to which the peasant movement might be put, Mao continued his work with the Kuomintang peasant department even during the days which immediately followed the coup.[28] And as one who had been fascinated by the plots and stratagems which fill the pages of the *Romance of the Three Kingdoms,* he must have admired the strategy which Chiang Kai-shek had devised and executed with such skill—on the surface so simple, but so well designed to achieve multiple aims.

The Northern Expedition, under the overall direction of Chiang Kai-shek, began with the conquest of Hunan by forces under the field command of T'ang Sheng-chih, a Hunanese militarist who had transferred his allegiance to the Kuomintang earlier in the year. He had under his immediate command the Eighth Army, composed of six divisions of Hunanese troops. In addition he had overall direction of the Seventh Army, composed of Kwangsi troops commanded by Li Tsung-jen, and of two divisions drawn from the Fourth Army com-

mand of the Kwangtung general Li Chi-shen. These two divisions were
the 10th, under Ch'en Ming-shu, later to be expanded to form the
Eleventh Army, and the 12th, under Chang Fa-k'uei, also subsequently
expanded and given the name of the Fourth Army from which it had
been drawn. The Kwangtung divisions spearheaded the drive, and by
the beginning of August 1926, all Hunan was in Nationalist hands.[29]

In the middle of August these forces resumed their northward
drive, invading the centrally situated province of Hupeh, and on October 10 they completed the occupation of the Wuhan tri-city complex
of Hankow, Hanyang, and Wuchang. T'ang Sheng-chih's Eighth Army
was then left to garrison Hunan and Hupeh, while the other forces
moved southeastward to assist Kuomintang armies which had begun an
attack, the previous month, on the adjoining province of Kiangsi.
Kiangsi was part of the domain of the warlord Sun Ch'uan-fang, who
controlled five provinces of east central China and who had as his ally
Chang Tsung-ch'ang, the "dog-meat general" of Shantung. By early
November, Chiang Kai-shek's armies had inflicted a hundred thousand
casualties on Sun Ch'uan-fang's forces, which fell back in the direction
of Nanking and Shanghai.[30]

Chiang Kai-shek had been uneasy about leaving T'ang Sheng-chih,
a recent and presumably opportunist convert to the Kuomintang cause,
as garrison commander for Hunan and Hupeh. On October 22, in the
hope of preventing power there from slipping from his own hands,
Chiang had suggested that the central headquarters of the Kuomintang
should be transferred from Canton to Wuhan. Then in November,
after conquering Kiangsi and making its capital of Nanchang his headquarters, he wanted the principal organs of both the party and the
government transferred there, so that he might keep political as well
as military affairs under his direct supervision. The Communists initially resisted the move from Canton, but in November and December
the principal conservative leaders of the Kuomintang left Canton for
Nanchang. Chinese Communists and other left wing members of the
Kuomintang now saw fit to follow Chiang Kai-shek's original suggestion and moved to Wuhan. A government dominated by left wing elements, with Borodin the power behind the throne, was formally established there on January 1, 1927. Chiang Kai-shek now found himself
unable to entice the members of his Central Executive Committee to
meet in Nanchang, and he encountered a cool reception in Wuhan
when he visited there later in the month. Thereafter, his heart hardened, he declared that the Communists must be expelled from the
Kuomintang, and he began to take steps against them in areas under
his control.[31]

Although Mao Tse-tung had earlier been made the head of the
Peasant Department of the Communist party, he may have stayed in

Canton with the Peasant Movement Training Institute of the Kuomintang until October 5, 1926; only then did the institute's sixth session, which was held under his supervision, come to an end. Not long afterward he was back in his native province, and at the beginning of 1927 he spent a little over a month investigating the peasant movement in five counties of central Hunan. According to the report which Mao prepared at the conclusion of his investigation, the movement was being conducted under the leadership of the poor peasants, and particularly the poorest ones, and was releasing human energies on a scale sufficient to carry the revolution to early victory.[32] He wrote:

In a very short time, several hundred million peasants in China's central, southern, and northern provinces will rise like a tornado or tempest—a force so extraordinarily swift and violent that no power, however great, will be able to suppress it. They will break through all the trammels that now bind them and push forward along the road to liberation. They will send all imperialists, warlords, corrupt officials, local bullies, and evil gentry to their graves. All revolutionary parties and all revolutionary comrades will stand before them to be tested, to be accepted or rejected by them. . . . With the fall of the authority of the landlords, the peasant association becomes the sole organ of authority. . . . Whatever nonsense the people from the association talk in the meetings is considered sacred. . . . Supreme in authority, the peasant association allows the landlord no say and sweeps away his prestige. . . . At the slightest provocation they make arrests, crown the arrested with tall paper hats, and parade them through the villages, saying, "You dirty landlords, now you know who we are!" Doing whatever they like and turning everything upside down, they have created a kind of terror in the countryside. . . . A revolution is an insurrection, an act of violence by which one class overthrows another. . . . The rural areas need a mighty revolutionary upsurge, for it alone can rouse the people in their millions to become a powerful force.[33]

"To give credit where due," Mao continued, "if we allot ten points to the accomplishment of the democratic revolution, then the achievements of the urban dwellers and the military rate only three points, while the remaining seven points should go to the peasants in their rural revolution." [34] Whether or not this was a fair evaluation, it was not realistic to expect the armies of Chiang Kai-shek to maintain the momentum of the Northern Expedition with the country behind them in turmoil, properties being seized, and landlords killed, for most of the officers of the National Revolutionary Army came either from the landlord class or from bourgeois urban backgrounds. The peasant movement also endangered the Wuhan regime, for its immediate security depended on the loyalty of T'ang Sheng-chih's Hunanese army, and Hunan was probably the province in which the storm of the peasant movement raged most fiercely. Finally, the peasant movement threatened to split the Communist Party; Ch'en Tu-hsiu was trying to obey the Comintern, which had ordered the Communists to stay in the Kuomintang, whereas Mao Tse-tung was promoting a course which would help lead to their expulsion from it.[35]

In the early months of 1926, Borodin had opposed the launching of the northern expedition for reasons which probably included a reluctance to risk Russian national interests in north China and Manchuria. That this concern had been justified became clear during the early months of 1927. In January the Manchurian warlord Chang Tso-lin arrested the Soviet manager and several directors of the Chinese Eastern Railway. The Soviet Union secured their release by threatening to take military action against Chang Tso-lin, but this did not end his attacks on Russian interests. Such attacks extended to the Peking area, which now was under his control, and even to the lower Yangtze Valley. His henchman Chang Tsung-ch'ang, the "dog-meat general," was operating there in support of the east China warlord Sun Ch'uan-fang. In February Chang Tsung-ch'ang detained a Soviet ship bound for Hankow, took off Borodin's wife and several Soviet couriers, and sent them off to his headquarters in Shantung.[36]

In this situation, the concern for the early success of the Northern Expedition which Borodin presumably felt, as advisor to the Kuomintang, undoubtedly was reinforced by national considerations and personal motives. At any rate, Borodin wanted Chiang Kai-shek to drive immediately toward Peking, and Borodin mobilized opposition to Chiang when he refused to bypass Shanghai.[37] Chiang Kai-shek probably did not dare to press northward while the powerful armies of warlord enemies remained on his eastern flank. But his refusal may well have been due also to distrust of the intentions of Borodin, the Chinese Communists, and their Kuomintang allies at Wuhan. The coup which Chiang Kai-shek had mounted at their expense on March 20, 1926, had served his immediate purposes admirably. But a coup provides a narrow and unsteady base, as compared to a consensus. A coup is, after all, a blow, and those who are struck may be expected to strike back when the opportunity comes for them to recoup.

It accordingly must have come as no surprise to Chiang Kai-shek when the Central Executive Committee of the Kuomintang, meeting in Wuhan in mid-March, carried out a reorganization which was intended to restore the hierarchy as it had existed before his coup of the year before. In an attempt to subordinate him to the authority of the party, the Committee relieved him of his position as chairman of its standing committee and named Wang Ching-wei, still an exile in France, to head both the party and the government.[38]

Shortly afterward the Wuhan regime became party to a plot which must have widened the existing breach. On March 1, Chiang Kai-shek had appointed, as chairman of the political department of his field headquarters, a brilliant and versatile Chinese writer and intellectual named Kuo Mo-jo. Kuo Mo-jo accepted the appointment only after a secret exchange of telegrams with the authorities in Wuhan, waited until Chiang Kai-shek was absent, and then sent the entire staff of the political department to Wuhan. On March 30, adding insult to injury, he wrote for publication a vitriolic essay in which he called Chiang Kai-shek a reactionary counterrevolutionary and demanded that he be executed.[39]

One of the Communists arrested in the course of Chiang Kai-shek's coup of March 20, 1926, had been Chou En-lai, then deputy director of the political department of the Whampoa Military Academy. He was not detained long, and after his release he worked for compromise measures intended to preserve the Kuomintang-Communist alliance. With the launching of the Northern Expedition, Chou En-lai had gone to Shanghai to engage in underground work against the warlord Sun Ch'uan-fang. This work, conducted among labor unions and other groups, culminated in a general strike and worker uprising. This movement came in two waves, the first during the second half of February 1927, when Chiang Kai-shek's troops first got within striking distance of Shanghai, and the second one month later, after many of the workers had obtained arms. This second time they were victorious, and the troops of Chiang Kai-shek were able on March 22 to occupy Shanghai with very little fighting.[40] The occupation of Nanking two days later by Chiang's Sixth Army was marred by troop attacks on foreigners and their properties, for which its Communist political commissars subsequently were blamed. But the whole of the lower Yangtze Valley now was in Chiang's hands.[41]

Shanghai was the port through which about half the foreign trade of China flowed, a great commercial and industrial metropolis, and the principal banking center of China. In the past, Chiang had been dependent on the flow of financial assistance from the Soviet Union, with Borodin in a position to turn off the spigot. Shanghai was now available as an alternative source of support, and Chiang knew how to tap it. It had been his home base since 1911, when he had served under Ch'en Ch'i-mei. Ch'en was a Kuomintang general who had ruled this area, off and on, until he had been assassinated on the orders of Yüan Shih-k'ai. Through Ch'en Ch'i-mei, Chiang had become acquainted with an older generation of party leaders who had provided Sun Yat-sen with financial support—men who now still wanted political change, but not social revolution. After the death of Ch'en Ch'i-mei, Chiang Kai-shek had been one of a group which had founded and managed a commodity exchange in Shanghai, the profits of which had gone to Sun's cause. During this latter period, too, Chiang Kai-shek had formed close connections with Tu Yüeh-sheng, leader of the Green Gang of Shanghai's underworld, but also a prominent banker and industrialist.[42]

If Chiang Kai-shek were to break with the left, he would need loans to tide him over until he could set up a government of his own with mechanisms for tax collection. He and his associates had the contacts through which they could and did obtain the needed loans from the financiers of Shanghai.[43] In accepting those loans Chiang Kai-shek assumed at least an implied obligation to exert a restraining influence on the left, for the moneyed interests of Shanghai, like conservatives elsewhere in the country, had become alarmed by the strikes, political demonstrations, and antiforeign riots which the organizers of the Communist party were promoting in the cities of east and central China.

On April 1, Wang Ching-wei arrived back in China from the year-long exile which Chiang Kai-shek had forced upon him. He debarked in Shanghai and remained there for a few days, during which he saw Chiang Kai-shek and conferred with Ch'en Tu-hsiu. On April 5, Wang Ching-wei and Ch'en Tu-hsiu issued a joint statement expressing the intention of maintaining collaboration between the Kuomintang and the Communist party. Shortly afterward Wang left for Wuhan to resume charge of the party and the government.[44]

By the time Wang Ching-wei left for Wuhan, it must have been apparent to the warlord Chang Tso-lin that no love was lost between Chiang Kai-shek, in Shanghai, and Borodin, the Chinese Communists, and the left wing of the Kuomintang, in Wuhan. The Kuomintang organization in Peking had worked against Chang Tso-lin for two years and had been under Communist control for over a year. When Chang Tso-lin's forces had occupied Peking in December of 1926, the Communist Li Ta-chao and his comrades had simply moved into the compound of the Soviet embassy and continued to run the Kuomintang from there. On April 6, having perhaps drawn encouragement from the widening split between Chiang Kai-shek and the people in Wuhan, Chang Tso-lin carried out a raid on the Soviet embassy—during which his gendarmes and police seized several truckloads of documents in Russian and Chinese—and arrested Li Ta-chao and his associates. Many friends and sympathizers petitioned for Li Ta-chao's release, but on April 28, Chang Tso-lin had him and nineteen of his comrades hung.[45]

Meanwhile, Chiang Kai-shek struck a similar blow at the far more potent Communist apparatus in Shanghai. He assigned the tasks of disarming the workers and purging the Communists to Pai Ch'ung-hsi, the Nationalist commander from Kwangsi who had captured Shanghai, and to Tu Yüeh-sheng, the head of the Green Gang, to whom he gave the temporary rank of major general. During this purge Chou En-lai, who had helped direct the worker uprising against Sun Ch'uan-fang, managed to get away, but many other Communists and leftists were less fortunate. An undetermined number of them—the estimates ranged from some hundreds to upwards of five thousand—were either killed outright or arrested and later executed.[46]

On April 18, 1927, Chiang Kai-shek established his own national government at Nanking, which was to remain the capital city throughout the following ten years. Chiang's new government was headed by a five-man standing committee, which included Hu Han-min and other leaders who had opposed the alliance with the Communists, and it continued Chiang's purge of the Communists in all areas under its control.[47] Those areas did not, of course, include the provinces of Hunan and Hupeh. They also did not include the neighboring province of Kiangsi. Kiangsi was garrisoned by an army commanded by Chu P'ei-te who, as a close friend of Wang Ching-wei, was now unwilling to take his orders from Chiang Kai-shek.[48]

The Chinese Communists convened their Fifth Party Congress at Wuhan on April 27, 1927, in the wake of the disaster they had just suffered at Shanghai. Such disasters are bound to create discontent with the leadership under which they occur. The policy of working as a bloc within the Kuomintang had made the purge possible, and Ch'en Tu-hsiu was blamed for the policy—although he had accepted it with reluctance and followed it at the insistence of the Comintern.

There was also much dissension at the congress over the issue of imposing restraints on the peasant movement, and on this issue Mao Tse-tung had the support only of Ch'ü Ch'iu-pai, Liu Shao-ch'i, and a few others in the leadership. Wang Ching-wei had expressed anxiety about regulations which Mao Tse-tung had wished to see adopted. Mao had been advocating the death penalty or life imprisonment for those who engaged in counterrevolutionary activities, and he had argued that all landlords and peasant proprietors who owned as much as five acres were uniformly counterrevolutionaries. Ch'en Tu-hsiu had in March refused to permit Mao Tse-tung's report on the peasant movement in Hunan to be published in a Communist party journal, and at this congress he deprived Mao of the right to vote. The congress decided that only very large holdings of reactionary landlords should be confiscated; it also decided that relationship to officers in the revolutionary army should be accepted as demonstrating that a landlord was not reactionary. As might be expected, Mao became discouraged and stopped attending the congress, offering the excuse that he had fallen ill.[49]

Wang Ching-wei attended the congress and may well have drawn encouragement from its decisions to place restraints on the peasant movement and not to confiscate the lands belonging to the relatives of officers in the revolutionary army. It seemed likely, at that point, that the differences between Wuhan and Nanking might be settled through armed conflict, and the armies which were loyal to the Wuhan regime held the key to its survival. Wang Ching-wei could, however, hardly have taken comfort from a speech made at the congress by a newly-arrived representative of the Comintern named M. N. Roy. In the presence of Wang Ching-wei and other luminaries of the Kuomintang, Roy declared that the Communist party was participating in their government "in order to use the state machinery for achieving hegemony." [50]

At about the time that the Fifth Party Congress began, military forces of the Wuhan regime under T'ang Sheng-chih and Chang Fa-k'uei began a drive to link up with the supposedly friendly armies of Feng Yü-hsiang, the "Christian general." His armies had recently occupied the northern part of the adjacent province of Honan. While its main forces were off on this expedition, Wuhan itself became endangered, and there were serious troubles between Communist-led organizations and Wuhan's garrison troops in the neighboring provinces of Hunan and Kiangsi. On May 18, a general in western Hupeh rose in revolt, at the instigation of Chiang Kai-shek, and advanced on Wuhan. He was stopped, when only twenty-five miles away, by a hastily assembled force under command of a Communist general named Yeh T'ing. On May 19, an "inspection brigade" of the General Labor Union in Changsha ransacked the home of one of the generals who was off on the Northern Expedition and arrested the general's father. Two days later the Changsha garrison retaliated by disarming the local workers and suppressing their organization. The Communists' Hunan Provincial Committee then mobilized the peasants for a march on Changsha, an attack which the garrison repulsed with great loss of life. During the immediately following weeks, the military authorities extended this counteroffensive, and the Communist-led peasant associations and labor unions were suppressed throughout the provinces of Hunan and Kiangsi. [51]

At the beginning of June, the Communists in Wuhan received a telegram from Stalin in which they were told, among other things, to stop depending on unreliable generals, to organize a revolutionary court to try reactionary officers, to raise new armies composed of twenty-thousand Communists and fifty thousand workers and peasants, and to draw a large number of working class and peasant leaders into the Central Executive Committee of the Kuomintang. The Communist leaders in Wuhan, seeing no way of implementing such instructions, did not propose to try, but the Comintern delegate Roy was more obedient. Perhaps he had been deceived by some polite words of agreement which Wang Ching-wei had uttered—in response to Roy's revealing speech at the party congress—and assumed that Wang Ching-wei would help him enforce the discipline of the Comintern. At any rate, Roy showed Wang Ching-wei a copy of the telegram from Stalin. In consequence, Wang and his colleagues learned, from the most authoritative of sources, that the Comintern intended to deprive them of the control of their own party.[52]

About this same time the Wuhan forces under T'ang Sheng-chih and Chang Fa-k'uei made a junction with those of Feng Yü-hsiang in northern Honan. Wang Ching-wei and some of his associates hurried there, hoping to enter into an alliance with the "Christian general." Feng Yü-hsiang was willing to negotiate and accepted the offer of the Wuhan government to turn over to him the southern part of Honan Province. But in the end, all that the "Christian general" offered in return was advice, and he gave that only after he had reached an agreement with Chiang Kai-shek. He recommended that Borodin should go home and that the members of the Kuomintang Central Executive Committee in Wuhan should either join the Nationalist government at Nanking or go abroad.[53]

Stalin, finally realizing that the situation was desperate, sent new instructions about the middle of July. The Chinese Communists still were not to withdraw from the Kuomintang, but they were to develop their own illegal fighting apparatus, withdraw from the Wuhan government, arm the workers and the peasants, prepare the workers for decisive action, and develop the agrarian revolution. On July 15, at about the same time that these instructions arrived, the Wuhan Nationalists expelled the Communists from the Kuomintang and the government; two days later the suppression of Communist, worker, and peasant organizations in Wuhan was underway. General Galen and some other Russian advisers remained, but Borodin and Roy left Wuhan for the USSR. Stalin sent Besso Lominadze to replace them, and some Chinese Communist leaders stayed on in Wuhan for awhile. But their existence became more precarious and some fled or went into hiding. All this opened the way for Wang Ching-wei and his associates to follow Feng Yü-hsiang's advice: to go abroad or join the Nanking government of Chiang Kai-shek. The Wuhan government did not come apart all at once, but by autumn it had ceased to exist and a "unified" national government was functioning in Nanking.[54] Meanwhile, the expulsion of the Communists from the Wuhan regime had opened the way for Mao Tse-tung to try to stir up, in his native province of Hunan, the peasant uprising which he had predicted would smash all trammels and sweep away all enemies of the revolution.

3
Mao Takes to the Hills

THE CHINESE COMMUNISTS reacted to their expulsion from the Wuhan government, in the summer of 1927, by trying to take over the provinces which were the domain of the Wuhan government. This was to be achieved through a peasant revolt staged in the four provinces of Hunan, Hupeh, Kiangsi, and Kwangtung. Because this revolt was to begin at the time of the autumn festival, it came to be known as the Autumn Harvest Uprising.[1]

This project obviously was an ambitious one, considering the extent to which the party apparatus had been disrupted and its peasant and worker organizations suppressed. To have had maximum chances of success, the peasant revolt should have been supported, under a coordinated plan, by whatever military forces the Chinese Communists could muster. However, they were concerned about the likelihood that the expulsion of Communists from civilian posts under the Wuhan government would shortly be followed by similar moves against Communist officers who held military commands. Evidently acting under the spur of this concern, the Communists decided to carry out a military revolt before they were ready to start their peasant insurrection. Perhaps realizing that the Autumn Harvest Uprising might fail, they also decided to move the revolting forces southward in an effort to seize and hold the original Kuomintang-Communist base of Kwangtung.[2]

At this point the military forces of the Wuhan government were concentrated in three provinces of south central China: Hupeh, the northernmost of the three, which contains Wuhan itself; Hunan, to the south; and Kiangsi, lying east of Hunan. The three top commanders were T'ang Sheng-chih, whose three armies occupied Hupeh and Hunan; Chu P'ei-te, with one army of troops—from the southwestern province of Yunnan—which was garrisoning the province of Kiangsi; and Chang Fa-k'uei, a Cantonese general whose three armies had just been deployed into Kiangsi in expectation of hostilities with the forces of Chiang Kai-shek.[3]

The Communists could hope to detach major units from the armies of only one of these three commanders, those of Chang Fa-k'uei. He was not himself a Communist, but a number of the higher-ranking officers in his armies were. Among them were Yeh T'ing, who was in charge of Chang's branch headquarters at Nanchang and commanded the twenty-fourth division; Yeh Chien-ying, chief of staff of the Fourth Army; and Chou I-ch'un, political commissar of the Twentieth Army and a relative of Ho Lung, commanding officer of the Twentieth Army.

Ho Lung's early career had been like that of the outlaws in the novel *All Men Are Brothers*. In 1912, during a famine in western Hunan, a peasant rebellion had broken out. Ho Lung had armed himself with a cleaver, killed an official, and taken to the hills. He was only sixteen at the time, and only a few followers fled with him. However, his father was influential in a widespread secret society known as the *Ko-lao-hui*, and many of its members flocked to Ho Lung's side. Moreover, Ho Lung proved to be a capable leader, and by the time he was twenty he commanded a force of several thousand men. That force controlled an area consisting of eight counties, in the region where the borders of Hunan, Hupeh, and Szechwan meet, and his raids extended beyond this area and into the neighboring province of Kweichow. In 1918, because it was unable to defeat him, the government of Hunan gave him a commission in the provincial army and made him garrison commander of an area through which opium caravans passed. By taxing this traffic, he had been able to live comfortably, and he had only switched his allegiance when the planning for the Northern Expedition was underway. When the expedition had reached Hunan, Ho Lung had joined the National Revolutionary Army; his Communist relative Chou I-ch'un had been appointed his political commissar.[4]

Although Chu P'ei-te was not aware of it, one of his key subordinates was a member of the Communist party: Chu Teh, a fellow Yunnanese, director of the public safety bureau at Nanchang (the capital of Kiangsi), and commander of Chu P'ei-te's officer-training regiment. Chu Teh had been Chu P'ei-te's senior at the Yunnan Military Academy and in the provincial army during the early days of the revolution against the Manchu dynasty. By 1921, Chu Teh had attained the rank of brigadier general and had become addicted to the smoking of opium, which then was one of the principal crops in the highlands of his native province. He had also become dissatisfied with his military career, for he had recently been forced out of the post of commissioner of public security in the Yunnan provincial government. In the winter of 1921 he went to Shanghai. There he talked with Sun Yat-sen and Ch'en Tu-hsiu, decided to begin a new career, and broke himself of the opium habit. He then went to Europe where he studied for two years, became acquainted with Chou En-lai and other young Chinese who had come to France under the work-study program, and joined the Communist party. After his return to China, Chu Teh had par-

ticipated in the Northern Expedition as a political officer. He had
kept his membership in the party secret, but when the commander under whom he served began to execute leftist cadres, he and a Communist general named Liu Po-ch'eng both hastily deserted. In January
1927, Chu Teh had showed up in Nanchang, and his old friend Chu
P'ei-te had given him his new posts.[5]

With Yeh T'ing's headquarters at Nanchang and Chu Teh in
charge of its police force, that city was the logical center for the revolt.
The first meeting of the intended participants was held in a small village on July 19. By the last week of July, military preparations were
well underway and a party front committee had been set up, under the
leadership of Chou En-lai, to provide political direction. The principal
forces were to be Ho Lung's army and Yeh T'ing's division. There
were a few smaller units in Hupeh and Kiangsi which were also under
Communist commanders, and the party ordered them to march to Nanchang in order to take part. Neither Liu Po-ch'eng, who had come in
from Szechwan, nor Yeh Chien-ying, chief of staff of the Fourth Army,
had troop commands of their own to contribute, but both participated
in the military planning.

Before the end of the month some leaders of the Wuhan regime
—such as Eugene Ch'en, its Foreign Minister, and Soong Ch'ing-ling,
the widow of Sun Yat-sen—had already left Wuhan for Shanghai, en
route to the Soviet Union. It accordingly must, by then, have been apparent to Chang Fa-k'uei that the Wuhan regime was headed for dissolution. Chang Fa-k'uei was unwilling either to abandon his troop
command and go abroad or to make his peace with Chiang Kai-shek,
and on July 26 he told Galen that he intended to take his armies back
to Kwangtung.

Galen passed this information on to Chinese Communist leaders
that very evening and raised the question of whether this did not make
it unwise to go ahead with the military revolt. If Chang Fa-k'uei really
were going back to Kwangtung, and if he did not require his Communist subordinates to leave the party, then it might be better to postpone
the break with him until they had all reached Kwangtung. This might
obviate the need for Communist-led elements of his army to fight their
way back and make it possible for them to arrive intact. However,
Galen offered this only as his personal opinion, perhaps because it was
not in complete accord with a telegram which had just been received
from the Communist International. That telegram read, in part: "If
there is no chance at all of victory, then it will be all right not to start
the Nanchang revolt." This seemed to imply, of course, that the revolt
should be carried out if there were any chance of success. The others
present had nodded after Galen had expressed his own opinion, as

though they agreed, but the telegram from the Comintern evidently left them without the courage of their convictions. In this indeterminate situation, Chang Kuo-t'ao was directed to go to Kiangsi, apprise the comrades there of these developments, and participate in the decisions to be made.

Chang Kuo-t'ao got to Nanchang on July 30, less than two days before the revolt was to be started. Once there, he tried to get it postponed or called off. In support of this position he is alleged to have said the Comintern had telegraphed that the revolt should be started only if its success could be guaranteed. Otherwise, he urged, it would be best to reach an understanding with Chang Fa-k'uei, or, failing that, to withdraw the Communists from his armies and dispatch them to various regions among the peasants. However, Chou En-lai and the others refused to listen. Perhaps they had put too much effort into their preparations to contemplate calling the revolt off and were under too much tension to endure the delay required for sounding out Chang Fa-k'uei. As one of them put it, the arrow was already on the bowstring and had to be shot. Moreover, Ho Lung commanded the largest single body of the troops which would be involved, and he had set his heart on taking over Chang Fa-k'uei's position.

The Nanchang revolt began during the early hours of August 1, 1927, with Ho Lung in command and Yeh T'ing as deputy commander. Thereafter, August 1 would be celebrated as the anniversary of the founding of the Red Army, and Chu Teh's connection with the revolt and later accomplishments would lead to his being regarded as its founder. By dawn the local garrison had been disarmed and Nanchang was entirely in rebel hands. That evening a meeting was held to decide on the route to be taken for the return to Kwangtung.

The first elements of the revolting force left Nanchang on August 3, and all were on their way by August 5. They were accompanied by the tenth division of the Eleventh Army under Ts'ai T'ing-k'ai, and they took with them the money of the Kiangsi Provincial Bank and all the arms and ammunition they could carry. However, by the time the troops had reached the borders of Kwangtung, their numbers had dwindled from twenty-one thousand to about eight thousand. Ts'ai T'ing-k'ai evidently had come along unwillingly, and he managed to detach his command from the line of march and escape with it. Most of the other losses were due to the circumstances under which the march was conducted. It took place in the heat of summer, the troops were short on animal transport and heavily laden, and a fast pace was maintained during the first days in order to elude pursuit. Moreover, since the route chosen was over secondary roads which went through mountainous and sparsely populated terrain where food and water were scarce, the men went hungry and were reduced to drinking the polluted water which stood in irrigation ditches. In consequence, many men dropped from exhaustion, fell ill, or deserted.

The force of only eight thousand men was clearly inadequate for seizing and holding the major Kwangtung center of Canton, but it did succeed in taking the coastal port of Swatow. Several days later the force was attacked by a large concentration of troops and suffered a disastrous rout. Most of the leaders abandoned the scene of this defeat and escaped to Hong Kong by small boats. Yeh T'ing and Yeh Chien-ying stayed in Hong Kong long enough to help plan an uprising, staged in Canton in December, which was put down with considerable loss of life. A Communist peasant leader named P'eng P'ai escaped from Swatow with a few hundred men and made his way to his home district. There he established the small Hai-lu-feng soviet, which survived until the following spring. Ho Lung went to his home district in western Hunan to raise another army, and Liu Po-ch'eng went to the Soviet Union, where he enrolled at the Frunze Military Academy. The only real survivor, in the immediate military sense, was Chu Teh. He salvaged a force of perhaps two thousand men and led them on a road which eventually brought them to a rendezvous with another remnant force led by Mao Tse-tung.

Chou En-lai was sick with malaria at the time of the defeat at Swatow, but he was among those who escaped to Hong Kong by small boats. After he had recovered, he went surreptitiously to Shanghai, where he went back to work for the party center. Forty years later, talking to some young Red Guards, Chou En-lai was to make a statement implying that Chang Kuo-t'ao had been at least partly right, and he wrong, at the time of their argument in Nanchang.

It was right at that time to engage in armed struggle. The problem was that we should have united with the peasants. If after the uprising we had dispersed to build bases in the rural areas of Kiangsi, our strength would have been very great. Instead we tried to seize cities with our armed forces, a policy which was based on a purely military viewpoint. We went from Kiangsi to Kwangtung; our first object was to capture Swatow in order to win foreign [Soviet] aid. On the one hand we wanted to seize cities, on the other we wanted to rely on foreign aid. Influenced by these two ideas, we did not unite with the local peasants . . . I began to make mistakes when I was only twenty-nine. I am sixty-nine now, but still make mistakes.[6]

The expulsion of the Chinese Communists from the Wuhan regime did not find the responsible leaders of the Comintern ready to admit their mistakes. Stalin had insisted that the Chinese Communists should remain within the Kuomintang right up to the time of the final break. But after it had come, it served the purposes of his faction in the Kremlin to place the blame for the failure of Comintern policy in China on Leon Trotsky and to make Ch'en Tu-hsiu the scapegoat. Ch'ü Ch'iu-pai and Ch'en Tu-hsiu's other enemies in the party were only too glad to cooperate. It was impossible at this time to muster a quorum of the Central Committee; many party leaders were with the forces which had just left Nanchang for Kwangtung, and Ch'en Tu-hsiu and his supporters had left central China for Shanghai. Nevertheless, on August 7, 1927, an emergency conference was convened at Kiukiang, in northern Kiangsi. At this meeting Ch'en Tu-hsiu was censured, deposed from his post of general secretary, and replaced as leader of the party by Ch'ü Ch'iu-pai.[7]

At this same meeting Mao Tse-tung was appointed secretary of a new front committee, created for the purpose of directing the Autumn Harvest Uprising in Hunan and Kiangsi. Provincial party leaders from Hupeh were given a parallel assignment for that province. (The peasant risings in Kwangtung presumably were to be sparked by the party leaders who were en route there with the forces which had staged the revolt at Nanchang.) The Autumn Harvest Uprising was intended to result in the capture of Wuhan, but Wuhan was to be taken through the occupation of main cities along the transport routes leading to it rather than by direct attack. These cities were to be occupied through coordinated attacks launched simultaneously from within and without, but the main force for the operations against each city was to be supplied by the peasantry of the surrounding countryside.

The men who were assigned to conduct the uprising in Hupeh evidently realized that they lacked the resources—in leadership, numbers, training, discipline, and weapons—to carry out so ambitious an undertaking. At an earlier stage, peasant enthusiasm might have helped make up for some of these deficiencies, but that enthusiasm had been drained away in consequence of the vigorous suppression of the peasant associations during the previous spring. At any rate, the front committee for Hupeh, overwhelmed by the disproportion between its assigned task and the available means, never made more than a half-hearted effort which it bungled badly.

Mao Tse-tung was one of the party leaders who had helped formulate the plans. But after he arrived in Hunan, Mao drastically reduced the scope of his operation and made other important changes. He decided, for instance, to limit his objective to the occupation of Changsha, the provincial capital, and to raise and utilize a body of troops instead of relying primarily on the peasant masses. By the first week of September, Mao had available four military units: a Communist-led guard regiment from Wuhan, which had set out for Nanchang intending to participate in the August 1 revolt there but had been unable to

complete its journey in time; a ragtag outfit of deserters from a Kuomintang army; a body of spear-armed peasant marauders; and a mixed
body of unemployed miners and of peasants from the P'inghsiang-
Anyüan region of Kiangsi.

Mao Tse-tung planned to take two satellite towns near Changsha,
in an operation which was to start September 11, and to begin the
drive against Changsha itself on September 15. This plan may have
had the disadvantage of prematurely alerting the garrison at Changsha.
But it had become impossible to achieve complete surprise: the press
had already carried an item saying that the garrison commander had
captured two secret orders to party cells in Changsha, telling them to
mobilize and assassinate government leaders during the autumn festival.

A Russian agent who was assigned as an advisor to the front committee, and who was present during the attempted uprising in Hunan,
later reported that some aspects of the operation were nothing short of
hilarious, and it is true that almost everything went wrong. Mao Tse-
tung was arrested by some local police shortly after leaving Changsha,
and although he eventually succeeded in escaping, he was absent
throughout the military phase of the operation. The ragtag outfit of
Kuomintang deserters, jealous of the superior equipment of the guard
regiment, caught it in an ambush in order to seize its weapons. The
spear-armed peasants had some initial successes against militia posts
around Changsha; they captured quantities of guns from the posts
but were unable to put them to effective use. During one attack, a
peasant who did not know how to use a gun disorganized his unit by
accidentally shooting and killing one of his comrades. Moreover, the
commander of the Changsha garrison, having anticipated their attacks,
had disposed his troops on high ground outside the city walls and soon
surrounded the peasants with a superior force. The mixed regiment of
miners and peasants was the only one which gave a good account of
itself. It started out on time, captured one of the satellite towns, and
held it for awhile. However, without support from other units and
with no uprising underway in Changsha itself, the regiment was soon
surrounded and decimated. By the time Mao Tse-tung was able to
join his men, there was little left for him to do but pick up the pieces
and make for the hills.

Shortly before launching the Autumn Harvest Uprising in Hunan,
Mao Tse-tung had informed the party center that he intended to dis-
pense with the use of the Kuomintang flag; to call for a "complete
solution" of the land problem through sweeping confiscations; and to
declare, as the goal of the insurrection, the establishment of worker-
peasant-soldier soviets. These were new departures from the established

party line. Moreover, he had departed from the plan approved at the August 7 meeting by arbitrarily reducing the scope of his operation, and he had violated its underlying strategy by placing primary reliance on troops rather than on the peasant masses. Because a man who both disobeys orders and fails in his mission is doubly wrong, it is not surprising that the party censured Mao Tse-tung and removed him from his party posts, including his positions as member of the Central Committee and alternate member of its provisional Political Bureau. However, long before Mao learned of this action he had reorganized his remnant force, numbering less than a thousand men, marched them to the border between Kiangsi and Hunan, established them in a secure base, and set up a local soviet in the nearby town of Ch'aling.[8]

Mao Tse-tung undoubtedly had absorbed enough of the lore of outlaws to know what sort of territory is best for bandits and for guerrillas. It should be in rugged terrain with plenty of cover, which those who know it well can use for purposes of ambush or evasion. It should straddle a political boundary, so that one's band can slip across a border when things get too hot in one jurisdiction and require transfer to another. Although difficult of access for outsiders, it should be accessible to the outside, because foodstuffs, other supplies, and new recruits can be obtained only from inhabited areas.

The base which Mao Tse-tung chose met these requirements well. It was located in the middle section of the Lo Hsiao range, which marks the boundary between Kiangsi province and Mao Tse-tung's native Hunan, in the vicinity of a mountain known as the Chingkangshan. A region of towering crags, clothed in mists much of the year, and of slopes forested with fir and bamboo, its character is well-suggested by the name of the mountain range: *lo* may be translated as curtain, and *hsiao* as darkness. Chingkangshan, or wells ridge mountain, took its name from five nearby farm villages, each situated at a well, and the Chingkangshan base was in a broad and circular valley surrounded by wooded slopes.[9]

The Chingkangshan stronghold was already occupied, when Mao arrived in the area, by a gang of bandits commanded by a leader named Wang Tso, also known as Tiger Wang. The nearby county center of Ningkang was the base of a local strongman named Yüan Wen-ts'ai, with whom Tiger Wang was allied. Mao Tse-tung sent a couple of handguns and other presents to Yüan Wen-ts'ai, and having made friends with him, was introduced to the bandit chief. The upshot was that Wang and Yüan became subordinate commanders under Mao Tse-tung, their bands were added to his, and he gained control of the Chingkangshan base. There he passed the winter, and people thereabouts called him Commander Mao.[10]

In the spring of 1928, Mao Tse-tung had a rendezvous with Chu Teh. The force under Chu Teh had changed somewhat in composition, but it still had a substantial component of veterans of the Northern Expedition and the Nanchang uprising and was a more professionally military force than that of Mao Tse-tung. Chu Teh was, of course, an experienced commander. His ranking political commissar was Ch'en Yi, who had been an instructor in the political department at the Whampoa Military Academy under Chou En-lai. And his subordinate commanders included Lin Piao, then only twenty-one, but a Whampoa graduate who had emerged from the debacle at Swatow with his unit's equipment intact, and who in a subsequent encounter had defeated an enemy unit much larger than his own.[11]

Chu Teh and some of his officers were meeting Mao Tse-tung for the first time, and one of them named Kung Ch'u later recounted his initial impressions. Mao Tse-tung was wearing a uniform of badly faded grey cotton, cut in the style which Sun Yat-sen had popularized and which Kuomintang and Chinese Communist civilian cadres still wear today. Mao's hair was disheveled, and his beard had long remained unshaven—half concealing the big, black mole on his chin. Kung Ch'u noted that Mao spoke with a thick Hunanese accent, and that his voice lacked resonance. However, his speech was crisp, his language flavorful, and he quickly got to the key point of any question. Moreover, his manner was genial, and after talking with him for a short time one had the feeling of long acquaintance. Mao Tse-tung was the sort of person, Kung Ch'u concluded, who made people feel impelled to follow his leadership.[12]

Mao Tse-tung and Chu Teh decided to combine their forces and reorganize them into an army of three divisions. They named theirs the Fourth Red Army—commemorating the parent army of Chang Fa-k'uei, which had gained fame under the designation of the Fourth Army. Chu Teh became the commander in chief, Mao the army's political commissar, and Ch'en Yi the head of the political department. Each of them took as a concurrent responsibility the command of one of the three divisions. They and their subordinates fortified the passes; established headquarters offices, an ordnance department, a uniform workshop and hospitals; and drew up plans for establishing a soviet, intended to cover six counties, which they proposed to use as the base for further expansion.[13]

In April 1928, which is to say about the time that Mao Tse-tung and Chu Teh were deciding to combine forces, Chiang Kai-shek was beginning the second phase of the Northern Expedition. For this campaign he had not only the forces under his immediate command, but also those of Feng Yü-hsiang—the "Christian general," of Yen Hsi-shan

—long-time ruler of the northwestern province of Shansi, and of the Kwangsi leaders Li Tsung-jen and Pai Ch'ung-hsi. Chiang Kai-shek's opponents were the warlord Chang Tso-lin, with headquarters in Peking, and his associate Chang Tsung-ch'ang, who occupied the nearby province of Shantung.

Chang Tso-lin's principal base of power was Manchuria, which he had ruled for a decade as a virtually independent state. Its autonomy served the interests of Japan, which enjoyed a variety of concessions in south Manchuria. Moreover, Chang Tso-lin had maintained with the Japanese a cooperative relationship which extended back to the days of the Russo-Japanese war of 1904–1905, when Chang had fought with a band of pro-Japanese irregulars. The Japanese may have acquiesced in his involvement in the politics of China proper, during the warlord period. But after the Kuomintang armies had conquered central China, the Japanese saw the potential danger in the linkage of Manchuria and China proper which was inherent in Chang Tso-lin's continued occupation of areas below the Great Wall. If his forces were defeated there, then the armies of the Kuomintang—pursuing its aim of reunifying all China—might be expected to follow up on their victory and carry the campaign into Manchuria. And the extension of Kuomintang power and policies into Manchuria would threaten the interests enjoyed there by the Japanese.

In the summer of 1927, the Japanese government, motivated by these considerations, had urged Chang Tso-lin to withdraw his armies from north China into Manchuria and to consolidate his position there. However, he disregarded this advice, hoping that his position in north China would be saved by the split between the Wuhan and Nanking factions of the Kuomintang. Actually, the split interrupted the northward drive for substantially less than a year, and within a month after its resumption it became evident that Chang Tso-lin's forces were not up to the task of stemming the Kuomintang advance. In May 1928, the Japanese government sent identical notes to the governments at Nanking and Peking in which it warned that it would, in the interest of peace and order in Manchuria, prevent the entrance into that region of "defeated troops and those in pursuit of them." This was no empty threat, as the Japanese maintained a powerful army in their strategically-located Kuantung[14] leasehold at the tip of Manchuria's Liaotung peninsula. On June 3, Chang Tso-lin finally left Peking for Mukden. A group of staff officers in the headquarters of Japan's Kuantung Army saw to it that he did not arrive safely. Early the next morning a bomb wrecked his private railway car, and he was fatally wounded.

Chang Tso-lin's son Chang Hsüeh-liang, who succeeded him,

quickly reached agreements with the Nanking government which provided for the peaceful withdrawal of his forces from north China and
the raising of the Kuomintang flag over all Manchuria. Chang Tsung-
ch'ang tried to hang on, but by mid-September his troops too had been
withdrawn into Manchuria.[15]

The Northern Expedition was over, but the unification of China,
which it had been intended to achieve, eluded the grasp of Chiang
Kai-shek. He invited the other leaders of his coalition to a conference
at which the disbandment of troops was discussed, but they put less
confidence in his gratitude than in the forces on which their power was
based. In consequence, the disbandment of their armies did not take
place, and the three years which followed were marked by sporadic
warfare between the forces of Nanking, where Chiang Kai-shek held
the reins of power, and those of his erstwhile allies.

The preoccupation of Chiang Kai-shek and other major leaders,
first with the Northern Expedition and then with their internecine
struggles, was important to the Communists who had taken to the hills;
it left them facing only lesser enemies and gave them the opportunity
to establish bases and build up armed forces. The Chingkangshan was
only one of a number of base areas, varying in size and degree of permanence, which were established in southwest, central, and northwest
China in the years immediately following the break between the Communists and the Kuomintang. Armies of considerable size were supported in the Hunan-Hupeh soviet area, built up by Ho Lung, with
the assistance of a warlike sister named Ho Hsiang-ku and their relative Chou I-ch'un—the young Communist who had been the political
commissar of Ho's Twentieth Army. Large Communist forces were also
created in the Oyüwan soviet, situated in the Hupeh-Honan-Anhwei
border area. The two most noteworthy military commanders there were
Hsü Hsiang-ch'ien and Hsü Hai-tung, both veterans of the armies of
Chang Fa-k'uei. Beginning in 1931, they worked under the political
leadership of Chang Kuo-t'ao.

As Mao Tse-tung remarked in October 1928, the prolonged existence of "several small areas under Red political power amid the encirclement of White political power" was possible only because of two particular circumstances. One was "the prolonged splits and wars within
the White regime." The other was the fact that China had a "localized agricultural economy" instead of "a unified capitalist economy." [16]
The peasants, in other words, did not depend heavily on the market
for the sale of their produce and the purchase of goods. If cut off from
city markets, they could meet almost all their needs through sub-
sistence agriculture and from handicraft production. The cities were
in nearly the opposite position, because they were heavily dependent

on the agricultural produce of the countryside. Moreover, as in imperial China, formal government organization still stopped with the office of the district magistrate, established at the county seat. This meant that the countryside was a semivacuum which the Communists could fill by organizing the people—organizing them on the basis of occupation, sex, age, degree of ideological development, and capacity to bear arms.

This combination of circumstances was leading Mao Tse-tung and his comrades to formulate the strategy through which they eventually would conquer all mainland China. To oversimplify: They would mobilize the peasants of the countryside against the landed gentry—who were the local supporters of the status quo—by means which included the seizure and redistribution of the land. They would arm the peasants, who would have to fight if they were to protect their gains. They would use the armed peasantry to help defend and extend the areas under Communist control. And, when the process had been carried far enough, they would utilize the countryside and its resources to surround and attack the cities, which were the centers of non-Communist political power.

However, the year 1928, in which Mao advanced his analysis of why small areas of Red political power could survive, was one in which his own political power underwent a dangerous challenge. From early spring until autumn the Hunan party committee tried to bring him under its control. In March it abolished the front committee, through which Mao had exercised authority since the time of the Autumn Harvest Uprising. In June the Hunan party committee sent two emissaries with orders, to which Mao was strongly opposed, for the Fourth Red Army to conduct operations in southern Hunan. While Mao was away mustering the support of local committees for his proposal that these orders be rejected, Chu Teh and most of the army—which then numbered about ten thousand men—marched off to southern Hunan in obedience to them. During the ensuing campaign Chu Teh's forces suffered serious losses, and while they were away the Chingkangshan was attacked by elements of two Kuomintang armies. Mao Tse-tung put up a stubborn guerrilla defense, but the odds were too great. He had at his disposal only one regiment of regulars and local Red Guards and would undoubtedly have lost both his forces and the whole of the base area if the two Kuomintang armies had not finally fallen to fighting among themselves. This gave Mao Tse-tung a breathing period which he used to go off into southern Hunan. There he had a rendezvous with Chu Teh and persuaded him to return to the Chingkangshan. On November 6, after they had recovered part of the base area and stabilized the situation, Mao Tse-tung reconstituted the front committee,

with himself at its head, as the body to which other party committees
of the army and the base area were subordinate.[17]

On November 25, Mao sent the Central Committee a report in
which he described the consequences of having followed the orders of
the Hunan Provincial Committee: "The Red Army lost about half its
men, and countless houses were burned down and innumerable people
were massacred in the border area; county after county fell to the
enemy and some of them have not been recovered to this day." [18]

Chu Teh and Mao Tse-tung, in their efforts to recover and hold
these counties, were not entirely dependent upon the forces under their
own command. They are said to have had some assistance, in September and October, from Communist partisans commanded by Li Wen-
ling and Tuan Liang-pi—both Whampoa graduates and veterans of
the Nanchang Uprising. Li and Tuan had left the disintegrating
forces of Ho Lung and Yeh T'ing to return to their home districts in
Kiangsi, where they had recruited guerrillas and established small bases.
And in November Chu and Mao had been joined by P'eng Te-huai, a
towering man of peasant stock from Mao's own home district, with a
force known as the Fifth Red Army.[19]

In December 1928 the Chingkangshan base was attacked again,
this time by a powerful concentration of troops drawn from both Hunan and Kiangsi. In January 1929 Mao and Chu abandoned the Chingkangshan, leaving P'eng Te-huai and the former bandit Wang Tso to
put up a last ditch defense, and marched their army eastward into
Kiangsi. P'eng and Wang, with less than a thousand men who were fit
to fight, defended the base as long as they could and then retreated.
P'eng made his way eastward, hoping to rejoin Chu Teh and Mao
Tse-tung, but Wang Tso was unwilling to leave his native region. During a later period, after the Communists had regained control of the
area, both Wang Tso and his old comrade Yüan Wen-tsai were killed.
According to Mao Tse-tung, they had returned to their bandit ways,[20]
but another Chinese Communist account suggests that the charge for
which they were killed was that of "rebellion." [21]

4
Building the Kiangsi Soviet

SHORTLY after leaving the Chingkangshan in January 1929, Chu Teh and Mao Tse-tung destroyed a Kuomintang division in a desperate battle which cost them half their remaining force. They then drove onward to the Tungku-Hsingkuo region of south central Kiangsi, which was the base of Li Wen-ling and Tuan Liang-pi, the partisan leaders who had come to their assistance the previous autumn. After resting their men and getting reinforcements, Chu Teh and Mao Tse-tung drove eastwards to the Kiangsi-Fukien border area, where they occupied the town of Changting (Tingchow), Fukien.[1]

While Chu Teh and Mao Tse-tung were campaigning in Fukien, P'eng Te-huai was leading the remnant of his army across Kiangsi in search of them. Early in the spring he occupied the town of Juichin, Kiangsi—which soon was to become the capital of the Chinese Soviet Republic—and there he presently was joined by Mao Tse-tung and Chu Teh. While the three leaders conferred in Juichin, they received an important letter from the party center at Shanghai, now under a new leadership which had been chosen in Moscow the previous summer.[2]

The Chinese Communist party had held its Sixth National Congress in Moscow in the early summer of 1928, at the same time that the Comintern was holding its Sixth Congress there. At the party congress, Mao Tse-tung was elected *in absentia* to membership in the new Central Committee, but he was not among those chosen to form the Political Bureau. That was to be composed of Ch'ü Ch'iu-pai, Chou En-lai, Chang Kuo-t'ao, Li Li-san, Ts'ai Ho-sen, Hsiang Ying, and Hsiang Chung-fa.

The Chinese Communists and their Comintern mentors may have had a difficult time deciding who, among these seven men, should serve in the position of general secretary. Ch'ü Ch'iu-pai could not continue as top leader because of the failure of the putschist line he had followed so enthusiastically; he was not even allowed to return to China until somewhat later. Chou En-lai was, of course, closely associated with that line and with the failure of the uprising launched at Nanchang. Chang Kuo-t'ao was censured in Moscow for opportunism, perhaps because he assertedly had misrepresented the contents of instruc-

tions from the Comintern, on the eve of the Nanchang revolt; he too
was detained for awhile in Moscow. Li Li-san and Ts'ai Ho-sen were
opponents, and it may be that this made it seem desirable to choose a
third person as a compromise candidate for the post of general secretary. This left Hsiang Ying, a labor organizer who had been in the
Soviet Union for a year, where he probably had been receiving military
training, and Hsiang Chung-fa, another labor organizer. In any event,
Hsiang Chung-fa was chosen. A onetime coolie, his proletarian origins
were hardly open to question. However, the same could not be said of
his qualifications as leader, and the new Political Bureau soon fell
under the control of Li Li-san.[3]

Li Li-san—and those of his associates who left Moscow at the conclusion of the congress—were returning to a party which was suffering
from the consequences of widespread and vigorous suppression and
from the defeats it had suffered during the previous year. It had undergone a precipitous drop in membership, its surviving cadres had been
scattered, many of its unions and other front organizations in the cities
were defunct, and its existing strength was largely confined to the rural
bases with their peasant armies.

One of the resolutions which had been adopted by the Comintern,
reflecting a recognition of this situation in China, had declared that
the most important condition for the further development of the Chinese revolution was the strengthening of the Communist party, its
cadres, its periphery, and its center. The party was, in other words, to
build up its membership, strengthen contacts between the party center
and local organizations, and create an effective apparatus.[4] This did
not mean, of course, that the rural bases—with their peasant armies—
were to be neglected. Indeed, it was asserted in a resolution of the
party congress that one of the foremost tasks facing the party was the
development of a regular revolutionary army of workers and peasants.[5]
However, one is entitled to doubt that the leaders meeting in Moscow
placed the word "workers" before "peasants" by oversight. Instead,
they undoubtedly were reflecting both their own personal backgrounds
and orientation, which were predominantly urban, and the orthodox
view that the workers were more reliably proletarian than their peasant allies. It was, after all, logical to assume that the dictatorship of
the proletariat should be established primarily through reliance upon
the proletariat itself.

Mao Tse-tung and Li Li-san had first met during their student
days in Changsha. In 1917, Mao had put a want ad in a Changsha
newspaper for patriotic young men with whom he might exchange
ideas. In response, he had received "three and one-half replies." The
half reply had come from Li Li-san, who listened to all Mao had to

say and then went away without committing himself. As Mao later commented, their friendship never developed.[6] After those student days, they had taken different paths. Li Li-san was one of the students who had gone to France while Mao had stayed in China. Li Li-san had risen to leadership—and come to the attention of Moscow—as a labor organizer; Mao had devoted himself primarily to the organization of the peasants. Li Li-san's attitude toward peasants was manifested at the Sixth Party Congress. The peasants, he said, had petty bourgeois illusions about socialism. Those who had been dispossessed were attracted to socialism because they wanted to regain the land, and for this reason they demanded equal distribution of the land. This obviously was not socialism, but many Chinese comrades working in the peasant movement were not clear on this point. "I think," he asserted, "that such a comrade is Mao Tse-tung." [7]

If Li Li-san's first task, on returning to China, was restoring a party apparatus responsive to the center, it was also one which was bound to involve a conflict between him and Mao Tse-tung. Undoubtedly one of the reports coming to his attention, after assuming his responsibilities in the party center, was one from Mao Tse-tung. Mao had addressed this report to the Central Committee on November 25, 1928, from the Chingkangshan, as secretary of its newly-reconstituted front committee. In this report, besides placing blame for the defeats of the preceding summer on the Hunan party committee, Mao had complained that the Central Committee "instructed us to develop guerrilla warfare in much too large an area . . . probably due to an overestimation of our strength." Drawing a distinction between the Red Army and the Red Guards—local auxiliaries who were armed but not expected to give up their normal productive occupations—he explained: "The principle for the Red Army is concentration and that for the Red Guards is dispersion. . . . In our experience, the dispersion of forces has almost always led to defeat, while the concentration of forces to fight a numerically inferior, equal, or slightly superior enemy force has often led to victory." Mao Tse-tung was serving notice, in other words, that he did not propose to follow instructions with which he strongly disagreed.[8]

The important letter which Mao Tse-tung and Chu Teh received at their new base of Juichin, in the early spring of 1929, had been sent them on February 9 by Li Li-san. Instead of withdrawing the earlier instruction from the Central Committee about which Mao had complained, Li Li-san repeated it in strengthened form. In order to arouse the masses and preserve the strength of their forces, Chu and Mao were to divide their army into very small units, disperse them over the countryside, and then withdraw from the army. Li Li-san also complained that the revolutionary struggle in the countryside was creating within the party a "peasant mentality" which, if not corrected by proletarian leadership, might destroy both the party and the revolution.[9]

Li Li-san's instruction regarding dispersal, as a means of rousing the masses and preserving the strength of the Red Army, ran directly against the observations and conclusions which Mao Tse-tung had reported the previous November. Small and widely dispersed bands, constantly on the move, would not succeed in rousing and organizing the populace. As Mao had observed in that report: "Wherever the Red Army goes, the masses are cold and aloof, and only after our propaganda do they slowly move into action." Dispersal would also leave the Communists' base area without protection, and Mao had commented: "Wherever such an area is located, it will immediately be occupied by the enemy if armed forces are lacking or inadequate, or if wrong tactics are used in dealing with the enemy." [10] Even with a base, Chu and Mao had encountered difficulty in preventing homesick peasants from leaving the ranks. An army without a base would be like the body of a man who had no buttocks: it could not be set down to rest.

Mao Tse-tung undoubtedly saw—behind Li Li-san's instructions—a wish to subordinate the revolution in the countryside to that in urban areas and to remove him from his own base of power to the party center at Shanghai, where he could readily be brought under control. On April 5, 1929, Mao sent Li Li-san a letter rejecting his instructions on the grounds that they were based on an unrealistic view. Division of the army into small units, he explained, resulted in weak leadership and the danger that units would be crushed one by one. Accordingly, it was only during favorable periods that the army could be dispersed for guerrilla operations, and it was only during such periods that the top leaders did not need to stay in the ranks all the time.

In addition, Mao rebuked Li Li-san for his remarks concerning peasant consciousness—remarks Mao undoubtedly recognized as directed at himself—and read him a short lecture on revolutionary strategy. He wrote:

Proletarian leadership is the sole key to victory . . . but at the same time the major prerequisites for helping the struggle in the cities and hastening the rise of the revolutionary tide are specifically the development of the struggle in the countryside, the establishment of Red political power in small areas, and the creation and expansion of the Red Army. Therefore, it would be wrong to abandon the struggle in the cities, but in our opinion it would also be wrong for any of our party members to fear the growth of peasant strength lest it should outstrip the workers' strength and harm the revolution. For in the revolution in semicolonial China, the peasant struggle must always fail if it does not have the leadership of the workers, but the revolution is never harmed if the peasant struggle outstrips the forces of the workers.[11]

Mao Tse-tung's rejection of the orders of the party center, early in April 1929, marked the beginning of a period during which he worked hard and accomplished much in building and expanding his new base centered at Juichin, but also a period in which he stirred up opposition and created enemies for which he would later have to pay. As Mao may have learned or surmised, Li Li-san was employing harsh and sometimes sinister means to suppress or eliminate all sources of opposition which were within his reach. Refusing to go to the party center, in order to avoid falling under the control of Li Li-san, meant that Mao Tse-tung had to guard also against Li extending his hand into Mao's own area for the purpose of undermining his control of its party organizations and armed forces.

There was nothing new, of course, about Mao's determination to grasp power and hold it firmly, any more than there was about his opposition to orders with which he disagreed. What apparently was new was his riding roughshod over other Communists who were not his henchmen, in his efforts to expand and consolidate his own power, and employing against comrades an apparatus which used methods of terror and physical liquidation, in order to preserve that power.

According to Mao Tse-tung's own account, the partisans under Li Wen-ling, and under another leader named Li Su-chu in the same general area, were reorganized early in 1929, designated the Third Red Army, and placed under the command of Huang Kung-lüeh.[12] Huang had been the deputy commander of the Fifth Red Army under P'eng Te-huai. This suggests that the reorganization was carried out only after Mao Tse-tung and Chu Teh, linking up with P'eng Te-huai and the remnants of his army at Juichin, had received Li Li-san's letter of February 9, discussed its contents, and decided how to deal with the problems it presented. The fact that Li Wen-ling and some of his associates soon emerged as bitter enemies of Mao Tse-tung suggests that they resented bitterly his having taken over the base areas in which they had so recently given him a needed refuge, and his having deprived them of their independent commands.

It seems likely that Chu Teh, like Mao Tse-tung, was angered by Li Li-san's request that he withdraw from the army, and that he concurred in Mao's decision that they should both reject it. It also should not be assumed that Chu Teh was incapable of acting in cold blood. However, he was sufficiently endowed with human juices to be influenced by comradely feelings, and he evidently was out of sympathy with the treatment Mao Tse-tung began to accord to fellow Communists. Chu Teh was later quoted, at any rate, as saying that there were repeated struggles within the army, after the descent from the Chingkangshan and the move to Fukien, in which he had found himself caught in the middle. One faction would call for supporting Mao and opposing Chu, another for supporting Chu and opposing Mao. Chu Teh's subordinate Lin Piao—"that no good piece of work"—had come out openly in opposition to Chu, and he had been forced to exercise great forbearance in order to avoid an open break. For these struggles, which were accompanied by bloody purges in which many "good comrades" were sacrificed, Chu Teh put all the blame on Mao Tse-tung.[13]

In the course of 1929, Mao Tse-tung twice returned to western Fukien; and there he conducted another operation reminiscent of that carried out in the base of Li Wen-ling and his fellow partisan leaders. A former Whampoa cadet named Teng Tzu-hui, together with other Communists who were native to the area, had built up guerrilla bands and established a soviet which exercised jurisdiction over a fairly extensive area. Mao Tse-tung added these bands to a nucleus of regular troops, creating a force called the Twelfth Red Army, and placed it under the command of one of his own men. He also converted the administration built up by Teng Tzu-hui and his fellows into a satellite of his own soviet at Juichin. At these tasks Mao Tse-tung quite literally worked night and day. It is related that he began his "office hours" late at night, by the light of an oil lamp; that he became seriously ill in November; and that he would have lost his life if it had not been for the effort of a Dr. Nelson Fu of the Baptist Mission Hospital in Changting.[14]

By the end of 1929, Mao Tse-tung was well enough to convene a conference of party representatives from the Fourth Army. At this conference, held at Kut'ien, Fukien, he attacked the positions on major issues taken by Li Li-san and his supporters; advanced his own ideas on revolutionary strategy; and asserted the supremacy of his political leadership over Chu Teh's military command.

Mao Tse-tung's attack on the views of Li Li-san and his supporters was contained in two documents. The first and less explicit was a paper avowedly prepared for presentation at the conference; the second was a letter of January 5, 1930, which purportedly was addressed to Lin Piao, then a regimental commander in Chu Teh's Fourth Red Army. In both, the views which Mao attacked were attributed merely to "some people," but in his letter Mao made his target clear through the quotation of long passages from his April 5, 1929, reply to the Central Committee's instruction of the previous February—which, he complained, "was not in the right spirit." In the letter of January 5 to Lin

Piao, Mao wrote: "Some comrades in our party . . . seem to think that, since the revolutionary high tide is still remote, it will be labor lost to attempt to establish political power by hard work. Instead they want to extend our political influence through the easier method of roving guerrilla actions, and, once the masses throughout the country have been won over, or more or less won over, they want to launch a nationwide armed insurrection which, with the participation of the Red Army, would become a great nationwide revolution."

Mao went on to assert that the revolutionary high tide could not be accelerated by such guerrilla actions but only by "the policy of establishing base areas; of systematically setting up political power; of deepening the agrarian revolution; of expanding the people's armed forces by a comprehensive process of building up first township Red Guards, then district Red Guards, then county Red Guards, then local Red Army troops, all the way up to the regular Red Army troops; of spreading political power by advancing in a series of waves . . . only thus is it really possible to create a Red Army which will become the chief weapon for the great revolution of the future." [15]

Many years later, when Maoists were attempting to belittle the accomplishments of Chu Teh, one of them declared that comrades who had made mistakes were not publicly criticized, at the Kut'ien conference, but that many of the resolutions adopted there were directed at Chu Teh, who had opposed Chairman Mao as early as the period when they were together on the Chingkangshan.[16] It indeed was true that they often campaigned separately, perhaps because neither found it easy to subordinate himself to the other in their respective roles of military commander and political commissar. When it came to command decisions, the one would be likely to consider the matter military, the other to accuse him of refusing to see military matters in their wider political context.

Although Mao may have left the identity of those he was criticizing in this particular connection obscure, the points he made were crystal clear. He wrote:

The purely military viewpoint is very highly developed among a number of comrades in the Red Army. . . . These comrades regard military affairs and politics as opposed to each other and refuse to recognize that military affairs are only one means of accomplishing political tasks. . . . They think that the task of the Red Army, like that of the White army, is merely to fight. They do not understand that the Chinese Red Army is merely an armed body for carrying out the political tasks of the revolution. . . . The Red Army fights not merely for the sake of fighting but in order to conduct propaganda among the masses, organize them, arm them, and help them to establish revolutionary political power. Without these objectives, fighting loses its meaning and the Red Army loses the reason for its existence.[17]

Mao Tse-tung had accepted the fact that the Communists could not fight a conventional civil war, which can be waged only by those who control a well-defined territory and substantial population, and he had grasped the essential difference between conventional and revolutionary civil war. In conventional warfare there may be a division of labor between the military in the field, who do the fighting, and political leaders at the center, who direct its strategic course, formulate policies which may affect the outcome, and disseminate propaganda directed at the people of the respective sides. But a revolutionary civil war, as a campaign waged to cause the people to change sides, has their minds and feelings as its most important objectives, rather than features of terrain or pieces of territory. Because the revolutionary side fights for the purpose of being able to reach, influence, and organize the people, the practitioners of revolutionary warfare must be able to use and orchestrate all means of persuasion at the grassroots, tactical level.

In his so-called letter to Lin Piao, Mao Tse-tung criticized "comrades who suffer from revolutionary impetuosity," and Li Li-san was certainly one of them; he lacked the patience for the long, hard road which Mao saw as the way to power. If he had been unduly pessimistic when he had called for Chu Teh and Mao Tse-tung to disperse their forces and withdraw from the army, as Mao professed to believe, the events of the first months of 1930 filled him with undue optimism. Feng Yü-hsiang, Yen Hsi-shan, and the Kwangsi generals Li Tsung-jen and Pai Ch'ung-hsi—the leaders who had joined with Chiang Kai-shek to wage the second phase of the Northern Expedition—formed a coalition directed against their commander in chief. With the encouragement of Wang Ching-wei and the participation of Chang Fa-k'uei, who controlled two armies, they launched a military campaign intended to wrest the leadership of China from Chiang Kai-shek.

In February 1930, while this coalition was being formed, Li Li-san announced that the party center would, on May 1, convene a conference of delegates from the various soviet areas, and that this conference would be preliminary to an All-China Soviet Congress, to be convened in one of the soviet areas on November 7. He of course invited Mao Tse-tung to attend, but Mao did not deign to reply. Li Li-san followed up the initial invitation with repeated letters, and postponed the conference until May 31, hoping that Mao could be persuaded either to attend or to send a representative; the hope proving vain, Li Li-san reluctantly proceeded without Mao.

At this conference, and at a June 11 meeting of the Political Bureau, Li Li-san unveiled plans which, he hoped, would enable the Communists to seize control of the provinces of central China on which the power of the Nationalist government was based. He professed to believe that the time was ripe for a revolutionary upsurge in which principal cities could be seized through worker uprisings, encouraged and supported by Red Army attacks from without, and that warlord troops could be incited to mutiny and destroy their masters.[18]

Li Li-san's plans, which the Political Bureau approved, provided that the various Communist armies should be reorganized, with Chu Teh as overall commander and Mao Tse-tung as political commissar. All weapons were to be concentrated in the Red Army, which meant that armed Red Guards and local forces were also to be incorporated in army units. The forces directly under Chu Teh and Mao Tse-tung, re-designated the First Army Corps, were to take Nanchang and then move on Wuhan via Kiukiang. Ho Lung's troops, renamed the Second Army Corps, and those of Hsü Hsiang-ch'ien, as the Fourth Army Corps, were also to move on Wuhan. P'eng Te-huai, commanding the Third Army Corps, was to occupy Changsha, after which he was to join the general offensive against Wuhan. These attacks would be coordinated with uprisings of the workers in the cities and the peasants in the countryside; meanwhile, Kuomintang and warlord troops were to be immobilized through mutinies.[19]

Having been named commander in chief and political commissar of the combined forces, called upon to implement a plan to which the Political Bureau had given formal approval, and in the absence of opposition to the plan by leaders of the other armies involved, Mao Tse-tung and Chu Teh could hardly refuse to take part.

P'eng Te-huai captured Changsha on July 28. He proclaimed a soviet government, with Li Li-san its chairman *in absentia,* but was forced to withdraw from the city after holding it for ten days. Chu Teh and Mao Tse-tung attacked Nanchang on August 1, the anniversary of the ill-fated uprising which had been launched there three years before. They maintained the assault for twenty-four hours and then withdrew. Ho Lung and Hsü Hsiang-ch'ien put Wuhan in apparent peril but did not succeed in entering it. There were small demonstrations in some cities but no uprisings of the workers, and no significant mutinies occurred within the Kuomintang or warlord armies. With his revolutionary hopes and political future hanging on the outcome, Li Li-san ordered a renewed attack on Changsha. Chu Teh and Mao Tse-tung joined P'eng Te-huai for the attempt, which began on September 1 and lasted until September 13. At that point Mao Tse-tung persuaded his two colleagues that they should abandon the campaign and return together to Kiangsi. This forced the party center to call off the offensive against Wuhan, bringing Li Li-san's effort to carry out a nationwide uprising to an end.[20]

In the wake of the Communist withdrawal from their siege of Hunan's provincial capital of Changsha, the Kuomintang governor of that province initiated a roundup of residents who were believed to have Communist connections. Among them were Mao Tse-tung's wife Yang K'ai-hui—who had remained behind with their two small sons, Mao An-ying and Mao An-ch'ing, when Mao Tse-tung had taken to the hills after the failure of his Autumn Harvest Uprising—and his sister Mao Tse-hung. Both Yang K'ai-hui and Mao Tse-hung were executed, and Mao Tse-tung lost track of his two sons for many years.[21]

Mao Tse-tung had undoubtedly fallen in love with Yang K'ai-hui before their marriage, and he was to bemoan his loss of her in a poem written more than a quarter of a century after her death.[22] It should not be assumed, however, that his love for her had caused him to lead a monogamous existence, or that communism was for him a religion which enabled him to sublimate his sexual drives. Kung Ch'u, then a young officer in Chu Teh's command, describes a conversation he had with Mao Tse-tung in the spring of 1928 which bears upon that point. Kung Ch'u had a number of girls in his unit, which was then in training, and Mao Tse-tung was paying it a visit. Kung Ch'u quotes Mao as making suggestive remarks about the girls, and as asking him about his relations with them. Kung Ch'u replied that the girls were revolutionary comrades; that everybody in his unit had endless work to do; and that feelings of love between males and females in his unit simply did not arise. Mao then remarked that Kung Ch'u was, of course, a younger man. But he could not himself look on female beauty without having voluptuous feelings, and he did not believe that Kung Ch'u was not similarly affected. Mao Tse-tung then laughed mysteriously, as though cherishing some secret of his own.

Not long afterwards Kung Ch'u learned that Mao Tse-tung had "a pretty comrade" named Ho Shih-chen.[23] She was not one of the female comrades of the Red Army, but a middle school girl whose father had a bookstore in one of the towns of the area. A photograph, taken of her with Mao Tse-tung, portrays a girl of lively but delicate beauty whose appearance suggests that she had been gently bred. Mao met her in consequence of her duties with the Communist Youth Corps, of which she was a branch secretary, and became better acquainted by detaining her after a meeting on the grounds that he had important matters to discuss with her. The next day she came to help Mao with his work; she did not go home that night, and she stayed with him thereafter. In taking a "revolutionary sweetheart" Mao Tse-tung was not atypical of senior Chinese Communist officials of the revolutionary period. Chu Teh, for instance, had drifted away from his wife in consequence of his participation in the revolution, and he took another wife in 1928; she was killed not long afterwards, and early in 1929 he married K'ang K'o-ch'ing, a broad-faced, sturdy, teen-aged girl of peasant stock, and the leader of a partisan band. But the fact remains that Mao Tse-tung had for two years been living with a second wife at the time that Yang K'ai-hui was killed.[24]

As Mao Tse-tung had undoubtedly anticipated, the failure of Li Li-san's efforts to conduct a nationwide uprising led to a campaign which was aimed at repudiating what was known as the Li Li-san line. The campaign broke the hold of Li Li-san and his supporters on the party apparatus and replaced them with a new set of leaders. The key figure in this campaign was Pavel Mif, the recently appointed Comintern representative to China. He had the support of a group of young Chinese Communists who had been his students at Sun Yat-sen University in Moscow and who came to be known ironically as the "Twenty-eight Bolsheviks." Not all of them were to make their individual marks in Chinese Communist history, but included in their ranks were the next three general secretaries of the party: Ch'en Shao-yü (better known as Wang Ming) and Ch'in Pang-hsien (also called Po Ku), both in their early twenties, and a somewhat older man named Chang Wen-t'ien (alias Lo Fu), who had once worked on a Chinese newspaper in San Francisco and who was asserted—perhaps erroneously—to have studied at the University of California in Berkeley. In the aftermath of the struggle against Li Li-san, Hsiang Chung-fa was allowed to remain on as general secretary; Chou En-lai, who had made the shifts required by changing circumstances, was retained in the Political Bureau; and Mao Tse-tung was probably elected to it *in absentia*. However, at the close of the fourth plenary session of the Sixth Central Committee, held at Shanghai in January 1931, most of the key positions at the party center were in the hands of the Twenty-eight Bolsheviks.[25]

The fall of Li Li-san, however, came well before that session. He had been expelled from his positions in the party center in November; by the latter part of December 1930, he was already in Moscow undergoing interrogation in connection with charges of deviationism and beginning an exile that would last for fifteen years. By the early days of December, too, Mao Tse-tung had arrested and imprisoned Li Li-san's principal supporters in the party apparatus of Kiangsi Province. Mao evidently took this action on his own responsibility and in his own interests, perhaps calculating that the campaign which was toppling Li Li-san left them without the protection of the party center.

The men whom Mao Tse-tung had arrested were the leading members of the Southwest Kiangsi Special Committee—a regional branch of the Central Committee—and of the Kiangsi Provincial Action Com-

mittee, one in a network of bodies which had been set up for the purpose of carrying out the plans for a nationwide uprising. The Southwest Kiangsi Special Committee had been a thorn in the side of Mao
Tse-tung, and he must have regarded the Provincial Action Committee
in the same light, because the same men dominated both committees.
Moreover, he evidently did not see them as men who had opposed him
merely in obedience to the party center, and who could be depended
upon to be more cooperative after that center was under new leadership. They were continuing to oppose him in matters of military strategy and agrarian policy, and they undoubtedly were antagonistic to
him on personal grounds as well: The general secretary of the Kiangsi
Provincial Action Committee was Tuan Liang-pi, and one of the leading members was Li Po-fang, also known as Li Wen-ling. These were
the men who had given Chu Teh and Mao Tse-tung a refuge the previous year—in the Tungku-Hsingkuo area of Kiangsi—and had then
been deprived of control of the partisan bands they had built up.[26]

The headquarters of the Kiangsi Provincial Action Committee
was located in the town of Fut'ien at the time that Mao Tse-tung had
its leading members arrested, and that is where he had them imprisoned. When he did so, he may have anticipated trouble from nearby
troops of the Twentieth Army; many of the troops were natives of the
area from which Tuan Liang-pi and Li Wen-ling came, and some of
the officers had been their followers.[27] Perhaps in the expectation of
thereby preventing its interference, Mao Tse-tung also had the political commissar of the Twentieth Army arrested and imprisoned. If that
was his intention, Mao's maneuver did not wholly succeed. On or
about December 8, a battalion political commissar of the Twentieth
Army led his men from Tungku to Fut'ien and set the imprisoned
leaders free. They fled to an area beyond easy reach of Mao Tse-tung's
party machine, where they declared their continued loyalty to Chu
Teh, P'eng Te-huai, and Huang Kung-lüeh, evidently hoping for their
support against Mao Tse-tung. However they may have felt, none of
the three came out openly against Mao Tse-tung, and the names of all
three were appended to open letters issued on December 17 and 18
which declared their continued support for Mao Tse-tung. Although
some of the rebels were still resisting more than two months later,
they and their cause now were doomed.[28]

In trying to justify the arrest of the Kiangsi party leaders, Mao
Tse-tung charged that they were liquidationists—the name used to
describe adherents of Ch'en Tu-hsiu, who had been expelled from the
party not long before—and secret agents of an A-B Corps, or Anti-
Bolshevik League, created by the Kuomintang for struggle against the
Communists. In presenting the alleged basis for this charge, Mao Tse-

tung revealed that more than 4,400 officers and men of the Red Army had been arrested as members of that league, and asserted that some of them while under questioning had identified the arrested party leaders as being among the principal members of the league.

The final suppression of the Fut'ien rebels probably cost the lives of some 2,000 or 3,000 men. One of the men to whom Mao Tse-tung assigned a role in the liquidation of the rebels was Ch'en Yi, whom Mao had originally displaced as political commissar in Chu Teh's army, and who had originally sided with Mao's opponents. In doing so, Mao Tse-tung was demonstrating deep guile and a capacity to devise strategies designed to serve more than a single purpose. According to one account, Ch'en Yi had in 1929 journeyed to Shanghai in order to inform the party center of the situation in the Fourth Red Army, and of the conflict between Chu Teh and Mao Tse-tung. But since Chu Teh was unwilling to oppose Mao Tse-tung openly, Ch'en Yi could hardly refuse the task of helping Mao liquidate the rebels. Nevertheless, his role in this affair was not something which Mao's other opponents would readily forget, and in carrying out his assignment Ch'en Yi became committed to Mao's side.[29]

When Mao Tse-tung discussed the Fut'ien incident with Edgar Snow a few years later, he described it in terms of his struggle with adherents of the Li Li-san line.[30] This suggests that his original charge that the Fut'ien rebels were agents of the Anti-Bolshevik League represented a smoke screen designed to deceive, among others, the leaders of the party in Shanghai. One of the first acts of the new party leadership there was to send Hsiang Ying to set up a branch office in Kiangsi called the Central Bureau. At first Hsiang Ying appears in the main to have accepted Mao's version of the Fut'ien incident, but soon he was asserting that the Li Li-san line had been the central factor, deploring the use of trumped-up charges, and calling for an end to intraparty conflict.[31] However, it appears that Mao Tse-tung continued, through most of the rest of 1931, to use the local apparatus of the party's Political Security Bureau to carry on his purge of opponents, real or imagined. According to Kung Ch'u, who had been absent during the Fut'ien incident but who returned to Mao's base area in the late summer or early autumn of 1931, the purge was still going on when he got there. He quotes friends as having explained to him that suspects, charged with membership in one or another of a variety of anti-Communist organizations, were forced under torture to make confessions and implicate acquaintances. In this way the purge evidently had acquired a momentum of its own, much like a fire which creates its own draft, and many innocent army personnel and party cadres lost their lives.[32]

Meanwhile, Chu Teh's armies had been defending the base area against the forces of Chiang Kai-shek. In 1930, Chiang had succeeded in defeating the offensives launched against him by the warlord coalition. Then, alerted to the growing Communist menace by Li Li-san's abortive attacks against the cities, he had launched three successive campaigns against the Kiangsi-Fukien base. In each case, the Communists allowed Chiang Kai-shek's troops to make deep penetrations into their own territory. This enabled the Communists, moving on interior lines, to pit fresh troops against tired ones, in the area which they knew best, and in which they enjoyed the benefits of a widespread intelligence network and popular support. In each of the first two offensives the Kuomintang forces were defeated, and they were withdrawn from the third before any decisive battle had been fought. Mao Tsetung was supreme within his base, and Chiang Kai-shek seemed powerless to dislodge him.

5

The Party Center Moves in on Mao

THE FIRST of the offensives which Chiang Kai-shek launched against the Kiangsi base had been begun late in 1930 and been defeated in January 1931. That spring, in the evident belief that the root of the trouble lay in Shanghai, where the Communist party center was located, Chiang Kai-shek began to devote increased police effort to the task of ferreting out the leaders. Before long his agents scored a coup. One of the "special affairs units" of the party apparatus in Shanghai was headed by a man named Ku Shun-chang, who was notorious for his ability to strangle his victims with one hand. During a visit to Wuhan, Ku Shun-chang was taken into custody by the police, to whom he gave a list of the names and addresses of prominent leaders of the party in Shanghai. Not long afterward Hsiang Chung-fa, the general secretary of the party, was seized and executed. However, most of the other leaders were warned in time, and succeeded in evading capture.

Ku Shun-chang had served under Chou En-lai, and according to more than one account it was Chou En-lai who punished him for his defection. Shortly afterward, according to one story, a servant in Ku's Shanghai household, returning from an errand, saw Chou En-lai standing on a balcony with some other men. From inside the house she heard the loud music of Peking opera and the popping of firecrackers. The servant recognized Chou En-lai, who had been a frequent visitor to the house, but not the other men with whom he was talking and laughing; becoming frightened, she ran away. Later when Ku returned home, he found the house blood-spattered and the whole family dead. Chou En-lai was himself an amateur performer of Peking opera, and its raucous music and high-pitched singing would have provided an excellent means of masking the sounds which accompanied killings. But whatever the true details of the drama, he was generally credited with having devised the plot and ordered its execution.[1]

After the arrest and execution of Hsiang Chung-fa, the party center was headed briefly by Wang Ming; after Wang was transferred to Moscow as the party's representative to the Comintern, the party center was headed by Ch'in Pang-hsien. However, the party center now operated in an atmosphere of greater insecurity, and a decision was soon made to reduce the status of the Shanghai headquarters to that of a central bureau—leaving Liu Shao-ch'i in charge—and to transfer the party center to Mao's base. The transfer of personnel may have been accomplished gradually, but at least some of the principal leaders had arrived in the central soviet by late autumn, when the First All-China Conference of Soviets was held at Juichin. The conference was convened on November 7, 1931—the anniversary of the Russian revolution and one year later than Li Li-san had proposed holding it—and established a Provisional Central Government of the Chinese Soviet Republic, with Mao Tse-tung as chairman.[2]

Election to this post gave Chairman Mao much face but little power. The various soviets were geographically dispersed, and they accordingly could not be administered from a single center.[3] Moreover, it was the party which determined policy for the civil administration as well as for the army. Prior to the move of the party center to Juichin, Mao's party position as secretary of the General Front Committee had made him supreme—that and the sheer force of his personality, intellect, and will, which evidently made him the dominating figure in any personal confrontation. But as Chu Teh is said to have remarked in December 1931: "With the coming of the center to the soviet area, everything will be settled by the party and not decided by just one person." [4]

The Chinese Communists had the Japanese to thank for the fact that they were able to meet at Juichin, in the late autumn of 1931, and hold their congress without having to worry about the likelihood of an attack from Chiang Kai-shek. Chiang had pitted only miscellaneous forces against them in the first and second campaigns, and those had been badly chewed up. But he had used some of his own crack divisions in the third campaign and he had directed it himself. They had advanced rapidly, and by the middle of September it appeared that nothing the Communists could do would prevent his occupying Juichin itself. But on the night of September 18, 1931, elements of the Japanese Kuantung Army—the force which garrisoned the Japanese leased territory in south Manchuria and guarded the lines of the South Manchurian Railway—staged an incident which it made the excuse for occupying Mukden, the governmental center and most important city of Manchuria. This incident required Chiang's full and immediate attention, and he accordingly broke off his campaign against the central soviet.[5]

Chiang Kai-shek was anxious to avoid a war with Japan. He accordingly asked Chang Hsüeh-liang, the heir and successor of Marshal Chang Tso-lin, to follow a policy of nonresistance, evidently hoping that the incident could be localized. Chiang's hope proved vain, and on September 23 he announced that China was entrusting its case to the League of Nations. Chang Hsüeh-liang obeyed the instructions of Chiang Kai-shek, with the consequences that he saved much of his army but quickly lost Manchuria.

Chiang Kai-shek's policy of nonresistance was still in force in January 1932, when Japanese marines made a landing at Shanghai. However, the Nineteenth Route Army under Ts'ai T'ing-k'ai—the commander who had participated unwillingly in the initial phase of the march back to Kwangtung during the Nanchang Uprising—put up a sturdy resistance. His army was joined, in its disobedience to orders, by two of Chiang's own divisions; the Japanese were stopped in their tracks; and in May they signed an agreement which brought the hostilities at Shanghai to an end.[6]

In the interval between the outbreak of the fighting in Shanghai and its termination, Manchuria had been declared independent of China, and the puppet state of Manchukuo had been established there.[7] The Japanese decision to detach Manchuria suggested that they had no immediate intention of extending their conquests into China proper, and their willingness to bring the hostilities at Shanghai to an end confirmed that. Accordingly, Chiang Kai-shek was freed to resume his attacks on his Chinese Communist enemies.

The Chinese Communists made good use of the period of respite which began immediately after the Mukden incident. That respite enabled them to expand the central soviet until it covered many counties with a total population which Mao estimated at 2,500,000, and to increase their armies both by drawing on the manpower of the base area itself and by winning over and reorganizing enemy troops. Meanwhile Ho Lung similarly increased the area under his control and expanded his forces, as did Hsü Hsiang-ch'ien, with Chang Kuo-t'ao as his political commissar. In consequence, the total strength of the Red armies reached an estimated 200,000 men.[8]

The apparent success of the Communists in repelling Kuomintang offensives, Chiang Kai-shek's preoccupation with the problem of Japanese aggression, and the growth of the Red armies had led the new leaders of the Communist party to conclude that the guerrilla phase was over. They accordingly adopted a forward, aggressive line in military affairs, which envisioned attacks on major centers, and on January 1, 1932, they called for the winning of a preliminary victory in one or several provinces.[9]

In response to this call, the troops under Ho Lung poured out from their base and menaced western Hupeh. This put Wuhan in danger of being caught in a pincers between Ho Lung's forces and those of Hsü Hsiang-ch'ien and Chang Kuo-t'ao, which became active around their Hupei-Honan-Anhwei base. Mao Tse-tung opposed the new policy but was overruled. In March 1932, Lin Piao, who had not long before been made commander of the First Army Corps, was given command of an Eastern Front Army composed of his own force and the Fifth Army Corps. That spring he launched an offensive in Fukien which carried the Communist flag all the way to Changchow, just short of the seaport of Amoy.[10]

Chiang Kai-shek began the fourth anti-Communist campaign in June. Dealing with first things first—which is to say the threat to the strategic center of Wuhan—he defeated the armies of Ho Lung, which were driven back to their borderlands base, and of Hsü Hsiang-ch'ien and Chang Kuo-t'ao, which retreated westward into Szechwan. Chiang was then ready to turn his attention to the less pressing if more important problem of conquering the main base area centered around Juichin.[11]

In August 1932, the Communist leaders of party, army, and government held a conference at Ningtu to discuss the strategy to be employed in defending the central soviet against the expected onslaught. Chou En-lai, chairman of the party's Military Commission, and Liu Po-ch'eng, now returned from military studies in the USSR and serving as chief of staff, both favored a strategy designed to defeat the enemy beyond the borders of the soviet. Mao Tse-tung, who came to the conference direct from the victory at Changchow where he is said to have led troops which destroyed a Kuomintang division, argued that the Communists follow the strategy they had employed in Chiang's three previous campaigns: Permit the enemy to penetrate the base area and fight them there.[12]

Mao Tse-tung presumably argued, as he later wrote, that the Communists, although numerically inferior to the enemy in overall terms, could nevertheless win by concentrating superior forces for each of a succession of battles with individual parts of the enemy's total force. As he put it: "Our strategy is 'pit one against ten', and our tactics are 'pit ten against one'—this is one of our fundamental principles for gaining mastery over the enemy." [13] He must also have argued that his tactics and strategy could be applied most successfully within the base area, where the Communists knew every road and trail and where their organization of the populace would enable them to move in secrecy and learn of every movement by the enemy. Operating there on interior lines, they were in the position analogous to the spider within his web, the strands of which quickly told him when and where any part had been touched, permitted him to move with ease both outward and laterally, and yet entrapped invaders who might try to move on them.

We do not know what arguments Chou En-lai and Liu Po-ch'eng

advanced. They may have pointed out that Mao Tse-tung's strategy had worked well against miscellaneous forces and their commanders during the first two campaigns, but not against crack divisions commanded by Chiang Kai-shek in the third. They may also have pointed to the destruction which repeated invasions inflicted upon the base area, its resources, and its inhabitants. And they may have asked whether the allegiance of the people could be permanently held by a government which made it a policy to permit penetrations of the base area instead of endeavoring to protect its populace.[14] But the clinching argument probably was that the Communists were in possession of Chiang Kai-shek's military plans and hence in a position to defeat his forces "beyond the gates."

The Chinese Communists had captured some radio sets during the first so-called encirclement campaign in 1930. In January 1931, Mao Tse-tung and Chu Teh had set up a special radio unit, and before long the Communists were intercepting and trying to decode enemy messages. The cryptographic capabilities of the Chinese Communists undoubtedly were enhanced during 1931, when experienced intelligence agents like Li K'e-nung moved from Shanghai to the central soviet, and in 1932 they were able to decode the radio messages of the Military Affairs Commission of the Nanking Government. This enabled them to read the traffic between Nanking and the military commanders who were to take part in the fourth campaign, and to devise battle plans based upon a knowledge of the enemy's dispositions and intentions.[15]

The strategy of Chou En-lai and Liu Po-ch'eng, designed to defeat the enemy beyond the gates, was based on more than knowledge of enemy military plans. It also was in accord with the aggressive and forward policy which had been adopted by the Political Bureau under the leadership of the Twenty-eight Bolsheviks. In consequence, when Mao Tse-tung argued against the application of that strategy, one of the Twenty-eight Bolsheviks—Chang Wen-t'ien, alias Lo Fu—subjected Mao to a bitter attack during which he evidently demanded that Mao Tse-tung should be expelled from the party. At any rate, some years later Mao Tse-tung recalled: "At the Ningtu conference, Lo Fu wanted to expel me, but Chou and Chu objected."[16]

After the Ningtu conference Mao Tse-tung went to Changting, in western Fukien. Complaining that he felt ill, he consulted Dr. Nelson Fu, the Chinese Christian who ran the Fuyin (Gospel) Hospital there. Dr. Fu diagnosed Mao's trouble as the consequence of physical exhaustion, decided that he needed daily treatments, and entered him in his hospital. Mao remained there for four months.

When he was deeply engaged, as he doubtless had been during

the recently concluded Fukien campaign, Mao Tse-tung was prone to extend himself for prolonged periods during which he took little rest. He must have gone to the Ningtu conference feeling keyed up, been under considerable tension during the struggle which went on there, been deeply chagrined at the outcome, and departed with an acute sense of letdown. It accordingly would probably be unfair to conclude that Mao's illness was entirely political.

However, Mao was not too exhausted, while in the hospital, to ask a multitude of questions about the details of its administration. Learning that it had only six physicians on the staff, recalling the needs of the Red Army, and pointing out that conditions were relatively peaceful, he urged Dr. Fu to use the period of comparative tranquility to train a batch of army doctors. When Dr. Fu told him that it took several years to train a doctor, Mao impatiently declared: "Several years is too long, one or two years is enough!" Somewhat later Mao told Dr. Fu that the Kuomintang would soon be carrying out military operations in western Fukien and persuaded him to transfer his hospital from that area to Juichin. Mao also got the name Fuyin Hospital—with its missionary connotation—changed to Central Red Hospital.[17]

The part of Chiang Kai-shek's fourth campaign which was directed against the central soviet and against nearby Communist-held areas had an inauspicious beginning. In a night ambush of one of Chiang's columns, the Communists decimated two whole Kuomintang divisions. Chiang resumed the offensive a month later, only to meet a devastating defeat which brought the offensive to an end.[18]

However, in Fukien, and perhaps in immediately adjacent areas of eastern Kiangsi and northern Kwangtung, the Communists did not follow the strategy of attempting to defeat the enemy "beyond the gates." In Fukien, the acting provincial secretary of the party—a man named Lo Ming—evacuated the inhabitants from a number of towns and nearby areas, and the Communists fought the invaders there in accordance with the guerrilla strategy which had been favored by Mao Tse-tung.

The party center reacted to his apparent breach of discipline by firing Lo Ming. Designating the strategy followed in his area the "Lo Ming line," the party center also initiated a "struggle," or campaign of attack, designed to discredit that line and to punish its supporters. Mao Tse-tung supposedly had left military affairs to others during the months which followed the Ningtu conference, but there seems little doubt that the struggle against the Lo Ming line was intended to weaken Mao's influence within the army and over subordinate elements of the party apparatus. Mao Tse-tung's own secretary was probably expelled from the party during the struggle, for he dropped from sight and never reappeared. He had, incidentally, played a prominent role during the Fut'ien episode—an affair which the leaders of the party can hardly have forgotten or forgiven. Among those subjected to criticism were Mao's own brother, Mao Tse-t'an, and three other men who later rose to high position: Teng Hsiao-p'ing, described as Mao Tse-t'an's "confederate"; T'an Chen-lin, commander in chief of the Fukien Military District; and Hsiao Ching-kuang, commander in the Fukien-Kiangsi border area. Finally, a short time after the struggle against the Lo Ming line had begun, Chou En-lai assumed Mao's former position of political commissar of the forces commanded by Chu Teh.[19]

In the autumn of 1933, the Communists lost an opportunity, presented by a rebellion centered in Fukien, to alter the course of their war with Chiang Kai-shek. Afterward, Mao Tse-tung and his opponents in the leadership apparently each tried to place the blame on the other's doorstep. It is doubtful that the accounts of Mao or of his critics can be taken at face value, but the circumstances leading up to the rebellion and its military course and outcome all are clear. During February 1933, the Japanese had extended their aggression against China by invading the Inner Mongolian province of Jehol; in April their forces passed through the Great Wall and entered China proper; and in May Chiang Kai-shek agreed, as the price of a truce signed at Tangku, to demilitarize a wedge-shaped piece of territory which began at Peking and ran north and east to the Great Wall. This concession lent force to a groundswell of discontent over the course being pursued by Chiang Kai-shek: Each aggression by Japan seemed to lead to an act of appeasement, and each act of appeasement to be followed by a fresh aggression.

This groundswell lifted the hopes of some of Chiang Kai-shek's old rivals in south China, who wished to present themselves as alternatives to his rule. Several of them allied themselves with Ts'ai T'ing-k'ai, commander of the Nineteenth Route Army and hero of the previous year's battles with the Japanese at Shanghai but since then transferred to Fukien to fight the Communists. Beginning in the spring of 1933, these leaders sounded out the Chinese Communists, and in October the two sides reached a preliminary agreement for an alliance directed against Chiang Kai-shek and calling for resistance to Japan. The following month the rebels declared the establishment at Foochow, capital of Fukien province, of a People's Revolutionary Government. Then two weeks later the Communists issued a statement denouncing it, and when Chiang Kai-shek initiated a military campaign against it, they stood idly by.[20]

Chiang Kai-shek had begun his fifth campaign against the Chinese Communists about the same time that they were reaching their preliminary agreement with the Fukien rebels. He put down the Fukien rebellion within a few short weeks, and his fifth campaign got well underway early in 1934. In planning and conducting this campaign, Chiang had the assistance of a group of German advisers headed by General Hans von Seeckt. They had devised a strategy of blockade, conducted by a huge force of about 700,000 men. Thousands of small fortifications were built from which the intervening areas could be covered by machine gun and artillery fire. More such works, with supporting roads, were gradually built inwards in concentric rings. This military strangulation was supported by an economic blockade, and even salt—so necessary, in the long run, in man's diet—became scarce.[21]

In this situation the ability to decode the enemy's radio traffic, which assertedly had provided the foundation for the success of the forward and offensive strategy employed by the Communists in the fourth campaign, was of limited use. It was also a situation which would have afforded little scope for the application of Mao's strategy of allowing enemy columns to penetrate deep into the Communist base area and destroying them there. Chiang's forces did not push forward in columns this time, but only in a way which forced the Chinese Communists to fight positional battles they could not win. Chiang's forces advanced gradually and methodically, covered by artillery fire and with their flanks well-guarded. This left the Chinese Communists with only two alternatives to surrender: to go down fighting in the defense of the base area and its populace, or to abandon them in the hope of surviving through flight.

In 1936, in discussing this period, Mao Tse-tung wrote:

At the time of the Fukien incident, two months after the commencement of our fifth countercampaign, the main forces of the Red Army should have thrust into the Kiangsu-Chekiang-Anhwei-Kiangsi region, with Chekiang as the center, and swept over the length and breadth of the area between Hangchow, Soochow, Nanking, Wuhu, Nanchang, and Foochow, turning our strategic defensive into a strategic offensive, menacing the enemy's vital centers, and seeking battles in the vast areas where there were no blockhouses. By such means we could have compelled the enemy, who was attacking southern Kiangsi and western Fukien, to turn back to defend his vital centers, broken his attack on the base area in Kiangsi, and rendered aid to the Fukien People's Government—we certainly could have aided it by these means. As this plan was rejected, the enemy's fifth "encirclement and suppression" campaign could not be broken, and the People's Government in Fukien inevitably collapsed.[22]

This "plan," of course, represented precisely the sort of adventure to which Mao Tse-tung had objected in 1930, at a time when conditions had been relatively favorable: Chiang Kai-shek then was under attack from a powerful coalition, and the forces of Ho Lung and Hsü Hsiang-ch'ien were still in central China and available to take part in the Communist offensive. In 1934, a campaign capable of threatening Chiang Kai-shek's capital and other major cities would undoubtedly have required all the forces the Communists could muster, and this would have run counter to Mao's earlier warning that base areas would immediately be occupied by the enemy if they were left without armed forces adequate for their defense. Accordingly, by conveying the impression that he favored such a campaign at the time of the Fukien rebellion, Mao Tse-tung was implying that he had been acutely aware of the consequences which would flow from a failure to give military support to the Foochow regime.

It is difficult to square this implication with the record. On January 13, 1934, when the tide of battle was clearly running against Ts'ai T'ing-k'ai's Nineteenth Route Army, the Chinese Communists sent the rebel leaders a telegram urging them to arm the masses in defense of Foochow and other strategic cities, and expressing the opinion that this was "the only way out." The nearest thing to an offer of military assistance, which this telegram contained, was the statement: "It should be proclaimed to the Nineteenth Route Army that the only way to fight Japan and Chiang would be to cooperate throughout with the Soviet government and the Red Army, supported by a concerted military action." The telegram was sent by the Provisional Central Government of the Chinese Soviet Republic, of which Mao Tse-tung was chairman, and his name was appended at the end of the text.[23] Moreover, a little later that same month Mao Tse-tung declared that the Fukien regime represented a portion of the reactionary ruling class which regarded the Communists as an enemy and the Kuomintang as rotten. In order to save themselves, the participating leaders had set up their People's Revolutionary Government, intending to deceive the masses into believing that there was a third road between those of the Kuomintang and of Communism.[24]

It might be argued that Mao Tse-tung may not have agreed with the line taken in the telegram sent in his name, that he had merely been acting as the mouthpiece of the party center when he gave a hostile analysis of the character of the Foochow regime and its leaders. But almost two years later, at a time when he had achieved a dominant position within the leadership, Mao again criticized the Fukien People's Revolutionary Government for "failing to arouse the people to struggle" and expressed the opinion that the Nineteenth Route Army led by Ts'ai T'ing-k'ai represented the class interests of sections of the bourgeoisie and of the landowning classes.[25]

Although Ts'ai T'ing-k'ai clearly did not want to fight the Communists while Japanese aggression remained unchecked, Mao Tse-tung was correct in his evaluation insofar as it applied to the other principal leaders of the Fukien regime; most of them, at base, were men who regarded the Communists as their enemies. Holding that view, it would have been natural for Mao to urge the line taken in his telegram; it represented an attempt to take advantage both of the leaders of the Fukien regime and of their rebellion. The proposal for concerted military operations against Chiang Kai-shek undoubtedly was sincere, but that involved the question of who would do the concerting. Mao Tse-tung would certainly have opposed putting elements of the Red Army at the disposal of the political leaders of the Fukien regime. The proposal concerning the Nineteenth Route Army made in his telegram was, however, a scarcely-veiled effort to detach that army from its allegiance to the Fukien regime and bring it under Communist control.[26]

If Mao was indeed the author of the strategy which the telegram embodied, it would hardly have been accepted if it had not had the support of other leaders as well.[27] However, it represented a position which was sufficiently subtle, if not ambiguous, to be readily misrepresented—as it undoubtedly was later, both by him and by his enemies. And if Mao was the author or most vocal advocate of the underlying strategy, then he was liable to be made the scapegoat for its failure once the Communists had absorbed the consequences of Chiang Kai-shek's victory over the Nineteenth Route Army. A friendly regime in Fukien would have given the Communists access to its seaports and its markets and relieved them of the need to protect their western flank. Instead, the Communists now were ringed in by enemy forces and under tight blockade.

In August 1934, Mao Tse-tung—suffering from malaria, in political eclipse, and perhaps even ordered under house arrest—took up residence in the small town of Yütu, Kiangsi. Kung Ch'u was at that time commander of the South Kiangsi military area, with headquarters at Yütu. According to his account, he was surprised one afternoon to have Mao Tse-tung ride up to his gate in the company of two men of the Political Security Bureau. Kung Ch'u invited Mao into his headquarters, noted that his skin was yellow and his appearance haggard, and inquired about his health. Mao replied that he had been low in health and spirits. After he had washed his face to refresh himself after the journey and lit a cigarette, Mao explained that he would henceforth be conducting the affairs of the government from Yütu. Apparently the Political Security Bureau personnel who had accompanied Mao Tse-tung had immediately made his wants known, for an official of the party's county committee came hurrying in at this point, saying that a house and garden nearby were being put at his disposal.

During the days which followed, Kung Ch'u thought it strange that Mao Tse-tung seldom had a visitor. Accordingly, the next time he was in Juichin he asked Chu Teh why Mao was directing the government from Yütu. Chu Teh laughed, as though enjoying another man's misfortune, and indicated that Mao was being punished by the party. However, Chu Teh seemed disinclined to say more, so Kung Ch'u sought out a friend whom he believed to be well-acquainted with the affairs of the party center. According to this friend, Mao Tse-tung had been put on probation for his role in the Fukien affair. When the question of supporting the Fukien rebels came up for discussion in the Political Bureau, Chou En-lai, Ch'in Pang-hsien, and Chang Wen-t'ien had wanted to send two army groups into Fukien with the missions of backing up the Nineteenth Route Army and helping carry out a purge of wavering elements. However, Mao Tse-tung had stubbornly opposed this course, urging that the Communists should wait until the Nineteenth Route Army had proven its will to fight. Actually, the Nineteenth Route Army had been defeated more quickly than any of them had anticipated, but when it became evident that it was too late to back up that army, the blame had been placed on Mao Tse-tung.[28]

The month before Mao Tse-tung moved to Yütu, the Chinese Communists directed an army commanded by Fang Chih-min—with Su Yü as chief of staff—to attempt a breakthrough and march north, perhaps as a diversionary operation. The army succeeded in breaking out, but not in taking the pressure off the central area; it was soon cut up, its commander was taken prisoner, and the remnants of the force thenceforth operated as guerrillas under the command of Su Yü. In August another army, with Hsiao K'o, Wang Chen, and Jen Pi-shih as leaders, broke out and headed west for the Hunan-Kweichow border area. This operation was successful, and in October Hsiao K'o and his comrades succeeded in linking up their army with the forces of Ho Lung.[29]

By October 1934, the central soviet had been reduced to a small fraction of its former area, and the Communists were forced to the conclusion that they could not save their main force without abandoning the Kiangsi base. This conclusion led them to make some brutal decisions. Only thirty-five women would be permitted to accompany the hundred thousand persons—about 85,000 of them soldiers and the rest cadres of the party and the government—who would take part in the attempt to break out. Mao Tse-tung's wife Ho Shih-chen, then well advanced in pregnancy, was one of them; so was Chu Teh's wife

K'ang K'o-ch'ing. But most of the men with wives would have to abandon them. There were about 20,000 wounded soldiers who would have to be left behind, together with a force of regular and other troops which were to mount a last ditch defense in order that the others might get away. A number of leaders—including Hsiang Ying, Ch'en Yi, and Mao Tse-tung's brother Mao Tse-t'an—were to direct the defense and then escape with whatever remnants they could salvage, organizing them for guerrilla warfare. Ch'ü Ch'iu-pai, a former general secretary of the party, was also left behind because he was believed to be slowly dying of tuberculosis. (After the loss of Juichin, the Nationalists killed Mao Tse-t'an; Ch'ü Ch'iu-pai was captured and later executed.)[30] It was decided that a number of military officers and political commissars whose trustworthiness was in doubt would be permitted to take part in the breakthrough, but only in the custody of Political Security Bureau guards.[31] In advance of the breakthrough there was a purge, according to Kung Ch'u, during which many cadres of the army and the government who were adjudged to be wavering or reactionary elements were taken to a restricted area and liquidated.[32]

6

Long Marches, and
the Road to War

THE MAIN BODY gathered, one morning in the middle of October 1934, for the beginning of the march. Those who were setting out could not know that the retreat they were beginning would last a whole year, that they would have to travel five or six thousand miles to reach their destination, and that only about one in ten would complete the journey. One of the participants in this terrible retreat, which was to become known as the Long March, later told of watching Chu Teh and Chou En-lai ride in with the personnel of general headquarters, followed by members of the Central Committee. Among the members of the Central Committee was Mao Tse-tung, looking thin and emaciated from his illness. Armies under the command of Lin Piao and P'eng Te-huai went ahead to open the way; they were followed by a training regiment, the headquarters staff, party and government cadres, the supply department, an arsenal unit, printers with printing presses, the government mint, doctors and nurses, and even the tailors of the uniform factory with their sewing machines. Additional army units protected the flanks and brought up the rear.[1]

The success of Hsiao K'o's breakthrough of the previous August evidently had told the Communists what direction to take; they too would move westward and attempt to link up with the forces of Ho Lung. Until the Communists reached the first line of fortifications, they traveled only at night. In consequence, the advance elements of the Communist armies were able to launch a surprise assault, occupy a string of fortifications and entrenchments, and open the way for the others to pass through. After that they moved as rapidly as they could, marching four hours and resting four hours, day and night. Beyond the first ring lay three other rings of blockading forces. When they broke through the last one at the end of November, about half their troop strength had been lost through desertions and battle casualties. By this time they were on the Hunan-Kwangsi border. But Chiang Kai-shek had divined their intention, and he interposed powerful armies between them and the forces of Ho Lung and Hsiao K'o. The Communists accordingly abandoned their original plan and moved into the sparsely populated and lightly defended province of Kwei-chow.[2]

In Kweichow the Chinese Communists were able to interrupt their flight long enough to rest and confer. It will be recalled that each of the major setbacks of past years had been followed by changes in the top leadership. In Kweichow, the Political Bureau held a meeting at Lip'ing in December 1934, but it produced no change in top leadership. Evidently the majority was standing together behind Ch'in Pang-hsien, the general secretary. If he were to be unseated, it would take a meeting like that held at Kiukiang in 1927. It is doubtful that there had been a quorum at that party conference, and some of the participants then were not even members of the Central Committee, but it had repudiated Ch'en Tu-hsiu and enabled Ch'ü Ch'iu-pai to assume the leadership of the party.

Mao Tse-tung accordingly agitated for the holding of a meeting of the Political Bureau which would be enlarged through the inclusion of ranking military leaders. He also undertook a campaign to line up supporters among the intended participants. The top leaders of the party were loath to call such a meeting, but they did not need to be told that survival depended, as never before, upon the army. Accordingly, after the matter had been raised and had become a burning issue, they capitulated. Moreover, they evidently agreed that the military participants would be allowed to vote along with the members of the Political Bureau itself.

The meeting took place at Tsunyi, Kweichow, in January 1935. It represented a turning point, in Mao's rise to power, which was later treated as though it had marked his arrival at the summit. Before Tsunyi his upward climb had been interrupted by reversals—he had probably been expelled either from the Central Committee or its Political Bureau three times and been given the lesser punishment of a reprimand eight times.[3] At the Tsunyi conference he scored an important if a limited victory, but whether it would be followed by further reversals could not then be judged. In later years it came to be asserted that Mao Tse-tung was elected the chairman of the party at the Tsunyi conference—an assertion which seems consistent with the official history of the party, until the relevant passage of that history is read with care.

The sharp edge of the wedge which Mao used to split the leadership necessarily had a narrow range of targets. He directed the main force of his blows against Otto Braun, a representative of the Comintern who had succeeded in slipping into the central soviet, and against Ch'in Pang-hsien, alias Po Ku, the general secretary of the party. Policies cannot be brought under attack without touching those who have espoused them, and here again Mao attacked only on a narrow front. He asserted that the party's political line and the instructions it had received from the Comintern had both been correct, and that conditions for a decisive victory had existed at the beginning of the enemy's fifth campaign. Victory had not been achieved—despite the bravery and skill of the Red Army, the high standard of work in the rear, and the support of the broad masses—simply because the military leadership could not follow the correct strategy and tactics which had been employed in the earlier campaigns. They could not follow them because Otto Braun "monopolized the work of the Military Commission," and was committed to a strategy of pure defense.

This was a rationale which was bound to appeal to almost everyone present: to the leading cadres of the party, whose political line was praised and whose evaluation of the objective situation at the start of the fifth campaign was reaffirmed; to the leaders of the government, who had been responsible for rear area support; and, above all, to the military commanders, because it lifted from them the imputation of blame for a catastrophic defeat. It was also a rationale which reaffirmed the correctness of Mao's own strategic and tactical concepts. If accepted, it would enable him to speak with authority about the decisions—mostly military in nature—which faced the Chinese Communists then and would face them for some time to come.

In his report, delivered at the beginning of the Tsunyi conference, Ch'in Pang-hsien had refused to admit that there had been misjudgment on the part of the military leadership. Having endorsed the strategy and tactics which had been employed, he had to take responsibility for the defeat which was attributed to employing them. At Tsunyi he was deposed, and Chang Wen-t'ien succeeded him as general secretary of the party. A measure of the blame must, at least by inference, have attached also to Chu Teh and Chou En-lai: Chu Teh, as chairman of the Military Commission of the soviet government, for allowing Otto Braun too much authority; and Chou En-lai, as chairman of the similarly-named commission of the party, for allowing that body to become overshadowed instead of maintaining a moral ascendancy. After Tsunyi, it is said, Mao exercised the decision-making powers, in the military field, which had earlier been exercised by Chou En-lai and the discredited Otto Braun. But whether he formally replaced Chou En-lai as chairman of the party's Military Commission at Tsunyi or somewhat later is a question on which available sources do not agree.[4]

When the American writer Edgar Snow visited the headquarters of the Chinese Communists in 1936, they mentioned to him the military operations they had conducted in the vicinity of Tsunyi. But if they then thought of the conference held there as one which had produced momentous changes in the leadership, they evidently did not see fit to tell him of it.[5] Nym Wales spent some months with the Chinese Communists in 1937, and in a record of that visit she wrote: "Mao Tse-tung is chairman of the Military Committee (nothing else now)." [6] Yet in 1945 the Central Committee adopted a resolution which read in part as follows: "The Tsunyi Meeting . . . inaugurated a new central leadership, headed by Comrade Mao Tse-tung—a historic change of paramount importance in the Chinese Communist party." [7]

In 1945, the outcome of World War II was no longer in doubt and the Communists were anticipating a period during which they would again challenge the hegemony of the National Government of the Kuomintang headed by Chiang Kai-shek, now a prestigious figure who had led the nation through the eight long years of China's war with Japan. It accordingly served the interests of the Communist party—as well as of Mao Tse-tung and his close supporters within the party—to build up Mao's image as a comparably great and farseeing figure. It also served their purposes to portray the party as one which had for a decade enjoyed unity under wise and stable leadership. But the question of the exact position to which Mao Tse-tung had been elected at Tsunyi—if, indeed, he had been elected there to any additional position whatsoever—had to be evaded. It had to be evaded because in 1935 the position of general secretary—to which Chang Wen-t'ien had been elected—was the top one in the hierarchy.

In 1967, at a time when violent feuds had broken out in China between rival factions, each of which sought to be recognized as the leadership core about which a new organization was to be formed, Mao Tse-tung was quoted as saying: "They are fighting for the position of being 'the core.' That is not worth fighting for. The core is formed in the midst of struggle. At the Tsunyi conference some people would have had me as the core, but I would have nothing of the kind. I thought I had better let Chang Wen-t'ien do the job." [8] The Chinese Communists then were still under the direction of the Comintern, Mao was only a "native Communist" whereas Chang Wen-t'ien was one of the Twenty-eight Bolsheviks, and as Mao remarked of them on another occasion: "They were indispensable at the time." [9]

After the Tsunyi conference, the Communists abandoned much of the heavy equipment which had slowed their march, complicated the tasks of the defending troops, and predisposed the Communists to taking the most direct routes towards their objectives. With the way to Ho Lung's Second Front Army in Hunan blocked, they now were attempting to link up with the Fourth Front Army of Hsü Hsiang-ch'ien and Chang Kuo-t'ao, in the western province of Szechwan. In order to mask their intention and defeat Chiang Kai-shek's efforts to bring them to bay, they took an indirect route. It was marked by many feints and reversals, and it took them through Kweichow, Yunnan, and Sikang provinces—extremely rugged areas of southwest and west China inhabited largely by Miao, Lolo, Tibetan, and other minority peoples.

Perhaps the most dangerous portion of the route was in western Szechwan, where they had to cross the Tatu River, a rushing torrent which runs through deep chasms. As both Chiang Kai-shek and Mao Tse-tung were aware, this had been the site of decisive battles during the period celebrated in *Romance of the Three Kingdoms,* and in the nineteenth century, when a great army of the Taiping rebels had been wiped out by imperial forces. Chiang Kai-shek tried to trap the Communists here, but they managed to escape through a series of heroic exploits. After they crossed the Tatu River, the only important obstacle between them and their fellow Communists in Szechwan was one high, snow-covered pass. Tired, frozen, and with some of them ill— Mao Tse-tung had to be carried on a stretcher—they crossed the pass late in spring and soon linked up with elements of the Fourth Front Army.[10]

In Szechwan the army rested for some weeks while the leaders conferred. According to an account given to Edgar Snow a short time later, Chang Kuo-t'ao and Hsü Hsiang-ch'ien, whose Fourth Front Army was somewhat the larger of the two, favored remaining in Szechwan and trying to reassert Communist power south of the Yangtze. Mao Tse-tung insisted on continuing northward to the Shensi-Kansu border area just below the Great Wall, where Kao Kang and Liu Chih-tan had set up a soviet. Neither Mao Tse-tung nor Chang Kuo-t'ao would yield to the other, and in consequence the Communists split into two groups. Mao Tse-tung, Lin Piao, P'eng Te-huai and Chou En-lai led the smaller group northward; Chu Teh and Liu Po-ch'eng, with part of the First Front Army, remained behind with Chang Kuo-t'ao and Hsü Hsiang-ch'ien.[11]

Beyond northwestern Szechwan lies the province of Tsinghai, a part of China's high, cold, Tibetan borderlands. Much of it is a wind-swept, desolate land of arid wastes, great swamps and scanty vegetation through which the traveler may pass for days and days without seeing a human habitation. Other portions are inhabited by tribespeople who live in a mixed pastoral and agricultural economy. The men, colorfully clad, fur hats worn at a rakish angle and rifles with long fork-rests slung across their backs, often make a dashing appearance, particularly when on horseback. But the Communists found that these

Tibetans were the enemies of all Chinese, and many of the Chinese lost their lives in consequence of the hardships of the march and the hostility of the people they encountered.[12]

Once out of Tsinghai and into Kansu, the Communists had to fight several more battles against Kuomintang and provincial Moslem troops, but on October 20, 1935—a year after they had set out from Kiangsi—Mao Tse-tung and some thousands of his comrades finally entered the soviet which had been established by Kao Kang and Liu Chih-tan. Here they found a refuge, and here—first in the small town of Paoan and later in Yenan—the party leaders made their headquarters.

Some time after the end of the Long March, Mao Tse-tung, following his usual practice, brought under his own control the forces of the base in which he had found refuge. The Fifteenth Army Corps, which had been based in the Shensi soviet, was incorporated in the command of his faithful follower Lin Piao.[13]

The Communists of the Second Front Army, under Ho Lung and Hsiao K'o, began a long march of their own about the time that Mao Tse-tung and his comrades were settling down in Shensi, and it took them equally long. In the spring of 1936, one of the armies under Hsü Hsiang-ch'ien and Chang Kuo-t'ao drove southward to open the way. Thereafter the Second Front Army, the Fourth Front Army, and the portion of the First Front Army which had stayed with Chu Teh and Liu Po-ch'eng all set out for the Communist base in Shensi. When all had arrived, in the autumn of 1936, the total strength of the Communist forces there was perhaps almost as great as that of the First Front Army which had left the Kiangsi soviet two years before.[14]

However, Chang Kuo-t'ao, still unwilling to subordinate himself to Mao Tse-tung, evidently wished to establish a soviet of his own farther on in the northwest. He ordered Hsü Hsiang-ch'ien and two other commanders to press onwards; but they met heavy defeats at the hands of Moslem cavalry and Kuomintang troops, and the remnants finally returned to Shensi.

There can be little doubt that the most authoritative voice at the base to which Chang Kuo-t'ao returned, late in 1936, was that of Mao Tse-tung. Chang Kuo-t'ao later related that he went to see Mao, about that time, found him berating Chang Wen-t'ien, the general secretary of the party, in the most obscene language possible, and saw Chang Wen-t'ien slip out of the room, ashamed and humiliated.[15] Chang Kuo-t'ao had himself already undergone the humiliation of having to return in defeat to the camp of his opponent, but early in 1937 he suffered the further indignity of being put on trial for his mistakes. The verdict was that he—who had been chairman of the meeting at which the party had been founded, and one of its principal leaders ever since—was to study until he had rectified his errors.[16] It accordingly is small wonder that he later left both Yenan and the Chinese Communist party, an outcome which undoubtedly gave considerable satisfaction to Mao Tse-tung.

In central China the Communists had been able to exploit, as motive power for their revolution, the discontent of the peasantry. At the root of this discontent lay the fact that an expanding population was pressing against limited and fixed amounts of arable land. In consequence of this pressure, tenant farmers had to pay high rents. Often they were forced to borrow, and if the attendant risks to the lender were high, so were the rates of interest. To cap it all, it was the agrarian populace on which the chief burden of taxation fell. The Communists could appeal to the peasant with policies which bettered his lot at the expense of the landlord. They also gained wide respect by enforcing in their armies, which provided the spearhead for their political work, standards of behavior toward the populace which were unexpected—if not unique—in a land where men with guns often took whatever they wanted.

In the northwest, the Communists were in a position to exploit another powerful force of more general appeal; but for this circumstance they might never have been able to survive, much less rise to power. This second motive force was Chinese nationalism, directed against the Japanese—who were then encroaching on north China from their base in Manchuria. As early as 1932 the Chinese Communists had reacted to that encroachment by adopting a declaration of war against Japan. Then in 1933 they had offered to make common cause with "any armed force," meaning any dissident commander, provided he agreed to the cessation of attacks on soviet areas, the granting of "democratic rights" and the arming of the masses against Japan. Coming from a relatively small force far removed from the areas of Japanese encroachment, this was not an impressive offer. However, once the Communists were in northwest China, such proposals no longer had the appearance of mere propaganda gestures. Moreover, they had an attraction for people of all classes throughout China.[17]

One of the first to respond to the logic of the Communist appeal for a united front was General Sung Che-yüan, who administered the Peking area, standing under the immediate threat of Japanese forces just to the north. In 1936 Liu Shao-ch'i, then working underground as head of the Northern Bureau of the Chinese Communist Party, was able—working through an intermediary—to reach an agreement with General Sung. Under this agreement, Sung Che-yüan released from prison a substantial number of Communists who had earlier been picked up by his police. Perhaps to cover himself if the releases were questioned by the Nationalist authorities in Nanking, he required that each man so released should first sign a pledge to renounce Communism. The pledge was one which generally was not kept, and perhaps neither side expected that it would be. And before the arrangement was consummated, Liu Shao-ch'i first cleared it with the secretariat of the party, headed by Chang Wen-t'ien. Nevertheless, the agreement was, three decades later, to be the basis for charges of treason to the party leveled against Liu Shao-ch'i and the men whose release he arranged.[18]

The Communist appeal for an anti-Japanese united front had special meaning for the troops which Chiang Kai-shek brought in to reinforce the units already facing the Communists in their new base area. They were homesick natives of Manchuria, driven out by the Japanese, and they were commanded by Marshal Chang Hsüeh-liang, the former ruler of that area. The Chinese Communists put to them a simple appeal: Why should Chinese be fighting Chinese when it was the Japanese who were occupying Manchuria and threatening to conquer the rest of China as well?

On December 7, 1936, Chiang Kai-shek flew to Sian, the Shensi headquarters of the commanders of the Manchurian troops and provincial forces facing the Chinese Communists. The purpose of his mission was to direct those commanders to begin on December 12 what was to be the sixth "bandit-suppression campaign." Chiang Kai-shek knew that Marshal Chang Hsüeh-liang wanted him to stop the civil war, establish a united front, enter into an alliance with the Soviet Union, and undertake a program of resistance to Japan. The Young Marshal had made such proposals two months earlier and Chiang had rejected them—as he had rejected similar proposals from other military and political leaders—because he was intent on pursuing what he regarded as first things first. What Chiang evidently did not know was that Chou En-lai had persuaded the Young Marshal to enter into a *modus vivendi* with the Communists, and that they were in constant liaison. Indeed, the Young Marshal had taken Communists into his headquarters and had a Communist representative on his staff.[19]

Near Sian there is a small hot spring resort which had been famous since the days of the T'ang dynasty, when Sian was China's capital. On the grounds of the resort there is a willow-lined pool beside which a T'ang emperor used to watch Yang Kuei-fei, his favorite concubine and the most famous beauty of Chinese history, while she bathed. There, too, they were sometimes joined by a general of whom she was fond, and who finally betrayed the emperor and undertook a devastating rebellion. It was in the guest house of this resort that Chiang Kai-shek was lodged upon his arrival at Sian. On the night of December 11–12, Marshal Chang Hsüeh-liang, Chiang's general—abetted by a provincial commander named Yang Hu-ch'eng—also staged a rebellion. In the early morning hours Chiang's guard detail was attacked and he had to flee—barefoot, in his nightshirt and without his false teeth. In scaling a wall he fell, hurt his back, and was unable to get very far before he was captured.[20]

There is an old saying that if you would strike a king, you must strike to kill. Undoubtedly both Chiang's immediate captors and the Communists, who quickly learned of his capture, considered whether he should not be executed. A few years later Liu Shao-ch'i, who had risen to a rank just below Mao Tse-tung in the party hierarchy, mentioned in a speech the Sian incident, when the fate of Chiang Kai-shek was being decided. Without going into detail, he cited it as an instance when the minority ultimately turned out to be right.[21] It may have been Mao Tse-tung who was the leader of a majority which wanted to deal harshly with Chiang. According to an observer who was in Yenan at the time, a huge meeting was held at which Mao Tse-tung and others spoke. Amidst great jubilation, a resolution was passed demanding that Chiang Kai-shek should be subjected to a trial by the masses as a traitor.[22]

Meanwhile Moscow had, of course, learned of the Sian incident. *Pravda* denounced Marshal Chang Hsüeh-liang, depicting the Sian coup as a Japanese plot, and Stalin sent Mao a telegram giving the Chinese Communists an ultimatum. Either they would use their influence with Chang Hsüeh-liang to effect Chiang's release, or they would be denounced by Moscow as bandits and repudiated before the world. On receiving the telegram, Mao Tse-tung is said to have flown into a rage, swearing and stamping his feet.[23]

If this indeed was Mao Tse-tung's reaction, Liu Shao-ch'i may have had him in mind when he subsequently observed that during this period "certain comrades" had failed to apply Marxism–Leninism correctly. "They did not understand," he asserted, "that the contradiction between the Chinese nation and Japanese imperialism had become the principal one while the contradiction among the different classes and political groups within the country had become secondary. As a result they opposed the Party's policy of . . . uniting with the Kuomintang to fight Japan." [24]

Molotov later credited the Russian intervention with saving Chiang Kai-shek's life.[25] Those Chinese Communists who wanted to treat him as a traitor, it seems clear, were running squarely against the policy of the Comintern. In 1935 it had directed member Communist parties to strive by every means possible to establish an "anti-imperialist united front" on a national basis as well as on an international scale.[26] And in the then prevailing situation, Japan could only be defined as imperialist by both the Chinese and the Russians. From their Manchurian base the Japanese were not only encroaching on China; they had already clashed with Soviet forces along the uneasy borders which separated them, and from Manchuria they posed a potential threat to the whole Soviet position in the Far East. If there was to be a united front in China, Chiang Kai-shek's life had to be spared; and if Chiang was to lead his country against Japan, his prestige had to be preserved.

And so one day, while Chiang was being held captive, into his room walked his old subordinate from Whampoa days—Chou En-lai. Undoubtedly Chiang Kai-shek took this as an ominous sign. Chiang's during his days in the Shanghai underground; and even in 1936 he subordinates had twice narrowly missed killing or capturing Chou, had a price of $80,000 on Chou's head.[27] But Chou En-lai, the Communists' negotiator *par excellence,* had come not to turn the tables on his former superior but to work out a complicated deal. Possibly the most difficult part of his task was to preserve Chiang Kai-shek's prestige. This was accomplished by reversing the roles of captor and captive. On December 25, Chang Hsüeh-liang accompanied Chiang Kai-shek back to Nanking for trial and punishment. He was to remain Chiang's captive throughout the war, and when the Nationalists left the mainland in 1949 for Taiwan, Chang Hsüeh-liang, still Chiang's captive, was taken along. He accordingly has never been in position to give the world an unvarnished account of the negotiations at Sian.[28]

Whatever the precise agreements reached, one thing is certain. After the Sian incident, the policy of appeasing Japan was abandoned. On July 7, 1937, there was a clash near the Marco Polo bridge, outside Peking, between a Chinese garrison and some Japanese troops conducting maneuvers. The incident might have been settled, like similar ones in the past, but this time the government at Nanking refused to sanction a settlement reached at the cost of concessions. The Japanese responded by pouring troops into north China. On August 8 they seized Peking, and the following month the Kuomintang and the Communists announced that they had formed a united front to oppose Japan. There now could be no doubt: the incident at Marco Polo bridge had marked the beginning of a war of resistance against Japan. It was not to end until Japan's surrender in August 1945.[29]

7

United Front and People's War

YENAN, which had become the Chinese Communist headquarters, is situated in the unique landscape of China's loess country.
The loess is fine silt, deposited in places to a depth of some hundreds
of feet, by winds blowing in from nearby desert lands. It is highly
porous, and capillary action draws to its surfaces water which carries
a heavy load of soil chemicals. When the water evaporates in the dry
air of the northwest, it leaves behind a cementlike surface coating,
which covers the soft soil inside. This soil tends to cleave vertically,
giving the country the aspect of a land of plateaus interrupted by
steep-sided canyons where the water has coursed or where roads, in use
for ages, have bitten ever deeper into the land.

Because the loess beneath the surface is unconsolidated, it is easy
to dig into the vertical faces of these canyons to make cave dwellings,
the interior walls of which soon harden. A home dug into the side of
a loess plateau leaves the land above free for cultivation. One might
not even know of the house beneath, unless one saw a column of smoke
rising through the hole in the ground provided for the chimney shaft.[1]
Mao occupied such a cave house during his first years in this area, and
some of his fellows lived in them throughout the period of the war
against Japan and for some time thereafter. In this setting—one of
mountains, plateaus, and canyons—they began their part of the war
against Japan.

In the interest of achieving the united front against Japan, the
Communists had agreed to discontinue their policy of forcibly con-
fiscating lands owned by landlords, renounce the aim of overthrowing
the Kuomintang by force, and place the Red Army under the control
of the National Government's Military Affairs Commission. To sym-
bolize this change, it was renamed the Eighth Route Army. This army
was to be composed of three divisions, designated the 115th, the 120th,
and the 129th, with a total strength of forty-five thousand men.

Chu Teh remained in Yenan as commander in chief of the Eighth
Route Army, and P'eng Te-huai became his deputy and commander of
its front line headquarters. Lin Piao became commander of the 115th
division, with Nieh Jung-chen as his deputy; Ho Lung of the 120th
division, with Hsiao K'o as deputy commander; and Liu Po-ch'eng

took over command of the 129th division, with Hsü Hsiang-ch'ien as second in command.[2]

The Communists did not reduce their armies in size, in consequence of their redesignation as divisions, nor did they stay within the authorized strength of forty-five thousand men. Indeed, each of the divisions eventually grew into a great field army, as did two other Communist forces. One of the two was an offshoot of the 115th division commanded by Nieh Jung-chen. The other, named the New Fourth Army in honor of the force under Yeh T'ing which had taken part in the uprising at Nanchang, was formed in east China in 1938. It was built by gathering together the guerrillas under Hsiang Ying, Ch'en Yi, and other leaders who had been left behind at the time of the Long March, and Yeh T'ing came out of retirement to command it.

Moreover, the Communists did not honor their pledge to put their forces under the command of the Nanking Government and its Military Affairs Commission. In August 1937 the Political Bureau, at a meeting held at Loch-uan, Shensi, decided that their forces should remain under the control of the Communist party and wage an independent campaign based upon a strategy of their own. When conditions were favorable they would engage in mobile operations, but the basic strategy would be one of waging guerrilla warfare.[3]

In September 1937, Eighth Route Army troops under Lin Piao ambushed and defeated a large column of Japanese troops in the battle of P'inghsing Pass. Soon after this battle Lin Piao was so severely wounded that he had to relinquish his command for the duration of the war, and the Communists did not again engage in large-scale operations until 1940. That summer P'eng Te-huai mustered about four hundred thousand men, drawn from all three divisions of the Eighth Route Army, and conducted the major offensive known as the "Battle of the Hundred Regiments."[4] But for the most part the Communists watched while Japanese columns advanced along transport lines and waited until they had defeated government troops. Then they moved in and organized the people of the countryside against the Japanese and under their own administration.

By the end of the war there would be nineteen Communist enclaves sandwiched in between the more or less permeable barriers presented by the strong points which the Japanese garrisoned and the connecting transport lines which they guarded. The total population of these Communist enclaves was estimated at ninety million.[5] Each enclave provided a separate base and a recruiting ground.

The government's forces also waged the war against Japan in their own style. They fought tenaciously in positional warfare in the environs of Shanghai, suffered heavy losses, and were forced to withdraw westward. In advance of this withdrawal, the capital was moved first to Hankow, one of the three Wuhan cities, and then to Chungking, above the Yangtze rapids in the mountain-girt province of Szechwan.

During the first year or so of the war against Japan, the Kuomintang and the Communists maintained reasonably cooperative relations. The Communists, wanting the support of all anti-Japanese elements of the populace, and perhaps remembering that the first united front had broken down in consequence of their pursuit of the social revolution, kept their pledge to discontinue their radical agrarian policies in favor of ones which featured the reduction of rents and of interest rates. Chiang Kai-shek, for his part, allowed the Communists to establish offices in his capital and to publish a daily newspaper there. The principal Communists who initially were assigned to duty in Nanking were the same ones who had negotiated the united front: Chou En-lai, Ch'in Pang-hsien, and Yeh Chien-ying. In 1938, after the capital had been removed to Hankow, the liaison group was joined by Wang Ming, alias Ch'en Shao-yü, who had returned to China from Moscow the previous year and been made the head of the party's united front department.[6]

The new relationship between the two parties made it possible for the Chinese Communists, among other things, to initiate a search for children who had been left behind with peasant families at the time of the Long March. Ho Shih-chen's could not be found, but Chou En-lai did succeed in locating Mao's two sons by Yang K'ai-hui, and in sending them to Yenan.[7]

However, the cooperative relationship between the Kuomintang and the Communists came under increasing strain, as the areas under government control contracted and those under the Communists expanded. After 1939 the government, anxious to prevent the southward and westward extension of Communist influence, maintained a blockading cordon of troops along the border between the main Communist base and government territory. In October 1940 the government, concerned about the expansion of the New Fourth Army in the east China region which had been its own principal prewar base of power, ordered that army to move north of the Yangtze river. By the end of the year the headquarters element of the New Fourth Army was still south of the river, and during the first days of January 1941 it was surrounded and attacked by government troops. In this attack Yeh T'ing, the commander, was captured, his deputy Hsiang Ying was killed, and most of the headquarters force of ten thousand men was annihilated. The government then demanded that the rest of the New Fourth Army should be disbanded; instead, the Communists ordered Ch'en Yi to assume command and sent Liu Shao-ch'i, in the role of political commissar, to help him reorganize the New Fourth Army and expand it further. This brought to an end, for most practical purposes, the period of Kuomintang–Communist collaboration.[8]

Simultaneously carrying on warfare against the Japanese and revolution against the Kuomintang, under the circumstances which prevailed, posed two seemingly incompatible requirements. One was to maintain discipline and direction over widely scattered administrative entities and military units. The other was to decentralize control. There was no overall central government of the Communist areas of wartime China. Decentralized civil administration was necessary because of the fragmented character of the Communist domain. Military control had similarly to be decentralized in order to give individual commanders freedom to make their own tactical decisions in the light of conditions which could not be known to any central headquarters.

Disciplined adherence in each area to a set of doctrines which applied to all was necessary if communications were to be mutually intelligible and if efforts were to be coordinated. This was especially true of military units because they were dual-purpose instruments. They were not only fighting forces but also political instruments of the party. They made the initial contact with the populace and began the process of organizing the people against the Japanese and under Communist control. Because they served a dual purpose, they had to have a dual system of command. Each unit had a military commander and a political commissar. The commissar was both a teacher and a leader. As teacher, he was responsible for the ideological indoctrination of the troops and the party's organizational work among them. As leader, he shared responsibility with the commander, passing on all military decisions of political significance.[9] In the process, he also became a student of war and sometimes became a skilled commander of troops.

Because the party guided the civil administration of scattered territories and laid down the tasks for far-flung forces, its operations also had to be decentralized. Beyond the barrier of Japanese troops facing the Yenan area, regional bureaus of the party carried on, in the war base areas, the work of the Central Committee. Indeed, they served as Central Committees in miniature, with their own subordinate units and party schools.[10]

The wartime expansion of Communist base areas, by opening new recruiting grounds, made it possible for the party to grow enormously. According to Mao Tse-tung, party membership grew from forty thousand in 1937 to "several hundred thousand" in 1942.[11] The increase in the party's work necessitated this growth, but its rapidity posed problems. Some of the new recruits were ill-chosen and most of them were poorly grounded in Communist doctrine. The party, in short, needed massive doses of indoctrination and the membership needed pruning.

In addition, Mao Tse-tung was ready, by the end of 1941, to extend and consolidate gains he had been scoring at the expense of his opponents. Otto Braun, the representative of the Comintern, had left China in 1937. Chang Kuo-t'ao, his power already gone, had renounced the party in 1938, when a mission to government-held territory made it possible for him to leave Yenan for good. However in 1937—perhaps because of the withdrawal of Otto Braun—Wang Ming had been sent back from Moscow. It will be recalled that he had been leader of the Twenty-eight Bolsheviks and general secretary of the party prior to his 1931 assignment as its representative to the Comintern. In Moscow he had risen to membership in the Executive Committee of the Comintern, and had become Stalin's principal expert on matters relating to China. If Stalin had not anticipated that Wang would resume leadership of the party upon his return to China, he must at least have expected that Wang Ming would stiffen the spine of General Secretary Chang Wen-t'ien and other Moscow-oriented leaders, and that he would work for close collaboration between the Communists and the Kuomintang as necessary to the successful prosecution of the war.

Mao Tse-tung was soon criticizing Wang Ming, during party meetings at Yenan, and it seems likely that he arranged to have Wang Ming assigned to duty in the Nationalist capital in order to minimize his opportunities to influence other members of the leadership. However, this evidently had not ended the widespread acceptance of Wang Ming's line, nor ensured that Mao Tse-tung would be consulted on all important matters and that his views would necessarily prevail. After P'eng Te-huai and his fellow military leaders had launched the 1940 campaign of the hundred regiments, for example, Mao Tse-tung complained: "It is regrettable that P'eng Te-huai should have carried out a thing of so great a magnitude without consulting me." P'eng Te-huai, it was subsequently alleged, had initiated the campaign in order to divert Japanese strength from a multiprong attack directed at government-held centers, and under the influence of the Wang Ming line.[12] In this context, the annihilation of the headquarters element of the New Fourth Army was, for Mao Tse-tung, a blessing in disguise, because it enabled him to discredit the Wang Ming line.

Wang Ming had come representing the line of the Comintern, shaped under the influence of Stalin and designed to serve the interests of the USSR. Mao Tse-tung was determined that his party should be an autonomous one, based on his own brand of sinicized Marxism and following his unchallenged leadership. If he could establish his own ideological supremacy, it would cut the ground from under his

Moscow-oriented competitors and enable him to consolidate his position as leader of the party.

Early in 1942 Mao Tse-tung called Liu Shao-ch'i to Yenan to help conduct a massive campaign for the rectification of the party. At that point Liu had served as political commissar of the New Fourth Army for only a year, but his acceptance of the post and accomplishments in it undoubtedly combined to recommend him to Mao Tse-tung. The decision to reorganize and build up that army, in defiance of government orders for its disbandment, obviously ran exactly counter to the Wang Ming line, and it was hardly a decision which Moscow might have been expected to approve. A Moscow-oriented Communist might have accepted the task of implementing it out of a sense of party discipline, but Liu Shao-ch'i performed as though his heart were in the job. Before 1941, the New Fourth Army had neither established Communist-governed base areas nor tried to promote Yenan's agrarian reforms in the regions in which it carried on operations. After the reorganization carried out by Liu Shao-ch'i and Ch'en Yi, it did both.[13]

Mao Tse-tung and Liu Shao-ch'i were men of dissimilar character, bent and experience. Liu Shao-ch'i's forte had been organizing labor unions; Mao Tse-tung had engaged in such work for awhile, but his preference, of course, was for organizing the peasants. Liu had operated predominantly in the underground, Mao with the army. The nature of Mao's leadership was personalized; Liu was an organization man. Mao had never willingly accepted any authority which was not self-imposed. Years as a Red working in so-called White areas had taught Liu that organizational discipline could be essential to survival. In this campaign, the dissimilarities of the two men enabled them to complement each other.

Mao Tse-tung launched the campaign, which lasted two full years, shortly after Liu Shao-ch'i's arrival in Yenan. In his speeches, Mao attacked those comrades who merely parroted the phrases of Marx, Engels, Lenin, and Stalin, and he insisted that China's Communist movement must be guided by a practical Marxism which had been adapted to Chinese conditions. Indeed, the rectification movement marked the beginning of stress within the party on the "thought of Mao Tse-tung." [14]

Liu Shao-ch'i, in his speeches, put great emphasis on the requirements of party organization, solidarity, and discipline. In the documents covering this campaign, it was stressed over and over again that the individual must obey the organization, the minority must obey the majority, lower echelons must obey higher ones, and all must obey the principles laid down by the Central Committee.[15] The body of doctrine which emerged was Mao Tse-tung's "mass line"—the concept that workable policies are ones which are based on ideas current among the people, and which the masses can be persuaded to embrace as their own and translate into action—wedded with Liu's more orthodox principles of organization. Each of the two leaders went some distance towards acceptance of the other's approach, in a compromise which was to last the better part of two decades.[16]

The 1942–1944 rectification campaign greatly strengthened Mao Tse-tung's position as *de facto* head of the party, gave Liu Shao-ch'i wide recognition as a party ideologue and leader ranking close to the top, and undermined further the authority of Mao's Moscow-oriented opponents. By this time, of course, the actual locus of power within the party was far different from what it had been in 1928, when the last party congress had been held, or even in 1938, when the Central Committee elected at that congress had last met in plenary session. If Mao Tse-tung's gains were to be consolidated through a formal realignment of the hierarchy, it would be necessary to hold another party congress.

In April 1945 the party held an enlarged plenary session of the Sixth Central Committee at which Mao Tse-tung secured the adoption of a long resolution which contained his own version of party history. It criticized as erroneous the lines pursued by such leaders as Li Li-san, Wang Ming, and Ch'in Pang-hsien, and praised the positions which Mao Tse-tung had taken in opposing them. It also characterized as entirely correct the leadership he had given the party over the preceding decade and credited the rectification campaign conducted under his auspices with having corrected erroneous thinking of both the right and the left, thereby achieving for the party an unprecedentedly high level of unity and solidarity.

Immediately after the conclusion of this plenum, the Seventh Party Congress was held, a new party constitution was adopted, a new Central Committee was elected, and the party hierarchy was reorganized. The new constitution was well-tailored to serve Mao's purposes as the prospective *de jure* leader of the party. It did not provide for continuing the post of general secretary; indeed, its retention might have created confusion as to who was the top leader and called attention to the fact that Mao Tse-tung had not, over the previous decade, been occupying what had been intended to be the highest position in the party. Instead the constitution provided for the post of chairman of the Central Committee, and specified that its incumbent should serve concurrently as chairman of the policy-making Political Bureau, and also as chairman of a Central Secretariat through which the routine work of the party should be conducted.[17] Mao Tse-tung had long been known as Chairman Mao by virtue of his 1931 election as chair-

man of the Provisional Central Government of the Chinese Soviet
Republic. Creating for him the top party position of chairman of the
Central Committee would obviate the need to change his title, thereby
contributing to an impression of continuity of leadership.

Mao Tse-tung was, of course, elected chairman of the new Central
Committee. Chu Teh's name came next, on its rank-order list, and Liu
Shao-ch'i was third. The three leading members of the Twenty-eight
Bolsheviks all were elected regular members of the Central Committee.
But Chang Wen-t'ien's name appeared half-way down the list, and
Wang Ming and Ch'in Pang-hsien occupied the forty-third and forty-
fourth positions in a list of forty-four.

Mao Tse-tung had been able to humble his opponents, in part at
least, because he had learned from his mistakes. In Kiangsi, by physically liquidating real and presumed opponents, he had created more
problems for himself than that elimination of enemies had solved. As
he later observed, a different principle had been initiated at Yenan:
There some people were not executed, not because their crimes did
not justify their execution, but because it would serve no useful purpose. "Furthermore," he remarked, "the head of a man does not grow
like the leek, and once it is cut, another will not come out. If a head
is wrongly cut, there would be no way to correct the mistake." [18] Wang
Ming was later to charge that Mao Tse-tung had attempted to poison
him, but it was the political degradation of Wang Ming and Ch'in
Pang-hsien which was important, and that was achieved through the
rectification campaign and confirmed at the Seventh Party Congress.[19]

Mao Tse-tung had also learned, as demonstrated by the composition and adoption of his version of the party history prior to the convening of the Seventh Party Congress, the importance of carefully preparing his position before entering an important meeting. In 1932, he
had gone to the Ningtu conference direct from a victorious military
campaign, only to suffer a sickening political defeat. After the Long
March he had left the actual fighting to others, and stayed in Yenan
where he could hold forth as top leader and keep the affairs of the
party center constantly under his watchful eye.

There is little doubt that Mao Tse-tung towered head and shoulders, in political authority, above everybody else who spent the war
years in Yenan. However, the circumstances of life, in this rural setting
and under conditions of Nationalist blockade, imposed on all a lev-
eling simplicity. Willingness to accept austerity as a common necessity
became an individual virtue. Moreover, no matter how Spartan the life
and how simple the needs of the people, certain things had to be provided: food, clothing, household items, and simple implements. For the
great part they had to be locally produced, and the Chinese Commu-

nists perforce became jacks-of-all-trades. Each man might have his main task, but he was expected in his spare time to turn his hand to whatever else was required—whether it was raising vegetables, knitting socks, or helping run a small workshop. Avoidance of such tasks would have been regarded as a selfish refusal to be bound by the near egalitarianism which joint survival required; specialization of any narrow sort was not merely impermissible—it ran against the moral code. In Yenan, Mao Tse-tung set an example by using his spare time in the cultivation of a garden. But it seems unlikely that he did so merely for effect: authoritarianism and egalitarianism were simply different facets of his contradictory nature.

Yenan was a relatively secure and peaceful base—a fact which made it possible for Mao, during his years there, to do a great part of the writing which now comprises the works of Mao Tse-tung. By the time the Yenan years were over, he had matured: attitudes, views, values, and techniques he had acquired in these and earlier years had been not merely molded; they had become hardened into permanence. His whole adult life had been one of unremitting and often violent struggle, and he consequently regarded struggle as man's normal condition. The great feats he had repeatedly seen men accomplish, when their bloodstreams were coursing with adrenalin, had set his standards of accomplishment at heroic levels. The willingness with which people accepted austerity in furtherance of a war for national salvation led him to expect they would be capable of continual self-denial on behalf of his other goals. Campaigns led among a mobilized people in time of war had yielded successes he was to attempt by similar means in time of peace.

To the extent that most men prefer periods of peace to constant struggle, comfort to unending self-denial, opportunity for leisure to continual campaigns of frenetic activity, Mao's people were bound—after peace came—to fall short of his expectations. For this, Mao was to put the blame not on the people but on their leadership. If one may generalize, the leaders just under Mao were men who had shared similar experiences and who felt themselves approximately his equals. When peace came they took on changed jobs with different requirements and adjusted to changed circumstances. Mao was never to lose his predilection for mass movements as opposed to methodically planned programs. He was always to retain a dislike for specialization which ripened into a distrust of specialists; they were too much in the class of intellectuals to suit his taste, and too far removed from the jacks-of-all-trades who were his ideal. These attitudes and preferences, carried over to times of peace, were to cause Mao's fellows to accuse him of still being dominated by a guerrilla mentality, and to see him as a leader trying to apply old solutions to new problems. But Mao, with his enormous will for domination and capacity for aggression, would try to bend both men and objective circumstance to his will. In this lay the seeds of future conflict between Mao and those who were more directly to lead the cadres in postwar years.

In Yenan, too, Mao Tse-tung loosed the bonds which attached him to Ho Shih-chen, a woman of essentially gentle nature, and formed an alliance with another partner whose taste for conflict was at least as well developed as his own. In doing so he incurred the disapproval, by all accounts, of some fellow leaders of his own generation. But members of a younger generation of Chinese did not merely disapprove; many of them were shocked.

The Long March had been hard on Ho Shih-chen. A photograph taken of her after its conclusion depicted a woman whose clothes were hung on a frame which was scarecrow thin.[20] In Yenan she probably filled out again, but she bore on her body the scars left by fourteen bomb fragments.[21] By 1937 she had borne him at least three children—probably all of them girls, since the only sons he is known to have had were both by Yang K'ai-hui.[22] Bearing children both during the Long March and soon afterwards may have sapped her physical vigor, and not giving Mao Tse-tung a son may have depressed her spirits, because it is on sons that Chinese custom puts great value.

At any rate, by 1937 Mao Tse-tung was evidently ready for someone else. Nym Wales, who spent some time in Yenan that year, told of preparing an informal supper for several guests, including Mao Tse-tung and a movie actress named Lily who had recently arrived and was cutting a wide swathe in Yenan. Mao spent the evening holding hands with the movie actress, while she leaned on his knee in a familiar way, both of them protesting that they had drunk too much.[23] The relationship may not have gone beyond that which Nym Wales described, but against the background of Chinese social custom, which frowns on public display of sexuality, the message which each was conveying was that of readiness for a liaison. Ho Shih-chen's marriage with Mao Tse-tung evidently was breaking up, and not long afterwards—exactly when is uncertain—he sent her off to Moscow to undergo prolonged treatment for what was described as a nervous disorder.[24]

Meanwhile, Yenan was becoming famed as a place where men and women led lives of monastic simplicity in the interests of a "war of national salvation." For many of the youths of China, to whom this was a holy war, Yenan was a place which exerted a quasi-religious attraction. As such, it drew large numbers of patriotic and idealistic young people from the colleges and universities of China. The largest concentration of such institutions was in Peking, the country's intellectual capital. Peking had, of course, fallen into Japanese hands at the very beginning of the war, and Japanese armies dominated that part of the north China plain on which the city is situated. However, it is near the edge of that plain, and within sight of the foothills of a mountain chain which extends to the Yenan area and beyond. Indeed, two of Peking's best universities were located outside the city walls and within easy walking distance of the foothills. In the early years of the Sino-Japanese war, students from Peking slipped out, made their way to the Western Hills, were soon in touch with Communist guerrillas, and made their way to Yenan. Predominantly of good family backgrounds, they brought to Yenan trained minds, patriotic fervor, youthful enthusiasm, and high ideals.

A young woman of quite different background came to Yenan, in the late 1930s, and soon became the third wife of Mao Tse-tung. This young woman had been born into a poor family named Luan, which then lived in Chuch'eng County in the province of Shantung. Her father is said to have died a few years after she was born, and the mother took the child to live with her own relatives in Tsinan, the capital city of the province. Perhaps to please her maternal grandfather, whose surname was Li, her name was changed, and as Li Yün-ho she attended primary school. According to one account she also went to lower middle school, which would have carried her through nine grades. If a different account is to be believed, she was lured away from home when she was about fifteen and spent something over a year with a theatrical troupe.

Li Yün-ho was next enrolled in a provincial boarding school, where the theatrical arts were taught, known as the Provincial Experimental Drama Academy. Chao T'ai-mo, the principal of this academy, divided his time between it and National Tsingtao University, where he held a professorship. However, while Li Yün-ho was a student in the academy, Chao T'ai-mo was promoted at the university to the positions first of dean and then of chancellor, and in consequence he moved his residence to Tsingtao. Li Yün-ho followed him there, and he got her a job as junior assistant in the university library. In Tsingtao, Chao T'ai-mo married a famous beauty named Yü Shan, and Li Yün-ho became a frequent visitor to their home. There she met Yü Shan's cousin Yü Ch'i-wei, who was then a student at National Tsingtao University. By all available accounts, Li Yün-ho fell in love with Yü Ch'i-wei and lived with him until he left Tsingtao for Peking, later in the year. Yü Ch'i-wei was a nephew of Yü Ta-wei, best known as defense minister in the Nationalist government, but nevertheless was a

Communist working in the underground under the alias of Huang Ching.

In 1934, a movie director from Shanghai took a trip to Tsingtao, where he paid a visit to Chao T'ai-mo and his wife. They introduced Li Yün-ho to the director, and through him she got a job with a new motion picture company which had been established in Shanghai. Both the company and a group of movie critics set up for the purpose of writing favorable reviews of its films were offshoots of the Alliance of Leftist Writers, which had been established under the leadership of Ch'ü Ch'iu-pai. Well-known authors like T'ien Han, Hsia Yen, and Yang Han-sheng wrote the scripts and helped direct the films. Li Yün-ho played in some of these films under the stage name of Lan P'ing, but in none of them did she have more than bit parts.

Late in 1934 or early in 1935, Li Yün-ho married a talented young man named T'ang Na, who worked in Shanghai's film industry in the varied roles of script writer, actor, director, and motion picture critic for the press. He is said to have found her promiscuous—she is alleged to have had affairs with a succession of actors and directors—and possessed of a terrible temper. He must nevertheless have been in love with her, because he did not ask her for a divorce, and during one particularly stormy period in their relationship he made an unsuccessful attempt at suicide.

However, their marriage advanced Li Yün-ho's career by making her better known, and by enabling her to move from one company to another at a crucial point. In 1935, the government closed down the company by which she had originally been hired, and threw both T'ien Han and Yang Han-sheng in jail. T'ang Na then helped her get a job with another company, and during 1936 and 1937 she appeared in three of its films; in two she had bit parts and in one a supporting role. Actually, she could not reasonably expect to rise much higher. She would have been accounted somewhat less than beautiful even if her looks had not been marred by slightly protruding teeth, and by most accounts she was not long on talent. This did not, however, prevent her from trying to achieve stardom.

It should not be assumed that Li Yün-ho sought to advance her career as an actress only by making herself physically available to directors and fellow actors. While she was well-endowed physically, she was also well-endowed with sheer brass. An account bearing on this point has been given by one of the founders of the well-known Chinese picture magazine *Liang-yu*, which then was being published in Shanghai. He tells of Li Yün-ho appearing in its offices one day, seeking an interview with the editor, and asking him to use her photograph on the cover of one of its issues. The editor assertedly asked her why

Liang-yu should put the picture of a third-rate actress on its cover, whereupon she left in a big huff.[25]

It seems likely that the party's Public Security Bureau began to keep a dossier on Li Yün-ho at the time she was first hired by the left wing film company at Shanghai. At any rate, it contained derogatory information, and by 1967 it had become an uncomfortable dossier to hold, for she had risen by then to a position of great power. Yet the dossier could hardly be destroyed, for one is supposed to be kept on every member of the party. That year a search was made in order that it might be located and sent to her office in Peking. It had been kept in a special box, and the deputy director of the Public Security Bureau at Shanghai, who had it in his safekeeping, had been heard to say that this box contained important materials which were so secret that he might be executed if they were divulged. The box had been kept locked, and the key had to be fetched, because it was kept in a separate place. When the box was opened another box was discovered inside. In this box there were three parcels, and only after they were opened was the dossier found.[26]

With the outbreak of hostilities around Shanghai, in August 1937, the major film companies making patriotic pictures moved inland. This was during the initial period of the united front of the Communists and the Kuomintang, and T'ien Han and Yang Han-sheng had been released from jail and put in charge of film enterprises of the government. Li Yün-ho was one of the actors who moved inland, first to Hankow and then to Chungking, and who worked for the government's Central Film Studio. However, she was given parts in only a couple of films. In 1939, it is asserted, she was unable to conceal her jealousy of more successful actresses and unhappy about being left out of the film then being shot. She accordingly left Chungking for the northwest, where there were two studios—one in Sian and the other in Yenan. Rejected by the studio in Sian, she traveled onward to Yenan.

The director and female star of the company with which Li Yün-ho had first been associated, when she arrived in Shanghai, were now working with the Yenan Motion Picture Group, but she was not invited to join it. However, there was one leader in Yenan to whom she could turn for help: K'ang Sheng, head of the party's Central Intelligence Department. K'ang Sheng was a native of Chuch'eng County, in which Li Yün-ho had been born, and in China fellow provincials tend to look to each other for help when they are away from home and need assistance. Moreover, there is some reason to think that Li Yün-ho may have been involved, before coming to Yenan, in K'ang Sheng's network of secret intelligence agents. At any rate, K'ang Sheng was one of those who introduced her into membership in the party, and he arranged for her to be given a job as instructor in drama at Yenan's Lu Hsün Academy of Art.[27]

In Yenan, Li Yün-ho dropped the stage-name of Lan P'ing and adopted the new name of Chiang Ch'ing. Chiang is a common surname, and it also means river. Ch'ing means green and is a homophone for the "ch'ing" which means pure—or, as applied to a woman, chaste. In Yenan, too, Chiang Ch'ing demonstrated an unabashed determination to call attention to herself. A former party leader who then was in Yenan has been quoted as saying that when cultural shows were held there, the first few rows were reserved for leading officials. Chiang Ch'ing, he said, would always sit immediately behind them, and call out her expressions of approval or disapproval of the performances in bellowing tones. On cold nights she would gather with others around the warm stove in this party leader's cave. When other party officials came in for consultations, those already around the stove would tactfully withdraw—but not Chiang Ch'ing.

One day Mao Tse-tung came to the Lu Hsün Academy to make a speech, and Chiang Ch'ing was of course a member of the audience. She had chosen a seat directly in front of him, and at the conclusion of his speech she rose and asked Mao a question. He praised her for being diligent and inquisitive, and undoubtedly made a mental note that she also was physically attractive. The rest was a repetition of the events—in another locale and with a different young woman—which had led to his marriage with Ho Shih-chen. Whether at his invitation or on her own initiative, Chiang Ch'ing went to his place in order that they might discuss certain ideological problems. This visit was repeated; finally she moved into his cave; in due course she became pregnant; and in the spring of 1941 she gave birth to a baby girl whom she named Li Na. Li had, of course, been Chiang Ch'ing's surname, but people inevitably have speculated that she chose the second part of the child's name in sentimental remembrance of her husband T'ang Na. If Mao ever taxed her with it, she made it up to him later; when they had a second daughter she named the child Mao Mao.

Viewed apart from his position, one might have thought Mao Tse-tung to have been an unattractive catch for a young woman. It was not merely the large wart on his chin. Edgar Snow reported that Mao still had the personal habits of a peasant, was completely indifferent to his appearance, and was apt absent-mindedly to turn down the belt of his trousers and search for "guests." Snow concluded it was doubtful that Mao would ever command great respect from the intellectual elite of China, who would consider him uncouth.[28] His build, too, was not entirely in his favor—a pelvic structure somewhat out of proportion to his shoulders and chest suggested, if only faintly, the pear shape he was to assume as he put on more weight.

A pro-Communist American journalist named Agnes Smedley, who visited Yenan, found plain, flat-nosed Chu Teh more attractive than Mao Tse-tung. She was taken to her first call on Mao at midnight because he slept in the daytime and worked at night. On arriving at the entrance to his cave, she had pushed aside the padded cotton drape across the entrance and stepped into a dark cavern. Directly in the center of this darkness was a rough-hewn table on which stood a tall candle, its light falling on piles of books and papers and touching the low earthen ceiling above. In this sinister gloom a man's figure, covered by a mass of dark clothing and a loose, padded greatcoat, stood beside the table, one hand leaning upon it. The face was obscured in shadow, and the section of earthen floor on which he stood was raised, accentuating his height. She wrote:

The tall, forbidding figure lumbered towards us, and a high-pitched voice greeted us. The two hands grasped mine; they were long and sensitive as a woman's. Without speaking we stared at each other. His dark, inscrutable face was long, the forehead high, the mouth feminine. . . . I was in fact repelled by the feminine in him and the gloom of the setting. An instinctive hostility sprang up inside me and I became so occupied with trying to master it that I heard hardly a word of what followed.

Initial hostility later gave way to friendship, but the revulsion inspired by his handshake, which she tried to avoid as much as possible, remained.[29]

Given all the circumstances, one is entitled to speculate that Chiang Ch'ing attached herself to Mao because he was the principal actor in a great political drama in which she might become the leading lady. Although she got the part, it was at the cost of a big storm and subject to conditions designed to minimize her role.

Mao Tse-tung and Chiang Ch'ing, of course, each had a living spouse. Because some of the moving picture people in Yenan were Chiang Ch'ing's former associates, her past behavior and reputation were bound to become common knowledge there. In addition there was widespread sympathy for Mao's wife Ho Shih-chen among the people with whom she had shared the dangers and hardships of the Long March. Moreover, Yenan was not a remote guerrilla base with only a local peasant and semirural populace, like the Chingkangshan or the Kiangsi-Fukien border area, and Mao was no longer a leader of secondary rank. Yenan was full of idealistic youngsters from China's universities and Mao was a famous leader—and his attachment to Chiang Ch'ing was a scandalous affair.

In addition, it was not only during dynasties of the remote past that ambitious and self-willed women had brought disaster. In the lifetime of Mao and his fellows, the Empress Dowager Tzu Hsi had usurped power, brought humiliations upon China, and contributed much to the fall of the imperial regime. When the Communists came to power, Mao Tse-tung might become the modern equivalent of the Emperor. Then Chiang Ch'ing, whose self-assertiveness and ambition must have been evident to all, would be in a position to exercise great influence.

Given all the attendant circumstances, including Mao's own self-willed character, it is hardly strange that there should have been a debate among the party elders in which a majority objected to his taking Chiang Ch'ing as his wife, and during which he is said to have threatened to "go back to my native village and become a farmer" if they did not relent. Finally—perhaps after it was apparent that Chiang Ch'ing had become pregnant—a compromise was reached. Mao Tse-tung and Chiang Ch'ing might stay together on the understanding that she would remain in the background as a housewife and not involve herself in political affairs.

In the dangers which they evidently foresaw in this marriage, the party elders were prescient, as Lenin is said to have been on his deathbed when he warned against letting Stalin inherit the mantle of his leadership. Chiang Ch'ing was indeed kept in the background for more than a decade, and as one who craved the limelight this was a period of great bitterness and frustration. In later years old Chu Teh, and more particularly his wife K'ang K'o-ch'ing, would be punished for having "spread false rumors about Madame Mao." Equating opposition to her marriage with enmity for Mao Tse-tung, she would assert: "When Liu Shao-ch'i was opposed to me in Yenan, he actually pointed the spearhead at Chairman Mao." [30]

Before Chiang Ch'ing emerged from obscurity, there was a period of ten years during which Liu Shao-ch'i was chairman of the government, and his wife Wang Kuang-mei occupied the stage as China's first lady. Wang Kuang-mei, as a glamorous "golden girl" and the daughter of a wealthy family, had been educated in the best schools of Peking. After postgraduate studies she had become an assistant on the faculty of one of Peking's Christian universities. She had gone to Yenan only in 1946, joined the party in 1948, and married Liu Shao-ch'i a short time later.[31] The contrast between the backgrounds of the two women could only have intensified the jealousy which Chiang Ch'ing came to harbor for Madame Liu.

However, in the early 1940s all that remained in the future, and victory over Japan would not be in sight until there were other powers fighting on China's side. While everyone knows that the United States became a belligerent against the axis powers consequent to Japan's attack on Pearl Harbor, it is less commonly remembered that Japan launched that attack because the United States was trying to block Japan's efforts to conquer China. In the spring and early summer of 1941, the United States froze Japanese assets; put an embargo on exports of petroleum products to Japan; made a loan to China; signed a lend-lease agreement with China; supplied one hundred P-40 fighter planes; and released an equal number of men from the armed forces to fly them for China as members of Colonel Chennault's American Volunteer Group, known as the Flying Tigers.[32] The Japanese reaction was understandable even if—as in any conflict which cannot be won—it ultimately proved unwise.

Once at war with Japan, the United States necessarily became concerned over the preoccupation of each Chinese side with its enmity for the other. This concern did not end when it became certain that the United States would be able to defeat Japan, for the prospective costs in terms of American dead and wounded loomed large. Meanwhile several hundred thousand Nationalist troops were being used to seal the Communists off from Nationalist areas. Chinese forces fought the Japanese less, because men and resources were being conserved with an eye to the resumption of the civil war, and when either Chinese side did fight the Japanese it was without coordination with the other. Finally, the United States government—which hoped that a strong, united and democratic China could be built after the victory over Japan—was loath to harvest instead the bitter fruit of a China sunk in the chaos of civil war.

In consequence, the United States attempted to promote command arrangements which would make a unified Chinese military effort possible. Early in the summer of 1944, at a time when the military picture in China appeared to be going from bleak to nearly hopeless, President Roosevelt urged Chiang Kai-shek to give the operational control of China's forces to General Joseph W. Stilwell, then commander in chief of American forces in the China-Burma-India theater. The Chinese Communists, who had much less to lose and more to gain from such an arrangement, expressed willingness to serve under allied command. Generalissimo Chiang Kai-shek agreed in principle, but stalled. He had originally indicated that he did not want a commander assigned to his theater who had previous experience in China, and General Stilwell had been an old China hand. Their personal relationship, moreover, had become strained. But the essential point was that Chiang Kai-shek could hardly surrender the command of the armed forces he controlled to anyone else, because his political power depended on that control. He would not surrender command to another Chinese, much less to a foreigner, and most certainly not to one who, like General Stilwell, wanted to supply the Chinese Communists with American arms.[33]

During the spring of 1944, President Roosevelt had sent Vice President Wallace to China with the mission of doing what he could to bring to an end the fighting between the two Chinese sides. While Wallace was in Chungking, Chiang Kai-shek—although rejecting the suggestion that the Chinese Communists could play a useful role in the war against Japan—did finally assent to a request which President Roosevelt had made to him, and on which he had previously been un-coöperative: He agreed to the establishment of a United States Army Observer Group in Yenan. But he also complained to Vice President Wallace about his relations with General Stilwell and asked that a top emissary be sent to Chungking to serve as the liaison between himself and President Roosevelt.[34]

In the summer of 1944, President Roosevelt, in response to this request, sent Major General Patrick J. Hurley to China. For good measure, and to serve other purposes of his own, Roosevelt also sent along Donald Nelson, erstwhile chairman of the War Production Board. They arrived in Chungking early in September, prepared to talk tough. However, their coming undoubtedly told Chiang Kai-shek that there was more give in the American position than in his own. Later that month he not only rejected renewed urgings to give Stilwell the command of Chinese forces; he also requested that Stilwell be withdrawn.[35]

The American effort to secure the coordination of government and Communist military effort through the appointment of an American commander having failed, the United States government reverted to the effort to promote formation of a joint council of all Chinese parties for the joint conduct of the war. That inevitably led—because neither Chinese side would trust its fate to the other—to the question of Communist participation in the government. Accordingly, from the autumn of 1944 onwards, General Hurley took on the task of endeavoring to bring the two Chinese sides together in a coalition government.

In assuming this to be a feasible project, Hurley evidently was encouraged by the recollection of what he and Nelson had been told by V. M. Molotov during a stopover they had made in Moscow on their way to China. Molotov had virtually disclaimed any interest in the Chinese Communists—much as Stalin had in a talk with Averell Harriman the previous June—and seemed to portray them as not being true Communists at all. Hurley apparently accepted this expression of disinterest at face value.[36] He may have done so out of naïveté, but in doing so he was not far wrong. Stalin, as events were to prove, set less store by the revolutionary prospects of the Chinese Communists than on Soviet relations with the government of Chiang Kai-shek. In consequence, had Chiang Kai-shek been right in his assertions that the Chinese Communists were the tools of Moscow,[37] persuading them to take part in a coalition government, on terms acceptable to Chiang Kai-shek, probably would have been a feasible project. It was not, however, because Mao Tse-tung was just as determined to achieve power as Chiang Kai-shek was to hold it, and no more disposed to permit a foreign power to stand in his way.

On November 7, 1944, in pursuit of the American objective of achieving the unification of Chinese parties by peaceful means, General Hurley flew to Yenan. The United States Army Observer Group, sent there pursuant to the agreement which Vice President Wallace had extracted from Chiang Kai-shek, had been there for over three months. There its members, under the command of an old China hand, Colonel David D. Barrett, were using the facilities put at their disposal by the Chinese Communists in order to gather intelligence about enemy armed forces and Japanese-occupied areas. They also were endeavoring to learn all they could about the Chinese Communists, their capabilities and their intentions. The arrival of General Hurley in Yenan has been best described by Colonel Barrett himself:

The arrival of the plane from Chungking was always a big event in Yenan, and on the afternoon of the 7th of November, Chou En-lai and I were among a large crowd of Chinese and Americans on hand to greet it. After it had landed and the doors opened, there appeared at the top of the steps a tall, gray-haired, soldierly, extremely handsome man, wearing one of the most beautifully tailored uniforms I have ever seen and with enough ribbons on his chest to represent every war, so it seemed to me, in which the United States had ever engaged except possibly Shay's rebellion. It was Major General Patrick J. Hurley, Special Emissary of the President of the United States, of whose intention to visit Yenan apparently no one had thought to inform us. He had come, so I was soon to find out, to act as a mediator between the Nationalist Government and the Chinese Communists.

Visibly startled by this picture of soldierly bearing and sartorial splendor was Chou En-lai, who at once asked who the distinguished visitor was. I told him it was General Hurley, whom I had once seen years before in New York when he was Secretary of War. "Please hold him here until I can bring Chairman Mao," said Chou, as he disappeared in a cloud of dust.

In a shorter time than I would have thought possible, Mao and Chou appeared in the Communists' only piece of motor transport in Yenan, at least as far as I ever saw, a beat-up truck with an enclosed cabin. Close behind them came a company of infantry, evidently hastily mustered at a barracks near the airfield. While Mao greeted the general with due ceremony, the company lined up in guard of honor formation and the general reviewed them. After the general had returned the salute of the officer commanding the company, he drew himself to his full impressive height, swelled up like a poisoned pup, and let out an Indian warwhoop. I shall never forget the expressions on the faces of Mao and Chou at this totally unexpected behavior on the part of the distinguished visitor.

After the review, Chairman Mao and the general climbed into the cab of the ancient truck and I squeezed in with them to act as interpreter. This was a task of some difficulty, due to the saltiness of the General's remarks, and the unusual language in which he expressed himself. His discourse, in addition, was by no means connected by any readily discernible pattern of thought. Seeing country people on the road would remind him of anecdotes—which probably meant nothing to Mao—about old friends back in Oklahoma. One old farmer having trouble with a balky mule which had been frightened by our truck elicited a yell from the General, "Hit him on the other side, Charley!" These and other spontaneous remarks required quick thinking and free translation on my part in order to give the chairman and Chou En-lai some faint idea of what the talk was all about.

When General Hurley left Yenan three days later, he took with him a draft, worked out by him and the Chinese Communists, which later came to be known as the Communist Five-Point Proposals. It of course provided for the unification of all military forces in China and the establishment of a coalition government embracing all anti-Japanese parties. All anti-Japanese armed forces were to carry out the orders of this coalition government, and supplies acquired from foreign powers were to be equitably distributed among them. The coalition government was to support the principles of Sun Yat-sen, which were interpreted in terms of government of the people, for the people, and by the people. It was to "promote progress and democracy and to establish justice, freedom of conscience, freedom of the press, freedom of assembly and association, the right to petition the government for the redress of grievances, the right of writ of *habeas corpus,* and the right of residence." Finally, it also was to "pursue policies intended to make effective those two rights defined as freedom from fear and freedom from want."

"The fine Italian hand of General Hurley in the above terms," Colonel Barrett has remarked, "is clearly apparent." There can be little doubt that this is true. On November 9, General Hurley, on reading the proposals originally submitted to him by the Chinese Communists, had remarked that they seemed entirely fair to him, but that they did not go far enough. He accordingly made some suggestions which were incorporated in the final draft. Then just before he emplaned, he turned to Mao Tse-tung and declared: "Chairman, I think it would be appropriate for you and me to indicate, by signing these

terms, that we consider them fair and just." As Colonel Barrett recounts: "And this they did, placing copies of the terms on a flat stone
of convenient height. I distinctly recall that Mao signed his name as
an American would a check, not by placing his seal (chop) upon the
two copies of the document. A blank space was thoughtfully left with
the typed signature of Chiang Kai-shek below, in which the Generalissimo could indicate his approval later—should he so desire." [38]

"In fairness to General Hurley," Colonel Barrett added, I wish
to note here that as he and Mao were about to sign, the former said:
'Chairman Mao, you of course understand that although I consider
these fair terms, I cannot guarantee the Generalissimo will accept
them.' " The Generalissimo, of course, did not. Indeed, after General
Hurley had returned to Chungking, Chiang's brother-in-law, T. V.
Soong, remarked to him: "The Communists have sold you a bill of
goods." [39] Again, in fairness to General Hurley, it is worth recalling
that this blunt comment did not keep him from continuing to try—
right up to the day of Japan's surrender, and even after that—to bring
the two Chinese sides together in a coalition government.

By 1945, with the outcome of the war no longer in doubt, each
Chinese side became concerned about the immediate situation it would
face after the defeat of Japan. Their civil war, damped down in the
face of a common enemy but not extinguished, was almost certain to
flare up in full vigor after Japan's surrender. Then one side or the
other could get an advantage, depending on the extent to which it was
able to take the surrender of Japanese troops, occupy the territories
those troops were to vacate, and fall heir to their arms and ammunition. The Communists were the better placed geographically, particularly in north China, because they had established "liberated areas"
in close proximity to the Japanese. This advantage, however, was only
a potential one. The government of the Nationalists was the one which
enjoyed diplomatic recognition and the transport advantage inherent
in the logistic support of United States forces. Communist hopes, therefore, would turn in part on the acceptance or rejection of the thesis
that they should be permitted to take the Japanese surrender in those
areas where theirs was the predominant Chinese force.

The Communist forces, which had numbered about 80,000 in
1936, had grown enormously. According to conservative estimates, the
war's end was to find the Communists with 600,000 regular troops and
a militia of 400,000. If their own figures are to be accepted, the Communists then had over 900,000 regular troops, a militia of 2,200,000—
and a party membership of 1,210,000. The Nationalist government,
at this juncture, was credited with an army of 3,00,000 combat troops
which were better-armed than those of the Communists.[40] The respec-

tive figures seemed to indicate that the government forces should have the edge in any postwar military contest.

While the war continued, Mao Tse-tung had been demanding that the Nationalists agree to the establishment of a coalition government to replace their one-party rule, and Stalin and Molotov had been saying that the two Chinese sides should get together.[41] On August 14, 1945, the Soviet Union went one step further. It negotiated with Chiang Kai-shek's government a Sino-Soviet Treaty of Friendship and Alliance.[42] Subsequently Stalin advised the Chinese Communists that their insurrection "had no prospect" and that they should join Chiang's government and dissolve their army.[43]

On the same day that the Nationalists concluded their treaty with the Soviet Union, Chiang Kai-shek—at the urging of General Hurley—invited Mao Tse-tung to visit Chungking for joint discussions. Mao's initial response was rude in tone and demanding in content. But shortly thereafter General MacArthur, as Supreme Commander of the Allied Powers in the Pacific, issued an order designating the National government of Chiang Kai-shek as the sole agency for accepting the Japanese surrender in all parts of China except Manchuria—where it was to be taken by the Russians. Meanwhile a report had come to Hurley's ear that it was being said in Yenan that the Chungking government, while inviting Mao to visit Chungking, was declining to guarantee his safety while he was there. Accordingly Hurley sent word to Mao that he was willing to fly up to Yenan, then fly back to Chungking with the Communist leaders, and take responsibility for their lives while in Chungking. Then Chiang invited Mao again, and Mao accepted the renewed invitation. And so it came about that General Hurley, once again in sartorial splendor but this time in the civilian dress and Homburg hat appropriate to his changed status, which was now that of ambassador to China, once more flew to Yenan. The next day, August 28, 1945, Mao Tse-tung flew back with him to Chungking, to begin a period of negotiations.[44]

During this flight, presumably his first, Mao Tse-tung composed a poem descriptive of the vast land which unrolled below and of the heroic emperors who had ruled it during notable periods of the past. It concludes with the lines: "If great heroes you would find, look in the epoch of today." A Chinese scholar has pointed out that this line is evocative of another—perhaps the best known one in all the literature of China—which is to be found in *Romance of the Three Kingdoms*. In it, the redoubtable if treacherous Ts'ao Ts'ao says to Liu Pei, scion of the imperial house of Han: "The only heroes in the world are you and I." Liu Pei had ruled the state of Shu, which had later become the province of Szechwan, in which Chiang Kai-shek's capital of Chungking was located. The domain of Ts'ao Ts'ao, like that of Mao Tse-tung, was situated to the north of it. Liu Pei, like Chiang Kai-shek, regarded himself as China's legitimate ruler; Ts'ao Ts'ao and Mao Tse-tung were challengers. Accordingly, Mao Tse-tung evidently was likening himself to Ts'ao Ts'ao and Chiang Kai-shek to Liu Pei. By implying that they were the only heroes in the land, Mao suggested that he was looking forward to finally inflicting on Chiang the defeat which Liu Pei had suffered in the end.[45]

While Mao Tse-tung was in Chungking, Chiang Kai-shek gave a banquet in his honor. A memorable photograph has recorded the occasion. The two leaders are raising their glasses to each other in a toast; Chiang is shaven-headed—looking as hairless and as slender as a serpent, and Mao is rumpled and burly—the mongoose in their confrontation.[46]

Mao Tse-tung and Chiang Kai-shek entered into negotiations with each other under a certain compulsion, not all of it applied by Moscow and Washington. After eight long years of war the Chinese people yearned for peace, and many of them hoped that Communist participation in a coalition government might provide the means of avoiding civil war. In addition, the prospect of a coalition government had wide appeal because the rule of the Kuomintang was increasingly seen as having become inefficient, corrupt, and oppressive. Finally, many people hoped that, through the inclusion of a number of third parties in the coalition, it might be possible to end one-party rule by the Kuomintang without merely replacing it with the one-party rule of the Chinese Communists. In these circumstances, neither the Communists nor the Kuomintang wanted to take public blame for the failure of negotiations, and each wanted to win the third parties to its side.

But negotiations between Chiang and Mao could hardly be fruitful because each knew the other too well. As Mao Tse-tung had written: "Chiang Kai-shek has . . . held firmly to the vital point that whoever has an army has power and that war decides everything. In this respect we ought to learn from him. . . . A few small political parties with a short history, for example, the Youth Party, have no army, and so have not been able to get anywhere. . . . Every Communist must grasp the truth, 'Political power grows out of the barrel of the gun.' " Mao conceded that things were different between the bourgeois parties in other countries, but asserted that in China the proletariat had to take its environment into account and see clearly to the heart of the matter. "Where there is naïveté on the question of military power," he said, "nothing whatsoever can be achieved." [47]

During September and October, while negotiations went on in

Chungking, American marines were landed at principal ports and airfields which they secured, and American transport planes moved three
large Nationalist armies to key areas of east and north China. Meanwhile Communist forces swarmed throughout the countryside of those
same areas, blocking roads and cutting railways.[48] Mao Tse-tung nevertheless stayed in Chungking until October 11, 1945. Then he returned to Yenan, leaving Chou En-lai to carry on negotiations. But by
the end of November Chou too had left, and Ambassador Hurley had
resigned in frustration.[49]

President Truman selected General George C. Marshall to take
up the task at which Ambassador Hurley had not succeeded. For
slightly over a year General Marshall tried to bring about a lasting
truce and a coalition government. The United States did not pursue
this objective by maintaining the role of impartial middleman. It remained American policy to support the Nationalist government and
to help that government establish its authority insofar as its military
capabilities and limited American assistance would permit.[50] Nevertheless, by the end of January 1946, both sides had agreed on the cessation of hostilities, to be monitored by truce teams. But a contest for
possession of Manchuria had begun the previous autumn, and Chiang
Kai-shek would not agree to the dispatch there of truce teams—which
might have helped implement the cessation of hostilities there—until
the following March.

The Soviet Union had entered the war against Japan just in time
to take part in the kill. Soviet forces had swept into Manchuria, and
there had disarmed both Japanese troops and a 320,000-man "puppet
army" composed principally of Manchurian Chinese. When Soviet
forces withdrew, they apparently took with them all the heavy equipment of the forces they had disarmed but left at least some light
ordnance and ammunition behind. Accordingly, there was on hand in
Manchuria a reservoir of over 300,000 well-trained men, who were at
loose ends, and weapons with which they might be rearmed. The Chinese Communists, who had begun moving skeleton units into Manchuria immediately after the Japanese surrender, fleshed out their units
by recruiting, and they had no trouble laying their hands on needed
weapons. Chiang Kai-shek was determined to take over Manchuria for
the National government. He evidently counted on being able to do
so by military means and was willing to discontinue the attempt only
on terms which the Communists would not accept. In consequence
the Marshall mission failed, and that failure opened the floodgates to
full-scale civil war.[51]

In July 1946, the Chinese Communists gave symbolic recognition
to the fact of final break. Abandoning the designations which had been

assigned their forces by the government when the war against Japan had broken out, they adopted the new name of the People's Liberation Army.[52] Despite the Communists' subsequent acquisition of air and naval forces, this designation—often abbreviated to "the PLA"—has been the collective title for their forces ever since. On July 20, Mao issued an inner-party directive expressing confidence in Communist ability to win what he called a defensive war. Two months earlier Communist forces in Manchuria had suffered heavy losses in trying to hold the Manchurian town of Ssuping in a positional battle—a defeat for which P'eng Chen, the political commissar, rather than Lin Piao, the military commander, was later to be blamed. Now Mao Tse-tung outlined a strategy of temporarily abandoning all cities which could be defended only by a heavy concentration of troops. Instead, all possible forces would be made available for mobile operations designed to destroy enemy forces. Chiang Kai-shek, Mao evidently felt sure, would not adopt a similar strategy; rather he would take cities and tie down a large proportion of his forces in their defense—cities which the Chinese Communists need not directly attack. By these and other means Mao Tse-tung counted on overcoming the advantages his opponent enjoyed in terms of numbers, military equipment, and United States assistance.[53]

Pursuant to this strategy, and in the face of a strong Nationalist offensive in the spring of 1947, the Chinese Communists even abandoned Yenan. Their leaders split into two groups, with Mao Tse-tung and Chou En-lai leading one group which hid out in the countryside north of Yenan. Chiang Ch'ing accompanied Mao Tse-tung, taking with her their daughters Li Na and Mao Mao. The other group, headed by Liu Shao-ch'i and Chu Teh, went to a small place in the north China province of Hopeh, where they established a Central Committee office.[54]

Liu's handling of affairs, during the year or so Mao was in hiding, became the subject of a disagreement which is of interest chiefly because it was an early instance of their differences, which eventually would split the party. Liu Shao-ch'i held a party conference at which a new and more radical land law was adopted. Mao Tse-tung later criticized the law as representing an ultra-leftist policy which "failed to make a sober analysis and raised the sweeping slogan 'Do everything as the masses want it done.'" But while this was an early case of dissension between them, it was not one to which the Maoists would call much attention when they took up the offensive against Liu Shao-ch'i. By then he was being portrayed as no leftist at all, but as a rightist renegade who long had sought to follow the capitalist road.[55]

While Mao Tse-tung was in hiding, Chiang Kai-shek was justify-

ing Mao's prediction with respect to Nationalist strategy by taking and
garrisoning city after city, until his forces were badly overextended.
Within a year the tide had turned: Nationalist forces in Manchuria
were under siege; P'eng Te-huai had defeated the Nationalist divisions
in the Sian area; and the line of retreat of Chiang's garrison in Yenan
was cut off. Mao Tse-tung had been more concerned about strategy
than the symbolic or psychological importance of Yenan. Chiang Kai-
shek, however, proceeded to airlift twenty-three thousand more men
to Sian—the key to Yenan—from the Chengchow-Loyang sector further south. Chengchow is a vital junction of east–west and north–south
railway lines, and the area contained huge stocks of military supplies.
PLA commanders Ch'en Yi, Liu Po-ch'eng, and Ch'en Keng massed
two hundred thousand troops nearby, launched a general offensive at
the beginning of June, and captured Chengchow less than three weeks
later. Then in September, Chiang's forces lost Tsinan, another railway
junction town farther east.[56] Major General David Barr, head of a
United States Army Advisory Group in China, had urged withdrawing
the garrison from Tsinan while there was yet time to save it. Instead
the order was to fight to the last, and the Tsinan garrison was destroyed.[57]

Beginning in early March of 1948, General Barr had advised
Chiang Kai-shek to evacuate Manchuria while he could still save the
Nationalist armies there. By the end of October they were in critical
danger. Chiang Kai-shek was in Peking trying to direct the Manchurian
operations alone, without reference to his supreme staff. Predictably,
his final decision to withdraw them coming months too late, those
armies were all destroyed, and only a few thousand troops succeeded
in escaping. In November Communist forces under the overall command of Ch'en Yi, with Jao Shu-shih as his political commissar, began
a giant battle of annihilation in east central China. By January 12,
1949, they had destroyed Nationalist armies totaling over half a million men.[58]

That was the beginning of the end. The Nationalist government
expressed the wish for a peaceful settlement, but it was too late; the
Communists saw no need to settle for half a loaf when the whole loaf
was within their reach. They captured the capital at Nanking in April;
by autumn most of mainland China was in their hands. On October
1, 1949, they established their own government of the People's Republic of China in Peking, with Mao Tse-tung as its chairman.

Before the year was out, the seat of the Nationalist government—
after brief sojourns in Canton, Chungking, and Chengtu—had been
transferred to the island of Taiwan (commonly known to non-Chinese
as Formosa). With one exception, the foreign diplomats of ambassa-

dorial rank all remained in Nanking instead of accompanying the government when it evacuated the capital and moved to Canton. Of this one exception Mao Tse-tung was later to make the sour observation that the last ambassador to take leave of Chiang Kai-shek was that of the Soviet Union.[59]

8

Leaning to One Side and
Walking on One Leg

IN 1949 China's economy, after seven years of resistance to Japan and four years of civil war, was near collapse. China was going to have to lean on someone while it got on its feet, and later when it took its first steps on the road of economic development.

The Chinese Communists appear initially not to have considered the Soviet Union as the prospective nation on which to lean. All the assistance which the USSR had extended to China during the war had gone to the government of Chiang Kai-shek. Mao Tse-tung had sometimes flouted the advice of the rulers of the Kremlin, and his experiences with them had undoubtedly left a sour aftertaste. During the war, Stalin and Molotov had remarked that Mao Tse-tung and his fellows were "margarine" Communists rather than genuine ones.[1] These remarks may not have been insincere. After all, real Communists were supposed to accept Moscow's direction and to base their revolutions on the proletariat, not on the peasantry. Indeed, Mao was later to remark that Stalin had distrusted them even after they had come to power.[2] But beyond the question of willingness was the question of ability to be leaned upon. In the immediate postwar period it appeared that the war-ravaged Soviet Union's own problems of postwar reconstruction would rule it out as the donor of any substantial aid.

Throughout the last years of the war against Japan, it was principally the United States which assisted China to survive, and it was to the United States that Chinese looked for massive aid in their postwar reconstruction. The Russians came into the war against Japan only for the final kill, and during their occupation of Manchuria they stripped its industries of equipment for their own use.[3] With the Soviets taking, the Americans looked like the only prospective givers. This was certainly the way the situation looked to non-Communist Chinese; apparently it did not look much different to the Communists.

In 1944, Mao Tse-tung was himself saying that a postwar China would have to industrialize, that it would need the aid of foreign capital, and that this assistance would necessarily come from the United States. Moreover, he averred, China's industrialization should be carried out under a system of free enterprise rather than bureaucratic capitalism.[4] While this may sound odd if not incredible from today's perspectives, there was nothing so odd about it at the time.

Mao Tse-tung evidently then hoped that American influence in China might open the way to Communist participation in a postwar coalition government. It was not that he was surrendering the goal of total power. It was rather that participation in such a government seemed the preferable road to its attainment. He recognized that the Chinese people were war weary and would want, after victory, a period of the peace they craved; because the Nationalists were superior at least in numbers and equipment, he could not be certain of the outcome of a civil war; and if a period of trial proved participation in coalition government an unsatisfactory route to power it would be possible, after a period of peace, to renew the civil war. If the Communists were to participate in a coalition government, some time still would necessarily pass before they gained predominant power. Meanwhile they would have preferred to see Chinese industry built through private enterprise rather than see it become the power base of a state bureaucracy not subject to Communist control. Indeed, during this period the Communists may not yet have settled the question of whether China, still an agrarian country, should or should not pass through a "capitalist phase" during which industries would be built and a proletarian base would be developed.

The American effort on behalf of a coalition government having failed, the only road to power left was that of civil war. During the war against Japan, American military support had gone only to the Nationalists. Thereafter it was the Nationalist government that had been named to take over the territories and arms of the surrendering Japanese, and the Nationalists had been assisted by the provision of American airlift and sea transport. The United States had indeed imposed an embargo on shipment of military supplies to China from August 1946 to May 1947. But even before that period had expired, the United States had turned over some thousands of tons of ammunition, held by American forces then in China, to the National government forces. If this sort of mediation was leaning to one side, its character could have been overlooked if the mediation had been successful. But after mediation had clearly failed and the two sides were locked in combat, United States military and economic assistance continued to go to the Nationalists, along with the services of a United States military advisory group.[5] Looked at objectively, it is not strange that Mao Tse-tung had by 1949 given up any thought he may have earlier harbored about postwar Sino-American collaboration.

The first clear sign of a total reversal in this regard came in No-

vember 1948. The Communists had occupied the Manchurian city of
Mukden at the end of September. The incoming Communist authorities shortly thereafter assured the American consul general in that city
that the new regime was interested in mutually advantageous trade
through which it might obtain the equipment needed for the rehabilitation of Manchurian industry. Accordingly, they indicated, they would
welcome the continuance of his office. Then on November 14 the
American consul general received a notification (as did his French and
British colleagues) that he must within forty-eight hours surrender any
radio station in his possession; moreover, the communication was addressed to him as the "former American consul." He sent a report to
Washington and asked for instructions, but the forty-eight hours passed
and he had not received them. Upon the expiration of the deadline,
the Communist command in Mukden surrounded the consulate with
troops, cut off the electricity and water, and placed everyone inside
under incommunicado house arrest. There they remained until October 1949, when the consul general was jailed and word of his arrest
got out. Thereafter the whole American staff was accused of espionage
and deported in December.[6]

The evidence is strong that the change in the treatment accorded
the consul general in Mukden represented a unilateral policy decision
by Mao Tse-tung himself. The notification addressed to the "former"
consul general on November 14 was signed by General Wu Hsiu-
ch'üan, chief of staff under Lin Piao of the Communist Northeast
Region. He was part of the hierarchy of Communist officials in Manchuria which had shown a quite different attitude during the earlier
days of the month. Thus one is led to assume that his regional headquarters had, in the interim, received a new policy directive from the
party's central headquarters. That the directive had emanated from
Mao himself is suggested by two circumstances. The first is that the
essence of General Wu's notification was reiterated in a circular communication which Mao Tse-tung issued in March 1949. In it he instructed all party cadres that they should, upon entering major cities,
refuse to recognize the legal status of any foreign official establishments
and personnel. He explained: "The imperialists, who have always been
hostile to the Chinese people, will definitely not be in a hurry to treat
us as equals. . . . As long as the imperialist countries do not change
their hostile attitude, we shall not grant them legal status in China."
A second bit of evidence bearing on the same point is the different
attitude assertedly held about the same time by Liu Shao-ch'i, the vice
chairman of the party. If Radio Peking is to be believed, as late as
1949 Liu Shao-ch'i was advocating a favorable reaction to a statement

by Secretary of State Dean Acheson that the United States wanted only friendship with the Chinese people.[7]

On June 30, 1949, Mao Tse-tung set forth his position publicly. Remarking bitterly on American supply of arms to Chiang Kai-shek, he accused the United States not only of being an imperialist power—which he described as the biggest one remaining in the world—but also of wanting to enslave the world. The Chinese people had learned, he claimed, that they should "lean to one side"—they should ally themselves with the Soviet Union and the "People's Democracies." [8]

In December 1949, this leader of the so-called margarine Communists went to Moscow seeking both a formal alliance with the Soviet Union and economic assistance for his new regime. He remained there until February of the following year. The fruits of his visit were the Sino-Soviet treaty of alliance and subsidiary economic agreements. Under these latter agreements the Soviet Union extended to China $300 millions in credits, to be supplemented by a supply of blueprints and expert advisers. It would be interesting to know whether Stalin also discussed with Mao any plans relating to South Korea, which the North Korean Communists were to invade the following June.

The amount of economic assistance Mao Tse-tung had obtained was obviously small and the form—credits rather than grant aid—less than generous. Later Mao Tse-tung was to explain, perhaps in self-justification, the difficulties he had faced. Stalin had distrusted the Chinese Communists, he declared, even before they had undertaken their victorious campaign against the Nationalists. That campaign had been undertaken in the teeth of Stalin's orders to cooperate with Chiang Kai-shek instead of making revolution against him. After the Chinese Communists had come to power, that mistrust remained. "Stalin," Mao explained, "feared that China might degenerate into another Yugoslavia and that I might become another Tito." In consequence they had "struggled" over the question of the 1950 treaty of alliance, which Stalin really had not wanted to sign.[9]

With the assurance of at least limited Soviet support behind them, the Chinese Communists undertook what was to be a three-year period of internal rehabilitation and consolidation. It had little more than begun, however, before they faced an external crisis. During the autumn of 1950, it became apparent that the Chinese Communists had to be ready to go to war in Korea or be willing to witness the destruction of a fellow Communist regime and the extension to China's northern border of what they considered an enemy power.

If we are to believe later accounts, circulated for the purpose of placing some of his fellow leaders in an unfavorable light, it was Mao who proposed that Communist China should "resist America and aid Korea," and he succeeded in having this proposal adopted in the face of opposition from several if not all his principal subordinates. P'eng Te-huai, who had been the field commander throughout the war against Japan, and who was to become the commander of the so-called Chinese People's Volunteers in Korea, was later represented as having declared that "whether it is the 37th or the 38th parallel, it would be better not to fight." Vice Premier Ch'en Yün, chairman of the government's Financial and Economic Committee, is said to have taken the view that "to fight against the Americans and to continue with economic construction were two incompatible policies." The attitude of Vice Premier Kao Kang was also important, for he held the concurrent post of chairman of the Northeast People's Government in Manchuria, which borders on Korea and which would necessarily be a major base for Chinese operations there. P'eng Te-huai was later quoted as having said that Kao Kang "gave the only vote in support of Chairman Mao when the Korean war broke out." But the same account which quoted P'eng Te-huai to that effect declared that his statement had been untrue. "Actually," it explained, "Kao Kang opposed the dispatch of forces to aid Korea." [10]

Whatever the truth of these accounts, the Chinese Communists seem to have decided not to react if only South Korean troops invaded North Korea, but to intervene if they were joined by United Nations forces. On October 1, 1950, General MacArthur called upon the North Koreans to lay down their arms, and South Korean troops crossed the 38th parallel into North Korea. On October 3, Chou En-lai warned that China would intervene if forces of the United Nations Command also crossed the 38th parallel. In disregard of this warning, an American division invaded North Korea a few days later, and UN forces commenced a drive towards the border between Korea and Manchuria. Before the month was out the Chinese had intervened.[11]

The Chinese Communists were able to claim a victory—when the war ended three years later—because the war left the government of North Korea intact and in possession of approximately the same territory it originally had held. The successful prosecution of the war against powerful enemies enhanced the authority of the Chinese Communist government, thereby contributing to its ability to consolidate its control over the length and breadth of China. The costs of the war, both in human and economic terms, had been substantial, but not beyond China's ability to bear. In fact, economic rehabilitation proceeded successfully, and the war helped the Chinese Communists to solve the problem of what to do with Kuomintang armies left on the mainland at the end of the civil war. They were sent to Korea, and expended there.[12]

The Chinese forces which fought and took casualties in Korea were, of course, not confined to the surrendered armies of the Kuomintang. Indeed, one of the Chinese killed in Korea was Mao An-ying, elder of the two sons of Mao Tse-tung. According to a story which gained currency in China, Mao had arranged for his son to serve as the secretary of P'eng Te-huai who, thinking to advance the young man's career, had him reassigned to the headquarters staff of the Chinese Second Army. Its headquarters subsequently were bombed by United States planes, and most of the members of the staff were killed —among them, Mao An-ying. In consequence, although P'eng Te-huai won additional prestige through his command of Chinese forces during the Korean war and became minister of national defense the year after its end, he may also have won the lasting enmity of Mao Tse-tung.[13]

By intervening in Korea and thereby saving Stalin from the consequences of an enormous miscalculation, the Chinese Communists placed themselves in a position to seek the greater Soviet assistance needed for their country's longer-term development. In the autumn of 1952, they set up a State Planning Committee, which was to draft a five-year plan covering the period 1953–1957, and they sent a delegation headed by Chou En-lai to Moscow to negotiate for Soviet aid. The mission was successful, but the negotiations took a whole year. In consequence, it was not until the second half of 1953, when the Korean war had ended, that the extent of the Soviet commitment was known and the principal members of the State Planning Committee gathered in Peking.

As chairman of the committee, the Chinese Communists had named Kao Kang, the head of the Northeast Bureau of the party and their top administrator in Manchuria. Because Manchuria was the chief base of China's heavy industry, as well as an agriculturally important area, Kao Kang had become experienced in dealing with the problems of economic reconstruction. Kao apparently found a kindred spirit, among the members of the committee, in Jao Shu-shih. He had been holding similar positions in the East China Bureau of the party and as administrator of a region which included the industrial and commercial metropolis of Shanghai, as well as its primarily agricultural hinterland. Not long after they took up their new duties in Peking, the two men found themselves involved in a dangerous struggle with Mao Tse-tung.

It would appear that this struggle had its roots in the problems which the Chinese Communists had faced during the immediately pre-

ceding years, while they were consolidating their hold upon the mainland. They had then been engaged both in the urgent task of rehabilitating the economy, which had been crippled by twelve years
of war and civil strife, and in initiating and carrying forward the socialization of its private sector. These two tasks were, of course, partially contradictory, and hence a source of contention within the leadership.

The government, moreover, had been hastily organized, with an
unwieldy structure based on a system of committees, and the Communists conducted important programs largely by mobilizing the
masses in big campaigns, each aimed at achieving one or more related
objectives. However, in 1952, the same year in which they had established the State Planning Committee, they began drafting a constitution under which the government was to be reorganized. That year
they also appointed Jao Shu-shih as the new head of the Organization
Department of the party. The expectations of change which were entertained by some of the leaders may be judged from a remark made
by Tung Pi-wu, one of the twelve founders of the party. Tung Pi-wu
had been educated in the law while a student in Japan. He now was
a vice premier of the government and the chairman of its Political and
Legal Committee. In discussing the draft constitution with P'eng Chen,
the mayor of Peking and concurrently a vice chairman of that committee, Tung Pi-wu remarked that the Chinese Communists had in the
past lived by movements, but after the constitution had been adopted
they would live by the law.[14]

The expectation expressed by Tung Pi-wu undoubtedly reflected
the hope of all government leaders who liked orderly procedures, but
it was not one which would have been shared by Mao Tse-tung. He
liked to operate through mass movements, which he could stir up and
guide by issuing directives to the cadres in his capacity of party chairman. Working primarily through the government would have cramped
his style, and abiding by the rule of law would have limited his power.

One of the principal programs initiated during the early months
of Communist rule was that under which land holdings were to be
equalized. Mao Tse-tung and Liu Shao-ch'i both spoke on this aspect
of land reform at a plenary session of the Central Committee which
was held in June of 1950. Both leaders took the same line. Mao spoke
of the need for "preserving a rich-peasant economy" in order to promote the early restoration of production. The work of agrarian reform, he said, "should be carried forward by stages in an orderly manner." Liu Shao-ch'i went on to say that "the policy we have adopted on
the preservation of the rich-peasant economy is of course not a temporary but a long-term one." [15] Land reform was to go ahead slowly,

he announced, and subject to central control. Disruption of the villages in the name of class war, where it had occurred, was to cease.[16]

Two weeks later the Chinese Communists adopted a Land Reform Law which provided for the confiscation from all landlords of the land, draft animals, and farm implements, which were to be redistributed on an equal basis. The former landlords might share in this redistribution, however, with but one qualification: Landlords who were "enemies of the people" were excepted. Yet when it was applied, the 1950 Land Reform Law was carried out in bloody fashion. It is widely believed that several million landlords were adjudged enemies of the people and executed.[17] Those shown being executed, in photographs of the period, were roughly-clad, gnarled, and obviously work-worn peasants; perhaps the fat, sleek ones had fled before the storm.

It is fairly clear that the regime's economic planners, like Liu Shao-ch'i himself, had not intended that land reform should be handled in this way. As late as 1951, Po I-po—a top official in the economic sphere—was criticizing the cadres for entertaining "utopian" ideas about the imminence of socialism in the countryside instead of encouraging the peasants to produce more and thus "get rich." [18]

In 1967, the Maoists were to charge that Liu Shao-ch'i's 1950 statements on land reform constituted one example of his black record of revisionism.[19] The allegation was cynically unfair, because his statements had differed from those made at the same time by Mao Tse-tung only in the sense that they were more detailed and more emphatic. Indeed, one is entitled to wonder whether Mao, with similar cynicism, had been responsible for the brutal application of what was, on its face, a relatively mild law. If so, it would help explain why Mao's critics were to allude to him as a man who quickly forgot what he had said, went back on his word, and behaved capriciously. In any event, the destruction of China's landlords was no less thorough and brutal than the destruction of the aristocratic families carried out two millennia earlier by the first emperor of the Ch'in dynasty, the man whom Mao Tse-tung had so admired in his boyhood.

The implementation of the Land Reform Law was largely completed in 1952, and in August Liu Shao-ch'i reassuringly declared: "Big movements are not possible again hereafter. The main thing is to concentrate energy on economic construction." The similarity of his remark to that of Tung Pi-wu suggests that the expectation of a shift to orderly rule was widely shared in the upper echelons of the party. However, Liu Shao-ch'i may also have had in mind one of the assumptions of the regime's economists about the organization of the agricultural sector. They believed that to proceed successfully from privately-owned to collectivized agriculture would require mechanization, and that China would for some time be insufficiently advanced in the industrial sphere to make that possible.[20]

Liu Shao-ch'i, as vice chairman of both the party and the government, should have been able to speak with authority, and doubtless would have if the regime had been operating under a system of unified and collective leadership. But Mao Tse-tung was determined to carry out a speedy collectivization of China's agriculture. In other words, the land which had just been distributed among the peasants was to be taken away from them in favor of a system of joint ownership by agricultural producers cooperatives. This precipitated a policy struggle, beginning in 1952, in which Mao Tse-tung did not gain the upper hand until three years had passed.[21]

During the first phase of this struggle it was regional leaders— alerted by widespread opposition from the peasants to the loss of their land—who mounted the most effective resistance to speedy collectivization. Most of the top regional leaders, and some of their immediate subordinates—men like Ch'en Yi and T'an Chen-lin, who were serving in east China under Jao Shu-shih—had been military commanders or political commissars of the forces which had conquered their respective areas for the Communists. After victory, they had been kept on there to administer the affairs of the party and of the government. With Communist rule still largely decentralized, they exercised great power. Many of these men wore two hats: As leaders in the regional and lower bureaus of the party they made decisions, and in their roles as government officials they supervised the implementation of those decisions. They had become habituated to the autonomous exercise of authority, and in 1953 some of them exercised it by dissolving many of the hastily-organized cooperatives. This aroused the wrath of Mao Tse-tung, who demanded that they undergo the punishment of self-criticism.[22] It may also have helped persuade Mao that the regional bureaus had become bastions of resistance to his will and ought to be abolished.

There are few experiences more exasperating than to serve under a leadership which issues conflicting orders but exerts heavy pressures for compliance. It accordingly is not strange that some of Mao's fellows concluded that the qualities, practices, and habits of thought which had made him a genius at waging revolutionary war unsuited him for the tasks of government administration. It will be recalled that Mao Tse-tung was the chairman of both the party and the government, and that a reorganization was impending which would afford an opportunity to make changes in the leadership. By the early part of 1953, a group had emerged which hoped to use this opportunity to reduce the power of Mao Tse-tung.

At least two of Mao's oldest comrades openly participated in the attempt to reduce his power. One of them was T'an Chen-lin, now a high official in Jao Shu-shih's east China regime; he had taken part in the Autumn Harvest Uprising and then followed Mao to the Ching-kangshan. The other was Chu Teh, commander in chief of the army, who had joined Mao Tse-tung the following year. In 1953, it was later disclosed, T'an Chen-lin "took the lead in sending a joint letter asking our great leader Chairman Mao to 'take a rest,' " and Chu Teh tried "to become the leader himself . . . advocating the idea of becoming chairman in turn." The group also sent an emissary to consult Kao Kang, while he was still in Manchuria, to solicit his opinions on the selection of vice chairmen and cabinet ministers and to inquire about his own desires. After an initial disclaimer of personal ambition, Kao Kang is said to have expressed an interest in the positions of vice chairman or general secretary of the party and of premier in the government. Somewhat later, it is alleged, Kao Kang sought to enlist the support, for his ambition to attain these posts, of T'ao Chu, one of the regional leaders in south China.[23]

The group which wanted to reduce Mao's power was perhaps too numerous and too influential to be dealt with successfully through a direct attack. Indeed, some of them were individuals who were too powerful to be purged. In consequence, Mao Tse-tung had to adopt a strategy designed to divide the opposition and achieve the purge of some who were vulnerable in order to provide object lessons to the others. Choosing Kao Kang and Jao Shu-shih as potential victims fitted into this strategy very well. They had just been removed from their power bases, which were regional, in order to take up their new positions in Peking. The central charge which was to be the basis for purging them was that they had used conspiratorial means which were designed "to split our party and to overthrow the leading core—the long tested Central Committee of the party headed by Comrade Mao Tse-tung—with the aim of seizing the supreme power of the party and the state." [24] This charge of conspiracy made it unnecessary to take up directly the challenges implicit in T'an Chen-lin's letter of advice, and Chu Teh's effort to succeed to the chairmanship. T'an Chen-lin had acted in the open, and the charge of conspiracy accordingly did not apply to him; and Chu Teh, with his revolutionary record and position as commander in chief of the armed forces, was not someone to attack head on.

In expressing the ambition to become vice chairman or general secretary of the party and premier of the government, Kao Kang had invited the opposition of Liu Shao-ch'i and Chou En-lai, the occupants of the positions which he sought for himself. Accordingly, the choice of Kao Kang as one of the two principal leaders to attack was an adroit move, well-designed to attract the support of Liu and Chou. And if Mao was also determined to end the exercise of autonomous power by regional leaders, he could hardly have chosen a more appropriate target. In his governance of Manchuria, Kao Kang had behaved with notable independence. He had, for instance, negotiated international agreements with Soviet officialdom, much as though Manchuria were a separate state. Moreover, Mao Tse-tung, with his own record of resistance to Moscow's direction and advice, and seeing Kao Kang apparently enjoying Moscow's favor, may have looked on Kao as a potentially dangerous, Soviet-backed rival.

Mao Tse-tung undoubtedly considered Jao Shu-shih's east China region a hotbed of the opposition. It almost certainly was one of the regions in which many of the agricultural cooperatives had been the dissolved. Moreover, he may have considered Jao Shu-shih partly responsible for the joint letter inviting him to "take a rest." The names of only two signers of that letter have been revealed—T'an Chen-lin and a lesser leader named Ch'en P'ei-hsien—but both of them were Jao Shu-shih's subordinates. Then, after Jao Shu-shih had come to Peking to take up his duties as head of the Organization Bureau of the party, he allegedly made personnel shifts designed to assist Kao Kang in his quest for power.

Kao Kang and Jao Shu-shih apparently had their first open clash with Mao Tse-tung shortly after they arrived in Peking in 1953. They were among the officials who took part in a National Financial and Economic Conference which was held that year, and it later was asserted that at this conference the "Kao-Jao clique" had "madly assailed Chairman Mao." [25] The two men, coming fresh from jobs outside Peking in which their voices unquestionably carried much authority, may well have spoken their minds and found themselves in an altercation with Mao Tse-tung. If so, it may also have been an altercation which Mao had sought, to afford him the pretext for initiating his own campaign against them.

About the beginning of 1954, the cases of Kao Kang and Jao Shu-shih were taken up in the Political Bureau and then laid before a plenary session of the Central Committee.[26] Very shortly afterward, Ch'en Yi gave an account of what allegedly had transpired, to a gathering of lesser leaders at Shanghai. In his account of the misdeeds of the two men, he outlined in general terms the more serious charges, and supplied specific details which might have seemed trivial had they not involved disrespect for Mao Tse-tung. Mao charged, for instance, that Jao Shu-shih, who had spent some time in the United States, had frequently expressed the view that the world's greatest political leaders had been Abraham Lincoln and Franklin D. Roosevelt. This clearly indicated, of course, that Jao Shu-shih had less than highest regard for the leadership of Mao Tse-tung. Kao Kang had remarked, in the context of having given Mao and his people the hospitality of his base at the end of the Long March, that they had arrived like "beggars in rags," with nothing to eat. "If I had not taken him in then," Kao asked rhetorically, "where would Mao be today."

According to Ch'en Yi, Kao Kang and Jao Shu-shih had each been called in separately, at the meeting of the Political Bureau, and had been confronted with the results of an investigation of their cases. Kao Kang, refusing to admit any wrongdoing, had pulled out a pistol and pointed it at his head. According to this story, the man sitting next to him had struck his elbow, and the bullet had gone into the ceiling.[27]

The rhetorical question which Kao Kang had asked was, of course, the same one which might have been posed by Wang Tso and Yüan Wen-ts'ai, the onetime bandit chiefs of Chingkangshan, and by Li Wen-ling and Tuan Liang-pi, the partisan leaders who had taken Mao and the remnants which had fled with him from the Chingkangshan into their Kiangsi base—had any of them been alive to ask it. It might have made no difference in the end, but before he voiced the question, Kao Kang might have reflected that it may be more comfortable to give than to receive. The donor may enjoy the sense of superiority which often accompanies the act of giving, but the recipient will hardly appreciate being made to feel inferior. And if he is a man of strong ego, the position of inferior may be intolerable. In such a case, gratitude may be dissolved in resentment, and the resentment directed at those to whom one feels indebted.

The punishments meted out to Kao Kang and Jao Shu-shih, as well as to some of their supporters, were not announced until the spring of 1955. Both men, the announcement revealed, had been deprived of all their posts and expelled from the party. At the same time it was asserted that Kao Kang had committed suicide, and his act was described in terms designed to rob it of the respect which suicide traditionally enjoyed in China. It had been regarded highly as the ultimate form of protest available to a conscientious official against the wrong policies of a willful ruler, or any person who had suffered grossly unjust treatment. As such, it had enabled a man to leave life in a morally superior position, and to put those against whom he was protesting in the wrong. As if attempting to deprive Kao Kang of this morally superior position, the announcement declared: "Kao Kang not only did not admit his guilt to the party, but committed suicide as an ultimate expression of his betrayal of the party." [28]

This purge was the most conspicuous feature of the trial of strength within the leadership, but not its only consequence. The anticipated reorganization of the structures of the party and government began shortly after Mao Tse-tung had won his battle against the two regional leaders. In 1954 and 1955, the several regional governments and the regional bureaus of the party were all abolished, inaugurating a period of centralization which was to last for several years (after which new regional bureaus of the party would again be set up). Mao Tse-tung continued to hold the dual position of chairman of the party and of the government, and his power over the central apparatus was fortified, rather than diminished. The new government constitution, proclaimed in 1954, provided: "The chairman of the People's Republic of China commands the armed forces of the country, and is chairman of the Council of Defense." [29] And in the 1954 reorganization of the government, P'eng Te-huai became the minister of national defense. In consequence of these changes, Chu Teh, who is supposed to have wished to become "chairman in turn," was divested of his position as commander in chief of the People's Liberation Army, and given no place in its professional chain of command.

That same year the committee which Kao Kang had headed was reorganized as the State Planning Commission. As its chairman the Communists appointed Li Fu-ch'un—a fellow provincial of Mao Tse-tung, participant with Chou En-lai in the work-study program in France, veteran of the Long March, and since Yenan days a specialist in economic affairs. By 1955 his commission had completed the drafting of a first five year plan. Under it, China carried out a program of economic development which stressed industry; and within this sector of the economy, primary emphasis was placed on extractive and heavy industries—on steel, coal, electric power, petroleum, cement, machine building, and armaments. And the results, by the end of the Five-Year Plan, were impressive. Steel output rose from 1,350,000 tons in 1952 to 5,350,000 tons in 1957. Meanwhile production of coal, electric power, and cement doubled or more than doubled, and the output of petroleum tripled. These accomplishments—and expectation of continued Soviet aid—led the Chinese Communists to envisage two more five-year plans which were to put them in a position such that they would no longer have to depend on outside assistance. By 1967, they would have completed the socialist transformation of their economy and be in possession of a large modern industrial sector and the trained workers, technicians, and scientists to run it. On that base they expected to build towards the status of the world's third superpower, a status they hoped to achieve by the end of the century.[30]

The results obtained during the first Five-Year Plan, however, were results obtained under forced draft. Quantity was often obtained at the expense of quality and at the cost of damaged machinery and equipment. Moreover, since the stress was on extractive and heavy industries, light industry and agriculture were slighted. Thus the effort was one to obtain increasing worker output without providing the encouragement and support which might have been supplied by a proportionately increased flow of consumer goods and foodstuffs. To use a Chinese expression, the country was not walking on two legs; rather, it was trying to run, and on only one leg. In fact, additional and new demands were being placed on the agricultural sector. Industry was to some extent dependent on agriculture for raw materials; in addition, the latter sector had to provide the exports of grain and raw materials with which to repay the USSR for its assistance. And meanwhile China's own population was growing by at least twelve millions each year.[31]

Given the additional burdens which the regime was putting on agriculture, there were good reasons for following moderate agrarian policies throughout the period of the first Five-Year Plan. If it was necessary to produce large agricultural surpluses, then the peasants should not be alienated and the agricultural sector disrupted by rapid and radical socialization. This clearly had been the assumption of Teng Tzu-hui, director of the Rural Work Department of the party; toward the middle of 1955, with the concurrence of Liu Shao-ch'i, he ordered some two hundred thousand hastily-organized cooperatives dissolved. It evidently was also the assumption of Li Fu-ch'un, in July 1955, when he discussed the Five-Year Plan before the National People's Congress, a body composed of several thousand party and nonparty representatives which the new constitution described as "the highest organ of state power." While talking about the portion of the plan dealing with the formation of Agricultural Producers Cooperatives, Li Fu-ch'un declared that implementation must and would proceed slowly. Only a third of the peasants would be organized into cooperatives by 1957. Moreover, the cooperatives into which they would be organized were of the so-called lower-level, semisocialist type. The peasants would contribute to the cooperatives their lands, draft animals, and farm equipment, but they would be reimbursed for them through dividends, drawn in proportion to their respective contributions, as well as by payment for their labor.

Li Fu-ch'un assured the congress that the plan had been "drawn up under the direct leadership of the Central Committee . . . and Chairman Mao Tse-tung." It had also been approved by a national conference of the party and adopted by the State Council of the government. Accordingly, when the congress approved the plan on July 30, the closing day of its session, it undoubtedly was under the impression that moderate agrarian policies would prevail.[32]

The next day Mao Tse-tung spoke on this same subject of agricultural cooperatives before a meeting of party secretaries of provincial and lower levels. In his speech he angrily accused "some comrades" of tottering along "like an old woman with bound feet," and demanded a speedup in collectivization. He ordered these men—mostly lower-level leaders who could not be expected to resist the authority of Mao Tse-tung—to go back home and "work out a program suited to the situation." Referring to the leaders, as yet unnamed, who had been responsible for dissolving the two hundred thousand cooperatives, and apparently equating himself to the party center, Mao declared, "As early as April 1955, the party center gave the warning: Do not commit the 1953 mistake of mass dissolution of Agricultural Producers Cooperatives again, otherwise self-criticism would again be called for. But certain comrades preferred not to listen." [33]

Mao Tse-tung demanded that half rather than a third of the peasants should be organized into cooperatives by 1957, and the remainder by 1960. In consequence, by October 1955, when the Central Committee next met, a leap in the collectivization campaign had already become an accomplished fact. Mao Tse-tung had pulled a coup: He had reversed a policy adopted by the regular decision-making bodies of the party and the government, using the prestige of his position to get lower-level officials of the party to do his unilateral bidding. Moreover, the meeting of the Central Committee which Mao Tse-tung called in October was an enlarged meeting; in other words, officials who were not members of the Central Committee also attended the session. Undoubtedly he had invited officials on whom he could count for support, and had calculated that the larger the forum the smaller the chances of a full and frank debate. And the Central Committee agreed, at this meeting, that the formation of cooperatives should proceed even faster than Mao had earlier demanded; under this speeded up program it was to be basically completed by April 1958.[34]

But Mao remained satisfied neither with this advanced timetable nor with the semisocialist nature of the lower-level cooperatives which the Central Committee had authorized. In 1956, against opposition from Premier Chou En-lai and ranking Vice Premier Ch'en Yün, he pressed for still speedier implementation and more radical measures. By the middle of 1957 almost all peasant families had been organized

into higher-stage cooperatives—a type in which the peasants were required to contribute their land, animals, and implements without being reimbursed for them.[35]

It accordingly is apparent that the early years of the regime were
ones during which Mao scored a series of successes. They also were
ones during which he enjoyed the taste of success. Chow Ching-wen,
one of the third-party leaders and democratic personages whom the
Communists had chosen as ornaments with which to adorn the facade
of their regime, has told a story bearing on this point. It concerned
an occasion in which Mao was to participate, held in the Huai-jen
Hall, and the protocol governing such affairs, which required those
present to greet Mao's entrance by rising to their feet and applauding.
At this affair, Chow Ching-wen was in the seat nearest a door, in the
back row. Accosted by the director of the government's Bureau of
Ceremonies, who asked him to get up and clap as soon as the chairman
entered, Chow Ching-wen realized that Mao would come in through
the nearby door. The protocol director was seeing to it that the man
in the best position to see Mao enter would alert the rest of the audience, and that the chairman would be greeted by applause from the
moment he first appeared. Chow Ching-wen of course did as he had
been directed, and in consequence of his location he could watch Mao
Tse-tung at close hand. A more modest leader might have deprecated
the adulation, and a matter-of-fact one would have advanced at a
normal pace. But Mao Tse-tung, Chow Ching-wen observed, walked
slowly past, obviously prolonging and drinking in the applause.[36] Not
long afterwards, however, events were to enable Mao's fellow leaders
to take steps designed to tone down such manifestations of adulation.

9
Fragrant Flowers and Stinking Weeds

IN CHINA's long history there have been but two revolutions which radically changed the structures of both society and state.[1] The first was that of Shih Huang-ti, who in 221 B.C. succeeded in bringing the feudal era to an end and in founding a centralized empire. The second was the revolution which began in 1911 with the overthrow of imperial rule and culminated in 1949 in the establishment of the People's Republic of China.

The centuries immediately preceding Shih Huang-ti's revolution, the turbulent age of the "Warring States," were also the golden age of Chinese thought. With numerous kingdoms competing for primacy, political theorists and social philosophers were in demand. And so many sages arose, each with his own disciples, that the era of the "Warring States" came to be known also as that of the "Hundred Schools" of thought. But after Shih Huang-ti had unified the land, only one way of thought remained permissible, scholars who had served other rulers fell under suspicion, and the books which were the classics of their various schools were ordered burned.

In the latter years of Kuomintang rule, a number of third parties were formed in the expectation that their representatives might participate in a prospective coalition government. Many of the leaders of these parties were university professors and other leading intellectuals —the modern counterparts of the scholars of the era of the "Warring States." Because the third parties were intent on seeing one-party rule brought to an end, they were regarded as enemies by leaders of the Kuomintang and as political allies by the Communists. Moreover the Communists had found it expedient, after they had conquered the mainland and while they were seeking the broad support which would facilitate the consolidation of their regime, to rule through what was professed to be a united front of all democratic elements. For this purpose they maintained a body called the Chinese People's Political Consultative Conference, which included in its membership the representatives of third parties.[2]

In the summer of 1953, when Mao Tse-tung was engaged in a struggle with more conservative leaders of his party over the pace of agricultural collectivization, he attended an enlarged meeting of the

National Committee of the People's Political Consultative Conference. The meeting was a large one, attended by about one thousand persons. Among the speakers was Liang Shu-ming, one of the top leaders of the China Democratic League and a scholar with a background of practical experience in the field of agrarian reform. In his speech, Liang Shu-ming remarked that the life of China's peasants was very hard and that, in comparison with factory workers, they were ill paid. Indeed, insofar as remuneration was concerned, the factory workers were in the ninth level of heaven, and the peasants in the ninth level of hell.

Apparently Liang Shu-ming's remarks did not seem out of order to the audience, as it did not react to them in any way. But they led Mao Tse-tung to reach for the microphone and vent a stream of sarcasm. Referring to a famous concubine of the T'ang period, who had been noted for her great beauty, he said: "I suppose you think you are very beautiful, more beautiful . . . than Yang Kuei-fei. But to me you stink." Liang Shu-ming seemed thunderstruck and at a loss to account for Mao's fury. Pointing a finger at him, Mao continued: "The radio in Taiwan says you are a man of character and principles. But to me you stink! You have stinking bones!"

Soon the hall was filled with abusive shouts and Liang Shu-ming, unable to continue, was forced to leave the platform. After this outburst an old anti-Kuomintang general named Ch'en Ming-shu arose, asked for permission to speak, and tactfully suggested that "we should not have become so excited today." Mao Tse-tung did not pursue the matter further at the time, but Liang Shu-ming was subsequently hounded out of public life and General Ch'en Ming-shu was brought under attack and forced to undergo a period of self-criticism.[3]

Mao Tse-tung's attack on Liang Shu-ming was, however, an insignificant affair when compared with a campaign, begun late in 1954, in which a writer named Hu Feng was the central target. In his 1942 "Talks at the Yenan Forum on Literature and Art," Mao Tse-tung had decried the demands of writers that literature should be motivated by a love of mankind, be concerned with universal aspects of human nature, and be created under conditions of freedom. He had declared that there should, in a class society, only be class love; that literature should be created to serve the workers, the peasants, the soldiers, and their allies; and that it should be subordinate to politics. After the Communists had come to power, Hu Feng had dared to criticize the "mandarins" of the Communist party who wielded authority in the sphere of literature and who interpreted the 1942 Talks in ways which suffocated creativity.

The counterattack against Hu Feng culminated, in 1955, in his being accused of being more than just an ideological deviationist. It was declared, in a series of critiques which appeared in *People's Daily*, that he was the leader of a secret service organization which was working in the underground for the imperialists and the Kuomintang. Hu Feng was arrested and put it prison, where he was rumored to have gone insane, but his arrest did not mark the end of the campaign. Mao Tse-tung had said that 95 percent of the people were good, and a search now went on to identify the 5 percent who might be counter-revolutionary or guilty of unorthodox thinking. Intellectuals were, of course, particularly suspect; before the campaign died down, the nerves of many of them gave way, and suicides were frequent.

The principal front man for the campaign was Chou Yang, the party's literary czar. However, it was rumored at the time, and subsequently confirmed, that the writer of the critiques concerning Hu Feng, which had appeared in *People's Daily,* was none other than Mao Tse-tung himself.[4]

Yet less than a year after the campaign against Hu Feng had died down, Mao Tse-tung was urging a greater and continuing role for the third parties and inciting the intellectuals to voice their criticisms of Communist rule. This may seem strange, when viewed against the background of his role in the affair of Liang Shu-ming and the campaign against Hu Feng. But in the interim there had been a radical change in his own personal position. The challenge to his primacy, which had been mounted in 1953, had been defeated by 1955. Kao Kang and Jao Shu-shih had been purged, and Chu Teh had been deprived of his position as commander in chief—in a defeat which had been softened somewhat in 1955, when Chu and nine other veteran commanders had been given the title of marshal. Seemingly secure in his dual position of chairman of the party and the government, Mao had flouted the consensus within the leadership and forced the pace of agricultural collectivization. But during the spring of 1956 he came under a new and more dangerous challenge within the party, and he was in search of outside forces which he might be able to muster against his fellow leaders.

Early in 1956, the Chinese Communist party had sent a delegation headed by Chu Teh to Moscow to attend the Twentieth Congress of the Communist party of the Soviet Union. On February 25, at that party congress, Khrushchev made the famous speech in which he denounced the crimes of Stalin and the role of the secret police under Beria.

Khrushchev revealed that Stalin had "acted not through persuasion, explanation, and patient cooperation with people, but by imposing his concepts and demanding absolute submission to his opinion." He went on to explain,

Whoever opposed this concept and tried to prove his viewpoint and the correctness of his position was doomed . . . Stalin, using his unlimited power, allowed himself many abuses, acting in the name of the Central Committee, not asking for the opinion of the committee members nor even of the Central Committee's Political Bureau; often he did not inform them about his personal decisions concerning very important party and government matters.

Stalin's unlimited power, Khrushchev said, resulted in part from the growth to monstrous size of the cult of Stalin's personality. Actually, Khrushchev asserted, "It is impermissible and foreign to the spirit of Marxism–Leninism to elevate one person, to transform him into a superman possessing supernatural characteristics, akin to a god. Such a man supposedly knows everything, sees everything, thinks for everyone, can do anything, is infallible in his behavior." This cult of the personality of Stalin became, as Khrushchev observed, "the source of a whole series of exceedingly serious and grave perversions of party principles, of party democracy, of revolutionary legality." [5]

Naturally, the contents of Khrushchev's speech were quickly made known to leaders of the Chinese Communist party back in China, and they took stock of its applicability to their own situation. In the years immediately past, Mao Tse-tung too had acted not through persuasion, explanation, and patient cooperation with people. Rather, he had acted by imposing his own concepts and demanding absolute submission to his opinion. Kao Kang had recently opposed him and maintained the correctness of his own position; in consequence he had lost his life. Sometimes Mao Tse-tung had acted unilaterally in the name of the party center, not asking for the opinions of the committee members nor even of its Political Bureau. He, too, sometimes did not inform them about his personal decisions concerning important party and government matters. After they had spoken and gone on the record on such matters, as had Vice Chairman Liu Shao-ch'i in 1950 on land reform and Planning Commission Chairman Li Fu-ch'un in 1955 on collectivization, Mao Tse-tung had quickly and abruptly pulled the rug out from under them.

After his years in the wilderness, Mao Tse-tung had in 1949 entered Peking, as a photograph of the period reveals, looking like a tramp who had for some time been sleeping in his rumpled clothes— which he probably had. Later photographs of him reviewing successive national day parades showed him as an exalted figure, somehow removed from his fellow leaders, standing atop the ramparts of Peking's imperial palace which had once been the preserve of China's semi-divine Son of Heaven. On such occasions all eyes turned to him as they had to Stalin, reviewing similar parades atop the Kremlin. His fellow leaders were aware of his feet of clay. But he was on the way to attaining—in the eyes of the rank-and-file of the party and of the populace—the status of a god.

The party Constitution of 1945 contained a phrase about the thought of Mao Tse-tung which seemed to put him on a level with Marx and Lenin. It read, "The Chinese Communist party takes the theories of Marxism–Leninism and the unified thought of the practice of the Chinese Revolution, the thought of Mao Tse-tung, as the guideline for its actions." There had been opposition to its insertion at the time from Marshal P'eng Te-huai, and perhaps from others as well.[6] Being guided by Marxism–Leninism was one thing; Marx and Lenin were dead, and they could be reinterpreted. To be guided by the thoughts of a living man was another thing; his thoughts went on and on, and were unpredictable. In the constitution of the party, such a sentence could be used to justify Mao's "imposing his concepts and demanding absolute submission to his opinion." Such, at least, may have been the thoughts of Mao's fellow leaders.

Finally, among those near Mao Tse-tung was a thin-faced man with thick glasses, an unpleasant half-smile, and the look of a fox, sometimes referred to as China's Beria. This was K'ang Sheng, seventh-ranking man in the Political Bureau, a man who had been trained in police, security, and intelligence techniques during several years spent in Stalin's Russia.[7] Mao Tse-tung was already in his sixties; what role might K'ang Sheng play during Mao's later years, and upon his demise?

Such may have been the situation as seen by some of Mao's fellows, when they gathered at an enlarged meeting of the Political Bureau in April of 1956 to discuss the Stalin era and the implications for China of what Khrushchev had revealed.[8] What must be done, they must have asked themselves, to avoid a repetition in China of mistakes of the Stalin era? And how could this be done? Mao Tse-tung himself had undoubtedly become furious that Khrushchev had opened this Pandora's box. Moreover, some may have told themselves, while Mao could be a trial to those who worked with him, his prestige was an asset to the regime. For both these reasons, they should endeavor not to cause undue loss of face to Mao Tse-tung.

The solutions decided upon were quite far reaching, on paper at least, and they would have been so in practice if Mao had remained bound by them. It was decided to alter the party constitution so that it would give less encouragement to the development of the cult of Mao Tse-tung and would tend to ensure collective leadership rather than one-man rule. The drafting of a new party constitution was begun, and when it was completed the following changes had been made: (1) References to the thought of Mao Tse-tung, as a guiding principle and as something all members were enjoined to study, were eliminated;

(2) the statement that nobody is free of shortcomings or mistakes in his work was inserted; (3) a provision, missing from the old constitution, for the new elective positions of vice chairmen of the party was incorporated; (4) the provision, contained in the old constitution, that the chairman of the party should hold the concurrent post of chairman of its Central Secretariat, was deleted; (5) the new elective position of general secretary of the party was created; (6) supervision of the work of the Secretariat, which was empowered to conduct the day-to-day business of the party, was entrusted to the Political Bureau, and within the Political Bureau, to a newly-created Standing Committee; and, (7) it was specifically stated that "all important issues are to be decided collectively." [9]

This draft constitution, before coming into effect, required the approval of a party congress, the theoretically supreme source of party authority.[10] However, large bodies are subject to manipulation from the top. In 1956, the party leaders took an unprecedented step which may have been designed to prevent Mao Tse-tung from claiming that the draft constitution represented only the will of leaders at the center, rather than that of the party as a whole. The selection of delegates to the new party congress was for the first time accomplished from the grass roots upwards, rather than from the top.[11]

In September 1956, the Communists convened their Eighth Party Congress. During that same month they held two plenary meetings of the Central Committee, one before the holding of the party congress and the other after it had met and elected a new Central Committee. At these meetings the new constitution was discussed and ratified, and a number of changes were made in the leadership. Teng Hsiao-p'ing, who had made a name for himself as army commander and political commissar during the decades of war and revolution, became general secretary of the party and a member of the Standing Committee of the Political Bureau; this placed him in a position to exercise, over the newly-created party Secretariat's conduct of day-to-day business, a measure of the supervisory authority vested in the Standing Committee of the Political Bureau.[12] Four men were elected vice chairmen of the party and thereby became ex officio members of the Standing Committee of the Political Bureau: Liu Shao-ch'i, Chou En-lai, Chu Teh, and Ch'en Yün. K'ang Sheng—"China's Beria"—was dropped from full membership in the Political Bureau and became the fifth among six alternate members. At about this same time it was apparently agreed that the Standing Committee should be divided into two lines, or groups, with Mao Tse-tung dropping into semi-inactive status, in the second line. Finally, a new position was created but left vacant, that of honorary chairman of the Central Committee. It obviously was meant to provide an honorable but empty role for Mao Tse-tung when an appropriate time for him to step down might come.[13]

It seems likely that the general outlines of the foregoing reforms had emerged during the meetings of the Political Bureau which had been held in April 1956. Facing de-Stalinization, Mao Tse-tung undoubtedly feared that a new and more dangerous effort to deprive him of the chairmanship was in the offing. He is believed to have been seriously ill in 1954, and he may have calculated that his health might be advanced as the reason for asking him to step down. Shortly after the April 1956 discussion of Khrushchev's speech, Mao made the first of his highly-publicized swims across the Yangtze River—as much as to say, "Look how healthy I am!" That summer he repeated the swim a second and a third time.[14]

Mao may also have known, as early as April 1956, that his fellow leaders contemplated the creation of bureaucratic mechanisms and arrangements designed to dilute the authority of the party chairman. He could, of course, be expected to work within the party against such changes, but he may have realized that he might prove unable to muster sufficient support within the party to prevent those changes. If so, it would help explain the fact that he began at this time to seek, not only inside the party but outside as well, support which might be used against his opponents in the party.

In April 1956, as was revealed a decade later, Mao Tse-tung gave a speech before party cadres from the provinces in which he said: "I suggest that the party and government organs be retrenched on a large scale and cut away by two-thirds." In that same speech he also declared that it would be desirable to have a multiparty system of rule until the time when all parties had withered away. "We should," he added, "allow the democrats to state their views. We should accept anything which is reasonable regardless of who the speaker is. This is advantageous to the party, the state, the people, and socialism." [15]

Such pronouncements touched on the most sensitive points of party policy. When made within a party forum, the party's rules concerning outside discussion and its control of the press and other media could combine to ensure that their circulation remained limited. But Mao Tse-tung's dual chairmanship gave him an additional means of issuing pronouncements. The 1954 state constitution provided, as one of the organizations of "united front" rule, a Supreme State Conference, to be called by the chairman of the government for the purpose of discussing and deciding important affairs of state. This gave Mao Tse-tung a forum which he could use without referring the matter to the party; he could convene meetings at his own discretion, and invite almost anyone he wished. Once he had made a speech before this forum, oral discussion of its contents could hardly be prevented. The party might then be constrained to publish an official version of the speech. It could be altered, but this version would necessarily have to bear some resemblance to the original speech.[16]

On May 2 Mao Tse-tung made a speech before the Supreme State Conference in which he appears to have spelled out views which he had advanced at the party meeting of the preceding month. The speech is not known ever to have been published; but some of the ideas which he expressed, and some of the language he employed, are believed to have been used in a talk made later that month by Lu Ting-yi, Director of the Propaganda Department of the Central Committee, before a selected group of intellectuals.

Lu Ting-yi began by recalling China's era of the "Warring States," when a phrase had emerged about "letting all schools contend in airing their views." The history of the country had shown, he said, that academic development would stagnate if independent thinking were not encouraged, and if free discussion were not allowed. Such freedom should be denied to counterrevolutionaries. But within the camp of the people, he declared, the party advocated the line of "letting all flowers bloom together and all schools contend in airing their views." During the ensuing weeks "blooming and contending" became a slogan about which party spokesmen themselves contended. Meanwhile the third-party and nonparty people, to whom the slogan was addressed, failed to respond. September came, the new constitution of the party was adopted, and its structure and hierarchy were realigned —all with scarcely a mention of the policy of "blooming and contending." [17]

Indeed, it might have become a forgotten phrase if it had not been for the secondary consequences of Khrushchev's famous speech. That speech did not merely cast discredit on the concept of one-man rule. It also raised the question of whether anything short of drastic change in the nature of the Communist system could prevent a repetition of the crimes of the Stalin era.[18] As between states and parties within the Communist system, it shook the assumption that one state or party should have the right to dominate the others. In individual countries that speech lit the spark of hope for an end to repressive governance. Mao Tse-tung had once observed that a single spark can light a prairie fire. In Hungary the spark of hope ignited the uprising of October 1956.

Our world is so composed that strong vibrations emanating from one part will set up sympathetic vibrations in others. Similarly, an explosion in one country sometimes sets off similar explosions elsewhere, in chain reaction. The one which had occurred in Hungary reverberated in Peking, confronting the leadership with the question of whether there were dangerous pressures under the lid which they had clamped down on Chinese society. In this situation, it could persuasively be argued, public expression of dissatisfaction might serve as a safety valve, providing a controlled release of pressures. Indeed, as Mao argued, public criticism was necessary if rightful grievances were to be revealed and corrected and if misunderstandings were to be cleared up through the use of explanations and persuasion.

The Hungarian uprising may have reinvigorated Mao Tse-tung's efforts to persuade other party leaders to accept his proposed policy of inviting public criticism of the party and its performance. However, when they remained unpersuaded he nevertheless went ahead, trying through his individual efforts to get a campaign of criticism underway. Late in 1956 he held a four-hour meeting with the leaders of third parties. There he voiced the hope that they would all express their opinions openly and assured them that nobody would be punished for it. And on February 27, 1957, he again addressed the Supreme State Conference, criticizing and rebutting "the opinions against the policy of a hundred flowers." It is clear from the treatment accorded this speech, entitled "On the Correct Handling of Contradictions Among the People," that there was a conflict of opinion, or contradiction, between him and other leaders of the party. The speech was not published in China until June 18, five days after a summary and long extracts—leaked to the press in Warsaw—had been printed in the *New York Times*. And even then the version published in China was one which admittedly had undergone revision.[19]

The problem of conflict within a society, Mao Tse-tung observed in this speech, is not eliminated by communism. There are two kinds of conflicts, or contradictions: antagonistic contradictions, with counterrevolutionaries and other enemies of the people, which require the use of force; and nonantagonistic contradictions among the people, including the bourgeoisie, for the resolution of which force should not be used. Contradictions among the people should be corrected through persuasion, by the rectifying of mistakes, and by the satisfying of rightful grievances. Stalin's mistake was in not differentiating between the two, in treating all contradictions as antagonistic ones which required the use of terror. The tragedy of Hungary, like everything else, had two sides, one bad and one good. Its positive result was that it made us conscious of the mistakes which spring from great power chauvinism and taught us to beware of those mistakes.

Marxism–Leninism, Mao continued, is not afraid of criticism and does ont fear discussion.

[It] must come out to meet criticism head on because only in this way can it be strengthened and become a really great power and not a new

religion or taboo. . . . The opinions against the policy of a Hundred
Flowers are the result of a fear of criticism, fear of losing the monopo-
listic position. They are an example of dogmatism. Marx never said
that he should not be criticized. To those who do not follow that teaching of Marx I would address an old saying: "He who does not allow
himself to be criticized during his life will be criticized after his
death."

"There need be no fear," Mao asserted, "that the policy of a
Hundred Flowers will yield poisoned fruit. Sometimes it is necessary
even to have this poisoned fruit to know what it is that we are fighting against. . . . It is not enough to attack reactionaries. We must
know exactly what the reactionaries want and what they represent." [20]

The third-party leaders were pleased by Mao Tse-tung's apparent
determination that their own groups and the Communist party should
enjoy a prolonged period of peaceful coexistence and mutual guidance.[21] This seemed not to be the same Mao Tse-tung as the one who
—in their presence—had greeted a criticism by Liang Shu-ming with
spiteful sarcasm, or who had played a decisive role in the campaign
against Hu Feng and others suspected of dissent. But some of the
third-party leaders soon sensed that they were in danger of becoming
pawns in a struggle which was half hidden from them, and while they
held back the masses did not respond. Although they did not completely understand the issues in this struggle, they did see the danger
of being caught between the two sides of a Communist party which
was split. According to a story circulating in Peking, the majority of
the members of the Communist party attending the Supreme State
Conference had gotten up and left the hall when Mao Tse-tung made
his famous speech on "Contradictions." As one of the third party
leaders remarked, " 'blooming and contending' is not good because it
is not supported by the line of Liu Shao-ch'i through P'eng Chen." [22]

Liu Shao-ch'i and P'eng Chen may be taken as representatives of
those within the party who did not share Mao's view that conflict was
necessarily a force for progress—it might, instead, promote an unac-
ceptable degree of disruption, or even chaos. And in the present instance, they evidently surmised, Mao wanted to stir up a storm in
which their own positions would be undermined, in order to recover
the ground he had lost through de-Stalinization. But Mao Tse-tung
was asserting that the "driving wind and rainburst form of mass class
struggle has basically concluded," and in May they agreed to the
launching of a rectification movement which was to be carried out "as
gently as a breeze or light rain." Amidst assurances that party cadres
who were willing to correct their mistakes would "generally be ex-
empted from disciplinary measures, particularly disciplinary measures

of a grave nature," the party apparatus was put behind a campaign designed to elicit public criticism.[23] There ensued, that spring—in response to renewed assurances and strong pressures—a brief period during which the Hundred Flowers of open criticism bloomed throughout the land.

Some of the attacks made on the policies and performance of the party undoubtedly reflected the true views of those who made them. General Lung Yün, who had been governor of Yünnan Province during pre-Communist days and who had become an official in the Communists' Peking government, may have been speaking for himself when he criticized the Maoist policies of "leaning to one side" and of alliance with the Soviet Union. He pointed out that the Russians had removed "huge quantities of industrial equipment" from China's Manchurian provinces after World War II, and he asserted that they were requiring China to "pay all the expenses of the Korean War." The United States had "given up her claims for loans granted during the first and second world wars, yet the Soviet Union insists that China must pay interest on Soviet loans." [24]

It would be interesting to know whether Chang Po-chün, a third-party leader who was serving as minister of communications, was speaking only for himself, or at the instigation of Mao's critics within the party, when he declared: "Socialist democracy ought to exceed capitalist democracy. The president of a capitalist country has a term of three or four years, and how many years had Stalin? And who knows how many years Chairman Mao will want?" [25]

At Peking University, the students bloomed and contended in open-air meetings, and each day they put up hundreds of posters written in the big Chinese characters designed to catch attention and make for easy reading. Some of them demanded that the writer Hu Feng should be released from prison, and that innocent people who had been wronged during the anti-Hu Feng campaign should be rehabilitated. One young man began his first poster with a quotation from Heraclitus which read: "In Ephesus all adult men should die and government of the city should be handed over to beardless young men." On May 31, 1957, *People's Daily*—perhaps in a party effort to cast discredit on Mao's policy of inviting public criticism—published a letter from a young lecturer in Peking University who allegedly had written: "China belongs to the six hundred million people. . . . It does not belong to the Communist party alone. . . . If you carry on satisfactorily, well and good. If not, the masses may knock you down, kill the Communists, overthrow you. This cannot be described as unpatriotic, for the Communists no longer serve the people." In the Wuhan cities, if Mao's own later account is to be believed, the stu-

dents tried to stage a Hungarian-style uprising, party leaders mobilized the workers, and there was a two-day struggle in the streets.[26]

Among the Hundred Flowers which may have sprung up during
this campaign there also were many stinking weeds, and some of them
had perhaps produced the poisonous fruits of which Mao Tse-tung
had spoken. On June 26, Chou En-lai warned non-Communist Chinese
that they would be classified as enemies of the people if they continued
to criticize the government. However, on July 12, *People's Daily* published an article—believed to have been written by Mao Tse-tung—
pointing out that "demons" could be wiped out only after they had
"come out of their cage" and shown themselves. Nevertheless the party
moved quickly; the flood of criticism was dammed up, rightists were
compelled to recant and confess their errors, and numbers of "demons"
were executed. Within the government an antirightist campaign was
launched, and several non-Communist political figures were brought
under fire. On July 15, two of the "democratic personages" who headed
government ministries "confessed" that they had conspired to attack
the Communist party and its leadership in order to "replace the proletarian dictatorship with bourgeois democracy," which "would have
inevitably led to a capitalist comeback." Later in the year the antirightist campaign was extended, first in the state and party bureaucracies and then to conservative professionals and enterprise managers.[27]

Among the rightists brought under attack were officials in the
Ministry of Control, an organization responsible for accounting, audit-
ing, investigating, and maintaining the economic controls required for
the orderly management of a planned economy. Accusations were first
leveled against subordinates, and they in turn implicated their superiors. Through this process, Deputy Minister Wang Han, leader of the
Communist party group within the ministry, became a target. He was
accused of resisting party discipline, attacked for having criticized the
state's economic plan as "reckless," and charged with insisting on retaining the authority to halt the expenditures of financial and economic agencies—that is, with defending his accountants in the performance of their duties as laid down by state regulations. In addition,
a number of seemingly extraneous accusations were leveled against
him. It was, for instance, alleged that he had been guilty of serious
misbehavior during the war, when he had been the deputy political
commissar of a division in the field.

In the autumn of 1957, sixteen mass meetings against Wang Han
were held within his own ministry, and thousands of wall posters were
put up containing criticisms of him. Finally Wang Han, a party member of a quarter century's standing, was driven to confess: "My crimes
are terrible; my soul is evil; I am an antiparty, antipeople, rightist

element." Thereafter he was fired, becoming an object lesson for any successor who might consider standing up for the right to carry on in independent fashion the control functions which his ministry existed to perform.

Just as accusations against lesser officials had led to Wang Han, the charges laid against him might similarly have led to the implication of still higher officials. The commander of the division in which Wang Han had been deputy political commissar had been General Li Hsien-nien. At the time of Wang Han's disgrace, Li Hsien-nien was director of the government's Office of Finance and Trade. Like Wang Han, whose duties were closely related to his own, he was an advocate of conservative economic and financial policies. Accordingly it seems likely that the charges of wartime misbehavior made against Wang Han were intended to threaten Li Hsien-nien. This is a tactic which the Chinese call "killing the chicken to intimidate the monkey." [28]

The part played by Mao Tse-tung in initiating the Hundred Flowers movement is clearer than his role during the period after its 180 degree reversal, when China's intellectual garden was so assiduously weeded. However, two years later Mao cast additional light on the whole affair in a conversation with visiting leaders from Communist Hungary. At the time of the uprising in their country, he said, he had sent an urgent message to the Kremlin asking Khrushchev to take military action against the Hungarian revisionists. The Hundred Flowers movement had been designed to release the tension which had built up in Chinese society after the death of Stalin. At first it had produced constructive criticisms, and it was only later that the rightists began to take an open part in the public debate. Some party leaders then had wanted to cut the movement short. But he decided to wait awhile, and in consequence the party leadership had learned who its friends were, and who were its enemies.[29]

It may be expected, in politics as in physics, that each action will produce an equal and opposite reaction. As Mao Tse-tung may have calculated, when he moved party policy far in the direction of tolerance, its reverse swing created conditions favorable to intolerant attacks on elements which he regarded as rightist enemies. The victims of the reversal were, of course, not only people. Pragmatic attitudes were discredited and moderate policies were jettisoned. Earlier in 1957 Mao Tse-tung, perhaps fearful that he was soon to be deprived of the chairmanship, had been talking of voluntarily stepping down.[30] Before the year had ended he felt sufficiently secure to leave Peking for Moscow. There he tried to enlist the support of Soviet leaders for a belligerent course which he evidently hoped would lead, among other things, to Communist conquest of the Nationalist-held island of Taiwan.

The East Wind Blows

IN THE PURSUIT of their external aims and ambitions, the Chinese Communists had before 1957 twice found themselves at a disadvantage because the United States had nuclear weapons and they did not. The first time they met what they term "nuclear blackmail" was in the context of the Korean war. The Chinese Communists proved difficult to deal with, during the negotiations intended to bring hostilities to an end on acceptable terms, and early in 1953 the United States began applying a new kind of pressure—the threat to extend the war to the Chinese mainland and to use nuclear weapons.[1]

Stalin had, in August 1952, agreed to a greatly increased program of military aid to enable the Chinese Communists to carry on the Korean war. But he evidently had given them neither nuclear weapons nor the right to invoke Soviet nuclear capabilities as a counterthreat. Consequently this new form of American pressure produced an immediate reaction from Peking. On February 24, 1953, the Chinese Communists sent to Moscow a delegation headed by Ch'ien San-ch'iang, China's leading nuclear scientist. Presumably the purpose of the delegation was to persuade Stalin to fill this important chink in Peking's armor. Stalin, however, suffered a fatal stroke shortly after this delegation arrived in Moscow. In consequence Ch'ien San-ch'iang had to draw what cold comfort he could from his appointment as one of China's official mourners at Stalin's funeral.[2] With other urgent problems on their minds, Stalin's successors were probably in no mood to make decisions of the sort the delegation wanted. Within a relatively short time the negotiating logjam at Panmunjom was broken and the Korean armistice was signed.

The issue of China's offshore islands, and the related one of Taiwan, provided the occasion for another such confrontation with the United States. The Chinese Communists, victorious everywhere on the mainland, had run into trouble when they tried to extend their triumphs to islands off China's southern coast. The island of Quemoy, lying athwart Fukien's port of Amoy, proved a particularly hard nut to crack. Their first attempt was defeated by troops under a brave Nationalist general named Hu Lien, who decimated the seasick and disorganized Communist troops which landed on Quemoy's beaches.

Subsequently the Communists put their troops through a course of amphibious training, which involved much swimming, in China's inland waters. But the intention of using these troops was thwarted by a fluke—the schistosome. It is common in the waters where the troops were trained, and great numbers of them became incapacitated by the liver disease which it causes.[3]

In August 1954, Chou En-lai had publicly urged the "liberation" of Taiwan and warned that "foreign aggressors" who interfered would face "grave consequences." Shortly thereafter the Chinese Communists had begun shelling Quemoy in a campaign which lasted well into the following year. In response, the United States Congress in January passed the "Formosa Resolution" authorizing the President to commit American forces to the defense of the offshore islands if he judged a Communist attack on them to be part of an attack on Taiwan itself. The Chinese Communists nevertheless maintained their pressure against the offshore islands, and on March 8, 1955, Secretary of State Dulles pointed out that our forces were "equipped with new and powerful weapons of precision, which can utterly destroy military targets without endangering unrelated civilian centers." [4]

Shortly after this second reminder of American nuclear power, the crisis in the Taiwan Straits ended. In April, Chou En-lai went to Indonesia, where he attended the Bandung conference of Asian and African nations. There he asserted that the "will of the Chinese people" to liberate Taiwan was a just one. But he also expressed the willingness of the Chinese government to enter into negotiations with the United States in order to discuss the relaxation of tensions in the Far East generally, "and especially in the Taiwan area." [5]

China had turned toward policies of moderation, in its relations with neighboring Asian states, even before the Bandung conference. In April 1954, China and India had concluded a treaty based upon principles of peaceful coexistence and mutual noninterference in each other's internal affairs. At the Bandung conference, China joined with other Asian and African nations in reaffirming such principles as suitable for general observance. The final communique of that conference also contained the following passage: "Pending the total prohibition of the manufacture of nuclear and thermonuclear weapons, this Conference appealed to all the powers concerned to reach agreement to suspend experiments with such weapons." [6]

On January 18, 1955, the Soviet Union had announced the intention of assisting Communist China and four European Communist countries to develop programs of research in the peaceful application of atomic energy. In the spring of that year the USSR, in pursuance of its announcement, agreed to provide China with an experimental nuclear reactor and various related forms of assistance. That same year the Chinese Communists had reorganized their Academy of Sciences, and early in 1956 they set up a Scientific Planning Committee and initiated a twelve-year plan for scientific development. They also undertook to contribute 20 percent of the cost of operating the Joint Institute of Nuclear Research, established at Dubna in March 1956 to train bloc scientists. Their contribution was second only to that of the Soviet Union.[7]

By some time in 1957, if not before, the Chinese Communists became anxious to use Soviet assistance in the nuclear-sharing field for the purpose of creating a nuclear weapons capability of their own. In May they set up an Institute of Atomic Energy, and on October 15, 1957, China and the Soviet Union signed an agreement under which the USSR promised to provide China with a sample atomic bomb and technical data concerning its manufacture.[8]

Mao Tse-tung should have been, and doubtless was, gratified by this development, which held forth the promise of shortening the period of years China would need to create its own nuclear-weapons capability. But Mao, with the impatience which had come to characterize him, was thinking also in terms of existent power and its immediate uses. The spirit of moderation which had characterized the Bandung period and the time of the Hundred Flowers movement had become a victim of China's subsequent antirightist campaign. In this respect China and the Soviet Union were out of phase. Closer acquaintance with nuclear weapons had caused Soviet leaders to conclude that the only alternative to peaceful coexistence would be the most destructive war in history. At the same time, evidently considering that nuclear weapons imposed restraints also on the west, they held that there was an enhanced likelihood that the transition of individual countries from capitalism to socialism could be effected peacefully. In consequence, Khrushchev had in 1956 declared that Soviet adherence to peaceful coexistence was a "fundamental principle" rather than a temporary expedient.[9]

In August 1957, the Soviet Union successfully launched an intercontinental ballistic missile, and on October 4 it put Sputnik I into orbit around the earth. Meanwhile the current news accounts of American efforts in the space field seemed to represent dismal failures in a lagging program. Global communism, some would have said, had begun to seem the wave not of some distant future, but something much closer at hand. Mao Tse-tung's assessment was that the USSR had achieved for the Communist world a decisive strategic advantage, and he wished to exploit it for Chinese purposes. This might be accomplished if he could persuade the Soviet leadership to abandon Khrushchev's policies of peaceful coexistence.

If the Soviet leadership could be so persuaded, Soviet capabilities might be utilized to China's benefit in one or more of several ways. If the USSR were to give more militant support to third-world countries which had conflicts of interest with western powers, that would tend to divert the attention and resources of the United States and its allies to theaters distant from China, thereby giving Communist China more freedom of action. If the USSR with its great military capacity would undertake overtly to support China in future crises, it might thereby deter the United States from intervening in future campaigns directed against the offshore islands and Taiwan. Finally, China would obtain an enhanced power position in its own right if the USSR were to make available to it increased amounts of military assistance and a greater range of weapons.

With some such thoughts and hopes in mind, Mao Tse-tung for the second time left China and journeyed to Moscow—ostensibly for the purpose of participating with other Communist leaders in the November 1957 celebrations of the fortieth anniversary of the Russian revolution. On landing at the Moscow airport, he paid tribute to Soviet achievement in the space field, expressed appreciation for past assistance to China from the Soviet Union, and declared, "there is no force on earth which can separate us." [10] At the same time he had in mind ideas which were to lead to just such a separation.

On November 17, Mao Tse-tung met with a group of Chinese students who were studying in the Soviet Union. The Russians had launched Sputnik II just two weeks before this meeting, and Mao commented that the two satellites marked a new turning point. In the struggle between the socialist and capitalist camps, he said, it was no longer the West wind that prevailed over the East wind, but the East wind that prevailed over the West wind.[11] The next day, taking his turn to speak before the gathering of the leaders of the world Communist movement, he set forth and developed his assessment that the East–West balance of forces had been changed, thereby opening new opportunities for the advance of communism.

In his speech, Mao disputed Khrushchev's thesis that conditions in the world had become favorable to a peaceful transition of individual countries to socialism. He conceded that it was tactically useful to talk of the hope for such transition, but held that Communist parties should not tie their hands by committing themselves to following only the parliamentary road to power. At some stage along that road, he held, resistance would be encountered which would make it necessary to resort to armed force in order to smash the old state machinery and overcome the armed forces which supported it.[12]

While he evidently held that the risks inherent in the policy line he urged were made acceptably low by growing Communist-bloc superiority, Mao did not merely dismiss without discussion the objections based on the dangers of nuclear war. First of all, he emphasized that the socialist countries would never themselves be the first to unleash such war. But if one were to be unleashed by the imperialists, "if worst came to worst and half of mankind died, the other half would remain while imperialism would be razed to the ground and the whole world would become socialist." [13] Thereafter, in Mao's opinion, "the victorious people would very swiftly create on the ruins of imperialism a civilization thousands of times higher than the capitalist system and a truly beautiful future for themselves." [14]

Mao Tse-tung was joined in Moscow by a Chinese Communist military delegation, which was headed by Defense Minister P'eng Te-huai and which included General Su Yü, chief of staff of the People's Liberation Army. The delegation stayed in the Soviet Union for about three weeks, during which it engaged in discussions with Marshal Malinovsky and other Soviet leaders. However, the contents of the 1957 Declaration, which emerged from the Moscow meeting of Communist leaders, and of the statements that Marshals P'eng Te-huai and Malinovsky each issued at the conclusion of their talks, suggest that Mao Tse-tung had failed to convince the Soviet leadership of the accuracy of his assessments and that his military delegation did not get important new military aid commitments.[15] Indeed, at this point Soviet leaders may have already concluded they had made a dreadful mistake in negotiating the agreement—on which the signatures were scarcely dry—to give China the atomic bomb.

Subsequent developments proved that each side held to its original views. Soviet leaders remained convinced that local wars would pose the danger of becoming wider wars, that those in turn might escalate into nuclear conflict, and that the Soviet Union would be likely to suffer grave damage in any nuclear exchange with the United States. Mao Tse-tung, for his part, held to the view that powerful enemies should be respected only tactically; strategically, they should be despised. That is to say, he held that a powerful opponent could be defeated through a series of small encounters if one took care always to oppose him, in the areas of conflict, with tactically superior forces. This might be accomplished, for instance, through encouragement of and support for so-called wars of liberation to be waged in various countries and areas, as conditions became ripe or could be made to become so. Such wars would, of course, be waged against "the imperialists and their lackeys"—meaning all those opposing Communist efforts to gain power.

Mao Tse-tung returned from Moscow believing that China's own "war of liberation" was still incomplete. Taiwan remained in the hands of the National Government of the Republic of China, which was allied to the United States and receiving military assistance from it. The offshore islands also remained in Nationalist hands—proclaimed stepping-stones for Chiang Kai-shek's return to the mainland, bases for commando operations against coastal areas, spots from which subversive agents could be sent ashore, and outposts the Nationalists used in endeavoring to enforce a blockade of Chinese Communist ports.[16]

Garrisoning these islands for the Nationalists were large concentrations of troops, including both men who had come with the government when it had evacuated the mainland and Formosan Chinese recruits. If the Chinese Communists could eliminate those garrisons, they probably believed, they would thereby deal the government on Taiwan a military, psychological, and political blow which would dash Chiang Kai-shek's hopes for returning to the mainland and would also bring Taiwan itself more nearly within their reach.

In May 1958, following Mao's return from Moscow, he and his party's Military Affairs Committee began a series of meetings which lasted eight weeks. These meetings were interrupted briefly at the beginning of August when Khrushchev, accompanied by Marshal Malinovsky, paid a short visit to Peking. There the two Soviet leaders conferred with Mao Tse-tung and Minister of National Defense P'eng Te-huai. The joint communique issued on August 3, at the conclusion of their talks, contained the assertions that they had had a full exchange of views on major questions confronting their two countries in the international field, and had reached unanimous agreement on the measures to be taken to safeguard peace. Nevertheless, on August 24 the Chinese Communists, evidently hoping to force the Nationalist troops on Quemoy to surrender through artillery fire directed against it and vessels coming to resupply the garrison, opened a heavy and prolonged bombardment of that offshore island.

In this second Taiwan Straits crisis Mao Tse-tung, a man notably adept at creating strategies intended to serve several purposes at one time, undoubtedly had three opponents in mind. The obvious ones were the Government of the Republic of China and the United States. A local defeat of the former would weaken the international prestige of the latter; and even if the campaign were not pressed to a successful conclusion, it would put strains on the Sino-United States alliance at its weakest point—for the offshore islands played an important role in the politico-military strategy of Chiang Kai-shek but were at best of only peripheral military interest to the United States. Mao Tse-tung's less obvious and third antagonist was Khrushchev. On December 21, 1957, after the Moscow meetings at which Mao had tried to change bloc policies, Khrushchev had publicly stated before the Supreme Soviet: "We say to the representatives of the western countries, and especially the United States . . . let us recognize the status quo . . . renounce any attempt to alter the existing situation by force." [17] Accordingly Mao now was placing Khrushchev in the difficult position of having to support in practice a high-risk strategy which he had rejected in principle, or of appearing to the world to have let down a Communist ally.

In response, Khrushchev tried to run a middle course. He gave verbal support to the Chinese Communists, but that support was so phrased and timed as to minimize the risks to the Soviet Union. At the end of August and the beginning of September the American press carried stories of a United States military build-up, in the Taiwan area, in which nuclear capabilities were several times mentioned. Then on September 4, Secretary Dulles indicated that the United States would help defend the offshore islands if Chinese forces proved unequal to the task. (The direct assistance which actually proved necessary was chiefly in the realm of resupply. Vessels of the United States Navy convoyed Nationalist ships, and United States aircraft escorted Chinese Nationalist cargo planes to the islands.) On September 6, two days after Secretary Dulles had made his statement, Chou En-lai signaled Chinese Communist willingness to quiet down the crisis. This he did by offering to resume Sino-American ambassadorial talks—periodically held meetings, originally begun in consequence of the suggestion Chou had made towards the end of the earlier Taiwan Straits crisis. Only after Chou En-lai had taken this initiative, making further escalation appear unlikely, did Khrushchev make his most belligerent statements.[18]

This he did in two letters to President Eisenhower, dated September 7 and September 19. It had become known on the latter date that the United States had sent to Quemoy eight-inch howitzers capable of firing atomic shells. Khrushchev accused the United States of resorting to atomic blackmail against China and declared that an atomic attack on China would be rebuffed by the same means. Then in a statement of October 5, without receding from the position that the Soviet Union would come to the aid of the People's Republic of China if it were attacked from without, he made it clear that he regarded the Taiwan Straits matter as an internal one of the Chinese people in which the Soviet Union did not intend to interfere. The following day the Chinese Communists suspended their bombardment of Quemoy.[19] With Khrushchev disengaging the USSR from the outcome, nothing more was to be gained by continuing the venture.

Although October 6 marked the end of the 1958 Taiwan Straits crisis, it did not close the matter insofar as Khrushchev was concerned. Mao Tse-tung evidently had behaved towards the presumed leaders of the world Communist movement much as he did towards his own Central Committee. He had proposed new policies and, when they had encountered a hostile reception, he had gone ahead and implemented them anyway. He had sought to commit the bloc in a context of gravest importance: that of war and peace in the nuclear era. And he was fully aware how his exercise in "brinksmanship" would be regarded by his Soviet allies. Indeed, Mao knew, before he began his 1958 venture against the offshore islands, that it ran against the grain of the Soviet leadership's continuing policies, and also that the Russians were having second thoughts about helping the Chinese Communists acquire nuclear weapons. On April 4, 1958, before the Chinese Communists had even begun the eight weeks of military meetings which preceded the attack on the offshore islands, the Soviet Union had made that evident. It had sent a note, addressed to both to the United States and China, urging the desirability of instituting a ban on nuclear weapons tests before such weapons might come into the possession of additional powers—meaning, among others, Communist China.[20]

Moreover, it is virtually certain that Khrushchev's August visit to China was motivated by a determination to prevent Mao Tse-tung from creating a dangerous crisis in the Taiwan Straits. Five years later the Chinese Communists published a statement alleging: "In 1958 the leadership of the Communist party of the Soviet Union put forward unreasonable demands designed to bring China under Soviet military control." [21] In a speech of September 24, 1962, before the Central Committee, Mao Tse-tung had explained: "Beginning in the second half of 1958, Khrushchev had thought of sealing off the China coast, and he wanted to blockade us by forming a joint fleet in our country to control the coast. Khrushchev came to China precisely for the purpose of discussing this question." [22]

In describing Khrushchev's efforts to that end as having begun in the second half of 1958, Mao Tse-tung seems to have suggested that the Soviet leader did not take the shelling of Quemoy as a final answer. If there were subsequent negotiations on the subject, Khrushchev undoubtedly sought to use the threat of withdrawing military aid as a bargaining lever, and found it insufficient to move Mao Tse-tung. At any rate, on June 29, 1959, the Soviet Union, as the Chinese Communists later put it, "tore up the agreement on new technology for national defense concluded . . . on October 15, 1957, and refused to provide China with a sample of an atomic bomb and technical data concerning its manufacture." [23] The Soviet Union also began, during 1959, to cut back on its aircraft deliveries to China.[24]

During the latter part of 1959, Khrushchev visited the United States, traveled across the country, and went away impressed. The Chinese Communists obviously resented Khrushchev's visiting the United States, just as they resented the Soviet abrogation of the agreement covering military technology. Indeed, they were later to link the two, describing Khrushchev's "tearing up the agreement" as a "ceremonial gift" to President Eisenhower, made "to curry favor with the U. S. imperialists and create the so-called 'spirit of Camp David.' " [25]

Just as the celebrations of the fortieth anniversary of the Russian revolution had given Mao Tse-tung the opportunity to go to Moscow and lecture Soviet leaders, the tenth anniversary of the founding of the Chinese People's Republic afforded Khrushchev an occasion to visit Peking and lecture the leaders of Communist China. Because this anniversary occurs on October 1, Khrushchev was coming fresh from his September visit to the United States. At the state banquet which marked the anniversary, he made a speech in which he remarked that President Eisenhower was a man who wanted peace, but that some exponents of the cold war were pushing mankind toward a new world war. He warned that "those who ignite it will be the first to be consumed in its fire." Although the Communist camp was strong, he said, it nevertheless would be wrong to "test the stability of the capitalist system by force." Indeed, "the peoples would not understand and would never support those who took it into their hands to act in such a way." [26]

It was of course clear to his listeners whom Khrushchev had in mind. Indeed, he went on to discuss the Chinese Communist ambition to gain control of Taiwan. Given American support for Chiang Kai-shek's government on Taiwan and the Soviet alliance with mainland China, he said, that ambition was an incendiary factor which resulted in the atmosphere of an imminent great war. What the Soviet Union wanted was to ease international tensions and eliminate war. After the October revolution in the USSR, a Far Eastern Republic had been set up on what had been Russian territory in the Far East, and Lenin had recognized it. But later it was reunited with Russia. Why should China not pursue a similar course toward Taiwan? [27]

The Chinese Communists later portrayed this suggestion as Soviet connivance in the "United States plot to create two Chinas." Khrushchev, for his part, unquestionably was intent on trying to prevent Communist China from pursuing courses which might bring catastrophe to his own country. However, in the process he had very neatly repaid Mao Tse-tung for his behavior in Moscow two years earlier.

I I

Great Leap and Resounding Fall

MAO TSE-TUNG and his military mission undoubtedly knew, when they returned from Moscow late in 1957, that China was not likely to get from the Soviet Union enough additional military aid to ensure the rapid modernization of China's armed forces. Without such aid, those forces would for some years remain defensively quite strong —but incapable of projecting power very far beyond China's land and sea frontiers. Had the Taiwan Straits venture of 1958 been militarily successful, its outcome might have been used to support Mao Tse-tung's contention that conditions were ripe for more venturesome bloc policies. The venture might also have served Mao's purposes if it had embroiled the Soviet Union with the United States. By the autumn of 1958, of course, it was clear that the gamble would not succeed on either count. Indeed, it would not have taken much imagination for Chinese leaders to anticipate the subsequent cutbacks in military assistance which the Soviet Union imposed as the penalty for Mao's audacity.

All this meant, as Mao Tse-tung undoubtedly had feared even before he went to Moscow, that Chinese aims would have to be sought predominantly through the use of Chinese power. If China were to become a great modern power, that would have to be accomplished, in greater degree than the Chinese Communists had hoped, through Chinese efforts. To accomplish it in Mao's own lifetime would require a great leap—an early takeoff into self-sustaining economic growth.

It is not surprising, given Mao's impatience, that the subject of a possible great leap was raised at party meetings held in the weeks immediately following his return from Moscow.[1] It must have thrown China's economic planners into consternation. China's second Five-Year Plan was due to begin January 1, 1958, and that was only a few weeks off.

The plan had been under consideration for more than a year. As early as September 1956, Liu Shao-ch'i, in an address before the Eighth Congress of the Chinese Communist party, had described the plan in general terms. It envisioned the continued development of heavy industry, relatively high development of light industry, and increases over the five-year period of one-quarter or more in wages and in the income of the peasant population.[2] In other words, relatively more consumer goods were to be made available, and standards of living were to be raised substantially. The congress was addressed also by the economist Ch'en Yün, the first-ranking among the government's vice premiers. "We must be prudent and practical," he said, "go forward slowly, gather experiences, push ahead gradually." Drafting of the actual plan was begun that year and continued in 1957.[3] The period of planning thus corresponded roughly with the moderate period of the Hundred Flowers, and the contents of the plan reflected Ch'en Yün's pragmatic approach.

This pragmatic approach also counseled against further disruption of agriculture. Accordingly, in September 1957, the regime issued a reassuring directive referring to the Agricultural Producers Cooperatives, which had just been set up. It stated: "Once the size of the . . . cooperatives has been fixed, it should be proclaimed that there will be no more change for the next ten years." [4]

Meanwhile, however, the antirightist campaign, which had followed the period of the Hundred Flowers, had undermined the position of the economic pragmatists. Before the government had a chance to implement the second Five-Year Plan, Mao was able to have it put aside. Before 1958 was out, he and his followers had also radically altered the system of agricultural organization, in which there was to have been "no more change for the next ten years."

Mao Tse-tung approached the problems of economic development with the realization that China was short on capital but long on manpower. He intended, therefore, fully to mobilize and utilize China's great population in the creation of new plants and the production of exportable surpluses. In pursuit of these aims he unfurled, one after another, what became known as the "Three Red Banners" —the "General Line," the "Great Leap Forward" and the "People's Communes."

The General Line was a concept rather than a program. Explicitly attributed to Chairman Mao, it called for "going all out, aiming high and achieving greater, quicker, better, and more economical results in building socialism." [5] It provided the slogan, first of all, for a vast program under which many tens of millions of people were mobilized to work on water conservancy projects. The showpiece among them was the large Ming Tombs Reservoir, near Peking. It was constructed by "volunteers" ranging from Premier Chou En-lai on down, and it was completed in the brief span of six months.[6] These were projects well suited to the substitution of manpwer for capital equipment. They were also the sort to which the people were accustomed —the Chinese peasants have from time immemorial been mobilized for irrigation and flood control purposes. But the success of this campaign encouraged the extension of the General Line to other projects as well—specifically, to the Great Leap Forward and the inauguration of the People's Communes.

Mao Tse-tung did not unveil the targets of the Great Leap Forward as parts of a single, completed plan. One set of targets, more ambitious than those of the discarded five-year plan, was set up in February 1958, and they in turn were radically raised in midsummer.[7] Meanwhile, a struggle went on within the leadership. There was an inherent contradiction in the General Line. Trying to achieve "more and quicker" results was inconsistent with seeking "better and more economical" ones, because emphasis on quantity and speed was likely to lead to waste and inattention to quality. Just as Mao's approach was illogical, the specific goals he set were unrealistic. The chief burden of telling him so would naturally first fall on Ch'en Yün, because he was the only economic specialist on the Standing Committee of the Political Bureau. The evidence suggests, however, that two other members of this six-man body may have supported Ch'en Yün. In May Lin Piao was added to the membership of the Standing Committee, perhaps to break a tie vote in favor of Mao Tse-tung.[8]

That same month Liu Shao-ch'i, addressing the second session of the Eighth Party Congress, announced the Great Leap Forward on behalf of Mao Tse-tung.[9] It was, of course, Liu Shao-ch'i who had outlined before the first session of that congress the moderate objectives of the 1958–1962 Five-Year Plan. In effect, Liu Shao-ch'i had been called on to reverse himself, rejecting the plan he earlier had advocated before the same body. That plan had called for raising industrial production between 14 and 15 percent a year.[10] The Great Leap Forward called for raising levels of production throughout the economy by 100 percent during a single year.[11]

If this objective was unrealistic for the industrial sector, it was irrational as far as agriculture was concerned. With more than three-quarters of China's populace in rural areas, the 10 percent of the land suitable for agriculture was already under highly intensive cultivation.[12] Nevertheless, an official organ of the Communist party attributed to Mao Tse-tung himself the prediction that grain production would not only be doubled in 1958 but doubled again in 1959, completely solving China's perennial food problem.[13] Simultaneously, the rural populace was expected to build thousands of small-scale industrial establishments throughout the countryside. When completed, these workshops were intended to utilize peasant labor during agricultural slack seasons, thereby increasing the supply of needed goods.

Why did Mao Tse-tung lay his personal prestige on the line for the quick attainment of such far-reaching results? The answer must be found in his mystic faith in the masses, in his own power to mobilize them, and in what the mobilized masses were capable of accomplishing. This faith was perhaps, in part at least, an outgrowth of his long experience of warfare in which men, whose blood streams are filled with the adrenalin of combat, accomplish the seemingly superhuman. He approached the problems of peacetime construction in the manner and spirit in which he had undertaken military campaigns. Natural obstacles would have to yield to his implacable will. Once infused with his spirit, China's mobilized millions would sweep all before them.

In 1958, Mao wrote: "The decisive factor, apart from the leadership by the Party, is our six hundred million people. The more the people, the more the views and suggestions, the more intense the fervor, and the greater the energy." [14] Indeed, during the Great Leap many suggestions were put forward, advocated with fervor and applied with energy. They also were applied en masse, without sufficient advance consideration.

There were, for instance, the campaigns for close planting and deep plowing. The amount of available land could not be greatly or rapidly increased, but if two stalks of grain could be raised where one grew before, then grain production could be doubled. This had been accomplished on demonstration plots, to which generous quantities of fertilizer had been applied. It did not work on a nationwide basis, for which adequate fertilizer was lacking. The idea behind deep plowing, using a system of cables and winches to pull deep-cutting plows, was that it would bring up the supposedly richer soils which had not been deprived of their nutrients by centuries of cultivation. The usual result was to turn under the topsoil on which the peasant had expended his fertilizer and to turn up infertile subsoils.

Another campaign was that for backyard steel furnaces. People everywhere were given the plans for building them and urged to participate in a campaign to raise steel production. They used whatever iron ores and scrap were at hand and sometimes, in excesses of enthusiasm, threw in the family cooking pots—which presumably would no longer be needed, as the people were all to be well fed in communal mess halls. Upwards of six hundred thousand such furnaces were constructed, and they turned out great quantities of metal which soon clogged the transport system but which turned out to be too low in quality for use at industrial centers.

Beginning in the spring of 1958, the amalgamation of the co-operatives into large-sized agricultural communes was begun. During the summer, Mao Tse-tung made extensive and well-publicized tours of China's rural areas in order to push the movement forward. In the course of the rest of the year, in a vast administrative and agricultural upheaval, China's three-quarters of a million cooperatives were amalgamated into about twenty-six thousand rural communes, and their lands declared nationalized.[15] In addition, communes were also set up in the cities. Each commune was intended to be an all-around, basic-level unit for purposes of government administration, economic activity, social control, and militia organization.

Under the commune system, agricultural tasks were tackled by great groups of people, so that each individual field was no longer tended by the peasants who knew its particular characteristics and requirements. The small, privately-held plots and the pigs and chickens which had provided a large share of the vegetables, meats, and edible oils were turned over from the individual families to the communes. Meanwhile, so much labor was being mobilized for the construction of rural workshops and small industrial plants, and so many meetings were being called to work up popular enthusiasm, that regular farm work had to be done hurriedly and little time and labor were left for tending the subsidiary plots and caring for farm animals. Working harder and sleeping less, the people needed more calories to keep going. Under the illusion of plenty and believing that the communism of "to each according to his needs" was at hand, the communal mess halls served generous meals and wasted food.

The whole gigantic effort was run much as military affairs had been handled during Yenan days. It was not merely that it was treated as a series of campaigns for water conservancy, back yard production, and so on. Abandoning central direction and control, the regime reverted to the decentralization practiced in guerrilla days. It set objectives at the top and delegated responsibility for other decision making and for the direction of effort to local levels. Party cadres, many of whom knew relatively little about industry or agriculture, largely took over the responsibilities which had been discharged by specialists, technicians and managers. Under the pressures which the party cadres transmitted, people tried to meet quantitative targets by working harder and completing each task in the shortest possible time. People were driven beyond endurance, the upkeep of machinery was neglected, materials were used wastefully, and quality control was abandoned for quantity production.[16]

At the same time the statisticians were warned that their work showed a lack of "political consciousness" and that emphasis on professional standards was "doctrinairism." To use a Maoist phrase, "politics were in command," and it was the political duty of statisticians to produce figures which would encourage the masses and spur them on to greater efforts.[17] Those who produced the statistics obliged. The figures they turned out reflected not only the upsurge in production which actually occurred during the early part of the Great Leap Forward but also covered the gaps between actual performance and the much higher targets. Evidently believing the statistics which flowed in, and encouraged by weather which was exceptionally favorable for agriculture, the authorities in Peking asserted, at the end of October 1958, that food production had been raised from 185 million tons in 1957 to an estimated 350 to 400 million tons. Similar claims were made for industry; it was asserted that steel output, to cite one category, had been raised to eleven million tons, or twice 1957 production.[18]

This same period witnessed also a great leap in the promotion of the cult of Mao Tse-tung. Even before 1958, Mao's every utterance was being publicly treated with an awed reverence worthy of the divine word. But early that year Ch'en Po-ta, political secretary to Mao Tse-tung, was made editor in chief of the party journal, *Red Flag*. In disregard of the 1956 decisions concerning the cult of personality —decisions reflected in the revised constitution which the party had adopted—Ch'en Po-ta undertook a campaign which built the cult of Mao to still greater proportions. *Red Flag* began to eulogize Mao as a Marxist–Leninist theorist who had discovered a special road providing a shortcut from socialism to communism.[19] *People's Daily* and other organs of news and propaganda joined in chorus.

The public was told that "Chairman Mao is like the sun giving light wherever it shines." His "thought" had the miraculous power of creating a spirit of self-sacrifice which in turn generates a "great material force." Indeed, "today in the era of Mao Tse-tung, heaven is here on earth . . . Chairman Mao is a great prophet . . . Each prophecy of Chairman Mao has become a reality. It was so in the past; it is so today." Mao Tse-tung complemented this description of his spiritual powers by demonstrating his physical vigor. In less than one month, if the regime's media are to be believed, he swam the broad and swift Yangtze River no less than seven times. He also made extensive tours in the provinces which were given widest publicity.[20]

The calculated timing of Mao's well-publicized swims and tours suggests that they, and the adulation they helped inspire, had purposes additional to those of giving him pleasure and building up the stock of those who so publicly praised him. The cult of his personality enhanced his authority and made his personal position more secure. He revealed that this latter consideration was not absent from his mind during a conversation, subsequent to the fall of Khrushchev, which he had with Edgar Snow. Stalin, he observed, was said to be the center of such a cult, whereas Khrushchev had none at all; perhaps, he suggested, that was why Khrushchev fell.[21]

At the same time, Mao's elevation, so far above men who had for many years been his approximate equals, must have set their teeth on edge. Marshal Ho Lung revealed this sourness when he observed sarcastically to members of the Hunan party provincial committee: "Hunan is the home of our emperor. It won't do to bungle things here." [22] The remark evokes a comment made by Mao's opponents during the Fut'ien revolt of 1930; they had accused Mao of behaving like a "party emperor." [23]

Mao's self-willed spirit, which inspired such remarks, was evident in his conduct of affairs leading to the adoption of the programs for the Great Leap and the People's Communes. An examination of the sequence of events suggests he employed the methods which were habitual with him when he could not persuade others willingly to accept his policies and plans. Proper procedures, under the provisions of the constitutions of the party and the government, would make it appropriate for the Political Bureau of the party to formulate proposals and, in important matters, to submit them to a plenary meeting of the Central Committee for its approval. Thereafter, in the case of sufficiently important matters, they would be passed on also by the Party Congress and submitted to the National People's Congress for ratification. This procedure had been followed in dealing with a proposal Mao Tse-tung had made in 1956 regarding a grandiose twelve-year program for agriculture, making possible delay of acceptance of the proposed program while it underwent revisions.[24]

Mao had undoubtedly raised the matter of a Great Leap at meetings of the Political Bureau late in 1957 and early in 1958. However, as we have already noted, there are grounds for speculating that he met opposition to the idea, within that body—opposition which he did not succeed in overcoming until May of 1958. Later in May the full Central Committee met, a party congress was held, and the decision to launch the Great Leap was announced; but it was already underway.[25] Thus the regime was, in effect, committed to the Great Leap before the Central Committee met and the party congress was held, rather than in consequence of their deliberations.

The first people's communes were established in the spring of 1958, and Mao Tse-tung gave the program his explicit approval in June. By August communes had been established throughout several provinces. But it was only in August that the Political Bureau approved the program. It accordingly would appear that the Political Bureau had been faced with a *fait accompli,* as was the Central Committee when it was next called into plenary session that autumn.[26]

Getting the Great Leap started and the People's Communes established, before they had been approved at the national level, was accomplished only by overcoming widespread opposition at the provincial and local levels. Indeed, this resistance to the Great Leap—with its new and heavy burdens on the populace, and to the People's Communes—which would further upset the peasant economy, existed in every province of China. It found its most effective expression through the party's provincial and local secretaries, many of whom were purged in consequence.[27]

The agricultural province of Honan, where the People's Communes were first initiated, provides an illustration. Principal members of the party's provincial committee were accused of objecting that "famine has occurred continuously," that "the peasants are beasts of burden, human beings are harnessed in the fields, girls and women pull harrows with their wombs hanging out," and that "the peasants will revolt and reject the leadership of the Communist party." Events in Honan were to justify the prediction of revolt, but from the standpoint of their careers, those who made it were right at the wrong time. In May, P'an Fu-sheng, first secretary of the party's provincial committee and political commissar for Honan Military District, was discharged for opposing agricultural collectivization, socialist construction, and Chairman Mao.[28]

In September 1958, Mao Tse-tung admitted that "a few comrades" still were unwilling to see industrial development handled as a mass movement. They were, he said, disparaging it as representing "a rural style of work" and "a guerrilla habit." He asserted, however, that it provided a foundation on which "it is possible to accomplish any task whatsoever." [29] Before 1958 was out, this assessment of Mao's was to be proven wrong. By November the populace had begun, consequent to the strain of frenetic work and constant meetings, to show signs of exhaustion. That month the Political Bureau met in Chengchow, in the agricultural heart of China, and decided to make on-the-spot checks in various provinces. These checks revealed that all was not well in the communes, and that the statistics covering accomplishments had been badly inflated. How badly inflated they were could not be determined at once, because the statistical system had collapsed in chaos.[30]

At the end of November, the full Central Committee, which had been presented with the Great Leap as a *fait accompli* and circumvented on the decision to launch the People's Communes, was convened at Wuchang. The outcome of its deliberations would give comfort to those who hold that the principles underlying politics cannot in the end be nullified through the practice of one-party rule; that the other side of the coin of authority is responsibility; and that the leader who embarks on fateful courses without the support of a consensus must prove right or suffer for it. Mao Tse-tung had forced the hand of the collective leadership; now it forced his. In December 1958, he was removed from the position of chairman of the government of the People's Republic of China, and it was decided that Liu Shao-ch'i should succeed him. Consequent to his elevation to that post, early in 1959, Liu Shao-ch'i became also the chairman of the government's National Defense Council and commander in chief of the armed forces. For outside consumption, the change was described as having been made at Mao's own request and in order that he might be free to devote his full time to party affairs. In actual fact, he was later to recall, during a recital of accumulated grievances, his dissatisfaction over the Wuchang conference.[31]

Mao Tse-tung of course continued to hold the chairmanship of the party, and the party controlled the government. Mao's dignity was preserved even to the extent of suggesting to the public that Liu Shao-ch'i's position depended on Mao's favor. This was implicit in the public description of Liu Shao-ch'i as Mao's "closest comrade in arms." [32] Whereas it had been sufficient in the early days of the regime to refer to him simply as "Comrade Mao Tse-tung," it became increasingly *de rigeur* to call him "Chairman Mao."

The Central Committee did not, at the plenary session which decided to relieve Mao of his government position, go so far as to decide to abandon the Great Leap or dissolve the People's Communes. However, it did reverse the trend towards full communism, which involved policies under which the land was to be state property rather than held by the cooperatives, supply was to be "to each according to his needs," and wages were no longer to be keyed to work done. It was decided that the workday should not exceed twelve hours, in order that people might get their needed eight hours of sleep, and that they should not be compelled to eat in mess halls instead of at home. Commune industries were to be continued, but on a more restricted basis; rural industries thereafter were to be primarily related to agriculture, and the backyard steel furnaces were abandoned. About ten thousand investigators were assigned to commissions which were to look into the communes and see to the weeding out of those cadres "who showed a bad style of work." [33] In addition, during the last part of 1958 and the early months of 1959, a number of the members of the Political Bureau made investigatory tours in the provinces.[34]

Marshal P'eng Te-huai was among the members of the Political Bureau who made such tours. According to his own account, one of the places he visited was the commune of Chairman Mao's native vil-

lage in Hunan province. While there, he checked up on reports of a
great increase in production which supposedly had been scored there
in 1958. However, on the basis of his investigation he concluded that
there had been an increase of only 16 percent, which was much smaller
than the gain which had been reported. He had also discussed the
matter with Chou Hsiao-chou, first secretary of the party's Hunan
Provincial Committee, who told him that the commune had raised its
production by only 14 percent, and only with much assistance and
large loans from the state. Mao Tse-tung also visited this commune,
and P'eng Te-huai subsequently asked him what his findings on its
production figures had been. Mao Tse-tung may have sensed that
P'eng Te-huai was trying to put him on the spot. At any rate, in recounting this conversation, P'eng Te-huai recalled: "He said he had
not talked about the matter." P'eng then added: "In my opinion, he
had." 35

By the spring of 1959, P'eng Te-huai had evidently become thoroughly disenchanted with the road down which Mao had been leading China. As minister of national defense, his professional interests
were being affected adversely by the consequences of Mao's policies in
both the sphere of foreign relations and that of internal affairs. In the
external field, those policies had led the Soviet Union to reduce its
military aid to China and to consider canceling its agreement to provide China with a sample atomic bomb and details concerning its
manufacture. Within China, the army had been diverted to construction projects and other economic tasks—as its contribution to the
Great Leap Forward—with the result that military training had to be
curtailed. In consequence of the failures attendant on the Great Leap,
the troops were on short rations. Moreover, P'eng Te-huai's soldiers
were learning, through letters from and visits to their homes, about
the privations which their families were suffering, and this was affecting troop morale.

P'eng Te-huai was not a man who kept his thoughts and feelings
to himself, and Mao Tse-tung had sensitive antennae. Accordingly, it
is likely that Mao Tse-tung's confidence that he enjoyed the personal
loyalty of P'eng Te-huai was eroding. That this may have been so is
suggested by a comment P'eng made shortly after his return to Peking
from a party conference in Shanghai, early in the spring. He complained: "Comrade Mao Tse-tung had mainly criticized me at the
meeting." 36

Shortly afterwards, P'eng Te-huai left China as leader of a delegation which spent the period between April 24 and June 13, 1959,
visiting the Soviet Union and other Communist countries. During this
period he saw Khrushchev and wrote a letter to the Soviet party in

which he criticized Mao's policies, including those of the Great Leap and the People's Communes.[37] Khrushchev shared his dislike for these policies, and wished to see China abandon them. Soviet aid was being devoted to China's program of economic development and Soviet prestige would be involved in its failure—and the Great Leap, as a formula for economic development, seemed bound to come a cropper. Peking was hailing the People's Communes as a Chinese discovery which provided a shortcut from socialism to communism, which China was soon to enter. To Khrushchev it was unthinkable that underdeveloped China should emerge from socialism before the more highly-developed USSR; to claim that China had discovered a new road to communism, along which it was showing the way, was to challenge the Soviet Union's role as the leader of world communism.

It would have been out of character for P'eng Te-huai to conceal his views from the members of his delegation or from members of the staff of the Chinese embassy in Moscow, and it may be that Mao Tse-tung was promptly made aware of the tenor of P'eng's conversations with Soviet officials and of his letter to the Soviet party. In any event, important personnel changes made in his military establishment, while P'eng Te-huai was on his tour, suggest that an effort to undermine him may already have been underway.[38]

On July 3, 1959, about three weeks after P'eng Te-huai's return to China, an enlarged meeting of the Political Bureau was convened at Lushan, a mountain resort in Kiangsi Province, and it was immediately followed by a plenary session of the Central Committee which lasted until August 16. On July 14, P'eng Te-huai circulated, among those present at the meeting of the Political Bureau, a "letter of opinion" addressed to Mao Tse-tung in which he criticized the way in which the establishment of the communes had been handled and questioned whether the Great Leap should be continued.[39]

On July 18, four days after P'eng had circulated his letter, *Pravda* and Moscow radio publicized a speech made by Khrushchev in which he too criticized the People's Communes and described the communes as reflecting a "poor understanding" of how communism was to be built. Khrushchev undoubtedly had learned that the meeting at Lushan was underway through messages from Soviet diplomatic personnel in China. They were reported to have shown great interest in obtaining news of the conference, and Khrushchev can have been in little doubt about the main subjects which would be under discussion there. The publicizing of Khrushchev's speech at that juncture was interpreted as an intervention in Chinese affairs, intended to strengthen the hands of P'eng Te-huai and other critics of Mao's policies.[40]

One of P'eng's principal supporters, during the discussions at

Lushan, was Chang Wen-t'ien, one of the group of twenty-eight Bolsheviks which had once dominated the party with the backing of the Comintern and at one time the holder of the top party position of general secretary. Mao Tse-tung undoubtedly saw, in the role played at Lushan by Chang Wen-t'ien, a second piece of evidence suggesting that he faced a Soviet-backed challenge to his policies, and hence to his position as leader of the party.

P'eng Te-huai's letter of July 14 was composed as though written only in his capacity as member of the Political Bureau—it contained no more than passing reference to military matters. But Mao Tse-tung, with his strongly held views about the relationship of the barrel of the gun to political power, would hardly have forgotten that P'eng Te-huai held the position of minister of national defense, and that he led the daily work of the Military Affairs Committee of the party.

In his letter, P'eng cited figures which credited the Great Leap with raising production in 1958 by almost 50 percent; conceded that the popular campaign for producing steel by indigenous methods had stimulated a nationwide geological survey and trained many technical personnel; and predicted that the rural communes would enable the peasants of China to free themselves from poverty and would speed both the building of socialism and the transition from it to communism.

However, P'eng said, there had been losses as well as gains. Principally because of inexperience, too large a proportion of resources and of effort had gone into capital construction, with the consequence that highly necessary commodities were unavailable. The campaign to refine steel in backyard furnaces, based as it was on a superficial understanding of what was required for the development of an iron and steel industry, had created imbalances and exacted a high cost in terms of misspent resources and wasted labor. In P'eng's view, the outstanding problem was that of tension and strain. Disproportions were affecting the relations between rural peasants and urban workers and between the various strata in the city and the countryside. In this situation, they faced the political problem of whether the broad masses could be mobilized to continue the Great Leap Forward. There were still people who did not have enough to eat, the cotton cloth required for clothing was in short supply, and the people were urgently demanding a change in the situation which prevailed.

In summing up experiences in their work, and the lessons to be learned from them, P'eng Te-huai observed that the habit of exaggeration had been bred and extended rather universally in the various areas and departments, and this had been reflected in reports. "This caused not a few comrades to become dizzy . . . and . . . for a rather long period of time, it was not easy to get a true picture of the situation." He himself, he said, was no exception. "Petty bourgeois fanaticism," he added, "renders us liable to commit 'left' mistakes. . . . As a result, divorced from reality, we failed to get the support of the masses." Some comrades, he said, believed that "putting politics in command" would solve everything. But it was "no substitute for economic principles, still less for the concrete measures in economic work." What was required, besides a systematic summing up of achievements gained and lessons to be learned, was to unite the whole party and work hard. "On the whole," he said, "there should be no investigation of personal responsibility. Otherwise, it would be unfavorable to unity, unfavorable to our work." On the basis of unity and hard work, he concluded, the targets for that year and the years ahead could surely be fulfilled.

In the entire letter, P'eng Te-huai made only two direct references to the chairman, both in the context of the failure of others, including himself, to heed Mao's injunctions and to understand the long-range nature of his policies. But this could not obscure the fact that Mao Tse-tung was closely associated with the policies and programs which P'eng Te-huai had criticized. Moreover, in personal conversations and smaller gatherings, held outside the hours in which the full meetings were taking place, P'eng and his supporters were not so circumspect. In a conversation which subsequently became known to Mao Tse-tung, Chang Wen-t'ien remarked that Mao was brilliant but, like Stalin in his later years, "very strong-handed in rectifying people." P'eng had agreed, and added the comment that throughout Chinese history the first emperor of every dynasty had been characterized by both brilliance and strong-handedness. At one gathering, P'eng Te-huai was heard to complain, in the context of the wasteful use of resources, that many provinces had built villas for Chairman Mao. And he repeatedly remarked in the meetings, if the charges subsequently made against him are to be believed, that "if the Chinese workers and peasants were not as good as they are, a Hungarian incident would have occurred in China and it would have been necessary to invite Soviet troops in." This implied, of course, both that wrong policies had created hardships which were well-nigh intolerable, and that the People's Liberation Army, which P'eng led, could not be depended on, in the case of a popular uprising, to side with the regime.[41]

On July 23, Mao Tse-tung made a long speech of rebuttal directed at P'eng Te-huai and other critics. In this speech he introduced the question of the loyalties of the armed forces in a seemingly offhand way, and in dealing with it he made a distinction between the

People's Liberation Army, which was commanded by P'eng Te-huai, and the Red Army, which was its revolutionary predecessor of guerrilla days. He believed, Mao remarked, that if it came to a showdown, the People's Liberation Army would follow him. If not, he would go back to the countryside, raise a Red Army, and lead the peasants to over-throw the government.

To judge from his speech, one particular shaft, which had been directed at Mao Tse-tung, must have penetrated to a particularly sen-sitive spot. In a school maintained for training party cadres in Kiangsi Province, and in the Intermediate Party School, there had evidently been bitter comments about the enormous wastage of human effort which had characterized the campaign for making steel through meth-ods of mass mobilization. In identifying Mao as the author of that campaign, and in suggesting that he should be punished for it, his critics had apparently had recourse to a saying of Confucius which indicated disapproval of the notion of human sacrifice, even in the symbolic form of making pottery figurines representing people and burying them with the dead. The saying went: "He who first made human images to bury with the dead should have no posterity." Mao Tse-tung had, of course, put his eldest son in the service of P'eng Te-huai during the Korean war; P'eng had given him an assignment near the front, and while serving there he had been killed. His other son, Mao appears to have believed, would have no progeny; this meant that Mao would have no male heir to carry on his line. In his speech, Mao referred repeatedly to the Kiangsi Party School, to the campaign for making steel, and to the saying of Confucius—before finally link-ing all three together.

On reading the text of Mao's speech, which does not permit one always to sense when he was employing an oral tone of sarcasm, one may gain the overall impression of defiance softened by a familiar jocularity. The jocularity is there, but beneath its surface Mao's lis-teners undoubtedly felt a sense of menace, and they realized that his hackles had been raised. A translation of his remarks, from which long-winded digressions have been omitted, still conveys something of the rambling quality which characterizes a typical speech by Mao Tse-tung.

Now we are jointly attacked by those inside and outside the party. The rightists say: What made Ch'in Shih Huang Ti fall? Because he built the Great Wall. Now we are about to collapse because of what we have done. . . . All utterances of the rightists have come into print. . . . Gentlemen, turn your ears to them! All they say is that things are in a mess. . . . Why should people be allowed to say such things? Because the divine continent [China] will not sink and the sky will not fall down. . . . It is merely that for a period vegetables and hairclips were in short supply, and there was no soap. With stocks unbalanced, the market became tight. With the market tight, everybody became tense. I think there is nothing to be tense about. If I say I am not tense it would not be true. I am tense before midnight, but after taking some sleeping pills, I am not tense during the second half of the night.

They say we are detached from the masses. But the masses still support us. I think that this was a temporary phenomenon lasting two or three months before and after the Spring Festival. . . . The cadres are leading hundreds of millions of people. At least 30 percent of them are activists, another 30 percent are pessimists. . . . The other 40 percent follow the tide. . . . In short, 30 percent plus 40 percent makes 70 percent. For a time, 350 million people were full of fanatical enthusiasm. They wanted to get things going. But during about two months before and after the Spring Festival they were unhappy and changed. When the cadres went to the countryside, the people did not talk to them; inviting them to eat, they gave them sweet potatoes and rice gruel, with faces that were unsmiling.

This was because of the "Communist wind." . . . The "Communist wind" was principally whipped up by cadres at the county and the commune level, especially some commune cadres who fleeced the production brigades and teams. . . . One month between March and April was spent to suppress this wind. Things that ought to be returned were returned, and the communes settled accounts with the production teams . . . and within the short course of one month they learned that "egalitarianism" didn't work and that "equalization, adjustment, and transfer of funds" were impracticable. I am told that the majority have now been transformed, and only a small number of them still linger after "communism" and are reluctant to part with it. . . . It was right for the government of Sung Chiang [leader of the band of outlaws in the novel *All Men Are Brothers*] to rob the rich to help the poor. . . . It is a long time since we were attacking the local bullies, dividing up their land, and turning everything they had robbed over to the people. That was all right too, because what we took was ill-gotten gains. But in "blowing the Communist wind" we took the funds, the fat pigs, and the big cabbages from the production brigades and production teams and walked away. That was wrong. Even in dealing with the properties owned by imperialists we had three ways: requisition, purchase, and squeezing them out through pressure.

Why was it that we were able to suppress this gust of wind in little more than a month? This demonstrates that our party is great, wise, and correct. . . . During the months of March, April, and May, several million cadres and hundreds of millions of peasants received an education. . . . The chief reason had been that the cadres had been unable to tell what were ill-gotten gains. They were unable to draw a clear line of demarcation, had not studied political economy, and had no understanding of the law of value, exchange of equal values, or distribution according to work done. . . . They may not understand the textbooks, but they can be taught to read them. It won't do for those at the commune level to know nothing about political economy. Things can be explained to the illiterates, and through educating them with facts, they can be made to understand things without reading books . . . it is easier for them to understand things than for the intellectuals. I have not read the textbooks, and I must read a little before I'll have the right to speak. . . . I think some problems cannot be solved at this meeting because some people will not give up their viewpoint. . . . It won't do to shut your ears to strange talk. You must get used to it. What your ears have to tolerate are nothing more than abuses directed at your ancestors. This also is difficult. When I was young, and even when I was a middle-aged person, I always felt enraged when I heard wicked words. I shall not attack unless I am attacked; if I am attacked I will certainly counterattack. Up to now I have not given up this principle. I have now learned the art of listening. I always listen with a stiffened scalp for one or two weeks before I hit back. I advise you comrades to heed what others say. You may agree or disagree with me; that is your business. If you disagree, I'll make a self-criticism if I am wrong.

Second, my advice to another section of comrades is that they must not waver at so critical a juncture. According to my observation, a section of comrades are wavering. They also say that the Great Leap Forward, the General Line and the People's Communes are correct, but we must see to which side their talks are ideologically oriented or addressed. . . . For example, they say "there are losses and gains." To place "gains" in the latter position is obviously done after much deliberation. . . . Suppose nine out of ten things we have done are bad, and all of them are published in the newspapers, then we certainly should be and will be wiped out. Then I'll leave, go back to the villages and lead the peasants to overthrow the government. If your Liberation Army doesn't follow me, then I'll look for a Red Army. But I think the Liberation Army will follow me. . . .

Among the questions I have raised, there should be added the question of unity. . . . Hold aloft the banner of unity—the unity of the people, the unity of the nation, the unity of the party. . . . People of both sides must heed what others say . . . I was not in a hurry to speak, and I bore up with a stiffened scalp. Then why don't I continue to bear up with a stiffened scalp? I have done it for twenty days, and the meeting will soon disperse. . . . Let's carry on with the meeting until the end of this month.

About the question of mess halls. Mess halls are a good thing. . . . The Investigation Group of the Academy of Sciences attacked the mess halls, attacked them on one point and neglected the rest. . . . Everybody has his shortcomings. Even Confucius. I have also seen Lenin's manuscripts which had been made a mess by changes. If there had been no mistakes, why should he have changed them? The experiment should last one or two years. I figure they will be a success.

The People's Communes will never collapse. At present, not a single one has collapsed. If they are not run properly, they will definitely collapse. The Communist party has to run things well, run the communes well, run all the enterprises well, and run well agriculture, industry, commerce, communications and transport, culture, and education. Many things you simply cannot foresee. . . . At present the planning organs do not take care of the plans. . . . The State Planning Commission and the Central Ministries had carried on for ten years. Suddenly . . . they gave up. Before August last year I devoted myself mainly to the revolution. I am absolutely no good at construction and do not understand industrial planning. But, comrades, in 1958 and 1959 the main responsibility fell on me . . . and I am to blame. "He who first made clay images of human beings to bury with the dead should have no posterity." I have no posterity (one son was killed, one son went mad). Is the inventor of taking up iron and steel smelting on a large scale K'o Ch'ing-shih or I? I say it is I. . . . In June, I talked of 10,700,000 tons, and later this was carried in the communique at Peitaiho . . . from then on we ran into trouble. The campaign was waged by ninety million people. So they say that he who first invented human images should die without posterity . . . I have read many reports discussing the matter, and most of them said that it could still be done. But the quality must be raised, the production costs and sulphur content must be lowered, and really good iron must be produced. . . . People hem and haw because they have various kinds of misgivings. People had a lot of misgivings in the first half of the month, but are outspoken now. Tell me what you want for the record. Verbal statements must be testified. Tell me what you want, and if you are able to get hold of me, purge me! Don't be afraid . . . I said at the Chengtu Conference that we must not be afraid of being thrown in jail, getting beheaded, or being expelled from the party. The reason that a high-ranking cadre has so many misgivings is that he is afraid that what he says might not be proper and he might be purged. This is what we call "being wise and protecting yourself."

Diseases enter by the mouth and all disasters come through the tongue. I'll be in great trouble today. . . . Those who disagree with me should refute me. . . . In point of fact, I am being refuted though I am not named. These views of the Kiangsi Party School and the Intermediate Party School are refutations. They say: Was he not without posterity who first made images to bury with the dead! The target of 10,700,000 tons of steel was suggested by me, and as a result, ninety million people were thrown into the battle. . . . Next the People's Commune. The People's Commune was not invented by me, but I suggested it. When I was in Shantung a reporter asked me: "Is the people's commune good?" I said: "Good," and he published a report on the strength of this in a newspaper. From now on, I must shun reporters. . . . You endorsed smelting iron and steel on a large scale and made me share what you endorse. . . . There is also the General Line, and you should share it in theory and in practice. It has been put in action in industry and agriculture. As to other tall talks, they must also be shared by others. . . . Will our current work fail in the same way as the 1927 revolution? Or will it be like the 25,000 *li* Long March with the greater part of our bases lost and the soviet region shrinking to one-tenth of its size? We cannot put things in this way. Have we failed now? All comrades present at the meeting have learned that ours is not a complete failure. We have paid too high a price, but . . . the people of the whole country have learned a lesson. . . . This trouble brought by me is a big one, and I hold myself responsible for it. Comrades, you must also analyze your own responsibilities, and you will feel better after you have broken wind and emptied your bowels.[42]

In the whole of this speech of July 23, Mao Tse-tung had not once mentioned P'eng Te-huai by name. If his challenge to P'eng Te-huai had remained implicit, he made it explicit very shortly afterwards. At the Lushan meetings he endeavored to portray P'eng and his supporters as members of a right opportunist, antiparty clique which was intent on creating a party split. P'eng was accused of having made "vicious attacks and spreading slanders inside the party and the armed forces against Mao Tse-tung, the leader of the party." The activities of his group were described as "a continuation and development of the case of the antiparty alliance of Kao Kang and Jao Shu-shih." Indeed, it was asserted that investigations had now disclosed P'eng Te-huai and Huang K'e-ch'eng, his chief of staff, to have been important members of that alliance.[43] In punishment, Mao Tse-tung insisted, P'eng Te-huai, Huang K'e-ch'eng, and their principal supporters should be dismissed.

At this point old Marshal Chu Teh is said to have demurred. He too had spoken up for less radical approaches to economic development and had observed that "the People's Communes were too early." Now, recalling the long years of guerrilla struggle they all had shared, he is reported to have observed of P'eng and his supporters: "They are comrades who ate rice cooked in the same pot." [44] Perhaps it was because of Chu Teh's intervention that the case of P'eng Te-huai and his supporters was not, like that of Kao Kang and Jao Shu-shih, treated as though it involved an antagonistic contradiction with enemies of the people. None of them were deprived of their respective positions as members or alternate members of the Central Committee or its Political Bureau. However, P'eng Te-huai was dismissed from his post as defense minister and replaced by Marshal Lin Piao. General Huang K'e-ch'eng, the chief of staff, was relieved of that job and succeeded by General Lo Jui-ch'ing, who had been serving as minister of public security. Chang Wen-t'ien was fired from his position of ranking vice minister of foreign affairs, and Chou Hsiao-chou—who had revealed to P'eng Te-huai his estimate of the true production figures in the commune which had been Mao's native village—was relieved of his post as first secretary of the party's Hunan Provincial Committee.[45]

On the day before the meetings at Lushan finally came to a close, Mao introduced for discussion a document written by an unidentified comrade who had quoted "several passages from me and Lenin," and who had taken pot shots at his "right-deviationist friends at the Lushan Conference." In submitting the document, Mao wrote:

Those friends of the splittist faction within the party who have deviated too much to the right to go any further, have you heard the

gunfire? Have your vulnerable spots been hit? You are unwilling to
heed what I say. I have 'come to the declining years like Stalin.' I am
'despotic and dictatorial' giving you neither 'freedom' nor 'democracy.'
I am 'craving for greatness and success' and being 'partial.' I have
'set a bad example to those under me.' I am also one who 'would not
change direction until he has come to the end of his wrong course,'
and 'once he turns, he turns 180 degrees.' . . . You have bombarded
me with these accusations, and nearly half of Lushan has been leveled
by your bombardment. . . . Have you seen how Lenin criticized and
repudiated renegade Plekhanov, those 'capitalist lords and their lackeys, the dying bourgeoisie and those swine and dogs dependent on it
and the petty bourgeois democratic faction'? If you have not done so,
please take a look. All right? . . . Since the secessionists and friends
of the right both cherish Marxism–Leninism, let me suggest that this
. . . document be put up for discussion by the whole party. I think
you probably will raise no objection! [46]

This was but one of a number of initiatives which Mao Tse-tung
took, at about this time, to take his side of the story to the rank and
file of the party. At the same time he agreed that high targets for
steel, coal, grain, and cotton which did not tally with realities should
be discarded. After the meetings at Lushan, the regime admitted that
its estimate of 1958 grain production had been substantially inflated.
But it claimed to have met the 1958 goals for other prime items, such
as coal and steel. The targets it announced for 1959 were set to exceed by about 10 percent the achievements claimed for 1958. The
Great Leap still was not entirely abandoned.[47]

After the Lushan plenum, Khrushchev remarked that his good
friend P'eng Te-huai, like Kao Kang before him, had committed no
offense save opposing Mao's incorrect policies towards the Soviet Union.[48] Mao Tse-tung would hardly have agreed, but on September 11,
in commenting on the case of P'eng Te-huai, he observed: "We can
never betray the fatherland and work hand-in-glove with a foreign
country. . . . At the same time, we are also not permitted to sow
discord behind the back of the Central Committee according to the
bidding of a foreign country." [49]

The dismissal of P'eng Te-huai was announced in September
1959. At the end of that month, it will be recalled, Khrushchev visited China to attend the October 1 celebration of the tenth anniversary of the founding of the Chinese People's Republic. In Mao Tse-
tung's view, Khrushchev undoubtedly came as a thrice-proven enemy.
In the spring he had torn up the agreement to provide China with
an atomic bomb; in the summer he had supported P'eng Te-huai's
challenge to Mao's authority; and in the autumn he had paid a
friendly visit on the president of the United States. Then to cap it all,
Khrushchev had proceeded, at what was intended to be a festive ban-

quet, to lecture Mao Tse-tung and his colleagues for pursuing a course towards Taiwan which endangered world peace.

Khrushchev had added insult to injury, and while Mao may have listened "with stiffened scalp," to use his phrase, it must have set his temper aboil. It accordingly is not surprising that he now turned from internal affairs—which were developing in ways he did not like but could not control—and engaged himself in open and bitter polemics with the Soviet leadership. In these polemics Mao Tse-tung reverted to the theses he had pushed during his 1957 visit to Moscow, and he developed them further. In April 1960, Mao and his propagandists loosed a particularly heavy volley which took the form of one important speech and a series of published articles, ostensibly released in celebration of the ninetieth anniversary of the birth of Lenin. In effect, these articles accused Khrushchev of "revising, emasculating, and betraying" Leninism and selling out the cause of world revolution.[50]

The counterattack by the Soviet leadership took a less public form. It took the form of a secret letter of June 12, containing an indictment of Chinese Communist policies and views. The letter was first sent to Peking, and then later in the month copies of it were distributed at an impromptu meeting of world Communist leaders who had gathered in Bucharest to attend a congress of the Rumanian party. This led to an acrimonious exchange between P'eng Chen, who headed the Chinese delegation, and Khrushchev. During this exchange Khrushchev is asserted to have likened Mao Tse-tung to Stalin, and to have denounced the Chinese leaders as "madmen" who wanted to unleash a nuclear war. P'eng Chen replied with a bitter attack on the Soviet party, and on Khrushchev himself.[51]

In the wake of the Bucharest conference, there appeared in the Soviet press a spate of articles suggesting that the Chinese Communists were inviting exclusion from the Communist bloc. The Chinese Communists were characteristically quick to sense the threat which that comment implied. Exclusion from the bloc might be expected to lead to the cutting off of Soviet economic assistance and, at least to the extent that it depended on bloc membership, to the withdrawal of Soviet military protection as well. The defiance of their reply had a ring which suggests Mao Tse-tung had a hand in its composition. The modern revisionists of the Soviet Union, the reply declared, were trying to isolate China, "but they will only isolate themselves"; the Chinese, who were prepared to rely on their own strength, would respond with "rage" and "heroism." [52]

Thereafter the Soviet Union, as the Chinese were to put it, "lost no time in taking a series of grave steps to apply economic and politi-

cal pressure, even to the extent of perfidiously and unilaterally tearing up agreements and contracts . . . to be counted, not in twos and
threes, but in hundreds." [53] In August of 1960, the more than one thousand Soviet advisers and technicians in China were withdrawn and
went home, taking their blueprints with them.[54] Now it was up to the
Chinese to make their own blueprints, complete joint construction
projects by themselves, and operate their new plants without the help
of Soviet engineers.

While Mao Tse-tung and his fellow polemicists were indulging
in this feud, China continued to sink deeper into the difficulties
caused by the Great Leap and the People's Communes. The regime
claimed a further 8 percent gain in the harvest for 1959, perhaps because its announced goal had been an increase of "about 10 percent."
But hunger soon became too apparent and widespread to be denied,
and the Chinese Communists began to complain that the country had
suffered natural disasters in 1959 and was meeting more of them in
1960—for which no agricultural production figures were released.[55]
By the winter of 1960–1961 malnutrition was widespread, diseases due
to dietary deficiency were breaking out throughout the country, some
people were dying of actual starvation, and popular discontent was
rising.[56]

Meanwhile industry, like agriculture, had become disorganized
through the application to it of the policies of the Great Leap Forward. To this disorganization were added the effects on industry of
agricultural shortfalls. The supply of those industrial raw materials
produced by agriculture was reduced, and a labor force already weakened by prolonged overwork was suffering also from the inadequacy
of its diet. Then came the termination of Soviet aid and the withdrawal of Soviet technicians which had been provoked by the polemics and defiance of Mao Tse-tung. As the result of these multiple
blows, factory chimneys all over China stopped smoking and the country settled into a deep industrial depression.

As early as the latter part of 1959 or the first part of 1960, armed
rebellions broke out in at least five of China's provinces, and it took
over a year to suppress them. P'an Fu-sheng, who had objected to Mao
Tse-tung's policies two years earlier, was proven right about the readiness of the people of Honan to revolt. In that province, and in Shantung to the east of it, members of the militia stole weapons, set up
roadblocks, seized stocks of grain, and engaged in widespread armed
robbery.[57]

The sufferings of the people, and reductions in troop rations which
left soldiers with less than 2,600 calories a day when they needed
4,000, combined to infect the armed forces with discontent. One sol-

dier was quoted by his superiors as remarking, in reference to pre-Communist days which he could not himself remember, "Some people are saying in China there once appeared a Sun Yat-sen and the grain was piled sky-high." Another was reported as asserting, "At the time of my discharge I shall not want anything but a rifle." He was asked, "Why a rifle?" His reply was: "To fight the party." [58]

The party, having drawn back too little and too late from Mao Tse-tung's Great Leap and other policies, had ridden China to a resounding fall. In January 1961, the members of the Central Committee met in plenary session. At this meeting, it would appear, Mao was unable effectively to use his tactic of isolating his principal opponents by equating their opposition to his policies with disloyalty to the party. The need for change was too self-evident, the opposition was too general, and it ran too high in the leadership. One of the principal spokesmen for those who insisted on a change was Teng Hsiao-p'ing, the secretary general of the Central Committee. It was later asserted that in 1961 Teng attacked the policies of the General Line, the Great Leap and the People's Communes, and remarked: "Any idea which cannot be carried out and does not hold water ought to be rectified regardless of who initiated it. There is no room for face-saving in this regard." [59] The majority evidently shared his view, for at this session the Central Committee decided on a far-reaching reversal of policies.[60]

In name, Mao's "three red banners" were retained. But some commune functions were quietly abandoned; small private plots were returned to the peasants, who were encouraged again to engage in sideline occupations; and free markets were expanded. In both industry and agriculture, the party cadres lost the production roles they had taken over from managers and technicians; and efforts to stimulate production through propaganda and exhortation gave way to the incentives of more pay for more work.[61]

In Kwangtung province the authorities took an additional step to help relieve the problem of unemployment—which had grown to serious proportions. They relaxed restrictions on emigration for people who wanted to go to the nearby British colony of Hong Kong in search of work. The exodus apparently began on a small scale late in 1961 or early in 1962, with a liberalization of the policies governing the issuance of exit permits. By April it had assumed the proportions of a tidal wave, with many people who held no valid exit permits flooding across the border into Hong Kong. As word of the exodus spread, people in provinces neighboring Kwangtung began to make their way towards Hong Kong in order to join in. With Hong Kong being inundated by a human flood, the British authorities made diplomatic representations in Peking, and Chou En-lai was moved to order the exodus stopped. Apparently this was easier said than done. On June 1, thousands of people, who wanted to buy tickets to the border station of Shumchun, rioted at the Canton East Railway Station, forcing the authorities to impose martial law. When quiet finally returned along the border between China and Hong Kong, that colony was left with the tasks of providing employment, housing, and social services for an estimated 142,000 illegal immigrants.[62]

In 1961 the Chinese government imported almost six million tons of grain. This was the first of a series of annual increments which were to help the people—whose average caloric intake had probably dropped to less than 1,500 per day—to regain the vigor needed for productive work.[63] The populace responded, and by the end of 1965 total production, although not per capita output, was back to the level which had prevailed before the beginning of the Great Leap.

The recovery, the beginnings of which became clearly discernible in 1962, admittedly was achieved through methods which stressed practical results rather than ideological purity. As Teng Hsiao-p'ing is supposed to have remarked at a conference that year, it does not matter whether cats are black or white; if they catch mice, then they are good cats.[64] From the standpoint of Mao Tse-tung, to follow such methods was to tread the revisionist road of his hated Soviet rivals. In his view, the life and death conflict between the proletariat and the bourgeoisie did not end with the establishment of Communist political power; this class struggle would not stop until all classes had been eliminated.[65] But with the reversal of his policies Mao had been placed in a position which for him was unusual. There was nothing unique about his being in the minority, but he was unaccustomed to being in a situation in which his strong will did not override that of a less determined majority.

12

"A House Divided"

IN THE LATTER YEARS of the Manchu dynasty, the Viceroy of Shensi—while on a trip abroad—purchased a quantity of exotic animals and birds, at the reputed cost of a million silver taels, and had them shipped to China as a present for the empress dowager. She had this menagerie, together with a few keepers he had hired, installed in a pleasure garden. Situated outside the northwest corner of Peking's city wall, the garden belonged to a younger brother of the emperor. After the overthrow of the Manchus, these imperial zoological gardens became the Peking zoo.[1]

One day in 1961 something more than a dozen men and a number of bodyguards arrived at the zoo and installed themselves in the superintendent's building. There they spent nine days in secrecy, making a study of a large collection of official documents which had been moved there for their use.

The men had been selected for this task by P'eng Chen, mayor of Peking, first secretary of the Peking Municipal Committee of the Chinese Communist party, member of the Political Bureau, and ranking member after Teng Hsiao-p'ing on the Secretariat of the Central Committee. The head of the group was Teng T'o, then only a secretary subordinate to P'eng Chen on the party's Peking municipal committee; but until 1959, he had been editor in chief of the *People's Daily*, the principal newspaper of the Chinese Communist party. The documents, on which they were to make a detailed report, comprised the instructions sent to officials of the county level and upwards—in the name of the Central Committee—during the years 1958–1961. The men were to pay special attention to those documents never formally discussed but nevertheless approved for distribution by "an individual." P'eng Chen assertedly had set up the project on the authority of an official who ranked even higher than himself. Nevertheless, it was deemed necessary to warn those engaged in the study: "Don't talk when you go out. If you talk, you alone will be responsible. No one else will take responsibility for you." They were sworn to secrecy because the "individual" whose unilaterally-issued instructions they were examining was, of course, Mao Tse-tung.

It was later charged that the purpose of the study had been to unearth sufficient evidence against Mao Tse-tung to enable other top leaders to force him to step out of his position as chairman of the party. Consequent to the arrangements made in 1956, the position of honorary chairman had been established and left vacant for his possible occupancy. As ranking vice chairman, Liu Shao-ch'i stood next in line of succession. P'eng Chen, it was alleged, expected to become prime minister. Whether or not members of the leadership hoped to bring about Mao's formal retirement to a purely honorary position, it seems clear that they wished, to the extent possible, to put him on the shelf. As one member of the study group is supposed to have observed, the history of the party showed that no mistakes in the party line had been corrected by those who made them.

To bring about the country's economic recovery would, of course, require more than the initial decision to correct wrong policy lines. It would also require control of the machinery for implementing the newly adopted policies and the ability to keep them in force long enough for them to bear fruit. As a disciplined and loyal subordinate, Liu Shao-ch'i had in 1958 proclaimed and defended Mao Tse-tung's programs, whether he believed in their wisdom or not. After the Central Committee had discarded them, loyalty to the organization required that Liu Shao-ch'i should support and defend the new policies which the Central Committee had adopted.

To do this in party meetings against so formidable an opponent as Mao Tse-tung, Liu Shao-ch'i needed as complete and well-documented a case as possible. The excerpts and commentaries prepared in the Peking zoo constituted part of that documentation. Other parts were supplied by trusted party officials who went on missions of investigation to communes, factories, mines, commercial centers, and schools in different parts of the country; the visits were made under a variety of pretexts.[2]

In addition, the other top leaders—bearing in mind the fact that Mao had not come by his title of "Great Helmsman" undeservedly—took what precautions they could, in their administration of internal affairs, to keep his hands away from the tiller. In 1956, as Mao Tse-tung was later to recall, they had "divided the standing committee of the Political Bureau into a first and second line, and set up the secretariat." "I retreated to the second line," Mao explained. "Liu Shao-ch'i and Teng Hsiao-p'ing were in the first line. Liu, as vice chairman, managed a portion of the important meetings, and Teng handled everyday affairs."[3] But Teng Hsiao-p'ing, Mao's supporters were later to charge, "consistently monopolized power, made arbitrary decisions" and, perhaps most unforgivable of all, "met Chairman Mao on equal terms and without ceremony."[4]

Mao himself later complained, "Teng Hsiao-p'ing is deaf, but when we had a meeting, he always sat in the place farthest way from me. Since 1959, he has not briefed me on the work of the Central Committee Secretariat." Teng Hsiao-p'ing and Liu Shao-ch'i, Mao asserted, had tried to pigeonhole him. They had "treated me like I was their dead parent at a funeral." [5]

The effort to strengthen the position of Liu Shao-ch'i and to weaken that of Mao Tse-tung was furthered by the publication in 1962 of a revised edition of Liu's book *How to Be a Good Communist.* Between that year and 1966, fifteen million copies of it were sold— compared to about a million and a half sets of the four-volume *Selected Works of Mao Tse-tung.*[6] The consequence was bound to be an enhancement of Liu's prestige among millions of cadres and other Chinese who studied his volume, with his name and the concept of being a good Communist tending to be equated in their minds.

In Liu's book, Chairman Mao is nowhere identified by name as the object of criticism. But Liu did attack those who "regard themselves as 'China's Marx' or 'China's Lenin,' posed as such in the party, and had the impudence to require that our party members should revere them as Marx and Lenin are revered, support them as 'the leaders,' and accord them loyalty and devotion. They went so far as to appoint themselves 'the leaders' without being chosen, climbed into positions of authority, issued orders to the party like patriarchs, tried to lecture our party, wilfully attacked and punished our party members, and pushed them around." [7]

Mao Tse-tung's thought had been equated with Marxism–Leninism before his setback of the de-Stalinization period. Then during the Great Leap Forward he had been lifted to a still higher pedestal. He had certainly demanded unquestioned loyalty and devotion. Had he appointed himself 'the leader' in 1935, without being specifically chosen? The fact that he was not elected party chairman until some years later suggests that his issuance of orders, during the intervening period, may have represented a usurpation of the authority which earlier had been exercised by the incumbent of what had been the party's top position, that of general secretary. Mao certainly had "wilfully attacked and punished" party members, "and pushed them around." Indeed, Liu Shao-ch'i's words suggest that he had been among those who had been pushed around, and that he had become sick and tired of it.

It was the foregoing criticisms which led to the subsequent charge: "What is most intolerable is that when the revised edition of *How to Be a Good Communist* was published in 1962, the spearhead of a pas-

sage in it was directed straight at our greatest leader Chairman Mao." [8]
If that passage was a spearhead which went straight to its mark, the
following additional one may have seemed a sharply pointed arrow
shot in a similar direction: "The 'left' opportunists were clearly wrong
in their attitude towards inner-party struggle. According to these almost hysterical people, any peace in the party was intolerable—even
peace based on complete unanimity on matters of principle and on the
party line. Even in the absence of any differences of principle in the
party, they deliberately hunted out targets, dubbed some comrades
'opportunist,' and set them up as 'straw men' to shoot at in inner-party
struggle." Liu continued, "We should not break with comrades who
have committed errors but who are nevertheless loyal. . . . We should
not castigate or expel them unless they persist in their mistakes and
prove incorrigible." [9]

The struggle against P'eng Te-huai and his supporters was still
fresh in people's minds when this revised edition of Liu's book was
published. It could not be seriously asserted that that struggle had
been waged at a time when there was unanimity on the party line,
but it had certainly been waged in the spirit which Liu Shao-ch'i decried.

The case of P'eng Te-huai was obviously and intimately related
to the issue of Mao Tse-tung's political power. Communist China had,
of course, three major bases of political power: the party, and the
other two bases it was supposed to control—the military establishment
and the civil administration. The majority of the party's Central Committee had sided with Mao's opponents in the top leadership and discarded his policies. This was a severe blow to his prestige, but the
defeat was not necessarily final since the new policies might at some
propitious time be reversed. But the defeat would be converted to
probably permanent loss of power if the Central Committee—which
had voted to deprive P'eng Te-huai of his post—voted to restore him
to it. In that event, power over the defense establishment, the second
of the three power bases, would pass to one of Mao's staunchest opponents. The civil administration, the third of the power bases, could
not be expected thereafter to side with Mao Tse-tung. Liu Shao-ch'i
was its chairman, and he was allied with Mao's opponents. The civil
administration would obey the party, as represented by its new majority, which would be fortified by its control of the army.

Mao Tse-tung appears to have recognized from the start that
Marshal P'eng Te-huai, discharged from his ministry of defense post
but still a member of the Political Bureau, would remain a source of
potential danger. After the Lushan plenum, an office was set up, under

Marshal Ho Lung, for the purpose of conducting a detailed investigation of P'eng Te-huai's past behavior and preparing recommendations for further action in his case. Undoubtedly Mao hoped thereby to eliminate the likelihood that P'eng might stage a comeback.[10]

Marshal Ho Lung, if subsequent revelations are to be believed, had been one of the leaders who had encouraged P'eng Te-huai in his opposition to Mao Tse-tung. If this charge was true, then Ho Lung might seem to have been a poor choice for the job. But Mao Tse-tung may have selected him for it as part of a deliberate strategy aimed at multiple objectives. It will be recalled that Mao Tse-tung, thirty years earlier, had given Ch'en Yi the task of liquidating a group of his opponents—party comrades with whom Ch'en Yi was probably in sympathy—during the affair known as the Fut'ien incident. Ch'en Yi had executed them and thereby placed himself irrevocably on Mao's side.

Mao Tse-tung had in effect presented Ho Lung with the old proposition of "heads I win, tails you lose." If Ho Lung refused the task or performed it unsatisfactorily, he would stand convicted of opposing Chairman Mao. If he carried it out to the chairman's satisfaction, he would thereby alienate Mao's opponents and place himself in Mao's camp. But if he had indeed encouraged P'eng Te-huai, then he would also be placing himself at Mao's mercy. The more serious the case he constructed against P'eng Te-huai the more damaging the indictment he would be preparing against himself.

In the event, Ho Lung accepted the assignment but stalled for over a year. Meanwhile it became obvious that the Great Leap was a disastrous failure, and Mao Tse-tung's position became correspondingly weakened. Ho Lung, it is asserted, then prepared a report in which he tried to vindicate P'eng Te-huai.[11]

The effort to vindicate P'eng Te-huai and to further undermine Mao's authority evidently was pushed forward at various official levels, and carried on—in thinly disguised fashion—even in the public press, the field of literature, and on the stage. It was overtly encouraged in the field of literature by an official immediately responsible to Chou Yang, the party's deputy director of propaganda, and it evidently was supported covertly by still higher-ranking ones.[12]

Three of the most noteworthy participants in the cultural sphere were immediate subordinates of P'eng Chen, the party boss of Peking. One of them was Teng T'o, whom P'eng Chen had entrusted with the task of conducting the studies at the Peking zoo, and who had thereby come into possession of a rich fund of information about party and governmental affairs. Teng T'o had a personal stake in bringing about a reversal of the 1959 verdicts. He had himself been one of the victims;

it was in 1959 that he was discharged from his influential position of editor in chief of the *People's Daily*.[13] A second was Wu Han, vice mayor of Peking, noted historian and famous playwright. These two men sometimes collaborated with a third, named Liao Mo-sha, who was an official on P'eng Chen's Peking party committee. Many of their satirical stories and essays, published under the titles "Notes from the Three-Family Village" and "Evening Chats on Yenshan," were intended as criticisms of Mao Tse-tung's qualities of leadership, his external policies, and his internal failures. Wu Han wrote at least one essay and a number of plays which were intended as attacks on Mao Tse-tung's treatment of P'eng Te-huai and as pleas for P'eng's reinstatement in office.

In these articles, the policies being ridiculed were dealt with in double-talk, and in neither them nor in the plays was Mao Tse-tung or P'eng Te-huai identified by name. Teng T'o's language sometimes was Aesopian, and Wu Han's plays dealt with past dynasties. But intelligent Chinese readers would not have trouble in identifying Mao Tse-tung as the boastful athlete—in one of Teng T'o's stories—who bragged he had once broken the Olympic record for the broad jump. It would be obvious to them what Teng T'o had in mind when he ridiculed the assertion by a neighbor's child that "the East Wind is our benefactor and the West Wind is our enemy." "Such cliches," Wu Han said, were examples of "big empty talk." Only less perceptive members of the public needed later to be informed by Mao's supporters that the one reference constituted "vilification of our Great Leap Forward" and that the other was an attack on Chairman Mao's "scientific thesis" that "the East Wind prevails over the West Wind" in world affairs. Similarly, sophisticated theatergoers, attending *Hai Jui Dismissed from Office*, were sure to see—in that play by Wu Han about the loyal minister of a past dynasty, punished by his sovereign for his honest criticisms—the parallel case of P'eng Te-huai's dismissal by Mao Tse-tung.

Teng T'o's satire was far from gentle. In an article entitled "A Special Treatment for Amnesia," he wrote that people suffering from this disease often forget what they have said, go back on their word, and do not keep their promises. The disease also leads to abnormal anger, losing one's temper, and finally may end in insanity or idiocy. "Thus if anyone finds . . . these symptoms present in himself, he must promptly take a complete rest and say nothing and do nothing, and if he insists on speaking and acting, he will come to grief." A cure, he suggested, might be effected by hitting the patient over the head with a special club, to induce shock. And it was imperative that treatment be administered by a competent doctor. "The family of the patient must not make any decision on its own, and, in particular, the patient himself must not interfere."

In *Hai Jui Scolds the Emperor,* Wu Han portrays the loyal but outspoken minister as upbraiding his sovereign in the following terms.

You did a fairly good job in your early years, but what has happened to you now? . . . by suspecting court officials, you are mean to your subordinates . . . the peasants begin to revolt everywhere. . . . Your shortcomings are numerous: rudeness, short-temperedness, self-right-eousness, and deafness to honest criticism. But worst of all is your search for immortality. . . . The most urgent problems today are the absurdity of imperial policies and the lack of clarity of official respon-sibilities. If you do not tackle these problems now, nothing will be accomplished.

For such advice the minister Hai Jui had been dismissed from office; but after the emperor died, he was deservedly restored to his previous position.[14]

P'eng Te-huai's own initial reaction had apparently been one of resignation to his lot. Even before his 1959 clash with Mao, he told his wife: "I am old. The chairman doesn't like me. . . . I have defeated Chiang Kai-shek and imperialism. My wish has been fulfilled. I can go home and plow the land. I don't care whether he likes me or not!" After the Lushan plenum he said to her, "Now that I am out of office, I feel free." [15]

But by 1962 the atmosphere, as the essays of Teng T'o and the dramas of Wu Han would suggest, had undergone a marked change. In January, Liu Shao-ch'i, in addressing a Central Expanded Opera-tions Conference of seven thousand cadres, is stated to have supported reversal of the verdicts by expressing his disapproval of past "ruthless struggles," as well as of the "merciless blows" administered to the vic-tims.[16] In June 1962, P'eng Te-huai—assertedly with the backing of P'eng Chen—circulated a long document in which he requested the reconsideration of his case and the nullification of the decision reached against him.[17]

However, P'eng Te-huai's case was flawed by the circumstance of his having criticized Mao's policies while in the Soviet Union, which enabled Mao to charge that he should be regarded as guilty of treason. If the Maoists were to be believed, "P'eng Te-huai is a man who main-tains illicit relations with a foreign country and who, in coordination with the Khrushchevian modern revisionists, aims to overthrow the dictatorship of the proletariat in China." Again, if they were to be believed, Liu Shao-ch'i "tried to help P'eng Te-huai rise again and resume command of the armed forces, so as to realize his . . . plot of usurping the leadership." [18]

As things turned out, Liu Shao-ch'i might have been wise to dispute this harsh interpretation of P'eng Te-huai's relations with the Soviet leadership, and to have helped him fight his case through to a conclusion. Instead, perhaps too cautious, too prone to compromise, and too unlike Mao Tse-tung—with his fighter's instinct for the jugular—Liu appears to have shied away from the struggle this would have entailed. In his speech of January 1962, Liu asserted that opposition to Mao Tse-tung constituted opposition only to an individual; that it was no offense for anybody to speak his mind at party meetings; and that those sharing P'eng's viewpoint might be rehabilitated providing they were not guilty of treason.[19] Thus he seems to have stood by those who had supported P'eng Te-huai, but to have given up the battle in the case of P'eng himself.

If Liu Shao-ch'i yielded in the case of P'eng Te-huai, he and his colleagues nevertheless held stubbornly to their defense of the policies intended to promote the country's economic recovery. Mao Tse-tung realized, of course, that his opponents' support arose from assessments that the country had suffered a debacle that had resulted from his own policies. When the new policies had been in effect for only a year, he was alleging that the situation was "extremely favorable." At the January 1962 conference, Teng Hsiao-p'ing in effect contradicted Mao. Teng told the seven thousand cadres in attendance: "It was the political situation which the chairman found extremely favorable . . . not only can you not describe the economic situation as being favorable, but it is extremely unfavorable." [20] For outside consumption, the period was described as one of temporary difficulties caused by natural calamities —which had resulted in three bad crop years—and by the withdrawal of Soviet aid. But at the same January meeting, Liu Shao-ch'i expressed the opinion that China's troubles had been "70 percent man-made" meaning, presumably, that Mao Tse-tung's policies had been largely responsible.[21]

Early in 1962, Liu Shao-ch'i arranged for Vice Premier Ch'en Yün, who had opposed Mao's adventurist policies beginning in 1957 and had been inactive since the beginning of the Great Leap, to assume the post of chairman of the Central Committee's subcommittee on financial affairs. Working in collaboration with Teng Hsiao-p'ing and P'eng Chen, the two top members of the Secretariat, Ch'en Yün and his subcommittee found that the government had a huge budget deficit. They submitted their report in May, after which Liu Shao-ch'i and his colleagues confronted Mao Tse-tung with Ch'en Yün's findings—in order, according to later and unfriendly accounts, "to blackmail Chairman Mao." Mao Tse-tung made known his displeasure that Liu Shao-ch'i had arranged for Ch'en Yün to be given this position, but he was evidently unable to rebut Ch'en's report. According to Chou En-lai, in view of the budget deficit Mao Tse-tung "gave us five years as an adjustment period." [22] This suggests that Mao perhaps agreed, at this point, to the continuance during that period of the economic policies which Liu Shao-ch'i and his supporters were endeavoring to maintain.

Mao Tse-tung's policies having been reversed in 1961, the agreed five-year period of adjustment would not expire before 1966. If Mao were nevertheless to attempt the early overturn of the regime's economic policies, he probably would have been prevented from doing so by his opponents. They controlled the party Secretariat and presumably enjoyed the support of a majority of the members and alternate members of the Central Committee. These circumstances may explain the fact that Mao Tse-tung called that committee into plenary session only once in the years between 1961 and 1966. However, the party constitution adopted in 1956 provides that the Political Bureau, of which Mao was chairman, shall call such sessions at least twice a year; that the National Party Congress shall elect a new Central Committee each five years; and that the party congress itself shall, except under extraordinary conditions, be called into yearly session. Under these provisions, new elections to the Central Committee should have been held in 1961. The "extraordinary conditions" which prevented its meeting for that purpose then and in immediately subsequent years were, one may presume, those which involved a split leadership.

Thus the constitutionally prescribed term of the Eighth Central Committee had expired in 1961, but Mao Tse-tung nevertheless called it into plenary session in September 1962. P'eng Te-huai had made a formal request for the reconsideration of his case. Since it had been the Central Committee which had adopted the verdict in that case, it presumably was only the Central Committee which could reverse or reconfirm it. Mao Tse-tung probably could not hope to induce the committee also to remove P'eng Te-huai from the Political Bureau. But with Liu Shao'ch'i evidently unwilling to support P'eng's reinstatement as minister of defense, Mao Tse-tung could realistically expect to have the original verdict reconfirmed. If it were reconfirmed, then it might also prove possible to remove two of P'eng's supporters from their positions on the party Secretariat. These were General Huang K'e-ch'eng—who had been relieved of his position as chief of staff of the armed forces at the Lushan plenum, but not from his concurrent post in the Secretariat, and General T'an Cheng—who had served under P'eng Te-huai as chief of the General Political Department of the People's Liberation Army. Finally, if Mao Tse-tung could not reverse the economic policies in force, he at least could attack the revisionist ideology on which they were based.

At this 1962 session Mao Tse-tung was, as usual, the presiding offi-

cer, and it would appear that he got his way insofar as the reinstatement of P'eng Te-huai is concerned. The communique released at the
end of the session stated: "The great historic significance of the Eighth
Plenary Session of the Eighth Central Committee held in Lushan in
August 1959 lies in the fact that it victoriously smashed attacks by right
opportunism, that is, revisionism, and safeguarded the party line and
the unity of the party." That communique also announced the removal
from the Secretariat of General Huang K'e-ch'eng and General T'an
Cheng, and the appointment to that body of General Lo Jui-ch'ing,
Lu Ting-yi and K'ang Sheng.[23] Lo Jui-ch'ing had succeeded Huang
K'e-ch'eng as chief of staff. It was K'ang Sheng, "China's Beria," who
had been demoted during the 1956 period of Mao's de-Stalinization.
And Lu Ting-yi was the director of the Propaganda Department of
the party's Central Committee. On the face of it, these appointments
may have appeared to strengthen Mao's influence within the Secretariat. In actual fact, K'ang Sheng was the only one, among the three,
who proved to be a loyal supporter of Mao Tse-tung.

At some point in the proceedings, Mao Tse-tung referred to the
semi-overt campaign of propaganda being conducted against him. In
an undoubtedly sarcastic vein, he remarked: "The use of novels to
carry out antiparty activities is a great invention. In order to overthrow
a political power, it is always necessary to create public opinion, to do
work in the ideological sphere." Perhaps with the thought in mind of
the work in that sphere which he himself would undertake, he added,
"This is true for the revolutionary class as well as for the counter-revolutionary class." [24]

Given Mao Tse-tung's character, it must be assumed that he had
put up a strenuous fight, at the earlier plenum of January 1961, against
the new policies which it adopted. In all likelihood he objected that
they would create a situation favorable to a comeback in China of
"unregenerate landlord and capitalist elements." The communique released following that plenum did concede that "an extremely small
number of landlord and bourgeois elements . . . are always attempting to stage a comeback" and that there were, within the regime, a
small percentage of functionaries drawn from such elements who had
not been sufficiently remolded, and others who had "degenerated owing
to the influence and corrosion of the reactionary classes." At the other
end of the spectrum, it noted, were some functionaries who "lack sufficient understanding of the distinction between socialism and communism . . . and of the socialist society's principles of . . . 'to each according to his work' and more income for those who work more." In
view of all this, a rectification movement was being carried out, it
noted, among the functionaries in rural and urban areas.[25]

At the September 1962 plenum, Mao endeavored to turn rectification more predominantly to his purposes, reinforced his warnings about the dangers of revisionism, and set forth theses which foreshadowed the "Great Proletarian Cultural Revolution" which he was to launch several years later. In a speech entitled "Never Forget the Class Struggle," Mao Tse-tung held that it would be necessary to guard against the overthrow of the proletariat by the bourgeoisie throughout the period of the transition to communism. Yugoslavia had undergone a qualitative change, with control passing from the workers and peasants and into the hands of "reactionary nationalists." The USSR was pursuing Khrushchev's "revisionist policy line," was praising Yugoslavia as Marxist–Leninist, and was criticizing China as adventurist, doctrinaire, and sectarian. Thus history had proven that classes still exist in a state which is under socialism and that a revolution can be overthrown even in a Communist country.

In the world arena, it would be necessary for China to support the "national liberation movements of the broad masses of Asia, Africa, and Latin America." Internally, China was not itself free from revisionism. Recognizing that there is a "spontaneous tendency towards capitalism" among the people, whereas "scientific socialism" is created only through conscious effort, Mao held that revisionism posed the danger of the revival in China of a capitalist and hence "reactionary" class. It accordingly would be necessary to educate the youth well. If the younger generation were to become revisionist, maintaining socialism in name but restoring capitalism in fact, then the succeeding generation would be forced to wage a new revolution against its parents. It would be necessary, Mao Tse-tung held, also to educate the masses, the cadres, and even the old leaders.[26]

In this speech Mao Tse-tung implicitly challenged Liu Shao-ch'i and his supporters on the basis of the policies they were following and the policy views, different from his own, which they had expressed. Liu Shao-ch'i allegedly had expressed the opinions that it would be desirable, in the interest of truthful reporting, that the New China News Agency should not be officially run; that stressing "standpoint" led to subjective and one-sided rather than objective news; and that it was important both to report about "imperialism"—meaning the United States and its friends—"as it is," and to report "about the mistakes of the Communist parties as they are." [27] To do this, in Mao's view, would be to forget the class struggle, because nothing can be considered independent of class viewpoint.

Following the cutting off of Soviet aid and the recall of Soviet experts in 1960, Liu is asserted to have stated: "Because we are preoccupied with our own cares, how can we [afford to] provoke United States imperialism or Soviet revisionism by aiding the struggle of the revolutionary people of the world?" During the "three difficult years" Liu is supposed to have advocated the reduction of Chinese external assistance programs.[28] In view of Liu Shao-ch'i's cautious and pragmatic nature, it is likely that there was truth in these accusations. To the extent that there was, Mao Tse-tung's insistence that Communist China support the "national liberation movements of the broad masses of Asia, Africa, and Latin America" was a rebuke to Liu Shao-ch'i.

In the sphere of internal policy, Mao Tse-tung's insistence on the need for a continuous class struggle had, as one of its corollaries, repudiation of the trend towards individual farming which assertedly had been promoted and defended by, among others, Liu Shao-ch'i and party Secretary General Teng Hsiao-p'ing.[29] In holding up Yugoslavia as the horrible example of a state which had deserted the Communist road, Mao was perhaps pointing an accusatory finger at both Liu Shao-ch'i and Vice Premier Ch'en Yün. Ch'en Yün had favored "democracy" at the production-unit level, and this would have led China in the direction of a Yugoslav-type economy.[30] Liu Shao-ch'i reportedly had complained that the cooperatives, like everything else, were being officially managed, and that a high degree of state intervention in the economy led to undesirable bureaucratism.[31]

Mao clearly meant that all within the leadership who approved a policy of allowing the operation of a substantial private sector were wrong. A private sector might fill in the gaps inevitably left by the socialist, planned sector; but it would encourage the spontaneous tendency towards capitalism. Those who enjoyed the fruits of that sector would seek to expand it, and China would tend to revert from communism to capitalism. His speech implied that the leadership was falling down on the job of providing proper socialist education for the next generation of revolutionary successors, and that not only the ordinary cadres but also the older leaders themselves needed remoulding.

Conditions in China had improved, by September 1962, but not enough to provide a margin which could be risked by any substantial change in the policies which were evidently promoting recovery. In the spring of 1962 millions of idle workers in the cities had been urged to go to the countryside, where they could help raise food and where they would be closer to its source. They were, of course, generally unwelcome; the peasants regarded them as so many additional mouths to feed. It was to escape from this dilemma that some hundreds of thousands from the Canton area tried to cross over into the nearby British colony of Hong Kong in search of work. Despite the efforts of the Hong Kong authorities to prevent their entry, and to round up and send back those who succeeded in crossing the border, over 140,000 remained in Hong Kong at the end of the exodus.[32] Meanwhile a similar movement had been underway among ethnic minorities in the far western province of Sinkiang, or Chinese Turkestan. There some tens of thousands crossed the border and sought refuge among ethnically similar peoples in adjacent parts of the Soviet Union.[33] It accordingly is not surprising that the communique of the September 1962 plenum announced no significant changes in economic policy.

The communique did, however, note that "some of our work is not well done. For instance, because of the incompetence of leading cadres, some production teams, some factories, and some business establishments have produced less or become unwelcome to the masses. We should endeavor to change this state of affairs and improve the work of those units without delay." [34] As this suggests, the rectification started earlier was to be continued if still underway or resumed if it were not. Mao Tse-tung had urged the need for proper socialist education of the youth, the ordinary cadres and the old leaders. As it unfolded in the following months, the program of rectification came to be known as the Socialist Education Movement. If the Central Committee had specifically agreed to the undertaking of this movement, it was evidently an agreement in principle, with the guidelines left for the top leaders to work out among themselves. If Liu Shao-ch'i had forebodings about the channels into which Mao would try to direct it, Liu may have taken reassurance from the fact that he and his supporters controlled the party machinery which would carry it forward.

During the approximately four years which the Socialist Education Movement lasted, four sets of instructions were issued for the guidance of those who directed it. The Chinese Communists have attributed the first and the last to Mao Tse-tung and the other two to Liu Shao-ch'i and members of the party Secretariat.[35] Their style and content are consistent with this attribution.

Mao Tse-tung's initial document, dated May 20, 1963, was described as a "draft resolution" and contained ten points. They were preceded by a section in which Mao complained that existing problems in the party's conduct of work in rural areas had been pointed out in the past but "were not presented in a clear-cut and systematic way." It was, he said, therefore "necessary that these problems be explained again in a manner which is both clear and systematic." Since 1960, he asserted, "we have worked hard to draft this resolution." In a succeeding and very long paragraph Mao delivered a philosophical lecture on the subject, "Where do correct ideas come from?" He then posed and proceeded to answer the question, "What exactly are the ten problems of current rural work?" However, he hardly achieved his aim of setting them forth and explaining them "in a clear-cut and systematic way."

Mao first identified the Central Committee documents dealing with agriculture which had been issued during the preceding two years, and indicated their general purposes. Next he asserted, "Conditions of agricultural production are becoming better each year . . . producing great impact on accelerating the development of the national economy." Then, without citing any other reason for his conclusion, he stated: "All this serves to explain that it was groundless for some comrades to entertain pessimistic views in the past towards the rural situation and the conditions of agricultural production. All this also proves the total correctness and greatness of the party in raising high the Three Red Banners of the General line, the People's Communes, and the Great Leap Forward."

In the immediately succeeding paragraphs Mao repeated his view that class struggle provided the means for "uniting the people in order to carry out smoothly socialist reforms and socialist construction." In this struggle, the party should "rely on the poor peasants and lower-middle peasants," and it should organize them. It should also base its policy on unity. "By unity," he stated, "we mean unity of more than 95 percent of the masses and of more than 95 percent of the cadres for the struggle against the class enemy and nature."

It will be recognized, on the basis of the foregoing, that Mao Tse-tung was a man who was not made uncomfortable by contradictions. Some of the remaining paragraphs contain specific injunctions as to the procedures to be followed, but organization men like Liu Shao-ch'i and Teng Hsiao-p'ing could hardly regard the draft as a whole to be a satisfactory basis for conducting a mass campaign. Nor could they believe that class struggle conducted by "a revolutionary class army" of poor and lower-middle peasants would benefit agricultural production.

Accordingly, a second document of ten points was prepared which was intended to set forth concrete policies. It contained numerous provisos designed to ensure that production would remain undisturbed and that such economic freedoms as the right to till private plots, engage in sideline occupations, and enjoy access to rural free markets might be preserved. Its drafters evidently also endeavored to ensure that the class struggle would be tempered through the observance of such laws and regulations as promised some measure of protection to individual human rights.

Mao Tse-tung could not have been pleased with this draft. The concern of Liu Shao-ch'i and his supporters for prescribed procedures, due process, and legal safeguards was probably as distasteful to Mao Tse-tung as was their anxiety to preserve a private sector in the economy. The record suggests that they had quite different attitudes on

the subject of the rule of law. In 1956, during the de-Stalinization period, Liu had declared: "One of the urgent tasks facing our state at
present is to begin the systematic codification of a fairly complete set
of laws and to put the legal system of the country on a sound footing." [36] In the spring of 1959, when Mao Tse-tung had been riding
high, the Ministry of Justice had been abolished.[37]

In June 1964, at a meeting of the Standing Committee of the Political Bureau attended also by the first secretaries of the party's regional bureaus, Mao Tse-tung discussed the Socialist Education Movement and laid down what were, in his opinion, the proper standards
for evaluating the movement.[38] He must, at this meeting or elsewhere,
have expressed his discontent with this second ten-point document.
Within about three months Liu had prepared a revised version. His
wife later declared that Mao Tse-tung had told him to do so, and the
changes he made in this revision are consistent with an effort to meet
the kinds of objections Mao might be expected to raise. In this version
Liu incorporated the set of standards Mao Tse-tung had advocated;
he also omitted or reversed the purport of some passages of his earlier draft, passages which had been designed to mitigate class struggle
and maintain small areas of freedom in the economy. The Maoists
later criticized this version as "outwardly 'left' but essentially
'right.' " [39]

In January 1965, Mao Tse-tung called a National Work Conference at the conclusion of which another document was issued. This
was the fourth in the series and was described as having been prepared
under Mao's direct supervision. Its "Twenty-Three Articles" left the
situation in such a muddle that the regime's media were flooded with
inquiries requesting definition of the line between legitimate side-line
occupations and ones associated with "spontaneous tendencies towards
capitalism." The editors could only reply that such occupations had
a dual nature. They served a "progressive economic function" but still
were "potentially ruinous." [40]

At least some portions of Mao's two documents read like transcripts of his impromptu speeches and remind one of Teng T'o's essay
on "Great Empty Talk." In a perhaps unfairly sweeping criticism of
Mao's semi-opaque and verbose style, Teng said: "Some people have
the gift of gab. They can talk endlessly on any occasion, like water
flowing from an undammed river. After listening to them, however,
when you try to recall what they have said, you can remember nothing." He went on to complain, "Making long speeches without really
saying anything, making confusion worse confounded by explaining,
or giving explanations which are not explanatory—these are the characteristics of great empty talk." Perhaps recalling that it may enable

great men to dominate the meetings of lesser beings which they attend and often chair, he conceded it had its uses. "Still," he said, "it will be quite awful if great empty talk should be made into a prevalent fashion indulged in on every occasion and even cultivated as a special skill. It will be still more disastrous if our children should be taught this skill and turned into hordes of experts in great empty talk." In conclusion he offered a piece of advice which Mao certainly would have rejected. It was, "I would advise those friends given to great empty talk to read more, think more, say less, and take a rest when the time comes for talking, so as to save their own as well as other people's time and energy." [41]

It would, however, have been no waste of the time and energy of Mao's opponents had they pondered well and taken adequate countermeasures against the threat contained in one of his twenty-three articles. "The key point of this movement is to rectify those people in positions of authority within the party who take the capitalist road . . . some are out in the open and some are concealed. Of the people who support them, some are at lower levels and some are at higher levels. . . . Among those at higher levels, there are some . . . even in the work of provincial and Central Committee departments, who oppose socialism." After much verbiage, he added, "In the movement, we must boldly unleash the masses; we must not be like women with bound feet." [42]

By the time these passages had been written, Teng T'o, Wu Han, and the other critics were no longer writing and publishing their criticisms of Mao Tse-tung. Teng T'o had sensed the shift of winds early. During the same month that the Central Committee had met in 1962, he announced the discontinuance of "Evening Chats on Yenshan." His last essay was entitled "Thirty-Six Strategems." In it he commented, "Of all thirty-six strategems, to depart is best." [43] Departing, however, was not a strategem Liu Shao-ch'i could use, and his opposition to Mao Tse-tung had brought the two leaders to a parting of the ways. It has been reliably reported that Liu Shao-ch'i refused, in January 1965, to accept the twenty-three article directive, and that Mao Tse-tung then decided that "Liu had to go." [44]

13
The Barrel of the Gun

WHEN Marshal P'eng Te-huai challenged Mao Tse-tung's policies in 1959, he apparently attempted to do so in his capacity as member of the party's Political Bureau, rather than in his role of minister of national defense. He initiated his challenge at a meeting of that bureau, held just before the Central Committee's plenum. However concerned he may have been about the impact of Mao's policies on his defense establishment, the concerns P'eng voiced were ones related primarily to the country as a whole. Nevertheless Mao Tse-tung, who liked to observe that "political power grows out of the barrel of the gun," evidently gave priority to Peng's removal from the Ministry of National Defense, rather than from the Political Bureau.

In succeeding P'eng Te-huai, Marshal Lin suffered under the twin handicaps of unimpressive public presence and impaired health. Somewhat under average height, gaunt and pale, his appearance would have been quite undistinguished but for bushy eyebrows and a nose which is, for a Chinese, unusually prominent. He had led an apparently charmed life from the time of his graduation from the Whampoa Military Academy until the outbreak of the war with Japan, and during the intervening decade he had established a legendary reputation as a successful military tactician. In 1937, however, he had been so seriously wounded that he had to be sent for treatment to the Soviet Union, where he remained until 1942. Lin held a major command during the civil war which followed the defeat of Japan, but his recovery from his wounds reputedly remained incomplete, and it had been P'eng Te-huai who had been given command of the Chinese troops who fought in the Korean war.

Lin appears nevertheless to have brought drive and determination, as well as outstanding ability, to the tasks of reorganizing the military establishment and making it responsive to his will. What he willed, of course, was determined in part by the circumstances under which he had become minister of national defense. Because he had come to the post consequent to Mao's contest with powerful opponents, their subsequent efforts to break Mao's power were implicit threats to his own position. This circumstance of shared interest in political survival ensured that Lin Piao would be the dependable ally of Mao

Tse-tung. Indeed, in his first published article, after assuming his post, he pledged "the unconditional loyalty of the People's Liberation Army to the party and Comrade Mao." [1]

Lin Piao evidently considered that his initial task, in ensuring the defense establishment's responsiveness to his will, was the thorough eradication of the influence of his predecessor. In theory, perhaps, the transfer of loyalties within an organization should occur automatically when one chief leaves and another succeeds him. In practice, a complete transfer of loyalties seldom occurs immediately. Especially at levels where there is close contact with the chief, the response accorded him by virtue of his position becomes reinforced by the regard he wins on a personal basis. When his successor takes over, the organizational loyalty due that successor may be diluted by enduring feeling for the former chief. In pre-Communist China, the importance of personal relationships was both greater than among people in other countries and more generally recognized. Supposedly all this had been changed, in Communist China, by the new cement of a shared ideology. But the treatment Lin Piao accorded ranking officers who had worked long and closely with P'eng Te-huai suggests that he did not overestimate the differences between Communist China and the old society out of which it had been born.

Of seven officers in the Ministry of Defense who had held the rank of vice minister before Lin Piao took over, four were reappointed. Their influence was diluted, however, in consequence of the appointment of six additional vice ministers. Further, the military records of the four who were reappointed suggest that none of them had risen through previous close association with P'eng Te-huai. On the other hand one of the four, T'an Cheng, had served under Lin Piao during the 1930s, and in the late 1940s he had been director of the political department of Lin's Fourth Field Army.[2]

The changes which Lin Piao made in the General Headquarters of the People's Liberation Army came very close to being a clean sweep of the supreme command. Seven departments were reorganized into three: The General Staff Department, General Political Department, and Rear Services Department. As the new chief of staff, Lo Jui-ch'ing took over the first of those departments. Vice Minister T'an Cheng was initially kept on in the concurrent post of director of the General Political Department. However, the head of the Rear Services Department, who had handled logistics for P'eng Te-huai during the Korean War, was replaced by Ch'iu Hui-tso, who had served with Lin Piao's Fourth Field Army. The former heads of the other departments either left the headquarters or stayed on in subordinate positions.[3]

The General Political Department was responsible for the chain of

command represented by the political commissars and their subordinates. Under the party constitution, it had charge of the ideological
and organizational work of the party in the army "under the general
direction of the Central Committee." [4] Mao Tse-tung was evidently
determined that this direction should be exercised through a body
which he believed he could control. That body was the Military Affairs
Committee, a *de facto* body nowhere provided for in the party constitution. It is generally assumed that Mao is its ex officio chairman
and the minister of defense its operational head.[5]

The Military Affairs Committee had existed before Lin Piao assumed office. But it apparently was then not a very active body, and
little was heard of it before 1958. P'eng Te-huai, who had felt uncomfortable in Mao's presence ever since 1953, evidently preferred
using his minister of national defense hat to working through Mao's
Military Affairs Committee. When Lin Piao became minister, however,
he and Mao established a "new" Military Affairs Committee, with at
least seven of China's ten marshals and two senior generals on its
standing committee. Marshal P'eng, of course, was not one of the
seven, nor was the aging Chu Teh, who had spoken up in his defense
at the Lushan plenum.[6]

Within the first year after he had assumed office, Lin Piao began
efforts to convert the armed forces into a political base for Mao Tse-
tung. Despite all the staff changes so recently made in the high command, this apparently brought Lin Piao into immediate conflict with
the directors of the two departments most immediately concerned.
According to work papers circulated within the People's Liberation
Army in the autumn of 1960, General T'an Cheng opposed Lin Piao's
proposal that his General Political Department should use "Chairman
Mao's works as the principal subject of our study." [7] There is also
evidence that Chief of Staff Lo Jui-ch'ing supported his position, declaring that to "make Chairman Mao's books the supreme directive
for all kinds of work in our army" would "not conform to the system
of our state." [8] That, of course, was true. The party constitution provided that "the Communist party of China takes Marxism–Leninism
as its guide to action." [9] The phrase equating Marxism–Leninism and
the thought of Mao Tse-tung had been deliberately removed when the
party constitution was revised in 1956. At the same time, as if to drive
the point home, there was inserted a sentence which pointed out that
"no . . . person can be free from shortcomings and mistakes in
work." [10]

General T'an Cheng, apparently in consequence of his opposition,
was relieved of his duties as director of the General Political Depart-

ment, and Marshal Lo Jung-huan, a former director, was brought back to supervise its operations. The whole matter was handled so quietly, however, that T'an Cheng's dismissal did not become generally known until several years later, when—Marshal Lo having died—General Hsiao Hua was formally designated director of the General Political Department.[11] General Lo Jui-ch'ing was not similarly dismissed, but his opposition may have marked the beginnings of a split between him and his minister of defense.

The opposition which Lin Piao had encountered did not, of course, deter him from pressing ahead with his proposal. At an enlarged conference of the Military Affairs Committee, which lasted from September 14 to October 20, 1960, Lin Piao demanded a "breakthrough" in ideological work. In response, the committee adopted a resolution which declared that Mao Tse-tung's thought was the "basis for our army in the past, present, and future" and called for a radical overhaul both of the content and of the machinery of political education in the armed forces.[12] At about this same time, Mao Tse-tung brought out the fourth volume of his *Selected Works*.[13] It seems unlikely that the timing was purely coincidental.

One aspect of this new stress on political work was the recruitment within the armed forces of new party members. In 1961 the General Political Department reported that over 229,000 such members had been recruited during the preceding year.[14] Efforts were made to maintain this momentum, and again in 1965 it was reported some "hundreds of thousands" of officers and soldiers joined the party.[15] It could be argued that this campaign was designed to strengthen party control over the army. But it may have been intended also to justify a bigger voice for the military in party affairs. Another campaign, begun in 1962 to the accompaniment of a directive from Mao Tse-tung, called for the building up of the militia. It doubtless was motivated in large part by concerns no different from those which had caused him, in 1958, to launch an "Everyone a Soldier" movement. But it also brought many civilians under a measure of control by the army, which now was to attach political cadres to militia organizations and to carry out their political and ideological education.[16]

If the first three years of Lin Piao's incumbency were marked by the politicizing of the military, the second three were characterized by efforts to militarize the party. Between 1963 and 1965, military region commanders in chief were appointed secretaries in five of the six regional bureaus of the Central Committee. During these same years the ranking secretaries of the party committees of at least half of China's provinces were made political commissars of the forces of their respec-

tive provincial military districts, thereby bringing them directly under
a second chain of command—that of the General Political Department
of the People's Liberation Army.[17]

In December 1963, Mao Tse-tung started a major campaign which
brought important segments of the government and economy under the
influence of the General Political Department. He began this campaign
by issuing a call to "Learn from the PLA." The People's Liberation
Army was held up as a model of both party loyalty and operating efficiency; all political, economic, and social organizations in China were
called upon to study its organizational, operational and ideological
training methods.[18]

The distinctive organizational feature of the campaign, as it developed in 1964, was the creation of a new political apparatus. This apparatus reached from basic-level establishments, in the fields of industry, commerce, and communications, up to and including the relevant
bureaus and at least fifteen ministries of the government. This apparatus was modeled after the political control system of the army, as it was
exercised through the General Political Department, and it called for
"putting politics in command" of all work. Like any new organizational structure of similar dimensions, it required a huge staff. In part,
the personnel were provided by putting some existing party cadres and
incumbent officials through "refresher" courses in military training
schools and giving others temporary training assignments with the
army. Other personnel were found among PLA officers and men who
either had already been discharged or who were detached for the purpose. Soon more than two hundred thousand such officers and men
were at work in China's trade and finance sector.[19] Many of the documents covering the training these men had received, under the aegis of
Lin Piao, are available for study. They eulogized and sanctified Mao
Tse-tung, but none contained substantive reference to Liu Shao-ch'i,
the titular commander in chief, or to Teng Hsiao-p'ing, the secretary
general of the party.[20] In the nonagricultural sector of the economy and
in the government, these men served as a transmission belt for Maoist
thought and policy.[21]

It would, of course, properly fall to Liu Shao-ch'i to take the lead
in meeting and if possible repelling this military incursion into the
government of which he was chairman. His opposition appears to have
taken a form which reminds one of the indirect approach Mao Tse-
tung's mother had advocated in their joint opposition to his father, the
ruling power in their family. It will be recalled that Mao had described
her as deprecating open rebellion, saying that it was not "the Chinese
way." Liu was subsequently charged not with opposing the whole
project, but only with having insisted that the new political depart-

ments in economic establishments should be placed, not under the General Political Department of the army, but under economic departments of equivalent level. Teng Hsiao-p'ing is quoted as having pointed out that "factories must produce, schools must run their classes, and commercial firms have their business to do—they are different from the PLA." [22] In keeping with this approach, four political departments were set up under the Central Committee itself. They covered the fields of industry and communications; trade and finance; agriculture and forestry; and—evidencing a spread of the system beyond the economic sector—foreign relations.[23] Subsequently the system was extended to the Central Committee's regional bureaus and to the provincial party committees.[24]

While the political departments were being set up in ministries of the government, some ministers opposed efforts to staff them with military men. Minister of Petroleum Yü Ch'iu-li, although himself a military officer of lieutenant general rank who had been in active service until 1958, was among those who objected. Chief of Staff Lo Jui-ch'ing again demonstrated his independence by saying that to place army cadres in national defense industries was "an expression of distrust for the party and the masses." [25]

Indeed, the very slogan of Mao Tse-tung's campaign—"Learn from the PLA"—suggested that he did not trust the party. He did not trust it to do its job properly, and believed that it needed to learn from the army how to do its job. The party paid lip service to his ideas, but the policies the party followed, especially in the economic sphere, were at variance with them. Accordingly the campaign, started in that sphere, laid heavy stress on the application of Mao's thought in actual practice. The PLA did not, however, slight the more general task of spreading the thinking of Mao Tse-tung beyond its own ranks, thus invading a sphere which more properly belonged to the Propaganda Department of the Central Committee.

In 1964, the PLA made available for public distribution two series of selected readings, taken from the works of Mao Tse-tung, which had originally been published by the General Political Department for the indoctrination of the armed forces.[26] In May 1964, on the eve of the Chinese Communist Youth League Congress, that same department first published a small, red-covered book entitled, *Quotations from Chairman Mao Tse-tung*. It was, from the start, distributed widely as a reward for meritorious study of the chairman's works.[27] But its distribution during the early years was nothing compared to that which it was later to attain. By the end of 1968, almost three-quarters of a billion copies were reported to have been printed and distributed.[28]

Mao Tse-tung conducted a sporadic campaign, during this period, against the government's Ministry of Culture. Actually, this campaign had been begun before he had launched his "Learn from the PLA" movement, and it did not culminate in success for him and his military supporters until that movement had faded. As it turned out, his staunchest ally in his efforts against the ministry was his wife, Chiang Ch'ing. When the party elders had consented to the marriage it was, of course, made conditional upon their agreeing that she would stay in the background as a housewife and not engage in political affairs. She had, however, begun to disregard that agreement, before the Peking government was a year old, by taking a more than housewifely interest in the affairs of the Ministry of Culture.

Even in Yenan days, Chiang Ch'ing had taken up the cause of revolutionizing the traditional Peking opera, which is dominated by historical plays in which the chief actors, dressed in the gowns of past epochs, play the parts of monarchs, generals, scholar-officials, and famous beauties. It provides a form of entertainment to which many Chinese are addicted, and it also serves as a school of behavior. The Chinese child, watching performances with his parents, learns how people comport themselevs in such roles as those of warrior or official, which he may himself play in later life. If the stage is a school, Chiang Ch'ing reasoned, then it should be used to inculcate the values not of past imperial times but of a present-day proletarian society. Chiang Ch'ing again took up this cause in 1949 in Peking, but she was at first unsuccessful. Her reforms were opposed by Mei Lan-fang, who had been a nationally-recognized star before Chiang Ch'ing was born and an internationally famous one while Chiang Ch'ing was playing bit parts.[29]

In 1950, however, Chiang Ch'ing had been appointed a member of the Motion Picture Guidance Committee of the Ministry of Culture.[30] The party's officials may have wished to divert her attention from the traditional stage to the modern screen, which was more in the field of her professional experience. By 1952 they undoubtedly were regretting the appointment. At a meeting that year, she lectured Propaganda Director Lu Ting-yi and his ranking subordinates in an effort to get them to withdraw a long list of films which she found objectionable. As Chou Yang, Lu Ting-yi's deputy remarked: "When Comrade Chiang Ch'ing is present, work becomes difficult." Moreover, she did not abandon her attempts to reform the Peking opera. At one point she used her old connection with K'ang Sheng, the long-time chief of secret police, to warn officials of the Ministry of Culture that they should deal with the "serious problem" of the "bad plays" appearing on the opera stage. If Mao did not himself pay much attention at first, he did after *Hai Jui Dismissed from Office* appeared. Chiang Ch'ing was credited with having seen it, pointing out the "serious political mistakes" embodied in it, and ordering it withdrawn.[31]

Having become exercised, and taking Chiang Ch'ing's side in urging reform of the traditional opera, Mao Tse-tung is supposed, in November 1963, to have complained: "The Ministry of Culture is the ministry of emperors, kings, commanders in chief and prime ministers, talented men and beautiful women, foreigners and dead people." [32] His estimate of his own place in history may be inferred from his poem *Snow*, written in 1945 and published in 1964, which compared the heroes of China's founding and conquering dynasties with those of his own lifetime. The following is a translation of the pertinent portion:

> The beauty of these broad rivers and towering peaks,
> Moved countless heroes to bow low.
> Founding Ch'in and warring Han,
> T'ai Tsung of T'ang and T'ai Tsu of Sung,
> Hands skilled to wield the sword,
> Not in the leisured arts of peace.
> Genghis Khan, towering o'er his age,
> Who knew only to draw the bow,
> And shoot great birds of prey.
> All are gone.
> If great heroes you would find,
> Look in the epoch of today.[33]

The epoch of the living Mao Tse-tung, one may surmise, was what he had wanted the theater to celebrate. Meanwhile Chiang Ch'ing was forging ahead with her plans for the theater. In 1963 and 1964 several operas on contemporary themes—such as *The Red Detachment of Women* and *The Red Lantern*—were staged, and in June of the latter year a Festival of Peking Operas on Contemporary Themes was held. Lu Ting-yi, as the party's propaganda director, opened the festival with an appropriate speech, but he can hardly have been speaking from the heart when he praised the reform of the Peking opera which the festival represented.[34]

The wife of a high official may get her way, but she can interfere in the business of her husband's subordinates only at the cost of provoking a resentment which is all the more bitter because of the risks attendant on expressing it. Secretary General Teng Hsiao-p'ing is supposed to have expressed his own feelings in a meeting of his Secretariat, held while the festival was in progress. "Some persons want to make themselves known," he said, "through criticizing and repudiating other people." Evidently recalling Chiang Ch'ing's lowly official position and her use of her husband's rank in order that she might play a prominent role, he continued, "They step on the shoulders of other people so that they may go on the stage." P'eng Chen, his ranking subordinate on the Secretariat, expressed his feelings with an allusion to the utilitarian Chinese custom of leaving an open seam in the back of the pants of small children. The plays on contemporary themes, he observed, were "still at the stage of wearing trousers with a slit in the seat." [35]

That same month Mao Tse-tung, at a meeting of the All-China Federation of Literary and Art Circles, charged that China's literary workers had been failing to carry out the party's policies. They were, he said, "on the brink of revisionism." If they did not reform, they "would inevitably become an organization like the Petofi Club of Hungary," which had paved the way for the 1956 uprising in that country. It would therefore be necessary "to launch a rectification campaign . . . on the front of literature and art." [36]

To lead this rectification campaign, which was soon being referred to as a "cultural revolution," Mao Tse-tung appointed a "cultural revolution group" of five persons headed by P'eng Chen. Director of Propaganda Lu Ting-yi was appointed a member of the group, as were two of his deputies. The fifth was K'ang Sheng, the former head of secret police.[37]

P'eng Chen's star had appeared, during the two years preceding this assignment, to be almost spectacularly in the ascendant. He is said then to have become, in practice if not by formal designation, a member of the Standing Committee of the Political Bureau. He also had acquired the designation, accorded only to a very select few, of being Mao's "close comrade in arms." Since Mao himself did not address large public gatherings, it might fall to P'eng Chen to read the principal speech at mass rallies which the chairman attended in Peking. It has been speculated that Mao Tse-tung was trying, during this period, to win P'eng Chen over to his side.[38] One might speculate, too, that by seeming to cast P'eng Chen in the role of crown prince, he was reminding others near the apex of power of his ability to change the order of their preferment.

This new assignment, however, placed P'eng Chen in a cleverly constructed trap. As head of the group, he became responsible for purging the party of its intellectual dissidents, the purge to be based on a screening of their literary and artistic output of preceding years.[39] The most objectionable of their works, from Mao Tse-tung's point of view, were the output of P'eng Chen's own subordinates within the Peking party committee and municipal government. If he indicted them, he would thereby be accusing himself. He would similarly be indicting the other high officials who had encouraged or permitted their subordinates to attack Chairman Mao. He would, in effect, be defecting from the ranks of his allies and placing himself at the mercy of Mao Tse-tung.

His position, then, would be like that of Ch'en Yi at the time of the Fut'ien incident, except that he was more clearly and deeply part of the opposition and had correspondingly less chance of merciful treatment at Mao's hands.

The alternative was to seek to thwart Mao's purposes, using tactics of evasion rather than outright defiance. This was the course which Lu Ting-yi, as director of propaganda, must have hoped P'eng Chen would choose. Lu and his deputies were in the trap too, because they were responsible for what went on in the sphere of culture which, in a communist state, is virtually inseparable from that of propaganda. They were, moreover, less well placed than P'eng Chen to choose the course of defecting because it was he who was to direct the work of the group. Only K'ang Sheng could remain personally indifferent to P'eng Chen's decision. He had not been responsible for what went on in the fields of culture and propaganda. He was responsible to Mao only for spying on the others and reporting what they did.

The chain of responsibility in the party and the government, like the chain of command, naturally did not reach from P'eng Chen's subordinates to him and stop at that level. It went upwards to Liu Shao-ch'i. Moreover, as a great new rectification movement, this cultural revolution was not narrowly focused on those subordinates, even though they provided a key to Mao's attainment of his objectives. As a broad torrent, it could undermine Liu's position by washing away key members of a broad stratum on which his leadership largely rested.

To prevent this, Liu would have to use his party apparatus to control and channel the campaign, mobilizing his subordinates and forming them into work teams, as he had done on a smaller scale during the socialist education movement. These teams went into the multitude of China's educational institutions, cultural organizations, and other bodies where, the Maoists later charged, "they attacked the many to protect the few."

The Ministry of Culture was bound, of course, to be one focus of the campaign. It would appear to provide an example of Liu Shao-ch'i's sacrificing victims but endeavoring to retain control. Since 1949 that ministry had been headed by Shen Yen-ping, famous long before the Communists had come to power as an author writing under the pen name of Mao Tun—which means "contradictions," a favorite word, of course, in the vocabulary of Marxists. Among Shen Yen-ping's vice ministers was the noted playwright Hsia Yen, who had converted some of Mao Tun's works into dramas for the stage and screen. Shen Yen-ping was relieved of his ministerial post in January 1965, as were Hsia Yen and two other vice ministers the following April. Four new vice ministers were appointed after those dismissals, two of them arm officers—Hsiao Wang-tung, transferred from the post of director of the political department of Nanking Military Region, and Yen Chin-sheng, who had been deputy director of the political department of Wuhan Military Region. Hsiao assumed the concurrent post of secretary of the ministry's party committee, and Yen assumed the post of director of the ministry's political department. But immediately upon the dismissal of Shen Yen-ping, Director of Propaganda Lu Ting-yi was given the concurrent post of minister of culture.[40]

Meanwhile Lin Piao's power was being increased. By 1965 a reorganization had been carried out which placed all public security forces under his control. In December 1964 or January 1965, he was raised again in the governmental hierarchy, becoming the first-ranking vice premier in place of the economist Ch'en Yün. Lin Piao already outranked all the other marshals on the Political Bureau excepting Chu Teh, who had been dropped from his post of vice chairman of the government in 1959, and who had not been included when Mao and Lin had formed their "new" Military Affairs Committee.[41]

Then, in May 1965, all military ranks were declared abolished; thereafter a man's post or command determined his status within the military establishment. None of the nine surviving marshals still held a troop command, and with the abolition of ranks and insignia of rank they were shorn of status and its symbols. This new change also put officers in the armed forces more completely at the mercy of the top command. Without personal ranks, an order relieving a man of his command would leave him with no remaining status in the military establishment: No court martial or trial would be necessary.[42]

The abolition of distinctions of rank was described as a reversion to the army's revolutionary practice intended to promote closer relations between officers and men, and between soldiers and civilians.[43] But differences of position remained. On April 5, 1966, officers holding high positions were warned not to assume that these positions would afford them any protection. The warning was contained in an editorial in the *Liberation Army Daily*, a paper published by the General Political Department, and it specified that the higher one's military position the more dangerous it was. Accordingly, those concerned were urged to "thoroughly remould their world outlook"—that is, to completely subordinate themselves to the thinking of Mao Tse-tung.[44]

Some insight into the thinking of Mao Tse-tung during this period, and of the atmosphere surrounding his relations with others in the leadership, is provided by interviews he granted then to two foreigners. In January 1965, Edgar Snow found Mao thinking about his own mortality and pondering philosophically about his country's future. Death so far had many times passed him by, but now he was getting ready to see God very soon. In China there might be continued development of the revolution towards communism, or the youth might negate it and make peace with the imperialists and the counterrevolutionaries. Future events would be decided by future generations.[45]

In August 1965, André Malraux, a close observer of the Chinese Communists' revolution in its early stages, was visiting Peking. In view of Malraux's status as the minister of culture in France, President Charles de Gaulle had given him a letter to deliver which was addressed to his own opposite number, Chief of State Liu Shao-ch'i. French Ambassador Lucien Paye made the arrangements for the two of them to pay an official call on Chairman Liu at his office, located in the Great Hall of the People.

It had been intimated to them, when the arrangements were made, that someone else might be present during the audience. On arrival they found a large group of ministers awaiting them and, somewhat apart from the group, Mao Tse-tung. Malraux recognized the equine face of Liu Shao-ch'i, and made his way to him in order to present the letter. In doing so, he described it to Liu Shao-ch'i as one in which de Gaulle had empowered him to serve as spokesman with both him and Chairman Mao Tse-tung. With the mention of his name, Mao Tse-tung took charge, apparently not even giving Liu Shao-ch'i an opportunity to make an appropriate reply. During the ensuing audience a secretary came in on three occasions to take up one matter or another with Liu, and each time Liu in turn consulted Mao Tse-tung in low-toned conversation. But never, during a long interview, did Liu Shao-ch'i raise his voice in participation.

Mao Tse-tung evidently expressed more forcefully to Malraux than he had to Edgar Snow the doubts he entertained about the revolutionary staunchness of China's younger generation. He introduced the subject by alluding to the intellectuals and describing them as anti-Marxist in their thinking. The trouble was that they had children, and that they had much influence among the young. This led Ambassador Lucien Paye, who had been minister of education prior to his diplomatic assignment, and who had visited many Chinese universities, to assure Mao Tse-tung that the youth of China were deeply committed to his cause. Mao disputed this, in effect asserting that the students in the universities were dissembling, that their apparent devotion to communism was mere lip service. "Whatever your ambassador may think," he told Malraux, "this youth is showing dangerous tendencies." But the fate of the world, he held, depended on the youth of China. Therefore, he asserted, they must be put to the test.

As Mao said this Malraux sensed, in the stillness of the others, a change in the atmosphere. It was, he said, as though the talk were

about secret preparations for an atomic explosion. He recalled the
period of Mao's campaign of the Hundred Flowers, when both the
intellectuals and the party had been put to the test. The repression
which followed had eliminated both those who had protested and the
party members who had let them criticize—two birds with one stone.
What cataclysmic new campaign was Mao planning? That it would
involve the youth was clear. Beyond that Mao revealed nothing—unless
one infers that he had been a shade too prompt in his response to a
comment Malraux had made about the army. In the Soviet Union,
Malraux observed, it had been the party which had created the Red
Army; in China, he thought, it was the army which had developed the
party. Mao Tse-tung, before acknowledging the role which the army
had played, had protested, "We will never allow the gun to rule the
party."

At the end of the audience Mao Tse-tung and his interpreter accompanied Malraux on his way out, Mao walking stiffly as though he
were not bending his knees, somewhat as Malraux had seen the aged
Churchill do. They were followed by a white-clad nurse, who had been
in attendance on Mao, with the others some distance ahead or behind.
As they proceeded, Mao talked of the unrelenting struggle which
needed to be fought against the forces and traditions of the old society.
Through such struggle the thought, the culture, and the customs of the
old China must be eliminated, and those of the proletarian China,
which did not yet exist, must be born. Otherwise there would arise new
classes and a new inequality; equality was not important in itself, Mao
said, but it was essential to the preservation of necessary contact with
the masses. China could be restored to greatness only if no deviation
from right methods was tolerated. In that battle, he asserted, he was
alone—alone, with the masses.

There appears to have been a contrast between the Mao Tse-tung
of Snow's interview and the Mao who received Malraux, just as there
was a contrast, illumined by Malraux's observations, between Mao Tse-
tung and Liu Shao-ch'i. In the first interview, Mao had seemed preoccupied by thoughts of mortality, philosophically admitting that in a
thousand years Marx, Engels, and Lenin might appear rather ridicu-
lous, and leaning heavily on the arm of an aide as he retraced his steps
after seeing Snow to his car. In the other interview, Mao Tse-tung
seemed determined that his vision for China should be projected
through an indefinitely lasting epoch; resolved that China must struggle down the Communist path until there was no danger of a return
to the past; and, though he walked with uncertain equilibrium, he
held himself like a bronze emperor. In part, the disparity may reflect
the facts of Mao's medical history, which has been marked by bouts of

illness which a hardy constitution enabled him each time to surmount, and of his temperament, which leads him into alternating periods of eruptive activity and recuperating quiescence. It may also be that Mao Tse-tung had, between the two interviews, passed from hesitation to decision, and settled on a course of action.

The contrast which Malraux had observed, between the dominating Mao Tse-tung and the dominated ministers gathered about Liu Shao-ch'i, helps explain how Mao, who had conveyed a sense of isolation even in the Yenan days, had come himself to feel alone and isolated from his fellows. One can sense that he would find it intolerable not to have the commanding voice in everything; that preventing him from doing so, when he and his fellows became at cross purposes, could be accomplished only by not including him in their deliberations; and that he nevertheless might often get his way in consequence of deeply-ingrained habits—his of demanding obedience, and theirs of yielding it when in his commanding presence.[46]

Mao Tse-tung was being sincere—when he told Malraux that the Chinese Communists would never allow the gun to rule the party—in the sense that he equated himself with the party and was determined to control his military colleagues. A few weeks after Mao had talked with Malraux, a Japanese correspondent was watching him through binoculars while he reviewed the October 1 national day parade from a platform atop the T'ien An gate to Peking's Imperial City. There were about thirty high-ranking officers and officials with him on the platform. When the parade had ended, Mao began to walk away. At this point, the correspondent observed, "these officers, led by the foreign minister, Field Marshal Ch'en Yi, formed up in two lines and saluted him." Mao glanced at them but did not return the salute. The scene was enough to tell the correspondent that "Mao was superior—much superior—to Ch'en Yi and other field marshals." [47] At least he confidently felt himself much superior; they now were, after all, really only ex-marshals. It was Mao who held the barrel of the gun.

14

The Gathering Storm

IN THE EARLY YEARS of the decade the cloud forming over Vietnam appeared, on the Chinese horizon, too distant and insubstantial to cause great concern. In the mid-1960s it loomed like the front of an oncoming tempest, approaching a China which was increasingly isolated and dangerously exposed. The reasons for this isolation are to be found, in large measure, in Mao Tse-tung's conduct of China's external affairs during the intervening period.

By the end of 1950 the Chinese Communists had extended their control over the western province of Sinkiang and reextended Chinese control over Tibet; both Sinkiang and Tibet border on India. In subsequent years they built a motor road, connecting Tibet and Sinkiang; part of that road passes through the desolate wastes of the Aksai Chin, a region along the western frontier between China and India. Meanwhile Communist China and India had reached no formal agreement as to where the national boundaries ran in this area, in adjacent Ladakh, or in some sectors farther east.[1] The Chinese themselves later admitted that the area had remained tranquil between 1950 and 1958, and it would appear that their construction of the road in 1956 and 1957 went unchallenged and that the Chinese military posts in nearby areas remained undisturbed.[2] But before the decade ended, Sino-Indian relations had soured.

While Mao was preoccupied with his Great Leap Forward within China, India had begun to infiltrate and outflank the Chinese frontier positions along the western section of the disputed border. In 1962, with the conduct of internal affairs largely in other hands, Mao Tse-tung turned more of his attention to external concerns, including China's relations with India. India was neutralist, and its neutralism was of the wrong kind. India maintained friendly relations with his American enemies and his Soviet antagonists; it favored peaceful coexistence; and it was a competitor of China for leadership among the uncommitted nations of the world.[3] From February 1962 onward, with Mao focusing on the continuing Indian infiltration, the verbal Chinese response became increasingly threatening.[4]

Chou En-lai, who had built a special relationship with Nehru during the 1950s, had attempted to use that relationship to bring the trouble to an end, but had not succeeded. There is evidence that he and Ch'en Yi tried to dissuade Mao and others from resorting to armed conflict. But even Liu Shao-ch'i is said to have sided with Mao, and they overruled Chou En-lai and Ch'en Yi. The October–November 1962 Chinese invasion of northern India followed, and it was a military triumph.[5]

The aim of the operation, however, was not the military occupation of such invaded territory as was indisputably Indian, but the gaining of political and diplomatic advantage. And Mao was right when he later commented, in the different context of his admiration for Napoleon, "I am not a diplomat. I am a soldier." [6] Chou En-lai, a perceptive diplomat to his fingertips, had undoubtedly foreseen the consequences. Indian prestige endured a shattering blow, but in the process Indian nationalism had been aroused, Indian communism had suffered a bad setback, and India was even less disposed than before to negotiate what the Chinese would regard as an acceptable border settlement. In addition, distrust of China had been widely sown among small, new nations which China had been seeking to woo and influence.

The campaign against India also resulted in the further exacerbation of relations between China and the Soviet Union. After initial hesitation, the USSR adopted an attitude of disapproval which the Chinese interpreted as condemnation. They in turn professed to find it unprecedented that one socialist state should side against another in a conflict with "reactionaries of a capitalist country." [7] A renewed cycle of mutual recrimination had been engendered, and by early 1963 the Chinese Communists had become so vituperative that the USSR engaged in jamming their radio broadcasts. The Chinese reaction to this interference was in a style so characteristic of Mao Tse-tung as to leave little doubt that he was taking a personal hand in the polemics. Accusing Khrushchev of "wallowing in the mire" of Yugoslav-type revisionism, the Chinese Communists taunted him and his fellows and challenged them in peremptory tones.

"You have no faith in the people," the Chinese asserted, "and the people have no faith in you. . . . That is why you fear the truth. We publish all the 'masterpieces' in which you rail at us. . . . You, modern revisionist masters! Do you dare do the same? If you are men enough you will. But . . . outwardly as tough as bulls but inwardly as timid as mice, you will not dare. We are sure you will not dare. Isn't that so? Please answer!" [8]

At the end of the same month in which the Chinese Communists issued that diatribe, the Central Committee of the Communist Party of the Soviet Union sent a letter to the Central Committee of the Chinese Communist Party, inviting it to send representatives to Moscow to discuss their differences. The Chinese Communists decided to accept, and in preparation Secretary General Teng Hsiao-p'ing drafted a paper setting forth views on the "general line" by which the international Communist movement should be guided. Evidently Teng Hsiao-p'ing and Mao Tse-tung found themselves in disagreement on this fundamental subject. It later was asserted that Mao Tse-tung, finding Teng's paper completely useless, had drafted his own twenty-five point "Proposal Concerning the General Line of the International Communist Movement." This proposal was incorporated in a letter of June 14, 1963, and sent to Moscow as an exposition of Chinese Communist positions.[9]

In effect, Mao's letter declared that the Chinese Communists could not accept the ideological leadership of the Soviet party because its internal and international policies constituted treason to Marxism–Leninism. It was in essence a call for the defeat of Khrushchev and his associates, and for carrying the world revolution through to the end under Chinese Communist leadership. On the face of it, the letter was addressed to the leadership of the Soviet party; in actuality, it was directed over the heads of that leadership. On June 16 the Chinese Communists began the mass distribution of the Russian-language text of the letter in Moscow and elsewhere in the USSR, allegedly even scattering copies from the windows of the train running between Peking and Moscow.[10]

The Chinese officials chosen to go to Moscow for the forthcoming discussions were Teng Hsiao-p'ing and P'eng Chen.[11] It is scarcely conceivable that Mao Tse-tung did not have a hand in the choice, and highly probable that the relevant decision was his. It might seem strange that Teng Hsiao-p'ing should be chosen to fight for propositions with which he presumably had differed. However, this forced Teng Hsiao-p'ing to disassociate himself from contrary positions he may have believed in, and publicly to espouse those of Mao Tse-tung. Moreover, if he and P'eng Chen failed to advocate Mao's positions vigorously, once they had been advanced as official Chinese Communist policy, they would thereby open themselves to the charge of violating party discipline. From these standpoints, Mao Tse-tung could hardly have made better choices.

Teng Hsiao-p'ing and P'eng Chen appeared at the Moscow talks as scheduled on July 5, 1963, and they remained there until July 20. However Khrushchev probably had needed no more than one reading of the June 14 letter, which in effect called for his overthrow, to tell him that the talks offered no prospects for a mending of the split.

Otherwise he might not have jeopardized them by proceeding with another project—which resulted in his regime's simultaneously serving as host, during an overlapping period, to a delegation of leading Chinese Communists, to the American statesman Averell Harriman, and to the British envoy Lord Hailsham.[12]

This was a project for a nuclear test-ban treaty intended to serve, among other things, as an obstacle to further nuclear proliferation. Khrushchev announced the willingness of the Soviet Union to enter into such a treaty, with the United States and Great Britain, on July 2. Those countries promptly accepted the invitation and sent the two envoys named above to Moscow as their representatives. Khrushchev participated in the opening of the negotiations on July 15, and they proceeded swiftly. Before the month had ended the partial test-ban treaty had been drafted and initialed.[13]

The Chinese had, of course, promptly denounced the American purpose as designed to prevent China from building nuclear weapons, and the treaty as a trap intended "to manacle the socialist countries." After it had been concluded, the Chinese declared that the leadership of the Communist party of the Soviet Union had "allied itself with U.S. imperialism . . . against socialist China . . . in flagrant violation of the Sino-Soviet Treaty of Friendship, Alliance, and Mutual Assistance." [14] If the earlier diatribe from Peking had been in the pugnacious style of Mao Tse-tung, the Soviet reply was in the homely metaphor characteristic of Khrushchev. The Chinese expression of doubt that their security still was guaranteed by Soviet arms was countered with the warning: "Don't foul the well; you may need its water." [15]

The warning did not deter the Chinese, and by autumn of 1963 the Soviet leaders were making efforts to arrange a conference of Communist parties at which the Chinese might be forced to capitulate or face expulsion from the international Communist movement.[16] Either outcome would strengthen the Soviet position of leadership, which the Chinese were challenging. Chinese expulsion, if that were the alternative, would free the Soviet Union, in the eyes of fellow members of its bloc, from the moral obligation to support Communist China's objectives—with all the dangers that might entail—by underwriting its military security. The Chinese Communists naturally refused to attend any such meeting, protesting that it would only make their split permanent. At the same time, they declared that a split with the Soviet party was inevitable because it had become revisionist, thus betraying Marxism–Leninism. This left China free to compete with the Soviet Union for leadership, and provided the rationale for encouraging the formation

of new "Marxist–Leninist" groups in countries where the existing
Communist parties preferred the leadership of Moscow to that of
Peking.[17]

In July 1964, Mao Tse-tung went so far as to solicit the support of
third countries, non-Communist as well as Communist, in his quarrel
with the Soviet Union. That month he gave an interview to a visiting
delegation of Japanese socialists who were concerned about continued
Soviet occupation of the Kurile Islands. In the course of the interview
Mao agreed that those islands should be returned to Japan and revealed that China itself had claims against the Soviet Union for Russian territorial acquisitions going back to Tsarist days—for which, he
ominously declared, "We have not yet presented the bill."

"There are too many places occupied by the Soviet Union," he
commented. "In accordance with the Yalta Agreement the Soviet
Union, under the pretext of assuring the independence of Mongolia,
actually placed the country under its domination. . . . In 1954, when
Khrushchev and Bulganin came to China, we took up this question but
they refused to talk to us. They also appropriated part of Rumania.
Having cut off a portion of East Germany, they chased the local inhabitants into West Germany. They detached a part of Poland, an-
nexed it to the Soviet Union, and gave part of East Germany to Poland
as compensation. The same thing took place in Finland. The Russians
took everything they could. Some people have declared that the Sinkiang area and the territories north of the Amur River must be included in the Soviet Union. The Soviet Union is concentrating troops
along its border." [18]

It would have been natural that Mao Tse-tung should weigh the
possibilities of a Soviet intervention in China. His challenge to Soviet
leadership was tending to loosen the bonds of Soviet authority throughout the bloc. As a belated effort to deal with the consequences of that
loosening, the 1968 intervention of Soviet troops in Czechoslovakia is
illuminating. It suggests that the Soviet failure to intervene in China,
in the earlier years of the decade, was the result of realistic calculation
rather than Soviet forbearance. It was also natural that Chinese concern about Soviet intervention should have been focused on Sinkiang
and on China's Manchurian territories—whose borders along the
Amur were in dispute. The Soviet Union had exercised *de facto* control over Sinkiang as recently as the period 1934–1942. Since the turn
of the century Manchuria had been the object of conflict, with either
the Japanese or the Russians occupying territory and enjoying special
rights. Indeed, renewed Soviet concessions there, which the USSR
gained at China's expense in 1945, had been surrendered only in 1954.

In addition, it was in Sinkiang's deserts that the Chinese were, about three months later, to set off their first atomic explosion.

After Mao's interview had been reported in the Japanese press, *Pravda* supplied the Soviet riposte. It commented that to raise the issue of existing boundaries, which had been established by history, would inevitably raise a whole series of irreconcilable demands and give rise to insoluble conflicts. Then it turned the tables on Mao, asking whether the Chinese had really inhabited Sinkiang since time immemorial. The native populace, it observed, was made up Uighurs, Kazakhs, Kirghiz, and other people whom the Chinese emperors had subjugated. The implication seemed clear: the USSR had the capability of stirring up trouble for China in Sinkiang. Indeed, the Chinese accused it of having done just that in connection with the 1962 exodus of tribespeople to the USSR, and the Soviets in turn accused the Chinese of having violated Soviet frontiers in incidents which totaled in the thousands.[19]

Whether or not Khrushchev harbored "wild ambitions" with respect to Sinkiang, as the Chinese asserted in the summer and autumn of 1964, the successors who removed him from power in October evidently did not. Indeed, they appeared ready to resume extensive Soviet economic and technical assistance to China. At this point Mao Tsetung—perhaps believing that his chief opponent had fallen because of Chinese pressures—seems to have anticipated that Khrushchev's internal and external policies might be reversed, and there was a temporary cessation of polemics. But in a speech of November 6, 1964, Brezhnev made it clear that the new Soviet leadership intended to give consumer goods priority over heavy industry; allow collective farmers to till private plots; treat the USSR as a "state of the whole people" rather than one in which the "proletariat" exercised dictatorship; support the partial test-ban treaty; and pursue the line of peaceful coexistence. This was, of course, the opposite of the things for which Mao stood. He accordingly would not accept the appeal, which Brezhnev made in the same speech, that China and the USSR should improve interstate relations and tolerate differences of method in building socialism. Instead, the Chinese began attacking Soviet policies as "Khrushchevism without Khrushchev." [20]

By the spring of 1965, the war in Vietnam was casting a shadow across China, and as the year advanced that shadow lengthened. The United States had initiated the bombing of bases and supply lines in North Vietnam, and greatly increased its participation in the ground fighting in the south. To judge from their statements, Chinese Communist leaders feared that the war might escalate to China in one of two possible ways. According to one view, the United States involvement in Vietnam was intended as a prelude to an attack on China, and southeast Asia was to serve as the jumping-off point of the American forces being deployed there. According to the other theory, escalation to China might result from United States involvement in a vicious cycle. Each increase in the quantities of men and materiel employed, in the types of weapons and other means resorted to, or in the geographic area involved led not to a solution but to frustration. This, in turn, led to further escalation. Sooner or later, according to this reasoning, the widening scope of the conflict would bring about its extension to China.[21]

As this conviction of looming danger took hold, it lent sharper focus and added urgency to Chinese policy pursuits. The existing general policies of promoting situations favorable to the cause of revolution and creating pressures against the United States would now be pursued for the more specific purpose of lighting backfires to divert United States efforts which might otherwise be expended in Vietnam. Other nations should be brought into conflict with the United States, if possible. Then China might, at best, not have to fight at all or, at worst, would not have to fight alone.

These concerns undoubtedly gained immediacy in consequence of the risks the Chinese Communists were taking to maintain the morale and capabilities of their Communist friends in Vietnam itself. The Chinese are prone to observe, in situations like that which faced them and the North Vietnamese, that neighboring states are as closely related as the lips and teeth. "If the lips are removed," they ask, "will not the teeth feel the cold?" In keeping with this logic and in competition for influence with their Soviet adversaries, who sent air defense missiles and military technicians to Hanoi, the Chinese Communists gave both generalized pledges of support and various types of concrete assistance. They were reported to be building airfields near the border, putting jet fighter planes into North Vietnam, and supplying anti-aircraft guns. They also sent some tens of thousands of Chinese troops to assist with the repair of damaged roads, bridges, and railway lines, and to help provide anti-aircraft fire.[22] Putting troops in North Vietnam was doubtless intended also to deter the United States from invading it. If the United States were to invade North Vietnam, it presumably would also have to take on the Chinese.

At the same time the Chinese tried to deter the invasion of North Vietnam by asserting that, if it occurred, the war would be extended to the rest of southeast Asia, and would become a conflict without limits. This was a threat, of course, made at the prospective cost of the other nations which might become involved. In April 1965, the Hong

Kong edition of the Communist *Ta Kung Pao* warned, "Remember the 38th parallel when crossing the 17th parallel. If the United States expands the war in Vietnam, the front line will extend from Vietnam to Korea." [23] Because there no longer were Chinese troops in North Korea, and because North Korean troops would necessarily become involved in any reopening of hostilities on that peninsula, the issuance of the threat could hardly have been pleasing to Pyongyang. If the North Koreans had been ready to stand back of such a threat, they doubtless would have preferred to speak for themselves. Indeed, the choice of the Hong Kong *Ta Kung Pao* to issue the threat, rather than a paper in Peking, suggests that the Chinese Communists wished to be able to disown responsibility, in their conversations with Korean officials, while being sure that the threat reached the attention of the United States.

At this point Chou En-lai was on a diplomatic tour in Africa, where the Chinese Communists were attempting to pursue two courses which were mutually inconsistent. One course was designed to take advantage of the revolutionary turbulence to be expected in emerging nations, and particularly ones whose territorial configuration might reflect the outcome of past competition between colonial powers rather than consideration of cultural, tribal, and linguistic boundaries. Particularly in the areas of such turbulence, the Chinese Communists were playing the role of supporters of revolutionary violence. At the same time, they were wooing the leaders of new governments in the context of more normal state-to-state relations. Chou En-lai is too subtly perceptive not to have been aware of the contradiction, and the difficulties he got into on this trip suggest that he was playing his role as cast for him by a peremptory Mao Tse-tung.

Chou En-lai's 1965 trip to Africa was made in connection with a "Second Bandung" conference of Asian and African states to be convened June 29 in Algiers. The Chinese Communists wished to use the conference to line up an impressive number of African and Asian states in support of a resolution condemning the United States intervention in Vietnam. In addition, Communist China and Sukarno's Indonesia had been talking about the possible formation of a new "revolutionary United Nations" free of United States and Soviet influence, and they may have hoped that the Algiers conference might provide the basis for such an organization. However, from the start of Chou En-lai's tour until the end of 1965 almost everything went wrong.[24]

Two weeks after Chou En-lai arrived in Africa, President Kenneth Kaunda of Zambia let newsmen know he was asking Communist China whether a pamphlet accusing him of being an imperialist stooge "carries the official backing of the Peking government." Kaunda also said he wanted to know whether the authors of a pamphlet, being circulated in Zambia but published in Albania—Communist China's one close collaborator in Europe—were planning a revolution in his country. "Zambia would fight like hell," he was quoted as saying, with anyone who tried to interfere in its internal politics.[25]

In Dar Es Salaam, Chou En-lai made a speech, perhaps intended primarily for his Tanzanian audience, in which he observed that "an exceedingly favorable situation for revolution prevails today not only in Africa but also in Asia and Latin America." In neighboring Kenya the government officials took note, and their spokesman observed, "It is not clear to Kenya what type or form of revolution Chou En-lai had in mind. But the Kenyan government intends to avert all revolutions, irrespective of their origin or whether they come from inside or are influenced from the outside." [26]

Chou En-lai's estimate of the revolutionary prospects in Africa, and the suspicion of Chinese motives which his remarks engendered, both seemed to be confirmed when pro-Chinese rebels came to power at Brazzaville, in the Republic of Congo. But elsewhere the operations the Chinese Communists supported were unsuccessful, and in Burundi their diplomats were expelled. Indeed, by the end of 1965, Chinese influence in Africa seemed largely confined to the Republic of Congo, to Tanzania, and to Ghana.

Meanwhile the whole project for holding an Afro-Asian conference in Algiers was turning into a confused nightmare which Chou En-lai probably would like very much to forget. While he was en route to Algiers to meet the Chinese delegation and attend the conference, Algerian President Ben Bella was overthrown by Defense Minister Boumedienne. Most of the foreign ministers of the participating countries, who had arrived for a preparatory meeting, wanted the conference postponed until there might be a more settled atmosphere. The Chinese argued for going ahead, creating considerable ill will through their seemingly dictatorial tactics. But in the end the conference was postponed until November 5.

The Soviet Union had made a bid to participate in the conference, pointing out that the USSR is an Asian as well as a European power. And before the November 5 date of the conference, it became apparent that the Soviet bid was almost certain to be accepted. Considerable sentiment had also developed in favor of the attendance, as an observer, of United Nations Secretary General U Thant. China wanted both to be excluded, especially since it had been talking about the creation of a body which might compete with the United Nations and from which the Soviet Union was to be excluded. Worst of all, the prospects of securing wide backing for a strong resolution condemning United States "imperialism" had dwindled along with Chinese influence. At the end of October the foreign ministers gathered for another preparatory meeting. With the opening date only a few days away, they again found themselves at cross-purposes with the Chinese. This time the Chinese Communists were insisting that the conference be postponed indefinitely. At the cost of considerable wrangling, and of exchanges of recriminations with their Algerian hosts, the Chinese got their way.[27]

The isolated position in which the Chinese Communists had found themselves, on the eve of the meeting which was to have taken place in Algiers, was the result in part—but only in part—of Chinese behavior on the continent of Africa itself. Their isolation was due in some measure also to China's behavior during the undeclared war over Kashmir, which broke out between Pakistan and India in August of 1965.[28] The Chinese Communists unquestionably hoped for either a Pakistani victory or a prolonged war on the Indian subcontinent. The United States had supplied considerable assistance to India subsequent to the Sino-Indian border conflict of 1962, and a Pakistani victory would have humbled not only India, but in some measure the United States as well. If the war were long and bitter, it might have diverted considerable amounts of United States attention and materiel from Vietnam to India.

In order to support Pakistan and add to India's military problems, Communist China carried out, beginning in the latter days of August, a campaign of intimidation against India. In a series of notes addressed to Delhi, China charged India with armed violations of the Chinese border and other offenses, made a variety of demands related to those alleged offenses, and warned that if the demands were not met "India must bear responsibility for all consequences." In the culminating note of September 16, the Chinese delivered an ultimatum, setting a three-day time limit and threatening "grave consequences"—a euphemism for war if the Chinese were using the language of traditional diplomacy.[29]

At this point the United States warned Communist China that if it engaged in large-scale military action against India, it might in turn face extensive retaliation from American forces. Whatever its real intentions had been, China now postponed the effective date of its ultimatum and then, in effect, withdrew it.[30]

At the same time Great Britain, the Soviet Union, and the United States were attempting, through actions taken both within and outside the United Nations, to bring a halt to hostilities. Once the Indians had frustrated Pakistani thrusts toward Kashmir, the efforts to halt hostilities were crowned with success, and both sides accepted an invitation from Kosygin for a meeting in Tashkent.[31] Peking had sought to pour oil on the flames. Moscow, at cross purposes with China as usual, proved largely instrumental in putting out the fire.

In the course of 1965, the Chinese Communists, in evidently increasing fear that the war in Vietnam would escalate to China, had taken a number of precautionary steps within their borders, including the partial evacuation of some of the cities of south China. But concurrently they had undertaken a series of external measures that had ended in demoralizing failure. Their most recent adventure had faced them, in the context of Indian–Pakistani hostilities, with the prospect of the very thing they had feared in connection with Vietnam—they had encountered the threat of American military attack.

Meanwhile their quarrel with the Soviet Union stood at a point such that they no longer counted on the Sino-Soviet treaty of alliance. Indeed, a Soviet intervention in China—otherwise impracticable and hence improbable—would, in case of war with the United States, become more than a theoretical possibility. Then a beleaguered China might have to fight on more than one front against the world's two most formidable powers.

One can infer that this was their analysis from statements which Foreign Minister Ch'en Yi made at a press conference held for Chinese and foreign journalists on September 29, 1965. Ch'en Yi observed that his hair had turned grey during sixteen years of waiting for an American invasion. Evidently excited, he declared: "If the United States imperialists are determined to launch a war of aggression against us, they are welcome to come as soon as they want, to come tomorrow. Let the Indian reactionaries, the British imperialists, and the Japanese militarists come along with them! Let the modern revisionists from the north act in coordination with them! We will still win in the end." [32]

At this point the Chinese Communists were holding a work conference, which was initiated in September and carried on into October, attended by principal members of the Political Bureau and of the regional bureaus of the Central Committee.[33] Ch'en Yi's remarks at the press conference may well have reflected the tone, as well as the content, of some of its discussions. And while the conference was in session, Communist China suffered its worst setback of the year—the reversal in Indonesia.

In August 1964, D. N. Aidit, the leader of the Communist party of Indonesia, had urged the formation of a "Djakarta-Phnom Penh-Peking-Pyongyang axis" to oppose "imperialism." That year and the next his party, the largest Communist party in the non-Communist world, intensified its efforts to infiltrate the armed forces of Indonesia, bring about the arming of a people's militia, and push Sukarno ever closer to Peking. In this latter aim they were assisted by the fact that Sukarno's policy of confrontation against Malaysia was clearly designed to destroy that commonwealth partner of Great Britain through efforts at internal subversion and the infiltration of armed bands. In effect, Indonesia was serving as the southern arm of a pincers directed against non-Communist countries of southeast Asia.

In August 1965, Aidit visited China, where he was received by Mao Tse-tung.[34] Whether they discussed plans which were to be put into effect in Indonesia the following month we do not know. But on the night of September 30, a coup was mounted during which six generals of the Indonesian army command were murdered. On October 2, before the outcome was known, the Indonesian Communist party endorsed the coup in *Harian Rakjat,* the party organ. Unfortunately for the Communists, the perpetrators of the coup failed to kill General Nasution, the chief of staff. He and other ranking survivors proceeded to ban and destroy the Communist party, and to neutralize Sukarno.[35] This stunning reversal marked the end of any thoughts of a Djakarta-Phnom Penh-Peking-Pyongyang axis and, for all practical purposes, of Indonesia's campaign against Malaysia.

The series of failures, which culminated in the reversal in Indonesia, undoubtedly widened the split between Mao Tse-tung—who had been largely responsible for the direction of external affairs—and his opponents in the leadership. The September–October party conference accordingly came at a most critical point, with the war in Vietnam serving as a catalyst. At this conference the leaders assessed the dangers and debated what should be done.

The contending elements in the leadership could pursue divergent aims in more normal circumstances but they could not safely do so while facing the threat of war. To fight effectively they would require, first of all, an agreed military strategy. This in turn would have to be supported by a whole range of external and internal policies. If China had become increasingly isolated in the world arena, what changes in external policies were called for to correct that situation? China was due to initiate a new five-year plan at the beginning of 1966. What changes in it, and in prevailing economic policies, would be needed to support the military strategy which might be chosen? And what measures in the fields of ideological indoctrination of the populace and of internal security?

We know that in 1965 all these questions represented areas of disagreement, and that some if not all of them were debated at the September–October conference. It is likely, because the choices were between sets of policies, that the differences coalesced in two sets of opposing views. It is certain that Mao Tse-tung found himself unable to make his views prevail on matters he professed to consider crucial.

Between spring and autumn, an open split had emerged over defense strategy and the related issue of external policy. The spokesman for one strategy was Chief of Staff Lo Jui-ch'ing. In an article published in May, ostensibly celebrating the anniversary of Germany's defeat in World War II, Lo Jui-ch'ing advocated for China a strategy similar to that which had been applied by the Soviet Union during that war. He envisioned preparations in advance, joining combat against the attacking forces as far forward as possible, and the defense of "cities and other places." For a defense of the sort Lo Jui-ch'ing contemplated, the professional army would have to supply the backbone, because only it could utilize the requisite weaponry. Chinese industry could supply some of it, but the rest presumably would have to come from the USSR. Indeed, Lo called for "uniting the socialist camp" in the "broadest possible united front against United States imperialism"; he declared that "we pay high tribute to and express our full confidence in the great Soviet people and the great Soviet army"; and he asserted that "we are deeply confident that we will . . . fight shoulder to shoulder against our common enemy, United States imperialism." [36]

In September Lin Piao published an article, commemorating the twentieth anniversary of victory in the war against Japan, entitled "Long Live the Victory of the People's War!" In this article he asserted that the Chinese people's victory against the invading Japanese had been won by following a primarily guerrilla strategy supplemented, when conditions had been favorable, by mobile warfare. The Communist base areas had been states "in miniature," with the army performing a threefold task: serving as a fighting force, a production corps, and an instrument for mobilizing the populace. The victory of the Chinese people had been won not as the result of outside help, but mainly through their own efforts. They had formed a united front embracing all the people who were genuinely anti-Japanese, but excluding the pro-Japanese sector of the "compradore bourgeoisie." If the United States were to engage in a large-scale ground war on the Asian mainland, the several hundred million Chinese people, with "everyone a soldier," would drown them in a People's War similar to that with which the Chinese had defeated the Japanese.

What the Chinese people had done, Lin asserted, the Vietnamese and other people could also accomplish, country by country, if they used the strategy through which the Chinese Communists had won their revolutionary war—the strategy of organizing the rural areas to surround and bring down the cities. Indeed, this same strategy might be applied by analogy, he said, to the world as a whole.

Taking the entire globe, if North America and Western Europe could by analogy be called "the cities of the world," then Asia, Africa, and Latin America constitute "the rural areas of the world." In this sense, the cities of the world were being surrounded by its countryside. The cause of world revolution depended on the outcome, and it was therefore the international duty of the socialist countries to encourage and support the revolutionary struggles in Asia, Africa, and Latin America. Just as the Chinese people had formed the broadest possible united front against the Japanese, so the socialist countries should form a united front against "United States imperialism." However, it would not be possible, Lin Piao indicated, to include the Soviet revisionists in this united front, just as it had not been possible for the Chinese Communists to include unpatriotic elements in their united front against the Japanese. The pro-Japanese sector of China's "compradore bourgeoisie" had been capitulators and traitors. The Soviet revisionists feared revolution, opposed People's Wars and were "working hand in glove with the United States imperialists." [37]

The two articles reflect not only the classic argument between Communist China's military professionals and the adherents of Mao Tse-tung's theories of revolutionary warfare, but also the continuing struggle for top political leadership. Lin Piao obviously was speaking not only for himself, as minister responsible for the army at the political level, but also for Mao Tse-tung, whom he quoted extensively and cited by name scores of times in the course of his exposition. Lo Jui-ch'ing, with his implication that Communist China should depend on the Soviet Union as ally and supplier of weaponry, was reflecting both military professionalism and the views of Liu Shao-ch'i, who wanted to mend relations with the Communist party of the Soviet Union and to reactivate the Sino-Soviet alliance.[38]

The case of Lo Jui-ch'ing illustrates the truism that a man is what he does. A profession is a mold which shapes a man, and the prevalent values of the organization with which he identifies himself tend to become his own. The Ministry of Public Security and later the professional armed forces had shaped Lo Jui-ch'ing. The organizational interests of those establishments, and the values they tended to adopt, helped determine his alliances within the party and its government.

Because Lo Jui-ch'ing had been responsible in matters of state security for the previous decade, it was natural that he should object, when first coming to the army, to making Mao's works the basis for all

its political work. He undoubtedly considered that doing so would
tend to subvert the collective authority of the party, which had but
recently amended its constitution to remove all reference to the
thought of Mao Tse-tung as a guiding principle, and as something all
members were enjoined to study. This made Lo Jui-ch'ing the natural
ally of Liu Shao-ch'i, whose constitutional position as commander in
chief was being undermined. In succeeding years, Lo's responsibility
for the professional training of the armed forces undoubtedly influenced him to see a professional army as an element more important
for China's defense than part-time militia and untrained guerrillas.
The greater dependence of regular forces on materiel would naturally
lead him to favor a strategy which involved the defense of the "cities
and other places" where that materiel was produced. This in turn
made his interests accord with those of the economic planners and industrial technicians who had built China's modern industrial sector,
and who would want to see it saved from destruction.

Lo Jui-ch'ing unquestionably knew that the strategy he advocated
ran against Mao's theories of revolutionary warfare. More important
still, he undoubtedly realized it would work only if there were a genuine rapprochement with the Soviet Union. Since Mao was too stubborn, too combative, and too committed to antirevisionism to give up
his feud with the Soviet leadership, Lo was in effect calling for the
party to deprive Mao of his remaining power to make important
policy.

Mao Tse-tung's defense strategy, as set forth by Lin Piao, would
require wartime dispersal of industry from centers vulnerable to military occupation or aerial destruction and a decentralization of the
economy. With local industries serving local needs, there would be no
centers so vital that their destruction would ensure China's military
defeat. But the requirements of such a strategy would have run directly counter to efforts which Liu Shao-ch'i and the economists had
been making, at least since 1963, to create integrated industrial com-
plexes under a centralized economy.

The framework which they had been setting up involved, first of
all, a shift from large, self-contained factories which attempted to
fabricate and assemble all the component parts of complex products.
These "all-purpose" plants were to give way to smaller ones, perhaps
manufacturing one single component or a set of related ones, in which
machine tools and other equipment could be kept in continuous use
and the workers could gain the proficiency which came from specialization. These factories in turn were to be integrated in "vertical" corporations covering their respective fields. Such corporations were set

up in a dozen fields, with agricultural machinery and pharmaceuticals receiving particular attention.[39]

At the same time, standards of quality were set up with which local industries would have to comply. Po I-po, chairman of the State Economic Commission, had remarked in January 1964, "When local people produce their own cigarettes and soap, they often make poor cigarettes out of good tobacco and bad soap out of fine oil-bearing crops and spices. For this reason, we must set a standard, and only when the local factories are able to meet this standard will they be allowed to use these raw materials." [40]

Mao Tse-tung and Liu Shao-ch'i had been in disagreement over some of the concepts involved in this economic planning long before the Vietnam war began to preoccupy the leadership. As far back as 1958 Mao had been insisting that the peasants should be required to depend on local factories, financed from their own resources, for production of their farm tools and machinery. The economists under Liu Shao-ch'i are asserted to have pigeonholed proposals Mao made that year in regard to agricultural mechanization. In 1959, Po I-po, one of these economists, had advanced his own plan, which envisaged not just mechanization but also electrification—required for such purposes as widest possible use of irrigation pumps—and production of chemical fertilizers. Such plans could not be carried out through local self-reliance, and one of Liu Shao-ch'i's first national corporations was set up for production of agricultural equipment.[41]

The Maoists opposed these corporations as "trusts" intended for the transformation of China's economy from a socialist to a capitalist basis. They were objectionable to Mao Tse-tung in part because the individual plants were run by specialists and technicians, operating under centralized planning done by the economists in Peking. Despite the lessons to be drawn from the failure of the Great Leap Forward, he evidently still preferred its methods. Economic development should be accomplished not in an orderly atmosphere but in one of struggle, through methods of mass mobilization. He wanted "politics in command" instead of economics, and leadership in the hands of local party cadres rather than managers and technicians. But while some of the issues involved were of long standing, the dispute undoubtedly was intensified by the looming problems of defense strategy, which in Mao's view required decentralization. Indeed, it was later charged that Liu's plan for the creation of centralized "trusts" was designed to counter Mao's strategic thought on the "geographical distribution of industry." [42]

That Mao Tse-tung favored dispersion of facilities important to the country in time of war is further illustrated by a plan he proposed for shifting the center of medical and health work to the countryside. He is supposed to have proposed this plan on June 26, 1965, and it came up for discussion at the September–October party conference. Mao Tse-tung had asserted that medical services in rural areas were either unavilable or inadequate, which was doubtless true. He is also said to have demanded that all doctors, except recently-graduated ones and others "whose ability is not high," be sent to rural areas. Liu Shao-ch'i evidently did not reject the plan out of hand, for in July he is said to have asked officials of the Ministry of Health whether half the doctors of urban centers could not be sent to rural areas, and if not half, then a third. Subsequently he is supposed to have argued, both before and during the party conference in September, that the relevant problems could be solved only in the context of broad measures which envisaged the "revolutionization of urban medical and public health work" as well.[43]

Mao Tse-tung also used the occasion provided by this party conference to press, as part of his "cultural revolution," for radical changes in the educational system. His doing so reflected his continuing concern about the reliability of a younger generation, which had never known a war or been hardened in its crucible but which would have to supply the successors to his own group of aging revolutionaries.[44] His attack on the prevailing system evidently ranged from an allegation that Peking University—China's most outstanding educational institution—was a "rotten" university, to demands for the abandonment of full-time courses of study at the country's universities, colleges, and technical schools. He preferred reliance on the part-work, part-study system, with all students working part-time on farms and in factories and workshops. Both the full-time and part-time systems were in use at the time, and the proportion of reliance on each evidently was geared to requirements for trained personnel anticipated under the third Five-Year Plan. At this same meeting Secretary General Teng Hsiao-p'ing, who advocated maintaining full-time courses at major institutions, is supposed to have "coldly dissociated himself from Mao Tse-tung" and to have "made a speech in which he declared he was against any cultural change and against changes in the schools." [45]

Two other members of the leadership had made speeches, outside this meeting but during the same month in which it began, in which they too went some distance towards dissociating themselves from Chairman Mao. At a national conference of provincial party propaganda cadres, Lu Ting-yi is reported to have made a speech which was ostensibly a criticism of Stalin but which was understood to be intended as disparagement of Mao Tse-tung. At that same conference

P'eng Chen had declared that "everyone in the face of truth was equal," and that even Chairman Mao should be criticized when he was wrong.[46]

The September–October meeting of the Political Bureau and the party's regional secretaries had, in short, been called at a time when there was a widened split in the leadership and when there was deep fear of war. If China was on the verge of another epic struggle, like that against the invading Japanese, then divisions in the top leadership might bring similar consequences. During that other war Wang Ching-wei, Chiang Kai-shek's competitor within the Kuomintang, had gone over to the invading Japanese, and headed a puppet regime in Japanese-occupied Nanking. Mao Tse-tung may have been alluding to this precedent when he referred, at this September–October meeting, to "revisionism" at the party center and asserted "this is the greatest danger." [47] Later he was, of course, to charge Liu Shao-ch'i with being a traitor and "lackey of imperialism." [48]

What Mao Tse-tung wanted done about revisionism at the party center, first of all, was to have Wu Han, the author of *Hai Jui Dismissed from Office* and the subordinate of P'eng Chen, criticized and repudiated. Undoubtedly Mao's opponents saw all too well where this might lead, and they refused.[49] Mao Tse-tung had tried to insert this needle and been rebuffed. He would have to try again from another vantage ground.

Assault on the Watertight Kingdom

PEKING had been converted into a "kingdom" which was so watertight, as Mao later complained, that it "could not be penetrated even by a needle." He had tried, during the September–October 1965 meeting, to arrange for the publication of a criticism of *Hai Jui Dismissed from Office,* which represented the sharp point of his needle, and he had failed.[1] After the conference ended, he and Chiang Ch'ing left the capital—initially for the more friendly surroundings of the Shanghai area. The public was not informed where he had gone; for over half a year it was left in ignorance of both his whereabouts and his activities, and in consequence rumors sprang up that he was seriously ill or had died.[2] It may be that the public was left uninformed because Mao's opponents were trying to put him on the shelf, and because his activities were not of the sort which made news of them suitable for dissemination to the populace.

These activities were aimed, first of all, at regaining control over key elements of the party apparatus that was centered in Peking. Successful assaults on those parts of the apparatus would be important to the outcome, but not finally decisive. This was so because any key personnel changes Mao could bring about would remain provisional until they were ratified or reversed by the Central Committee meeting in plenary session. But that committee was dominated by his opponents to an extent such that he had not seen fit to call it into session for over three years. Accordingly it too, at an appropriate point, would have to be brought under his control.

The key members of his opposition—each holding several posts concurrently—functioned as an interlocking directorate, and the effort to crack it open would require a series of complicated and interrelated moves. Mao's ostensible targets in Peking were members of the party's municipal committee, and this led to P'eng Chen, as leader of that committee. However, it was not the municipal posts held by P'eng Chen which made it necessary that he should be purged, but his national-level position in the party's Secretariat. Within that body, P'eng Chen was in charge of political and legal affairs. This meant that he conducted the day-to-day business of the party as it related to control over the public security establishment, which is to say the Public

Security Force, the police, the public prosecutors, and the courts. In addition, if Mao were to capitalize fully on his authority with the rank and file of the party throughout the country, and on his prestige with the populace, he needed to gain unimpeded access to the media of communication. This meant that he would have to make the party's Department of Propaganda, which exercised control over press, radio, and other media, responsive to his will. Most important of all, he would have to make sure that the armed forces stood solidly behind him.

At this point, Mao Tse-tung appears to have felt himself to be almost alone, or to use his phrase, "alone with the masses," at least in the sense that he lacked intimate confidants other than his wife. But he had allies on whom he could rely, in varying degrees, because he and they depended on each other for mutual support against common enemies. The most obviously important, because of his position over the armed forces, was Lin Piao. Almost as important, perhaps, was K'ang Sheng. As "China's Beria," he undoubtedly could instill a fear which would exact compliance from almost anyone on whom Mao Tse-tung might choose to put the finger. In addition there were men who owed their positions almost entirely to Mao, such as Ch'en Po-ta, whose earlier service with Mao as political secretary had led to his becoming editor in chief of *Red Flag,* and also Wang Tung-hsing, who had started as Mao's bodyguard and become vice minister of public security. Mao also had friends and supporters in the Shanghai area, where he often spent the winter months.

Among the party propagandists in Shanghai was a relatively obscure writer named Yao Wen-yüan, who had made such reputation as he had by attacking authors of more liberal stripe. Even fellow propagandists described him as "crude and brutal," a "big stick and a strait jacket." These qualities undoubtedly recommended him to Mao Tse-tung and Chiang Ch'ing. Under her guidance, Yao Wen-yüan prepared an article criticizing *Hai Jui Dismissed from Office*.[3] Mao read it through three times, judged that "it would do basically," but thought that other friends such as K'ang Sheng should see it. However, after further discussion he was persuaded not to take even that chance and to have it published just as it was. Accordingly he arranged through Chang Ch'un-ch'iao, a secretary of the Shanghai party committee, to have Yao's article published in the Shanghai *Wen-hui pao*.[4]

Yao Wen-yüan's article appeared on November 10, 1965, and it served the purpose for which it was intended—that of starting the process of smoking out P'eng Chen. In consequence, that date is generally regarded as marking the beginning of what was later called the "Great Proletarian Cultural Revolution." A cultural revolution was supposedly already underway, but it was being conducted by a group headed by P'eng Chen. The adjectives "great" and "proletarian" served to differentiate the revolutionary torrent loosed by Mao Tse-tung from that earlier and paler version.

The fury which Mao's campaign was to attain belied, of course, the mild connotations of the word "cultural." However, his revolution did have cultural targets, for one of its aims was the destruction of old culture, ideas, customs, and habits. It was to transform everything in what the Communists call China's superstructure—its culture, in the broad sense of that word—which was incompatible with the socialist character of the economic base.

It should also be said that the Chinese ideograms for "culture," which in their narrow sense mean "literature," carry a strongly political connotation. They referred originally to literature in the sense of the Confucian classics, embodying the orthodox ideology of imperial China under which the society was ordered and the state was governed. So that they might serve this dual function, the classics had been made the principal subject matter of education in traditional China, and of the examinations for entry into the imperial civil service. There was a continuity linking the scholar-officials of imperial times with the leaders of Communist China in the sense that both were determined to direct the thinking of the people in the channels of their respective orthodoxies. The bitterest struggles are apt to be those waged over the question of what shall be considered the true faith, or those fought for political power. Since Mao's Cultural Revolution involved both those issues, it was bound to be harsh and violent.

P'eng Chen undoubtedly suspected, as soon as Yao Wen-yüan's article came to his attention, that Mao Tse-tung was behind it. P'eng phoned the party's Shanghai committee headquarters but evidently got no satisfaction, for he was moved to ask: "Where is your party spirit?" He and his colleagues in the Department of Propaganda were able to prevent the reprinting of Yao Wen-yüan's article in much of the nation's press, but not in some of east China's newspapers or in the nationally circulated *Liberation Army Daily,* organ of the General Political Department of Lin Piao's military establishment. In reprinting the article, the paper pointed out that Wu Han's drama was "a great poisonous weed." Since the fat now was in the fire, Yao's article was, on November 29, reprinted in the *Peking Daily,* but with editorial comments intended to convey the impression that the debate concerned the evaluation of historic personages rather than current political figures.[5] On December 12, the same paper published an article, assertedly written by Teng T'o using a pseudonym, defending Wu Han on the grounds that "before truth, all are equal." [6]

Mao Tse-tung could not allow the matter to be diverted into channels of academic discussion, nor could he accept the thesis that others were his equals before the truth. On December 21, P'eng Chen was summoned for three days of discussions during which Mao confronted him in the presence of a number of Mao's own supporters. Among them were K'ang Sheng, perhaps ostensibly in his capacity of member of P'eng Chen's five-man group in charge of the cultural revolution; Ch'en Po-ta as responsible editor of *Red Flag;* and acting Chief of Staff Yang Ch'eng-wu, probably included in order to remind P'eng Chen that the military establishment stood back of Mao Tse-tung. Mao began by praising Yao Wen-yüan's article, as well as another by the writer Ch'i Pen-yü which had appeared in *Red Flag.* Its only defect, he remarked, was its failure to get down to the matter of naming names. Mao made it clear that he equated Hai Jui, the dismissed minister of Wu Han's play, with P'eng Te-huai. (That meant, of course, that the tyrannical, incompetent emperor, who was not right in his mind, was Mao Tse-tung.) The key question, Mao said, concerned the dismissal. P'eng Chen tried to evade the point by asserting that investigations had disclosed that Wu Han had not had any organizational connection or direct contact with P'eng Te-huai.[7]

Mao Tse-tung, of course, was not to be put off. He undoubtedly made it clear, in their three days of discussions, that he wanted Wu Han and other party intellectuals to be criticized, repudiated, and forced to make self-criticisms—which is to say confessions—and that he was holding P'eng Chen responsible for seeing that this was done.[8] Thereafter P'eng Chen was allowed to return to Peking and to resume his duties as head of the cultural revolution group—under the watchful eye, of course, of K'ang Sheng.

On February 7, 1966, P'eng Chen and his group issued, for circulation throughout the party apparatus, a document entitled "Outline Report Concerning the Current Academic Discussion of the Group of Five in Charge of the Cultural Revolution." Its very title, characterizing the issue as "academic," undoubtedly made Mao's blood boil. But its contents must have made him erupt. The authors of the document maintained that the struggle against people like Wu Han should be conducted in accordance with the "basic principle that all men are equal before the truth"; warned against public and unauthorized naming of names; and forbade seizing and holding people. Struggle was to be conducted by "opening discussion wide," as Chairman Mao had advocated during one of his Hundred Flowers speeches in 1957. In ostensible reference to the browbeating methods of the scholar-officials of China's Confucian past, but doubtless intending reproof of Mao Tse-tung, they held: "We must not behave like scholar tyrants who are always acting arbitrarily and trying to overwhelm people with their power." [9] The document was, in effect, as much an implicit criticism of Mao's style and methods as it was an explicit guide for conducting a struggle against the party's intellectuals.

In the interval between P'eng Ch'en's return to Peking and the issuance of his "Outline Report," Mao evidently had turned his attention to the task of purging Lo Jui-ch'ing. Besides being chief of staff of the People's Liberation Army, Lo was secretary general of the Military Affairs Committee and a member of the standing committee of that body. As long as he remained in those positions, Mao could not count on the firm backing of the armed forces. In addition, as a member of the party Secretariat, Lo was in a position to give advice and assistance to P'eng Chen in his dealings with the Ministry of Public Security and the Public Security Forces. For a whole decade Lo had headed both organizations, and he undoubtedly still exercised influence over both through personal relationships with former subordinates.

On September 3, 1965, Lo Jui-ch'ing had given a speech which conveyed the impression he had abandoned positions, taken in his article of the previous spring, which were at variance with ones set forth in Lin Piao's piece entitled, "Long Live the Victory of the People's War!" In his speech, Lo abundantly praised the thinking of Mao Tse-tung, condemned the Soviet revisionists, advocated defending China through the strategy of people's war, and endorsed Lin Piao's article—which had been published on the morning of the day in which he gave this speech—as providing a textbook on the theories of such a war.[10]

However, a speech by a Chinese Communist official, made under such circumstances, obviously cannot be taken to represent his true convictions. If Lo expected his September 3 speech to bring him forgiveness, he was mistaken. He made an appearance in his official capacity again in November, and then disappeared from public view. We may speculate that Mao Tse-tung and Lin Piao initiated the formal struggle against Lo Jui-ch'ing at an enlarged meeting of the Military Affairs Committee, held in Shanghai in January 1966. It was subsequently asserted that "at the beginning of 1966 the meeting in Shanghai fully exposed Lo's features," [11] and that a "big struggle took place not long ago"—comparable to one Mao had fought at an enlarged meeting of the Military Affairs Committee in 1958, while P'eng Te-huai was minister of national defense—over the issue of "regularizing" and "modernizing" the army along foreign, "bourgeois military lines." [12]

In March 1966, a Central Committee "work group" held sessions at which Lin Piao attacked Lo Jui-ch'ing, who was asserted to have attempted to usurp power in the PLA, and Liu Shao-ch'i, Teng Hsiao-p'ing, and P'eng Chen attempted unsuccessfully to defend Lo. On March 12, Lo was forced to make a self-examination. On March 18, he jumped out of an upper-story window, and was injured, in an unsuccessful attempt to commit suicide.[13] His fall illustrated a point made by the *Liberation Army Daily* on April 5. Unless military leaders thoroughly remoulded their world outlook, it observed, the higher their positions the more dangerous they were.[14]

The purge of Lo Jui-ch'ing, it must be emphasized, involved important issues of policy, as well as of personal power. Underlying demands for regularizing and modernizing the armed forces of China, as we have already noted, was a defense strategy which Mao Tse-tung could not accept. In war, you pit your strengths against the weaknesses of your enemy, not vice versa, and you should not attempt to fight the kind of war you cannot win. China was strong in terms of manpower, and if it fought on its own terrain it could employ the strategy of a "people's war." If the similar war being waged by the Communists in Vietnam were any indication, the enormously vaster populace inhabiting the land mass of China, if properly led, should prove unconquerable.

China was, on the other hand, still weak in terms of the industries which could supply the materiel which a "modernized" regular army would need to fight a conventional war against a major power. This was the kind of war which China could not be sure of winning and therefore should not enter. If it did, China would undoubtedly be forced into dependence on the USSR, the only available source of outside supply. That would require China to mend its relations with the Soviet Union—at the prospective cost of concessions which Mao would not even want to contemplate.

This same complex of issues, given immediacy by the war in Vietnam and the possibility that it might extend to China, helped produce a split which extended beyond the Chinese Communist party itself, producing enmity between the Chinese Communists and the Communist party of Japan. Party leaders there had been making their own assessment of the situation created by the struggle in Vietnam, and this assessment was reflected in an article published in the February 4, 1966, issue of *Akahata,* organ of the Communist party of Japan. The article asserted that there was increasing advocacy, within American military and governmental circles, of a war to smash China before it could perfect nuclear-armed missiles. There was, it held, increasing danger of a large-scale war in Asia, and no guarantee that it might not develop into a world war. This did not mean that there should be a suspension of polemics, based on principle, against modern revisionism—meaning

Soviet policies which the Communist party of Japan also found objectionable. (Its leaders resented Soviet interference in their party's internal affairs, and they too disapproved of the relative moderation
which characterized the Soviet attitude towards the United States.)
What the situation did require, according to *Akahata,* was for all Communist countries and parties to form a strong united front to carry out
effective and coordinated measures against "American imperialist aggression." Thus the article was calling on Communist China to cooperate with the Soviet Union in joint support of North Vietnam.

Three days after this article was published, a delegation of Japanese Communist party leaders, headed by Secretary General Kenji
Miyamoto, left on a two-month trip during which it sought support
for this position from the Communist leaders of North Vietnam and
North Korea and its acceptance by Communist China. The delegation
paid visits of ten days each to North Vietnam and North Korea, each
preceded and followed by a period of one to two weeks spent in China
conferring with practically all top Chinese leaders other than Mao Tse-
tung.

One gains the impression that the Chinese Communist leaders
with whom the Japanese delegation dealt in Peking went as far as they
dared towards the Japanese position. They could agree on the need for
an international united front against the United States, but they were
unwilling to go on record as stating that it should include the Soviet
Union. Indeed, to have done so would have called down on their heads
the wrath of Chairman Mao. According to a subsequently published
Japanese Communist account: "Our party took the attitude of strengthening militant solidarity between the two parties, on the basis of points
in agreement, leaving points of difference to settlement by the development of history, practice, and verification. The Chinese Communist
party delegation also agreed to study and discuss points of difference in
the future, giving plenty of time to it." [15]

During the third and final stay of the Japanese delegation in
Peking, the Chinese Communist leaders proposed the preparation of
a joint communique which should cover those matters on which agreement had been reached but would omit the others.[16] Among those who
helped draft the communique on the Chinese side was K'ang Sheng.
He was the member of the party Secretariat who specialized in relations
with other Communist parties, and who had been among those meeting
with the delegation on each of its three stops in China.[17] It seems fair
to speculate that he covered himself by communicating the contents of
the proposed communique to Mao Tse-tung, who was then wintering
in the south, and that Mao sent word to Peking that he wished to

receive the Japanese delegation before it left Canton for Hong Kong, en route back to Japan.

Mao Tse-tung received the representatives of the Japanese Communist party, on March 28, at the Tsungfa hot spring resort not far from Canton. Also present on the Chinese side were K'ang Sheng; T'ao Chu, first secretary of the party's Central-South Bureau, whose headquarters were in Canton; and Teng Hsiao-p'ing, who had conferred with the Japanese leaders in Peking, but who had been away when the actual drafting of the communique took place. Mao Tse-tung made his dissatisfaction with the communique abundantly clear to all, including the embarrassed Japanese, by shouting at Teng Hsiao-p'ing and the other Chinese: "You weak-kneed people in Peking!" He demanded that the communique, instead of being directed only against the United States, should call for a united front against both "United States imperialism" and "Soviet revisionism." The Japanese refused to agree, whereupon Mao declared that no communique would be issued.[18]

Mao Tse-tung, the Japanese learned, professed to expect both an American attack and Soviet intervention.

A war between China and America is inevitable. This year at the earliest or within two years at the latest such a war will occur. America will attack us from four points, namely the Vietnam frontier, the Korean frontier, and through Japan by way of Taiwan and Okinawa. On such an occasion, Russia, with the Sino-Russian defense pact as its pretext, will cross the frontier from Siberia and Mongolia to occupy China, starting at Inner Mongolia and northeast China. The result will be a confrontation across the Yangtze of the Chinese Liberation Army and the Russian Army. . . . It is a mistake to say that in the world today there are war powers and peace powers confronting one another; there only exist revolutionary war powers and antirevolutionary war powers. World revolution cannot come about by the evasion of war.[19]

In this situation, Mao Tse-tung indicated, the Japanese Communist party should be prepared to take up arms. As Miyamoto later explained, "The Chinese side was of the view that preparedness for a United States–China war—a third world war—was necessary, and that to arm thousands or tens of thousands of people would be more effective to hold in check the fighting power of imperialism than the mass activities by a million party men." Mao Tse-tung had not expressed the opinion that an armed uprising should be started immediately, he added, but it was clear that Mao wanted the Japanese Communist party to accept violent revolution and "people's war" as the only appropriate road.[20]

This was a road which the international faction of the Japanese

Communist party, led by Miyamoto, had taken over a decade earlier, when the United States was using Japan as the base from which to fight the Korean war. In 1951 and 1952, in consequence of Soviet and Chinese Communist urging, Japanese Communists threw Molotov cocktails and attacked police stations in the cities and tried to set up guerrilla bases in the countryside. Most of the youths who engaged in urban violence either were arrested and sentenced to long terms in prison or were forced to flee to China; no guerrilla base lasted for more than the briefest period; members dropped out of the party in great numbers; and public support for the party fell disastrously. By 1953, the Japanese Communist party was ready to modify its policies, and in midyear the ending of the Korean war provided additional justification for doing so. In 1955, party leaders resolved to abandon ultraleftism and give up the theory that revolution was imminent in Japan, and Communist China itself entered on the Bandung period in which it preached peaceful coexistence.[21]

Miyamoto and his colleagues, having set forth on that road over a decade before with disastrous consequences, were not about to give it another try. They had learned then that modern Japan was not prerevolutionary China. Moreover, the Japanese of 1966 were no longer living under an occupation regime. Their industry and commerce were booming, and their peasants had become prosperous farmers who owned the lands they tilled. This meant that the Japan of 1966 was even less ready to respond to calls for revolutionary violence than the Japan of the early 1950s. Finally, the Japanese Communist party had before it the lesson of Indonesia, an agrarian country which had much more in common with prerevolutionary China than did industrialized Japan. Its Communist party had embarked on a course of revolutionary violence, presumably in response to Chinese encouragement if not urging, and in consequence it was undergoing decimation.

The Japanese delegation accordingly returned home, still convinced of the desirability of a broad united front to oppose "American imperialism," and feeling that Mao Tse-tung's view of American and Soviet intentions towards China was neurotic.[22] But they were quite properly disposed to keep hidden from the public view any knowledge of what had transpired between the Chinese party and themselves. Mao Tse-tung and his supporters, however, were not motivated by similar considerations of what was proper in the relations between Communist parties. In the summer of 1966, strained relations between the Japanese and Chinese parties were publicly dramatized in connection with a Twelfth World Congress against nuclear weapons, due to be held in Hiroshima from August 5 to August 7. Pro-Peking delegates blew the conference apart, to the accompaniment of loud applause from Communist China.[23] Thereafter the photographs of Mao Tse-tung began to disappear from the walls of party headquarters all over Japan.[24] This set the stage for a period during which Chinese students in Japan would stage riots directed against Communist party offices in Tokyo, and representatives of that party in China would be made the victims of mob violence.[25]

K'ang Sheng evidently stayed on at Tsungfa for some days after the Japanese delegation had left. Between March 28 and March 30, Mao Tse-tung called K'ang in twice to discuss the related cases of P'eng Chen and his five-man group, and of Lu Ting-yi and his Department of Propaganda. Mao wanted the February "Outline Report" revoked, the five-man group disbanded, and a new group set up to take its place. Evidently equating himself with the "central authorities," and calling Lu Ting-yi the "king of hell," Mao asked why the Propaganda Department should have expected Yao Wen-yüan to get its permission before publishing the article attacking Wu Han's drama, *Hai Jui Dismissed from Office*. Could it be that a decision of the central authorities was not enough? It might be necessary, he indicated, to dissolve the Ministry of Propaganda, and P'eng Chen's Peking Municipal Committee, as well as his five-man group.

A few days before Mao Tse-tung gave to K'ang Sheng his instructions concerning the case of P'eng Chen, Liu Shao-ch'i had left the country on state visits to Pakistan, Afghanistan, and Burma. This left Chou En-lai the ranking member of the Political Bureau present in Peking. As such, Chou was responsible, together with Teng Hsiao-p'ing, for the supervision exercised over the party Secretariat by the Political Bureau. If Chou En-lai had not decided earlier to cast his lot with Mao Tse-tung, he evidently did so during the absence of Liu Shao-ch'i. On April 2, it is said, he informed Mao Tse-tung that he agreed with his instructions concerning P'eng Chen. Between April 9 and April 12, Chou En-lai, K'ang Sheng, and Ch'en Po-ta attended a conference of the Secretariat over which Teng Hsiao-p'ing presided. At this conference K'ang Sheng disseminated Mao Tse-tung's instruction, he and Ch'en Po-ta criticized P'eng Chen for his mistakes, and P'eng Chen attempted to defend himself. Finally Teng Hsiao-p'ing joined with Chou En-lai in pointing out that P'eng Chen's mistakes had been those of opposing Chairman Mao.

This disclosed that Teng Hsiao-p'ing was not prepared to stand up to Mao Tse-tung and opened the way for Chairman Mao's next step —consideration of P'eng Chen's case by the seven-man Standing Committee of the Political Bureau. Mao could now be sure of three votes— his own and those of Lin Piao and Chou En-lai—and probably that of Teng Hsiao-p'ing as well. With Liu Shao-ch'i still away, that gave him

an almost certain majority. He accordingly called the standing committee together on April 16, and it accepted his decision to dissolve
P'eng Chen's five-man group.[26]

Liu Shao-ch'i got back to Peking about April 20. If he was received
at the airport with the éclat appropriate to a chief of state returning from visits on foreign potentates, it was not reported by the *Peking
Review,* which usually dwells at length on such occurrences. Indeed,
it did not even mention the date of his return. If the circumstances of
Liu's reception seemed a bad omen, as well they may, his forebodings
must have seemed justified when he took up his tasks on April 21. Chou
En-lai and Teng Hsiao-p'ing had known how heavily Liu Shao-ch'i
depended on P'eng Chen, yet they had cast their votes against him;
now he could be sure, in the Standing Committee, only of Chu Teh
and Ch'en Yün.

Moreover, three days earlier an editorial had appeared in the
Liberation Army Daily which had been the product of collaboration
between Lin Piao, officers of the General Political Department of the
army, and Chiang Ch'ing. Since she had a hand in determining the
contents, it was full of condemnation of the "black antiparty and antisocialist line" which had existed in the field of propaganda, literature,
and art, as represented by those who had opposed her reform of the
Peking opera, defended bad motion pictures, and themselves produced
"poisonous weeds." But it also declared that the armed forces were the
chief instrument of the dictatorship of the proletariat, portrayed Mao
Tse-tung as the man who had created the People's Liberation Army,
and called on it to take an active part, in obedience to his instructions,
in the cultural revolution.[27] The barrel of the gun, from which political
power grows, had been openly invoked in support of Mao Tse-tung.

The target at which the gun was leveled, and the cause for which
it was invoked, were made clearer in another editorial published in the
same paper on May 6. That editorial declared that Yao Wen-yüan's
criticism of *Hai Jui Dismissed from Office* was the opening shot in an
effort to put down something which was much more serious than a
mere "scholar's rebellion"; the struggle was "a life and death one." Its
target was a group who had "put some departments and units of the
party and the government under their control." From these vantage
points they had "resisted the leadership of the party, and committed
antiparty and antisocialist crimes." They wanted "to have a trial of
strength with the proletariat," and the counterattack against them
represented a struggle over the issue of which would win, socialism or
capitalism. The armed forces did not "live in a vacuum," and all comrades would have to take an active part in this great struggle. They
accordingly were called on to "hold ever higher the great red banner

of Mao Tse-tung's thought" and to "carry the great socialist cultural revolution through to the end!" [28]

In the immediately ensuing period other papers under the control of Mao's adherents added their fire to that laid down by the army journal. Ch'en Po-ta's *Red Flag*, as well as the *Wen-hui pao* and *Liberation Daily* in Shanghai, joined in explaining to their readers the crimes of Teng T'o's group and its backers, who had perfidiously attacked Chairman Mao in "Notes from the Three-Family Village" and "Evening Chats on Yenshan." [29]

On May 16 Mao Tse-tung convened an enlarged conference of the Political Bureau. His recourse to an enlarged conference suggests that he was doubtful of being able to command a majority of the members of that body, and was endeavoring to create a favorable overall situation by including carefully selected nonmembers. On its opening day the conference was asked to adopt a draft circular which had been "formulated under the personal guidance of our great leader Chairman Mao." This draft declared: "The outline report by the so-called 'Group of Five' is actually an outline report by P'eng Chen alone. He concocted it behind the backs of Comrade K'ang Sheng, a member of the 'Group of Five,' and other comrades . . . P'eng Chen had no discussions or exchange of views at all within the 'Group of Five.' He did not . . . make it clear that it was being sent to the Central Committee for examination as its official document, and still less did he get the approval of Comrade Mao Tse-tung. . . . Employing the most improper methods, he acted arbitrarily, abused his powers and, usurping the name of the Central Committee, hurriedly issued the outline report to the whole Party." [30]

This was a gross misrepresentation of what had actually occurred. P'eng Chen may have written the "Outline Report," but it had been discussed on February 3 at an enlarged meeting of his group and endorsed on February 5 at a conference over which Liu Shao-ch'i presided. Mao Tse-tung had been duly informed, and subsequently Liu Shao-ch'i and Teng Hsiao-p'ing had approved the issuance of the document.[31] But Mao liked to say that a meal can only be eaten a bite at a time and that "in war . . . the enemy forces can only be destroyed one by one." [32] In his battle with Kao Kang and Jao Shu-shih, Mao had not pressed the case also against P'eng Te-huai, who allegedly had supported them. Again, in his contest with P'eng Te-huai and Huang K'e-ch'eng, no wide purge of higher-ranking opponents had occurred. Mao might not get his way, in the case of P'eng Chen, if he pointed his spearhead also at the others.

The operative portions of Mao's circular, which was adopted May 16, provided for the revocation of the February "Outline Report"; the dissolution of the "Group of Five" in charge of the cultural revolution; and the setting up of a new group to take its place. This new group was to be directly under the Standing Committee of the Political Bureau.

If Mao's opponents took comfort from the portions of the circular which seemed to make P'eng Chen solely responsible for the February report, the final paragraph of the circular held over them a threat. It read: "Those representatives of the bourgeoisie who have sneaked into the party, the government, the army, and various spheres of culture are a bunch of counterrevolutionary revisionists. When conditions are ripe, they would seize power and turn the dictatorship of the proletariat into the dictatorship of the bourgeoisie. Some of them we have already seen through, others we have not. Some we still trust and are training as our successors. There are, for example, people of the Khrushchev brand still nestling in our midst. Party committees at all levels must pay full attention to this matter." [33]

The same day this conference was convened, a second set of documents, covering the case of Lo Jui-ch'ing, was issued in the name of the Central Committee. It cited that committee as holding that Lo Jui-ch'ing was guilty of using the bourgeois military line to oppose the proletarian military line; using revisionism to oppose Marxism–Leninism and Mao Tse-tung's thought; opposing the party Central Committee, Chairman Mao, and Comrade Lin Piao; and usurping leadership in the army. Instead of making an earnest self-examination, Lo Jui-ch'ing had tried to commit suicide, thus cutting himself off from the party and the people. The Central Committee accordingly had decided to suspend him as secretary to the Secretariat of the party, and as vice premier of the State Council. A plenum of the Central Committee would later be asked to adopt a decision confirming such suspension. Meanwhile, relevant reports were being circulated in order that others might "learn lessons," and so that Lo's erroneous influence might be eradicated. [34]

The circulars covering the two cases of P'eng Chen and Lo Jui-ch'ing were to be sent to party committees down to the county level, and within the army down to that of regiment. Sending both out at the same time undoubtedly suggested that there was a linkage between the two cases. The circular covering that of Lo Jui-ch'ing was supported by other documents, one of which was a report to Chairman Mao by Yeh Chien-ying, director of the Armed Forces Inspectorate, Hsiao Hua, director of the General Political Department of the People's Liberation Army, and Deputy Chief of Staff Yang Ch'eng-wu. Undoubtedly those documents told the recipients that the Military Affairs Committee, of which Yeh Chien-ying and Hsiao Hua were members, and the military

establishment, under Yang Ch'eng-wu's operational direction, were supporting Chairman Mao.

The May 16 circular on the case of P'eng Chen, unlike that relating to Lo Jui-ch'ing, did not provide that he should be deprived of any
of his positions except that of head of the five-man cultural revolution
group. This would seem to have implied, despite the highly damaging
rebuke which the circular contained, that P'eng Chen's punishment
was to be limited to that rebuke and loss of authority over the conduct
of the cultural revolution. Moreover, because that circular exculpated
other members of his group, by placing on P'eng the sole blame for the
February "Outline Report," it provided no basis for proceeding against
the other members, such as Director of Propaganda Lu Ting-yi.

But before the conference ended, it was hit by the discharge from
Mao's second barrel. On May 18, Lin Piao made a speech in which he
said investigation had disclosed that Lu Ting-yi and Yang Shang-k'un,
director of the staff office of the Central Committee, had for some time
been engaged in underground activities. Linking their names with
those of Lo Jui-ch'ing and P'eng Chen, he asserted that all four cases
were closely related to the problem of preventing a counterrevolutionary coup d'etat. The case of Lo Jui-ch'ing already had been solved, and
the conference had initiated the task of solving that of P'eng Chen. It
now would be necessary to continue with that latter task, and to deal
with the problems of Lu Ting-yi and Yang Shang-k'un. "Chairman
Mao," Lin Piao disclosed, "has not slept well for many days." He had
been concerned about this problem of preventing a counterrevolutionary coup d'etat, and had discussed it first in connection with the case
of Lo Jui-ch'ing, and then again after P'eng Chen had been exposed.
In order to prevent the seizure of key points, as part of such a coup, he
had "dispatched personnel and had them stationed in the radio stations, the armed forces, and the public security systems." [35]

It would be interesting to know whether Mao Tse-tung's opponents
felt, at this point, that they had themselves been made the victims of a
coup d'etat, and how the conference responded to Lin Piao's speech of
May 18. Whatever the decisions it reached on the additional matters
Lin Piao placed before it, the conference issued no additional circulars
in the wake of those of May 16. The one which dealt with the case of
P'eng Chen, in the context of the dissolving of his five-man group, had
perhaps undermined his position sufficiently to prepare the public for
the steps subsequently taken in his case. But it would have been difficult to announce the related purging of Lu Ting-yi and Yang Shang-
k'un in terms which did not contradict the language of the earlier circular.

On June 3 the public was informed that P'eng Chen's Peking party committee was being reorganized. Li Hsüeh-feng, head of the party's North China Bureau, assumed P'eng's former position, and new men were named to replace subordinate members such as Teng T'o and Liao Mo-sha, both members of the "Three Family Village." The purge of the party committee was accompanied or followed by the reorganization also of the municipal government for which it was responsible. In this reorganization Wu Han, the third member of the "Three Family Village" and author of *Hai Jui Dismissed from Office,* lost his position as vice mayor.[36]

Lu Ting-yi was replaced, as director of propaganda by T'ao Chu, head of the party's Central-South Bureau, who assertedly had been recommended by Teng Hsiao-p'ing. No public announcement was made of this shift, but during the first days of June, the *People's Daily,* which was under the direction of the Department of Propaganda, showed unmistakable signs of having come under the control of Mao's supporters. In editorials of June 1 and June 2, it hailed the proletarian Cultural Revolution and its objectives. It not only described these objectives as the demolishing of old ideology, culture, customs, and habits, but also asserted that this was a revolution to determine the central issue of state power. On June 4 it warned that "no one who opposes Chairman Mao . . . can escape censure and condemnation, whoever he may be, whatever high position he may hold, and however much a veteran he may be. The only possible result is his total ruination." [37] While these articles suggested that *People's Daily* was under new supervision, the public did not learn that Lu Ting-yi had fallen until July 9. That day the press mentioned that T'ao Chu, whom it identified as director of the Department of Propaganda, had been among those present at an official reception.[38]

The elimination of Lu Ting-yi, like that of P'eng Chen, was accompanied and followed by a similar reorganization of the "watertight kingdom" over which he had presided—the realm of culture, education, and propaganda. Among the "monsters" who were swept out were three deputy directors of the Department of Propaganda who had opposed Chiang Ch'ing and offended Chairman Mao—Chou Yang, whom Chiang Ch'ing had denounced the previous February, and both Hsü Li-ch'un and Wu Leng-hsi, who had participated in the deliberations of P'eng Chen's five-man group in charge of the cultural revolution.[39] Hsiao Wang-tung, a former general who had entered the Ministry of Culture in the spring of 1965, took over the responsibilities which Lu Ting-yi had held in his capacity as minister of culture.[40] He also took over a concurrent job in the Ministry of Higher Education, where personnel changes were underway.[41]

The purging of Lo Jui-ch'ing, P'eng Chen, and Lu Ting-yi, all full members of the party Secretariat, inevitably changed its coloration. Former Marshal Yeh Chien-ying, who had helped Mao handle the case of Lo Jui-ch'ing, succeeded him on that body.[42] Replacements for P'eng Chen and Lu Ting-yi were not announced, but in other circumstances it might have been expected that Yang Shang-k'un, as alternate secretary and director of the party's General Office, would have been moved up to fill one of the vacancies. However, he too was being purged, as Lin Piao had in effect demanded. As director of the General Office, Yang Shang-k'un had several times angered Mao Tse-tung by making tape recordings of the chairman's speeches and other statements. Accurate transcripts of what the chairman said, when laying down instructions, were clearly necessary for the orderly conduct of public business. A stenographer, even if present, might have had difficulty in making such a transcript because of Mao's provincial accent, his voice's lack of resonance and his elliptical style. But Mao, from reasons of personal sensitivity, tactical guile, or paranoid suspicion, evidently did not want such recordings made without his knowledge. It is likely, too, that Mao held Yang Shang-k'un's party history against him. He had been one of the group of Mao's early opponents known as the Twenty-eight Bolsheviks; he had been a political commissar under P'eng Te-huai; and he had worked with P'eng Chen and under Liu Shao-ch'i in the Northern Bureau of the party.[43] In any case, he was quietly replaced by Wang Tung-hsing, the man who had risen from the status of Mao's bodyguard to that of vice minister of public security, and when the time came for explanations, it was charged that Yang Shang-k'un had spied on the chairman by hiding microphones in his personal quarters.[44]

Mao's May 16 circular had provided that a new Cultural Revolution Group should be constituted, and that it should be directly under the Standing Committee of the Political Bureau. He thus in effect made Liu Shao-ch'i, as the ranking member of that body in Peking, responsible for the further conduct of the Cultural Revolution. Liu and his subordinates proceeded to mobilize the maximum number of party officials, including some of their wives, into work teams. These teams were sent into government offices, schools, communes, and other organizations where they engaged in a vigorous rectification campaign. It was later asserted that Mao Tse-tung had on June 9 urged against hastily sending work teams everywhere.[45] It would not have fitted Mao's plans in any case, for the work teams to prove effective. They were intended to help conduct a movement among the masses and to keep it under control. He wanted a mass movement which broke down party control, and which he could redirect.

At the same time that Mao Tse-tung had transferred responsibility for the Cultural Revolution from P'eng Chen to Liu Shao-ch'i, he undertook measures designed to ensure that Liu Shao-ch'i, in trying to discharge that responsibility, would similarly come to grief. One such measure involved a woman named Nieh Yüan-tzu who was on the staff of Peking University. The surname Nieh, incidentally, is composed of three identical pictographs, written close together, each depicting the human ear. Besides serving as a surname, it has the meaning, appropriate for one who engages in intrigue, of "to whisper." Miss Nieh was rumored to be a friend of Chiang Ch'ing, and she had been in trouble with the president of Peking University. This helped ensure that she might lend a willing ear to a plot which had him as its intended victim.[46]

On May 25, Miss Nieh and six others put up at her university a poster, written in large Chinese characters and headed, "Bombard the Headquarters!" It declared that "the people of the whole nation, in a soaring revolutionary spirit" which manifested "their boundless love for the party and Chairman Mao," were engaged in the great Cultural Revolution. Its purpose was to defend the Central Committee and Chairman Mao against "the attacks of a sinister reactionary gang." But at Peking University, it declared, "something fishy" was going on. Lu P'ing, its president, was preventing the students from holding big meetings and from writing the big-character posters which might serve to arouse the people. He was trying to divert a life and death struggle into the channels of purely academic discussion because he wanted to sabotage that struggle and prevent a counterattack against "the sinister antiparty, antisocialist gang." The poster urged all revolutionary intellectuals to break down Lu P'ing's controls and rise up in a struggle to "wipe out all ghosts and monsters and all Khrushchev-type revisionists." [47]

The poster's appearance was well timed. It was spring, after a long, cold winter, when students are bound to be restless from spirits too long bottled up. It was also the period just before examinations, which some students will always dread and wish to see sidetracked. The unreleased tensions among the students of China were greater than among those of some other lands. The tensions resulted, in part, from the constraints which Chinese society places upon the youth, and also from the repression that comes with Communist controls. But in addition, there was a strong undercurrent of uneasiness shared with the society at large. Unusual things had been happening in the party and the government, Mao Tse-tung had been strangely absent from the capital for almost eight months, and odd rumors were afloat. Perhaps Mao Tse-tung and members of the Central Committee indeed were in grave danger. In the circumstances, Miss Nieh's poster, urging the students to rise in their defense, was bound to throw the university into an uproar of serious proportions.

Mao Tse-tung helped see to it that the uproar spread. On June 1, he ordered that the radio should broadcast an account of the poster, and on June 2 it was carried by the *People's Daily*.[48] The contagion of excitement quickly spread to other universities and schools, where the party's work teams endeavored to bring things under their control. But education inevitably ground to a halt, and the students, released from their normal routine, became an excited mass ready to be organized into a potent movement.

By the time the summer of 1966 came, Mao Tse-tung had solidified his control over the armed forces; broken P'eng Chen's hold within the nation's capital; destroyed opponents who had prevented his use of the propaganda apparatus; changed the complexion of the party Secretariat; and released much of the student population from the controls which the party had exercised directly through its own organization and indirectly through its Communist Youth League. But most of this he had accomplished from behind the scenes. After seven months, during which his whereabouts had been unknown to the public, he had on May 10 reemerged briefly into public view to receive a visiting Albanian delegation.[49] A photograph appeared in the papers the next day showing him with Premier Shehu of Albania and flanked by Lin Piao, Chou En-lai, and Teng Hsiao-p'ing.[50] But the site of the meeting was undisclosed, and this evidence that he was still alive had not dispelled rumors that he had been, and perhaps still was, gravely ill.

Mao undertook to dispel these rumors and prove his fitness, after everything else had been set in order, by his famous July 16 swim in the Yangtze River near Hankow. On this occasion, according to accounts which appeared in Chinese Communist publications, a healthy Mao Tse-tung, radiant with vigor and filled with buoyant spirits, swam a distance of almost fifteen kilometers in sixty-five minutes. Moving pictures taken on the occasion depict a Mao Tse-tung—whose buoyancy would be ensured by his build irrespective of his spirits—making occasional arm movements which were midway between those of a backstroke and a sidestroke. It is conceivable that he floated fifteen kilometers down the swift Yangtze, but the pictures did not bear out the assertion. When shown, he was accompanied by a great throng of people carrying poles between which were spread big banners with characters celebrating the great occasion.[51]

As those carrying the poles waded into deeper water they floundered, and others had to come to their aid. Among those who floundered, according to one account, was a swimmer who "became so excited when he saw Chairman Mao that he forgot he was in the water. Raising both hands, he shouted: 'Long Live Chairman Mao! Long Live Chairman Mao!' He leapt into the air but soon sank into the river again. He gulped several mouthfuls, but the water tasted especially sweet to him!" [52]

It was later charged in Peking that military and civilian opponents of Mao Tse-tung had made military dispositions and other preparations which were part of a plot intended to result in a coup scheduled for July.[53] However any unusual military deployments which actually occurred around the capital that month were probably part of precautionary arrangements, which Lin Piao later revealed he had made, intended to provide security during the period when Mao was re-establishing himself in Peking.[54] Mao returned there July 18, and a month later he reviewed the first uniformed contingents of what was described as a new "powerful reserve force" of the People's Liberation Army.[55] This force was composed of the student Red Guards, soon to number in the millions. However, it was not the Red Guards, but the army, which Mao intended to hold in reserve. It would not look well to use the army in overt attacks upon the party. The youthful Red Guards could serve as the spearhead of his attack, and once they had created sufficient chaos the army could step in to restore order—and with it, his authority.

The Red Guard Rebellion

MAO TSE-TUNG, reminiscing about his youth, once remarked: "What I enjoyed were the romances of Old China, and especially stories of rebellions. . . . I believe that perhaps I was much influenced by such books, read at an impressionable age." One of the romances he had read during his youth, he said, was *Hsi Yu Chi*.[1]

Sun Wu-k'ung, the impudent hero of this folk tale, was a red-bottomed monkey whose study of magic enabled him to perform prodigious feats. He stormed the gates of hell in order to cross his name from the books of the quick and the dead; stole and ate the peaches of immortality in the gardens of paradise; and made unsuccessful efforts to overthrow the heavenly emperor. Able to leap 108,000 leagues at a bound, he once traveled to what he took to be the boundary pillars marking the end of the world. There, impatient as always of limiting bounds, he urinated on one of the pillars as a mark of his disrespect.

When hard pressed in a fight, Sun Wu-k'ung would pluck a handful of hairs from his body, bite them into small pieces, spit them into the air, and cry, "Change!" Each fragment of hair then would change into several hundred small monkeys which would swarm to his support. When his enemies had been vanquished, another incantation would change the small monkeys back into their original form of fur, which he would replace.[2]

As we all tend to do with the heroes of tales which capture our imagination, the young Mao Tse-tung probably identified himself with Sun Wu-k'ung. In addition, Mao Tse-tung may have found the account of the monkey's magical capacity for self-multiplication peculiarly intriguing because the Chinese character romanized *mao* happens both to stand for his own surname and also to mean "fur" or "body hair," whether of man or animal.

In the spring of 1966, facing stubborn antagonists and feeling himself almost alone, Mao Tse-tung evidently recalled the folk tale and the method its hero used when badly in need of reinforcements. At the end of March he had called in K'ang Sheng and said, "We must overthrow the king of hell and liberate the little devils." He recalled that he had always believed in pitting local organizations against the authorities in Peking "whenever a central organization does something bad." Then he continued, "We need more Sun Wu-k'ungs from various localities to disrupt the heavenly palace." [3]

Because K'ang Sheng was a specialist in covert operations, and because he had once been director of the Organization Department of the Central Committee, he was a logical person to entrust with the covert tasks involved in instigating dissidence, liberating China's "little devils" from the bonds of school routine, and providing them with organizational leadership different from that of the Communist Youth League—which was dominated by Mao's opponents. According to one account, K'ang Sheng proceeded to establish groups of youths, devoted to the study of the "thought of Mao Tse-tung," which were to serve as forerunners of Red Guard organizations. [4]

For this purpose K'ang Sheng may have made some use of a network of secret agents who were responsible, if not directly to himself, then to Hsieh Fu-chih, the Minister of Public Security, who remained responsive to Mao Tse-tung throughout the ensuing years of turmoil and dissension. But it was personnel of Lin Piao's army who played the chief role in the organization and support of the Red Guards. [5] Numbers of such personnel had been attached to schools throughout the country pursuant to the "learn from the PLA" movement and the decision to establish PLA-type political departments in the colleges and universities. They accordingly were well placed to carry out the undercover organization of the first Red Guard units, accomplished in May or June. [6] Subsequently some hundreds of thousands of army personnel were overtly used to help promote, direct, and support the Red Guard movement. [7]

The student rebellion which began in Peking in the spring of 1966, and which soon spread to other cities, was directed in its initial stages against educational administrators who also served, in many cases, as party functionaries. To cite one instance, Peking University President Lu P'ing, against whom Miss Nieh's poster was directed, was also the head of that university's party committee. The party superiors of such functionaries naturally regarded attacks on them as antiparty activity. At some schools there already were work teams which Liu Shao-ch'i and the party apparatus had set up to carry on the Cultural Revolution. The members of these teams, coming to the support of the party's representatives in the schools, themselves became targets of attack. In other cases work teams were sent to schools, when unrest broke out, in order to bring it under control.

Wang Kuang-mei, the wife of Chairman Liu Shao-ch'i, was a member of one such team, which was sent to Tsinghua University. Her outstanding opponent there was a student named K'uai Ta-fu, and his opposition proved so stubborn that Liu Shao-ch'i was finally led to ask

K'ang Sheng about him. K'ang Sheng defended K'uai Ta-fu by describing him as "one of the revolutionary masses," whereupon Liu Shao-ch'i commented: "I consider him a demon. I think you are behind K'uai Ta-fu." [8]

By this time the first Red Guard organizations had appeared, and Liu Shao-ch'i had realized that he and his supporters faced a covert movement. He accordingly had issued a directive forbidding teachers and students from holding secret meetings, and he had declared Red Guard organizations to be illegal. Meanwhile, the party's work teams were succeeding in confining much of the student activity to the premises of the schools and in damping it down, but they were unable to extinguish it. Accordingly, Liu Shao-ch'i was forced to recognize that repression was an inadequate expedient. To provide a more adequate solution he ordered the party's Department of Propaganda, which supervised the education ministries, to undertake a reform of the country's educational system, teaching materials, and pedagogical methods.[9]

The task of devising and instituting such reforms would, of course, have been a long-term one, and Mao Tse-tung never gave Liu Shao-ch'i the time needed to get it off the ground. Returning to Peking on July 18, two days after his Yangtze River swim, he let things in the schools stew for a week while K'ang Sheng, Chiang Ch'ing, and Ch'en Po-ta assessed the situation. Then they ordered the work teams withdrawn, and Mao sent a warm letter of support to the Red Guards of the middle school attached to Tsinghua University; those students are supposed to have been the first to form such a group.[10] With the damper provided by the work teams removed, and with Mao expressing his support, conditions had been created which were to permit the movement to spread like wildfire.

Mao Tse-tung then settled down to other tasks immediately relevant to the calling into plenary session of the Central Committee. He needed its approval of the suspension from office of Lo Jui-ch'ing, as envisaged in his May 16 circular, for additional personnel changes made shortly thereafter but with less formality, and for still other organizational changes which he contemplated. In addition, Mao wanted the Central Committee's endorsement of substantive decisions he had made, and proposals he had advanced, since the last previous plenary session held in 1962, and particularly of his Cultural Revolution. That he wanted the Central Committee to serve as his rubber stamp is also clear. Before it ever met, he and his group prepared both the resolution it was to adopt and the communique it was to issue at the conclusion of its session.[11]

It appears that Mao Tse-tung, hoping to dominate the session,

managed to prevent the attendance of some of his opponents. It has
been estimated that upwards of half the regular and alternate members
of the Central Committee failed to attend this so-called plenary meeting, which was held from August 1 to August 12. If the circumstances
were irregular, this may explain the fact that the final communique,
unlike the communiques of previous plenary sessions, failed to mention the numbers in attendance.

As if to suggest that the People's Liberation Army stood behind
him, Mao convened the session on China's Army Day, which is August
1, and appeared clad in army uniform at ensuing public functions.[12]
Nevertheless, Mao Tse-tung evidently found himself in a minority
among those who did attend, and facing a hard struggle. Members of
the Central Committee who set much store on party principles could
hardly be expected willingly to approve Mao's stirring up the students
for his personal purposes, creating the Red Guards at the expense of
the party's youth corps, and using an extraparty movement against
officials of the party. That Mao came under attack for having done so
would seem implicit in an account which Chiang Ch'ing later gave of
a speech which her husband made at this plenum.

"You are too impatient," she quoted Mao as having told the members of the Central Committee. "You say that the situation is sharply
confused, or it is beyond control. But the masses have by no means
committed a big error. They will in short settle down in a correct direction. If you say that they are confused, then let them continue for a
few months. We can reach a conclusion when they have agitated to
their hearts' content." He then made an apparent effort to shift the
blame for confusion to "people within the Party Central" who had
sent out work teams, assertedly without his consent, and added, "At
any rate, if you reach a conclusion in haste nothing favorable will
come out." [13]

On August 5, Mao Tse-tung, following in the footsteps of Miss
Nieh, issued a "big character" poster of his own. It was entitled "Bombard the Headquarters," and its content suggested that the headquarters against which he was inciting the people were those of the
party itself. He asserted, "Some leading comrades from the central down
to the local party levels have . . . enforced a bourgeois dictatorship
and struck down the surging movement of the great Cultural Revolution
of the proletariat. They have . . . suppressed revolutionaries, stifled
opinions different from their own, imposed a white terror, and felt
very pleased with themselves. . . . How poisonous! Viewed in connection with the right deviation in 1962 and wrong tendency in 1964
which was 'Left' in form but 'Right' in essence, shouldn't this make
one wide awake?" [14]

In consequence the populace of Peking learned that a great struggle was in progress, and on August 10 a large number of gathered before party headquarters. Leaving the plenum Mao Tse-tung is reported to have gone out to the street, and told the assembled citizens: "You should be concerned about the national crisis, and you should carry out the Great Cultural Revolution to the last." [15]

Within the halls of the plenum the Maoists inhibited free debate, which the usual complete secrecy would have permitted, and created a pro-Mao atmosphere which was unrepresentative of sentiment within the Central Committee itself. This was accomplished by the unprecedented measure of packing the final sessions with "revolutionary teachers and students" and with officers from Lin Piao's People's Liberation Army. The implication is strong that Mao had either lost an important vote or was about to do so, and that he then violated the party's principle of "democratic centralism" in order to make his will prevail.[16] Evidently it did prevail, for the plenum adopted a sixteen-point set of "Decisions" dated August 8. These "Decisions" laid down guidelines according to which the Cultural Revolution was ostensibly to be conducted. The plenum also adopted a communique approving the policies Mao Tse-tung had advanced and the decisions he had made, on both the domestic and international fronts, during the four years since the previous plenum.

Taken together, these two documents suggest that Mao Tse-tung's Cultural Revolution was intended to serve the following principal purposes: first, the discrediting and overthrow of his major opponents within the party, identified not by name but as "those within the party who are in authority and are taking the capitalist road"; second, training and tempering through struggle a new generation of "successors in the proletarian revolutionary cause"; and third, achieving an ideological revolution among the whole populace by wiping out "old ideas, culture, customs, and habits" of the bourgeois past and replacing them with new ones derived from the "thought" of Mao Tse-tung, who was proclaimed "the greatest Marxist–Leninist of our era." By these means it was hoped to reverse the policies of Mao's opponents, thereby preventing a possible reversion to capitalism, and to create the new Chinese man who would need to emerge if China were to make the transition from socialism to communism. Such a man would not need the stimulation of material incentives, for he would be devoted to Mao's apparent conception of the good society—one of continuing struggle, collective enthusiasm, and individual self-denial.

The party, for its part, was called upon to persevere in giving correct leadership, to arouse the masses in support of the Cultural Revolution, and to cast out fear of the consequent disorders. The masses were to elect the members of various Cultural Revolution groups and committees, as well as the delegates to Cultural Revolution congresses, using a system of general elections like that employed by the revolutionary Paris Commune of 1871, and they were similarly to have the right to criticize those they had elected and to recall them if they proved incompetent. China was embarked, as pointed out in the Central Committee's "Decisions," upon a complex revolution that was to "touch people to their very souls." [17]

Mao Tse-tung was subsequently quoted as having said, in his speech at the closing ceremony, that the party's organization had been changed "slightly" in the course of the session. The changes were more than slight, for shifts had been made, as he admitted, in the bodies which formulated the party's policy and were responsible for its day-to-day business—in the Standing Committee of the Political Bureau, in the lists of the bureau's full and alternate members, and in the party Secretariat. These changes, he claimed, would guarantee the implementation of the decisions announced in the communique.[18]

The changes were not limited to the removal of P'eng Chen, Lo Jui-ch'ing, Lu Ting-yi, and Yang Shang-k'un from their respective positions in those bodies. But the other alterations only became apparent from the treatment accorded the various leaders at immediately ensuing public functions, the order in which their names were listed in published accounts of those functions, and seemingly casual mention in the press of their newly assumed positions. In consequence, people learned that the Mao-Lin faction in the Standing Committee of the Political Bureau had been strengthened by the addition to that body of Mao's two close associates, Ch'en Po-ta and K'ang Sheng; of Li Fu-ch'un, Mao's contemporary from Hunan, where both had been normal school students in Changsha, and later one of Chou En-lai's fellow students in France; and of T'ao Chu, who had risen to prominence during the latter years of civil war as deputy director of the Political Department of Lin Piao's Fourth Field Army. In addition, three members of the Military Affairs Committee had been newly named to the Political Bureau: former Marshals Hsü Hsiang-ch'ien, Nieh Jung-chen, and Yeh Chien-ying.[19]

On August 18, 1966, Mao Tse-tung celebrated his Cultural Revolution with a gigantic rally which filled the great square in front of Peking's imperial palace. Among those who attended were "tens of thousands of Red Guards," distinguishable in dress from army men only by the absence from their khaki uniforms and caps of identifying shoulder patches and stars, and by armbands bearing ideographs meaning "Red Guards."

A large proportion of those who filled the square and the reviewing stands on either side were students from Peking's concentration of colleges and universities and from its middle schools. During the rally they were led in cheers which, to judge from a lengthy color movie covering the day's events, hailed none of the leaders present save one—the distant but imposing figure, atop the ramparts, of Mao Tse-tung. With great sense of timing, the cheer leaders increased the pace, and with hypnotic effect. Soon young people could be seen jumping up and down; a youth with glazed eyes shouted hoarsely, girls wept, and one could be seen biting her sleeve. The color-filled square, the masses of people, the incantations of the cheer leaders—and above all, the presence of their incarnate leader—had created for them a psychedelic experience.

The great leader received numbers of people on the rostrum, he accepted a Red Guard armband, and he reviewed a parade assertedly composed of a million people. But most of the times the camera was focused on him his face was impassive and his gaze apparently unfocused. He may have felt gratified, but the many who were overjoyed because they could see him, and who hoped he too saw them, would hardly have felt their hope was being realized if they had been able to see that glazed look.

Those who paid attention to the externals, however, would have sensed the new order which had emerged from the just-concluded plenum. Lin Piao gave the first speech; he had become Mao's "closest comrade in arms," displacing Liu Shao-ch'i as second in rank and as Mao's presumed successor. In the pictures, Lin Piao appeared an unlikely choice—a wraithlike man of ashen complexion in a thick uniform which was too big for him by far, ill at ease, squinting in the bright sun at the tightly-clutched text of his written speech, which he shouted hoarsely in a high-pitched voice. His speech was half extravagant eulogy of Mao Tse-tung, the supreme commander, half strident call for sweeping away old things and striking down all "followers of the capitalist road."

Chou En-lai was the next to speak, and this suggested that he had, with the suppleness for which he is noted, preserved his position in third place. His speech was in the spirit of warm greeting to the throng, calling on the students of Peking to be good hosts to those who had come from the provinces, and telling them all that their main task was to carry out the Cultural Revolution in their own schools. His self-assurance was in striking contrast to that of Lin Piao, and the personality he projected made him stand out among the nearby leaders, hard of face or unappetizing of expression, looking wooden or self-important in their high-buttoned and ill-fitting uniforms. He alone was clad informally, but appropriately for a hot summer day, in a light-colored, open-necked, short-sleeved bush jacket. He alone looked bright-eyed and interested in everything that was going on; at one point he went down to join a crowd of young people, leading them in singing, and looking not unyouthful himself despite his sixty-seven years. On the record he is capable of much cold calculation. But clearly he is not a stuffy person, and obviously he can be immensely winning when he chooses.

Even Nieh Yüan-tzu—who had put up the celebrated poster at Peking University—was among the speakers, and Ch'en Po-ta—identi-fied as leader of Mao Tse-tung's Cultural Revolution Group—presided over the rally.[20]

But no role, other than that of being among those present on the rostrum, was accorded Liu Shao-ch'i, the chairman of the government. When the accounts of the rally were published it became apparent that Liu Shao-ch'i had fallen from second to eighth place. Liu Shao-ch'i, Chu Teh, and Ch'en Yün—whose names appeared in that order—now were outranked not only by Mao, Lin, and Chou, but also by T'ao Chu, who had replaced Lu Ting-yi as director of propaganda, by Ch'en Po-ta, by Teng Hsiao-p'ing, and even by K'ang Sheng.[21] At last that old secret policeman had gotten his revenge for the events of the period of de-Stalinization, ten years earlier, when Liu Shao-ch'i and the others had dumped him from the seventh place to which he had now returned.

The Red Guards had not been so much as mentioned by name in the documents adopted at the Central Committee plenum, but it soon became clear that they were to serve as a principal weapon of Mao's Cultural Revolution. The mass rally of August 18, at which they had been surfaced, had fired their revolutionary enthusiasm, and on August 20 they were loosed upon the populace. The first of the sixteen points, adopted on August 18, had contained the assertion that "the bour-geoisie . . . is still trying to use old ideas, culture, customs, and habits of the exploiting classes to corrupt the masses, capture their minds, and endeavor to stage a comeback." Accordingly, the first targets against which the Red Guards were launched were persons, objects, and prac-tices at which such a statement might seem to be directed.

That same first point also called for distinguishing between the people and the enemies of the people, and it specified that reasoning rather than force was to be employed in settling differences of opinion and conflicts among the people. But the youthful Red Guards, mostly students in their teens, were ill-prepared to differentiate between "con-tradictions among the people" and "contradictions with the enemy." They were better able to grasp the assertions, contained in the first, second, and fourth points, that this was a revolution; that "revolution-ary young people" were being called on to be its "pathbreakers"; and that, as "Chairman Mao has often told us . . . revolution cannot be so very refined, so gentle, so temperate, kind, courteous, restrained, and magnanimous." Moreover, it served Mao's purposes to create an atmosphere of fear and a widespread sense of individual helplessness which might paralyze his enemies.

During the ensuing days of August and into September, the Red Guards in Peking were encouraged to conduct a reign of terror. Persons who were deemed bourgeois were beaten in the streets or in their homes, which the Red Guards invaded at will. Houses were ransacked and possessions which Red Guards considered that a proletarian family would not need were destroyed or confiscated. The official *People's Daily* seemingly encouraged this simplistic violence, quoting Mao Tse-tung as saying, "In the last analysis, all the truths of Marxism–Leninism can be summed up in one sentence: 'To rebel is justified.' " [22] Whatever was said in the sixteen points, it quickly became evident that unbridled violence represented officially approved mass behavior, for neither police nor soldiers came to the help of those whom the Red Guards attacked. Indeed, as Chou En-lai later admitted, during this period the police and soldiers were under orders not to interfere. On August 23, Mao Tse-tung asserted that a few months of disturbances would be "mostly to the good." After a comment apparently deprecating publicity given to the proviso that struggle should be by reasoning and not by force, he remarked: "As I see it, the disturbances in Peking are not too serious . . . Peking is too civilized." [23] The tempering in combat—which Mao had told Malraux the youth of China required—was underway, with those who were most defenseless chosen as the initial victims.

In this revolution, described as "cultural," it was cultural treasures, institutions, and leaders that were the earliest to suffer. Books in homes and libraries were seized and burned or disposed of as waste paper. Because the culture against which this revolution was directed was primarily old culture, museums were closed down and old cultural monuments were defaced. On August 25, as the New China News Agency approvingly reported the following day, students of the Central Institute of Arts removed the institute's Chinese sculptures of ancient dynasties and art objects from abroad and "completely destroyed these by burning and crushing." [24] At the Central Academy of Music, "revolutionary students" seized Ma Sitson, the academy's president and China's most noted violinist, dumped a bucket of paste over his head, rammed on it a tall dunce cap, and then spat at and beat him.[25]

Ma Sitson was released after several months of imprisonment and degrading treatment, and he later succeeded in escaping from China. He subsequently told of other teachers being killed by their students and said he had heard Red Guards had invaded the Peking home of the noted novelist Lau Shaw and beaten him to death. These cases are merely a few among many. It is believed that tens of thousands of people in Peking and other cities were savagely beaten by Red Guards during August and September, and that many of them, like Lau Shaw, were beaten to death.[26]

If elements of the party leadership felt revulsion against such beatings and killings, they evidently were too intimidated to protest. But the first killing of a prominent official of the party was a different matter. In Tientsin, Wan Hsiao-t'ang, first secretary of the city's party committee, came in conflict with Red Guards, and some time in August he died after undergoing mistreatment at their hands. According to a wall poster, Chou En-lai declared that the killing was understandable, as Wan had "persecuted" Red Guards. Nevertheless he decried it as having been carried out under the incitement of bad elements; on August 31, Lin Piao told Red Guards they should not beat people—even "people in authority" who were "taking the capitalist road." [27] However, Mao Tse-tung, unlike Chou En-lai, evidently leveled blame rather at those who gave Wan a public funeral. "There are different ways of working," he is supposed to have said. "When Wan Hsiao-t'ang of Tientsin died, 500,000 people were organized in a funeral cortege. That is using a dead man for a political demonstration." [28]

In September, after the purpose of creating a widespread atmosphere of intimidation had been served, indiscriminate Red Guard terror was largely brought to an end, and Red Guard destruction of inanimate objects slackened off.[29] Ch'i Pen-yü, one of the members of Mao's group, later asserted that burning old and rare books had been a "revolutionary action," but that such destruction was "not necessary." [30] Such cultural objects, like the nonparty intellectuals, were secondary targets. It was the opposition within the party leadership which Mao especially wanted destroyed. That would require a campaign directed not only against opponents in Peking but also in the provinces, where many of them had their power bases.

The redirection of the major thrust of the attack and the extension of the offensive, which this required, were promoted by bringing millions of Red Guards from all over China to Peking. There they received indoctrination and guidance from Maoist leaders and attended one or another of a series of gigantic rallies.[31] According to official accounts, by the end of November, eight such rallies had been held during which Mao Tse-tung "received over eleven million revolutionary students, teachers, and Red Guards." [32] As the principal speaker at the rally held September 15, Lin Piao reminded the Red Guards that "the main target of attack" was "those within the party who are powerholders taking the capitalist road." Using the language of Mao Tse-tung's big-character poster of August 5, Lin Piao continued, "Bombard the headquarters and you bombard the powerholders taking the capitalist road." The headquarters which Red Guards from the provinces were to bombard were, it was made clear, the headquarters of the party in the provinces. It is also evident that Mao intended this attack to be destructive. As early as August 23, Mao had remarked: "It does not matter if there are no provincial party committees, we [will] still have the district and *hsien* [county] party committees." [33]

Meanwhile, those members of the Central Committee who had attended the plenum, and whose bases of operations were outside Peking, had returned home. They and their subordinates were under injunctions to "stand in the van" of the Cultural Revolution, to "arouse the masses," and to "persevere in giving correct leadership," as outlined in Mao's sixteen points. Many of them proceeded to lend encouragement to the formation of additional Red Guard and other mass organizations, and some set up local Cultural Revolution groups. In a few provinces they replaced the directors of the propaganda departments of their own party committees. However, the phrase "followers of the capitalist road" was too vague to be of much help in identifying Mao's intended victims; members of the Central Committee from outside Peking were reluctant to attack their own supporters, and none of them initiated a widespread purge.[34] Indeed, two powerful regional leaders, Liu Lan-t'ao of the party's Northwest Bureau and Li Ching-ch'üan of the Southwest Bureau, had opposed Mao's Cultural Revolution during the plenum and frankly said that they would be no readier to accept it after they had returned to their posts.[35]

In any event, the secretaries of the regional, provincial, and municipal bureaus of the party soon found themselves immersed in the tasks of receiving and taking care of heavy influxes of Red Guards. Often the first wave was composed of Red Guards from Peking, thousands of whom had by mid-September been sent out to spread Mao's gospel and make revolution.[36] The impromptu meetings for which the Red Guards gathered crowds—in order to read to them from the red-covered *Quotations from Chairman Mao Tse-tung* and lead them in singing songs in his praise, such as "Sailing the Seas Depends Upon the Helmsman"—might create no more problems than analogous activities by members of the Salvation Army. But the revolutionary activity of seeking out "followers of the capitalist road" and of "bombarding" their headquarters put party leaders in an anomalous position. They found themselves questioned, harangued, and often besieged in their own headquarters, perhaps by the same Red Guards

for whom they had been trying to provide food and temporary lodgings.[37] Accustomed to leading and unaccustomed to having their authority challenged, many of them defended themselves by calling on
troops of the local garrisons to maintain order or by pitting groups of
workers and local Red Guards against those from outside.[38]

Meanwhile, growing numbers of party leaders in Peking were
coming under Red Guard attack. Many of them had incurred student
ill will during the period when they were involved in the operations
of work teams sent into the schools shortly before the Central Committee plenum. Mao Tse-tung and his supporters, by condemning
those work teams for "repressing" the students, laid other leaders of
the party open to the charge of being "powerholders following the
capitalist road." Because such powerholders had been declared the
main targets of the Cultural Revolution, seeking revenge on them for
personal indignities suffered at the hands of the work teams appeared
to have revolutionary sanction.[39]

The basis for the attack on Li Hsüeh-feng, who apparently had
been raised earlier in 1966 to the rank of vice premier,[40] was typical.
He had succeeded P'eng Chen as head of the party committee for the
municipality of Peking, and thus he bore a share of responsibility for
the sending of work teams into the local colleges and universities. He
was, on October 14, forced to make a "self-examination" at a rally,
held at Peking Normal University, which was attended by fifty thousand people. His attackers, however, remained unsatisfied. His self-
appraisal was deemed ambiguous, and a second one was demanded.[41]

This new stage of the Cultural Revolution, however, produced
conflicts within the Red Guard movement itself.[42] That movement
had been begun in the context of an uprising against school administrators, and then expanded into a diffuse attack on the broad cultural
front. During those stages it did not seem to conflict with the self-
interest of any major segment of the student population. But this
ceased to be true when the Red Guard movement was refocused
against the leadership of the party apparatus.

Membership in the Red Guards supposedly was originally restricted to the offspring of members of five so-called classes comprising
workers, peasants, army personnel, revolutionary heroes, and revolutionary leaders.[43] In general, they presumably all shared a discontent,
arising from concern about their futures, because opportunities in
China were limited and advancement up the ladder was decidedly
slow.[44] But in effect the Red Guards had been drawn from only two
dominant classes, there was a profound disproportion in the degree
to which those drawn from each class had reason to share such con-

cern, and one should expect there to have been latent hostility between them. The revolutionary leaders had, for the most part, become the members of a new class of high civil officials and military officers. Their children, coming from relatively sophisticated family backgrounds, generally did well in school. Moreover, they might hope to benefit from their family connections, in terms of placement, once their educations had been completed. But the children of workers, peasants, and common soldiers, drawn from comparatively disadvantaged family backgrounds, were more apt to fail in school and, under the status quo which had prevailed, they faced bleak prospects.

The better schools and colleges, particularly in the Peking area, contained considerable numbers of the offspring of party leaders. Some of these youths had well-developed qualities and habits of leadership which they applied within the Red Guard organizations to which they belonged. When the effort was made to refocus the Red Guard movement, they faced a conflict of loyalties. Many of them, without ceasing to profess loyalty to Mao Tse-tung and to render lip service to his teachings, resolved the conflict in favor of their parents and the party apparatus to which those parents belonged. In consequence, the refocusing of the Red Guard movement set polarizing forces in motion and pitted many Red Guards drawn from privileged classes against others of more revolutionary bent.

The tendency in such cases is for those at the two poles to come into conflict for the leadership of those in the middle. There is little doubt that most of the students, when they were caught up in the Red Guard movement, lacked a firm grasp of the issues which had split the party leadership. Indeed, that doubtless had also been true of PLA personnel who had helped organize Red Guard units or had been attached to some of the others which had spring up, like mushrooms after a rain, consequent to student initiative. The students had been taught, most of them all their lives, to respect the party; in many of them, the habits of obedience to its leadership were deeply ingrained. With the top party leadership split and the guidelines laid down by Mao Tse-tung's sixteen points ambiguous, they were potential recruits for either side. The competition to gain their support added fuel to the conflicts which broke out between factions in individual Red Guard units, and between different Red Guard organizations.

These conflicts tended to grow because there was no generally available means of resolving them, within the Red Guard movement, through appeal to a recognized organizational authority. Efforts had been made to set up joint commands or general headquarters of Red Guards in major cities. But by the middle of September, three "headquarters" organizations had sprung up even in Peking, where they competed for the allegiance of the various Red Guard organizations of the capital's schools and colleges. And there was no overall organization for the Red Guards of the country as a whole.[45]

The case of the party was quite different. When its leaders in the provinces came under attack, they had available to them a central headquarters to which they were linked by a well-defined chain of authority and responsibility. It led to the central Secretariat, functioning under the direction of Teng Hsiao-p'ing.

For about two months, commencing with the August plenum, Mao's close associates were largely concerned, and perhaps preoccupied, with the giant rallies and indoctrination sessions held for the Red Guards, who had converged on Peking by the millions. Meanwhile Teng Hsiao-p'ing, who had spent a decade building up the apparatus of the party, evidently was trying to protect that apparatus from destruction by encouraging party leaders in the provinces to take measures through which Red Guard activity could be contained and controlled. Mao Tse-tung inevitably became aware of their resistance to the Red Guards, and early in October he convened a work conference at which leaders from the various regional, provincial, and municipal bureaus of the party were summoned to appear. This conference, originally due to last for three days, was repeatedly extended until it had gone on for almost three weeks.[46] The need to extend it arose from the fact that it was marked by a bitter struggle against stubborn opposition.

The conference probably reached a crisis on October 16, when Teng Hsiao-p'ing made a report which the Maoists attacked on the grounds that it embodied an "erroneous" line, presumably akin to that of Liu Shao-ch'i, who had wanted to keep the Cultural Revolution under party control.[47] Teng Hsiao-p'ing fought back so stubbornly that Ch'en Po-ta was moved to complain: "To discuss with Teng Hsiao-p'ing as equals is more difficult than to put a ladder against heaven." [48]

The first public hint that a desperate struggle might be underway came on October 17, when large wall posters appeared in various parts of Peking which read: "Let us pledge ourselves to defend Chairman Mao to the last." [49] Much stronger evidence came the following day, when one of Mao's great rallies was scheduled to take place. During the course of the day Director of Propaganda T'ao Chu, perhaps uncertain which side would win, changed the slogans to be used at the rally—according to one account—three times. In addition, there was a very long delay before Mao Tse-tung appeared. Finally he and almost all the other full and alternate members of the Political Bureau appeared, riding in nine open cars. However, instead of mounting the rostrum, they simply rode by, and the rally was dismissed without any of the speeches which had been a feature of previous rallies. This performance, which apparently mystified the Red Guards, suggested that there had just been a meeting attended by the members of the Political Bureau, that there had been a conflict over the line intended to be taken in speeches to be given at the rally, and that the conflict had not been resolved.[50] At a smaller rally held in the evening of the same day, Chou En-lai told the disappointed Red Guards that Ch'en Po-ta was tired, that Chiang Ch'ing was unwell, and that Lin Piao—for reasons which Chou En-lai did not disclose—had no prepared speech which he could give that day.[51]

It seems not unlikely that Lin Piao had, during that day's meeting, gone out on a limb which would not bear his weight, perhaps in the context of charges he made against Teng Hsiao-p'ing. It will be recalled that Lin Piao had, at the enlarged meeting of the Political Bureau held the previous May, described Mao Tse-tung as having been worried about the possibility of a counterrevolutionary coup d'etat. When his campaign against P'eng Chen had been launched, Mao had sent personnel to vital installations—in order, Lin said, to ensure against their possible seizure. This story, which Lin had related in connection with the struggles against Lo Jui-ch'ing, P'eng Chen, Lu Ting-yi, and Yang Shang-k'un, apparently led to the circulation of a much more specific account. According to this account, a coup had actually been plotted in February 1966, and it was to have taken place in July. It had, however, been forestalled by Mao Tse-tung through measures which included the shifting of some military units. Inevitably the Red Guards, in their meetings with party leaders, had asked questions about this story, and both Teng Hsiao-p'ing and T'ao Chu had denied its truth. Indeed, Teng Hsiao-p'ing had, on August 2, asserted that the story had been the subject of a formal inquiry, and had been found false.[52]

At some point during the October 1966 conference, however, Lin Piao related this story as fact, and dwelt on it at length. As he hardly needed to point out, the four alleged plotters all had been the subordinates of Teng Hsiao-p'ing, within the party Secretariat. This meant, if the story were true, that Teng could be charged with gross negligence. Lin Piao suggested that Teng might also have participated in the plot. "Liu and Teng have already been exposed," he said, "and it has already been made clear that they were the backers of the P'eng group. We must seek out the true facts of the February coup plot and

clarify why Teng and T'ao so hastily denied its existence and protected P'eng, and investigate whether they were connected with the
plot." [53]

Subsequent to this October conference, Chou En-lai denied the
truth of the story in the presence of K'ang Sheng, who should have
known the outcome of whatever investigations had been made, and
who concurred in Chou's assertion that there was no evidence to support it. (Nevertheless, K'ang Sheng asserted that it was "useful" for
the masses to have such suspicions.)[54] Moreover, even before the conference had ended, Mao Tse-tung himself affirmed: "Liu and Teng
have always done their work in the open." [55] These denials suggest
that Lin Piao, by having recourse to a story known to be untrue, in
an effort to discredit Liu Shao-ch'i and Teng Hsiao-p'ing, had discredited himself instead. In any event, there is reason to suspect that
he emerged from the conference under something of a cloud. He did
address a rally held on November 3. But pictures taken at a subsequent
rally of November 11 show Mao Tse-tung flanked by Ch'en Po-ta and
Chou En-lai, rather than with Lin Piao at his side, and for about five
months thereafter Lin Piao made no public appearances of note.[56]

Ch'en Po-ta's summation of the case against Teng Hsiao-p'ing was
much closer to the facts. At the August plenum, he remarked, the case
against Liu Shao-ch'i had been uncovered, but little had become
known about Teng's errors. "Actually, however, the problem of Teng
is clear and definite," he asserted. "It is important, too. Teng is the
spearhead of the erroneous line. The thought and style of Liu and
Teng are exactly opposite to those of Chairman Mao. At present, Liu
and Teng will not admit their errors but are still thinking of attempting attacks. Teng is more obstinate than the other." [57]

During this conference Mao Tse-tung asserted that Liu Shao-ch'i,
Teng Hsiao-p'ing, and their supporters had been trying ever since
1959 to put him on the shelf. They had treated him, Mao said, as
though he were their dead parent at a funeral—presumably meaning
that they had treated him with ceremony, but without communication.
"Teng Hsiao-p'ing is deaf," Mao complained, "but at meetings he
would sit far away from me. In the six years since 1959 he has not
reported to me about his work. He relied only on P'eng Chen for the
work of the Secretariat. Have you not said that he is quite capable?"
At this juncture someone interjected that Teng Hsiao-p'ing was lazy.
But that was not Mao's central point. "From 1959 to this date," Mao
was quoted as saying, "he had not at all had any intention of asking
for my instructions." [58]

By October 23, Teng Hsiao-p'ing had apparently abandoned his
resistance, for on that date he is reported to have made a self-criticism.

In it he acknowledged that he and Liu Shao-ch'i had represented the "bourgeois reactionary party line," and affirmed that he should himself take the responsibility for mistakes committed, in the various districts and in the different areas of work, during the period since the August plenum.[59]

Just before the conference closed, Mao Tse-tung made a speech directed largely at the party leaders he had called in from the provinces. If some of its passages were conciliatory, it nevertheless was not free from mocking irony. "It was I," Mao Tse-tung affirmed, "who kindled the flame of the Cultural Revolution." As soon as the contents of Miss Nieh's poster had been broadcast, he declared, the whole country had been aroused. "One blow, and you are in a fine mess! It was I who brought about this 'great calamity', and if you complain about it, it is not surprising." He had not been confident at the August plenum, he said, that his ideas would necessarily be carried out. "Sure enough, there were people who did not understand properly." Then came the Red Guards, "and it was no good not taking notice."

The trouble was, Mao explained, that when people had gone back home after the August plenum, they had failed to hold the meetings which might have prepared their subordinates ideologically for dealing properly with the Red Guards. In Honan, for example, seven or eight of the ten secretaries of the party's provincial committee had become engaged in reception work. But they had not been prepared to answer the Red Guards' questions, the Red Guards had become angry, and everything had been thrown into confusion.

Those participants in the conference who went back and still tried to operate as before, perhaps opposing one group of Red Guards with another, would be in for trouble. There was always a minority, he said, who take an opposing standpoint and in consequence "don't come through." However, "the broad masses of the cadres in the Central Committee bureaus, and provincial and municipal party committees can all come through . . . I believe that the majority can come through."

"After all," he said, "it's only a question of a mistake, just a mistaken line, once it's corrected, then all's well, isn't it? Who is striking you down? I have no intention of striking you down. In my view, the Red Guards don't want to either . . . You can't put all the blame on Comrade Shao-ch'i and Comrade Hsiao-p'ing. They have responsibility, I also have responsibility." Political and ideological work had not been done properly, but after this conference "things may be a bit better." [60]

Liu Shao-ch'i, like Teng Hsiao-p'ing, is reported to have made a self-criticism before the conference ended,[61] and Mao closed on a note which seemed to imply forbearance if not forgiveness. "We must not," he said, "get rid of Liu Shao-ch'i by a stroke of the pen. They [Liu and Teng] have committed mistakes, but let them correct themselves." [62]

During the immediately succeeding weeks, Liu Shao-ch'i and Teng Hsiao-p'ing continued to attend the mass rallies, and their names still were listed in the same order in which they had appeared since August 18. But it was observed, when they attended a November 12 celebration of the centennial of Sun Yat-sen's birth, that they sat stiffly and did not applaud or talk with leaders on either side of them.[63] Meanwhile Miss Nieh, who may have been included among the participants in the conference of the previous month,[64] was busy writing new attacks on Liu and Teng which doubtless were based in part upon accusations leveled at the two leaders while the conference was in session. The material she produced, attacking Liu Shao-ch'i and Teng Hsiao-p'ing by name, quickly found its way into wall posters and into Red Guard handbills.[65] Her essays soon proved to be more reliable indicators of Mao's intentions, toward the two leaders, than his conciliatory remarks at the close of the conference or the order in which their names continued to be listed on official occasions.

Some time after Mao Tse-tung convened his October conference, responsibilities which had been discharged by Teng Hsiao-p'ing's Secretariat were quietly shifted to another body known as the Cultural Revolution Group of the Central Committee. It will be recalled that Mao's circular of May 16, 1966, calling for the dissolution of P'eng Chen's five-man group, had provided that another body should be formed to take its place. The Cultural Revolution Group was its successor, and its leaders had been identified as such in connection with one or another of the public occasions held during the summer and early autumn. Ch'en Po-ta was its director, Chiang Ch'ing was its first deputy director, and T'ao Chu and K'ang Sheng were its advisors. Besides Chiang Ch'ing, there were three other deputy directors: Wang Jen-chung, who had worked with T'ao Chu in the Central-South Bureau; Liu Chih-chien, deputy director of the General Political Department of the People's Liberation Army; and Chang Ch'un-ch'iao, the secretary of the party committee for Shanghai who had helped Mao arrange for the publication of the *Wen-hui pao* article which had touched off the attack on the Peking party committee. It also became known, during the summer and early autumn, that the list of ordinary members of the Cultural Revolution Group included Yao Wen-yüan, who had written that article for the *Wen-hui pao*; Wang Li, Kuan Feng, and Ch'i Pen-yü, all three of whom were editors under Ch'en Po-ta of the journal *Red Flag*; and Mu Hsin, editor in chief of the newspaper *Kuang-ming jih-pao*.[66]

The full list of the members of the Cultural Revolution Group was not made public, however, until November 22. Perhaps it had by then both set up its offices, located with those of the Military Affairs Committee, and taken over the functions of the Secretariat. But the date on which this transfer of functions took place was not announced, and the fact that it had occurred was only acknowledged during the ensuing year.

The publication of the list of members of the Cultural Revolution Group coincided with the end of the period of Mao's Red Guard rallies, the last of which were held on November 25 and November 26. In announcing that these were to be the last rallies for the year, the authorities in Peking declared that "until the warm days of next spring, the . . . Red Guard fighters of universities, middle schools, army academies, and schools should stop coming to Peking or going to other localities by train, ship, or bus." The Red Guards who were already in Peking, and all other Red Guards who were away from home, were to depart by December 20 for the localities from which they had come. As from December 21, free rides on trains and free food would no longer be provided. PLA political personnel and soldiers were told to put their charges aboard their trains, and then return to their own units.[67]

It appears that Mao Tse-tung departed from Peking for the Shanghai-Hangchow area shortly after the November 26 rally,[68] leaving the responsibilities which once had been discharged by the Secretariat in the hands of the Cultural Revolution Group. The phase of his Cultural Revolution for which the Red Guards had supplied the spearhead had gone well enough in Peking, where the members of his entourage were best able to direct it. However, it had not dislodged important leaders of the regional and provincial bureaus of the party. Some of the Red Guards had been doing their best to "rebel against reactionaries," but others had been fighting among themselves or taking advantage of free food and transportation to take sightseeing trips to the beauty spots of China and to such historic "holy places" of Chinese Communism as Mao's birthplace at Shaoshan, the old headquarters of the Kiangsi soviet at Juichin, and Mao's wartime capital of Yenan.[69] The order for them to return home was not intended to put the Red Guard genii back in the bottle—Mao Tse-tung was to make further use of them. With potent reinforcements, and with most of them operating in the home localities they knew best, they might help bring down his remaining enemies. Alone, he seems to have concluded, they simply would not be up to the job.

17

The Unleashing of Madame Mao

IN THE TWELFTH CENTURY, the Golden Tartars conquered the northern half of China and established their capital at what is now Peking. According to tradition, their emperor had waters from the nearby Western Hills diverted to create a lake within his palace grounds. The Golden Tartars were in their turn conquered by the Mongols, and thereafter Kublai Khan enlarged the lake and created on its shores a hilly pleasure garden which Marco Polo saw and admired. Kublai Khan's death was quickly followed by the collapse of his dynasty and the return of the country to Chinese rule. The Ming Emperor, Yung Lo then rebuilt Peking and completed the creation on his palace grounds of three lakes known respectively as Pei Hai, Chung Hai, and Nan Hai, meaning north, middle, and southern seas.[1]

The Chinese Communists, as the new rulers in Peking, closed the area fronting on the middle and southern lakes to the general public. In this area, known as Chungnanhai, they established the offices of the party center and State Council, and the residences of the party's highest leaders.[2] The duty of ensuring the safety of its occupants was assigned to a division of troops. Officers of this division were posted at each of the many gates, and their men were quartered close at hand.[3]

The lakes, with their waters reflecting pleasure pavilions and drooping willows, and the background of red palace walls topped with roofs of golden yellow tiles, make the surroundings idyllic. But for those residents who reflected on its history, it must have seemed also a place haunted by the past. Passing through its main entrance, they might have been reminded of the suicide nearby of Hsiang Fei, the most famous beauty of the Manchu dynasty. Gazing out over the waters of Nan Hai, they would have seen the islet where, in the twilight years of that last imperial dynasty, the emperor Kuang Hsü had been kept confined by the strong-willed Empress Dowager.[4]

In the closing months of 1966, Chungnanhai may have seemed a confining place also to those officials residing there who had fallen under attack. Here they and their families had to live in close proximity to other high officials who had become their bitter enemies. Yet there was no better place, and certainly none which for the time being was as safe, to which they could move. The thick walls, about nine feet high, and the distance from the city streets, shielded them some-what from the distracting beating of gongs, the constant blare of loud-speakers, and the intermittent shouting of slogans which are the con-comitants of political demonstrations in Communist China. Moreover, the general rule against unauthorized entry protected them and their families from intrusions by people demonstrating against them beyond the gates, or by Red Guards intent on dragging them to some con-frontation.

None of the officials immediately below Mao Tse-tung was the object of a cult of personality, but they were nevertheless men of great prestige. The destruction of their prestige, among a populace long taught to revere its leaders, could in any case be accomplished only by degrees and over a substantial period of time. It was recognized that dragging them out prematurely would have greatly shocked the pop-ulace.[5] In consequence, Liu Shao-ch'i, Teng Hsiao-p'ing, and other high officials were allowed to continue residing in Chungnanhai long after they had ceased to participate in the day-to-day affairs of the party and the government.[6]

The destruction of the prestige of leaders marked for purge was nevertheless pursued relentlessly. In the late autumn of 1966, the prop-agandists in Mao Tse-tung's entourage had availed themselves of the thirtieth anniversary of the death of the famous writer Lu Hsün to illustrate their concept of the proper way to treat one's enemies. Lu Hsün had advocated never compromising with one's foes. He held that if a wild dog was chased and fell in the water, people should not help it out. Instead they should beat it to death while it was in the water and at a disadvantage, lest it survive to bite people again.

In a speech at a rally of seventy thousand people held on October 31, Yao Wen-yüan, who had once himself been described as crude as a cudgel, had advocated learning this lesson from Lu Hsün. Referring to Mao's known enemies and secret opponents, he remarked, "We must discover all the schemes and plots of those dogs that have fallen and all those that have not yet fallen into the water."[7] The known opponents of Mao Tse-tung, in the Peking hierarchy, were the dogs who had fallen into the water, and they were to be destroyed morally, if not physically. His secret opponents were to be hunted down, after which they could be similarly treated. These were to be the tasks of Chiang Ch'ing, Yao Wen-yüan, and the other members of the Cultural Revolution Group.

It seems likely that Ch'en Po-ta had been named the leader of the Cultural Revolution Group because he was both a trusted right-hand man of Chairman Mao and a member of the Standing Commit-tee of the Political Bureau of the Central Committee. It would have appeared inappropriate to appoint Chiang Ch'ing, who was not even an alternate member of the Central Committee, to head a body intended to purge it. Ch'en Po-ta proved to be an active participant in the work of the group, but he was at a relative disadvantage in meetings, through which a substantial proportion of its work was accomplished. While he is an incisive writer, he is reputedly of a retiring nature and a poor public speaker. Indeed, his Fukienese accent is so pronounced, and so different from ordinary Mandarin, that he sometimes uses an interpreter.[8] Chiang Ch'ing, by contrast, is clearly both self-assertive and a gifted rabble rouser. In consequence of these circumstances, and of the prestige accruing to her as the wife of Chairman Mao, she appears to have become the *de facto* leader of the Cultural Revolution Group.

To judge from the lists of the group's members who most frequently accompanied them to meetings, and other evidence, she and Ch'en Po-ta had a distinct preference for working with those who were farthest to the left. These were chiefly the editors from his journal *Red Flag* and the men who had assisted Mao Tse-tung and Chiang Ch'ing in Shanghai: Wang Li, Kuan Feng, Mu Hsin, Ch'i Pen-yü, Yao Wen-yüan, and Chang Ch'un-ch'iao. Some of the others appear to have been treated as though they had never been named members of the group.

The Red Guard organizations with which Chiang Ch'ing and Ch'en Po-ta chiefly concerned themselves were those associated with the Peking College and University Red Guard Rebel Headquarters, more commonly known as the Third Headquarters. This was the smallest of the three federations, at least during the early months of its existence, and Red Guard organizations affiliated with it were the most extremist. The leading ones were reputed to have been formed under the guidance of Chiang Ch'ing and other members of her group, and were admittedly responsive to their control.[9]

Chiang Ch'ing took the center of the stage almost immediately after Mao Tse-tung's departure from Peking. On the evening of November 28, she was the focus of attention at a rally attended by twenty thousand persons described as "militants in the field of literature and art." At this rally it was announced that Peking's principal opera companies, the Red Guard troupes of their respective schools, the Central Philharmonic Society, and the orchestra and ballet troupe of the Central Song and Dance Ensemble were all to become constituent parts of the People's Liberation Army, and that Chiang Ch'ing had been named its advisor on cultural work.[10]

One might have expected—in view of her long held interest in the theater, and the power over it which her new appointment gave her—

that Chiang Ch'ing might have made a graceful acceptance speech. She did indeed mention her deep interest in the theater, but did not date it back to her youth. "A few years ago," she said, "I was ill. My doctor advised me to spend more time in cultural pursuits so as to restore the functions of my organs of hearing and sight." In doing so, she had immediately been surprised by the reactionary nature of the Chinese theater, and had tried to assert her right to be a critic, but at that stage had been unsuccessful. Later she had received support in Shanghai, and thereafter she and others had produced several operas on contemporary themes. Later, if her poor state of health permitted, she might again be able to concentrate her efforts "on the question of what to destroy and what to foster in the whole field of literature and art." But now she was in a "continuing state of strain" and had to devote her attention to the affairs of the Cultural Revolution.

As she made clear in succeeding sentences, it was the purge aspects of this Cultural Revolution that were uppermost in her mind. She castigated members of the Number One Peking Opera Company, who had been reluctant to abandon traditional Chinese plays for her operas on contemporary themes, for their past sabotage of "Chairman Mao's instructions." She linked this resistance to their close relations with the heinous criminals of the former Peking Municipal Party Committee, Central Committee's Department of Propaganda, and Ministry of Culture.

However, despite their past resistance, the members of the company might still redeem themselves, and become good party cadres, by engaging in the struggle against the "bourgeois reactionary line." Struggle should, of course, be conducted by reasoning, and not by coercion or force. But it was necessary to struggle against and crush those in authority who were taking the capitalist road; to criticize and repudiate the bourgeois academic "authorities"; and to transform literature, art, and other parts of the "superstructure" in order that they might conform to the country's socialist economic base. In closing, she expressed the hope that all members of the company would join in this struggle.[11]

Because the leaders of the former Peking Municipal Party Committee, the old propaganda department and the former culture ministry had already been ousted from office, Chiang Ch'ing was in effect demanding that they be subjected to mass "struggle rallies" at which they would be denounced and humiliated. Students of the drama academy had already been incorporated in a Red Guard organization, and on December 3 they held a planning conference, brought P'eng Chen's house under surveillance, and on the grounds that they were engaged in "revolutionary actions," persuaded its guards not to interfere.

During the night of December 3 to December 4, they pushed into
P'eng Chen's house, turned on the lights in his bedroom, and called
on him to get up. "P'eng Chen's face," they reported, "turned ashy
color from surprise, and he could not even dress himself well." [12]

That same night, parties of Red Guards also seized men who had
been P'eng Chen's immediate subordinates in the Peking party committee and municipal administration; a former deputy director of the
party's propaganda department who had been a member of the original five-man Cultural Revolution Group headed by P'eng Chen; and
three men who had largely dominated the stage and screen world of
Communist China. Two of these three had been vice ministers of the
Ministry of Culture, one of them with the concurrent post of deputy
director in the propaganda department, and the third was a famous
playwright. Two of them had also been prominent figures in moving
picture studios in the days when Chiang Ch'ing was getting only
minor roles.[13]

About two weeks later, Red Guards announced that they had also
arrested two vice premiers of the State Council—former Propaganda
Director Lu Ting-yi and discharged Chief of Staff Lo Jui-ch'ing—as
well as Yang Shang-k'un, one of the Twenty-eight Bolsheviks, who
had served as director of the General Office of the State Council.
Taken into custody at the same time as Lo Jui-ch'ing were Liang
Pi-yeh, a deputy director of the General Political Department of the
People's Liberation Army, and Hsiao Hsiang-jung, director of the
General Office of the Ministry of Defense.[14] Then on December 24,
Red Guards from Peking arrested P'eng Te-huai, who had been re-
siding in Chengtu, and on December 27 they brought him to Peking.[15]

About two weeks before these series of seizures had been initiated,
the new Peking Municipal Committee of the Chinese Communist
party had issued a notice that no organization was allowed, in the
absence of authorization, to arrest and torture people, to set up a house
of detention, or to conduct trials. Any person or organization which
thereafter engaged in such illegal activities was immediately to be
dealt with in accordance with law. This notice had been dated November 18, and on November 20 a circular had been sent out, in the
name of the Central Committee, endorsing the notice and directing
that it should be given countrywide application.[16]

It may be surmised that this Central Committee circular had been
issued with the approval of Chou En-lai, and that it reflected his views.
With Mao Tse-tung and Lin Piao away, and Liu Shao-ch'i demoted
and presumably inactive, Chou En-lai was the ranking leader of the
Central Committee who was present in the capital. As prime minister
of the government, Chou necessarily placed the maintenance of or-

derly procedures high on the list of his priorities. The series of so-
called arrests which occurred subsequent to the issuance of the circular would seem to have contravened at least its spirit and the intent
which lay behind it. They would also appear to have been carried out
in disregard of Chiang Ch'ing's warning that there should be no coercion or use of force, whereas the seizures of high-ranking members of
the party had necessarily involved coercion.

Surrounding circumstances suggest, however, that the Red Guards
in question were guided not by Chiang Ch'ing's words, but by her
perceived intent. Those who participated in the arrest of P'eng Chen
subsequently described their action as having been taken "in compliance with . . . Chiang Ch'ing's call at the Literary and Arts convention." [17] The arrest of P'eng Te-huai was carried out by Red
Guards of the Peking Geological Institute and the Peking Aeronautical Institute. They were affiliated with the Third Headquarters,
which cooperated closely with Chiang Ch'ing, and they are reported
to have been flown to Chengtu in a special plane.[18] If Chiang Ch'ing
had disapproved of the arrests carried out on December 3, subsequent
arrests, and the continued use of coercion against those whom the Red
Guards had seized, could easily have been prevented.

Instead, P'eng Chen, Lu Ting-yi, Lo Jui-ch'ing, and Yang Shang-
k'un were on December 12 taken to the Workers' Stadium, in the eastern suburbs of Peking, where they were subjected to a public "trial"
before ten thousand Red Guards. The event was held under the spon-
sorship of the Third Headquarters, and the presence and participation
of army troops made it clear that the affair had official approval. A
photograph taken on the occasion shows the four prisoners standing
in a row, each with a huge placard bearing his surname hung across
his chest, and with a line of uniformed soldiers behind them. One
soldier can be seen twisting the arm of Yang Shang-k'un to force him
into a bowing position, and another is similarly holding the arm of
Lo Jui-ch'ing—once his ranking military commander. Lo's left leg
appears to be either in a white cast or covered with bandages, a reminder of the injuries he had suffered in his suicide attempt.[19]

On December 20, Lu Ting-yi was submitted to a second rally, this
time in the company of—among others—three deputy directors of his
Department of Propaganda and two former ministers of the Ministry
of Culture. Chou Yang, who had defended the Peking opera against
Madame Mao's assaults, was there wearing a dunce cap. Present too
were Hsia Yen and T'ien Han, bosses of the Shanghai film industry in
the days when Chiang Ch'ing was being given only bit parts, and leading figures in theatrical circles since then. Among Mao's enemies from
the literary field Teng T'o was notably absent. As leader of the "Three

Family Village" and as a poet guilty of a literary allusion which may have been intended to suggest that Chiang Ch'ing was a lady of easy virtue he can scarcely have been omitted through oversight. Rather, his absence seems to suggest that he had, as rumored, committed suicide. Wu Han and Liao Mo-sha, the two other members of the "Three Family Village," were both subjected to a struggle rally. So was Madame Fan Chin, the president of the *Peking Daily* and *Peking Evening News*, which had published "Notes from the Three-Family Village." There was an old link of sorts between her and Chiang Ch'ing. They shared the memory of Yü Ch'i-wei, alias Huang Ching, with whom Chiang Ch'ing had had a premarital love affair. He had left her and married Fan Chin, who was his widow. In a photograph taken at the rally, she appears with hair disheveled and arms twisted high above her back.[20]

The mistreatment accorded the victims was intended to accomplish their moral rather than their physical destruction. Their "face," or prestige in the eyes of the populace, and their self-respect, were intended to be destroyed. By causing the "masses" to participate, by witnessing the spectacle and hurling epithets at the accused, the people were made to become accomplices in this destruction. Since hate and aggression go together, the people would be induced to feel a justifying hatred for those they attacked, whatever their original attitudes towards them. In addition, the treatment accorded the victims might intimidate other officials, who otherwise might follow the "wrong line."

Merely executing the opponents of Mao Tse-tung would clearly have accomplished their purge, but it would have sacrificed the rest of the multiple ends at which the strategy of the Cultural Revolution Group was aimed. Similarly, seriously injuring the victims, before they had been thoroughly discredited, would prevent the completion of their moral destruction. It may have been for this reason that K'ang Sheng reproved the Red Guards for subjecting Lu Ting-yi to serious abuse. They had suspended him by ropes tied to his arms and legs, swung him about, and in the process had badly injured him—making it impossible to subject him to further struggle rallies.[21]

Intimidating as Red Guard treatment of their victims may have been, the terms of surrender for those who had followed the "wrong line" were not notably more attractive. As outlined in an editorial in *Red Flag*, the terms included confession to the so-called masses that they had executed the wrong line in the past; reversing actions which they had taken against members of the "revolutionary masses"; supporting the revolutionary actions of the masses in the future; criticizing their own mistakes and humbly undergoing the "active criticism" of the revolutionary masses; and not resisting any "excessive words or actions" of those who criticized them.[22]

At this stage in the Cultural Revolution "the revolutionary masses" constituted, for practical purposes, the Red Guards, and more particularly the Red Guard organizations responsive to the Cultural Revolution Group. Such Red Guards were, however, in the minority,[23] and their employment against high officials of the party evidently led to a great increase in Red Guard factional strife. The children of ranking officials, from those of Liu Shao-ch'i on down, had been early Red Guard leaders, and the arrest of P'eng Chen warned them what might be in store for their own parents. The very day after P'eng Chen's arrest, a group of them formed a new organization known as the United Action Committee. This organization, and others similar to it, assumed the tasks of attempting to defend the party organization and to protect its leaders.[24]

These Red Guards began a serious struggle against Red Guards affiliated with the Third Headquarters; leveled poster attacks at Chiang Ch'ing, who was supporting them; and circulated criticisms even of Mao Tse-tung and Lin Piao.[25] Chiang Ch'ing responded to this "adverse current" by instigating the arrest and imprisonment of Red Guards of the United Action Committee.[26] With Peking's Red Guard movement in turmoil, *Red Flag* was led to complain, in an item published December 12, that persons within the party were sowing discord among Red Guards and other mass organizations, creating splits, and instigating armed fights.[27]

The following day T'ao Chu made a speech which may have helped ensure his early fall from the high-ranking positions to which he had risen as successor to deposed Director of Propaganda Lu Ting-yi. In this speech, T'ao Chu identified "comrades" Liu Shao-ch'i and Teng Hsiao-p'ing, by name, as persons responsible for implementing a bourgeois policy line during fifty days preceding the August plenum. This line had already been exposed and criticized, he said, both at that plenum and at the following party conference. In various districts, there had been other advocates of that line, but if these people did not engage in conspiratorial activities, their cases could be treated as nonantagonistic contradictions rather than as contradictions with enemies of the people. Recently some people had been opposing the Cultural Revolution Group and advocating that it be "kicked out." Such activity was counterrevolutionary. People in some districts were even announcing slogans and making statements in opposition to Lin Piao, Chou En-lai, Ch'en Po-ta, and K'ang Sheng; they were, he said, absolutely unpardonable.[28]

T'ao Chu's speech contained apparently severe criticisms of both

Liu Shao-ch'i and Teng Hsiao-p'ing, but it also laid him open to charges of having attempted to sabotage Mao Tse-tung's Great Proletarian Cultural Revolution. T'ao Chu was deemed to have implied that Liu and Teng, like their supporters, had been guilty only of errors which constituted nonantagonistic contradictions; that they had been guilty of committing such errors only during a period of fifty days; and that their cases had been settled at the Eleventh plenum and the party conference which followed.[29]

Mao Tse-tung evidently was determined to treat the cases of Liu Shao-ch'i and Teng Hsiao-p'ing as ones involving offenses which required their being utterly crushed. Chiang Ch'ing was unquestionably reflecting his attitude, as well as her own, when she later declared that accounts should be settled for offenses committed during the fifty days, during the preceding seventeen years of Communist rule, and during the 1930s as well.[30] She also would hardly have been one to forgive T'ao Chu for omitting her name from the list of those who might not be criticized, and she may have resented his saying that those who criticized Chou En-lai were unpardonable. It later became evident that many of the attacks on Chou, which began to escalate during the immediately succeeding weeks, owed their inspiration to men close to her in the Cultural Revolution Group.

Chiang Ch'ing was later quoted as saying that the task, in the autumn of 1966, had been to blow a spark into a fire. By winter the flame had become a consuming blaze. First Chou En-lai and then T'ao Chu, it would appear, had tried to damp it down, and other high officials tried to fight it, or protect themselves against it as best they could. In more normal times, those who supported and faithfully implemented the party line could generally count on the backing of the party organization. But now the situation was reversed, and the top leaders of the party apparatus were unable to defend even themselves.

With the protection afforded by party status vitiated and party bonds loosened, other ties assumed increased importance. These more personal ties were those of family, by blood or marriage; of personal loyalty formed through past superior-subordinate relations; or of close friendship arising from shared experiences, interests, and points of view.

The party leadership had implicitly recognized that such bonds continued to play a role even among veteran Communists. On the one hand, it had preserved a rough balance, in appointments to high posts, between personnel drawn from one or another of the several field armies with which almost all high leaders had formerly been associated, either as military commanders or political commissars.[31] The party had, on the other, demanded that Communists draw a clear line of demarcation between themselves and relatives, associates, or friends adjudged to be antiparty elements. The Maoists attempted to apply this latter rule for their own purposes, asserting that opposition to Chairman Mao should be equated with opposition to the party. But, insofar as this assertion was not accepted at face value, they were working against the grain of party and of personal loyalties.

If Mao Tse-tung and his supporters had recognized the importance of webs of personal relationships under ordinary circumstances, they had even more impelling reasons to do so now. The relatives, associates, and friends of those purged or marked for purge were regarded with suspicion, sometimes with good reason, and became the objects of pressure or purge in their turn. In consequence, the purge tended to acquire a self-feeding momentum of its own. Moreover, those who were conducting it, since they inevitably encountered opposition and created enemies, did not themselves remain immune from the atmosphere of fear which they were creating, or from the exaggerated suspicions to which fear and enmity give rise. Some of these phenomena appear to have characterized relations, during the last weeks of December and the first days of January, between Chiang Ch'ing and some leaders of regular party organs in Peking.

With Mao Tse-tung and Lin Piao away, the Military Affairs Committee was under the leadership of Ho Lung. He was, in addition, the director of a Cultural Revolution Group, similar in purpose to that headed by Chiang Ch'ing but established for the purpose of separately conducting the Cultural Revolution within the People's Liberation Army. But Ho Lung's attitude toward that revolution was undoubtedly colored by his relationships with some of its prospective victims, and most particularly with Li Ching-ch'üan, first secretary of the party's Southwest Bureau and political commissar of the Chengtu Military Region. Li Ching-ch'üan had served under Ho Lung, who had commanded the First Field Army, and their families were intimately related.[32]

Li Ching-ch'üan was one of the party leaders who had most forthrightly opposed the policies of the period of the Great Leap Forward, and some of them he had simply refused to implement. The problem of Szechwan, he had declared, was the problem of grain, and it would not be solved by acceding to Mao's demands to "put politics in command." Rather than give prominence to politics, he had said, "We should give prominence to fertilizer." After P'eng Te-huai had been dismissed for opposing Mao's policies, Li Ching-ch'üan had given him refuge. When it became evident that those policies had failed, and when hunger was stalking most of the rest of China, Szechwan supplied grain from the surplus it had produced for distribution in other provinces. Evidently this had not saved Li Ching-ch'üan from Mao's criticisms, for Li had commented, "Some people eat Szechwan grain, and insult us too." [33] In the summer of 1966, while in Peking, Li had opposed the Cultural Revolution and had declared that he would be no readier to support it after returning to Szechwan. In consequence he was marked for purge, as Red Guard posters and Chiang Ch'ing's criticisms both made clear.

Associated with Ho Lung, as one of the deputy directors of the PLA Cultural Revolution Group, was his nephew Liao Han-sheng, who held also the concurrent posts of vice minister of national defense and political commissar of the Peking Military Region. Liao Han-sheng undoubtedly shared Ho Lung's attitude towards the purges which were so prominent an aspect of the Cultural Revolution. He was related by marriage to Yang Shang-k'un—their wives were sisters—and Yang had been humiliated in the same public rally as P'eng Chen, Lu Ting-yi, and Lo Jui-ch'ing.[34]

Evidently Ho Lung's other colleagues shared in some measure his distaste for the Cultural Revolution. A girl who belonged to Red Guards of the United Action Committee, in a letter to her parents, wrote: "Listening to the talks of the four vice chairmen of the Center Military Affairs Committee, we saw clearly that there is a great difference between what they say and what the Cultural Revolution Small Group says. That is why there are masses among the general public who stand on the side of the Military Affairs Committee, just as we do." [35] During this same period, if accusations made against him are to be believed, Ho Lung was directing and assisting anti-Maoist Red Guards, who included his son Ho P'eng-fei, Liu T'ao, one of the daughters of Liu Shao-ch'i, and Li Li-feng, son of Li Ching-ch'üan.[36]

However, the resistance of Ho Lung and his fellows in the Military Affairs Committee, insofar as effectiveness is concerned, compared poorly with their past records. One would not have supposed that Ho Lung had once been a swashbuckling bandit, or that they had led armies which had conquered substantial portions of what had been Kuomintang China. But he had grown fat through good living, and neither he nor they any longer commanded troops. The Military Affairs Committee was primarily a policy-making body; it was the Ministry of Defense and the Ministry of Public Security which could marshal forces, and both were headed by men responsive to Mao Tse-tung.

Behind the shield which that control provided, Chiang Ch'ing pressed ahead with the operations of her Cultural Revolution Group. On December 18, she held a forum in the Great Hall of the People. In attendance were representatives of the organizations affiliated with all three Red Guard headquarters. At this meeting Chiang Ch'ing and members of her group neatly solved the apparent contradiction between the November 20 circular, which forbade unauthorized arrests, and the behavior of her Red Guards. Specific authorization was given for the Red Guards to arrest anyone putting up posters attacking Mao Tse-tung or Lin Piao; those who, with evil intent, put up posters attacking Chiang Ch'ing, might also be arrested.

This of course left Red Guards free to put up posters attacking anybody else, and this was important to the operations of her group. The regular press, insofar as it still operated, was under a limitation, contained in the eleventh of the sixteen points adopted at the Eleventh Plenum. It provided that no individual might be attacked by name in the press until such attack had been approved by a party committee composed of persons of the same or higher level. To have flouted this rule would have been a flagrant violation of a widely-publicized resolution, adopted under the aegis of Mao Tse-tung by the party's Central Committee.

However, the same resolution provided a convenient loophole. It contained an injunction to rely on the masses and respect their initiatives, as well as praise for the use of wall posters. In consequence, posters and Red Guard newspapers provided a means for evasion, on a massive scale, of the restriction against attacking individuals by name. Members of the Cultural Revolution Group used the resolution freely, passing to friendly authors of the Red Guard press damaging materials from the party's dossiers on even its highest-ranking members.[37] These items were sometimes published verbatim, but were often interpreted and elaborated in ways most unfavorable to those under attack. On the other hand, the Red Guards flooded the streets of Peking; they were avid readers of whatever was posted on its walls, and authorizing them to arrest anyone putting up posters attacking the Maoist leadership ensured a preponderant advantage to its cause.

The Red Guards were not, of course, confining themselves to propaganda activities. Some Red Guard organizations included provost guard detachments, doubtless intended orginally for policing and protecting their own membership, but soon put to use in attacking and arresting rival Red Guards. Preeminent among anti-Maoist Red Guards of this category in Peking, some of them the sons of high officials like Ch'en Yi and Tung Pi-wu, were those known as the West City Picket Corps. At the December 18 forum Chiang Ch'ing asserted that they, and the similarly named East City Picket Corps, had official supporters who operated behind the scenes, and she identified six persons by name as among such supporters. One of these alleged supporters was Chou Jung-hsin, secretary general of Chou En-lai's State Council, and a second was Wang Jen-chung, one of the deputy directors of her own Cultural Revolution Group, but clearly no longer in her favor. All such corps, she said, should be disbanded. Members of the West City Picket Corps, she asserted, had killed many people. They should be identified, arrested, and shot.

The November 20 circular had forbidden the unauthorized maintenance of prisons, and Chiang Ch'ing dealt with this problem, too, in a way designed to favor the Red Guards responsive to the control of her group. Those whom the Red Guards arrested should henceforth all be turned over to the Ministry of Public Security for detention. It would make them available at any time for questioning by the arresting Red Guards, who would be allowed to come and go freely within the place of detention. She did not, of course, say whether such facilities would be available to all Red Guard organizations on an equal basis.

The answer to that question was, however, perhaps implicit in her explanation as to why those arrested were to be turned over to the Ministry of Public Security rather than to the Peking Public Security Bureau or one of its sub-bureaus. The Ministry of Public Security, she explained, was under the control of Vice Premier Hsieh Fu-chih, and "we trust him." The Peking Public Security Bureau "had problems," and it had been necessary to send fifty cadres to reorganize the West City Public Security Bureau. Indeed, the public security organs, as well as the Supreme People's Procurate and the Supreme People's Court, were all bureaucratic organs, introduced from foreign countries, which had "opposed the thought of Mao Tse-tung for several years."

Chiang Ch'ing might have explained, but apparently did not, that the Supreme People's Procurate, and its subordinate organs, owed their existence to regularly approved statutes, and that these statutes gave them the authority to supervise the operations of executive and judicial organs of the government, in order to ensure that such operations were conducted in accordance with law. Instead, she complained that the Supreme People's Procurate "investigates over our heads and censors our materials."

Besides such high organs of the state, there were lesser organizations which should be closed down because they were being used for similarly inimical purposes—the liaison offices in Peking of the party's provincial committees, and those Peking restaurants which catered to provincial tastes. "All Peking offices of the provincial committees," she asserted, "and the restaurants in Peking of the provinces have been secret service centers used for collecting intelligence information for those provinces. For example, the Szechwan Restaurant is supported by Li Ching-ch'üan and the Shansi Restaurant is operated by P'eng Chen. The Ministry of Public Security must shut them down, and Vice

Premier Hsieh Fu-chih agrees and says that he will talk with the Premier about it."

At this same meeting on December 18, Chiang Ch'ing implied that Ho Lung and Li Ching-ch'üan had been bracketed with Liu Shao-ch'i as officials soon to be purged. She challenged the members of her audience to do "ideological work" on their children Liu T'ao, Ho P'eng-fei, and Li Li-feng, in order to win them over so that they might "reveal information about their parents." Referring to Madame Liu Shao-ch'i's participation in the operation of the work team at Tsinghua University the previous spring and early summer, she said, "Wang Kuang-mei should be grabbed back to Tsinghua to make a confession." [38]

On December 26 Chiang Ch'ing held another conference in the Great Hall of the People. This time she met with representatives of a new organization, the All-China Red Worker Rebels General Corps. Among her entourage were Chang Ch'un-ch'iao and Yao Wen-yüan, temporarily back from Shanghai where they had been deeply involved in the affairs of a new local organization of somewhat similar name. The representatives who had come for the meeting were workers employed under the temporary and contract systems, and hence ineligible for membership in regular trade unions and inclusion in their comparatively superior systems of medical care, unemployment and retirement pay, and other benefits. Usually drawn from among the peasants near urban centers, they had to depend upon the agricultural communes for their long-term welfare. Accordingly they were available for recruitment into a new labor organization and motivated by grievances which enabled the Maoists to pit them against the Ministry of Labor and the long-existing All-China Federation of Trade Unions.[39]

That federation had been built largely through the efforts of Li Li-san, the Moscow-trained Communist who had dominated the Political Bureau during the late 1920s and part of 1930 when he had engaged in a prolonged struggle with Mao Tse-tung, and of Liu Shao-ch'i, a long-time specialist in labor union work. Liu Shao-ch'i had been elected chairman of the All-China Federation of Trade Unions in 1934, and had been its honorary chairman from 1948 through 1957. Li Li-san had been its *de facto* leader from 1949 to 1953, which is to say during formative years of the Peking regime, when the rapid growth of mass organizations was being promoted. Under his leadership the federation had acquired tendencies toward autonomy from the party and toward "economism," which is to say seeking material benefits for the workers, and it had continued to manifest such tendencies long after Li Li-san had lost its leadership.[40] Moreover, it undoubtedly continued to harbor leadership elements disposed to work with Liu Shao-ch'i in preference to Mao Tse-tung. Evidently the Maoists had concluded that they should not risk the continued operations in Peking of so large a nationwide organization which might be responsive to leaders who were antagonistic to Mao Tse-tung.

The systems under which peasants were employed for nonagricultural work, whether of the temporary or the contract type, apparently had been designed both to minimize the cost to the state of industrial development and to satisfy Mao Tse-tung's insistence on wiping out distinctions based on occupational specialization. Just as the half-work, half-study educational methods he favored were to break down the barriers between mental work and physical labor, the temporary and contract work systems were to minimize the differences between city and country, and between worker and peasant. Nevertheless, the worker representatives at this meeting tactfully represented those systems as having been developed by the Ministry of Labor at the inspiration of Liu Shao-ch'i.

This prompted Chiang Ch'ing to launch into a diatribe against Liu Shao-ch'i and his wife. Liu Shao-ch'i, she conceded, was the chief of state. "But," she asserted, "We should examine what kind of chief of state he is." The father of Wang Kuang-mei, his wife, had been a big capitalist, and "she has masterminded all this system." At this point Chiang Ch'ing summoned by telephone the minister of labor, whose offices had been sealed earlier that day by the representatives of the new labor organization. She also summoned personnel from the Secretariat of the All-China Federation of Trade Unions.

While awaiting their arrival, Chiang Ch'ing inveighed against the contract-labor system as "capitalist," and after officials of those organizations had come she reproached them in the following terms: "You have no class consciousness; nor do you bear in mind Mao Tse-tung, the party Political Bureau Standing Committee, or the masses. You have kept things secret from the party Central Committee. You have neglected the workers, and your guilt is extremely grave."

The representatives of the All-China Red Worker Rebels General Corps then recounted the "ruthless repression the workers had suffered under the temporary labor system." At this point, if the record is to be believed, "tears ran down their cheeks and they really sobbed." Chiang Ch'ing assertedly joined in and, with "tears rolling in her eyes," protested: "It isn't a sign of weakness that I cry. It's just because I have seen true comrades of our own." When they went back home, she instructed, they should spread the word that there was soon to be a big conference in Peking to condemn the contract and temporary work systems. She also would suggest the issuance of a circular ordering that workers dismissed since June 1, 1966, be reinstated and given retroactive payments of back wages. Because the representatives of the new labor organization came from out of town, they might sleep in the offices of the All-China Federation of Trade Unions, instead of sealing them up at once. Chiang Ch'ing also charged the Ministry of Labor and the officials of that federation with taking good care of the representatives, because they were "the guests of Chairman Mao." [41]

On January 2, 1967, a joint notice was issued by the All-China Red Worker Rebels General Corps, the Ministry of Labor and the All-China Federation of Trade Unions which presumably reflected Chiang Ch'ing's suggestions. It did not, however, end the attacks on the latter federation. One more issue of its organ, the *Workers' Daily*, was put out under a changed name, after which its publication was suspended. On January 3, demonstrators marched through the streets of Peking denouncing federation Chairman Liu Ning-yi and his chief subordinates, and papers were posted attacking also Li Li-san and other past leaders of the federation on the grounds that they had, over the previous seventeen years, followed the antirevolutionary line of Liu Shao-ch'i, Teng Hsiao-p'ing, and their allies. [42]

On December 27, the day after they had set in motion the operation against the labor federation, Chiang Ch'ing and some of her colleagues held another forum, this time with Red Guard groups affiliated with the Third Headquarters. At this forum, Ch'en Po-ta warned the Red Guards against their growing tendency toward anarchism, voiced the opinion that they should not try to take over the administration of their schools, and expressed the view that they would benefit from a period of training at the hands of the army—training which was, in fact, instituted under an order issued four days later. It provided that teachers and students should be organized into squads, platoons, companies, battalions, and regiments and subjected to periods of political and military training of between fourteen and twenty days. [43]

Chiang Ch'ing utilized the forum to renew her attack on Wang Kuang-mei, justifying it in the context of a 1963 state visit which Liu Shao-ch'i and his wife had paid to Indonesia. "Wang Kuang-mei," she said, "is a dishonest person. Before Wang went to Indonesia, she came to see me. At that time I was in Shanghai, sick. She said she wanted to wear a necklace and a flowery dress. I said, 'You are the wife of the chief of state of a great country. It is all right for you to take several dresses. But you are a member of the Communist party, and you cannot wear a necklace.' Because of this she didn't sleep well for several nights. Finally she agreed, saying, 'I accept your opinion and am not going to wear a necklace.' In the end, when I saw the film, it turned out that she had worn a necklace after all. She cheated me."

At this point Chiang Ch'ing paused to ask whether the film taken on the occasion of this state visit was still in existence, to describe it as

a "poisonous weed," and to urge that it should be shown at Tsinghua
University, where Wang Kuang-mei had led the work team during
June and July. Then she repeated her demand of December 18:
"Wang Kuang-mei should be dragged back to Tsinghua!" [44]

The time to take Liu Shao-ch'i himself to a struggle rally had not
come, but that evening a rally of one hundred thousand people was
held to denounce him and Teng Hsiao-p'ing *in absentia*.[45] A few days
later, papers the size of regular newspapers, carrying photographs taken
on the occasion of the state visit to Indonesia, were posted in Peking.
State visits almost inevitably involve toasts, and Sukarno was fond of
dancing. In consequence the photographs included ones of Liu Shao-
ch'i dancing with an Indonesian woman, Wang Kuang-mei and one of
Sukarno's wives posed arm in arm, and Wang Kuang-mei holding a
match to light Sukarno's cigarette. In the accompanying captions, Liu
Shao-ch'i and Wang Kuang-mei were described as depraved elements
whose behavior had disgraced China. Liu Shao-ch'i, the captions asserted, was a person of the Khrushchev type who had indulged himself
in alcohol and women; Wang Kuang-mei, while pretending to be a
woman of the new China, was actually the sort who sold her favors for
money.[46]

On January 6, Red Guards of Tsinghua University went to the
middle school where Liu P'ing-p'ing, a younger daughter of Liu Shao-
ch'i, was studying. They found that she was being put through an oral
"self-examination" before the students and teachers, so they waited
until it had been completed, after which they detained her at school.
Meanwhile a carload of other Tsinghua Red Guards drove to one of
Peking's hospitals, where they took control of the hospital's switch-
board. They then put through a call to Wang Kuang-mei, alleging that
Liu P'ing-p'ing had been run down by a car and critically injured, that
an immediate operation was necessary, and that Wang Kuang-mei
would have to come at once to authorize it in person.

In this way they lured Wang Kuang-mei out of Chungnanhai and
into their trap, as they had hoped. They also drew in Liu Shao-ch'i, his
army officer son Liu Ying-chen, Liu T'ing-t'ing, another of the daughters, and one of Liu's bodyguards, all of which they had not intended.
Nevertheless the Red Guards succeeded in turning the others away,
taking Wang Kuang-mei off to Tsinghua University, and subjecting
her to a hostile confrontation—the first of several she was to endure
that year.[47]

Wang Kuang-mei was allowed to return to Chungnanhai only
after she had signed a statement dated at 5 A.M. of the following day.
In this statement she undertook to bring to light all she knew about
her husband's political activities, organizational work, moral charac-

ter, and daily life. This information was to be included in written self-examinations, which she was to submit at ten-day intervals. In addition she promised to return to Tsinghua University, at any time her captors required, and to engage there in repeated self-examinations before students, teachers, staff, and workers, until she had made a self-examination which they found acceptable.[48]

In reviewing Chiang Ch'ing's performance in the role of the Cultural Revolution's grand inquisitor, during this period of Mao's absence from Peking, one might be reminded of a remark made about her by one of her apologists. Perhaps endeavoring to explain away the reputation she had gained, he remarked that many of her enemies had attacked her. By the end of 1966 she had, in turn, attacked many of her enemies. In doing so, she had proved a worthy mate and a good student of the thought of Mao Tse-tung. They shared enmity for the same persons, if perhaps in differing proportions, and as he had once remarked, "If others attack me, I always attack back." [49] It seems doubtful, moreover, that he would consider she had laid about her with too heavy a hand. It will be recalled that Chang Wen-t'ien had complained to P'eng Te-huai, at the time of the Lushan plenum, that Mao Tse-tung was very brilliant, but also very strong-handed in rectifying people. P'eng Te-huai had agreed, commenting that in China's history the first emperor of every dynasty had been strong-handed as well as brilliant.[50]

18

The Shanghai Storm

THE CHINESE COMMUNISTS have described the Cultural Revolution of Mao Tse-tung as an unprecedented thing. Viewed as a whole it was, like Frankenstein's monster, indeed a new thing. Looked at in detail, it may be seen as having been similarly created by assembling parts taken from bodies of previous revolutionary experience.

To begin the first, or mobilizational, phase of the Cultural Revolution, Mao Tse-tung took a leaf from his opponents' book. For half a decade they had been undermining him through literary works of veiled or half-veiled criticism. By sponsoring the writing and publication of Yao Wen-yüan's articles, beginning with the attack on the play *Hai Jui Dismissed from Office,* Mao Tse-tung turned the tables on them.

Mao's decision to use the student Red Guards, in the second phase of the Cultural Revolution, was undoubtedly inspired in part by the May Fourth Movement of 1919. That earlier movement, too, had featured massive student demonstrations, confrontations with officials accused of responsibility for objectionable policies, and recourse to violence against persons and property. The student demonstrations of 1919 had ended once they had attained their immediate objectives. But like a yeast, they had started a vast social ferment in which even laborers had participated, and which helped prepare the way for subsequent revolutionary change.[1]

The treatment suffered by victims of the Cultural Revolution, at Red Guard rallies and kangaroo courts, is reminiscent of that inflicted by the peasants on landlords and village gentry who had exercised authority at the local level, during the 1926 uprisings in Mao's native Hunan. In his 1927 report on those peasant uprisings, he wrote: "Every day the coarse, harsh sounds of their denunciations pierce the ears of the gentry. . . . The local bullies and evil gentry are crowned with tall paper hats bearing slogans such as 'Local bully so-and-so' or 'So-and-so, one of the evil gentry.' They are walked on a lead and escorted by big crowds both in front and behind them. Sometimes gongs are beaten and flags waved to attract attention. This form of punishment, more than any other, makes local bullies and evil gentry shudder with fear. He who has once been crowned with the tall paper hat loses face forever and can never hold up his head again." [2]

The Red Guard phase of Mao Tse-tung's Cultural Revolution, like the reign of terror conducted by the peasants of Hunan, was unquestionably destructive of the prestige and morale of those against whom it was directed. However, the process of actually removing Mao's opponents from positions of authority had, except in Peking, hardly been begun. In order to accomplish this task, Mao Tse-tung evidently was willing to destroy those portions of the power structure which had become their strongholds, or which he considered obstacles standing in his way.

In justifying such destruction, Mao Tse-tung's supporters appear to have looked to the experiences of the revolutionary Paris Commune of 1871. In the spring of 1966, an article had appeared in Ch'en Po-ta's journal *Red Flag*. The article praised the proletariat of Paris for having recognized that the state system they attacked, which had been "the political instrument of their enslavement," could not also serve "as the political instrument of their emancipation." In consequence of this recognition, "the Commune smashed the old judicial organs and liquidated reactionary legal traditions. It stipulated that judges should be elected by the people and that procurator-generals should be appointed directly by the Commune." [3]

It became apparent that such measures might be applied in China when Chiang Ch'ing made her verbal attack of December 18 on the country's public security and legal systems, and when Public Security Minister Hsieh Fu-chih later testified: "Thoroughly smash the public security, procurate and justice organs—this Chairman Mao has said to me, if not ten times, at least eight times." [4]

It is not clear whether Mao Tse-tung ever justified this demand—that Hsieh Fu-chih cooperate in destroying the public security system for which Hsieh was himself largely responsible—by reference to the Paris Commune or any other non-Chinese revolutionary model. Undoubtedly Hsieh recognized that this demand arose from the circumstance that the government at each level had been made subject to the guidance of the party. In every party committee there was a secretary in charge of political and legal affairs who controlled the public security police. If party committees in the provinces and municipalities were to be destroyed, it accordingly might be necessary first to put the public security departments of the government out of action. [5]

Mao Tse-tung did, however, give Hsieh Fu-chih an explanation, based upon an analysis of the 1949 Chinese Communist revolutionary takeover, which apparently was intended to justify smashing any part of the government which had fallen under the control of his allegedly revisionist opponents. Referring to the replacement by Communists of functionaries of the preceding government of the Nationalists, he said: "This government of ours was established through the dispatch of a small number of leaders to suppress the upper group and also through the selection of the great majority of people in the lower echelon from among the Kuomintang government bureaucrats." Under such circumstances it was clear that the "residue of feudalism" would corrupt the regime and the "buds of revisionism" appear. A new takeover had become "unavoidable" because this was "not a government established through a revolution of workers and farmers and through their seizure of the political reins." [6]

It was to the workers and peasants that Mao Tse-tung looked to provide the principal motive power for this new phase of his Cultural Revolution. Of the two, the workers might be more easily mobilized because they were concentrated in the cities, rather than dispersed in the countryside. Moreover, it was the cities which contained the main headquarters of party, government, and mass organizations from which his principal opponents were to be dislodged.

In planning this new phase, Mao undoubt dly referred again to his own revolutionary experience. It had been the support of the workers and the peasants which had helped ensure the military success of the Northern Expedition, launched in 1926 by the Kuomintang and its Chinese Communist collaborators. Friendly peasants had facilitated operations in the countryside, and a revolt of Communist-organized workers, timed to coincide with the approach of advancing forces, had delivered Shanghai into the hands of Chiang Kai-shek.[7]

"The May Fourth Movement," Mao later told visiting members of a foreign military delegation, "was started by intellectuals. . . . However, a thorough revolution like the Northern Expedition or the Long March can be accomplished only through workers, peasants, and soldiers—the masters of our time—as the main force. Workers, peasants, and soldiers are in fact only workers and peasants, because soldiers are merely workers and peasants in military uniform." During the earlier part of the Cultural Revolution, "criticism and repudiation of the bourgeois reactionary line was started by intellectuals and the broad masses of young students. . . . Intellectuals can always change quickly and have quick perception, but they have their natural limitations, lack the will for thorough revolution, and very often show a wavering character." [8]

The biggest concentration of workers was to be found in Shanghai, a city of about ten million inhabitants. Shanghai was accordingly selected as the place in which to launch what came to be known as the

"January storm," and it was probably in nearby Hangchow that Mao Tse-tung and Lin Piao spent most of the ensuing period of about forty days, following the November 26, 1966, reception for Red Guards, during which they apparently were absent from Peking.

The Shanghai party committee was led by Ch'en P'ei-hsien, one of the signers of a letter sent to Chairman Mao at the time of the Kao Kang–Jao Shu-shih affair, suggesting that he should "take a rest." The most prominent of his party committee colleagues was Ts'ao Ti-ch'iu, the mayor. Preparations for seizing power from them had been begun early in the autumn. By the initial days of September, the first contingents of some two thousand Red Guards from Peking had been sent to Shanghai, where they were intended to "establish revolutionary ties" and to engage in "struggle," and many more Red Guards followed on their heels.[9]

In Shanghai the various groups of visiting Red Guards set up local headquarters, or liaison stations, a process which was to be repeated elsewhere in China until whole networks of such stations had been created.[10] They also lost no time in besieging the municipal offices and demanding to see the mayor. At this point the Shanghai Red Guards were, for the most part, supporting the local party committee, as were the workers. After a few days the besieging Red Guards were roughly dispersed by a large group of workers mobilized by the party committee. (This defensive reaction was, incidentally, to prove far from unique. Rather, it was repeated in centers all over China, with the local authorities using workers, peasants, local Red Guards, or troops to break up demonstrations mounted by outside Red Guards from Peking or other places.) In Shanghai, the offensive of the Red Guards, after they had been administered this rebuff, degenerated into a war of words conducted by poster and through loudspeakers.[11] As Mao Tse-tung soon recognized, they were incapable by themselves of carrying the day against an entrenched opposition.

The task of creating Maoist worker organizations, which were to provide the needed reinforcements, was quietly begun at least as early as the first part of November. By November 17 the Cultural Revolution Group had prepared a directive calling on the workers to assume the leading role in the Cultural Revolution. It also authorized revolutionary student organizations to send representatives into factories, mines, and other enterprises in order to join forces with the workers. The command system for production was to remain undisturbed, and the workers were enjoined to stay at their posts during working hours. At the same time, a parallel leadership system was to be set up for purposes of carrying on the Cultural Revolution. Party committees at all levels, and the leaders in productive enterprises, were directed to encourage the establishment of this parallel leadership, which was to be chosen through elections conducted on the model of the Paris Commune. They were, however, not to interfere in the process, to be afraid of the rising of the masses, or to oppose it.[12]

On December 15 another directive was adopted which was to extend the Cultural Revolution also to the peasants of the countryside.[13] The two documents called on the workers and peasants to "grasp revolution and promote production"—dual requirements which were to prove incompatible. In practice, one or the other had to take precedence, and it was production which was to give way to revolution. The expectation, too, that managers might be both willing and able to guide the workers in setting up a second command system, based on the exotic model of the Paris Commune of 1871, also appears to have been unrealistic.

It seems fair to surmise that it was the theoretician Ch'en Po-ta who had been largely responsible for the formulation of the November 17 directive. Ch'en Po-ta and several leftist members of the Cultural Revolution Group discussed that directive, the day it was dated, with selected worker and Red Guard representatives,[14] but it appears to have remained unpublished until the latter part of December. Perhaps publication was held up in order not to alert Mao's opponents prematurely, and in order that his own adherents might gain as much lead-time as possible for the preparation of the next phase of his offensive.

In November, Nieh Yüan-tzu, the redoubtable female who had put up the poster attacking the president and party committee of Peking University early in the Cultural Revolution, descended on Shanghai. She arrived with a splash, putting up at the best hotel and passing out the news—startling, at this stage, to at least some people in Shanghai—that the ringleaders responsible for the antiparty "black line" were none other than Liu Shao-ch'i and Teng Hsiao-p'ing.[15] That same month two members of the Cultural Revolution Group, Chang Ch'un-ch'iao and Yao Wen-yüan, also came to Shanghai, charged with the task of directing operations against their fellow members of the party's Shanghai municipal committee.[16] Their comings and goings were unheralded, as befitted the movements of men engaged in conspiratorial tasks, but they played major roles in the events which followed.

The Shanghai to which Chang Ch'un-ch'iao and Yao Wen-yüan had returned had been substantially altered, in atmosphere and appearance. The streets were more than usually filled with people, some of them doubtless unemployed because of the disruptions incident to the Cultural Revolution. Moreover, its normal population had been swollen by about a million additional persons. Foremost in activity, though not in numbers, were the Red Guards from Peking. The air was filled with denunciations of their opponents, and their posters had begun to fill all available wall space. Large numbers of peasants, who had come from nearby rural areas either to participate in or to witness the excitement, had also flooded into the city. Perhaps the most numerous of the newcomers, however, were labor conscripts and recruits, drawn from Shanghai during preceding years, who had taken advantage of loosened official authority to return home.[17]

Most of them were former students, sent to agricultural villages— or to state farms and construction sites in border areas, some as distant as Sinkiang—because they had been surplus to the needs of the urban economy. Those who had returned from Sinkiang were particularly bitter. They had gone, in many cases, believing that they would work with "wonderful tractors and other things." Instead, they had become earth-coolies living in "fascist concentration camps," some of them allegedly enclosed with electrified barbed wire, as though they were offenders undergoing "reform through labor." [18] Even those recruited for work in the ordinary countryside complained: "The farm village is hell; it is a sea of bitterness." These evaluations of life on the frontier and in farm villages gave rise to the slogan: "Fight back to the cities! Demand human rights." [19] The first part of the Maoist injunction, to "grasp revolution," evidently fitted their temper; the second part, to stay on the job and "promote production," clearly did not.

From among the diverse elements of the permanent and temporary populations of Shanghai, the Maoists and their Red Guard helpers from other areas built a new organization. As early as November 9, such an organization, calling itself the Shanghai Workers' Revolutionary Rebel General Headquarters, was already in being. That day the startled inhabitants of Shanghai learned that some 2,500 of its members had commandeered a train and forced the crew to set off for Peking. They wanted, they explained, to visit Chairman Mao and complain about the evil mayor and his colleagues. The train was stopped at Anting, several stations beyond Shanghai, and Shanghai's mayor promptly labeled the new organization counterrevolutionary. At Anting, matters were at an impasse, with the Revolutionary Rebels occupying the station and refusing to budge, demanding that their action should be recognized as revolutionary and hence justifiable. The mayor refused, but at this point Chang Ch'un-ch'iao and Yao Wen-yüan suddenly appeared at Anting and signed their list of demands.[20] By this performance, the new organization was called to public attention in dramatic fashion, and given the overt blessings of leading members in the camp of Mao Tse-tung.

Before long a rival organization, known as the Workers' Scarlet

Guards, appeared. Its headquarters were located in the offices of the Municipal Federation of Trade Unions, and its formation no doubt had the approval of the mayor and other members of the municipal party committee. The Revolutionary Rebels immediately charged that the Scarlet Guards had been duped by reactionaries and were nothing more than the private bodyguards of Shanghai's mayor. Subsequently handbills were circulated in Shanghai asserting that Lin Piao had ordered the organization's dissolution.[21] The mayor could prevent such assertions from finding their way into the Shanghai press, but he was in an anomalous position which undoubtedly prevented his making vigorous use of the mass media. He had come out publicly in support of the Cultural Revolution in a public speech on the eve of China's October 1 National Day, perhaps hoping to win exemption from further attacks.[22] The tactic had not succeeded, but in the absence of support from a centrally directed and coordinated opposition to the Cultural Revolution, he could scarcely be expected to go on the offensive against Mao Tse-tung, or publicly to take issue with Lin Piao, Mao's ranking supporter and chosen heir.

It accordingly is not strange that public support for the mayor and his party committee, which seemed overwhelming in November, appeared to erode in the last days of December, with some of the local Red Guards shifting sides and affiliating themselves with the Revolutionary Rebels.[23] Meanwhile the contest between the rival worker organizations had extended from the sphere of propaganda, characterized by posters, mass demonstrations, and counterdemonstrations, to the realm of violence. The Scarlet Guards accused the Revolutionary Rebels of beating people with iron bars, pointing out, to no avail, that Mao's sixteen points had contained a clear injunction against the use of force.[24]

It was only on December 26, with the two labor organizations deeply engaged in bitter struggle, that the public officially learned from *People's Daily* of the Cultural Revolution Group's decision to extend the Cultural Revolution to the economy.[25] It can scarcely have been pure coincidence that December 26 was also chosen as the day on which to seal the Peking offices of the Ministry of Labor and to hold Chiang Ch'ing's meeting with the temporary and contract workers. Similarly, the presence back in Peking of Chang Ch'un-ch'iao and Yao Wen-yüan, on the day of the meeting, can hardly have been merely fortuitous. The promises Chiang Ch'ing made to those representatives were quickly made known in Shanghai, where they raised high hopes that the temporary and contract worker systems, disliked for different reasons by both permanent and temporary workers, would be abolished. Moreover, Chiang Ch'ing's promises did not remain entirely unfulfilled, for vast sums were paid out as back wages to the city's unemployed.[26]

If these developments enabled the Shanghai Revolutionary Rebels to draw large numbers of temporary and contract workers into their membership, it probably gave their organization a needed edge. Since so many of them were unemployed, they were able to devote their full time to propaganda, mass demonstrations, and street fighting. Their opponents, on the other hand, were predominantly drawn from among the regularly employed. The Scarlet Guards are said to have got the worst of it as fighting force, about this time, under circumstances which recall the first appearance of the Revolutionary Rebels. They too commandeered a train, and several thousands of them set off for Peking. Several stations down the line they were intercepted by Revolutionary Rebels and defeated in a mass encounter which is said to have cost over ten lives and to have left scores wounded.[27]

However, the Scarlet Guards, being drawn predominantly from among the regularly employed, had available to them the weapon of the strike. Their reasons for resorting to it undoubtedly were compounded of economic motives, resentment at the steps taken in Peking against the All-China Federation of Trade Unions and on behalf of workers affiliated with Chang Ch'un-ch'iao, and irritation over other grievances.[28]

The Shanghai-based railway workers had shared with their fellows throughout China the enormous extra task, discharged between August and the end of December, of shuttling an estimated fifty million Red Guards around China, eleven million of them to Peking.[29] For the time being many of them were traveling by foot in officially encouraged emulation of the Red Army's "Long March" from central China to Yenan, and Mao's series of giant receptions for the Red Guards had ended. But at the time it appeared that they had merely been suspended for the winter. On November 16 the regime had promised that "beginning from April next year . . . those university and middle school students who . . . have not come to Peking . . . will have the opportunity to make a free trip . . . to see our most respected and beloved Chairman Mao and to conduct studies and exchange revolutionary experience."[30] Meanwhile many other people were on the move, singly or in groups numbering sometimes in the thousands, and in Peking long rows of newly constructed worker houses had to be set aside for the lodging of visiting petitioners from the provinces.[31] Many of those on the move made trouble for the overworked train crews—the case of the Revolutionary Rebels from Shanghai who commandeered a train provides one example which was not unique. In consequence the railwaymen were in a mood themselves to make complaints and lodge demands.

According to one of the strike organizers, representatives of Shanghai workers in the railway, public utilities, finance, trade, postal, telecommunications, and other sectors met in the Scarlet Guard General Headquarters on the night of December 27. After debate, a majority voted in favor of a strike in which all should participate except nightsoil collectors and workers in the power plant and waterworks. Evidently they were excepted in order not to work undue hardship on the populace. However, the authorities could hardly permit a strike of the contemplated dimensions without running the risks of losing the support of elements of the general populace and seeing the emergence of a vacuum of power and authority. On December 29 they signed an agreement for the payment of substantial additional sums for wages and benefits.[32] But they appear either not to have met all worker demands in this agreement, or to have signed a second agreement which they promptly declared null and void on the grounds that it had been signed under duress, and to have left the workers angry and dissatisfied.[33]

The final decision to strike was reached in the early morning hours of December 30, and the work stoppage was immediately effective. Traffic on the two main rail lines stopped; transport on the inland waterways of the Shanghai delta, on which the city largely depended for food and raw materials, came to a virtual halt; port operations ceased; and many factories shut down.[34]

The reaction came within a week. On January 4, pro-Mao groups seized control of the Shanghai *Wen-hui pao,* and the next day they took over the *Liberation Daily.* These papers were then used to turn the issue of the strike against the mayor and his party committee. On January 5, the *Wen-hui pao* carried the text of an open letter to the people of Shanghai, issued the previous day in the name of the Shanghai Workers' Revolutionary Rebel General Headquarters and ten affiliated organizations, blaming those authorities for the disorganization into which the city had been plunged. The letter further accused them of intending also to cut off the vital supplies of water and electricity on which the populace depended. The people were called upon both to take a firm hold of revolution and to promote production, thereby smashing what was described as the counterattack of the bourgeois reactionary line.[35]

On January 9, the two papers printed the text of a telegram, from the rebel groups to Chairman Mao, alleging that the party officials of Shanghai were using material benefits to lure workers into "economism" in order to sabotage the cultural revolution.[36] This was followed by their issuance of a ten-point notice, in the name of thirty-two organizations, asserting that those officials had set themselves against Chairman Mao; had tried to shift the orientation of the struggle from the political to the economic sphere by wantonly increasing wages, benefits and allowances; and had fomented port, transport, and industrial strikes which jeopardized the national economy and the livelihood of the people.[37]

The roles of Chiang Ch'ing and other members of the Cultural Revolution Group, in using "economism" to turn the spearhead of struggle against their opponents, appear to have been conveniently forgotten. The conference to condemn the contract and temporary worker systems, of which Chiang Ch'ing had talked at the December 26 meeting, was never held. When workers from Liaoning Province arrived in Peking, believing that the conference was soon to start, they were told that they had been the victims of a hoax played on them by "bad eggs" in the provincial Department of Labor.[38] Demands for reforming the two systems continued, but they were met by statements that the matter was under study and that reforms might be considered at a later stage. Less than two months after Chiang Ch'ing had met with representatives of the All-China Red Worker Rebels General Corps, an order was issued abolishing the organization and declaring the benefits, extended under an agreement they had negotiated in Peking, to be illegal. The fact of the matter was that Mao Tse-tung approved of the temporary and contract worker systems and was opposed to raising the pay of workers hired under those or other systems.[39]

The seizure of the two principal newspapers early in January was followed by the takeover, on January 17, of the city's radio and television stations.[40] This gave the Maoists a virtual monopoly of the communications media. In consequence they were in position to turn the full force of those media against the party committee, which evidently still held out against them. It also gave the Maoists the ability to engage in selective suppression of information. This enabled them to be less fussy about the means they used to achieve the ends they sought.

However, the strictures of the Shanghai press against the evils of economism did not end the urge to practice it. The peasants pressed their demands, which included the abolition of the communes and a change in the land-ownership system. Workers continued the attempts to better their economic lot, and managers still tried to hold their loyalty by meeting their demands. On January 21, the Wen-hui pao complained that economism had "swept over the whole city and

quickly spread to the rural areas with temporary crushing success."
But it was not, by then, confined to Shanghai and neighboring rural
areas. The January 9, 1967, Peking *People's Daily* had already observed that economism had become the key problem of the Cultural
Revolution not only for Shanghai but for the entire country.[41]

The workers and the peasants had, in other words, failed to meet
the expectations of Mao Tse-tung, although he later excused them on
the grounds that they had been hoodwinked. Toward the end of
January the army was introduced, and it paved the way for the seizure
of power the following month.

An Australian student visiting Shanghai during the last week of
January has described the atmosphere then prevailing as one of great
excitement, with Red Guards, armymen, and workers speeding about
in decorated trucks, beating drums, clashing cymbals, and roaring slogans. The bund facing the waterfront was full of people participating
in the excitement, arguing, and scrambling for the propaganda leaf-
lets tossed from passing vehicles. So many layers of posters were pasted
on the doors and windows of shops that the visitor could not tell one
kind of shop from another, or a store from a public lavatory. On
January 27, he and fellow students from Australia and New Zealand
were entertained at Futan University, headquarters of Shanghai's main
pro-Maoist Red Guard organization, where they apparently were able
to talk freely with their Chinese hosts.[42]

The period during which these Red Guards were allowed to believe themselves freely-acting champions of the cause of Mao Tse-tung
was, however, drawing to a close. That same night, after their foreign
guests had left, they went out on a mission, arrested three writers who
had incurred their suspicions, and brought them to the university for
questioning. Unfortunately for the Red Guards, the writers were
friends of Chang Ch'un-ch'iao. When they got back to the campus,
they were met by a convoy described as consisting of military trucks
and motorcycles with sidecars, all filled with troops, and seventy men
of the police force, now apparently under military control. The prisoners were promptly released and troops armed with machine guns
took over the campus.[43]

Some troops were still there a year later, when a number of the
same Australian and New Zealand students came back for a return
visit, and one of them has reported that Futan University seemed a
different place. They were watched closely throughout their visit, had
few opportunities to talk to the friends they had made the year before,
and were tempted to conclude that they might have learned as much
by remaining in the antipodes and reading the *Peking Review*. They

ascertained, however, that the Red Guards had learned to recognize who was boss. The Futan University Red Guard who acted as their interpreter at a stage performance was observed, before announcing each new item on the program, to bow to a portrait of Mao Tse-tung.[44]

19
Strategy for the Seizure of Power

MAO TSE-TUNG and Lin Piao reappeared in Peking between the middle and the end of the first week of 1967. The Shanghai Municipal Committee had not yet been dislodged. However, the strikes gave evidence of the erosion of its authority, its Scarlet Guards had been defeated in a mass encounter with the rebel workers, and the *Wen-hui pao* was in rebel hands. Perhaps some new element might have to be injected into the struggle in Shanghai if authority there were to be seized rather than merely destroyed, but the circumstances were such that Mao Tse-tung now could turn attention to the problem in its larger context. More particularly, he could begin to apply the lessons of Shanghai in the nationwide seizure of power.

In the fourteenth point of his August 8, sixteen-point resolution, Mao Tse-tung had declared that the Great Proletarian Cultural Revolution was "a powerful motive force for the development of the social productive forces in our country." In a passage which evokes his Great Leap Forward, he had explained that the aim of the Cultural Revolution was "to revolutionize people's ideology and as a consequence to achieve greater, faster, better, and more economical results in all fields of work." If the masses were fully aroused, he held, and if proper arrangements were made, the revolution and production could be carried on simultaneously, without the one hampering the other.

This was not the way things had worked out in Shanghai. The workers and peasants had been aroused, but they had responded to their hopes, which were for improvements in their respective lots, or to their fears, which were that the Cultural Revolution would bring reduced pay and benefits to the workers and the loss of private plots and sideline occupations to the peasants.[1] The consequence had been that "economism" had, with "crushing success," swept over the city and spread to rural areas, and then became a nationwide phenomenon. It was a manifestation of the revisionism against which Mao fought, and if not checked it would defeat his Cultural Revolution. When the Red Guards had proved an inadequate main force, he had turned to the workers and the peasants. Now they too had disappointed him by allowing themselves, as he put it, to be hoodwinked temporarily by powerholders who followed the capitalist road.[2]

Mao Tse-tung professed to believe that the majority of leaders were good, and that the powerholders following the capitalist road were a mere handful. These professions, however, need to be viewed in the light of Maoist semantics. Chiang Ch'ing had stated that "one could not talk about 'minority' and 'majority' independently of class viewpoint," [3] and the *People's Daily* subsequently explained that "the 'majority' which goes against the interests of the broadest sections of the masses is in fact a minority, a handful." [4]

The handful of powerholders, in other words, were a numerical majority of leaders; they were, moreover, in authority throughout China. This meant that Mao Tse-tung needed to interpose, between them and the masses whom they had "hoodwinked," another body of leaders who were numerous, pervasive, and responsive to his control. The only source from which he could draw them was the army. Heretofore, it had played several roles in his Cultural Revolution, but the most significant one had been that of defensive shield. Henceforth it might have to become the spearhead.

In conversation later in the year with foreign visitors, Mao Tse-tung rationalized his recourse to the army by asserting that the soldiers were only workers and peasants wearing army uniforms.[5] It was true that the soldiers had been recruited from among the sons of workers and of peasants, but they obviously had to serve within a framework of military discipline. There was danger that this discipline might break down if the army had to be pitted against the workers and the peasants.

Moreover, as leaders in the upper echelons of the military establishment would be quick to realize, making the army the principal weapon of a nationwide purge of the party would endanger army unity at command levels. This was particularly true because of the extent to which the top leaderships of the party and the armed forces overlapped. The Military Affairs Committee, the Ministry of National Defense, and the headquarters staff each contained personnel who were also members of the Central Committee of the party. The members of those bodies could perhaps justify siding with Mao Tse-tung, as top leader of the party, against Liu Shao-ch'i, as chairman of the government and constitutional commander in chief, on the grounds that the party was superior to the government. But the same rationale could not be used to justify using the army to destroy the party's structure. It was the party which had provided a framework of rule which they would be abandoning in favor of an aging if charismatic leader.

For the politico-military leaders of China's various regions and

provinces the situation would be still more difficult. In almost every
one of China's thirteen military regions, either the commander or the
ranking political commissar—most commonly the latter—was also the
first secretary of either a regional bureau or provincial committee of
the party, and in two regions the same officer concurrently held the
three positions of commander, political commissar, and party secretary. Similarly, in the various provincial military districts, the majority
of the ranking political commissars also were secretaries, and usually
the first secretaries of the provincial committees of the party. Accordingly, the military positions of the political commissars, and of the
military commanders with whom they shared command and might
have close working and personal relations, would make them instruments of a purge in which the political commissars, in their party
capacities, themselves were presumptive targets.

If Mao Tse-tung was not to be hampered unduly in pursuing the
course on which he was determined, it would be necessary first of all
to clear out of the upper echelons of the military establishment those
leaders who had disclosed antagonism to his Cultural Revolution or
strong resistance to the army's involvement in it. Such attitudes had
risen to the surface within the Military Affairs Committee, the PLA
Cultural Revolution Group, and the General Political Department of
the PLA. Moreover, personnel of those bodies, consequent to the
practice of assigning leaders in one body to concurrent posts in another, also held important positions in the Ministry of National Defense, the General Staff Department, and the Cultural Revolution
Group of the Central Committee.

The prime example of an incumbent military leader who had
shown antagonism toward the purge aspects of the Cultural Revolution was Ho Lung, director of the PLA Cultural Revolution Group
and the ranking vice chairman, after Lin Piao, of the Military Affairs
Committee. Chiang Ch'ing had made remarks early in December
which suggested Ho Lung was intended to be purged, and Lin Piao
confirmed it at a meeting of the Military Affairs Committee held immediately after his own return to Peking. Ho Lung's obvious offense
had been to encourage, support, and perhaps help direct the pro Liu
Shao-ch'i Red Guards known as the United Action Committee. However, Lin Piao charged him with having been the wire-puller behind
discharged Chief of Staff Lo Jui-ch'ing.[6] Soon Ho Lung and his
nephew, Vice Minister of Defense Liao Han-sheng, were being accused
in wall posters of having been major participants—along with Lo
Jui-ch'ing, P'eng Chen, Lu Ting-yi, and Yang Shang-k'un—in the
alleged coup plot of February 1966. Both were purged, and after the
period of public denigration required to prepare the populace for

such action against so legendary and high-ranking a figure, Ho Lung was taken to a mass rally and "tried" in a kangaroo court conducted by Red Guards.[7]

The Maoists evidently felt that it would be dangerous to leave in positions of authority the close friends and associates of Ho Lung and Liao Han-sheng. If they had not been Mao's enemies before, the purge of Ho Lung and Liao Han-sheng might have converted them to enmity. Accordingly, Wang Shang-jung, director of the Operations Subdepartment of the General Staff and a veteran of Ho Lung's First Field Army, and Lei Ying-fu, his deputy, were both arrested.[8] Two officers holding the rank of deputy commander in the Air Force, Ch'eng Chün and Liu Chen, and Su Chen-hua, Political Commissar of the Navy, were all attacked as Ho's accomplices and purged.[9] Yang Yung, the commander of the Peking Military Region, was replaced,[10] perhaps because of his necessarily close association with Liao Han-sheng, who had held the concurrent post of political commissar in his command.

Liu Chih-chien, deputy director of the General Political Department of the People's Liberation Army and a deputy director of the PLA Cultural Revolution Group as well as of that under the Central Committee, was arrested. He was known to be opposed to the army's participation in the Cultural Revolution in local areas, and he was held to have been responsible for preparing speeches, delivered by four vice chairmen of the Military Affairs Committee, which took a line different from that being set forth by Chiang Ch'ing.[11]

The purging of Ho Lung, Liao Han-sheng, and Liu Chih-chien, as director and deputy directors of the PLA Cultural Revolution Group, opened the way for the reorganization of that body. It also afforded a convenient opportunity to modify the arrangement—provided in the sixteen-point resolution adopted by the Central Committee the previous August—under which the General Political Department of the People's Liberation Army shared with the Military Affairs Committee powers of supervision over the PLA Cultural Revolution Group.

On January 11, the old PLA Cultural Revolution Group was dissolved and a new one was set up. Its greater responsiveness to Mao Tse-tung was to be ensured in two ways. It was to be subject to the joint supervision of the Cultural Revolution Group headed by Ch'en Po-ta and Chiang Ch'ing, and of a Military Affairs Committee from which Ho Lung had been purged and which now was back under the control of Lin Piao. Moreover, Chiang Ch'ing was appointed its advisor, which gave her double authority over it. The top position of director was given to Hsü Hsiang-ch'ien who, like Ho Lung, had been a marshal of the PLA.[12] However, he had for some years been in semi-retirement because of ill-health,[13] and this may have put him at a disadvantage vis-à-vis Chiang Ch'ing; whatever her professed state of health, she could hardly be accused of a lack of vigor.

Circumstances related to those which led to the reorganization of the PLA Cultural Revolution Group dictated that changes should be made also in the Central Committee Cultural Revolution Group headed by Ch'en Po-ta and Chiang Ch'ing. The members of this body may have been chosen as early as May 16, 1966, when the earlier group headed by P'eng Chen was dissolved and the decision to set up a new one was adopted. If so, the complexion of its membership may have reflected the balance of political forces which then existed. By the time it emerged publicly on the scene as an operating body, a radical change in the balance of power had already occurred. This may explain why a high proportion of those identified as members never played discernible roles of importance in its affairs, and why some of them had become the objects of political attack as early as November of 1966.

The highest-ranking member to come under fire was T'ao Chu. Lin Piao had pointed the finger of suspicion at him during the party work conference held in October 1966, and on January 4, Ch'en Po-ta had complained of him: "In spite of his being advisor to the Cultural Revolution Group, he has not consulted us at all on the problems of the Cultural Revolution Group, he has not consulted us at all on the problems of the Cultural Revolution. He has carried out things in secrecy without informing the Cultural Revolution Group." Chiang Ch'ing had added to the indictment, charging T'ao with being "a behind-the-scenes leader of the Liu-Teng line and also a two-faced, false person." These accusations were the signal for Red Guard demonstrations, calling for T'ao's overthrow, which began the very next day.[14] As fourth-ranking man in the party, vice premier, and director of the Propaganda Department of the Central Committee, T'ao Chu was one of the residents of Chungnanhai.[15] But once so authoritatively branded for the hostile attention of the Red Guards, he could come out of that area only at his peril. Mao Tse-tung may have had this circumstance in mind when, in discussing the question of T'ao Chu with his colleagues, he commented: "I did not settle the matter, nor did you settle it. However, the Red Guards arose and settled it immediately." [16]

The fall of T'ao Chu and Liu Chih-chien appears to have led to the dismissal from the Cultural Revolution Group of several of their close associates. Soon, except for Chang Ch'un-ch'iao and Yao Wen-yüan who had responsibilities in Shanghai, there remained only seven of the original seventeen members.[17] The three leading members were, of course, Ch'en Po-ta, Chiang Ch'ing, and K'ang Sheng. Three of the others, Wang Li, Kuan Feng and Ch'i Pen-yü, were closely associated with Ch'en Po-ta as members of the editorial staff of his journal *Red Flag*. The remaining man was Mu Hsin, chief editor of the Peking *Kuang-ming jih-pao*. This left in the membership only men who shared Chiang Ch'ing's preoccupation with propaganda, agitation, and purge.

There was no lapse of time between the completion of these changes in organization and personnel, and the issuance of directives injecting the army into more active participation in the nationwide struggle for power, for which those changes had opened the way. On January 11, the same day that the PLA Cultural Revolution Group was reorganized and brought under different control, new instructions having that effect were issued.

The first, a "Message of Greetings to the Revolutionary Rebel Organizations in Shanghai," appeared on the front page of the January 12 *People's Daily* and was highly publicized in other media. It was issued in the names of the Central Committee, State Council, Military Affairs Committee, and Cultural Revolution Group, and it commended the revolutionary rebel organizations in Shanghai for having formed a "great alliance" which had "become the nucleus uniting all revolutionary forces." The concluding paragraph of the message called upon "party, government, army, and civilian circles, on the workers, peasants, revolutionary students, revolutionary intellectuals, and revolutionary cadres throughout the country to learn from the experience of the revolutionary rebel groups in Shanghai, to take concerted action and to beat back the new counterattack of the bourgeois reactionary line, so as to ensure that the Great Proletarian Cultural Revolution will forge ahead triumphantly along the proletarian revolutionary line represented by Chairman Mao." [18]

As a call to "revolutionary cadres" in party and government throughout China, this message implied that leaders who were deemed to be following the "bourgeois reactionary line" should be brought under attack by "revolutionary rebels" organized among their own subordinates. In demanding the formation of "great alliances," the message suggested that the organizations of workers, peasants, and students, if they wanted to be treated as part of the "revolutionary forces," should subordinate themselves to centers like that provided by the Shanghai Workers' Revolutionary Rebel General Headquarters, through which the Maoists could coordinate and direct their activities. Including the Military Affairs Committee among the four bodies issuing the call, and the army in the list of those addressed, carried the inference that the military were to assume an active role, in concert with revolutionary rebel groups, in the counteroffensive against the followers of the "bourgeois reactionary line."

Two other directives issued the same day gave the People's Liberation Army specific new tasks. The first stated that the PLA and the public security departments were to be responsible for the protection of the banks in all places.[19] The second conveyed a decision, assertedly reached by the Central Committee, that local PLA units should exercise military control over broadcasting stations in all places where the "revolutionary masses" were attempting to seize them from "those in authority who were taking the capitalist road." For the time being, such stations were to be allowed to carry only the rebroadcasts of the Central Broadcasting Station.[20] A third directive, issued January 14, specified that the local party committees must transfer to the military their important archives as well as the confidential personnel and communication staffs of their radio stations.[21]

The obvious purpose of these three directives was to prevent Mao's opponents from defending themselves through the use of public funds, local broadcasting facilities, and blacklist information gathered on the leaders and members of hostile mass organizations. The third directive would serve also to deny them the ability to communicate with each other by radio or to send secret messages by telegraph. This would hamper the lateral communications which might enable local party committees to cooperate with each other in their mutual defense, and help prevent the emergence of a coordinated countrywide opposition to the Maoist center in Peking.

Before January 14, however, events had been set in motion which were to involve the army in ways for which the directives provided no explicit authority. As at other major turning points in his revolution, Mao Tse-tung evidently was trying to gain over his opponents the advantage of surprise.

The sixteen-point resolution which Mao had submitted to the Central Committee in August 1966 cited "revolutionary students" in a passing reference, but at no point did it mention Red Guards. Indeed, the evidence suggests that Mao Tse-tung did not reveal to the Central Committee that the few Red Guards who had already appeared in Peking were intended to be but the forerunners of many millions, much less that they were to play a major offensive role in his Cultural Revolution, or that the schools would be ordered closed for a year to enable them to play it.[22]

Subsequently it was decided, at least at the level of the Standing Committee of the Political Bureau, that Red Guards would not be organized "in factories, offices, organizations, and individual units of enterprises." According to a statement attributed to Chou En-lai, both Mao Tse-tung and Lin Piao had agreed to this restriction.[23] The restriction was observed in name but violated in fact, with organized workers being called "revolutionary rebels" rather than Red Guards, and emerging en masse during the "Shanghai storm."

Similarly, the decision to use the army as the main instrument of takeover, at most hinted at in the January 11 "Message of Greetings to the Revolutionary Rebel Organizations in Shanghai," was not made explicit until its implementation had been begun in several provinces. Again, it was presumably in violation of understandings, reflected in standing directives to the army, that the PLA was not to be involved in the conduct of the Cultural Revolution in local areas.[24]

The first of these provinces was Heilungkiang. In that province Mao Tse-tung's principal allies were P'an Fu-sheng, first secretary of the Heilungkiang Party Committee; one Red Guard organization with which other Red Guards and some revolutionary rebels may have been affiliated; and cooperative commanders in the headquarters at Harbin of the Heilungkiang Military District.

P'an Fu-sheng had opposed Mao Tse-tung's Great Leap Forward when he was first secretary in Honan, charging that the peasants "were not equal to beasts of burden in the past," that girls and women were pulling plows and harrows "with their wombs hanging down," and that "collectivization is transformed into exploitation of human strength." In 1958 he had been discharged in consequence. After the Great Leap had failed, P'an Fu-sheng had begun a political comeback, and in May 1966 he had been appointed first secretary in Heilungkiang. Shortly after the August 1966 plenum, apparently unwilling to risk his hard-won position by again opposing Mao Tse-tung, he had recanted his "errors," pledged his loyalty, and in consequence won Mao's forgiveness.[25] On August 29, P'an had publicly demonstrated his new allegiance, at a mass rally in Harbin, by denouncing the "antiparty and antisocialist crimes" of other top leaders of the Heilungkiang Party Committee.[26]

The one so-called mass organization clearly responsive to P'an Fu-sheng's control was the Red Rebel Regiment of Harbin Military Engineering Institute. (The Shanghai Liaison Center of this organization was, incidentally, among the groups which were affiliated with the Shanghai Workers' Revolutionary Rebel General Headquarters, and which issued the January 4 open letter to the people of that city.)[27] It seems fair to surmise that it was PLA control of the Harbin Military Engineering Institute which ensured the pro-Mao alignment of the institute's Red Rebel Regiment, and of other Red Guard and rebel organizations affiliated with it.

With the break between P'an Fu-sheng and its other members, the provincial committee fell under the direction of its second secretary, who held the concurrent post of governor. The governor and his colleagues came under heavy if uncoordinated attack from Red Guards in August, and sometime in September he and two of his fellow secretaries were dropped from the committee.[28] Mao Tse-tung was doubtless gratified, for he was later to cite the governor as a prime example of an "antiparty" element.[29] But the victory was only partial, and the offensive against the rest of the party committee continued.

The campaign continued, but it was marked more by reverses than by progress. The majority of the Red Guards of Heilungkiang's universities and colleges were supporting the party committee,[30] and they proved to be thorns in the flesh of P'an Fu-sheng. If we are to believe his own account, at one point they harassed him for four days and nights, during which he was allowed neither to eat nor to sleep, and he was for a time hospitalized in consequence.[31] New mass organizations sprang up composed of factory hands, transport workers, discharged veterans, and displaced urban youths, but P'an Fu-sheng was not in a position to meet the demands of any of them. The discharged veterans and the former urban youths wanted a permanent change from the hardships of land reclamation, construction and farming work in the harsh climate of Heilungkiang's mountainous and border regions, while the industrial and transport workers, like those of Shanghai, wanted shorter hours and more pay.[32] Since P'an Fu-sheng could not meet their demands, their organizations remained basically hostile and beyond his control.

On December 5, the Red Rebel Regiment of Harbin Military Engineering Institute, the one mass organization under P'an Fu-sheng's control, was defeated in a clash with the organized industrial workers. Apparently most of the personnel of the Harbin Public Security Bureau were also unsympathetic to P'an Fu-sheng and his Red Guard friends. Indeed, in a subsequent discussion of this general period, P'an Fu-sheng asserted that the "reactionary organs" had arrested people and conducted a reign of "White terror." Beginning on December 5, the local garrison headquarters had to institute day and night patrols to protect P'an Fu-sheng's Red Rebels from further attacks.[33]

Such, then, was the general situation on January 12, 1967, when the call for a counteroffensive, issued in Peking January 11, was publicized. P'an Fu-sheng and top-ranking officers of the Heilungkiang Military District responded promptly to the call—indeed, they responded so promptly as to suggest that they had been given advance instructions and knew precisely what was expected of them. According to a purported account by participants, they went to the Harbin Red Rebels United Headquarters on January 12 to map out the actions to be taken, and on that same day they took over the *Heilungkiang Daily*, the *Harbin Evening News,* the provincial and municipal radio stations, and the public security departments. The power of the Harbin City Public Security Bureau was later described as having been taken over from above on down; the director of the Public Security Department of the Heilungkiang Provincial Government had come over to the side of P'an Fu-sheng.[34]

During the ensuing days, P'an Fu-sheng and his supporters, with the backing of the army, took over the Harbin Railway Bureau, where the employees were out on strike, and sent in their Red Rebels in an effort to restore rail traffic.[35] At the same time they were having to meet attacks launched against them by the principal mass organizations. Three of them combined forces to attack the offices of Harbin's two newspapers, and to attempt a counterseizure of the Public Security Bureau, and violent clashes ensued. On January 23, one of the hostile mass organizations encircled and attempted to storm the headquarters of the Red Rebels, from which P'an Fu-sheng's operation had been launched. But the Public Security Bureau remained under the firm control of his PLA-backed rebels, and the attacks were beaten off. The ringleaders of the five principal mass organizations were arrested and imprisoned, and one organization after another was forced to disband.[36]

By January 31, the situation in Harbin was sufficiently under control to permit the Red Rebels and units of the PLA to hold a mass oath-taking rally at which they declared that the party's Provincial Committee and the Provincial People's Council had been deprived of all their powers. In their places a nineteen-member Red Rebels Revolutionary Committee was inaugurated, and it became the new organ of power. Of these nineteen, five were officers of the PLA, five were cadres of party or government, and nine either were identified as the representatives of mass organizations or were persons of obscure background. But the distribution of positions within the committees makes it clear where the actual authority was intended to reside. P'an Fu-sheng became chairman and, like the few other nonmilitary leaders who subsequently became the chairmen of similar committees, he was promptly named to the concurrent position of first political commissar of the provincial military district. The commander of Heilungkiang Military District was named vice chairman. Three Standing Committee members were chosen, of whom two were ranking military officers. (The third Standing Committee member, a leader of student Red Guards, subsequently was dropped from the committee and reportedly arrested.)[37]

Mao Tse-tung and his close supporters appear to have anticipated that the call of January 11 would soon evoke throughout the nation responses similar to that which it had met in Heilungkiang.[38] However, only in Shansi Province was there a somewhat similar and equally prompt response. On January 14 a public notice was issued declaring that twenty-five revolutionary rebel organizations had agreed to form a Shansi Revolutionary Rebel General Headquarters, and claiming that it had on January 12 seized power from the party and government authorities of Shansi and its capital city of Taiyuan. The claim was, however, somewhat premature. This is clear even from the text of the announcement, which berated the provincial committee for refusing to surrender its archives.[39] The actual seizure of power was to require the assistance of the military, and they initially were reluctant to become involved. As the political commissar of Shansi Military District later explained, some of them were afraid that "it would draw fire to our door, create trouble for us, and adversely affect the stability of our units." [40]

A broadcast over Kiangsi provincial radio on January 20 claimed, in the name of thirty-two organizations, the establishment of a Kiangsi Rebels Revolutionary Committee.[41] However, other broadcasts and news reports of that and succeeding days made it evident that the Kiangsi Rebels Revolutionary Committee was not in control of the province. Indeed, about that time a great riot occurred in Nanchang, the provincial capital, with army reservists helping lead the peasants in what was described as a rollback of the revolutionary rebels. At about the same time clashes between Maoists and anti-Maoists were reported from major cities in various parts of the country.[42]

It would appear that Mao Tse-tung was particularly disappointed with the way things went in the province of Anhwei. In Peking, an example had recently been made of Li Pao-hua, first secretary of the Anhwei Provincial Committee, member of the Central Committee, and reputedly the son of Li Ta-chao—the director of the Peking University Library under whom Mao Tse-tung had once found humble employment, a man perhaps more instrumental than any other in bringing about the founding of the Chinese Communist party, and one of the party's earliest leaders. Li Pao-hua had been captured by Red Guards, taken to Peking on January 3, and paraded before the masses a week later—as though to prove that neither personal position nor illustrious antecedents could protect Mao's opponents from political downfall and public disgrace.[43] Nevertheless, Anhwei Province could not be brought under Maoist control. Railway operations at Pengpu, on the line between Peking and Shanghai, came to a halt—suggesting that economism was rife.[44] More important, Mao's remaining opponents apparently had under way a bogus seizure intended to camouflage their retention of power.[45]

On January 21, Mao Tse-tung, after reading a report on Anhwei, reportedly gave Lin Piao the following directive: "It is necessary to send the army to help the left wing revolutionary masses. The army should extend help wherever there are genuine revolutionaries and whenever they ask for such help. The so-called noninterference is false noninterference. It has long ago become interference. In connection with this, I ask that a new order be issued and the former one be rescinded." [46]

The impatience which Mao Tse-tung must have felt at this point was reflected in a *People's Daily* editorial of January 22, calling upon proletarian revolutionaries to form great alliances and seize power. "If the revolutionary masses want to control their own destiny," it read, "everything boils down to the matter of their holding in their own hands the seals of authority! If they have power, they have everything. If they lack power, they lack everything. Among a thousand things, among ten thousand things, the most important is to hold supreme power. . . . Join together and arise. Band together and rise up. Seize power! Seize power!! Seize power!!!"

On January 23, an order was issued which embodied the instructions which Mao Tse-tung had conveyed to Lin Piao. It also directed that "counterrevolutionaries and counterrevolutionary organizations who oppose the proletarian revolutionary leftists" were to be resolutely suppressed. "Should they resort to force, the army should strike back with force." In an apparent reference to military commanders who were supporting party colleagues and suppressing Red Guards and revolutionary rebels who engaged in violence, the directive warned that "the army must not be an air raid shelter for the handful of party powerholders taking the capitalist road and diehards who persist in the bourgeois reactionary line." It asserted that "the whole country should be given a penetrating education in the struggle between the proletarian revolutionary line represented by Chairman Mao and the bourgeois reactionary line represented by Liu Shao-ch'i and Teng Hsiao-p'ing." It ended with the injunction, "This directive must be transmitted in full to every fighter of the PLA." [47]

The results and repercussions of this directive were not long in coming. In Shansi they were both almost immediate and positive. On January 25, a Revolutionary Committee was declared established for the city of Taiyuan, and it proved to be the forerunner of a similar committee for the whole province which was inaugurated on March 18. Subsequently the political commissar of Shansi Military District gave an account of the part which its personnel had taken in the seizure of power. He asserted that the military authorities in Shansi had established day and night patrols and created an atmosphere conducive to seizure of power by broadcasting Chairman Mao's call for the PLA to support the left. They had helped promote the growth of revolutionary strength within individual party and government organizations, and thereafter had assisted the revolutionary cadres and revolutionary rebels within them to take over authority and exercise control. In some cases they had sent PLA representatives to lend the weight of their authority by being present at the seizure of power; in other cases armed men had been dispatched. Organs of particular importance, or in which revolutionary strength was inadequately developed, had simply been taken over by armed units of the PLA. The provincial public security department, court, and procurator's office were among the organs put under direct military control.[48]

Meanwhile, in much of the rest of China, the PLA had run into serious difficulties. The January 23 directive opened up to each of the multitude of contending organizations the opportunity to invoke the strength of the PLA for the suppression of its opponents. There is little doubt that commanders were quickly inundated with requests for help, and that the directive had placed them in a quandary. They had been given the unenviable task of deciding which ones among opposing sets of organizations represented the true left. In many cases one might appear to have as valid a claim as another. But to intervene on behalf of neither might lay commanders open to the charge of disregarding the instructions of Chairman Mao. If the commander made a choice, those against whom he intervened were almost certain to accuse him of suppressing the revolutionary masses. Either way he was bound to incur the wrath of at least a portion of the local people, and the consequence was a rash of assaults on military headquarters. Red Guards usually were involved in these assaults and, to make the pill still more bitter to swallow, commanders frequently found among them Red Guards from the PLA's own military schools and colleges.[49]

Having one's command headquarters besieged, invaded, disrupted, and perhaps occupied would, of course, upset commanding officers at any time. But these attacks came at a time when they had reason to fear war with the United States, perhaps compounded by hostile intervention from the Soviet Union. The United States had naval craft patrolling near China's coasts; it had forces on Taiwan, from which Chiang Kai-shek talked of returning to the mainland;

and it was engaged in a war in Vietnam, near China's southern borders. On its land frontiers, China faced Soviet forces along a 7,000 mile perimeter.

Finally, the January 23 directive posed, for commanders, new problems in maintaining discipline and unified command. The Cultural Revolution had been carried on within the PLA at the same time that it had been going on outside it. Undoubtedly it had been conducted within the armed forces only in modified form and, insofar as possible, separate from the Cultural Revolution in society at large. Nevertheless, it was bound to have affected army discipline to some extent, even before the January 23 directive was issued. But with the issuance of that directive came the danger that the boundaries which had contained the Cultural Revolution, as conducted within the army, would be eroded. Within individual units, contention was likely to arise over which mass organizations to support, thus affecting discipline. The same issue was likely to arise between units, and if they supported opposing sides they might find themselves fighting one another.

It would appear that only one full day elapsed between the time Lin Piao received Mao Tse-tung's complaint and the date on which the January 23 directive had been issued. It had been sent out in the joint names of the Central Committee, State Council, Military Affairs Committee, and Cultural Revolution Group. But the brevity of the intervening period suggests that Lin Piao had sent it out solely on his own and Mao's authority, and that they were impelled to discuss it with principal members of the military hierarchy only after reports of assaults on various military headquarters began to pour in.

At any rate, on January 27, we find Mao Tse-tung explaining the issuance of the directive at an enlarged session of the Military Affairs Committee. Both the tenor of his remarks and the contents of instructions issued in the following days suggest that he felt himself to be on the defensive and recognized the need to ease the problems he had created for the army. Nevertheless, he defended the issuance of the January 23 directive in his characteristically aggressive way. Originally, he conceded the army was not to intervene in the Cultural Revolution. But in fact it had already intervened before the directive had been issued. Thereafter the struggle had sharpened, and it was necessary for the army to support the left.

Perhaps in response to express or implied complaints and criticisms, unlikely to have come from any but senior members of the committee, he commented that most old leaders still did not understand the Cultural Revolution. They were still trying to live on the reputations gained through past services, whereas they were going to have to reform and temper themselves through the Cultural Revolution, and establish new reputations.

Discussing the offensive then unfolding, Mao commented that some people asked themselves whether or not to seize power. But this was no time in which to restrict oneself by seeking to differentiate between individual holders of power. If one spent time discussing matters, one would be forestalled by the opposition. Accordingly one should seize power and then report to the State Council, asking for its approval. Thereafter, the old cadres from whom authority had been taken should work under the supervision of the new cadres who had taken it. After the completion of the movement, judgment could be reached as to whether those from whom power had been seized were or were not followers of the capitalist road.[50]

Beginning January 28, several new directives dealing with the problems facing the army were issued in the name of the Military Affairs Committee. A short instruction, issued that day, directed that the Cultural Revolution within the army should be suspended entirely in seven of China's thirteen military regions. Six were regions facing the coast or border areas, and the seventh was the Wuhan Military Region, which contained central reserves to be used whenever they might be needed in any of the other regions. Elsewhere the Cultural Revolution should be carried out stage by stage and group by group, and only as directed by Chairman Mao and Vice Chairman Lin.[51]

The second and longer eight-point directive, also dated January 28, contained a notation indicating that it had been personally approved by Chairman Mao. It laid down further restrictions upon the conduct of the Cultural Revolution within the armed forces; declared that assaults on military leadership organs were forbidden; and attempted to lay down guidelines for handling cases which had already occurred. It directed that prosecution should be instituted if the assaults had been made by counterrevolutionaries, but that action need not be taken if they had been made by leftists. "Henceforth," it asserted, "no assault shall be permitted." [52]

The directive also attempted to deal with the problems created by Red Guards traveling about the country in order to "exchange revolutionary experiences" with other Red Guards. Such liaison often led to their involvement in local struggles, usually on the side of those factions which opposed the local leadership. The problem had become acute for military commanders, of course, when those struggles tended increasingly to be directed at themselves and their headquarters. Accordingly, this directive ordered that all students who had gone to outside areas to exchange revolutionary experience should return as quickly as possible to their home areas to engage in struggle. On February 3, the voices of the party center and the State Council were added to that of the Military Affairs Committee. A joint circular was issued in their names pointing out that many Red Guards, traveling on foot, were causing overcrowding and scarcity of food in the Ching-kang Mountains, Juichin, Yenan, and other places holy to Chinese communism. Moreover, infectious diseases had broken out and were affecting the health of the Red Guards. Accordingly, they should all return to their schools as quickly as possible, and make revolution there. Those whose homes were a considerable distance away might travel by rail.

These directives did not solve the problem of how to differentiate between true and merely self-proclaimed leftists. They did not end assaults on military headquarters either. Indeed, between January 30 and February 9, five directives had to be issued dealing with assaults on the headquarters of five different military regions and districts.[53] They also did not succeed in putting the Red Guard genii back in the bottle, but the task of doing so was under way.

Mao Tse-tung evidently had finally decided, by the early days of February, how to fit together the pieces of his evolving strategy. He had started with the Red Guards as his main force the previous August, put the workers in the forefront about the turn of the year, and had then called on party and government cadres to rise in rebellion later in January. In order to increase their effectiveness and responsiveness to his purposes, he had called on them all to form "great alliances." Finally he had been compelled to turn to the army to supply the requisite force and help provide direction, and now the army was in trouble.

Against this he could balance some accomplishments. Power had just been seized in the province of Heilungkiang as well as in Taiyuan, and in some other places progress was being made toward its seizure. In each such case power was being seized with the aid of some incumbent local leaders of party or of government. They could, in addition, provide in each place a nucleus of experienced leadership to help wield power once it had been seized.

The basis of his strategy would, in consequence, be a three-way alliance composed of the People's Liberation Army; those leading cadres of party and government who came over to Mao's side and whom he considered truly revolutionary; and the so-called great alliances, composed of leftist mass organizations. The three-way alliance would be used to seize power in all places and organizations of government within which such an alliance could be forged. Where the revolutionary forces were too weak, then power could simply be taken over by the army. It then could serve as the temporary organ of control while revolutionary organizations were being developed and formed into great alliances, and until suitable leading cadres stepped forward from within, or were assigned from outside. In either case, the objective would be the establishment, as the new organs of authority, of revolutionary committees comprised of representatives of each component of the respective three-way alliances.

If the three-way alliances were to govern, they would require subordinate instruments containing cadres experienced in administration. It was necessary that some indication be given to such cadres that they would have a future within the new regimes so that they would stay on the job and not go over to the opposition. Neither the army nor the mass organizations contained sufficient numbers of experienced personnel to provide a completely new administration.

With the January 31 seizure of power in Heilungkiang, it became desirable to reveal to the country how power was intended to be seized elsewhere, and necessary to indicate by whom it was to be exercised. The process of informing the country was begun with editorials in the February 2 issue of the *People's Daily* and in an early February issue of *Red Flag*. They acclaimed the example of the revolutionary rebels of Heilungkiang as one to be applied creatively in other parts of the country. The revolutionary rebels had united with those senior leading members of the Provincial Party Committee who followed Chairman Mao's correct line, and with leaders of the People's Liberation Army, to form a "three-in-one force to seize power." Having praised the revolutionary rebels, thereby suggesting the continuing role of great alliances, the editorials went on to emphasize the importance of the cadres. The large numbers of leading cadres in party and government who stood on the side of Chairman Mao were "more experienced in struggle . . . politically more mature and have greater ability in organizational work. Nurtured and taught by Chairman Mao, they are good cadres tested in long years of struggle, and a treasure of the party." Such cadres, the editorials asserted, "can certainly become the backbone and leadership of the struggle to seize power." [54]

These editorials, and succeeding statements contained in *People's Daily*, *Red Flag*, and other media, suggested that the three-way alliances were to be only provisional organs of authority. They did not specify that relevant provisions of the sixteen-point resolution of August 8, 1966 were to be abandoned. In that resolution it had been declared that "cultural revolutionary groups, committees, and congresses" were "organs of power of the proletarian Cultural Revolution." They "should not be temporary organizations but permanent." Moreover, it was "necessary to institute a system of general elections, like that of the Paris Commune, for electing members to the cultural revolutionary groups and committees, and delegates to the cultural revolutionary congresses."

It soon became clear that those provisions were widely assumed still to be relevant. On February 2, the *Shansi Daily* declared: "We have proclaimed the Paris Commune election method." [55] On February 5, with power finally undergoing seizure from the Shanghai party committee, a "Shanghai City People's Commune" was declared established. On that same day a "Preparatory Committee" to establish a "Peking Commune" was inaugurated. [56] But these moves evoked no approving reaction from Mao Tse-tung. Instead there was an embarrassingly long period of official silence.

If a system of general elections were to be followed, the leaders whom the masses would choose would be revisionist ones who had "hoodwinked" them by responding to the general wish of workers for better pay and shorter hours, and to the general wish of peasants for larger private plots and free access to city markets. And if all officials were subject to recall, as was supposed to have been the case with those of the Paris Commune, the consequence might be anarchy, rather than the continuance in office of experienced personnel.

That Mao Tse-tung had come to some such conclusions is apparent from a speech of February 9 by Wang Li, one of the leaders of the Cultural Revolution Group and an editor of *Red Flag*. It was Chairman Mao, he declared, who had decided to diffuse widely the experience of the power seizure in Heilungkiang. "It is not good to rely only on the Red Guards and workers after seizing power. Good leaders must be included in the new leadership organ without fail." [57]

On February 20, Mao Tse-tung called Chang Ch'un-ch'iao and Yao Wen-yüan to Peking to discuss their establishment of the Shanghai City People's Commune. According to wall posters purporting to report their conversation, Mao Tse-tung asserted that following the model of the Paris Commune would raise a whole host of new problems. For instance, establishing people's communes everywhere would necessitate changing the People's Republic of China to the Chinese People's Communes. That in turn would raise the question of whether foreign countries would recognize the new government. He then went on to outline what were undoubtedly his more basic objections. Leading cadres and specialists, he said, were needed. But the current attitudes in Shanghai toward those in authority bordered on anarchy. He had learned that the people there were even overthrowing the so-called "alley cadres"—the members of the party's lane and neighborhood committees. He had also heard that the Shanghai Public Security Bureau was just making a show of dealing with offenders taken into custody—that they were taken in the front entrance and then let right out through the back door. Such a commune, he said, would not be strong enough to put down counterrevolutionaries.[58]

On February 24 a "Shanghai Municipal Revolutionary Committee" was established in place of the Shanghai City People's Commune. Meanwhile, Mao Tse-tung's attitude having been made clear, plans for the establishment elsewhere of governing bodies modeled on the Paris Commune were quietly shelved.[59]

One may be entitled to speculate that the real enthusiasts for participatory democracy had been Ch'en Po-ta and his coterie of fellow editors from the journal *Red Flag*. Ch'en Po-ta's previous writings had contained a number of references to the Paris Commune, whereas Mao Tse-tung is said to have mentioned it, in his works, in only one passing reference.[60] Ch'en Po-ta, as Mao Tse-tung's political secretary and ghost writer, would have been in a good position to insert in the draft of the sixteen-point resolution, while it was under preparation, the provision for bodies organized on the presumed model of the Paris Commune. Mao Tse-tung may have merely accepted the insertion, either wholly or half-convinced at the time that it might prove useful.

Mao is a man at two extremes and of abrupt shifts. The Mao Tse-tung to whom participatory democracy would appeal was perhaps the remnant of the youthful Mao who had been interested in anarchism before he became converted to communism,[61] and who in Yenan had remarked: "There should be no government—the people should rule themselves." [62] It was Mao the antibureaucrat who had called for the mass criticism of the period of the Hundred Flowers, and Mao the opponent of economic planners and of specialists who had mobilized the people in the Great Leap Forward. This was the Mao Tse-tung who so frequently preached the line of "from the masses, to the masses"—learning what the people wanted and, on that basis, formulating policies the people could be persuaded to accept as their own. It was the Mao who liked spontaneity and voluntarism.

It was perhaps a different Mao Tse-tung who had remarked, of these masses, that they were poor and blank. Moreover, he had claimed that this was really a good thing. Being like blank sheets of paper, new and beautiful things could be written on them.[63] What would be written large on those blank sheets, one may assume, would be the thoughts of Mao Tse-tung. It was the dictatorial Mao Tse-tung who rejected the election of the Paris Commune, or indeed, any real elections at all. As he explained, in August 1967, to some foreign visitors: "Some people say that elections are very good and very democratic. I think that 'election' is only a civilized term. I myself do not admit that there is any true election. I was elected a people's deputy for Peking District, but how many people are there in Peking who really understand me? I think the election of Chou En-lai as premier means his appointment as premier by the center." [64] Moreover, this was the Mao Tse-tung who regarded "the center" and himself as synonymous, and who imposed his own strict discipline.

Mao Tse-tung was not unaware of the contradictions in his nature. The record of a talk he had with fellow officials on December 21, 1965 bears on this point. He asked them: "Do you have a dual character?" Then, apparently without waiting for an answer, he went on to remark, "I do." [65]

The Black Wind of February

CHINA and the adjacent inner land mass are a vast thermo-dynamic machine which sucks in the humid monsoons from the sea in summer, when heated air rises over the continent of Asia. When winter comes, the flow reverses, and dry winds from cold interior deserts are drawn across the land. Near the end of winter, the countryside about Peking lies parched and without crop cover. When the winds attain gale force, they carry with them heavy clouds of fine silt from the Gobi, lift powdery soil from nearby croplands and swirl up the dust from city streets and neighborhood lanes. In these storms, Peking's skies become so dark that homes may need lights even at high noon.

The dynamics of the Cultural Revolution evoked similar currents of ebb and flow, the most noteworthy of which was one which was dominant in Peking early in 1967, and which gained the designations of the February "adverse current," or "black wind." As the first of these two designations implied, it was a reaction to one of opposite direction which had been dominant prior to its coming.

In Peking, Mao Tse-tung's January 1967 demand that revolutionary activists seize power produced an immediate and well-nigh overwhelming response. T'ang P'ing-chu, the editor of *People's Daily*, and Hu Ch'ih, acting head of the New China News Agency, had been named to membership in the Cultural Revolution Group on January 11, and the organs they headed had faithfully publicized the call which Mao Tse-tung had that day issued. Nevertheless, one week later it was reported that Hu Ch'ih had been attacked in posters put up by revolutionary rebels of his own office and had been dragged through the streets, and similar treatment was subsequently accorded T'ang P'ing-chu.[1] Neither had been a member of Chiang Ch'ing's inner circle, and their fall from office opened the way for it to assume more direct control over the principal press and propaganda media.

The response within the ministries and commissions of the national government was similarly prompt, and in many cases equally effective. The officials in charge of government offices at the center, without means of self-protection comparable to those of leaders entrenched in provincial posts, and having to operate under the watchful eyes of Mao Tse-tung and his supporters, were in a poor position to defend themselves. Within the first ten days following the publication of Mao's call, revolutionary rebels seized power in twenty-three ministries of the government. Even the Scientific and Technological Commission, with its important responsibilities in the field of producing advanced weaponry, was not spared disruption: In February, five of its vice chairmen were overthrown.[2]

In the circumstances which prevailed in the capital, it might well have been possible for Mao Tse-tung to have effected far-reaching personnel changes within the government in an orderly manner. In the civilian ministries and commissions, tried and experienced but younger subordinates might have been appointed to replace those opponents he chose to send into retirement. There would doubtless have been some temporary loss of efficiency, but the unclogging of channels of promotion and consequent improvement of morale might soon have raised governmental effectiveness to higher levels.

It doubtless was Mao Tse-tung's aim to ensure that the government, to the extent that he had to depend upon it, should become more effective, in the sense of being more responsive to his will. But as he had told Malraux on the eve of the Cultural Revolution, the forces which create new classes are powerful and men left to their own devices, even under communism, tend to restore inequality. Equality was not important in itself, he believed, but it was natural to leaders who had not lost contact with the masses. Similarly, the raising of living standards was not the aim of communism, though it might be incidental to it. His aim was to restore China's greatness, and that could be achieved only if he tolerated no deviation. In this battle he was alone—"alone with the masses."[3]

The implication seems plain: Mao Tse-tung believed that his fellow leaders had lost the contact with workers and peasants, essential to the mass line, on which governmental effectiveness depended. They now constituted a new class, with their own class interests to protect. In consequence they were bound to oppose his will, and the organizations they headed were bound to distort his policies. It would not be possible to restore contact between leaders and led, he appears to have concluded, by merely removing and replacing those at the top. Only a process of struggle, in which he must depend upon the masses, would disclose who were his true followers, and who merely gave lip service to his thought; and only the leadership of the masses within government organizations could remove their bureaucratic character.

It would perhaps be inaccurate to say that Mao Tse-tung had identified himself with the masses, for he had not accepted as his own their order of priorities. Indeed, he seems to have denied that they had their own independent vision, for he had characterized China's people as poor and blank.[4] Rather, he had identified China's masses with himself, which is a subtly but substantially different thing. Being like blank sheets of paper, they were ready to receive his vision and his thought. Once they accepted his thought, right action would flow automatically, and once they shared his vision, their energies would be released for its realization. But this required that he eliminate from the government, which stood between him and the masses, the bourgeois revisionists who had hoodwinked and misled them.

Some of Mao Tse-tung's colleagues, faced with the undiscriminating attack which he had loosed against government leaders, may well have asked themselves whether he was out of his mind. It must have seemed to them incredible that he should intend power to be seized from all who held it. That he had little less than that in mind was, however, confirmed by his statements at the enlarged session of the Military Affairs Committee, held on January 27. This was no time, he had said, to restrict oneself by seeking to differentiate between individual holders of power. After the completion of the movement, judgment could be reached as to whether those from whom power had been seized were or were not followers of the capitalist road.[5]

The principal leaders whom Mao was addressing, at this meeting, were old revolutionaries. They included men like Ch'en Yi, who had built and commanded armies of hundreds of thousands of men, with which China had been conquered, and who since then had abandoned troop commands for government posts. If they wondered what might happen to them, Mao gave them their answer. Many of the old leaders did not understand the Cultural Revolution, he said, and were still trying to live on the reputations gained through past services. Instead, they would have to earn new reputations for themselves in the Cultural Revolution. The old leaders from whom authority had been taken would be expected to work under the supervision of the subordinates who had taken it from them.[6]

That Mao Tse-tung was not bereft of his senses was proved by the decisions, reflected in directives issued immediately after this meeting, which were designed to ensure that the Cultural Revolution, as conducted within the armed forces, should not disrupt military discipline. These decisions must have been gratifying to those at the meeting whose responsibilities were primarily military. They did not, however, immediately ease the situation faced by old leaders serving within the nonmilitary sector of the government. The most senior ones, as vice premiers of the State Council under Chou En-lai, may have comforted themselves with the reflection that it was to this body that those seizing power were subsequently to report, presumably for its approval or disapproval. But they may also have reflected that Mao Tse-tung probably would wish to have the final say, in all cases of importance, as to whether individual seizures of power were to be approved.

The pressures generated within the central government, by Mao's January decisions, necessarily were focused upon Chou En-lai, in his capacity as premier. Indeed, they put him in a position similar, in one important respect, to that in which Liu Shao-ch'i had been placed in the previous year: the organization which was his base of power had been put in jeopardy. Moreover, disruption in the government would be bound to extend to the economy, which the government managed, and to the framework of public order which it maintained. The consequences, of course, would be economic hardship for much of the populace, and its exposure to widespread and lawless violence.

The position of Chou En-lai, however, was decidedly different from that of Liu Shao-ch'i insofar as concerned his personal relationship with Mao Tse-tung. Chou En-lai had accepted a position of subordination to Mao as early as 1935 or 1936, when he yielded to Mao the leadership of the Military Commission of the party. Unlike Liu Shao-ch'i he had never, in the years since then, given evidence of wanting to deprive Mao Tse-tung of political power or to compete with him in the field of ideological leadership. Over the years, Chou En-lai had sometimes differed with Mao Tse-tung on policy matters, and he had on at least one occasion been disciplined in consequence.[7] But he had, in the main, devoted his great talents and unflagging energies to the tasks of government administration, and had thereby succeeded in making himself seem well-nigh indispensable.

It was this concentration on government administration which had set Chou En-lai somewhat apart from the men who were early targets of the Cultural Revolution. Indeed, it had doubtless made him sometimes regard Teng Hsiao-p'ing and P'eng Chen, the two leading figures in the party Secretariat, as adversaries. They were lower than he in the party hierarchy, but the government was subordinate to the direction of the party, and they had handled the most important of its day-to-day affairs. The brashness of Teng Hsiao-p'ing must occasionally have irritated Chou En-lai, and the widespread impression that P'eng Chen was being groomed for higher office may have led Chou En-lai to see him as a potential contender for his own position.

As chairman of the government and second-ranking leader of the party, Liu Shao-ch'i was Chou En-lai's immediate superior. But in a contest of wills between Mao Tse-tung and Liu Shao-ch'i, this consideration was vitiated by the subordination of government to party, and by Mao's top position within the party. If other considerations had been equal, Chou En-lai might have preferred the leadership of Liu Shao-ch'i, for they both were, unlike Mao Tse-tung, devoted to orderly procedure. But decades of observing the two men must have told Chou that the less assertive Liu Shao-ch'i, a man inclined to compromise, would be no match, in a test of wills, for the pugnacious and domineering Mao Tse-tung.

It accordingly is not surprising that Chou En-lai had gone along with Mao Tse-tung's Cultural Revolution, supporting it to the extent required to maintain Mao's confidence and retain his favor. But a reading of Chou's numerous speeches and instructions, to the Red Guards throughout the period in which they were the primary activists in the Cultural Revolution, and subsequently to revolutionary rebels, makes one thing clear. Within the limits imposed by a determination to retain his influence with Mao Tse-tung, Chou En-lai consistently raised his voice for moderation. At a public rally on January 8, for example, he criticized those who wanted to drag Liu Shao-ch'i and Teng Hsiao-p'ing out of Chungnanhai, and turned his back on the audience, to show his disapproval, when there were shouts of, "Down with Liu Shao-ch'i and Teng Hsiao-p'ing!" Only when there was a shout for the overthrow of the reactionary line of Liu Shao-ch'i and Teng Hsiao-p'ing, a different demand which he could support, did Chou En-lai turn around and again address the audience. "Liu and Teng," he explained, "are still members of the Standing Committee of the Political Bureau, and your calling for the overthrow of these two makes my position very difficult." [8]

Chou En-lai's role as the outstanding proponent of moderation made him the natural enemy of preponderant elements of the Cultural Revolution Group. The qualities of moderation and compassion were, of course, alien to the nature of its de facto leader, Madame Mao. She and Ch'en Po-ta had gathered around them a group of extreme left wing ideologues and propagandists who previously had been men of relatively little consequence. Suddenly they had found themselves members of a powerful if perhaps temporary organization which was engaged in the purge of old leaders, and it undoubtedly occurred to them that they might become the core group of a new generation of revolutionary successors. But if their present power were to be further enhanced and its permanence ensured, then the leaders who stood in their way must be subjected to a purge of great thoroughness.

The efforts of the Cultural Revolution Group to carry out a thorough purge of old leaders not only ran counter to Chou En-lai's preferences for moderation, it threatened to destroy his ability to keep the government running and the economy functioning. In consequence there emerged, between him and members of that group, a contest which resembled that between two well-matched wrist-wrestlers. Each sought to gain the upper hand, and the relative positions of the two sides appeared to shift back and forth as the ebb and flow of events lent new strength first to this side and then to the other.

The surface amenities were nevertheless preserved, and the mutual struggle remained unacknowledged almost to the end. In public, Chou En-lai made statements about Chiang Ch'ing which she undoubtedly considered eulogies. She sometimes gave him her verbal support, and she mixed praise with the criticisms she voiced of his State Council colleagues.[9] In consequence of this practice of the oriental art of not seeming to see that which it is inconvenient to recognize, Chou En-lai's opponents within the Cultural Revolution Group were not placed in the position of having to avow responsibility for attacks on him and his subordinates conducted by those whom they manipulated from behind the scenes. He, in turn, enjoyed the advantage of being able to avoid a showdown until he was prepared for it.

In earlier and less troubled times, the State Council had included upwards of twenty members, comprising Premier Chou En-lai and his vice premiers. At the outbreak of the Cultural Revolution the State Council was not up to that maximum strength, and the responsibilities of one or two vice premiers were primarily regional. Nevertheless, a dozen or so had been available to share the tasks of coordinating and supervising, through their respective ministers and chairmen, the many ministries and commissions subordinate to the State Council. During the early weeks of 1967 only six remained at work, and they were almost all under attack. As Chou En-lai remarked, "We are short of hands." [10]

The nature of the problems which he and the remaining vice premiers faced are well illustrated by his efforts to get the disorganized railway system back into proper operation. On January 13, he and Minister of Railways Lü Cheng-ts'ao had attended a meeting of revolutionary rebels of the railway system. At this meeting there had been a fight among the rebels themselves, and the meeting had ended with the rebels interrupting Chou's speech and dragging down the minister.[11] Chou En-lai himself was not uncritical of the ways in which Lü Cheng-ts'ao had dealt with his administrative problems, but Chiang Ch'ing did nothing to help either one of them when, at a Red Guard rally five days later, she accused Lü of being a sworn brother of P'eng Chen, of having instigated the railway strikes, and of being responsible for the disruption of the railway system.[12]

It was, of course, the Cultural Revolution which had disrupted the railway system, and factionalism among its revolutionary rebels stood in the way of the restoration of normal operations. On January 27 Chou En-lai and Vice Premier Li Hsien-nien met with the rebels who had seized power within the system, and who evidently were seeking the assistance of other departments in carrying on their work. Evidently Chou En-lai had decided that he should hold their feet to the fire by compelling them to accept the responsibility which went with the assumption of power. His answer was: "Let your twenty revolutionary rebel organizations of railway departments take up responsibilities first! Railway transportation can never stop for a single moment. . . . You must rely on yourselves for doing your work and emancipating yourselves. . . . You cannot relinquish power. You can neither assign it to a lower level nor submit it to me. I won't accept it even if you give it to me." Instead of buckling down to work, they had expended their energies in fights and quarrels, and he had to explain to them, "You must set up a practical work group. You must stand duty by turns. . . . I want to be answered when I ring up. . . . You should not go home to sleep after a quarrel. . . . In the future you will take complete charge of various fields in the Ministry of Railways." [13]

After ten meetings with the revolutionary rebels, the Ministry of Railways was still in a state of confusion, but an alliance was finally set up which Chou En-lai described as a model. Nevertheless, after about three months the alliance broke down consequent to factional strife among its members, and Chou En-lai, with the aid of the PLA, reluctantly took over control of the railway system. [14]

In unleashing his Cultural Revolution, Mao Tse-tung had observed: "There is no construction without destruction. . . . Put destruction first, and in the process you have construction." [15] Of the two, destruction naturally proved the easier, and construction failed to follow automatically in its train. In the other ministries which had been seized, as in the Ministry of Railways, the various power struggles proceeded along lines determined by the urgent nature and broadcast character of Mao's call, the motivations common to mankind, and the form which organizations tend to assume. The urge to better one's lot is broadly shared, whereas organizations are usually shaped like pyramids, with little room at the top. If many are encouraged simultaneously to scramble upward, struggles are bound to break out among them. Moreover, those who reach the top, in such circumstances, are unlikely to stay there very long. This latter fact, which lends zest to the game known as "king of the mountain," is well known to gangs of small boys fortunate enough to live near tall gravel piles.

As early as January 18, Mao Tse-tung had asked Chou En-lai how the taking over of power was doing. Chou had replied, "In some units power is taken over by one group, and then another, and passes backward and forward." [16]

This situation, which did not improve during the remainder of the month, gave Mao Tse-tung a firsthand illustration of the shortcomings of the revolutionary rebels. Meanwhile, the importance of support from senior leaders was being demonstrated both by results in Heilungkiang and the few other places where such cadres had joined hands with the revolutionary rebels, and by the lack of substantial progress in all the other provinces. Faced with a broad gap between expectation and accomplishment, and evidently goaded by impatience, Mao Tse-tung apparently reached another decision, about the end of January, which could only be implemented through continued reliance on experienced hands.

This was the decision to make the army responsible for provincial and local administration throughout China. The Central Committee's Northeast Bureau may have continued as a coordinating center in the three Manchurian provinces for some months longer, and in Shansi a new provincial party "core group" functioned, with the Revolutionary Committee as its administrative organ,[17] but after February 3 the Party Center stopped naming regional and provincial party committees among the addressees of its circulars. There was no concurrent announcement of the new decision, but on February 15, Chou En-lai remarked: "The current situation in the country is similar to the military control introduced in 1949." [18] This control was variously exercised—most obviously through military control commissions, less so through military domination of preparatory committees for the establishment of revolutionary committees, and of the revolutionary committees themselves.

This meant that the army was being made responsible for functions normally exercised by a party of perhaps twenty millions, with its host of cadres, and by the provincial governments subordinate to it. With only some three millions of men in the army, and with its regular responsibilities still to perform, the army would need the help of experienced civilian personnel. This need gave Lin Piao's army an interest in Chou En-lai's aims, as opposed to those of the Cultural Revolution Group.

The consequent reestimate of the importance of old leaders contributed, as we have seen, to the decision to set up, in various provinces and municipalities, revolutionary committees based upon the three-way alliance, rather than organs of power chosen through the electoral model of the Paris Commune. This decision was a heavy blow to the Cultural Revolution Group. Ch'en Po-ta, of course, had long been on record as being interested in that model. As recently as February 1, Chiang Ch'ing had declared: "The title 'chief' is to be smashed to pieces. There will be no need for 'chiefs' in the future. We will have the people's commune." [19] Its repudiation later that month accordingly was a partial repudiation of both the leader and the deputy leader of the Cultural Revolution Group. To their subordinates, the decision meant not so much loss of face as of hope for the thorough purge which would enhance their prospects.

This sudden reversal appears also to have gotten the Cultural Revolution Group into a contretemps with Mao Tse-tung. It centered about an editorial in an issue of *Red Flag* which appeared on February 2.[20] The editorial evidently was prepared while the line on old cadres was undergoing change and, as Mao Tse-tung is supposed to have remarked, one must be especially clearheaded when policy is being changed.[21] In any case, the editorial reflected what must have been a failure to grasp the full implications of the shift. Mao Tse-tung was involved in this failure because he was known to have reviewed the editorial and to have made changes in it. But when a leader joins his subordinates in an oversight or blunder, they are likely to suffer doubly for it.

In this case, the subordinate most directly concerned was Wang Li, as editor of *Red Flag*. But the Cultural Revolution Group was also involved because he was a member of the group and because it had just taken over responsibility for supervising the country's principal media of information and propaganda. This assumption of control had followed upon the overthrow by revolutionary rebels of the editor of *People's Daily* and the acting head of the New China News Agency, but it had been extended also to include such media as public broadcasting and the journal *Red Flag*.[22]

The editorial was, for the most part, in keeping with the violent mood, undoubtedly arising from Mao's sense of frustration, which had been so intensely manifested in his call of January 22, with its reiterated cry: "Seize power!" The struggle for the seizure of power, the editorial declared, was "a life-and-death struggle." The revolutionary masses had become clear as to who were "the chief figures among those in the party who are in authority and taking the capitalist road." The conflict with them was not a "contradiction among the people" but a "contradiction between ourselves and the enemy."

Having defined the deadly nature of the struggle, the editorial went on to declare that the most important condition for victory was the formation of the great alliance of the proletarian revolutionaries and the promotion of their unity with the broad masses. The greatest danger, once power had been seized, was the outbreak of dissension among the revolutionaries. Having placed its finger on the main weakness being displayed by the revolutionary rebels, the editorial proceeded, in a third section, to urge that they place their trust in those leading cadres who, "for quite a long time in the past, waged struggles within the party against the handful of people in authority taking the capitalist road." They were "the treasure of the party" and could provide the backbone and become the leaders in the struggle.

In this third section Mao Tse-tung was reported to have inserted two passages intended to strengthen the discussion of the role of old cadres. The first read: "When the revolutionary leading cadres rise up to join the masses in seizing power from the handful of persons within the party who are in authority and taking the capitalist road, the revolutionary mass organizations should support them. It must be recognized that they are more experienced in struggle, they are more mature politically, and they have greater organizational skill. The seizure and retention of power will be helped immeasurably by their inclusion in the core of leadership."

Mao Tse-tung's second insertion was placed after a passage which declared that even those cadres who had merely made errors should not be overthrown indiscriminately, but should be given a chance to correct their errors and make amends. Here he added: "To learn from past mistakes to avoid future ones, and to cure the sickness to save the patient is a long-standing policy of the party." [23]

A fourth section contained a discussion of the need to create entirely new forms of governmental organization. "In summing up the experience of the Paris Commune, Marx pointed out that the proletariat must not take over the existing bourgeois state machine, but must thoroughly smash it. . . . Since a number of units . . . have been turned into organs of bourgeois dictatorship, naturally we must not take them over ready-made, resort to reformism . . . and effect peaceful transition. We must smash them thoroughly." In creating new organizational forms for state organs, replacing those to be smashed, it would be necessary to "respect the initiative of the masses." The editorial then tied Mao Tse-tung to this proposition by saying: "On June 1 last year, Chairman Mao described the first Marxist–Leninist big-character poster in the country, which came from Peking University, as the Manifesto of the Peking People's Commune of the sixties in the twentieth century. Chairman Mao showed his wisdom and genius in predicting even then that our state organs would take on completely new forms."

If Mao Tse-tung was satisfied with this editorial when it left his hands and went into publication, he did not remain so very long. On February 9, Wang Li made a speech in which he declared that it was Chairman Mao who had decided to diffuse widely the experience of power seizure in Heilungkiang. The important problem at the moment was the problem of leaders. It had been placed only third, rather than first, in the *Red Flag* editorial, and for this mistake he was having to undergo self-examination. Then, upbraiding the revolutionary rebels, Wang Li declared: "You are overthrowing everybody simply because he used to work there, but is it not true that such an act leaves nothing behind but some vacant office rooms and official stamps?" Such acts, he continued, would "develop into moves to exclude and overthrow one another within the mass organizations, and will even overthrow oneself in the long run. . . . It is not good to rely on the Red Guards and workers after seizing power. Good leaders must be included in the new leadership organ without fail." [24]

Mao Tse-tung may well have become doubly displeased with the editorial when he realized that the third section, which foreshadowed adoption of the three-way alliance, was incompatible with the retention of the model of the Paris Commune, implied in the immediately following section. By invoking his name anew, in support of that model, the editorial had increased the awkwardness of his disengaging from it. In this situation it would be strange if his disgruntlement had not extended also to Ch'en Po-ta personally, as the man who presumably had pushed the concept in the first place, and to the Cultural Revolution Group as an organization which had continued to go in one direction after he had begun to shift to another.

The Cultural Revolution Group, in any case, went into a period of partial eclipse which began about the first of February and lasted until the middle of March. During this period, no less than forty documents concerning the Cultural Revolution are known to have been issued from Peking. A substantial number were sent out in the name of Chou En-lai's State Council, and it joined Mao's Party Center, Lin Piao's Military Affairs Committee, or both, in issuing many others.[25] Only one of these directives contained even a reference to the Cultural Revolution Group: it mentioned that that group had agreed that students, and workers from other units, were not to "exchange revolutionary experiences" with workers employed in industrial and mining enterprises, scientific research organs, and designing units of six of the ministries responsible for machine-building, since they were "important classified units of the state." [26] In possible deference to the special interest of the Cultural Revolution Group in Red Guard organizations subject to its control, one of several circulars demanding that students return to their own schools contained the phrase, "excepting those granted special permission by the Party Center." [27] But the directives preponderantly served the interests of Chou En-lai, as opposed to those of the Cultural Revolution Group, and none bore its name, as one of the issuing authorities—not even one which ordered working personnel of literary and art groups, in whom Chiang Ch'ing presumably had a special interest, to cease going out for "revolutionary exchange" and to return to their own units.[28]

Since the beginning of the Cultural Revolution Chou En-lai, as the regime's top administrator and one of its most approachable officials, had taken on tasks of receiving and addressing groups of Red Guards and dealing with the petitions and complaints of delegations of workers and peasants which poured into Peking from all parts of China. He had attended many of the extraordinary conferences incidental to the conduct of the Cultural Revolution, and carried on with his regular duties as well. Chou En-lai is a man of extraordinary energy who professes to need little sleep, but the extra burdens, imposed consequent to the attacks on his officials of January and early February, were forcing him to work until three or even five o'clock in the morning.[29]

The burden on Chou En-lai obviously had to be kept within bounds, and on February 15 there was a meeting at the Party Center at which it evidently was agreed that Chou might retain the services of such ministers of the government as could be salvaged. Two days later, with the backing provided by this assurance, he met with representatives of the revolutionary rebel factions in the fields of finance and trade, set forth some of the difficulties he had faced and laid down restrictions intended to limit the struggle to seize power within units subordinate to the state council.[30]

Seizures of power in government ministries which lacked the consent of the Party Center, Chou En-lai declared, would be disallowed. Even where seizure of power was not disallowed, the rebels were to exercise only general supervision instead of directing actual operations. Turning to seizure of power over specific ministries, Chou commented that Red Guards of the Peking Political Science and Law Academy had been permitted to take over the Ministry of Public Security as an experiment, but that the results had not been good. (They had feuded with other Red Guards, who had invaded the Peking Public Security Bureau, and a bloody battle had ensued inside that headquarters.) Neither that seizure of power nor ones in the Ministry of Foreign Affairs and the Ministry of Finance—headed respectively by Vice Premiers Ch'en Yi and Li Hsien-nien—would be recognized.

In the Ministry of Finance, Vice Minister Tu Hsiang-kuang had led revolutionary rebels in a seizure of power, taken over operational control of the ministry, and dissolved its party committee. By this time the position of the party's Central Committee had become am-

biguous, functions of its Secretariat and Propaganda Department had
been taken over by the Cultural Revolution Group, and its other
departments were in limbo. Nevertheless Chou En-lai, in censuring
those who had seized power in the ministry, demanded: "Are the
masses allowed to declare the dissolution of a party committee?" As
though to drive home his points, and perhaps to suggest where he
stood with the military establishment, Chou En-lai had PLA soldiers
arrest Vice Minister Tu Hsiang-kuang on the spot.[31]

In the future, Chou En-lai admonished, invasion of government
ministries by outsiders could not be permitted. The Cultural Revolution in the various ministries, he declared, should be centered in their
own respective rebel groups, for the movement would not develop
there if Red Guards or other outsiders came along and seized power.
Some of the Red Guards had become very famous, he commented,
and were putting up their posters in all parts of the country. In this
connection he mentioned three well-known Red Guard organizations
which were instruments of the Cultural Revolution Group: the Red
Flag Combat Corps of Peking Aeronautical Institute, the Chingkangshan Corps of Tsinghua University, and the Tungfanghung Commune
of the Peking Geological Institute. However there was a saying, he
remarked, that "famous names are not necessarily accompanied with
substance."

The grounds on which Chou En-lai justified the exclusion of
outsiders from participation in power seizures within the ministries
were well-designed to protect him from the accusation that he was
endeavoring to stifle the Cultural Revolution as a mass movement for
"self-liberation." At the same time, the rationale he advanced was
well tailored to his need to afford some protection to his ministers.
Subordinates could with impunity encourage outsiders to overthrow
their superiors. But they would be more cautious about themselves
engaging in a seizure of power, which might be disapproved after it
had been carried out, leaving them to work under the same superiors
whom they had attacked and offended.

That Chou En-lai was determined to temper the struggle against
his ministers is apparent from comments threaded throughout this
talk. "I invited Yao I-lin," referring to the minister of commerce,
"to Chungnanhai and am letting him take some rest. You have issued
a warrant of arrest with the intention of seizing him. This, however,
is like issuing a warrant of arrest against the party center. I support
your revolutionary spirit, but do you not think that there is need
to uphold organization and discipline? You members of the Ministry
of Commerce should retract the warrant of arrest against Yao I-lin,
apologize to him and exercise serious self-criticism."

At another point in this talk, Chou En-lai referred to the case of Chang Lin-chih, who had been the minister of coal industry. "I am not calm in my mind about the death of Chang Lin-chih," he declared. "He died suddenly after a struggle lasting for more than forty days." They had kept the chairman of the Commission for Economic Relations with Foreign Countries, who was doing excellent work, under attack for a whole month—a period during which agreements with twenty foreign countries had been signed. Chou had permitted them to attack a vice minister of petroleum industry, the minister of the First Ministry of Machine Building, and the first vice minister of commerce but, he implied, they seemed still not to be satisfied. "From what I have heard," he said, referring to the Vice Chairman of the State Capital Construction Commission, "you seem to be planning to drag Hsieh Pei-yi out to the rally of ten thousand and attack other leaders, one after another."

Mao Tse-tung, he pointed out, had said that the purpose of punishing past mistakes was to furnish lessons for the future, and that one treated the illness to save the patient. "However," he pointed out, "to carry out such struggles against leaders destroys both work and physical health." This was the way to deal only with the enemy, "and I am filled with pity. Do you not feel anything?" The old leaders, he said, were an asset of the party, and extremely few of them were really bad. "Such a way of treatment is unnecessary, even toward P'eng Chen. Struggles against leaders must be carried out in a civilized manner. Do you think that it is all right to let such a way become spread throughout the party?" [32]

The altered atmosphere of mid-February, in which Chou En-lai spoke so forthrightly, opened the door wide to the February "black wind," or "adverse current." The principal movers of this current were old leaders at the center who, in the words of Ch'en Yi, "tried to save each other and formed a group." [33] They were reacting to a situation in which a cabinet official, held in respect one day, might be cleaning out urinals the next, and in which Mao Tse-tung was being glorified while they, who had fought so many of the battles which had given him power, were being vilified.

Even old Chu Teh, taxed with having opposed Mao at every crucial juncture in the history of the party, and with having joined his wife in spreading "false rumors about Madame Mao," [34] had to undergo the indignities of having his house ransacked and his wife paraded through the streets. Long the commander in chief, he was now being described as a "big warlord and man of vaulting ambition who had sneaked into the party." He had "shamelessly distorted and falsified the histories of the party and the army . . . and advertised himself as 'the founder of the Red Army' . . . personally built by our great leader Chairman Mao . . . the real founder of the . . . Red Army of China." [35]

The black wind of February may have gained impetus as a reaction to such indignities inflicted on old leaders, but it arose as an effort to limit and control further personnel and organizational changes in various units of the central government. Then, if subsequent assertions are to be believed, what started as an attempt to hold the line developed into an adverse current, aimed at the rehabilitation of fallen leaders, which would carry China toward a "capitalist restoration." Chou En-lai obviously played a major role insofar as the first aspect of the movement was concerned, but it was Vice Premier T'an Chen-lin who became branded as the moving spirit who stirred and directed the black wind.[36]

The antagonists of T'an Chen-lin, in charging him with seeking a capitalist restoration, probably did not mean that he favored a return of the economy to private ownership, but rather that he and like-minded men would manage it in ways that Mao Tse-tung opposed, and turn it to purposes which were inconsistent with Mao's order of priorities. T'an Chen-lin was attacked as having said: "What is communism in essence? First, one must eat well. Second, clothes: one should have everything that is available, all kinds of colors and patterns, not just a great expanse of crow black, or a great expanse of blue. . . . Third, housing. One should be able to compare with modern cities. Fourth, transport. Except for people running races, everyone who goes by road should have means of transport. In broad outline communism is these few principles: food, clothes, house, job, plus cultural entertainment, scientific institutes, and physical education." [37]

Mao Tse-tung himself, for lack either of interest or imagination, had never painted a clear picture of what the achievement of a China restored to greatness should mean in terms of the life of China's people. In this respect, Mao the ruler resembled Mao the student in normal school, who contented himself with drawing an oval, calling it an egg, and turning it in as his examination paper in still life drawing.[38] In conversation with Malraux, Mao had dismissed Kosygin's statement that communism meant the raising of living standards with the deriding remarks: "Of course! And swimming is a way of putting on a pair of trunks! . . . It isn't simply a question of replacing the czar with Khrushchev, one bourgeois with another, even if it's called Communist." [39] To the Maoists, Liu Shao-ch'i was China's Khrushchev, and officials like T'an Chen-lin, who might wish to relieve the austerity of life in China, could be expected to choose his "bourgeois" leadership in preference to that of Mao Tse-tung.

In February, Ch'en Yi was defending Liu Shao-ch'i as a good Communist whose case should be treated as one involving merely contradictions among the people.[40] T'an Chen-lin, tied to him by their joint membership in the group of old leaders who were trying to save each other, was less outspoken but more open to suspicion. During an earlier period of discontent with Mao's leadership, that involving Kao Kang and Jao Shu-shih, T'an Chen-lin's name had been first among the signers of a letter to Mao Tse-tung, suggesting that he "take a rest." [41] Now he was open to suspicion of again wanting Mao Tse-tung to retire from leadership, and of working for the rehabilitation of Liu Shao-ch'i and Teng Hsiao-p'ing. Because they had been held responsible for formulating and implementing the "bourgeois reactionary line," and their supporters only for faithfully following it, rehabilitating Liu and Teng would logically have required that the reversal of verdicts be made general. Thus all that had been accomplished, by way of a sweeping purge, would be undone. This undoubtedly would have been the wish of some old leaders. As Ch'en Yi later said in one of his confessions: "I have always told comrades who were close to me that if I were to lead the great Cultural Revolution there would be no great Cultural Revolution." [42]

T'an Chen-lin became a target of the Cultural Revolution Group during February 1967. Between mid-January and early February, he had brought the agricultural and forestry section of the government, which was subject to his supervision, under his own tight control. He accomplished this by arranging for his confidants to organize conservative elements in the guise of revolutionary rebels, carry out sham seizures of power, suppress the leftists and cause the collapse of their organizations. Beginning about February 21, the Cultural Revolution Group began an effort—in which Wang Li, Kuan Feng, and Ch'i Pen-yü are supposed to have played prominent roles—to reverse this adverse current. Their first move was an attempt to stage counterseizures in organizations under T'an's supervision. For this purpose they used Red Guards, in defiance of Chou En-lai's insistence that power seizures within the government might not be conducted by outsiders. But T'an Chen-lin stood his ground, Chou En-lai supported him, and the initial effort was defeated.[43]

However, the Cultural Revolution Group renewed the attack during the first half of March, and its struggle against T'an Chen-lin became an issue at an enlarged meeting of the Military Affairs Committee, held from March 14 to March 18.[44] The committee had but

recently been reorganized, following the expulsion of former Marshal
Ho Lung, by new appointments to his place and to that left vacant
by the purge of Lo Jui-ch'ing,[45] but now it proved no more amenable
to the will of Mao Tse-tung than before its reorganization. In the
course of what was evidently a stormy session, a group of leaders
rose up in opposition to Lin Piao, defended T'an Chen-lin, and
challenged the position taken by the Party Center that the Red Guard
United Action Committee was a counterrevolutionary organization.[46]
The group which opposed Lin Piao, judging from subsequent accusations and personnel changes, included three of the other five former
marshals on his committee: Hsü Hsiang-ch'ien, Ch'en Yi, and Yeh
Chien-ying.[47] Because Hsü Hsiang-ch'ien had replaced Ho Lung as
head of the PLA Cultural Revolution Group, this opposition drew
into question Maoist control over that group, as well as over the
Military Affairs Committee.

There were rumors that a son of T'an Chen-lin had been arrested,
early in the year, as a member of the United Action Committee.[48]
Such action would have been interpreted by other leaders as part of
the campaign against T'an himself. But this would have been only
one among many arrests of the children of old leaders. Their arrests,
and the published decision that their organization was counterrevolutionary, bound old leaders together and pitted them against the
Cultural Revolution Group. A teen-aged son of Ch'en Yi, for instance,
had been accused of an act of violence for which he was sentenced
to life imprisonment, whereas many other Red Guards had committed similar acts with impunity. The difference evidently lay in the
organizations to which they belonged: Ch'en Yi's son had been a
leader of the West City Picket Corps, which was closely related to
the United Action Committee.[49] Moreover, upwards of 140 Red Guards
of the United Action Committee had been imprisoned, and only two
of them were accused of similar acts of violence. The chief offense of
the others had been opposing Chiang Ch'ing's Cultural Revolution
Group and trying to defend leaders whom it had marked for purge.

When Mao Tse-tung had given the army the tasks of supporting
the left and taking over the governing of the provinces, he had played
his last and highest card. The Military Affairs Committee was the
top body responsible for the political guidance of the PLA. Consequently, strong opposition to his policies within that body placed
both his policies and his position in jeopardy. He could not, in order
to quiet opposition, reverse the position taken on the United Action
Committee. Declaring it a counterrevolutionary organization had
been an indirect way of indicating that Liu Shao-ch'i and other fallen
leaders, whom the Red Guards of the United Action Committee had

tried to protect, were counterrevolutionaries, and hence that their purge would be justified. Mao had to maintain this position, for there was no longer room in the leadership for both him and them, but this did not mean he could not order the release of the imprisoned youngsters as an act of clemency.

A regime which keeps a large number of the sons and daughters of its own officials in prison for political reasons is a regime which is coming apart at the seams. Chou En-lai, who was trying to protect his subordinates and hold together the government of which he was prime minister, is obviously a man of extraordinary endurance. But by mid-March even that endurance had been tried very nearly to its limits. (A foreign dignitary, who had an appointment with him about that time, told of waiting until about an hour before midnight to be admitted, and then finding that an exchange of views was out of the question. Chou's hands shook so badly that his guest had to assist him in opening a cigarette box, and he was so exhausted that he was hardly capable of forming coherent sentences.) [50]

Chou En-lai had, in any case, to move warily. While the Military Affairs Committee had been in session, Miss Nieh had made a public speech in which she had said, "Watch carefully whether there is a person like T'an Chen-lin even among the persons whom the Center has defended." Miss Nieh had gained the reputation of speaking for persons much higher than herself consequent to having put up the famous poster at Peking University on behalf of Mao Tse-tung and because of reputed friendship with Chiang Ch'ing. The person to whom she undoubtedly referred in this speech was Chou En-lai, whose supporters responded by putting up posters defending him the very next day.[51]

Nevertheless Chou En-lai continued to afford T'an Chen-lin his protection for about three months after the Military Affairs Committee meeting.[52] He waited about a month in the matter of the imprisoned members of the United Action Committee, perhaps in order to give Mao Tse-tung's wrath time to simmer down. Then he went to Hangchow, where Mao had gone, as was his custom during Peking's cold months, and came back with Mao's order for their release. Both Chou En-lai and Chiang Ch'ing met with them the evening of the day they were freed. Accounts of the meeting represent Chou as saying that he had long been opposed to their arrest—clearly a rebuke to Chiang Ch'ing. It was undoubtedly an emotional meeting for the Red Guards, and it evidently was for Chiang Ch'ing as well. She was described in at least one account as having had tears in her eyes, but it is unclear whether the emotion which may have caused them to well up was contrition or chagrin.[53]

If Mao Tse-tung was willing, at least after some delay, to have the immediate issues which had been debated in mid-March smoothed over, he nevertheless faced the basic one, which so deeply concerned him, both squarely and without delay. Immediately after the Military Affairs meetings, a campaign was prepared and launched which had as its purpose the utter destruction of the moral authority and political position of Liu Shao-ch'i.

"National Betrayal"

The danger which Liu Shao-ch'i still posed to Mao Tse-tung could hardly arise from any activities which Liu himself would lead and direct. He could not leave Chungnanhai without being observed, and the servants of his household reported even the conversations of his family circle. The danger lay rather in his continued moral authority and availability as an alternative leader. Those who undoubtedly saw him in that light included old leaders who had been alienated by debasing treatment, accorded them while Mao Tse-tung was being elevated to the status of a living god. There was perhaps no danger that they would try to smash the image, but rather that they might try to place him, like a god, upon the shelf. This danger might be removed by giving the coalescing opposition new and intimidating reminders of Mao's power, and by so thoroughly discrediting Liu Shao-ch'i that he became useless to Mao's opponents.

Three days after the March 14 to March 18, 1967, session of the Military Affairs Committee, the Maoists announced the formation of a "Preparatory Committee for Thoroughly Smashing the Liu Shao-ch'i Renegade Clique." It was composed of the representatives of Red Guard and revolutionary rebel organizations, and it was evidently intended to help conduct the agitational and propaganda aspects of the campaign to denigrate Liu Shao-ch'i. This was to be accomplished by portraying him as an archcriminal, a renegade from the party, and a betrayer of his country. In Maoist language, he was to be converted into "a stinking heap of dog dung, spurned by mankind."

It seems reasonable to surmise that the security police were not idle during the days immediately following the decisions to launch this campaign, and to set up the *ad hoc* committee which helped conduct it. On March 27, that committee announced the arrests of thirty-five "turtles"—the Chinese equivalent of "bastards"—who were alleged to be members of Liu's "renegade clique." Among them were Vice Premier Po I-po, chairman of the State Economic Commission and alternate member of the party's Political Bureau; An Tzu-wen, director of the Organization Department of the party; Chang Wen-t'ien, who had been elected general secretary of the party in 1935; Yang Hsien-chen, who had lost his post as president of the Central Committee's Higher Party School consequent to his opposition to Mao Tse-tung's split with the Soviet Union; and Hsü Tzu-jung, first vice minister of Public Security.[1]

Liu Shao-chi's "renegade clique," the Peking Red Guard press promptly pointed out, owed its existence to his having "propagated a betrayal philosophy." On the eve of the outbreak of war against Japan, he had been in charge of the party's Northern Bureau. Pursuant to instructions of General Secretary Chang Wen-t'ien, in the Party Center in Yenan, Liu Shao-ch'i had negotiated through an intermediary with General Sung Che-yüan, then ruling in Peking, for the release of party members imprisoned there. But instead of insisting on their unconditional release, Liu is supposed to have accepted the condition that they first sign declarations renouncing communism. This was represented as a conspiracy, between Liu Shao-ch'i and Chang Wen-t'ien, on the grounds that they had failed to seek Mao's approval.

Sixty-one Communists imprisoned in Peking, and several hundreds jailed elsewhere, had signed declarations renouncing communism and had been released. Among them had been Po I-po, An Tzu-wen, Yang Hsien-chen, Hsü Tzu-jung, and others among the "thirty-five turtles already caught." Those who had been released in 1936 became members of an alleged clique, which Liu Shao-ch'i built up while in charge of the Northern Bureau, and they had banded together to support and protect each other. Liu Shao-ch'i, it was charged, had arranged at a Seventh Plenum of the Central Committee for the revision of a by-law prohibiting those who had once renounced the party from becoming members of the Central Committee, thus opening the way for appointment to that body of Po I-po, and of An Tzu-wen, who became head of the party's Organization Department in 1956. On the other hand, members of the clique had oppressed and mistreated Liu Ko-p'ing, chairman of the recently formed Revolutionary Committee in Shansi Province, who had refused to renounce communism and had remained in prison till 1944.[2]

This portrayal of supporters of Liu Shao-ch'i as renegades and traitors to the party was perhaps well designed to appeal to the unsophisticated, and particularly to the millions of Chinese too young to have been acquainted with the conditions which had faced party workers in so-called White areas. The unsophisticated could not be expected to realize that Sung Che-yüan probably did not take the professed renunciations at face value, but needed them for self-protection against possible charges that he had released enemies of the regime to which he was responsible. They also were probably unaware that Mao Tse-tung was not chairman of the party in 1936; that Chang Wen-t'ien then held what had been considered its highest office; and that Liu Shao-ch'i would have been derelict if he had not acted upon the orders of the Party Center.

The young, in particular, could not be expected to realize fully that those working in the underground had to pose convincingly as non-Communists to stay alive and out of jail, and, once in, could not be too fussy about how they got out. But men like Po I-po and An Tzu-wen, believing that the ends justified the means, would consider it their duty to renounce communism in order to emerge from prison and resume working for it, as many of them did, under newly assumed names.[3]

If there had been a party bylaw which prohibited the election to the Central Committee of persons who had once renounced the party, and if it was changed at a Seventh Plenum, it seems logical to suppose that Mao Tse-tung should have been aware of the purpose of the change. The relevant dates suggest that the Seventh Plenum in question could only have been that of the Sixth Central Committee, held in April 1945. Since Mao Tse-tung's *de facto* position of leadership had by then been firmly established, he should have been in a position to challenge any proposal for a change in bylaws which would have had the effect of admitting, to the leadership, men whom he regarded as traitors to the party.

This portrayal of the events of 1936 as a traitorous conspiracy must, in other words, be regarded in the same light as many other accusations leveled at Liu Shao-ch'i on the basis of words or actions which could be fairly portrayed only in the context of the times. His advocacy of preserving a rich peasant economy in 1950 was, to cite one instance, described as part of his "black record."[4] His accusers made no mention, of course, of the facts that the overriding consideration then was the restoration of agricultural production, that its restoration depended heavily on encouraging the more efficient producers, and that Mao Tse-tung himself, in a speech of November 6, 1950, had advocated "a change from the policy of requisitioning the surplus land and property of the rich peasants to one of preserving the rich peasant economy."[5]

It is recognized in China, perhaps more generally than elsewhere, that an attempt to destroy a person of consequence requires the cover of a moral justification, and that it should logically take the form of accusations of a gravity which is proportional to the status of the person being attacked. That which is recognized as required tends to become ritual. In consequence, a cover of justification is sometimes offered, as in this case, even when those directly concerned all recognize that its tissue is transparently thin. In this instance it served Mao's interests for other old leaders to see through to his purposes, one of which was to make clear the danger of contemplating any further close association with the cause of Liu Shao-ch'i. It helped him set the stage for a meeting of the Standing Committee of the Political Bureau, called late in March, at which its members apparently were called upon to vote on a proposal that Liu Shao-ch'i should be deprived of all official responsibility and authority.[6]

The meeting was held to the accompaniment of violent demonstrations against Liu Shao-ch'i and his associates, conducted outside the building in which the Standing Committee met, and undoubtedly intended to influence the votes of those who participated. Even so, Mao Tse-tung managed to muster only the necessary six votes—reportedly his own and those of Lin Piao, Chou En-lai, Ch'en Po-ta, K'ang Sheng, and Li Fu-ch'un against the five of Liu Shao-ch'i, Teng Hsiao-p'ing, T'ao Chu, Chu Teh, and Ch'en Yün.[7]

Vice Premier Ch'en Yün, as an economist who had opposed the Great Leap Forward, had been out of Mao's favor and relatively inactive ever since 1958, and Chu Teh had been in a similar position since the related affair of P'eng Te-huai. According to one report, Mao Tse-tung had but recently asked Chu Teh either to write some articles for publication in favor of the Cultural Revolution or to make a self-criticism for failing to support it, but Chu had declined, observing that if there were anyone who should criticize himself it was Mao Tse-tung.[8] Vice Premier Li Fu-ch'un, as chairman of the State Planning Commission, had followed the party main stream until the Cultural Revolution. Coming under Red Guard attack, he had reexamined his position.[9] Evidently this had led him to side with Mao Tse-tung. It may be assumed that Chou En-lai cast his lot with Mao Tse-tung, despite the contest waged against him by the Cultural Revolution Group, because he realized that the Standing Committee of the Political Bureau was not Mao's court of last resort. It would be the army which would be the final arbiter, and since Lin Piao commanded it, Chou's own chances of survival depended on playing the game out to the end. The lineup, in other words, was one in which those who had already fallen into Mao's disfavor opposed those who either were in charge of the Cultural Revolution or who still hoped to avoid becoming its victims.

With this victory behind him, Mao Tse-tung again reorganized the Military Affairs Committee and the PLA Cultural Revolution Group. Former marshals Hsü Hsiang-ch'ien, Ch'en Yi, and Yeh Chien-ying reportedly were dropped from membership on the Military Affairs Committee because of their opposition to Lin Piao and to policies of the Maoist Center, and former chief of staff Su Yü and Vice Premier Hsieh Fu-chih were appointed to two of the resulting vacancies.[10] Hsü Hsiang-ch'ien had been accused, as head of the PLA Cultural Revolution Group, of having ignored Chiang Ch'ing, its advisor, and of having refused to let her and Kuan Feng have a hand in its operations on the pretext that they were unacquainted with the actual situation in the military forces. It accordingly must have given her considerable satisfaction to be the person who announced that Hsü Hsiang-ch'ien had been dismissed also from his post as head of that group, and that Hsiao Hua, director of the General Political Department of the PLA, would act in his place. At least two other members were dropped from the PLA Cultural Revolution Group in this April reorganization, and acting Chief of Staff Yang Ch'eng-wu and Vice Premier Hsieh Fu-chih were added to it.[11]

Meanwhile, the campaign to destroy the moral authority of Liu Shao-ch'i was going ahead full blast. That authority had been substantially buttressed by Liu's authorship of a book on the self-cultivation of Communists, which has been translated under the title, *How to Be a Good Communist*. It had far outsold *The Selected Works of Mao Tse-tung*, and to the millions who had studied it, Liu Shao-ch'i had undoubtedly come to be associated with the virtues which the book inculcated.[12]

On April 6, the *People's Daily* published an article entitled, "Bury the Slave Mentality Advocated by China's Khrushchev." It described the book on the self-cultivation of Communists as "a big, poisonous weed," and attacked its author as having said: "The viewpoint of some people is, 'I am willing to subordinate myself to my superiors and to the majority, but my superiors and the majority must first be correct politically. However, if they are wrong politically I will not subordinate myself to them.' This makes the correctness or otherwise of the majority, or the superiors, or the Party's Central Committee the condition of subordination. It is incorrect to stipulate such a condition." Liu Shao-ch'i's position, said the author of the article, represented advocacy of a slavishness, in the name of party unity, which Mao Tse-tung had always opposed. "As early as 1930," the article declared, "Chairman Mao warned us that . . . 'it is quite wrong to take a formalistic attitude and blindly carry out directives, without discussing and examining them in the light of actual conditions, simply because they came from a higher organ.' "[13]

The statement attributed to Liu Shao-ch'i was, of course, in accord with organizational principles of Marxist–Leninist parties in general and with those of the Chinese Communist party in particular. It also was in harmony with a statement made by Mao Tse-tung in 1938, when he had declared: "We must affirm anew the discipline of the party, namely: (1) the individual is subordinate to the organization;

(2) the minority is subordinate to the majority; (3) the lower level is subordinate to the higher level; and (4) the entire membership is subordinate to the Central Committee. Whoever violates these articles of discipline disrupts party unity." [14] Finally, those principles had been and still were embodied in the constitution of the party.[15]

The real differences between Mao Tse-tung and Liu Shao-ch'i, insofar as party discipline was concerned, related to the applicability of the rules which Mao had enunciated to Mao Tse-tung himself. When Mao Tse-tung spoke in 1938 of discipline and unity, it was in the context of his rival Chang Kuo-t'ao's refusal to be bound by a majority which Mao Tse-tung himself controlled. Liu Shao-ch'i spoke of subordination of the individual to the organization, and the minority to the majority, as principles which applied even to Mao Tse-tung himself.[16] Mao Tse-tung, like Liu Shao-ch'i, was concerned about party unity. But as he was demonstrating, when it came to a choice between preserving that unity and enforcing his own will, then it was party unity which he chose to sacrifice.

Liu Shao-ch'i regarded the party, as believers do the church, as something greater than the sum total of its members, and its unity as resting on the doctrine of Marxist–Leninist ideology.[17] In 1942, Mao Tse-tung had declared: "Marxism–Leninism has no beauty, nor has it any mystical value. It is only extremely useful. . . . Those who regard Marxism–Leninism as religious dogma show . . . blind ignorance. We must tell them openly, 'Your dogma is of no use,' or, to use an impolite formulation, 'Your dogma is less useful than shit.'" [18] Mao Tse-tung's evaluation of the party was similarly utilitarian rather than mystical. "If there is to be revolution," he had declared in 1948, "there must be a revolutionary party." [19] If the party had in his opinion ceased to be revolutionary, one may assume, he put no more value on it than he did upon Marxist theory divorced from revolutionary practice.

If it had not been destructive of their thesis that Liu Shao-ch'i urged slavishness, the authors of the *People's Daily* article might have quoted Liu Shao-ch'i as also having said that party members should not "follow blindly," nor "flinch from any necessary innerparty struggle." Rather, they should "carry on an irreconcilable struggle in the party against ideas and views which are wrong in principle and against all other undesirable phenomena." [20] Again, although their words were similar, the standpoints of Liu Shao-ch'i and Mao Tse-tung were at variance. In Liu Shao-ch'i's view, the struggle against wrong ideas should be conducted within the party; Mao Tse-tung was using elements from outside of the party to attack its majority. Moreover, it was apparently not unthinking obedience, per se, to which Mao Tse-tung objected, but obedience to any will contrary to his own. In August 1967, Lin Piao was to remark, in Mao's presence: "I say that we must carry out Mao Tse-tung's ideas when we understand them and even when we do not understand them for the time being." [21] There is no indication in the record of the talk by Mao Tse-tung, into which Lin Piao interjected this remark, that it was displeasing to Mao Tse-tung. Indeed, injunctions to follow Mao Tse-tung's thought, whether or not it was fully understood, subsequently appeared in the regime's media with sufficient frequency to suggest that the reverse had been the case.

The Maoists appear, moreover, to have been intent not merely to portray Liu Shao-ch'i as opposed to Marxism–Leninism, which was to be equated with the thought of Mao Tse-tung, and as head of a clique of traitors to the party. In addition they sought to demonstrate that he and members of his family also were traitors to their country and betrayers of its people. The first member to be so branded was his son Liu Jung-jo, the leader of one of two revolutionary rebel organizations in the Seventh Ministry of Machine Building. He was arrested on January 19 on the charge of having sold state secrets to a foreign power.[22] It was doubtless intended that people should infer that the secrets were military ones, since his ministry was responsible for aircraft production, and that the foreign power was the Soviet Union, in which he had been a student. The further inference that Liu Shao-ch'i had endeavored to protect his son in such wrongdoing was possibly intended to be drawn from charges leveled against Hsü Tzu-jung, whose name had been on the March 27 list of members in Liu Shao-ch'i's "renegade clique." Hsü Tzu-jung, it was charged, had used his position as vice minister of public security to protect a spy.[23]

The theme that Liu Shao-ch'i was himself a traitor to his country and his people was introduced, in the seemingly innocuous context of reactions to a moving picture, in an article which appeared March 31, in an issue of *Red Flag*. The article was by Ch'i Pen-yü, a member of Chiang Ch'ing's group, and it was entitled, "Patriotism or National Betrayal? On the Reactionary Film *Inside Story of the Ch'ing Court.*" [24]

This film, widely shown in China during the early 1950s, dealt with a power struggle which occurred at the turn of the century within the Manchu court. The outstanding protagonists were the young Emperor Kuang Hsü and his favorite consort, who were supporting officials intent on introducing reforms, which they hoped would strengthen China and enable it to resist foreign encroachments, and the strong-willed Empress Dowager Tzu Hsi, who attempted to deal with foreigners by turning against them the fanatical members of the secret society known as the *I Ho T'uan*, or Boxers. In the film, as in the history on which it was based, Tzu Hsi's machinations culminated in the Boxers' siege of the foreign legations, the death of Kuang Hsü's consort at the hands of the Empress Dowager, the approach of the international force which captured Peking and lifted the siege, and the flight of the court to Sian.[25]

According to the article in *Red Flag*, Mao Tse-tung and Chiang Ch'ing had long ago condemned *Inside Story of the Ch'ing Court* as "a film of national betrayal" and she, as a member of the Ministry of Culture's committee for guiding film work, had demanded that it "should be firmly criticized and repudiated." Director of Propaganda Lu Ting-yi, Deputy Director Chou Yang, and other officials had demurred, citing Liu Shao-ch'i—identified in Ch'i Pen-yü's article by the circumlocution "the top party person in authority taking the capitalist road"—as being of the opinion that the film was patriotic. It might seem unfair to conclude that Chiang Ch'ing and Ch'i Pen-yü tended to identify themselves, respectively, with the Empress Dowager and with the fanatical and superstitious members of the *I Ho T'uan*. The first part of the conclusion would have to rest on inference, but not the second. Ch'i Pen-yü's treatment of the Boxers as patriots makes his approval of them evident. "At a crucial moment when our country was being partitioned among the imperialists," he wrote, "the *I Ho T'uan* heroes stepped forth bravely. . . . Demonstrating in the streets, the *I Ho T'uan* heroes often shouted the slogan, 'Kill the foreign devils!' . . . The patriotic, anti-imperialist struggle of the *I Ho T'uan* was closely linked with the antifeudal struggle. The battle cries of the *I Ho T'uan* were: 'Kill the foreigners and wipe out corrupt officials.' "

The same issue of *Red Flag* also contained an attack on Liu Shao-ch'i's wife.[26] It took the form of a report of the alleged misdeeds at Tsinghua University of the party work team to which she had belonged, and of the "so-called" Red Guards sympathetic to it, subsequent to the work team's withdrawal. Wang Kuang-mei was identified in the article only by the use of her surname, and the leaders of the "Red Guards" in question were merely called "Ho —— and Liu —." But her role as a member of the work team was well known in Peking, and readers undoubtedly identified the Red Guard leaders as Ho P'eng-fei and Liu T'ao, the children of Ho Lung and Liu Shao-ch'i. Finally, the publication of the article in so authoritative a party journal, controlled by the Cultural Revolution Group, was bound to suggest that the time had come to submit her to renewed personal harassment.

On the night of April 9, thirty-odd Red Guards of Tsinghua University's Chingkangshan Corps were admitted to Chungnanhai, obviously with official authorization. They proceeded to Liu's home, where four of them entered, went to the couple's bedroom, and roused them from their sleep. Wang Kuang-mei was forced to dress and accompany them to Tsinghua University.[27] There, on April 10, she was subjected to one mass struggle meeting and three so-called trials.[28]

Wang Kuang-mei can hardly have been in good shape for such an ordeal. She and her husband had undergone a long period of chronic worry, beginning in the spring of 1966, and more recently several periods of acute strain. On one earlier occasion, in December, she and her husband had been routed out of bed in the middle of the night, that time by their own servants, who had proceeded to hold a struggle meeting against them. There had been the affair of January 6, when she had been inveigled into leaving Chungnanhai in the belief that their young daughter Liu P'ing-p'ing had been critically injured, and then taken to Tsinghua to face long hours of abuse. On January 19 Liu's son had been arrested, and on January 26 she and her husband had been taken out into nearby Peihai Park where her husband had faced a small struggle rally.[29] There had been tension in the family between the parents and their eight children, four of whom had yielded to the mounting pressures to denounce their own parents.[30] Then, beginning early in April, there had been almost daily parades past Chungnanhai by big crowds which had been mobilized to demonstrate against Liu Shao-ch'i.[31] All these things, robbing their rest of repose and injecting into their bloodstreams adrenalin which could not be put to the uses which nature intended, were bound over time to take their toll. During her ordeal of April 10, Wang Kuang-mei several times asked for some of the tranquilizer pills she had been taking. She had, she explained, been tending Liu Shao-ch'i, who had been ill, and had herself become nervous, sick, and close to breaking down.

The first period of her interrogation, which began shortly after 6:30 of what apparently was a chill morning, was preceded by an episode perhaps intended to remind her that Chiang Ch'ing stood back of the whole affair, as she did behind the Chingkangshan Red Guards under whose auspices it was conducted. The interrogator insisted that she put on the silk dress she had worn in Indonesia "to flirt with Sukarno," and she was also asked to put on the jewelry for which Chiang Ch'ing had criticized her. She protested that it was too cold for a dress intended to be worn in the tropics, and finally she was put into it by force.

During the interrogations which followed, Wang Kuang-mei was addressed as "the stinking wife of a three-anti element," meaning a man opposed to socialism, the party, and the thought of Mao Tse-tung. Those who composed the audience chimed in with abusive chants, including the quotation about those who are to be reduced to "dog's dung spurned by mankind." The interrogations were wide ranging and clearly designed to draw forth admission of damaging facts about her husband and herself, and derogatory comments on Mao Tse-tung and the Cultural Revolution Group. In these respects they were not particularly successful, whereas she herself occasionally drew blood. She did not deny that her husband had made mistakes, but observed: "The achievements of the past seventeen years belonged to Chairman Mao, and because Liu Shao-ch'i was in the first line, all the mistakes were his." She praised the accomplishments of the Cultural Revolution Group in general terms, but commented that it, too, could make mistakes. What they had been she would not say, contenting herself with the observation that T'ao Chu had been a member of the group, and now he was "left to rot."

The interrogator reserved the subject in which he may have been most interested for the evening session. In doing so, he perhaps calculated that Wang Kuang-mei would by then have been suitably worn down by the preceding twelve hours, with its two periods of questioning and the struggle session with the so-called masses which had been held in between. At any rate, it was in the evening session that he queried her about her relations with American officialdom.

During the period of the Marshall mission, Wang Kuang-mei had served as an interpreter in Executive Headquarters, set up in Peking in January 1946 to supervise the military truce between the Nationalists and the Chinese Communists. It was disbanded consequent to the withdrawal of United States participation slightly less than a year later, but while it functioned it had a tripartite staff composed of American, Kuomintang, and Chinese Communist personnel. Wang Kuang-mei's interrogator questioned her in detail about her relations with American officials in the headquarters, and she readily admitted having dined with some of them, one exchange of inconsequential gifts, and traveling from Peking to Yenan on an American aircraft. However, all this was normal at the time, and she admitted to nothing more than these casual relationships.

Nevertheless, they were later to be reflected in charges that she had been sent to Yenan, where she in 1947 married Liu Shao-ch'i, as the secret agent of a "United States Strategic Intelligence Board." [32] Allowing for possible variant translations of the term used, it is possible that the reference was to the Office of Strategic Services, predecessor of the Central Intelligence Agency. However, the United States, during the immediate postwar period in question, had no organization with which the name can properly be identified. President Truman had ordered the OSS disbanded on October 1, 1945. There was yet no general agreement as to what, if anything, should replace it, and the CIA was not established until after the passage in 1947 of the National Security Act.[33] It seems most probable that Liu Shao-ch'i's enemies started from the premise that espionage on behalf of a foreign power was the gravest crime with which he might be connected, and then proceeded to seek out circumstances which might make his involvement in it seem plausible.

Being linked to Liu Shao-ch'i was the source of tragedy not only for the elegant Wang Kuang-mei and for high-level officials, but for cadres at every level of leadership. This was true, for example, even for Shih Ch'uan-hsiang, leader among the men who had as their occupation the collection of the contents of the toilets of the city of Peking. For generations, such men have made their nightly rounds throughout the capital, transporting that which they have collected to the suburbs. There it is dried in the form of rough cakes under Peking's bright sun, after which it is ready for use in fertilizing the garden plots which surround the city.

While the concept that physical labor is worthy of respect was brought to Chinese intellectuals by western tides of modernization, traditional attitudes that it was beneath the dignity of the scholar died hard. To combat these attitudes, Mao Tse-tung contended that it was the unreconstructed intellectuals who were unclean, and the workers and peasants who were clean, even though their hands were soiled and their feet smeared with cow dung.[34] In keeping with this teaching, Shih Ch'uan-hsiang had in 1965 been elected to represent Peking in the National People's Congress, and to celebrate his status his photograph had been taken shaking hands with Chairman Liu. Two of Peking's vice mayors had done stints of voluntary labor as temporary members of his crew. Shunned in the old days because his occupation had been held in bad odor, he now could brag of high contacts and tell foreign visitors: "Never before in the history of mankind has a mayor collected shit with a night-soil man." [35]

During the first months of the Cultural Revolution, visiting Red Guards were proud to go out with old Shih, who taught them how to handle the buckets and other equipment of his trade. He also was described as telling them that now, since the revolution, the workers had stood up and were cleaning up the muck of capitalism and revisionism under the leadership of the party and Chairman Mao.[36] His putting Chairman Mao and the party in the wrong order may have been overlooked, but the professions of loyalty toward Liu Shao-ch'i, for which he had become noted, could not be forgiven. In January

1967, Shih Ch'uan-hsiang was denounced as no member of the working class at all, much less a model worker, before a rally of one hundred thousand people.[37] *Sic transit gloria mundi.*

Old Shih was left to sink into odious obscurity, but not Liu Shao-ch'i. Investigations designed to produce further evidence against him, and to identify more of his supporters, were pushed apace. By May 28, according to a wall poster, twenty-five hundred members of his alleged faction had been uncovered by Red Guards working under the guidance of the Cultural Revolution Group.[38] The campaign to vilify Liu Shao-ch'i also went on and on, at varying levels of intensity.

It was important that Liu should be thoroughly discredited and repudiated so that the Central Committee, when it might again be called into session, would surely ratify the decision to deprive him of all official position and authority.[39] It was also useful, when presumed Maoists fell into bitter fighting among themselves, to point to Liu Shao-ch'i as the archenemy against whom they should all unite. At such times the campaign against him could be raised to new levels of intensity, in the hope that internecine disputes might be forgotten.

22

The Center of the World

No GREAT upheaval can be confined to the country in which it breaks out, and China's Cultural Revolution was no exception. During the twelve months beginning in August 1966, Communist China was involved in crises and incidents, at home and abroad, with a total of thirty-two countries.[1] In listing its foreign friends, in the autumn of 1967, it could point with approval to only two foreign states, Albania and North Vietnam.[2] This state of affairs was the consequence of applying the logic which underlay a remark which Mao Tse-tung made on July 7 that year. China, he said, had become the political center of the world.[3]

Mao's remark can be reconciled with reality only by proceeding from his world view, and accepting his assumptions. The crude outlines of his view of the world, and of China's proper place in it, undoubtedly were formed—however they may later have been modified—in the interior province of Hunan during the last days of imperial rule. The principal road to advancement in imperial China was provided by the civil service, entry to it required a mastery of the Confucian classics, and education was shaped accordingly. Mao Tse-tung was exposed also to elements of a modern education, and the Empire gave way to the Republic while he was still in school, but the influence of the Confucian classics did not die with the Empire.

Confucius had held: "Just as the sky has no two suns, so the earth has no two rulers."[4] During the following two millennia this assessment became deeply imbedded in the Chinese consciousness. Surrounded by broad oceans, high mountains, infertile deserts and arid steppes, imperial China was long protected by geography from the need to revise this view of the world.

The settled life of agricultural China had facilitated the development of a written language which served the needs of a political and cultural imperialism. It can, since it is based on ideograms rather than an alphabet, be used, as can our arabic numerals, without reference to differences of dialect or pronunciation. As such, it made possible the communication required for the governing of a far-flung empire, and facilitated the extension of Chinese rule to other sedentary peoples in what is now called China proper. Adopting the Chinese written language, in the absence of any of their own, they adopted Chinese attitudes and in effect became Chinese.

The nomadic life of the peoples of the neighboring steppes made their cavalry formidable but denied them comparable literary and political accomplishments. When at peace with China, they might send emissaries to Peking bearing the products of their pastoral economy, and receive generous gifts of Chinese goods in return. The products they brought were regarded as tribute, and the obeisances they made at court were treated as acknowledgment of Chinese suzerainty. When at war with China, they were regarded not as independent enemies but as rebels to be pacified. If suppression failed and they conquered Chinese territory, they could transmute military victory into political rule only by settling down, using the existing Chinese bureaucracy, and learning the written language in which its business was conducted. In the process, they ceased to be nomadic tribesmen, and they, too, became Chinese.

In consequence, the Chinese came to see their written language as a civilizing agent, to equate culture with Chinese culture, to regard themselves as innately superior, and to see China as the center of the world. In its political theory, the Chinese Empire denied the equality of other nations with itself, and even their rights to independence. In the nineteenth century, a Chinese viceroy could presume to issue orders to Queen Victoria and to demand that she "earnestly obey." [5] Subsequent experience proved that China's capabilities were insufficient to enforce the respect for equal treatment which western political theory seemed to promise in principle but often to withhold in practice, much less Chinese claims to paramount authority. To make practice accord with either Chinese or western theory required that China first be made sufficiently powerful.

It was the disregard of this requirement, in the days of Mao's childhood, which made the Boxer uprising so indisputably disastrous. Individual Chinese, however, might differ over the questions of whether the Empress Dowager should be regarded as benighted for holding to traditional views of China's world role, and inhumane for seeking to deal with troublesome foreign countries by encouraging the Boxers to kill off the foreigners within China's borders. That this is so is suggested at least by the disagreement between Mao Tse-tung and Chiang Ch'ing, on the one side, and the majority of the leadership on the other, over the question of whether *Inside Story of the Ch'ing Court* was a film of national betrayal. In the Maoist view, the Boxers were Chinese patriots who should not have been portrayed as misguided fanatics, and the reformist Emperor and his consort had not deserved to be treated as the hero and heroine of the story.

During the first decade of Chinese Communist rule, Mao Tse-tung was concentrating on building Chinese industrial and military power, and it was helpful to this end to work within the prevailing international system. Simultaneously, China was asserting its sovereign right to equal treatment by the "imperialist" powers. Thereby it gave implicit recognition to the theory of the equality of states, and its espousal of the Bandung principles, during the 1950s, made that recognition explicit.

During the first half of the second decade of Chinese Communist rule, Mao became preoccupied with his quarrel with the Soviet Union and intent on building Chinese power through policies of self-reliance. His overt criticism of the Soviet Union for its World War II territorial acquisitions was in effect an appeal to Communist states of Eastern Europe to join China in its anti-Soviet campaign. It was also an appeal to Japan and states of western Europe to support China against the Soviet Union. In neither case did it bring very significant results. The effort to mobilize Afro-Asian states against the United States, in the context of Vietnam, yielded similarly disappointing fruits. In consequence, there is little doubt that Mao Tse-tung began to downgrade the value of state-to-state diplomacy.[6] This process of downgrading undoubtedly was accelerated after Mao became convinced, early in 1965, that the war in Vietnam was a prelude to an American attack on China, and that the Soviet Union would join in that attack. Lin Piao's article, on so-called People's War, made publicly clear that there had been a fundamental policy change in response to this assessment. Western Europe, where some states had been appealed to as parts of the "third world," now was lumped with North America as an area to be surrounded by the hostile "world countryside" of Africa, Asia, and Latin America. There had, in short, been a shift of emphasis to revolutionary diplomacy and a downgrading of more normal state-to-state relations. Such relations were not to be broken at Chinese initiative; abroad, they provided channels through which Mao's gospel might be spread, and at home the diplomatic missions of foreign countries were useful as points on which Chinese pressure might be applied. But the primary touchstone of the value to China of other states had become their willingness to align themselves with China against the Soviet Union or to oppose the United States, and of nonruling Communist parties, it was their readiness to follow the Maoist path of armed insurrection.

In consequence, the only foreign states which the Maoists could still single out for praise became Albania, which was firmly aligned against the Soviet Union, and North Vietnam, which was engaged in a so-called war of national liberation against "United States imperialism

and its lackeys." Insofar as other countries were concerned, what really
counted was not the relationship of their governments to China but
whether there existed within their borders Communist parties or
splinter groups following the Maoist way. In this context the Maoists,
in November 1967, commended "the people of Laos, Burma, the Phil-
ippines, Thailand, India, Indonesia, and other countries" who were
"embarking on or persisting in the road of revolutionary armed struggle." In the vast areas of Asia, Africa, and Latin America, the Maoists
asserted, a democratic revolutionary movement was unfolding. The
orthodox Communist parties could not be praised and hence were un-
worthy of mention, but "the proletariat of Western Europe, North
America, and Oceania" were depicted as "plunging into the struggle
against United States imperialism and monopoly capital in their own
countries." [7]

There was little in Mao Tse-tung's background, as a Chinese or
as a Marxist–Leninist, which might predispose him to favor the long-
term perpetuation of the present international system. His new order
of priorities implied a downgrading of even its short-term value. In the
context of revolutionary diplomacy, which was what now really mat-
tered, he evidently felt justified in claiming that Peking had become
the political center of the world. For good measure he had, in his comments of July 7, 1967, added the assertions that it should also become
the world's military and technological center.[8] Consciously or uncon-
sciously, he was assuming the traditional Chinese view that Peking was
the rightful center of the world.

The government leaders immediately responsible for the conduct
of China's external affairs included men who, unlike Mao Tse-tung,
had been educated abroad and in the once sophisticated Peking, and
whose perspectives had benefited from extensive official foreign travel.
They did not fully share Mao's apocalyptic assessment of the imminence of a major war, his view of China's place in the world, and his
enthusiasm for revolutionary diplomacy. But the storm, into which
China's great helmsman had steered the ship of state, forced them to
look to their own survival. For them, the eye of the storm came in
February 1967, considered by those who helped stir up the storm a
month of adverse currents. It provided a period in which they could
begin restoring order, before the storm began at the end of March to
blow again with redoubled fury. The course Mao had set also made
external collisions inevitable, and their sounds reverberated back and
forth between Peking and other capitals.

In Peking, the twelve months beginning in August 1966 may be
divided into periods: the August eruption of the Red Guards; the
power seizures by the revolutionary rebels the following January; the

reassertion of authority by surviving old leaders beginning in mid-February; and a return to extremism, at the beginning of April, which attained a sharp peak in August 1967. In each period the conduct of foreign affairs was influenced by the relative positions of the three power centers which, with the party structure increasingly paralyzed, emerged as parts of the headquarters of Mao Tse-tung: the army, the civilian government, and the Cultural Revolution Group, represented respectively at the top echelons by Lin Piao, Chou En-lai and, for practical purposes, by Chiang Ch'ing. The relationships of these three power centers were two-faced ones. Ostensibly, and to varying extents in actual fact, they cooperated with each other, and in addition they acted in opposition to one another. The relative position of the power center represented by Chou En-lai depended heavily upon the degree to which Lin Piao sided with him or with Chiang Ch'ing.

August 1966 would appear to have been a period during which Lin Piao and Chiang Ch'ing were cooperating fully with each other and in which Mao Tse-tung had not taken Chou En-lai into his full confidence. In addressing the August 18, 1966, Red Guard rally, Chou En-lai told the assembled students and teachers that their main task was to carry out the Cultural Revolution in their own schools. The presumption that Mao Tse-tung had other and more important tasks for them was raised two days later, when they surged into the streets of Peking and began their reign of terror. It subsequently was confirmed when this particular talk was conspicuously omitted from a volume of speeches of the leaders distributed for the guidance of Red Guards,[9] and when the schools were ordered to remain closed for the academic year 1966–1967 so that the students might continue to make revolution in the country at large.[10]

The August 20 eruption of the Red Guards marked the beginning of a period of ten days during which the streets in front of the Soviet Embassy were jammed from morning to night with demonstrators. They impeded the movements of Soviet diplomatic personnel, plastered all the houses and walls of the neighborhood with antirevisionist slogans, and mounted huge loudspeakers which kept up a day and night din of anti-Soviet slander and abuse.[11] On August 31, Lin Piao, addressing another rally of Red Guards, redirected their attention by making it clear that the main target was "those in authority who have wormed their way into the party and are taking the capitalist road." [12] At that point the campaign against the Soviet Embassy died down.

Circumstantial evidence, buttressed by the subsequent statements of Chinese leaders themselves, strongly indicates that some members of the Cultural Revolution Group became intent, early in 1967, on overthrowing Chou En-lai. His survival at the apex of the governmental pyramid appears to have depended upon Mao Tse-tung's assessment that he was indispensable. This made an overt, frontal attack on him impractical, but suggested that he might be defeated by degrading his administrative effectiveness. Among the main keys to this effectiveness were the vice premiers and other subordinates who responded loyally and effectively to his leadership, and who in turn were largely dependent on his protection for their political survival. The effort to overthrow Chou En-lai by first bringing about the purge of his key subordinates was represented, in subsequent accounts, as a plot hatched early in 1967. The men eventually blamed for it may have not been the only ones involved, and the intention to attack Chou En-lai may have been harbored earlier, but the January movement to seize power opened wide the opportunity to push it vigorously.

Vice premiers Lin Piao and Hsieh Fu-chih were immune from leftist attacks, Lin because of his special position as Mao's "closest comrade-in-arms" and Hsieh because he had completely subordinated his will to that of Mao Tse-tung and was cooperating closely with the Cultural Revolution Group. But the several vice premiers who managed different sectors of the economy all came under heavy assault. Mao Tse-tung's sixteen-point directive, of August 8, 1966, had specified that scientists and technicians, who were engaged in atomic, rocket, and other important programs, were to be given special protection; and on August 13, Chou En-lai had taken Vice Premier Nieh Jung-chen's Scientific and Technological Commission, as well as the Academy of Sciences, under his protective wing.[13] Nevertheless, Nieh Jung-chen and the various scientific bodies were brought under heavy and persistent attacks and numerous scientists were purged.[14] Some of these attacks can be traced, if not to Chiang Ch'ing herself, at least to Red Guard organizations highly responsive to the influence of her group,[15] and to one of her two daughters.[16] But the heaviest and most prolonged attacks on any of the vice premiers were those against Ch'en Yi.

Chou En-lai had made a reputation in diplomacy before he had become a government administrator, and he had not given up its practice in 1958 when Ch'en Yi became foreign minister and director of the State Council's Foreign Affairs Staff Office. In consequence, attacks on Ch'en Yi and the conduct of China's foreign affairs were in a special sense attacks on Chou En-lai. In his dual capacities, and under Chou En-lai's direction, Ch'en Yi supervised an aggregation of agencies of which the Ministry of Foreign Affairs, with its foreign service, and the Overseas Chinese Affairs Commission, dealing with millions of Chinese living abroad, were the most important. But it also included the Commission for Cultural Relations with Foreign Countries; the Bureau of Foreign Specialists; the Foreign Language Publication and

Distribution Bureau; and three special schools, which were Red Guard hotbeds—Peking Foreign Language Institutes No. 1 and No. 2, and the Foreign Affairs Institute. Finally, Ch'en Yi's influence extended to the bodies controlling economic and other relations with foreign countries through several vice directors of his staff office, who held concurrent positions of leadership in relevant government bodies.[17]

A bluff figure, Ch'en Yi was bound to be a storm center of the Cultural Revolution, even if he had not been in a special relationship to Chou En-lai. His mind was too independent and his point of view too broad for confinement within any rigid ideological framework, and an open nature and impulsive temperament denied him the refuge of a pretended orthodoxy. Ch'en Yi was capable of playacting on occasion, and of giving out the current line, as from a record, for the benefit of foreign visitors. But true to his name—"ch'en" means "to state" and "yi" denotes "boldness"—he was almost compulsively prone to speak his mind, and his mind rejected the cult of the thought of Mao Tse-tung; Chiang Ch'ing's view on what she called literature and art; the demands of Red Guards and revolutionary rebels; the authority of the Cultural Revolution Group; and the Cultural Revolution itself.

The contributions which Ch'en Yi had made in the war against Japan and to the victory over the Kuomintang were perhaps greater than those of any other field commander, not excepting Lin Piao. But even this might not have saved Ch'en Yi from early purge had it not been for the determined protection of Chou En-lai—and for the same forthrightness which was also the greatest source of his difficulties. It gave Mao Tse-tung the assurance that Ch'en Yi was engaged in no secret plots against him, and it presented Mao with a challenge which he met by ordering that Ch'en Yi was to be criticized but not overthrown. He evidently decided, in other words, that Ch'en Yi's independent spirit was to be broken, and that he should be forced to accept the will of Mao Tse-tung as though it were his own.

The charges made against a man may tell us as much about the outlook of his attackers as they tell us about the man himself; Ch'en Yi's case provides no exception. In 1959, when the government of Indonesia was forcing out many of the Chinese who had dominated that country's economy, Ch'en Yi is alleged to have remarked to a visiting group of overseas Chinese: "We have chased off almost all Englishmen, Americans, and Frenchmen but when people chase us off we make a fuss about it. That is not altogether fair." [18] His detractors also taxed him for having told the 1961 graduating class of Peking's universities and colleges, while discussing the relative importance of being "red" and being "expert," that those who had expertise could make important contributions to their country even though they might not be able to attain complete redness. He had admitted that he himself was not "red through and through." His thinking was a mixture, he said, deriving from communism, the teachings of Confucius and Mencius, and even of bourgeois thoughts. The most that he could say, after forty years as a revolutionary, was that his Communist thoughts were dominant.[19]

He had subsequently objected to outside pressures designed to make him reform his thinking. In 1962, when there was a rising crescendo of exhortation to study the thought of Mao Tse-tung,[20] he is supposed to have remarked to colleagues that he originally had not intended to join the Communist party, but that a certain person had led him to do so. "That is O.K.," he was quoted as saying, "but thought reform is not." [21] He also objected to the Chinese Communist attempt to mold the thoughts of China's children through comic books filled with rigid political dogma. They would, he feared, breed a new generation of Chinese whose world views were crude and oversimplified. "Children should be given many fantastic and beautiful stories," he said, "fairytales, fables, and stories like *The Arabian Nights*. Because when children entertain many fantasies, their wisdom is widened and their horizon is expanded." [22]

In addresses to drama writers in 1962 and stage artists in 1965, Ch'en Yi had asserted that workers, peasants, and soldiers would be better served by plays they could enjoy than by plays of revolutionary realism filled with propaganda. China's writers, he complained, had been caught in a net of regulations which killed their creativity. He attributed some of these restrictions to Mao Tse-tung, who had held that it was impermissible to portray heroes with shortcomings, or to present tragedies—presumably meaning plays in which proletarian virtue did not emerge triumphant. With this view, Ch'en Yi said, he disagreed; the shortcomings of heroes served to highlight their virtues, and taught their own lessons, whereas oversimplified plays could have a propaganda effect contrary to that intended. He could see such a play once, but not for a second time; it was like being lectured every day. "When such revolutionization is carried out," he said, "there is no question about ideology, but there will be no plays." [23]

Ch'en Yi was, by implication, accusing Chiang Ch'ing of killing the theater through her campaign for its revolutionization, and it is no wonder if they sometimes argued, as she put it, "until our faces are red." [24] It should also be no wonder if she harbored resentment, in this same connection, against Chou En-lai. He had joined Ch'en Yi, at the 1962 forum of playwrights, in asking why classical plays could still draw full houses three hundred years after they were written, while modern plays flopped after three days if they were not subsidized through block bookings. He had also joined with Ch'en Yi in urging playwrights not to confine themselves to current political topics but to write as they pleased.[25]

In the spring of 1966, Ch'en Yi had sent some fifteen work teams into various organizations for which he was responsible,[26] and his wife had participated in one of them. This led to his being attacked the following autumn, like almost all the other leaders, for having tried to put the Cultural Revolution in a straitjacket. It was presumably in this connection that he is supposed to have commented: "We don't want all this talking about straitjackets. If you are talking about straitjackets, then Mao Tse-tung's thought is the biggest straitjacket." [27] Liu Shao-ch'i had helped Ch'en Yi rebuild the New Fourth Army and expand its guerrilla bases during a crucial period of World War II, and Ch'en Yi evidently was unwilling to turn his back on him in time of trouble. He was attacked, at any rate, for having supported Liu Shao-ch'i at the August 1966 plenum, and for speaking up thereafter in defense of him —and of Chu Teh and Ho Lung as well. Many of the charges against Liu Shao-ch'i, Ch'en Yi observed, were obvious fabrications, Liu's opposition to Mao Tse-tung had been exaggerated, and he had not been alone in it. "I have opposed Chairman Mao on several occasions in the past," he declared, "and I am not quite sure I won't do so in the future." [28]

Ch'en Yi blamed the Cultural Revolution Group for the early excesses of the Red Guards, which he openly deplored. "The Cultural Revolution Group," he remarked, "permits the students to go crazy." [29] Of the Red Guards of his two Foreign Language Institutes he sarcastically observed: "Originally there were twenty-one units, but after a week there were over fifty, and after another week, over seventy. Over four thousand people in over seventy units makes seventy cliques. The oceans are vast to behold: this is truly one hundred flowers blooming and one hundred schools of thought contending." [30]

This remark might, of course, be taken not merely as an explicit criticism of Red Guard factionalism, but also as implied criticism of that forerunner of the Cultural Revolution, Mao's period of the Hundred Flowers. Ch'en Yi did not, however, merely imply doubt about Mao's infallibility. "I am not," he said, "a person who in every matter takes Mao's words and puts them at the head." [31] At a time when Mao was being praised as the greatest Marxist–Leninist of the era, he remarked: "Marx came from Germany, and Germany produced a Kautsky and a Bernstein to modify him. Lenin came from the Soviet Union and there, there appeared a Khrushchev. Chairman Mao belongs to our country; there may also be someone to modify him. Wait and see." [32] His attitude toward the revolutionization of Chinese diplomacy may be gauged from his statement: "This Mao Tse-tung thought is downright Chinese stuff; let's not take it abroad." [33]

The revolutionization of China's external relations, however, was already under way. The effort to impose Maoist leadership on Japanese Communists was evident as early as the autumn of 1966, when some Japanese in Peking began to behave like Red Guards and make life miserable for representatives of the Japanese Communist party. On September 16, for example, a group of them went to the lodgings of Junichi Konno, newly-arrived correspondent for *Akahata,* beat him up, and then tortured him by pouring water down his nostrils, and on October 27 eight representatives of the Japanese Communist party, who had come to attend the third anniversary celebration of the China-Japan Friendship society, were dragged from a bus and beaten up.[34]

Toward the end of 1966, the government began to bring home most of its foreign service personnel, including all but one of its ambassadors, in order that they might be subjected to the Cultural Revolution. Mao buttons and little red books of his sayings became important export items, and Chinese diplomats who remained abroad began to behave like Red Guard militants.[35]

The first notable attacks on Ch'en Yi by the Red Guards came in the autumn, and his initial reaction was to deal with them in the common sense terms of a man too busy to waste time dealing with absurd demands of immature youngsters. "I come to the Foreign Ministry," he said on one occasion, "and people want me to lower my head and confess my crimes. What crimes have I committed? It is a joke." [36]

When he did have confrontations with the Red Guards, he sometimes treated them with the jocularity appropriate to a charade. At one encounter, following the Red Guard custom of opening meetings with the reading of a passage from *Quotations from Chairman Mao Tse-tung,* he pretended to find a passage in which Chairman Mao praised Ch'en Yi as "a man of nerve and a clear head." [37] When he was undergoing one of their kangaroo courts, and the time came for him to keep an appointment w .h a visiting foreign dignitary, he embarrassed the students by asking whether he should go wearing the dunce cap they had placed on his head, and then reduced them to laughter by begging them in mock seriousness to take good care of it, as he would need it later.[38]

The January 1967 period of the seizure of power was, however, no laughing matter. He now was faced not merely with student Red Guards, but also by the more mature revolutionary rebels of his own ministry. On January 18, they seized power, setting up a "Ministry of Foreign Affairs Revolutionary Rebel Station" through which to "carry on revolution and supervise work" within the ministry.[39] It may have

THE CENTER OF THE WORLD

been about this time that he complained, "All my heads of department have been removed. What sort of minister am I, anyway?" Mentioning a certain ambassador who had been out of the country only half a year, he asked: "What is the problem? As soon as he gets off the plane you take him out and struggle him." [40] Too many people were under attack toward whom he felt loyalty. "If you only believe Chairman Mao, Lin Piao, Chou En-lai, Ch'en Po-ta, K'ang Sheng, and Chiang Ch'ing," he said, "or if you are being especially generous and add in five deputy premiers, that only makes eleven people. Such a great party, does it only have eleven people who are clean? I don't want to be this sort of clean person. Take me out and show me to the masses." [41]

Ch'en Yi was, on January 24, taken out and shown, if not to the masses, at least to ten thousand personnel of the foreign affairs sector. On that day he made a self-criticism on which he had worked the previous seven days and nights.[42] It was accepted, but his wife was not so fortunate. She was three times required to make self-criticisms, all of which were rejected as insincere, and she was paraded in a three-cornered hat in punishment. Nan Han-chen, chairman of the China Committee for the Promotion of International Trade, was subjected to a kangaroo court, and on January 27 he committed suicide.[43] Early in February an official of the Commission for Economic Relations with Foreign Countries was taken out for struggle, and after it had gone on for seven days, Ch'en Yi was moved to protest. The man, Ch'en Yi recalled, had been in prison for seven and a half years during the Kuomintang period, and had undergone torture by electric shock. "He is a good comrade. After liberation, his work has been thorough. There is nothing here to accuse. One ought to have respect for this kind of comrade. I doubt whether you rebels have got this kind of spirit." [44]

The revolutionary rebels, in Ch'en Yi's view, were not engaging in the ideological struggle designed to correct errors and thus restore a soundly based unity, but in the destructive struggle which should be reserved for enemies of the people. In words which were to be vindicated by the subsequent course of the Cultural Revolution, he admonished: "Special attention should be paid to the form of struggle. You must not damage the feelings between comrades. Otherwise one will not achieve the aim of the struggle between the two lines. When a lot of people are injured, it is afterward very difficult for them to go back and work together. In this respect I have learned a bitter lesson. When feelings are hurt one cannot get together afterward. You simply look at each other with anger. There is no good in this. People remember you for a lifetime and when they have the opportunity they avenge themselves. This is not the ideological struggle." [45]

Some of Ch'en Yi's supporters within the Foreign Ministry, in apparent reference to the period beginning in mid-January when he was not in control and the revolutionary rebels were riding high, made the derisive comment: "When there is no tiger on the mountain, the monkey becomes king." [46] The appropriateness of the comment may be judged from the fact that this period was marked by a new campaign against the Soviet Embassy, the violence and duration of which suggested that Communist China was endeavoring to force the Soviet Union to break diplomatic relations.

The affair which led to this outbreak occurred in Moscow, but was clearly the consequence of the Cultural Revolution in China. Chinese studying abroad had been called home, and a group of them en route to Peking had arrived in Moscow on January 25. Feeling impelled to demonstrate their antirevisionist revolutionary spirit, they had gone to Lenin's tomb and staged a demonstration. Soviet police forcibly ejected them from its precincts, and the Chinese Embassy protested that nine of them had been so badly injured that they would be unable to proceed on the next day's plane.[47] The *People's Daily* of January 27 reported this occurrence as "a shocking and bloody incident" in which "Soviet troops, police, and plainclothesmen savagely attacked a group of Chinese students" whose only offense had been reading aloud *Quotations from Chairman Mao Tse-tung*. This constituted a new "blood debt," owed to the Chinese people. "Hit back hard," it demanded in an editorial, "at the rabid provocations of the filthy Soviet revisionist swine!" [48]

The demonstrations against the Soviet Embassy began so promptly as to raise question whether preparations had not been under way even before the demonstrators had read that day's report of events in Moscow and the editorial calling for revenge. The demonstrations were also too well organized to have been completely spontaneous. Red Guards were morning participants, but afternoons their numbers were swelled by unarmed troops trucked in from barracks in the suburbs, and even by peasants from nearby communes of the countryside.[49] After a few days, fervor might wane, only to be rekindled by some new development. First it was welcoming receptions for the returning students who had been injured at Lenin's tomb. According to a later account, they seemed lively to fellow-travelers during the flight home, but as the plane approached Peking they donned bandages. At the airport, motion pictures were taken of them being helped solicitously from the plane, some of them on stretchers.[50] A few days later the Chinese Embassy in Moscow posted offensive propaganda, about the January 25 incident, in showcases mounted near the street. The Foreign Ministry demanded that they be removed, and after the Chinese refused, the Russians themselves undertook the task. Members of the Embassy staff tried to resist the removal, a fracas developed, and thirty-one Chinese allegedly were brutally beaten.[51]

Back in Peking the personnel of the Soviet Embassy, harassed day and night by hostile demonstrators and blaring loudspeakers, arranged to send their dependents home. In the bus which took them from the Embassy, they later recounted, the children were made to repeat pro-Mao slogans, and at the airport the wives were forced to crawl under portraits of Mao and Stalin before being allowed to board their plane.[52] Many Soviet personnel took refuge in other embassies, only to be told that their safety would not be guaranteed if they did not stay in their own compound. With the Soviet Union threatening to break diplomatic relations and demonstrations being carried on also against other eastern European embassies, the Czechs followed the Soviet example by sending their families home, and the Poles and East Germans prepared to follow suit.[53]

Anti-Soviet demonstrations are reported to have been conducted that winter also along the border between Manchuria and the Soviet Union. *Pravda* later charged that groups of Red Guards numbering from several hundred to a thousand crossed the frozen Ussuri River south of Khabarovsk, in trucks and on foot, shouting slogans, persistently trying to overrun Soviet border guards, and calling on them to rebel against their revisionist masters. The account suggested that fighting broke out between the demonstrators and the border guards, who had to display considerable fortitude and tenacity in order to hold their ground without having recourse to firearms.[54]

On February 11, Chou En-lai attended an anti-Soviet "condemnation rally" at which he made a speech, broadcast live and heard by foreign correspondents, demanding that the demonstrations be halted and the Soviet diplomats guaranteed the protection essential to performance of their duties. In reporting the rally the next day, *People's Daily* portrayed Chou En-lai as having been present, but as not having been among the speakers. The motives of this misrepresentation are easy to surmise. Chou's speech was a rebuke to the extremists of the Cultural Revolution Group who controlled the *People's Daily*, who had used that control to stir up the populace, and who probably directed the demonstrations. They may have calculated that treating Chou's address as a nonspeech might improve the chances of appealing to Mao Tse-tung and getting Chou overruled. If they tried, they did not succeed, for the harassment of the Soviet Embassy stopped the following day.[55]

The new internal trend toward moderation, arising from a recognition of the continuing need for old leaders, had already begun to make itself felt before the demonstrations against the Soviet Embassy had ended. On February 8 the Military Affairs Committee had issued a directive specifying that "the liaison centers of the revolutionary mass organizations set up in various places must . . . be abolished without exception." [56] This meant, among other things, that the revolutionary rebels' liaison station in the Ministry of Foreign Affairs, set up January 18 for carrying on revolution there and supervising the ministry's work, would have to be disbanded. The power seizure in that ministry, as Chou En-lai indicated in his speech of February 17, would not be recognized.

The second half of February and the first weeks of March were the period of the "February adverse current," during which old leaders moved to regain ground lost during January, and to reassert control over agencies under their supervision. Surveying the situation on February 12, Ch'en Yi remarked, "If my advice had been followed earlier, things would not have come to this. Now the Foreign Ministry is in a mess, without organization and without discipline, and confidential material about foreign affairs has been taken off." [57] Feeling that he had been proved right, on February 20 he repudiated his self-criticism of January 24 as having been forced on him. "I have," he sorrowfully observed, "been a revolutionary for more than forty years; I never thought that it would come to this." [58]

Moving with the February current, Ch'en Yi took the offensive against the rebels, placed old officials back in their jobs and, with the aid of Liao Ch'eng-chih, chairman of the Overseas Chinese Affairs Commission, set up friendly power-seizure committees in that body and perhaps other organizations subordinate to his Foreign Affairs Staff Office.[59] But by the end of March, the February "adverse current" had been reversed and Ch'en Yi was back in trouble. On April 4, a mass rally against him and Liao Ch'eng-chih was held; on April 8, a new liaison station was set up, in defiance of the ban of February 8, to coordinate the attacks against him; and on April 17 about a thousand Red Guards and revolutionary rebels demonstrated outside his ministry. On the latter date, Ch'en Po-ta announced that Chou En-lai would thenceforth supervise the work of the Foreign Ministry, and two days later he asked the Red Guards to moderate their attacks against Ch'en Yi. Despite Ch'en Po-ta's instructions and Chou En-lai's efforts to protect him in the continued exercise of his duties, the attacks on Ch'en Yi continued and were again extended to his principal subordinates.[60]

The period of extremism which began in April 1967, like that of the previous January, was marked by demonstrations against the embassies in Peking of foreign governments. The first was against that of Indonesia, and again the immediate cause was an incident abroad which reflected the revolutionary spirit prevalent in China itself. A Chinese Communist resident of Indonesia, allegedly engaged in the clandestine distribution of pamphlets calling on fellow Chinese to oppose the Indonesian Government, was arrested and put in jail. Shortly thereafter he either was killed or committed suicide, depending upon the account one chooses to believe. This started a series of demonstrations and counterdemonstrations, in the respective countries, in the course of which Yao Teng-shan, the Chinese chargé d'affaires in Indonesia, was declared *persona non grata*.[61]

On April 30, Yao Teng-shan arrived in Peking, where he was accorded a hero's welcome and a reception by Mao Tse-tung. A photograph taken at the reception shows a ruffianly fellow with a broad grin, his arms familiarly linked with those of Mao Tse-tung and Chiang Ch'ing. Once back on duty, he began to make bold accusations against Chou En-lai and Ch'en Yi, both of whom he accused of suppressing the revolution in the Foreign Ministry, and before long he was a leader in its new Revolutionary Rebel Liaison Station.[62]

On May 12, Chou En-lai is reported to have met with Red Guards and revolutionary rebels of various factions from the foreign affairs sector, who demanded that Ch'en Yi should, as earlier decided by Ch'en Po-ta, be required to attend criticism rallies.[63] Chou En-lai was represented as agreeing, and saying that he would himself chair the meetings. It may be assumed, of course, that Chou En-lai proposed to attend and chair the meetings in order to keep them within bounds. Apparently some of the Red Guards and revolutionary rebels were dissatisfied with this arrangement. Beginning in the early morning hours on May 13, several hundred of them invaded the Foreign Ministry and occupied it for about thirty hours. During this invasion they smashed doors and windows, beat up PLA guards and Foreign Ministry officials, and broke into the confidential archives—presumably in search of materials which might buttress their case against Ch'en Yi.[64] There was in force a regulation, publicly announced on February 17, which specified: "No one shall be allowed to raid or occupy secret rooms and file rooms and seize secret documents and files." [65] But the quoted response of one of the rebels, when an official protested against their rifling of the archives, was: "What's so terrific about secrets? To hell with them." [66]

It is doubtful that the perpetrators of this invasion were apprehended and "punished according to law," as the regulation of February 17 prescribed. If so, the punishment did not serve as sufficient deterrent. On May 29, two or three hundred Red Guards and rebel workers broke into Chungnanhai and staged, at the Foreign Affairs Staff Office, a repetition of their May 13 rampage against the Foreign Ministry.[67] With the foreign affairs sector of the government in disarray, China's foreign relations entered upon a new period of extreme turbulence. Before this period ended, xenophobic outbreaks had strained relations with several countries to or beyond the breaking point, and the offices of the British Embassy in Peking had been put to the torch and lay in ashes.

This anti-British outburst was occasioned by events, in the British Crown Colony of Hong Kong, which were themselves the consequence of China's Cultural Revolution. What Lord Palmerston had called "a barren island with hardly a house upon it," when seized in 1841 to provide a refuge and a residence for British merchants driven from Canton, had since been enlarged to almost 400 square miles, first by the cession of the tip of the Kowloon peninsula just across the harbor in 1860, and then through a ninety-nine year leasehold, negotiated in 1898, covering an additional strip of mainland territory and numerous adjacent islands. By 1967 it contained a population of about 3,750,000, of whom approximately 98 percent were Chinese.

In 1967 Hong Kong seemed, in several respects, to be an anachronism. It existed as a colony, in an era of decolonization, on the doorstep of the world's most vocally anti-imperialist power. In an age of high taxes and deficit financing, it had low tax rates and had been producing, in most years, a budget surplus.[68] Almost entirely lacking in natural resources, it had a thriving economy, based on industry and trade, which was growing at a rate of roughly 15 percent per year.[69] Originally created for the benefit of the mother country and British subjects, it turned over no revenues to the treasury in London, although it did help cover the cost of maintaining British troops stationed in the colony. Instead, the substantial sums left over, after covering operating costs, were largely plowed back into public works, such as the low-cost housing projects in which over a quarter of the colony's population had been resettled.[70] The colony, in short, was being governed for the benefit of its inhabitants, and it was governed well. Hong Kong was not entirely immune to civil strife or exempt from the ills of urbanizations, as a mob outbreak in 1956[71] and a couple days of destructive disturbances by restless youths in the spring of 1966 had demonstrated.[72] But such occasions were the exception, as the decade between them would suggest. Hong Kong's normal atmosphere is one of amicable bustle, and it is a place where one ordinarily can walk the streets in perfect safety, day or night.

Communists could not expect to be among the Chinese appointed to the colony's Executive Council, an advisory body to the governor, and to the Legislative Council, which passes on the legislation which he enacts.[73] But in Hong Kong they could and did publish newspapers, run theaters which showed Chinese Communist films, conduct banking and shipping operations, maintain retail stores specializing in mainland goods, run schools attended by about 20,000 students, and control labor unions with a total membership of about 186,000.[74] They had, of course, set up unions for seamen, transport workers, and public utility employees, because strikes by such workers bring greater pressures to bear on a government than do work stoppages in other fields; but they had organized workers also in a number of the colony's ordinary industrial enterprises.

As might be expected, the Cultural Revolution on the adjacent Chinese mainland set standards of militant behavior to which Communist agents in Hong Kong felt impelled to conform. Adopting mainland practices, they began to distribute among the members of their labor unions, the students in their schools, and the employees of their enterprises, Mao badges and copies of that talismanic book, the red-covered *Quotations from Chairman Mao Tse-tung,* and to hold frequent meetings devoted to political indoctrination, patriotic songs, and the chanting of revolutionary slogans. The militant spirits aroused through such sessions were bound to find an outlet, and Communist agents in Hong Kong naturally sought to channel them into actions which conformed to the expectations, real or presumed, of their mainland masters.

It is unlikely that the Cultural Revolution Group in Peking actually planned a confrontation between the government of Hong Kong and local Communists. However, its members must have realized, if they gave any thought to the matter, that such an outcome was likely. Such a confrontation had occurred, late in 1966, in the small Portuguese enclave of Macao, on the opposite side of the Pearl River estuary from Hong Kong. They also might have reflected that the two cases could not be accorded comparable treatment, if only because Great Britain maintained diplomatic relations with Communist China, whereas Portugal did not. Peking had been relatively free to determine the extent to which it became committed in Macao, whereas it would have to become involved at the government-to-government level in the case of a confrontation in Hong Kong. Moreover, Hong Kong was not Macao, Great Britain was not Portugal, the Cultural Revolution was in a more advanced stage in 1967 than it had been in 1966, and a settlement like that reached between the authorities and the Communists in Macao[75] might not be possible in Hong Kong. With Hong Kong it might have to be a case of everything or nothing, and government policy had not envisioned recovery of Hong Kong before a take-over of Taiwan.[76]

The troubles in Hong Kong were touched off by a labor dispute between members of a Communist union and the management of a Chinese-owned plastics factory which manufactured artificial flowers.

It was not the first labor dispute in Hong Kong which had involved
behavior and demands reminiscent of the Red Guards and revolutionary rebels of the mainland, but it was the first in which the police
were called on to do more than just stand by. On May 6, picketing
workers used force to prevent the management from moving finished
goods out of the factory, and the management responded by requesting
police assistance. The police repeatedly warned the pickets, but they
persisted in efforts to prevent removal of the goods. In consequence the
police intervened and arrested twenty-one men, including the chairman
of the Hong Kong and Kowloon Rubber and Plastics Workers Union.[77]

It was a minor incident, and not one in which anybody was seriously hurt, but it led to major repercussions. The union published demands which its parent federation endorsed; Communist newspapers
denounced the government and accused the police of brutal attacks
on unarmed workers; pro-Communist organizations began to hold
meetings to drum up support for the arrested workers; and antigovern-
ment posters began to appear in public places. The union's demands,
moreover, were ones the government could not accept. It was called
upon to cease its brutality and ensure that it was not repeated; release
immediately all those who had been arrested; pay compensation for all
injuries and damage; punish those responsible; and refrain from further interference in labor disputes.[78]

The Chinese Communists in Hong Kong represented a distinct
minority, but they undoubtedly believed that a large proportion of
the populace was susceptible, as fellow Chinese, to involvement
on their side in a showdown with British imperialists. To get them
involved and aroused would, however, require a bigger incident than
the scuffle of May 6. The recollection of the mob violence which had
flamed up in Kowloon the previous year, after a brief period of agitation over a minor issue and without their participation, may have encouraged them to instigate a similar outbreak.

The plastic flower factory was made the center for further demonstrations and slogan chanting, and because it was located in a heavily
populated part of Kowloon, the demonstrators attracted big crowds of
curious spectators and idle mischief-makers. In consequence the makings of a mob was on hand May 11, when the Communist pickets
threatened to break into the factory and engaged in a further clash
with the police. The violence spread to other parts of Kowloon, with
paid participants helping to keep it going, and for three days mobs
battled the police, set fire to cars and buses, and looted government
offices. Yet in these three days of violence there was only one fatality.
A boy standing on a balcony was killed, not as a result of police action,

but probably by a brick thrown or dropped from above by one of the rioters.[79]

The police, mainly Chinese, were able to put down the disturbances without inflicting fatalities in consequence of excellent training, which stressed the importance of using no more than the necessary minimum of force. The training included anti-riot drills and developed rigid collective discipline and superb self-control on the part of individual men. But one additional factor should be mentioned: the laws and regulations of the colony narrowly restrict the importation and possession of firearms, and they are rigorously enforced. In consequence the police seldom are in danger of being shot and have less reason themselves to resort to use of their own firearms. Moreover, riot police are equipped with weapons, manufactured in the United States, firing nonlethal, wooden projectiles; these projectiles are about six inches long and an inch in diameter, are fired low so that they richochet off the pavement at shin or knee height, and inflict sufficient pain to put rioters out of action without doing them serious damage. In Hong Kong the police use ordinary firearms only as a last resort, and in the rioting from May 11 to May 13, they used no greater force than that of tear gas bombs and baton charges.[80]

The day after the rioting was initiated, delegations of employees from Communist newspapers and department stores, as well as representatives of Communist unions and other organizations, began to converge on Government House. They came asking to see the Governor in order that they might protest government "brutality" and reinforce the demands of the plastic workers' union. In Macao, late the previous year, similar groups demanding to see its governor had behaved so badly that they had to be ejected, and had subsequently charged that they had been trapped inside and beaten.[81] It was by then a well-worn trick of mainland Red Guards, who used it to provoke and justify attacks on the headquarters of those they sought to overthrow, and the Hong Kong authorities did not fall for it. The callers accordingly were met at the gate by an aide who offered to accept any petitions they might have, but who declined to admit them to the premises.

On May 15, a Chinese vice minister of foreign affairs in Peking called in Sir Donald Hopson, British chargé d'affaires, and handed him a statement in which it was asserted that the Hong Kong authorities had turned loose on the bare-handed workers, representatives of various circles, and young students, large numbers of armed troops and police who had committed against them "large-scale sanguinary atrocities." The note alleged that this was the result of long premeditation, and was "a component part of the British government's scheme of collusion with United States imperialism against China." In apparent reference to the calls at Hong Kong made by American naval vessels—in order to allow the crews periods of rest and recreation—and to organized leave travel by American military personnel from Vietnam, it was charged in the note that the British Government was "continuing to provide the United States with Hong Kong as a base for aggression against Vietnam in disregard of the repeated solemn warnings of the Chinese government." Moreover, the British authorities in Hong Kong were stepping up other hostile measures in a vain attempt to exclude from it the "great influence of China's Great Proletarian Cultural Revolution" which "they mortally fear and hate."

"The Chinese government demands in all seriousness," the statement continued, "that the British government instruct the British authorities in Hong Kong as follows: 'Immediately accept all the just demands put forward by Chinese workers and residents in Hong Kong; immediately stop all fascist measures; immediately set free all arrested persons (including workers, journalists, and cameramen); punish the culprits responsible for these sanguinary atrocities, offer apologies to the victims and compensate for all their losses; and guarantee against the occurrence of similar incidents.'" The British government and the British authorities in Hong Kong were to accept those demands "immediately and unconditionally." The Chinese government and people were "determined to carry the struggle through to the end." In a final warning, the note declared that should the British "cling to their perverse course, they must be held responsible for all the grave consequences arising therefrom." [82] The phrase "grave consequences" is, of course, one which was handed down from the days of traditional diplomacy and which then was used to threaten a break of diplomatic relations and a declaration of war.

The statement of the Chinese Ministry of Foreign Affairs was promptly published and immediately reinforced by three days of demonstrations conducted in front of the British Embassy, and by mass rallies held in Peking and Canton. At one of these rallies, held in Peking May 18, Minister of Public Security Hsieh Fu-chih declared: "All activities carried out by our compatriots in studying, propagating, applying, and defending Mao Tse-tung's thought are their absolute, sacred, and inviolable right." [83]

Shortly after the publication of the Foreign Ministry statement, the more conservative elements among Communist China's agents in Hong Kong fell into line with public support for the demands which had been set forth by their labor union colleagues. Each morning, beginning May 17, they drove up to the gates of Government House in their Mercedes-Benz sedans; demanded to see the Governor; were refused admittance; joined other demonstrators in waving the red book and chanting slogans; and drove away again. With all Communist organizations and enterprises committed, the numbers of demonstrators grew each day. They were obviously well organized: the men were almost all identically dressed in dark blue trousers and white shirts, the women in dark skirts and white blouses; they left their gathering places on an apparent schedule; they stepped along together in well-ordered ranks; and after they had demonstrated for a period and stuck up whatever posters they carried, they moved on to make room for those who followed.[84]

At first the demonstrations themselves were orderly, although they created a terrific pandemonium which only subsided close to the end of business hours, when everyone went home. But by May 20, they had begun to get rough and that afternoon the police, in order to control the crowds, had to cordon off the entry to the road in front of Government House. The next morning the demonstrators found their way blocked by police, who informed them that they might proceed only in groups of no more than twenty at one time. Apparently lacking orders covering this contingency but unwilling to submit to police orders, they went back downhill where some of them engaged in minor rioting.

The next day, May 22, they were back again in force at the Communist Bank of China building, which was their gathering place. The police were out in force too, drawn up about a hundred yards away, blocking the road leading up to Government House. From a window of the Bank of China building a loudspeaker, carrying a woman's strident voice, blared encouragement to the demonstrators and directed propaganda at the police. They were urged to turn their guns on their officers, and warned that they and their families otherwise would suffer when peoples' courts were established in Hong Kong.[85] The demonstrators advanced as far as the police line and suddenly began to strike, kick, and claw at the police. One of the policemen doubled up, kneed in the groin, and at this point they were given the order to strike back with their batons. They fell to with a will, and then began to hustle demonstrators into waiting police vans. At this point the propaganda uses of white shirts and blouses became apparent. They showed the gore from bashed heads, either one's own or that of a fellow demonstrator which could be rubbed on one's shirt. Some of the demonstrators suddenly produced and donned bandages which had been stained red in advance, and photographers from the Communist press soon had the makings of an impressive propaganda display.[86] Demonstrators not in the front ranks then went rioting through Hong Kong's downtown streets, and had to be brought under control through the usual police tactics and the declaration of a curfew.

Meanwhile the respective governments, in London and in Peking, had each moved to back up its own people. On May 18, the British Government had declared that it stood by Hong Kong,[87] and on May 22 the Foreign Ministry in Peking informed the British Embassy that the two British consular officers stationed in Shanghai, Peter Hewitt and his assistant, would have to be withdrawn within forty-eight hours, and their office closed. Red Guards had invaded the premises a few days before, smashing furniture, terrorizing Hewitt's wife and children, and frog-marching him around his own compound. On May 24, when they left for the airport en route to Peking, the two men were made to run a gauntlet by hooligans who jostled, kicked, and struck them, and daubed them with glue.[88] That same day Communists and their supporters in Macao, who had been demonstrating against the British Consulate there, forced the Consul to stand in the hot sun for seven hours while they chanted hate slogans at him; he closed his office the following day and took his staff to Hong Kong.[89]

In Hong Kong, the decisive police reaction of May 22 put an end to the Communists' mass demonstrations, and beginning the next day they adopted new tactics. A rash of inflamatory posters began to appear on streetcars, buses, ferries, and public buildings. On June 1, the government prohibited the use of such posters and began a campaign to remove them, which the Communists resisted tenaciously. The Communists also called strikes of transport, public utility, and dockyard workers, substantial numbers of whom responded to the call. At a few establishments they armed themselves with iron rods and similar weapons and barricaded the doors, in one case holding members of the management staff as hostages. The police moved in to evict such workers, and the government dismissed its striking employees. Then, in a move soon copied by transport companies and other employers, they rehired those who appeared to have been coerced and were willing to resume work.[90]

At this point Hong Kong Communists must have been feeling keen disappointment at the reactions of the populace as a whole. Many non-Communists, predominantly young mischief-makers and street riffraff, had participated in the initial rioting but did not take part in subsequent violence. Meanwhile, prompt and generous public response to a privately initiated fund, raised to assist the families of policemen who had become casualties, demonstrated that the suppression of violence had been widely appreciated. When it became apparent that the choice was between the government and a Communist-dominated Hong Kong, there was little doubt where popular preferences lay.

Most of the people were aware, in varying degrees, of conditions on the mainland, and many had come to Hong Kong in order to escape them. It was a populace which worked for a living and which found that the transport strikes made getting to work more difficult. Everyone had to eat, and when the Communists called on June 13 for a ban on food sales, the vendors did not respond—but the populace became still more aware of Communist willingness to sacrifice its well-being.[91]

The motivations of actual participants in Communist-led demonstrations, strikes, and violence were more complex. There is no doubt that some, in consequence of Communist indoctrination, because of dissatisfaction with individual private employers, or for other reasons, felt commitment to the cause. Others took part because they happened to work for Communist enterprises, or in the belief that a Communist takeover was imminent. The workers of one firm, for instance, seemed convinced that the People's Liberation Army was scheduled to move into Hong Kong on July 17 and that some of them would then become the managers of the company.[92]

But many workers took part in strikes consequent to intimidation. This conclusion is supported by much evidence based on individual cases, and the differing reactions of workers in dissimilar occupations. Local transport workers and ocean seamen were both called on by their Communist unions to go on strike. The local transport strikes were effective for at least the first days until the troublemakers were screened out, and bus company operations were hampered for some months. But seamen were in a different position from bus drivers. Once at sea they were among fellow seamen who had disregarded the strike call, and out of reach of Communist goon squads. In 1967, only two ships calling at Hong Kong had to delay sailings on account of difficulty in filling crews. The Communists had proclaimed that they would convert Hong Kong into a "dead and stinking port," but that year its exports increased by almost 17 percent.[93]

Once the Communists in Hong Kong had initiated their campaign and been administered an initial rebuff, leaders in Peking were faced with the question of what kinds and amounts of backing they should lend, and to what end. Each of the three main elements in Mao's headquarters was bound to view this question from the standpoint of its own interests and concerns. Hong Kong was China's best customer and the annual source of about U.S. $600,000,000 in convertible foreign exchange, which was about enough to pay for the approximately six million tons of food grains which China had been importing each year to help feed the population.[94] Hong Kong got most of its fresh foods from the mainland, and it would accordingly suffer from the interruption of their flow. But a prolonged stoppage would have complicated the problems also of government leaders on the mainland, and taking over Hong Kong would be killing the goose that laid the golden eggs.

The People's Liberation Army could undoubtedly have taken Hong Kong without much initial difficulty, although with longer-run consequence which might have been much more serious. But it also had its hands full already: it was having to support industry, agriculture, and the left, administer the provinces, and try to maintain public order in an increasingly disorderly land. This made the army the natural ally, in this matter, of Chou En-lai, who would have had to deal with the economic and diplomatic consequences of a military taking over of the colony.

The Cultural Revolution Group, on the other hand, undoubtedly looked at the matter from the standpoint of its commitment to revolutionary activism. Hong Kong's colonial administrators were persons in authority taking the capitalist road, and foreign imperialists to boot. The thought of Mao Tse-tung was for the whole world; he had held that to rebel is justified; and the Chinese of Hong Kong had a sacred right to apply his sayings.

In 1969, a Chinese refugee in Hong Kong, who claimed to have been a leader of Red Guards subject to the direction of the Cultural Revolution Group, asserted that the State Council under Chou En-lai, and the People's Liberation Army under Lin Piao, had opposed the campaign of disturbances in Hong Kong, but that the Cultural Revolution Group had participated in planning and directing them. In mid-1967, he claimed, that group had sent four hundred specially-trained Red Guards to Hong Kong to spearhead the violence.[95]

The actions and declarations of the government, the army, and the Cultural Revolution Group tend to lend credence to this story. There is no convincing evidence that the government in Peking ever ordered the interruption of food shipments into Hong Kong, which came by rail, road, and water. Interruptions did occur, but they appear to have been due chiefly to troubles on the mainland which halted rail traffic in the neighboring province of Kwangtung, and to disorders which sometimes flared at border-crossing points.[96] Disorders there were almost inevitable, given the incendiary influence of the Cultural Revolution, for some farmers cultivated land on both sides of the border, which ran down the main street of one village. Moreover armed militia, recruited from among the local populace, garrisoned this border village, and when fellow townsmen attacked Hong Kong police at the border, they undoubtedly felt some temptation to join in. They are generally believed to have been responsible for machinegun and sniper fire which killed five Hong Kong police and wounded eleven there on July 8.[97] But regular units of the People's Liberation Army were not involved. They subsequently took over border duty at that place, and they were sometimes seen restraining members of the local populace.[98]

Chou En-lai was probably speaking both for himself and the army command when he remarked, on June 24, that the destiny of Hong Kong would be decided by "our patriotic countrymen there and the seven hundred million Chinese people as a whole." [99] This seemed to imply that the struggle in Hong Kong was primarily up to the Communists there, and that a military takeover by the People's Liberation Army was not imminent. But members of the Cultural Revolution Group, in public speeches and through the media they controlled, proclaimed that Hong Kong's rulers would be given "a taste of the Chinese people's iron fist" if they did not lower their heads and admit their crimes, and called on the Chinese people of Hong Kong to rise and settle China's blood debts with the British imperialists.[100] It is also true that outsiders were sent into Hong Kong to carry out acts of violence, but evidence is not available to prove that they were sent in by the Cultural Revolution Group, or that they were Red Guards in the original sense of the term, as opposed to the loose usage denoting any revolutionary activists. The most hardened ones were men who spoke the dialect of the Amoy area, birthplace of most of the Chinese who had been expelled from Indonesia. Some of them had undoubtedly been involved in Communist activities there, and after their return to China they were at loose ends, ready to be recruited for dangerous tasks.[101]

Beginning late in June, it became increasingly evident that the Communists were treating the struggle in Hong Kong as a "war of national liberation" with Communist union headquarters, office buildings, goods emporiums, and schools serving as guerrilla bases. In these establishments they produced homemade weapons, and from them they sallied forth for hit-and-run attacks on police and other targets. As during the phase of mass demonstrations, the Hong Kong authorities waited awhile before taking decisive action, perhaps to give the local populace time to absorb the situation, and to see that the steps they were about to take were justifiable and necessary. Prior to July 12, they had met and contained the attacks, but on that day, which they later identified as the turning point of the struggle, the Colonial Secretary announced that the government was determined to seize and maintain the initiative.[102]

On that and following days strong parties of police, backed for the first time by military units, raided the principal Communist strongholds; seized stocks of homemade weapons and explosives, as well as inflammatory posters and literature; and took into custody occupants of the headquarters. The initial raids were strongly resisted by defenders using bottles, daggers, acids, and firebombs, but subsequent raids met with little or no physical opposition. Driven underground, the Communists continued their campaign of violence, relying chiefly on homemade bombs, sometimes thrown at the police but most often left to explode on the streets or in other public places. These terrorist tactics cost them additional public support, as did the killing of an anti-Communist radio announcer; he and a relative, driving in a car, were stopped, doused with gasoline and set afire.[103]

By early autumn the regime on the mainland had evidently written off the campaign in Hong Kong. Two payments each of HK $10,000,000 had been contributed from the mainland to help pay striking workers, but nothing was donated to cover the month of September.[104] During the second week of that month Communist China, in disregard of the boycott on ocean shipping to Hong Kong which it previously had tried to help enforce, sent four ships to discharge cargo there.[105] Later in the month one of Hong Kong's Chinese newspapers, implicitly recognizing that the struggle there was failing, put the blame on Communist China's failure to lend much more than verbal support.[106] But the terrorist bombings continued through most of the remainder of 1967, and by the end of the campaign they had inflicted fifteen of the fifty-one lives lost, and many injuries.[107]

The reporters in Hong Kong of the New China News Agency had not limited themselves to merely observing and reporting on anti-government incidents; they frequently were active participants. In consequence several of them were arrested, and on July 19 one of them was sentenced to two years in prison. In retaliation, the Chinese Communists put Anthony Grey, the correspondent in Peking of Reuters, under house arrest; it was not to be lifted until more than two years had passed and the last of the Chinese journalists sentenced in Hong Kong had served their terms and been released.[108]

Hong Kong's Communist press played a particularly incendiary role. The *Wen-hui pao*, for example, responded to the raids on Communist headquarters, begun by police backed by troops in mid-July, by recalling that the Boxers had used primitive weapons "to deal exterminating blows on the enemy, who had guns and artillery." It called on the people of Hong Kong to make all sorts of weapons, as well as to seize weapons from the enemy, and to "fight bloodily" in order to "exterminate the devil troops." [109] Finally, in August, the Hong Kong authorities suppressed three Communist newspapers, prosecuted two editors for sedition, and arrested additional reporters for taking part in illegal assemblies.[110]

On August 20, the Chinese Foreign Ministry responded to these steps with a note calling upon the British authorities to cancel the ban on the three newspapers and free all the arrested journalists within forty-eight hours; otherwise they would "be held responsible for all the consequences arising therefrom." [111] The British, of course, did not comply.

By this time the conduct of China's external affairs was under the control of extremist elements. They were cooperating fully with members of the Cultural Revolution Group, and that group was riding high. According to a wall poster account, Ch'en Yi had, on July 20, made a confession, admitting to having capitalist tendencies; to being an intellectual; to having made many mistakes; and to having opposed Chairman Mao on numerous occasions. But he also had said: "Who is there who had not opposed him? Out of 120 to 130 old cadres, there are scarcely twenty or thirty who have always remained loyal to him." [112] On August 12, Ch'en Yi was forced to attend a criticism rally held by revolutionary rebels of the foreign affairs sector,[113] and on August 19 Yao Teng-shan, the diplomat who had been forced to leave Indonesia, took Ch'en Yi's place in the Foreign Ministry. In doing so, he appears to have acted with the overt encouragement of Wang Li,[114] and perhaps with the more covert support of K'ang Sheng,[115] both leading members of the Cultural Revolution Group.

With Yao Teng-shan in control of the Ministry of Foreign Affairs and cooperating with members of the Cultural Revolution Group, the stage was set for the further escalation of the antiforeign demonstrations which had been going on in Peking earlier in the summer. They had been provoked largely by incidents abroad, some of them arising out of activities of Chinese diplomats, to which the Chinese responded by retaliating against the embassies and nationals of the respective countries in Peking.

In Burma, for instance, Chinese diplomats and aid technicians had succeeded in starting a Red Guard movement among the youths of Burma's large overseas Chinese community. The government of Burma attempted to deal with this movement through a variety of measures, such as forbidding the wearing of Mao badges, and some Chinese students responded to this prohibition by engaging in violent disorders. This, in turn, set off anti-Chinese rioting in the course of which the Chinese embassy was attacked by mobs and one Chinese technician was killed. In Peking, the Chinese did not content themselves with counterdemonstrations against the Burmese Embassy. They also openly avowed their support for the Peking-oriented Burmese Communist party (White Flag) which was engaged in armed rebellion, and called for the violent overthrow of the government of Burma.[116]

On August 3 Ichiro Sunama, a member of the Central Committee of the Communist party of Japan and its representative in Peking, and Junichi Konno, correspondent there for *Akahata,* had gone to the airport to catch a plane for Pyongyang, en route to Tokyo. When they arrived at the airport, they found numbers of Japanese waiting for them, carrying portraits of Mao Tse-tung and hostile placards. They also found that their plane's departure was being held up until the following day, perhaps in order to afford plenty of time for a thorough-going struggle rally. The treatment accorded to them during this rally was not merely degrading; it was so rough, according to subsequent accounts, that when the two men finally arrived in Pyongyang they had to be hospitalized.[117]

On August 5, Indonesian youths had attacked the Chinese Embassy in Djakarta and set one of its buildings on fire. The Chinese promptly retaliated by demonstrating against the Indonesian Embassy and burning its files and furniture. On August 9, the Mongolian Ambassador's chauffeur had refused to accept a Mao badge which Red Guards had tried to press upon him, and they responded by burning the Ambassador's car and invading the Mongolian Embassy. On August 11, the navigator of a Soviet ship anchored at Dairen had similarly refused a Mao badge. Red Guards at Dairen boarded and damaged the ship, beat up the crew, and paraded the navigator and the ship's captain through the streets. In Peking, the Chinese government issued to the Soviet Union a memorandum of protest, charging that the navigator had insulted the portrait of Mao Tse-tung, borne by the badge; the whole world, it asserted, "had entered the era of the thought of Mao Tse-tung." Also in Peking, Red Guards demonstrated outside the Soviet Embassy from August 14 to August 17, when they broke into the consular section, smashed its furniture, and burned its files. On August 15, the head of the Italian trade mission in Peking was detained in his office and the next day forced to face a hostile demonstration because Italian officials at Genoa had ordered a Chinese ship's captain to remove propaganda posters plastered on the outside of his vessel.[118] On August 18, Red Guards swarmed into the house in which Anthony Grey, the Reuters correspondent, was under house arrest. They wrecked the contents, killed the pet cat which shared his solitude, glued a poster to his back, and subjected him to what was known as the jet plane treatment—forcing him to lean forward with his arms jerked back behind him and to remain in that position so long that he could see his face in the pool of sweat which had dripped from his forehead.[119] On August 20, there were demonstrations against the embassy of Ceylon and on August 21, against that of Kenya.[120]

On the afternoon of August 22, British Chargé d'Affaires Sir Donald Hopson and his staff, eighteen men and five women, awaited the consequences which were to follow upon the expiry of the forty-eight hour deadline which had been mentioned in the Chinese note concerning Hong Kong. Chinese troops were lined up in front of the embassy; they presumably had come to provide it protection, but they were unarmed. Chinese demonstrators, drawn at least in part from the Foreign Language Institutes and other parts of the foreign affairs sector, began to gather. By early evening there were many thousands of them, sitting in the glare of floodlights, listening to speeches and recitations, and singing revolutionary songs. Then at 10:30 P.M. the crowd suddenly broke through the cordon of troops and came screaming into the embassy compound. Once inside, the demonstrators began overturning and burning cars, breaking the windows of the chancery, destroying furniture, and starting fires. Sir Donald Hopson and other members of the staff had just taken refuge in the embassy's strongroom, which housed the archives, but with smoke pouring through the air-ducts there was nothing they could do but go out and face the mob.[121] He later wrote his wife:

> I opened the door, and was first out followed by the others. There were perhaps five thousand in the courtyard. Immediately I was beaten black and blue with blows. Whoever could lay hands on me hit me with everything they had got. The women, in a fury, threw themselves on me and tried to knock me out with their batons. They dragged me by the hair and wanted to strangle me with my tie. I really do not know how I finally found myself a little further away in front of a door where, all of a sudden, a hand seized me by the arm. A Red Guard shouted to me in Chinese: "Come this way." He draggged me running towards the house of the Indians . . . where he hid me behind the big entrance doors.
>
> I was stunned by the blows I had received on the head, more or less unconscious and bleeding like a pig.

Eventually a military doctor bound up his head wound, and he was kept hidden in a police car while the crowd completed the destruction of his chancery. "I asked about the others. They told me the police were rounding them up one by one." [122] Most of the members of the staff, and their families, had been lined up, spat upon, punched, kicked, and otherwise mistreated in an effort to make them bow before a portrait of Mao Tse-tung. Some of the women had attempted to run from the scene, and two secretaries managed to escape to the nearby Finnish Embassy. Two others who sought asylum across the street in the Albanian Embassy were not so fortunate. The Albanians slammed the gate in their faces and then laughed and jeered at them when Red Guards began to manhandle them, pulling out hanks of hair and reaching down the fronts of their dresses.[123]

Sir Donald Hopson mentioned, in his letter to his wife, that the women and girls of his staff had been maltreated, but the more unpleasant details appeared in print only two years later, after Anthony Grey had been released from house arrest, spent a few days in the British Embassy, talked to friends who had been present on August 22, and returned to England. Then he wrote: "The Red Guards set out to humiliate them sexually by handling them in a most vulgar manner. In some cases the girls had their underclothes torn from them. Then they were interfered with in a revolting way." Male staff members, he recounted, had been similarly treated by female Red Guards. "One diplomat," he wrote, "was subjected to pain and humiliation by female Red Guards who took a fiendish delight in grabbing him by the genitals." [124]

The days following the attack on the British Embassy, Chou En-lai removed Yao Teng-shan from power within the Ministry of Foreign Affairs,[125] and shortly afterwards he issued a six-point directive which was to govern any further struggles with foreigners. The Red Guards and revolutionary rebels were forbidden to invade embassies, beat up foreigners, destroy buildings, set fire to buildings or cars, and obstruct diplomatic personnel in the performance of their duties.[126] The withdrawal of the Chinese government's support for the Communist offensive in Hong Kong, which became apparent in September, presumably was a further reflection of Chou's realization that Communist China had carried things too far.

The destruction of the offices of the British Embassy and the mistreatment of its staff, coming as a climax to all else that had transpired in Peking that August, produced a shock wave which reached to many foreign capitals. The government in London, of course, immediately took steps to select particular members of its embassy's official family for immediate repatriation. With Communist China's treatment of foreign embassies at a low reminiscent of the days of the Boxer Rebellion, other governments, and particularly those of countries whose relations with Communist China were badly strained, naturally felt impelled to consider the withdrawal of their own staffs. As Prince Norodom Sihanouk of Cambodia observed: "The Chinese . . . I do not know what is the matter with them. They are like persons falling into a state of exaltation and trance during the performance of annual ceremonies. At present they are off their heads. They have attacked some people and burned the embassies of others. They are making much noise." [127]

The Chinese government, however, evidently was anxious to prevent an exodus of foreign diplomats, and particularly unwilling that British personnel should return home and tell their full story while the destruction of their embassy was in the news and while feeling was still running high. However, the Chinese government lacked any pretext for forbidding the departure of British personnel. The retaliation imposed on personnel of the Chinese Embassy in London had been exceptionally mild: travel restrictions had been imposed on them, and they had been told that they might not use their radio transmitter, although there was probably no way to prevent their doing so, and they were still free to use commercial telegraph.[128] Police were of course stationed nearby, but this was doubtless done as much for their protection as to keep an eye on their movements and behavior. From the Chinese point of view, it would have been better if the British reaction had been severe and violent: because all things are relative, the Chinese then would not have looked so bad. Moreover, it then would have again become the turn of the Chinese government to protest and impose retaliatory measures. Such considerations undoubtedly led to what later became known as the battle of Portland Place.

On August 29, the members of the Chinese Embassy staff in London sallied forth, red books in hand and clenched fists raised high, evidently determined to stage a provocation. A news camerman was on hand, and he was able to record part of what followed. His first photograph shows shouting Chinese standing in the doorway. It also shows a London bobby, evidently inured to such performances, gazing the other way with a bemused expression; he evidently does not expect that which is to follow, for his arms are folded and he looks completely relaxed. In a second picture, more Chinese have emerged. They look like young men drawn from the Chinese student class, rather than toughies, and two of them have joined in awkwardly wielding in their four hands what looks like a baseball bat; another one stands, camera poised, ready to record the action which is to ensue. A third photograph was evidently taken after the skirmish had begun, for some Chinese can be seen swinging clubs and another has an axe at the ready; their opponents presumably are trying to keep their distance, for none are in view, though there is a fallen figure on hands and knees behind the axeman. The rest of the melee was not depicted, but it sent to the hospital three policemen, three Chinese, and one photographer.[129]

The following day Sir Donald Hopson was called in by a vice minister of Foreign Affairs to receive the "most serious protest" of the Chinese government. According to the Chinese version of events, a plainclothesman in the street had provoked the Chinese personnel by deliberately wearing a Mao badge upside down. They had gone out to make a serious protest and to warn him. At this point, "scores of truncheon-wielding police fell upon and brutally assaulted them." In view of these circumstances, the Chinese government demanded that the British government take immediate steps to prevent the recurrence of such outrages; punish the culprits; provide the injured with medical facilities; compensate them for all their losses; and remove the restrictions which had been placed on its embassy personnel. In conclusion, the vice minister told Sir Donald Hopson, starting from that day, no personnel of his office might leave Chinese territory without the permission of the Chinese Ministry of Foreign Affairs, and the exit visas already issued to some of them were canceled.[130]

On September 11, the Burmese Ambassador left Peking, and on September 13, Prince Sihanouk announced that he was withdrawing the entire staff of his embassy from Peking. The next day Chou En-lai assured the Cambodian Ambassador that his staff would be protected, emphasizing China's desire to maintain friendly relations with his country; Sihanouk accepted these assurances, and the withdrawal of the Cambodian mission was thereby averted. The Indonesian government also ordered all its personnel to leave, but their exit visas, like those of members of the British Embassy staff, were withheld until late autumn.[131]

Meanwhile the Chinese government, evidently anxious to inhibit full and frank reporting of events in Peking, was using quite different tactics towards foreign correspondents. The most numerous and effective group of such newsmen were the Japanese. There were nine of them; being Orientals, they could circulate unobtrusively; and their superior knowledge of the Chinese language, which is closely related to their own, enabled them to gather news with great facility. In September three of them were expelled from Peking for their allegedly unfriendly reporting.[132]

Shortly after these three newsmen had been ordered to leave, one of the Japanese correspondents was standing with his small son on the terrace of his apartment, which overlooked the British Embassy compound. The chancery, of course, was a charred ruins, but temporary offices had been set up in Sir Donald Hopson's residence. There had been another incident involving the Chinese Embassy in London, the day before, and some Red Guards came storming in to register their indignation. They called Sir Donald Hopson and half a dozen other diplomats out into the garden and read aloud to them their protest. Then one man, who seemed to be their leader, seized the chargé d'affaires by the hair and tried to force him to lower his head, shouting: "Bow and admit your crime." Sir Donald refused, and endeavored to remain erect, whereupon his head was given another push forward. At this point the newsman's small son began to cry, and his father hurriedly took him back into the building. But another Japanese correspondent, who had gone to the British Embassy to get his visa to pass through Hong Kong en route home, reported the sequel. At that point some soldiers of the People's Liberation Army intervened, and drove the Red Guards from the premises.[133] The Red Guards might not yet be obeying Chou En-lai's new directive, but at least the PLA was no longer allowing them to ride high.

23

"Put Destruction First"

THE MOST difficult set of problems facing Mao Tse-tung, throughout 1967, was that which involved the destruction of the power of the party in the provinces and the construction there of new governing apparatuses. At the beginning of the Cultural Revolution, he had talked as though his purge was to have a very narrow focus: "the handful of top party powerholders following the capitalist road." He never abandoned the use of that phrase, but it appears that he really contemplated, at least as early as August 1966, a purge of wide dimensions which was to extend down to the provincial committees of the party. This, of course, would mean that the purge would also extend to the provincial governments, since the same leaders commonly held key posts in party and government as concurrent positions.

At a work conference held a few days after the close of the August 1966 plenary session of the Central Committee, Mao Tse-tung discussed the disturbances of the student Red Guards then breaking out in various parts of China. "I firmly believe," he asserted, "that a few months of disturbances will be mostly for the good, and that little bad will result from these disturbances. It does not matter if there are no provincial party committees . . . workers, peasants, and soldiers must not interfere with the students in the great Cultural Revolution." [1]

Mao also appears to have anticipated that the construction of a new governing apparatus would be a simpler matter than the destruction of the old. Indeed, he may have thought that the new revolutionary movement, which would come into organized existence in response to his commands, could serve first as a destructive force and later as an instrument of government. This at least is suggested by the Central Committee circular of May 16, 1966, which had been prepared under his direction. It may be recalled that this circular contained a passage reading: "Chairman Mao often says that there is no construction without destruction. . . . Put destruction first, and in the process you have construction."

As things turned out, a few months of Red Guard disturbances did not suffice to overcome party leaders entrenched in the provinces. Much more time was required, and the workers, peasants, and soldiers, who originally were not to have taken part, were called upon to serve as reinforcements. Moreover, construction did not prove to be a by-product which arose spontaneously in the course of destruction. In consequence the army was required not only to assist in the process of destroying the party apparatus; it also was assigned the task of serving, throughout almost all of provincial China, as the interim governing authority.

Making army commands the successors of party committees, in guiding the administrations of China's provinces, gave those commands a set of interests which paralleled those of their party predecessors. These interests, of course, included a concern for order and stability, whereas the leftist mass organizations remained committed to revolutionary activism. This made for difficulties between army commands and mass organizations, and these difficulties in turn led to conflicts between army leaders in Peking and members of the Cultural Revolution Group. The two were of course cooperating in unseating old power-holders but had competing interests when it came to redistributing the power which had been seized.

It should also be noted that the Cultural Revolution, during which the army was given multiple and mutually incompatible sets of tasks, was bound to make trouble within the army itself. Some units found themselves responsible for protecting government properties and installations, or for discharging tasks within the economy which would normally have fallen to party and government cadres. At the same time other army elements, assigned to the tasks of supporting the left, became deeply involved in the activities of mass organizations and army men sometimes even became members. Those organizations not only fought each other but also engaged in activities which disrupted production and transport, and sometimes assaulted government installations and seized government property. In consequence, different army elements often found themselves in hostile confrontation with each other, to the detriment of unity of command.

Mao Tse-tung rode toward the goals of eliminating his opponents and creating a new governing system as though standing astride two horses. One was the Cultural Revolution Group, operating through the mass organizations of Red Guards and revolutionary rebels, and the other was the army, with its regional, provincial, and subdistrict commands. He could and did shift his main weight back and forth, but he had to hold these two supporting elements in alignment if they were to carry him to his goals.

Mao's countrywide campaign naturally had to be timed and conducted in the light of the circumstances peculiar to each of China's twenty-six provinces and so-called autonomous regions. They differed in proximity to sensitive borders, distance from the center, composition of the population, and extent to which political, governmental, and military authority was concentrated or dispersed. These factors determined both the risks which would be attendant upon campaigns against powerholders and the prospects for success.

The ancients had observed that the empire when divided tended ever to unite, and when unified tended always to divide. The Chinese Communists were well aware that the areas which historically had been first to yield to centrifugal forces were those distant from the center and inhabited largely by non-Chinese or minority peoples. Moreover, when the Communists came to power, they were determined to destroy the authority of religion, change local customs, transform the economy, and change racial balances by settling large numbers of Chinese in minority areas. All this had made it seem wise to strengthen the positions of their officials in minority areas by concentrating political, military, and governmental power in few hands, rather than by dividing it.

The areas in which top political, governmental, and military power was concentrated in the fewest hands included the autonomous regions of Inner Mongolia, Sinkiang, and Tibet, and the province of Szechwan. Each comprised not only a governmental unit, but also a separate military region. Szechwan was, in addition, the center of the party's Southwest Regional Bureau, exercising jurisdiction over the three provinces of Kweichow, Yünnan, and Szechwan itself. These regions and provinces, and several others as well, all contained substantial numbers of minority peoples.

In Inner Mongolia, Ulanfu held the four posts of military commander, political commissar, governor, and ranking party secretary. Power was only slightly less concentrated in Sinkiang, also known as Chinese Turkestan, where Wang En-mao held the three posts of military commander, political commissar, and party secretary, and in Tibet, where Chang Kuo-hua was military commander and party secretary. In Szechwan, Li Ching-ch'üan held the posts of political commissar for the Chengtu Military Region and first secretary of the party's Southwest Regional Bureau. In addition, he enjoyed close personal relations with Huang Hsin-t'ing, the military commander.

These leaders had wielded power in their respective areas ever since the conquest by Chinese Communist armies. This meant that each had enjoyed upwards of two decades in which to consolidate his position. Military force was available to each of them, and they showed themselves ready to use it, for the purpose of preserving their own power when it came under challenge from the center. During the Cultural Revolution each of them was overthrown, transferred from his base of power, or left in place but shorn of most of his authority.

But the process of cutting them down, or cutting them down to size, necessarily had to be pursued in accordance with individual circumstance and as opportunity presented.

In Sinkiang, Wang En-mao undoubtedly was regarded as suspect because of past close association with the disgraced Ho Lung; he had been the political commissar of Ho Lung's First Field Army. In addition, some of the officers and men in Sinkiang had been in Kuomintang armies until a point was reached, during the civil war, when changing sides seemed expedient; they accordingly could not be thoroughly trusted. As early as the beginning of 1967, some of the leading officers in Wang En-mao's command openly disobeyed orders from Peking, and harrowing tales of violence and torture, inflicted on Red Guards by the military in Sinkiang, filtered back to the capital.[2]

But Sinkiang was also the most sensitive of China's autonomous regions. Its deserts provided China's missile-range and nuclear-test areas; the borders between Sinkiang and India had recently been the scene of fighting; Sinkiang's western reaches contained restive pastoral peoples who could rely, in their troubles with the Chinese, upon the sympathy of closely related peoples just across the border in the Soviet Union; and the U.S.S.R. had a record of intervening in Sinkiang during times when the Chinese hold was weak. Moreover, Peking's problems were complicated by the outbreak, in January 1967, of armed rebellion involving the Sinkiang Production and Construction Corps. This corps was the responsibility of the Ministry of State Farms and Land Reclamation in Peking, and in putting down the rebellion it evidently had to depend on Wang En-mao's command.[3]

These circumstances combined to force Peking to deal carefully with Wang En-mao, limiting the application to his region of the Cultural Revolution. Indeed, no revolutionary committee was established for Sinkiang until such bodies had been set up in every other province and autonomous region except Tibet—where one was inaugurated the same day. The destruction of Wang En-mao's power was accomplished through a series of personnel shifts. The first ones occurred at various levels within his command, beginning as early as 1966. In 1968 another high officer was brought in to serve as chairman of the Sinkiang Uighur Autonomous Region's Revolutionary Committee, with Wang En-mao named as one of several vice chairmen.[4] Not long afterward he was relieved of his military post, and in early 1970 it appeared that he was no longer serving in Sinkiang in any capacity whatsoever.[5]

Tibet was an only somewhat less sensitive area. It had been the last region to be occupied by the PLA; subsequent Communist policies had led to a Tibetan uprising; China's Tibetan borders with

India, like those of Sinkiang, were in dispute; and the border area had been the scene of both heavy fighting and intermittent clashes. The Tibetan capital of Lhasa, like the Sinkiang capital of Urumchi, is separated from Peking by about two thousand miles of difficult terrain. Such considerations did not persuade Peking to exempt Tibet from the storms of the Cultural Revolution, but they did limit its will and ability to influence developments there. Chang Kuo-hua did eventually lose his position in Tibet, but he was removed by transfer rather than by purge, and only after the rulers of two adjacent provinces more accessible to Peking—Tsinghai and Szechwan—had been dealt with.

Before turning to the cases of Tsinghai and other provinces, it may be well to review the overall situation created by Mao's January 12, 1967, call for power-seizure. That call had precipitated a proliferation of revolutionary organizations at the level of the individual village, factory, school, or other institution, and from that level on up into the higher reaches of the government.[6] It was, of course, clear that seizures of power would be promoted by the unification of revolutionary organizations, which were called upon to form "great alliances." The importance of unification became all the more apparent when it was decided to set up revolutionary committees, at all levels, as the organs through which power was to be exercised.[7] It was, of course, to be the leaders of the great alliances who would represent the revolutionary masses in the three-way combinations—of revolutionary rebels, army officers, and "revolutionary cadres"—of which the revolutionary committees were to be composed.

Ideally, the process of forming revolutionary committees should have proceeded from the level of the grass roots upward, with each provincial revolutionary committee serving as the capstone on a new pyramid of power. In the hurly-burly which followed upon Mao's urgent call, attempts to seize power proceeded at all levels simultaneously, and without the unification of the participating revolutionary organizations.

At the higher levels, and particularly at that of the provincial center, the efforts to grasp power usually took the form of attempts to occupy key installations, most notably radio stations and the press, by one or another of the mass organizations or factional groups. Such takeovers were then followed by the issuance of proclamations declaring that power had been seized from the followers of the capitalist road. Each of the authorities who were the targets of these attacks reacted after his own fashion. Some moved overtly to repulse assaults on their installations, or to take them back after they had been seized; some bent before the storm, waiting to see what would happen next;

and others seized the initiative, staging sham power-seizures of their own, in which they sacrificed some of their more vulnerable subordinates in the hope that Peking might be satisfied or deceived.

Before the month of January was out, announcements of power seizures had been made in half of China's provincial capitals, and more were proclaimed soon afterwards. This faced Peking with the problem of distinguishing solidly-based claims from ones which were unduly optimistic, and real power-seizures from bogus ones. In the first months of 1967, Peking endorsed these claims only in the cases of the directly-governed cities of Shanghai and Peking and the provinces of Heilungkiang, Shansi, Shantung, and Kweichow. In one after another of the remaining provinces, Peking decreed that the army should assume interim authority. Peking's failure to respond to other claims was naturally interpreted as disapproval, and in several provinces the military authorities proceeded to suppress the revolutionary organizations which had occupied installations and professed to have seized power. In doing so, they incurred the lasting enmity of some organizations upon which the Cultural Revolution Group eventually put its stamp of approval.[8]

As things turned out, the four provincial revolutionary committees which Peking did approve were beset by difficulties. The pyramids of power, of which they should have been the capstones, were long abuilding. Meanwhile, Red Guards and revolutionary rebels fought among themselves. In consequence, the revolutionary committees remained without the authority to which they laid claim, and the factionalism which reigned below came to infect their memberships. As Chou En-lai was later to remark, in discussing the Shansi Revolutionary Committee: "The issue which confronts us in the past year or more is whether to topple or keep the revolutionary committee, which virtually exists only in name." [9]

The roots of the failure of revolutionaries to coalesce into great alliances may be traced, in substantial part, back to Mao Tse-tung himself. Preoccupied as he was with matters of ideology and attitude, he neglected to set forth a concrete program to which the masses might have rallied. Impatiently intent on bringing down his enemies, his call was issued before he had finally decided upon the revolutionary committees which were to serve as successor organizations. In his January appeal to the country, he proclaimed that with political power the proletariat had everything, and that without political power the proletariat had nothing. This was readily translated into an all-or-nothing struggle for position, first of all against old powerholders, but then among all who sought to fill the resulting vacuums. In this second phase, "blood debts" were to be piled up, and enduring enmities created. This made the voluntary formation of great alliances well nigh impossible, for they presupposed that some would lead and others accept subordination. But accepting subordination meant not only losing the prospect of exercising power; it also meant exposing oneself to revenge at the hands of one's bitter enemies.

These problems, however, did not immediately become apparent, as did those posed by outright resistance and sham power seizures. One of the first provinces in which a counterfeit seizure of power was carried out was Tsinghai. This province is adjacent to Tibet, and itself contains a substantial Tibetan population. The commander of Tsinghai Military District had risen to prominence within the particular field army system which had been commanded by Lin Piao: the Fourth Field Army and its predecessor, Lin's 115th division. However, he had but recently been transferred to Tsinghai from Manchuria, and real military power in the province may have been in the hands of his deputy commander and his political commissar. If so, military, political and governmental power were concentrated in few hands, for the political commissar was also a secretary of the provincial party committee and the governor of the province.

The sham power seizure in Tsinghai was engineered in February, and in March Peking identified it as a counterrevolutionary coup and charged the deputy commander with having usurped military power. He and the governor were ordered placed in solitary confinement, the governor so that he might "carry out introspection and wait for action," the deputy commander to await a trial which led to his execution. In a move which was to be repeated in one form or another in a number of additional trouble spots, Lin Piao's man, the recently appointed Commander of Tsinghai Military District, was directed to assume governmental authority as head of a Tsinghai Provincial Military Control Commission. Simultaneously the Lanchow Military Region, of which Tsinghai was a constituent part, was ordered to assist him in bringing all troops in the province under his direct command.[10]

The problem of Inner Mongolia was tackled shortly after that of Tsinghai. Its ruler was a sinicized Mongol who grew up speaking no language but Chinese. An early member of the Chinese Communist party, he had in his youth studied and worked as a translator in the Soviet Union; had adopted the pseudonym of Ulanfu, which is the Chinese transliteration of Lenin's family name; and, subsequent to the founding of the Peking regime, he had become vice president of the Sino-Soviet Friendship Association and president of its Inner Mongolian branch. When the Chinese Communists had moved into Inner Mongolia, just after World War II, Ulanfu's Mongol birth and Soviet connections made him an especially useful tool for establishing their power and consolidating their control.

During his long years of rule in Inner Mongolia, Ulanfu had learned the language of his people and become sympathetic with their efforts to preserve their cultural identity and resist assimilation. He had also seen them converted, in their own homeland, into a small and shrinking minority, consequent to Chinese immigration, and witnessed the encroachment of Chinese agriculture on their pastoral economy. The plowing up of their grasslands had been greatly accelerated during Mao's Great Leap Forward, and Ulanfu was one of the first party officials to go on record as favoring a retreat from its policies. With the subsequent embittering of China's relations with the U.S.S.R. and the Mongolian People's Republic, Ulanfu's Mongol birth and Soviet connections, once assets, turned into liabilities.

Ulanfu initially gave the appearance of going along with Mao's Cultural Revolution. He attended the first and second Peking Red Guard rallies in August 1966, sacrificed some of his more vulnerable subordinates during the latter half of that month, and on October 1, was back in Peking, where he was among the leaders joining Mao Tse-tung on the rostrum to celebrate National Day. In the interim, however, Red Guards from Peking had entered Inner Mongolia, establishing a liaison center in his capital city of Huhehot (Kweisui), and had begun recruiting local youths to form Red Guard units. They sought to penetrate schools, factories, the bureaucracy, and other organizations, and to counter them Ulanfu's supporters created rival "revolutionary" organizations among teachers, workers, peasants, and army veterans.

In Huhehot the Peking Red Guards and their local allies responded to Mao Tse-tung's January call for the seizure of power by occupying government buildings, the railway station, the telegraph office, the radio station, and the offices of the *Inner Mongolia Daily*. But Ulanfu quickly mustered his own supporters, backed them up with PLA troops, and went on the counteroffensive. By the middle of February, his troops had fired on and killed a number of student demonstrators, arrested over a hundred Red Guard leaders, and reoccupied all the facilities which they had seized.

When the deterioration of the Maoists' position in Inner Mongolia became evident, Chou En-lai requested the two sides to send delegations to Peking to work out a settlement. A truce was arranged there on February 16 under which the arrested Red Guards were released and their provocative activities were to cease, but the truce did not end Ulanfu's difficulties. Small-scale clashes continued, and Ulanfu evidently concluded that Chou En-lai's intervention had been intended chiefly to effect the release of the Red Guard agitators and to gain time. About March 1, Ulanfu ordered his troops to surround Red Guard headquarters and to rearrest Red Guard leaders who had been released two weeks before. Thereafter, his supporters, and the so-called revolutionary organizations which they directed, made preparations intended to result in the establishment of an Inner Mongolian Revolutionary Committee. They intended, in other words, to stage a false seizure of power, in an attempt to present Peking with a *fait accompli*.[11]

At this point Teng Hai-ch'ing, deputy commander of the Peking Military Garrison, was ordered to assume command of the 21st Army, which was stationed in Shensi Province not far from the Great Wall, to move it into Inner Mongolia, and to occupy key areas there. The 21st Army arrived in Huhehot early in April, and within a week it and following units were consolidating their positions. With martial law in effect and Teng Hai-ch'ing in control, Mao Tse-tung was in a position to announce the fall of Ulanfu.[12]

On April 13, a directive was issued, in the name of the Central Committee, ordering the reorganization of the Inner Mongolian Military Region; the establishment there of a preparatory group responsible for the formation of a Revolutionary Committee; the rehabilitation of Ulanfu's opponents; and the punishment of his principal supporters. Ulanfu was branded a "party person in authority taking the capitalist road," whose "problems" should be thoroughly exposed. The directive contained no indication, however, as to the fate of Ulanfu himself—an omission from which only ominous conclusions could be drawn.[13]

The next major object of Peking's attention was the province of Szechwan, domain since 1950 of Li Ching-ch'üan. Both he and Huang Hsin-t'ing, commander of Szechwan's Chengtu Military Region, had risen to prominence as officers of Ho Lung's First Field Army. There were, in addition, close family connections between Ho Lung and Li Ching-ch'üan; the two men were said to have married sisters, and two of Li's sons were brought up in Ho's household.[14] These connections were undoubtedly advantageous to Li Ching-ch'üan so long as Ho Lung remained one of the top leaders in Peking; after Ho Lung's fall, they could only be the source of Mao Tse-tung's suspicion and animosity.

In addition Li Ching-ch'üan, subsequent to his assumption of power in Szechwan, had insisted on adhering to what he considered to be pragmatic policies. In launching the Great Leap Forward, Mao Tse-tung had enjoined giving prominence to politics. Li Ching-ch'üan, it may be recalled, had dissented: "No, we should give prominence to fertilizer." The important thing, he had asserted, was to make a success of production; in Szechwan the problem of production was, first of all, the problem of grain; and this was one to which fertilizer was more obviously relevant than politics. Afterwards, Li Ching-ch'üan appears to have sensed that Mao Tse-tung blamed him for having proved right. With the Great Leap a failure and Szechwan's foodstuffs being shipped out to relieve hunger elsewhere, Li commented: "Some people eat Szechwan rice, and insult us, too." [15] After P'eng Te-huai had been dismissed from his post as Minister of Defense, for opposition to Mao's policies of the Great Leap period, Li Ching-ch'üan had welcomed him to Szechwan and given him a job.[16] Li Ching-ch'üan appears to have attended none of Mao Tse-tung's great receptions for the Red Guards, and when they entered his domain they found that Li Ching-ch'üan had created mass organizations of his own to oppose them.[17]

Mao Tse-tung evidently realized, in the autumn of 1966, that Li Ching-ch'üan's close relations with Huang Hsin-t'ing, the commander of the Chengtu Military Region, and Li's own status as its political commissar, would compound the Red Guards' problem of dislodging him. At the October 1966 conference, held in Peking and attended by party leaders from the provinces, he had taunted Li Ching-ch'üan, saying: "You yourself ran away. You were scared out of your wits, and went to live in the military region command headquarters." [18] Early in 1967, the long-standing relationship between commander and commissar was broken by removing Huang Hsin-t'ing from his Szechwan post, purging him, and replacing him by Liang Hsing-ch'u, a veteran of Lin Piao's Fourth Field Army.[19]

By this time Li Ching-ch'üan had built two mass organizations, the "Industrial Army" and the "Production Army," into a formidable force. In addition he may, during that period, have gained control of at least one of Szechwan's principal Red Guard organizations. During the February–March period of the "adverse current," PLA units and public security organs in Szechwan carried out a suppression of militant student groups, jailing many thousands of their members, and it soon became apparent that the shift in military commanders had not served to end army support of Li Ching-ch'üan.[20]

April marked the return of the Maoists to the offensive in Szechwan, as in the rest of China, and fighting between organizations supporting Li Ching-ch'üan on one side, and Red Guards from Peking and their local allies on the other, became especially violent during the first weeks of May. Up to this point the principal weapons had been wooden clubs, iron bars, and acids, but on May 6, the Red Guards appear to have made the mistake of tangling with workers at the Chengtu arsenal.[21] The PLA intervened but was unable to prevent several students from being killed by machine gun fire and a larger number from being wounded; the PLA also did not prevent the "Production Army" from escaping with hundreds of weapons.[22]

On May 7, Peking responded to these developments by ordering Li Ching-ch'üan relieved of his posts and reproving PLA units in Szechwan for having supported the wrong side. It directed that Chang Kuo-hua should succeed Li Ching-ch'üan as political commissar of Chengtu Military Region, and that he should head a preparatory group for a Szechwan Revolutionary Committee. In this task he was to be assisted by the new political commissar of the military region and by two long-time opponents of Li Ching-ch'üan, a husband and wife who held the posts of district and municipal party secretary, respectively, in Ipin, Szechwan, until 1962 when Li Ching-ch'üan had had them imprisoned.[23]

The transfer of Chang Kuo-hua, of course, had consequences which were not confined to Szechwan. It ended the situation in which he had exercised both military authority and political power in Tibet, and opened the way for the promotion of Tseng Yung-ya, a veteran of Lin Piao's 115th division and Fourth Field Army, to the command of the Tibet Military Region.[24] In Szechwan itself, the directive brought Li Ching-ch'üan's official career to a formal end, but it did not obliterate his influence or quickly bring Szechwan under Maoist control. Indeed, several reports indicate that Szechwan, between April and July, was in a virtual state of secession, with roadblocks established to keep traffic under surveillance and with entry and exit points well guarded.[25]

Szechwan was only one of the provinces in which the army engaged, during the months of February and March, in the large-scale suppression of leftists and their organizations. It seems unlikely that the army would have been allowed so free a hand, during that period, had the Cultural Revolution Group not been preoccupied with more urgent matters. In Peking the period was, of course, that of the February adverse current during which surviving senior leaders waged a battle against the Cultural Revolution Group. By the end of March, those leaders had been put on the defensive and the Maoists could turn their attention back to the affairs of the provinces.

The members of the Cultural Revolution Group evidently concluded that leftist organizations in the provinces would fare better if it were not for interference from the army, and demanded that the discretionary powers of army commanders should be sharply curbed. If this led to contention in Peking between military leaders and the

Cultural Revolution Group, as seems highly likely, then the army lost and Lin Piao had to accept the decision.

At any rate, on April 6 an order was issued to the army which stated: "In dealing with mass organizations, be they revolutionary or controlled by reactionary elements, or when the situation is not clear, shooting is forbidden." The order, implicitly recognizing that leftist organizations had antagonized the army by their assaults on military headquarters, forbade the army's making such assaults the basis for treating an organization as counterrevolutionary, and it specified that no action was to be taken against any organization which had carried out such attacks. Indeed, no organization whatever was to be declared reactionary, and no organization members were to be arrested without the approval of the center. Political work was to be employed instead of force, and mass organizations which made mistakes were to be helped through education.[26]

This order would appear to have been based on the assumptions that the majority of the masses were good, in the sense of being inclined to follow the path illumined by the thought of Mao Tse-tung; that those who did not follow it had been hoodwinked by bad leaders and could be won to the right path through political work by army cadres; that struggle by force between mass organizations would be won by the good majority if the army would only hold its armed force in abeyance; and that such "principled" struggles could be fought to a conclusion without unacceptably great damage to overall levels of peace and order.

These assumptions, however, were soon proven to be incorrect, and on June 6 an order was issued in the names of the Central Committee, State Council, Military Affairs Committee, and Cultural Revolution Group, which called for an end to "the sinister practices of beating, smashing, looting, ransacking, and arresting which have appeared of late." The order affirmed that only organs of the state might carry out raids, searches, arrests, detentions, and trials; that the properties of the state and of the collectives were not allowed to be occupied, seized, smashed, or sabotaged; that the files, documents, and seals of party, government, and army organizations were not to be seized or destroyed; and that armed struggles were prohibited.[27]

This new order evidently represented an unsatisfactory compromise between contending elements within Mao's headquarters, for its operative provisions were as weak as its language was strong. The army was made responsible for enforcement and authorized "to arrest, detain, and punish according to law those who instigate trouble." But those who were engaged in the practices which the army was called upon to suppress were principally the members of mass organizations, and the April 6 order governing the army's relations with them still remained in effect.

The army, it will be recalled, had been forbidden to use firearms against mass organizations and their members, and had been enjoined to use persuasion in place of force. But when nothing short of force proved persuasive, army commanders were caught between conflicting sets of orders. In seeking a way out of this dilemma, they naturally cast about for means of using force under circumstances such that they might be able plausibly to deny responsibility. Since mass organizations commonly fought each other in any case, the obvious solution was for army commanders to use amenable mass organizations, if they could be found or created, against those they found refractory.

The mass organizations which military commanders found amenable to their control were generally not ones which would be considered leftist by the Cultural Revolution Group. That group had sent bodies of Red Guards to important centers throughout the country, and they and the local Red Guards and revolutionary rebels with whom they made alliances naturally considered that their guidance came from Peking. They accordingly were prone to reject efforts of garrison commanders to bring them under control.

Garrison commanders sometimes could give the mass organizations which were amenable to their control certain decisive advantages. They might give them the ability to overcome their rivals by, for instance, building them up numerically and making weapons available to them. The personnel who were most readily available for this purpose, who had the most appropriate qualifications in terms of training and experience, and who had the readiest access to arms were likely to be men of the public security bureaus and members of the militia. Almost everywhere the public security bureaus had been placed under army control, and it was of course the army which was responsible for the training of the militia. Accordingly, in most places army commanders were in position to feed public security personnel and militiamen into the organizations which they wished to strengthen and control.

The public security bureaus throughout China had been staffed almost entirely by party cadres,[28] and party cadres had been responsible for the day to day direction of the militia.[29] Both sets of cadres had an uncertain future outside the party apparatus, within which they had found status and employment. This was particularly true in the case of those members of the public security bureaus who had made enemies in the course of discharging their police duties. With the Maoists attacking the party and threatening to destroy the public security system, these were men who would not be fighting for fun.

Public security and militia cadres accordingly gave both added weight and hard cutting edges to the mass organizations in which they were incorporated. As long as the interests of army commanders and party cadres ran parallel, mass organizations with large public security and militia elements were apt to be much more responsive to military control than they otherwise would be. Once those interests diverged, however, military commanders might find that such mass organizations were double-edged weapons which were cutting both ways.

The tendencies which led military commanders to support conservative organizations did not all originate in the dilemma posed by the April 6 order forbidding the army to use force and the June 6 order which urged it to reestablish order; that dilemma merely gave them powerful reinforcement. They also were not confined to particular geographic areas; nevertheless, their operation and consequences may be illustrated by recounting the events of spring and early summer in the Wuhan Military Region.

This military region consists of the centrally located province of Hupeh and the adjacent one of Honan, just to the north of it. Wuhan itself, located at the confluence of the Han and Yangtze rivers, is a tri-city complex consisting of Wuchang, the capital of Hupeh; the steel center of Hanyang; and the metropolis of Hankow. Because of its central location and command of transport routes radiating from it, possession of Wuhan has historically been crucial to the outcome of major military operations, and particularly of ones conducted along the country's north–south axis.[30] The Yangtze, flowing eastward toward Shanghai, is navigable for oceangoing vessels as far as Wuhan, where it is spanned by a bridge which permits through railway traffic from Peking to Canton. Chengchow, the provincial capital of Honan, is at the junction of the north–south Peking–Hankow Railway and the Lunghai line, which runs westward from the Yellow Sea, crosses northcentral China and penetrates deep into Sinkiang.

The central location of the Wuhan Military Region, and its access to rail and water transport, were undoubtedly considerations which led China's military authorities to station there not only the forces deemed appropriate to its own requirements but also those available for movement to other areas when reinforcements might be needed. In addition, Wuhan is important in its own right as a first-rate industrial center. Accordingly, with the possible exception of the Peking Military Region, no military region was more important to the Maoist cause.

Ch'en Tsai-tao, commander of the Wuhan Military Region, was an officer of rank and seniority commensurate with the importance of his command, which he had held since 1954. By 1967 he had a record of forty years of service, much of it under former marshal Hsü

Hsiang-ch'ien. Struggles had broken out early in the year in Hupeh, as in so many other provinces of China, in response to Mao's call for the seizure of power. Ch'en Tsai-tao later affirmed that it had at first been the policy of his headquarters to support the Red Guards from Peking and their local allies, but that this policy had to be abandoned because "they struggled against us." [31]

Meanwhile, developments in Peking and Wuhan were conspiring to disrupt Ch'en Tsai-tao's command and erode his authority. The political commissar of Wuhan Military Region had been Wang Jen-chung, first secretary of the Hupeh Provincial Committee of the party and second secretary under T'ao Chu in its Central-South China Regional Bureau. T'ao Chu's meteoric rise to high office in Peking had carried Wang Jen-chung to the position of second deputy head of the Cultural Revolution Group. By February, following T'ao Chu's fall, Wang Jen-chung too was undergoing purge.

That month the ranking deputy commander of the Wuhan Military Region, in collaboration with another deputy commander and a deputy political commissar, made a bid to seize the military leadership from Ch'en Tsai-tao. The move failed, and its ringleader was sent to Peking where he was subjected to criticism by Hsü Hsiang-ch'ien, Ch'en Tsai-tao's old commander and the new chief of the PLA Revolution Group.[32]

This punishment, however, could hardly have sufficed to restore Ch'en Tsai-tao to the self-confident exercise of full authority. It will be recalled that a deputy commander charged with a similar offense that same month in Tsinghai Military District, and against a commander who had risen within Lin Piao's field army system, was arrested, imprisoned pending trial, and later executed. Moreover, Hsü Hsiang-ch'ien, who administered the rebuke to the ringleader from Wuhan, was himself repudiated in April, when he was dismissed from leadership of the PLA Cultural Revolution Group.

Finally, Ch'en Tsai-tao's position vis-à-vis the authorities in Peking could hardly have been helped by events that spring in Honan Military District, which was subordinate to his Wuhan Military Region. In Honan there were two rival organizations, one made up of workers, which allegedly was under the control of a political commissar of the Honan Military District, the other consisting largely of Red Guards with some worker allies. The struggles between these two organizations came to a climax on May 26, when the workers' organization in the city of Chengchow assaulted a large building in which their enemies were barricaded. The attacking workers, according to circumstantial accounts, used cranes equipped with demolition balls, bulldozers, and steel bars to break into the building; thereafter they assaulted the defenders and finally set the building afire. The casualties at Chengchow were reported to have been so heavy that medical facilities and the local crematorium were both overtaxed. A number of PLA teams from outside were sent to Chengchow to stop the fighting, but the members of one were captured before they reached the city and the others allegedly were assaulted by local troops after their arrival.[33]

With Honan in turmoil and rail traffic through Chengchow disrupted, the authorities in Peking intervened. Holding that the PLA in Honan had supported the wrong side, they carried out a drastic overhaul of the military district. The commander was suspended, and the political commissar deemed most at fault was purged. The chief of staff, the director of the political department, the commander of Chengchow Garrison, and other commanding officers were dismissed or transferred.[34]

Meanwhile a similar situation had been developing in Wuhan itself. By June an organization of industrial workers known as the "Million Heroes" was confronting smaller organizations of Red Guards and steel workers; each had its strongholds; and the struggle between them was escalating. In consequence about 2400 factories had been forced to close down or curtail operations, and on June 14, the railway bridge over the Yangtze was closed.[35]

The headquarters of the Wuhan Military Region is reported to have been directly involved in supporting the Million Heroes and giving them direction. According to one account, the revolutionary rebels obtained proof of this on July 12, when they seized several high officers of that headquarters and confiscated the secret codes which the headquarters had been using in its communications with the Million Heroes.[36] Whether or not this particular story is true, there is little doubt but what PLA unit 8201, said to be a division of public security troops stationed at Wuhan, was intimately connected with the Million Heroes.[37]

Minister of Public Security Hsieh Fu-chih gave the following description of the Million Heroes organization:

It has great superiority in numbers, reputedly 1,400,000. In fact it does have several hundred thousand members. This is a mass organization. They wear steel helmets and carry in their hands large knives, poles, rifles, and even machineguns, and they have the killer instinct. Of the nine chieftains in the Million Heroes, four were from the people's militia. The militia in big factories were 100 percent Million Heroes. The Public Security Bureau, the People's Procurate, and the law courts were under military control, but it was the independent division (division 8201) that controlled them and of them some 70 or 80 percent were Million Heroes. . . . They had connections with the Szechwan Production Army and with conservative organizations in Honan, Hunan, and Kiangsi.[38]

Hsieh Fu-chih's account was not based on mere secondhand information. He and Wang Li, as a member of the Cultural Revolution Group, had been engaged in tours to centers such as Chengtu, where the PLA had been suppressing leftists, and early July had found them in Yünnan Province, where the Kunming Military Region headquarters had seized local control from the authorities of the provincial military district and gone into action against the Red Guards. After this crisis had been dealt with, the two men had proceeded to Wuhan.[39]

Hsieh Fu-chih and Wang Li arrived there on July 14. Their party included Yü Li-chin, political commissar of the Air Force, some Red Guards of the Peking Aeronautical Institute, and probably some miscellaneous aides and bodyguards.[40] Available accounts variously portray Chou En-lai as having been present in Wuhan to give them instructions the day they arrived, and as having been there July 18 or July 19, either to convey the directive of the center as to how it wanted matters in Wuhan settled, or to act as mediator.[41] However, those accounts do not portray Chou En-lai as participating in the investigations of the mission. If he communicated a directive to Wuhan after the mission had completed its investigations, it may be that he did so from Peking, by telephone or otherwise.

The members of the mission spent their first several days surveying the situation in Wuhan, spending the greater part of their time listening to and encouraging the Red Guards and their allies. According to the later testimony of Ch'en Tsai-tao, commander of Wuhan Military Region, he had wanted the members of the mission also to visit the organizations with which his command was on friendly terms, in order that they might "see the whole situation." In a criticism which undoubtedly was intended to include the Cultural Revolution Group, he had declared: "We have failed to carry out the great Cultural Revolution well. You may take a look for yourselves in the streets." [42]

Apparently Ch'en Tsai-tao's protests left his visitors unmoved. On July 19 they called an evening meeting attended by officers of the rank of divisional commander and above.[43] At this meeting Wang Li, acting as spokesman of the mission, set forth what was represented to be a directive from Chou En-lai. Wang Li told the assembled officers that the Red Guard and allied organizations were recognized as the true revolutionary faction; that the Military Region was guilty of errors of policy and direction; that a workers' organization which it earlier had suppressed should be rehabilitated; and that the Million Heroes was a conservative organization. According to one account, the commander of PLA unit 8201 rose to his feet, at this point, but Wang Li refused to allow him to speak; thoroughly angered, both the commander and his political commissar then stalked from the hall.[44]

Wang Li's words were received not only with anger, but also with apparent and perhaps genuine disbelief. The inclusion of Red Guards from Peking in the mission had suggested from the start that its members would favor the local Red Guards and their allies. By spending most of its time with them, the mission had confirmed the presumption that it was biased. Arrogantly refusing to let the divisional commander speak had also been a tactical error. It not only angered him but also lent justification to a remark attributed to the commander of the Wuhan Military Region: only the views of the students were listened to, and the views of the military were not heeded. Finally, the decisions would have stood a better chance of being accepted if they had been announced by Hsieh Fu-chih, who was both vice premier and deputy leader of the PLA Cultural Revolution Group, rather than by Wang Li, who had neither governmental nor military status and was undoubtedly regarded as an upstart. At any rate, some of the officers are alleged to have made an assertion, after the meeting, which they doubtless wanted to believe: that the instructions of Chou En-lai represented only a story made up by Wang Li.[45]

During the early morning hours of July 20, PLA unit 8201 occupied key points in the city and led an uprising of the Million Heroes. A mob composed of members of that organization surrounded the guest house in which Hsieh Fu-chih and Wang Li were lodged, and some of them, brushing past the guards, forced their way in and confronted the two men. Ch'en Tsai-tao learned of the commotion, hurried from his nearby quarters to the guest house, and was himself set upon by members of the mob. According to later accusations, he then shouted: "I am Ch'en Tsai-tao, not Wang Li." Shortly thereafter, truckloads of armed troops belonging to unit 8201 drove up, seized Wang Li, and took him to military headquarters. It was thronged with members of the Million Heroes who beat him up, and allegedly subjected him to the "jet plane" treatment—which so many victims of the Cultural Revolution Group had been accorded.[46]

Hsieh Fu-chih was variously reported as having been wounded by a stab in the back, bound, beaten, and marched through the street with Wang Li, both of them crowned with dunce caps. Not all of these reports can be accepted, and perhaps all of them represent an embroi-

dering of the story of what actually occurred. It is obvious from virtually all accounts that anger was directed chiefly at Wang Li. A number
of accounts indicate that Hsieh Fu-chih was left behind when Wang
Li was taken to military headquarters. At that point few people remained in the guest house, and Ch'en Tsai-tao was probably one of
those who stayed behind. He and Hsieh had worked intimately together in civil war days, when Hsieh Fu-chih had been the political
commissar of the army group which Ch'en Tsai-tao then commanded.
Against this background, it seems probable that Ch'en Tsai-tao arranged to have Hsieh Fu-chih escorted from the guest house to a place
of greater safety. This, basically, is the story of what happened at this
point, as related later by the political commissar of unit 8199, an airborne division stationed in the Wuhan area. He did not name the
high-ranking officer who had conducted Hsieh to safety, perhaps because Ch'en Tsai-tao by then was in disgrace.[47]

It accordingly seems likely that Hsieh Fu-chih was subjected to
little more than a threatening confrontation and possibly some minor
blows. The really painful blow must have been that to his self-esteem.
Here he was, the government's minister of Public Security, and unable
to afford protection to his own official party.

The authorities in Peking evidently learned of the mutiny at
Wuhan very shortly after it broke out. The acting chief of staff ordered
Ch'en Tsai-tao to guarantee the safety of Mao's envoys, but available
accounts credit their rescue largely to the airborne division and to
the air force at Wuhan, neither of which had participated in the mutiny. The political commissar of that division is asserted to have managed, through a combination of persuasion and ruse, to get Wang Li
moved to a barracks on the pretext that he needed a rest after his
ordeal; then to have slipped him out to spend the night in hiding on
the slopes of a nearby mountain; and finally to have moved him safely
to an airfield.[48]

During the last ten days of July, units of the East China Fleet
moved up to Wuhan and troops of the airborne division entered the
city, took over key points, and disarmed the Million Heroes and members of PLA unit 8201. Tseng Ssu-yü, a veteran of Lin Piao's 115th
division, was named the new commander of Wuhan Military Region,
and Ch'en Tsai-tao and principal officers deemed responsible for the
mutiny were brought to Peking for punishment. Meanwhile, leaders
in Peking put the best possible face on what must have been a highly
embarrassing situation. They organized great celebrations to mark
what was termed the "glorious return" to Peking of Hsieh Fu-chih,
Wang Li, and their party.[49] But a photograph taken on the occasion
of their welcome at the airport, with Chiang Ch'ing grasping the arm

of Wang Li on her right and that of Hsieh Fu-chih on her left, portrayed their faces as stony, or chagrined and angry, rather than triumphant. Wang Li clearly returned to Peking possessed by a vengeful mood. The other members of the Cultural Revolution Group undoubtedly shared it in some measure, for his mistreatment was an outrageous flouting of their collective authority.

In an atmosphere of purge, any regime's inquisitors are prone to see untoward happenings as the products of conspiracy. In consequence it was to be expected that the Cultural Revolution Group would not be satisfied with the punishment of Ch'en Tsai-tao and his immediate subordinates. Those who had been his close associates in times past were bound also to be the objects of their suspicion and revenge. Such considerations help explain the breadth of a purge, within the leadership of China's military establishment, initiated by the Cultural Revolution Group in the period which began with the outbreak of the Wuhan mutiny. The abduction and mistreatment of Wang Li evidently did not, however, precipitate the decision to launch this purge.

The members of the Cultural Revolution Group, even before the mutiny, must have seen the overall situation in China as one in which military commanders not only in Wuhan, but also in many other parts of China, were protecting and supporting enemies of the Cultural Revolution. In logic, such an evaluation would require that those commanders be put on all fours with powerholders within the party who were to be eliminated from positions of authority. In addition, since the Cultural Revolution Group functioned as the command post of Mao Tse-tung, and had been established for the overall conduct of the Cultural Revolution, its members undoubtedly saw themselves as representing a power center superior to the government or the army. In consequence, they evidently considered it within the scope of their authority to expand the list of targets to include powerholders within the military establishment.

The necessary targeting could be accomplished in part covertly, through Red Guard and other organizations which were directly under the influence of the group. But ensuring a really massive and coordinated response required that the call be widely publicized. For this purpose, of course, the group had available to it the principal regular media of news and propaganda, all of which had been made subject to its control.

On July 20 the *People's Daily,* allegedly on the initiative of Lin Chieh, a recently-appointed member of the group, carried a front-page lead article which identified "the small handful" of opportunists within the army, who were "following the capitalist road," as objects for purge. Like the similar power holders within the party, they were to be "criticized deeply and penetratingly, until they were overthrown and made to stink."

The day this article was published was, of course, the same as that on which the Wuhan mutiny broke out, but the appearance of the article on the same day would appear to have been coincidental. It was written in the context of alleged developments in Peking rather than Wuhan, and it appeared under a New China News Agency dateline of July 19, which is to say the day before the mutiny. Such evidence is not, of course, completely conclusive; the authorities in Peking appear to have clamped down an embargo on news about the mutiny which was not lifted until the safety of Hsieh Fu-chih and Wang Li had been assured. Any article written in reaction to the Wuhan mutiny would, in consequence, have had to be couched in a different context. But it seems highly unlikely that this would have required the assignment of a false dateline, or that Lin Chieh could have obtained a clear picture of events in Wuhan and composed an article in reaction to those events before that day's *People's Daily* went to press. It seems fairly safe, therefore, to accept the assertion later made that Lin Chieh had floated the slogan, "drag out the handful in the army," on July 19.[50]

The call for dragging out the "small handful" in the army was not dropped upon Wang Li's safe return to Peking. Instead, it was repeated almost daily in the press and on the radio. Since the "small handful" in the party had turned out to be a majority, the call seemed to signal the initiation within the armed forces of a purge of dimensions comparable to that launched against the party.

That this indeed was intended was more clearly suggested in the August 1 edition of *Red Flag*, Communist China's most authoritative theoretical journal and mouthpiece of the Cultural Revolution Group. This issue, which celebrated the fortieth anniversary of the founding of the People's Liberation Army, contained an editorial which declared: "A movement of mass criticism is now unfolding throughout the country against the handful of top-powerholders taking the capitalist road in the party and the army. This represents the general orientation of the struggle." [51]

Moreover, the editorial called upon the People's Liberation Army to join the proletarian revolutionaries of the whole country and take an active part in this campaign, in order to eliminate completely the pervasive and evil influence of the small group of counterrevolutionary revisionists within the army. This call, of course, came little short of inviting army personnel to revolt against superior officers. If it did not aim at creating a split within the army, it presumed that one already existed. Indeed, Wang Li, who later was alleged to have been responsible for the editorial, was in early August quoted as saying: "The nationwide and major contradiction at present is the dispute between the two headquarters within the military establishment." [52]

The highest ranking officer who was responsible on a full-time basis for matters relating to the political direction of the armed forces was Hsiao Hua, director of the General Political Department of the People's Liberation Army and head of the PLA Cultural Revolution Group. Posters attacking him had appeared on barrack walls and street boardings on July 20, the day on which the *People's Daily* had published the July 19 item which called for "dragging out" the handful in the army.[53] It accordingly seems likely that the decision to move against him antedated the Wuhan mutiny. In any case, with the outbreak of that mutiny he found himself, for the third time during 1967, in conflict with Chiang Ch'ing. In January she had accused him of looking down on the Cultural Revolution Group: when called to attend a conference he had pleaded inability to come, explaining that he had a prior engagement to meet with Premier Chou En-lai.[54] Underlying this expression of pique, however, there probably lay a difference between Hsiao Hua and the Cultural Revolution Group over important matters of policy, for their row came to a head on the eve of the issuance of the decision that the army should actively intervene in the Cultural Revolution. At that time Red Guards ransacked his home, and soldiers subordinate to Yang Yung, then deputy chief of staff and commander of the Peking Military Region, had distributed handbills attacking him. To avoid a deepening of the split, Chou En-lai had called an emergency conference attended by nine hundred members of the three services, after which he had put up a big-character poster calling for Hsiao Hua's reinstatement.

Hsiao Hua was finally reinstated in April, but before the end of May he was again in trouble. This time he was being criticized in connection with a sanguinary riot between factions which broke up a performance in Peking by the PLA Cultural and Art Troupe; given Chiang Ch'ing's special interest in the troupe, no more embarrassing occasion for a free-for-all could have been chosen. Hsiao Hua weathered this storm, but two months later he found himself being accused of having "blocked information concerning the Wuhan incident," and of being the "top person in authority taking the capitalist road in the General Political Department." The members of his own department, Chiang Ch'ing declared, "should criticize Hsiao Hua who is not promoting the Cultural Revolution, with his door closed." [55]

The charge that Hsiao Hua had worked with his door closed was Chiang Ch'ing's way of asserting that he had not consulted her sufficiently in her role of advisor to the PLA Cultural Revolution Group. Back of her use of that figure of speech, no doubt, there lay a decade of pent-up resentment. In the early 1950s, Chiang Ch'ing had been a member of the Ministry of Culture's Film Enterprise Guidance Committee, but she had been dropped from it on the occasion of its reorganization in 1954.[56] As Vice Minister Chou Yang had observed, when Chiang Ch'ing was present, "work becomes difficult." [57] The Cultural Revolution had made her enormously more powerful, but the intervening years had not made her less difficult. As Lin Piao tactfully put it, "Comrade Chiang Ch'ing . . . is full of revolutionary emotion. She is . . . sensitive to things. She is able to find problems and adopt measures to solve them." [58]

Chiang Ch'ing had demonstrated a determination to find and deal with problems, and a sensitive suspicion that she still was being shut out, from the very beginning of her accession to power. Early in the Cultural Revolution, to cite one example, she had visited the Central Broadcasting Station, complained that its doors were closed "tighter than the gates of Chungnanhai," and charged that they bore a sign indicating that she was not allowed to enter. Continuing to speak in figurative terms, she declared, "I want to protest: if you do not reform, I will paint your doors black." [59] The two immediate predecessors of Hsiao Hua, in the position of head of the PLA Cultural Revolution Group, had been discharged from their jobs to the accompaniment of charges that they had not consulted her and members of her group, or allowed them to have a hand in the army's Cultural Revolution.[60]

In August, Hsiao Hua similarly lost his post as head of the PLA Cultural Revolution Group, and for the third time in 1967 that group was reorganized. This reorganization was so complete that there remained, from the January 11 list which supposedly had been approved by Mao himself, only one member—Yeh Ch'ün, the wife of Lin Piao.[61] The group also ceased to be broadly representative of the People's Liberation Army as a whole, for the new roster included not a single officer drawn from the ground forces, which were its main constituent element. Hsiao Hua was also removed from his post as director of the General Political Department of the PLA, his principal subordinates were subjected to a virtually clean sweep, and his department went into limbo.[62]

Former marshal Hsü Hsiang-ch'ien, chief of the PLA Cultural Revolution Group from January until the reorganization of April 9, was brought under renewed attack at about the same time that the campaign against Hsiao Hua began. Hsü Hsiang-ch'ien, Wang Li asserted, was "the wire-puller behind Ch'en Tsai-tao," the top villain of the Wuhan mutiny. (The two men did, indeed, have a history of close professional relations. Ch'en Tsai-tao had joined Hsü Hsiang-ch'ien's force in 1929, when it had numbered only some two hundred men, and had worked his way up under Hsü from squad leader to general. Moreover, Hsü Hsiang-ch'ien had presumably been responsible for the appointment of Ch'en Tsai-tao as commander of Wuhan Military Region, for that appointment had been made when Hsü was chief of staff of the People's Liberation Army.)[63] On July 28, slogans appeared in the streets accusing the former marshal of being a supporter of the Million Heroes who deserved death. About the end of the month army lorries were driven through the streets of Peking bearing the slogan "Crush Hsü Hsiang-ch'ien," and on July 30 a mass rally to denounce the Wuhan rebels was turned into an attack on him.[64]

The attacks on Hsü Hsiang-ch'ien himself soon died down, and were transformed into a campaign against active commanders of military regions who had been closely associated with him and Ch'en Tsai-tao in the days of the civil war. Wang Li condemned the commander of the Nanking Military Region as being a member of what he described as the rebellious Hsü Hsiang-ch'ien faction.[65] He declared that the commander of that military region, which covers the provinces of Kiangsu, Chekiang, and Anhwei, and the commander of the Foochow Military Region, comprising Fukien and Kiangsi, both were engaged in a confrontation with the Center's Military Affairs Committee.[66]

Similar accusations were made against the leaders of Canton Military Region, covering the provinces of Kwangtung, Kwangsi, and Hunan, at a big rally organized by Lin Chieh, presumed author of the July 19 call for dragging out the "small handful" within the army. Soon thereafter a mammoth "investigation mission" was sent to Canton to participate in the great Cultural Revolution there and to drag out characters of the "Ch'en Tsai-tao type." [67]

These developments signaled deep trouble for the army authorities in the respective military regions. Members of rebel organizations in the Nanking and Foochow areas seized the two commanders there and subjected them to kangaroo courts, and bloody fighting—in which PLA troops reportedly were involved—broke out in both military regions.[68] The commander of the Canton Military Region could not be similarly treated because he was not present in his area of responsibility.

Huang Yung-sheng, the commander of the Canton Military Region, had suppressed the leftists during the period of the so-called February adverse current, earning thereby the sobriquet of "Canton's

T'an Chen-lin." In consequence he had been called to Peking early in the spring, ostensibly for "training," and he still remained there when the offensive which the Cultural Revolution unleashed in July hit his military region. Meanwhile the commander of the Shenyang (Mukden) Military Region (covering the three provinces of Manchuria), the acting commander of the Peking Military Region, and the deputy commander of the Foochow Military Region also were in Peking in similarly inactive status, and presumably for similar reasons.[69]

The overall situation accordingly was one in which the command of every military region along the north–south axis of China, from its frontiers with the Soviet Union and the Mongolian People's Republic in the north, to the border with Vietnam in the south, and along the central east–west axis provided by the Yangtze River system, from Szechwan to Shanghai, had been hit by the Cultural Revolution. The top commanders all, though variously, had undergone purge, were being kept in Peking, or were in their own regions and undergoing attacks called down on them by the Cultural Revolution Group.

If we are to believe statements later made by Lin Piao, the attacks on the commanders of the Nanking, Foochow, and Canton Military Regions, for which members of the Cultural Revolution Group had called, enjoyed the secret approval and encouragement of Yang Ch'eng-wu, the acting chief of staff. Yang did not feel secure, Lin Piao explained, because of the word "acting." In consequence he had distrusted and been unwilling to use officers who had not previously served in the same field army system and under his own command. He wished to eliminate the commanders of the three military regions because they had gradually been raised to the same rank as his own, and were potential competitors for his own position.[70]

The troubles which broke out in Canton, in the wake of the Wuhan mutiny and the call for dragging out powerholders in the army, took the form of struggles between organizations which the military had endeavored to suppress and others which they had favored and supported. The leftists used these struggles, which they reported in considerable detail, as ammunition for propaganda attacks against the army. Their accounts are full of accusations against officers of the command who remained in Canton and in charge, but they also suggest a persistent effort to focus on Huang Yung-sheng the ultimate responsibility for all the strife. Indeed, from a reading of these accounts one would suppose Huang Yung-sheng to have been present and in full command.

The struggles which broke out in Canton soon spread to other parts of the military region. Those which occurred in that city, and in neighboring portions of Kwangtung Province, were particularly well reported because Canton is a major exit-point for foreigners leaving China, and because many Chinese travel back and forth between Kwangtung Province and the adjacent British colony of Hong Kong. The first big clash took place on July 23, when several thousand Red Guards raided members of an opposing faction who were holding memorial services for comrades killed in a smaller encounter of two days before. Each side called up reinforcements, a bloody battle ensued, and the campaign was underway.[71]

The conflict which followed was fought with great violence, and sometimes was accompanied by considerable cruelty. According to numerous reports, the gouging out of eyes and the cutting off of ears and noses became frequent occurrences.[72] Such disfigurement was not, however, necessarily the consequence of mere wanton cruelty. Killings created "blood debts" and killers would be less likely to have to pay them if the bodies of the victims could be disfigured beyond recognition. But in spite of such efforts, the factor of revenge was constantly at work, tending to make conflict self-perpetuating, like a fire which generates its own draft.

The fighting corps, or "special action columns," of the mass organizations of the Canton area were armed, during the earlier battles, chiefly with daggers, spears, clubs, and iron bars. But the former soldiers and militiamen who frequently led the fighting corps were used to more effective weapons, and on August 9, the members of one faction robbed a freighter loaded with arms intended for shipment to North Vietnam. This raid was followed by others on freighters, warehouses, militia depots, army installations, and the naval base at Whampoa, downriver from Canton. In consequence, rifles, machine guns, and even heavier weapons came into play.[73]

On August 8, the municipal Public Security Bureau is reported to have suspended operations. Army troops, sometimes accompanied by public security personnel, were still seen on patrol, but they were unarmed and reluctant to interfere between fighting groups. On August 9, with the streets unsafe, buses and other means of public transportation ceased to function. Robbery and looting became problems, and people on residential streets organized themselves for mutual protection, set up roadblocks, and took turns manning them. Foreign travelers passing through Canton reported seeing corpses hanging from trees and lamp posts. It was surmised that some were the bodies of robbers, killed and hung up as a warning to other robbers, but usually the victims had themselves been stripped of all but their underclothes. By mid-August, with nobody in authority to take the initiative to remove them, the dead bodies began to decompose. There was fighting at the railway depots, the trains began to run irregularly, and the radio stations stopped broadcasting local programs.[74]

In the middle of August, the military authorities in Peking began moving troops of the 47th Army southward into Kwangtung, and Chou En-lai called representatives of the warring factions to Peking. An agreement designed to stop the fighting was signed, the representatives returned to Canton, and the agreement promptly broke down. More outside troops were sent in, and fresh negotiations were undertaken, but months were to go by before Kwangtung was to settle into even a temporary peace.[75]

Serious clashes, and in some places heavy fighting, reportedly broke out, during July and August, in every one of China's twenty-six provinces and autonomous regions. The fighting in Kwangtung undoubtedly was more serious than that which occurred, during that period, in most parts of the country. But it was not unique in terms of the weapons used, the violence of the fighting, or the damage inflicted on human beings, economic activities, and social order.

About August 8, the British Embassy in Peking received a long-distance telephone call from two British technicians working in Lanchow in the northwestern province of Kansu. They gave an eyewitness account of a pitched battle being fought in the streets outside their hotel in which industrial workers evidently were involved, for Lanchow's refineries, petrochemical plants and other modern industries stopped operating about this time. But the character of the encounter was not modern, resembling rather a battle between medieval armies: the two sides advanced on each other brandishing spears.[76]

The fighting in Lanchow was perhaps the last mass combat of that summer in which only primitive weapons were employed. In early August, reportedly on the orders of Mao Tse-tung, arms were issued to trusted Red Guard and revolutionary rebel organizations.[77] During this month, seizure of arms from the PLA assumed such dimensions that it was later described as a nationwide mass movement.[78] In Szechwan, possibly in consequence of a split within the armed forces stationed in the province, heavy fighting broke out in which even gunboats, tanks and artillery were involved.[79]

In Manchuria, bad disorders shut down the huge open pit coal mines at Fushun, disrupted production in the famous Tach'ing oil fields, and damaged the steel works at Anshan.[80] In this area, as in the Canton Military Region, fighting evidently was accompanied by considerable cruelty. In Peking, a Japanese correspondent encountered two Japanese women from an industrial city in Manchuria who told him: "Many people have had their noses clipped and their achilles tendons cut. We cannot tell who belongs to the revolutionary faction and who does not. We want to go back to Japan." [81]

The storm of extremism of which the two women complained, and which had in some degree infected all of China, reached a climax during August. It will be recalled that it was in this month that members of the Maoist camp lashed out, in their frustration, with attacks against one foreign embassy after another, culminating in the August 22 manhandling of the staff of the British Embassy and the burning of its chancery.

With professed supporters of Mao Tse-tung everywhere fighting one another, the Maoists made strenuous efforts to unite the masses by setting up well-identified villains, real or presumed, against whom all were invited to vent their spleen. P'eng Te-huai's offense against Mao Tse-tung was eight years past, but he nevertheless, was brought out for a kangaroo court trial,[82] and the campaign vilifying Liu Shao-ch'i, Teng Hsiao-p'ing, and T'ao Chu was thrown into higher gear.

By early August this campaign assumed the proportions of a siege of Chungnanhai, where the three men still were living along with the regime's current leaders. Some two thousand organizations had erected huts and tents, on the two sides of streets just outside the walls of Chungnanhai, to serve as liaison stations for the movement demanding that Liu Shao-ch'i and his two colleagues be "dragged out." [83] The atmosphere was one of much noise, confusion, and macabre carnival. Banners flapped in the wind, and effigies of the three leaders dangled from the trees. One liaison station had a huge plaster head of Liu Shao-ch'i, pierced by a pen, suggestive of his authorship of the now notorious book, *How to Be a Good Communist*. From inside the head, blinking electric lights shown through the eyes and mouth. There were also clay images of a kneeling Liu Shao-ch'i with a rope around the neck, modeled after the statue at Hangchow of an archtraitor of the Sung dynasty, upon which visitors to the site urinated, in manifestation of their contempt.[84] In early August the press of crowds was so great that cars could not pass through, and high officials found it difficult to enter or leave Chungnanhai.[85]

On August 5, a condemnation rally of a million people was held in Tienanmen Square, but Liu Shao-ch'i, Teng Hsiao-p'ing, and T'ao Chu were not taken out of Chungnanhai to attend it. Instead, loudspeakers were rigged up in the residences of the three leaders in order that they and their wives might hear a broadcast of the proceedings, and struggle meetings of manageable size were conducted against them in their individual homes.[86]

The August 5 proceedings were supposed to provide a climax,

after which the liaison stations were to be pulled down, but they were not immediately removed even after Minister of Public Security Hsieh Fu-chih demanded it.[87] On August 12, there was a conflict between rival groupings in one of the city markets, and each side called up reinforcements from allied organizations; thousands of people engaged in the melee, and under cover of the confusion others engaged in a looting of the market's shops and stalls. Eight days later the members of a rebel organization raided a government ministry and took away eleven truckloads of secret files.[88] Meanwhile, so many groups of petitioners, with their grievances and demands, had descended on the capital from the provinces that a row of newly-built housing two kilometers long, intended for local workers and their families, had to be used instead for accommodating the visitors.[89] The problems of the provinces had come to roost on a Peking which was losing the ability to deal successfully even with its own problems.

The Cultural Revolution Group had, of course, not been content to leave Chou En-lai and the several vice premiers free to deal with the problems it had created. It will be recalled that members of the group had, since early in the year, engaged in recurrent attempts to bring about Chou's downfall through attacks on his principal subordinates, much as one might bring down a tree by cutting its supporting roots. They had, previous to the month of August, made these attacks from behind the scenes, but that month two members of the group appear to have come into the open. On August 7 Wang Li, in an inflammatory speech, made a call for striking down Vice Premier Ch'en Yi, whose ministry had been Chou En-lai's original base of power within the government. Shortly afterwards, Ch'i Pen-yü is said to have published a letter in which he supported Wang Li's demand.[90] With their backing, Yao Teng-shan and other rebels in the Foreign Ministry seized power from Ch'en Yi, and exercised it in the several days which led up to the attack on the British Embassy. Meanwhile, however, trouble was brewing for Wang Li and his associates in another quarter, for they had made themselves the enemies of Lin Piao.

Lin Piao had been brought into conflict with the Cultural Revolution Group because it had placed him in a position similar to that of Chou En-lai. He had witnessed the unhappy fates of men who had led one or another of the army systems, other than his own, which had been built up during the two periods of civil war and the intervening years of the conflict with Japan, much as Chou En-lai had gone along with the purge of leaders who were not essential to the operations of the government. Ho Lung and P'eng Te-huai, who had led the First Field Army, had been the first to fall under attack; Hsü

Hsiang-ch'ien, who had shared with Liu Po-ch'eng the leadership of the Second Field Army, had been dismissed; and Ch'en Yi, formerly leader of the Third Field Army, was undergoing a protracted ordeal which threatened to break both his power and his health. Now, however, attacks launched by members of the Cultural Revolution Group had reached or were threatening key veterans of Lin's own Fourth Field Army system.

One of the highest-ranking of those veterans was Hsiao Hua. He had joined Lin Piao's forces in 1929; served as a political officer in his wartime 115th division; been political commissar of an army group which fought the Kuomintang in Manchuria; and then followed Lin Piao into North China for the campaign which had ensued there. After Lin Piao took charge of the Ministry of National Defense, he had placed Hsiao Hua in the highly sensitive position of director of the General Political Department of the PLA. If any officer could be regarded as a protege of Lin Piao, it was Hsiao Hua; but in the vengeful atmosphere following the Wuhan mutiny, and despite Lin's evident efforts to save Hsiao Hua, that officer had been dismissed.[91]

The commanders of Foochow and Canton military regions, who had also been brought under attack by members of the Cultural Revolution Group, were similarly high-ranking veterans of Lin Piao's own field army system. Han Hsien-ch'u, commander of Foochow Military Region, had served in the 129th division, predecessor of the Second Field Army, during the war against Japan. But during the ensuing period of the civil war he had been commander of an army under Lin Piao. The commander of the Canton Military Region, Huang Yung-sheng, had served under Lin Piao both during the war with Japan and in the civil war, and the forces garrisoning Kwangtung had been drawn from his Fourth Field Army.

Therefore the campaign to "drag out the handful in the army" was not only threatening the overall unity of the armed forces; it was also endangering the hard core of officers who presumably were personally loyal to Lin Piao. On August 9, Lin Piao gave a speech, at a reception for ranking officers, in which he asserted that good men were being attacked by bad people. As examples of good men under attack, he cited five officers—the director of the General Rear Services Department of the PLA, the commander of the air force, the political commissar of the navy, the director of the political department of the navy, and one of its deputy commanders—all of whom had served within his own field army system. Apparently addressing Huang Yung-sheng and other regional commanders who had been held in Peking for some months, consequent to accusations leveled against them, he said: "You must put up with it and control yourselves. . . . Bad people will be criticized and punished. Then you will straighten up your backs again." [92]

Among those also present, at this reception for military officers, besides Chou En-lai, with whom Lin Piao had implicitly aligned himself through this speech, were such members of the Cultural Revolution Group as Ch'en Po-ta, Chiang Ch'ing, K'ang Sheng, Wang Li, Kuan Feng, and Ch'i Pen-yü.[93] At least some of them were among the "bad people" to whom Lin Piao referred, and as he had predicted, some of them were soon to be criticized and punished.

Their offenses against Lin Piao's army were not, however, the only ones for which they were to be punished. These same people undoubtedly were behind a culminating effort, made that same month, to seize power from Chou En-lai. Subsequent to his 1970 trip to China, Edgar Snow reported that Chou En-lai's "most perilous moment" of the Cultural Revolution came at a time in August 1967 when both Mao Tse-tung and Lin Piao were absent from Peking. At that time Chou En-lai was besieged for two days and nights, in his offices in the Great Hall of the People, by half a million ultraleftist Red Guards. Their instigators, Snow explained, were intent on seizing both the files of the Central Committee and Chou En-lai himself. However Chou has a particularly winning way with young people, among whom he is greatly admired, and he survived this challenge through his supreme skill as a negotiator. By talking to small groups day and night, he told Snow, he gradually persuaded the Red Guards to disperse. Subsequently "some" of the leaders had been arrested as counterrevolutionaries.[94] If the others included Ch'en Po-ta and Chiang Ch'ing, the failure to arrest them is understandable: they were too high ranking and too closely associated with Mao Tse-tung.

24

Chairman Mao Takes a Trip

THE WUHAN incident unquestionably came as a stunning blow to leaders in Peking, and it ushered in a period of grave uncertainty. Heavy fighting, in which the PLA was involved, had been in progress in a number of provinces, and now the military region which contained the reserves—intended to be sent elsewhere in case of need—was itself out of control. What remained unclear was whether the troop uprising in the Wuhan Military Region would spread to other parts of the country, and whether the capture of Peking's emissaries was part of a wider plot, which might conceivably have originated in Peking itself.

It would have been strange if the Wuhan incident of 1967 had not evoked, in the minds of leaders like Mao Tse-tung and Chou En-lai, memories of the Sian incident of 1936. In each case rebellious officers at an important headquarters had carried out a kidnaping in order to force a change of government policy. In 1936 it had been Chiang Kai-shek who had been held captive. In 1967 the higher of the two officials who were detained was only a vice premier. But if high military officers in Peking were behind the incident at Wuhan, or if the uprising there spread and such officers were to give it their backing, then the parallel with the Sian incident might become complete. If the minister of public security himself had not been safe from capture in the greatest city of central China, then Mao Tse-tung might no longer be safe in the nation's capital, particularly since his presence there had but recently been highly publicized and hence was well known. It must accordingly have seemed wise that he should quietly leave Peking, and that he should remain in some other and undisclosed place until prevailing uncertainties might be resolved.

At any rate, Mao Tse-tung disappeared from public view about the time of the Wuhan incident. He left Peking unheralded, and his whereabouts remained a closely guarded secret during an ensuing period of about two months. Not unnaturally, his extended absence from the public view, during this critical period, itself became a factor which contributed to the prevailing uncertainty. It gave rise to speculation which, to get ahead of our story, continued even after he had returned to Peking and his presence there had been publicly an-

nounced. In consequence, a directive had to be issued, in an effort to
end the speculation, calling upon officials in the provinces to scotch
rumors "being circulated in all parts of the country" which "express
doubt about the health and existence of our leader." The directive
affirmed that Chairman Mao was "physically healthy," and asserted
that news to the effect that he had not been working had been disseminated "due to a misunderstanding." [1]

Mao Tse-tung may well have continued working throughout the
period during which he was out of sight, but it does not appear to
have been one during which China's great helmsman had a very firm
hand on the tiller. At any rate, the period of his absence was also that
during which the campaign to "drag out the handful of powerholders
in the army" was at its height.

According to Chou En-lai, the idea that China was about to undergo a capitalist and counterrevolutionary restoration had emanated
from Peking and been transmitted by telephone to all big cities in
the country. It had given widespread currency to the conclusions that
it was necessary to "seize political power by armed force" and "settle
issues by war." Since it was the PLA and the revolutionary committees
which exercised political power in the provinces, this would mean
seizing the military power and arms of the PLA and initiating a civil
war. In consequence, as Chou pointed out, seizure of arms and armed
struggles had occurred in all parts of the country, and "some people
who believed that Chairman Mao did not have majority support were
ready to follow Chairman Mao to the mountains to wage guerrilla
warfare." [2]

It is clear that Lin Piao did not intend to let others seize the military power on which his political position had been built. By early
August, as we have seen, the campaign against the army was threatening key officers who had risen to high rank through the field army
system he had commanded, and who presumably were personally loyal
to him. This had led him to insert in his August 9, 1967, speech the
passage which implied a challenge to the Cultural Revolution Group.
This was, of course, the assertion that his officers were good men undergoing attack from bad people, and that those bad people would
be criticized and punished.

It would appear that leaders of the Cultural Revolution Group
were quick to see the handwriting on the wall, as represented by Lin
Piao's words of August 9. They had been wielding great power, but
their authority derived from Mao Tse-tung, and Lin Piao had, in
effect, openly staked his future on the proposition that Mao Tse-tung
would side with him and Chou En-lai against the Cultural Revolution
Group. On August 11, Ch'en Po-ta and Chiang Ch'ing made speeches

which paved the way for their retreat. There was, Ch'en Po-ta alleged, "a secret and conspirational organization" which he identified as the "May 16 Corps." Its spearhead, he indicated, was seemingly directed at Chou En-lai, "but is actually directed against the Central Committee"—by which he evidently meant the headquarters of Mao Tse-tung. Chiang Ch'ing, too, alluded to the organization, declaring in her speech that it would not be tolerated.[3]

The next move would be up to Mao, but he had secretly gone to Shanghai, doubtless chosen as his temporary place of refuge because it was controlled by his supporters Chang Ch'un-ch'iao and Yao Wen-yüan.[4] Shanghai itself was not free of disorders, during the latter part of July and the early days of August, and Chang Ch'un-ch'iao later quoted Mao Tse-tung as having asked whether the disorders there could be brought under control.[5] Nevertheless Mao's stay in Shanghai appears to have been free of untoward events; by some time in September, if not before, the situation had become sufficiently clarified to permit him to make either one long tour or a series of inspection trips in several provinces; and when the time came to return to Peking, he was able to go by train.[6]

Mao had with him, on his travels, one person associated with each of the two contending sides: Chang Ch'un-ch'iao, who was a deputy head of the Cultural Revolution Group, albeit one who had been removed from its concerns in Peking since early in the year, consequent to his responsibilities in Shanghai; and Yang Ch'eng-wu, acting chief of staff of the People's Liberation Army. Air Force Political Commissar Yü Li-chin was also a member of the party; he may have been included primarily in order to facilitate Mao's travels by air, but both he and Yang Ch'eng-wu spent much of August in Shanghai, and both took part in some of Mao's discussions with provincial leaders. The two men doubtless felt honored to be members of Mao's party and to be at his right hand during important talks. But since the actors in one phase of the Cultural Revolution were apt to be the victims of the next, it was a dangerous honor.[7]

The security measures surrounding Mao's travels were in the hands of Wang Tung-hsing, vice minister of public security and Mao's long-time bodyguard. They apparently were stringent, for the public remained ignorant of Mao's travels until he had returned to Peking. However, security requirements alone would hardly suffice to explain the fact that the official media never listed the places Mao had visited and the respective dates. They revealed only that he had inspected parts of north China, central south China, and east China, and stated that he had made a study of the condition of the great Cultural Revolution in the provinces of Hopeh, Honan, Hupeh, Hunan, Kiangsi, and Chekiang, and in the municipality of Shanghai.[8] However, from the informal accounts which subsequently became available one gathers the impressions that Mao Tse-tung visited only the capitals of the five provinces of Honan, Hupeh, Hunan, Kiangsi, and Chekiang; that his visits to them were brief; and that the bulk of his time, while away from Peking, was spent in Shanghai. Obviously, however, the regime would have preferred to explain Mao's absence from the capital solely in terms of his inspection tour.

The available accounts of Mao's discussions make it clear that the position of the army, both as an agent of his Cultural Revolution and as a victim of the campaign against it, was high on his list of concerns. A chatty account given by officials in Mao's native Hunan suggests that army morale and discipline in that province had gone to pot. Mao's informants told him that army cooks no longer prepared meals for the troops because they spent all their time participating in the "four big" activities of the Cultural Revolution, referring to big contending, big blooming, big-character posters, and big or extensive democracy. They also said that PLA units stationed in the factories to ensure production, themselves forbidden to use arms, were being protected by armed workers.[9]

One gains the impression, from comments attributed to the Chairman in another account, that military discipline in some other provinces was even worse than in Hunan. In Nanchang, Kiangsi, Mao remarked that some people were inciting the soldiers to oppose their officers; he accordingly advised against allowing soldiers in the Kiangsi military district to practice the "four bigs" too intensively. Apparently referring to conditions within the military district of the province next door, he continued: "The fire will spread if the soldiers are roused. Struggles take place every day in Chekiang. In the struggle, the victims are made to wear dunce caps, hang black signboards on their necks, and kneel down on the ground and are subject to the jet-style torture. They won't stand these punishments. And neither are these punishments justifiable." [10]

On August 25 the authorities in Peking put out a notice calling for a mass movement to give effect to a current slogan, addressed to both civilians and the military, which urged: "Support the Army and Cherish the People." [11] This August 25 notice also reminded the populace that the arms, equipment, and materials of the PLA were supposed to be inviolable, and indicated once more that outsiders were not allowed to enter and occupy command organs.[12]

Sometime between August 25 and September 5, it would appear, Mao Tse-tung let it be known that he considered a stronger order to be required. Perhaps it was during this period that he issued an instruction, later published without date, in which he declared: "The army's prestige must be resolutely safeguarded and there can be no doubt whatever about that. Publication of editorials on the need to support the army and cherish the people is the center of the work. It is unavoidable that the army should have made mistakes in tackling for the first time the large-scale fighting task of supporting the left, supporting industry and agriculture, and carrying out military control and military training. The chief danger of the moment is that some people want to beat down the PLA! . . . There must be no chaos in the army." [13]

On September 5 a further, more detailed and much stronger order was issued. It attributed the call for the movement to "support the army and cherish the people" to Mao himself; it specifically prohibited seizures of arms and of military equipment and supplies, whether in the hands of the army, in arsenals, or in transit; it called for those which had been seized to be turned in, stored, and sealed; and it placed responsibility for enforcement on local garrison forces. By far the most important of all, it modified the April 6 order under which the army, in its dealings with mass organizations and their members, was forbidden to use its guns. Primary reliance was still to be placed on political work and persuasion, but when resisted or attacked, the army might now fight back.[14]

On September 1, and again on September 5, Chiang Ch'ing made speeches which undoubtedly reflected the way in which the wind was blowing. In these speeches she again alluded to the mysterious May 16 Corps which, she said, was centered in Peking and divided into a number of area armies. Superficially, it opposed the premier and concentrated its attacks upon him. "Actually," she declared, "it has collected black material to denounce every one of us, and it may throw it out in public at any time. . . . They had collected black material against me in the past, but only now have I discovered this." The May 16 Corps, she asserted, assumed the appearance of being ultraleft. But it really was "a demolition squad seeking to sway the party Central Committee headed by Chairman Mao from the 'left' and the right, and to bring disorder to our setup. The 'May 16' is a counterrevolutionary organization." [15]

Chiang Ch'ing's September 5 speech was made before the representatives of two warring factions from Anhwei, who had been brought to Peking to compose their differences. In it, she backed away somewhat from positions which she and members of her group had taken on the subject of armed struggle; spoke in support of the order which had been issued that day forbidding the seizure of weapons from the army; and praised the army for its forbearance in the face of provocation. Most important of all, she repudiated her own group's campaign to "drag out the handful in the army." This made her speech useful in bringing that campaign to an end, and it was in due course distributed far and wide, to her evident irritation, in both the form of taped reproduction and printed text.

On July 22 Chiang Ch'ing, evidently reacting to the events of previous days in Wuhan, had declared: "While the enemies possess weapons, we should by no means lay down our arms." In her speech of September 5, in an apparent effort to bring herself to deprecate armed fighting, she made the assertion: "Our struggle, too, is rather severe, although we do not use force. Nevertheless, I have let it be known that if some people insist on having a violent struggle with me, I will surely defend myself and strike back." Still speaking with forked tongue, she continued: "Comrades, I am not in favor of armed struggle, and you must not think that I like it, because I am firmly opposed to it. I resolutely support Chairman Mao's call for 'peaceful struggle, not armed struggle.' What I mean is: when the class enemies attack us, how can we afford not to have an inch of iron in our hands?"

At present, she continued, there was no need for that kind of struggle. Her previous advice of "attack by words and defend by force," she continued, "must not be deprived of its class content; it must not be viewed in isolation from definite circumstances and conditions. It would be too bad if, on your return, you stir up fights by wearing fighter's caps and raising spears."

At this point she was interrupted by K'ang Sheng, who observed: "Not spears. We now have machine guns." Still on the same tack, Chiang Ch'ing continued: "On the whole, I feel that the situation is excellent. It has tempered the younger generation and the young fighters. It has also tempered the revolutionary cadres as well as men of the older generation like old K'ang!" In apparent disgust, he interjected: "You people are tempering me every day."

Chiang Ch'ing's deprecation of attacks upon the army was somewhat more forthright. "Sometime earlier," she observed, there was this wrong slogan: Seize a 'small handful in the army.' As a result, 'a small handful in the army' was seized everywhere and . . . everywhere we seized their guns, beat them up, and scolded them. But they did not strike back, nor did they argue. Is there such an army in any other part of the world? Now we must not fall into others' trap and drag out the small handful in the army everywhere and indiscriminately." She did not, at this point, identify the "others" who had set the trap, but we assume that Chiang Ch'ing's hearers were intended to equate them with the leaders or backers of the May 16 Corps.[16]

Organizations spawned during the Cultural Revolution quite com-

monly used dates as parts of their names. These might be the dates of
their founding, or ones of wider revolutionary significance with which
the founders wished to associate themselves. The founding of the Cultural Revolution Group itself might be considered to have been May
16, for May 16, 1966, had been the date of the Central Committee circular which informed the party of the decision to dissolve P'eng Chen's
"Group of Five in Charge of the Cultural Revolution," and to set up
the new one headed by Ch'en Po-ta.[17]

Mao Tse-tung did not completely dominate the party at the time
the Cultural Revolution Group was established, and the original roster of the group's members necessarily reflected that fact. However, his
supporters played a dominant role in the group's activities from the
start, and by August 1967 it had been reduced, consequent to successive purges, to a small body of ten persons. It will be recalled that two
of them, Chang Ch'un-ch'iao and Yao Wen-yüan, had since February
been largely preoccupied with the affairs of Shanghai, in their respective capacities as chairman and vice chairman of its Revolutionary
Committee. This left in Peking a group composed of three leaders
and five members. The three leaders, of course, were Ch'en Po-ta,
Chiang Ch'ing and K'ang Sheng; the five members were Wang Li,
Kuan Feng, Lin Chieh, Mu Hsin and Ch'i Pen-yü.

Four of these five were closely associated with Ch'en Po-ta in a
related capacity as well, for they were members also of the editorial
staff of *Red Flag,* of which Ch'en Po-ta had been the editor in chief
since 1958. In addition Ch'i Pen-yü had been a favorite of Chiang
Ch'ing's since at least the early 1960s. The lists of the persons who had
accompanied Chiang Ch'ing and Ch'en Po-ta on their public appearances, both before and after the purges of other members of the group,
suggest that the five survivors were their trusted confidants.

Nevertheless, in the late summer and early autumn of 1967, Wang
Li, Kuan Feng, Lin Chieh and Mu Hsin were all arrested. The reason
advanced for the purge of each was either that he had been one of the
leaders of the May 16 Corps, or that he had been closely associated
with it,[18] and they were charged in Red Guard tabloids with responsibility both for the long-standing campaign against Chou En-lai and
his ministers, and for the short-lived one against the army.

The distinction between acts performed as members of the Cultural Revolution Group and deeds committed as leaders of an alleged
May 16 Corps was a fine one, and both Ch'en Po-ta and Chiang Ch'ing
seem to have recognized that the screen behind which they themselves
were attempting to withdraw was transparently thin. Ch'en Po-ta had
stated, in his August 11 speech, that it was not essential to lay hold of
the subordinate elements in the May 16 Corps. He then strengthened

that statement by asserting: "It is necessary . . . not to make such a mistake." [19] After it became known that Wang Li had been purged, Chiang Ch'ing warned Peking Red Guards: "Don't exaggerate the case of *Red Flag* magazine and the Central Cultural Revolution Group. Nor put your nose in the problem of Lin Chieh, Wang Li, and Kuan Feng. No big character posters should be posted and those already posted should be covered up." [20]

It was of course desirable, from the standpoint of the leaders of the Cultural Revolution Group, that the public should accept the thesis that the May 16 Corps, and not their own organization, had been the mechanism through which their own subordinates had carried out the activities of which they were accused. But even if nobody were actually to accept that thesis, it nevertheless was essential for it to be advanced: if the different elements of Mao Tse-tung's headquarters were to continue their association, the face of each had to be preserved. And since face is largely a matter of facade, what was necessary was that those concerned behave in public as though they accepted the story of the May 16 Corps at face value.

I do not know when Mao Tse-tung returned to Peking, but it evidently was some time before September 24, when the press first carried information about his tour, described it as having been made "recently," and revealed that he was back in the capital.[21] After his return he reportedly subjected both Ch'en Po-ta and Chiang Ch'ing to criticism and caused them to make self-examinations in which they confessed to errors of left-opportunism.[22] During September and October the surviving members of the group participated in a number of meetings at which Chou En-lai was usually the principal speaker, as though to suggest that they and he all stood solidly together.[23]

One gains the impression from transcripts of the proceedings, both of the meetings which she attended and those she did not, that Chiang Ch'ing found it distasteful to be expected to take a back seat and convey an impression of solidarity with Chou En-lai.[24] At one meeting, for instance, she interrupted his remarks to complain that on the previous day a group of fellows, who behaved like robbers, had ransacked the offices of the journal *Red Flag*.[25] It may be surmised that Chiang Ch'ing was protesting against investigations connected with the purge of members of her group—who, it will be recalled, were also members of the editorial staff of that journal. If she was concerned about the future of *Red Flag*, as a mouthpiece of the Cultural Revolution Group, her concern was fully justified: after one more issue, which came out in November 1967, it ceased to appear for over half a year. But it is hard to see how making her complaint in a semipublic forum could serve any purposes beyond expressing her pique and suggesting that no real solidarity existed between herself and Chou En-lai.

Insofar as organizational predominance is concerned, the late summer and early autumn of 1967 was a period in which the army won a victory at the expense of the Cultural Revolution Group. But this period marked a watershed of sorts in other respects as well, for Mao Tse-tung appears to have used the two months following the Wuhan incident to assess the state of the country and reassess the policies under which the Cultural Revolution was being conducted. By the time he had returned to Peking, he had determined to abandon the emphasis upon destruction, which had characterized the operations of the Cultural Revolution Group, and to get on with the tasks of construction. This would involve restoring order, setting up revolutionary committees for the twenty-two of China's twenty-six provinces and autonomous regions for which none had yet been established, and preparing for a Ninth Party Congress which would be expected to ratify a revised party constitution and elect a Central Committee which would be loyal to himself.

Mao Tse-tung is supposed to have remarked, towards the end of July: "The capital is full of workers. The leftist faction is as fierce as this, the rightist faction is as fierce as that. I don't believe it." [26] Not all the seeming ferocity of Peking's factions was playacting, as the casualties of the summer's disorders in the capital testified. But if Mao doubted that the lust for combat was universal, he was perhaps both right and more right than he knew. In truth, many people had grown tired of the hurly-burly of his movement and yearned for a more normal life. By early summer, householders had begun writing letters to the editor of *People's Daily* in which they complained that high-pitched loudspeakers, competing with each other until well past bedtime, or even throughout the night, were robbing workers of their needed sleep.[27] According to a Red Guard account, that summer the members of army families were complaining: "The Central Cultural Revolution Group had so shifted the veteran army cadres that they are separated from their wives and children, their homes broken up and their kin lost!" [28]

As complaints about workers being robbed of their sleep remind one, the reality of life is never the mere totality of all the crises with which governments are confronted and the crimes and catastrophes which fill the public prints. The need to earn one's living and the habit of doing one's job, if nothing else, are likely to ensure that much work is unobtrusively accomplished even amidst widespread disorders. Moreover, paradoxical as it may seem, the preoccupation of some with struggle may make it possible for others to find peace and pleasures through withdrawal.

After Mao Tse-tung's great August 18, 1966, rally for China's revolutionary students, but before they had been redirected against more serious targets, Red Guards had been defacing historic monuments and ancient buildings in the environs of Peking, as part of the attack on all old things, and conducting a campaign against non-utilitarian pursuits, on the grounds that they were bourgeois. On August 18, 1967, one year later, a Japanese correspondent reported that places of historic interest and scenic beauty, in Peking and its nearby countryside, again were being used as places of relaxation by citizens with carefree expressions, and as lovers' lanes by wandering young couples. The Red Guards had attacked the enjoyment of flowers, the keeping of goldfish, and the playing of cards. But now the florists were again doing a good trade, goldfish were back in the ponds at Peihai Park, and circles of workers were gathered around others who were playing cards.[29]

If Mao Tse-tung could have seen people enjoying themselves in Peking's Peihai Park, on a Sunday afternoon that summer, it might have told him that the time had come to start winding up his Cultural Revolution. A visit to Canton, where bodies lay rotting in the streets, might have led to the same conclusion. Mao Tse-tung could neither stroll unobtrusively through the one, nor safely visit the other, but the provincial centers he did visit in August and September were fairly typical of China as a whole. Upon his return to Peking he was quoted as asserting that "the situation was excellent in a big way," [30] a summary which was belied by much else which he had to say, and by the nature of the measures he instituted, during the immediately ensuing weeks.

Late in September Chou En-lai declared, "Chairman Mao said a few days ago that we were like a country divided into eight hundred princely states." [31] During his trip Mao had remarked, of the violent struggles underway, "I think this is a civil war." [32] As Mao Tse-tung's comment about the fragmented nature of his country suggests, it was not yet a civil war in which two sides each had its own directing headquarters and well-defined territorial base. However, the dynamics of the Cultural Revolution were tending to create such a situation.

As we have seen, Mao Tse-tung's party center had repeatedly called on revolutionary organizations to form great alliances, the leaders of which were to represent the masses as one of the three elements in the revolutionary committees. As we have also seen, this had raised the issue of who should lead the alliances, with its accompanying implication that those who did not lead should accept subordination. And the final acceptance of subordination might mean not only loss of the prospect of exercising power. It also meant, in many cases, placing oneself at the mercy of one's bitter enemies. In this situation, people everywhere wanted themselves and their own organizations taken as the nucleus around which the great and three-in-one alliances should be formed, and were unwilling to accept the permanence of ones which did not meet that criterion. As Chiang Ch'ing remarked in her speech of September 5: "At present a gust of foul wind is . . . being stirred up with the object of dissolving all revolutionary committees set up with the approval of the Central Committee." [33]

While organizations were not forming into the single groupings known as great alliances, the conflicts between them were nevertheless causing organizations to join alliances of another sort. If there were two contending factions within an individual office, factory or enterprise, the weaker was likely to seek outside allies whose fighting corps might help it win physical superiority, and through that superiority, organizational predominance.[34] By the middle of 1967, provincewide coalitions had been formed, and because similar groups are inclined to support each other, coalitions tended to have either a leftist or a rightist character.[35]

Mao Tse-tung must have observed this tendency for organizations to coalesce into two warring camps, one of the left and the other of the right, for beginning on September 14 and for some time thereafter the regime's media carried in bold type his assertion: "There is no fundamental clash of interests within the working class. Under the dictatorship of the proletariat, there is no reason whatsoever for the working class to split into two irreconcilable organizations." [36]

Mao also appears to have concluded—and this must have come to him as a deeply disturbing realization—that his own supporters among the people were less numerous than those who had been misled by capitalist-roaders "holding the banner of the party's Central Committee." [37] That conclusion seems to be implied, at any rate, by his own statement:

The broad masses of workers and peasants and the backbones of the party and the Communist Youth League have been hoodwinked in the course of the criticism and repudiation of the bourgeois reactionary line. . . . The broad masses of workers, peasants, and soldiers are practical workers, and so naturally they know very little about those in the upper levels. In addition, the broad mass of party and Communist Youth League backbones have unbounded love for the party and its cadres, and the powerholders who follow the capitalist road hold up a red flag to oppose the red flag. So they are hoodwinked, and some of them have been unable to disillusion themselves for quite a long time. . . . Those who are hoodwinked are all right once they see the light and change. They will be the main force again with the intensification of the movement.[38]

Mao Tse-tung conceded that the revolutionary spirit of the Red Guards was very strong. However, "when we do things some people have to assume command. Can the Red Guards assume command? They will certainly be toppled tomorrow once they are installed today. This is because they are politically immature. . . . The Red Guards are incompetent; they haven't been tempered. We can't trust them with things of such major importance." [39] Moreover, they and the revolutionary rebels were predominantly of the left faction, whereas circumstances were forcing a shift to the right. In consequence, "leaders of the revolutionary rebel faction and little generals of the Red Guards should be told that now is exactly the time when it is possible for them to make mistakes." [40]

Actually, Mao was giving up on the educated young, whom the Chinese Communists would call "intellectuals," many of whom were Red Guards. "Previously," Mao said, "I had the intention to foster successors among the intellectuals but now this plan is far from desirable. Intellectuals including young undergraduates inside and outside the party, in my opinion, in the main continue to embrace the bourgeois world outlook. This is because for seventeen years since liberation the field of culture and education has been dominated by revisionist elements." In consequence, bourgeois ideas had "been infused into their blood." Among the "bourgeois" traits which they demonstrated was a propensity for factionalism. "It is very important," Mao said, "to rally under one banner, under the Marxist slogan: Proletariat of the world, unite! However, they don't. They seem to favor a small group, with the fewer people the better." [41]

The problem of unity was closely bound up with that of the philosophical approach which had guided the theoreticians of the Cultural Revolution Group. A key element in this approach was expressed in the thesis, embodied in the May 16, 1966, circular which was the group's charter, and which had probably been drafted by Ch'en Po-ta, its leader: "Put destruction first, and in the process you have construction." What had led Mao Tse-tung to formulate this thesis, or to accept it if it was not his original formulation, and why had reliance upon it brought China to the brink of civil war?

That thesis summarized the way things undoubtedly seemed to work, as seen from the perspective of Yenan, throughout the eight years of the war against Japan. During those years, party leaders in Yenan necessarily left the work of organizing Communist enclaves elsewhere in China to the others who were on the spot. In those enclaves, beyond and between the Japanese lines, the destruction of enemy power and the construction of the organizational means whereby that destruction was accomplished went hand in hand, as mutually supporting activities. When the war against Japan was over, the party already had created the military and administrative capabilities which were to enable it to conquer the rest of China and which were to provide the nucleus for a new regime.

However, there were important differences between the way things had seemed to work during the war against Japan, and the way they had actually worked. Moreover, because the nature and the purposes of that war were profoundly different from those of the Cultural Revolution, the two were bound to have different dynamics and dissimilar consequences.

The war against Japan tended to unite all Chinese because the enemies were alien invaders. As a patriotic war for national survival, it had objectives which all could understand. This gave it the character of a mass movement with pronounced voluntarist aspects. Nevertheless, the party's political and military cadres played key roles, which were perhaps more pervasive than they were apparent, in stimulating, organizing, and directing this mass movement. Moreover, while the forces at their disposal might ostensibly exist only to fight the Japanese, force was available in the background for use also against uncooperative and disloyal Chinese.[42]

The Cultural Revolution tended to divide the Chinese people, instead of uniting them, because it was a pervasive struggle among their own leaders, of which the people were made the instruments. The struggle against the capitalist-roaders in the party, according to Mao Tse-tung, was the chief task of the Cultural Revolution.[43] But only the struggle itself, by putting the leaders within the party to the test, would disclose which were and which were not capitalist-roaders. This meant that the Cultural Revolution was an open-ended purge, and purges are in any case like conflagrations which generate their own draft. The destruction of the Cultural Revolution, in other words, tended to be self-perpetuating. And the party, which had been the organizing factor in Communist areas during the war against Japan, obviously could not play a constructive role during the Cultural Revolution because it was itself the object of destruction.

The purpose of the struggle against the capitalist-roaders in the party, Mao Tse-tung has said, was "to solve the problem of world outlook and eradicate revisionism." [44] This was too abstract to be firmly grasped by the majority of those who participated in that struggle. In the absence of anything more concrete, many of them were bound to play the game of "king of the mountain," fighting over the issue of who should succeed the leaders they had overthrown. The aphorism about victors and their spoils implies, of course, that those who fight only for spoils will fight as readily over them, among themselves. Some of the struggles of the Cultural Revolution, of course, were what might be called principled struggles, waged over matters which transcended considerations of personal ambition. But Mao Tse-tung's statements of his aims were as general as they were abstract, and hence of little use in preventing or settling such differences.

On September 28, Chang Ch'un-ch'iao, who had accompanied Mao Tse-tung on his travels and was well aware of Mao's complaints about the factionalism into which China had descended, made a speech in which he touched upon this problem. In this speech he asked: "When there are several 'mountain tops' in a unit, what can make them form an alliance and unite together?" Then, in answer to his own question, he said: "A program." [45]

This might have been a valid answer also for China as a whole, provided the program was a substantive one which met the aspirations of the people. But it has been observed that strong leaders are ones who raise a certain moral threshold against disagreement,[46] and it accordingly seems unlikely that Chang Ch'un-ch'iao pressed the point with Mao Tse-tung. A program which met the wishes of the Chinese people for less austerity would not have been in keeping with the will of Mao Tse-tung. About this time, speaking of his irregular methods in figurative language, he explained: "I personally favor the 'rustic style' and the 'practice of fighting guerrilla warfare.' Since we were victorious in twenty years of fighting, why is it this doesn't work out in socialist construction? . . . Until the early stage of liberation all party members by and large lived on an equal footing, carrying on their daily pursuits energetically and fighting quite bravely. All this has nothing to do with so-called material incentives; what really counts is the inspiration drawn from the revolutionary spirit." [47]

Mao Tse-tung has said that the fundamental law of the universe, according to Marxist philosophy, is the unity of opposites, and that internal contradictoriness exists in every single thing. "Between the opposites in a contradiction," he has held, "there is at once unity and struggle, and it is this that impels things to move and change. . . . In any given phenomenon or thing, the unity of opposites is conditional, temporary and transitory, and hence relative, whereas the struggle of opposites is absolute." [48] If he had seen the political process as a unity of the two opposites of destruction and construction, he was now shifting the emphasis to construction. If there was a contradiction involved in his principle of democratic centralism, he would now proceed with construction under central control. It might be unfair to assert that he had abandoned the democratic politics of the mass line, but he was determined to bring the masses into line with the thought of Mao Tse-tung.

At least as early as September, special courses for the study of the thought of Mao Tse-tung were initiated in Peking. Some of these courses, set up on the basis of military services and units, presumably had as their primary purpose the indoctrination of the participants themselves, and they might last no more than eighteen days.[49] Others apparently were directed at preparing the participants to serve in "Mao Tse-tung Thought Propaganda Teams" or other special-purpose units. Those teams were to help establish "Mao Tse-tung Thought Study Classes," to be conducted in municipalities, counties, communes, and smaller units throughout the country, so that Mao's thought and Mao's directives might be made known "to every household and everyone."[50] For the participants in courses held in Peking, the high point was a rally in the Great Hall of the People at which Mao Tse-tung himself was among the top leaders who appeared.[51]

Other courses were set up on a province-by-province basis, with as many as a thousand participants coming to Peking from a single province. They included people drawn from the three categories of which revolutionary committees were to be composed: representatives of the army, cadres drawn from party and government, and leaders of Red Guard and other mass organizations. Class supervisors were chosen from among the participants, and since this created a leader–follower relationship which might continue after the course had ended, the authorities in Peking were not above bringing pressure to bear for the choice of those they favored.[52] The participants were called upon to review their experiences in the light of Mao's directives, undoubtedly in the expectation that they would recognize their respective errors and come to terms with one another. From time to time key participants were called to special meetings held under the aegis of Chou En-lai and other top leaders, which were intended to resolve differences and culminate in agreements on the composition of preparatory groups for revolutionary committees, or of revolutionary committees themselves, at the municipal and provincial levels.[53]

Chou En-lai had for some time been bringing the representatives of warring groups to Peking for the purpose of working out agreements, and Mao Tse-tung had discovered that long periods of training had a cooling effect on hot heads. During his provincial tour he had remarked: "In Inner Mongolia there was an independent battalion comprising more than eight hundred men. It supported the conservatives and opposed the decision of the party Central Committee on the problem of Inner Mongolia. Coming to Peking, they acted arrogantly and made trouble, disobeyed the Premier's sayings and broke the furniture, so that the meeting could not go on. . . . Later, they were sent to Kaopeitien, Hsinch'eng, Peking, and trained for forty days. They all changed for the better. Returning to Inner Mongolia, they supported the left wing." [54]

Accordingly, the practices utilized in this process of constructing revolutionary committees cannot be described as new. What was perhaps new was their use in combination, with participants realizing that they might not be allowed to return to their home provinces until they had reached an agreement.

Mao Tse-tung clearly wanted this process of hammering out agreements, province by province and city by city, to move forward rapidly. A Tsinghai Revolutionary Committee had been established on August 12, which meant that such committees were in existence for five provinces and the two provincial-level municipalities of Shanghai and Peking. After his tour, Mao asserted that the problems of eight additional provinces had basically been solved, and that those of ten more were susceptible of solution by the end of the year. Thereafter, he said, the party organization should be restored, and party congresses held at various levels. It would not do to rush things, he conceded, but neither would it do to slacken efforts. "I see," he concluded, "that it will be about this time next year that the Ninth Party Congress is convened." [55]

The hammering out of agreements, province by province, under the auspices of the party center, implied that increased reliance should be placed on Chou En-lai, since he was its one outstandingly skilled negotiator. It accordingly was arranged that the Cultural Revolution Group, whose members had encouraged revolutionary organizations in their attacks on Chou En-lai, and the Peking Municipal Revolutionary Committee, as a body in which those organizations were represented, should take the initiative in calling off the attacks. Ch'en Po-ta, in his capacity of head of the Cultural Revolution Group, and Hsieh Fu-chih, Chairman of the Peking Municipal Revolutionary Committee, called the representatives of the offending groups to a meeting in which Ch'i Pen-yü, the one surviving ordinary member of the Cultural Revolution Group, also participated. Chiang Ch'ing evidently absented herself and thereby escaped having to take part in what would have been an unpleasant task: that of conveying to Red Guard and revolutionary rebel leaders Chairman Mao's instruction that the attacks on the Premier should stop.[56] The campaign conducted against Chou's subordinates, as exemplified by the case of Ch'en Yi, was also to be turned down, and here too Mao took a hand. It was made known that Chairman Mao had gone over a collection of "black utterances" attributed to Ch'en Yi, as compiled by the "Red Flag" rebel group of the Ministry of Foreign Affairs, and had then remarked: "The material isn't black at all; he is by temperament frank and straightforward." [57] Finally, on October 17 a directive was issued which contained the statement: "All propaganda posters about the slogan 'Down with Liu, Teng, and Ch'en' should be banned." [58] As Mao observed, "Ch'en Yi . . . has lost twenty-seven pounds in weight; I can't show him to foreign visitors in this condition." [59]

Banning the slogan "Down with Liu, Teng and Ch'en" meant, of course, that Ch'en Yi was not to be placed in the same category as Liu Shao-ch'i and Teng Hsiao-p'ing, and not that those two leaders had been forgiven. Indeed, according to one report, Mao Tse-tung had in September remarked: "Personally, I sense the portents of giving up the struggle against the enemy, the struggle against the highest authorities in the party taking the capitalist road." [60] It is clear that he deplored the tendency of the struggle to expand in scope and thereby become diffused. "We must," he said, "concentrate our efforts on the repudiation of the handful of top party persons in power taking the capitalist road. . . . We must topple the top capitalist-roader in power, overthrowing him not only organizationally but politically, ideologically, and theoretically as well. . . . Only a mere handful are diehard capitalist-roaders in power, but . . . their influence and the poison spread by them are far and wide." [61]

"In treating cadres," he said, "we must have faith in the fact that over 95 percent of them are good or comparatively good." [62] This reiteration of faith in the fundamental goodness of the majority of the cadres was needed, of course, because considerable numbers of them would be required for the formation of revolutionary committees. As Mao now pointed out, "The correct treatment of cadres is the key to creating a revolutionary three-way alliance, consolidating the revolutionary great alliance, and making a success of the struggle-criticism-transformation in each unit." [63]

This brought the dominant attitude towards cadres of the party and the government back to that which had prevailed early in the year, when it had been asserted that they were "a treasure of the party." In addition, a number of directives were issued in the autumn which were reminiscent of, but in most cases stronger than, ones which had been promulgated early in the year but left unenforced during the spring and summer months, when extremism rode high. In February it had been decreed that seizure of power was to be carried out by the revolutionaries of each unit, who were not to form alliances for that purpose with outside organizations. That injunction had been violated, with the consequence that revolutionary organizations had coalesced into sets of hostile coalitions, bringing China to the brink of civil war. In October it was prescribed that factories, schools, departments, and enterprises must bring about revolutionary great alliances on the basis of individual systems, trades, and classes.[64] In March workers had been called upon to "strengthen labor discipline" and "carry on the Cultural Revolution outside the eight hours of work." In September they were also told: "In the units which have stopped production as a consequence of armed struggle, wages should be suspended from the time when production stopped to the time when it is resumed." [65] In February the party center had directed that university and middle school students, excepting those granted special permission, were to return to their own schools, and in October an order was issued which began: "Universities, secondary, and primary schools in all places are to commence classes immediately and without exception." [66]

It would be naive to suppose that such orders would be univerally obeyed. The preconditions for an early resumption of classes, to cite but one example, were almost totally lacking: the morale of teachers and school administrators had been shattered, the old teaching materials had been discredited, and students had become accustomed to doing as they pleased. However, the new directives at least told people that there had been a change of line. Since many of those who created disorders were responding to signals from Peking, the new directives were bound to have some calming influence.

The agreements being hammered out in Peking, to be viable, had to cover not only the distribution of positions within the preparatory groups and revolutionary committees for the respective provinces. They also had to commit warring sides to cessation of mutual hostilities, and they had to contain provisions designed to ensure against resumption of hostilities. In the case of Kwangtung, for example, the agreements provided for the dismantling of roadblocks, the demolition of fortifications, and the surrender of arms and military equipment. They also covered the evacuation of factories, enterprises, state organs, newspaper offices, broadcasting stations, hospitals, and schools, as well as rural areas, which outside units of one side or the other had seized and held.[67] These agreements worked well enough to make it possible to hold the annual autumn trade fair for foreign businessmen, which opened in Canton on November 15, one month late,[68] and to establish a Kwangtung Provincial Revolutionary Committee on February 21, 1968.[69] By this latter date new revolutionary committees had also been set up for the municipality of Tientsin and the five additional provinces of Kiangsi, Kansu, Honan, Hopeh, and Hupeh.[70]

While Mao Tse-tung appears not to have participated in the negotiations which led to these agreements, he did give support to the

efforts, of which they were a part, to restore peace and order. Moreover, the nature of his statements on the subject suggests that he sought
more than a merely temporary cessation of disorders. "This nationwide disturbance," he was quoted as saying, "is the last one of its kind.
The army is also disturbed this time. After this disturbance, the whole
country will be at peace and become the regime of revolutionary rebels." [71] At about this same time he declared: "Henceforth whoever
seizes guns is a counterrevolutionary." [72] He asserted further:

> Hereafter, whoever kills people or commits acts of arson . . . will
> be identified with the fascist organization. A simple ruling will hence-
> forth be laid down with the stipulation that whoever assaults another
> will be primarily held responsible for the whole course of events and
> the degree of their deterioration. From now on, whoever stops pro-
> duction commits an offense. If he foments armed clashes and draws
> production workers into them, he will be labeled for that matter. . . .
> After one or two months we must mobilize the masses to uncover bad
> people who have looted state property, killed people, or committed
> arson. As the proverbial saying goes: one reaps what he sows. This is
> true in all such cases when the time comes.[73]

Mao Tse-tung was determined to deal also with those elements of
the populace which might have taken advantage of the Cultural Revolution to "get into our ranks through cracks and to undermine our
socialist cause." [74] If what he termed "errant cadres and bad leaders"
were not reformed or purged, they might be included within the memberships of revolutionary committees and end up in positions of leadership within a reconstituted Chinese Communist party. Moreover, if
the schools were now to be reopened and if party life were soon to be
resumed, it was time to subject school staffs and surviving party cadres
to a final screening.

However, the purge which began soon after Mao Tse-tung's return
to Peking, and which became known as "the cleansing of the class
ranks," was loosely defined as to purposes, procedures, targets and punishments. As such, it may have reflected both Mao's general habit of
issuing rambling and unclear directives, and the particular state of
mind induced by his summer's experiences and observations. The Cultural Revolution, by removing in large measure the controls normally
exercised over the populace, revealed how little the basic attitudes
of the people had been changed by seventeen years of Communist indoctrination and party rule. How was Mao Tse-tung to explain their
behavior? Their split into two mutually hostile factions must be due
to the fact that they had been misled by capitalist-roaders within the
party, including party cadres who had been imprisoned by the Kou-
mintang, and who had secretly turned renegade in repayment for
their release. The troubles which plagued the country must have been

caused in large part by unreformed class enemies—including those among the populace who had been inherited from the old society and had been assigned to the categories of landlord, rich peasant, counter-revolutionaries, bad elements and rightists, and who had not changed their class stand.[75]

Indeed, Mao Tse-tung appears to have seen himself as facing hidden enemies left behind on the mainland by the Kuomintang. "Emperors were extinct in France long ago," he pointed out, "but royalist forces still exist in France." [76] The Kuomintang was gone from the mainland, but Kuomintang forces were not. The Cultural Revolution itself, he was reported to have said early in 1968, was "a continuation of the prolonged struggle waged by the Chinese Communist party and the masses of revolutionary people under its leadership against the Kuomintang reactionaries, a continuation of the class struggle between the proletariat and the bourgeoisie." [77]

Chiang Ch'ing made some remarks, at a forum held on the evenings of November 9 and November 12, 1967, which deserve to be cited in this general context. In a speech which she made during this forum she alluded to the fifty days from the latter part of May to the middle of July 1966, when the party center, under the control of Liu Shao-ch'i and Teng Hsiao-p'ing, had sent out the work teams to conduct the Cultural Revolution; to the seventeen years from 1949, when the regime had been established, up to 1966, when the Cultural Revolution had begun; and to the 1930s and the 1920s, which had been years of struggle within the party and between the party and the Kuomintang. "Accounts must be settled," she said, "for the fifty days, for the seventeen years, and for the nineteen-thirties as well—the roots go a long way back. . . . The work teams in effect were meant to protect the seventeen years, to protect the thirties, even to protect the twenties." [78]

25
A Gift of Mangoes

In Chiang Ch'ing's speech at the Peking forum on literature and art, during which she had discussed the need to settle the
accounts of even the distant past, she also expressed the opinion that
the Cultural Revolution had not been carried out satisfactorily in
literary and artistic circles. It was necessary, she declared, to make a
penetrating investigation of those circles, and to deal harshly with the
many hidden enemies which they contained. The day after the forum
ended an order was issued, in the names of the Central Committee and
the Cultural Revolution Group, directing that Chiang Ch'ing's speech
should be rebroadcast, studied, discussed, and implemented in all units
of the country's literary and artistic circles, and in the mass organizations of all educational institutions, from the level of the universities
down to that of the primary schools.[1]

This order, coming on the heels of Mao's remarks about punishing people who had been guilty of looting, killing, and arson, signaled
a new extension of the Cultural Revolution. Heretofore the populace
had been used to purge the party and the government. Now the purge
was to be extended to the populace as well. And as with other new
departures during the Cultural Revolution, it was in Shanghai that
its application began.

Shanghai radio began reporting, at least as early as December 6,
that the purges of this new phase were already under way, and on
December 27, Chang Ch'un-ch'iao issued instructions concerning the
cleansing of class ranks among Shanghai's middle school teachers. In
April 1968 the Shanghai press was urging that leading figures in the
field of the drama in general, and the Peking-style opera in particular,
should be subjected to "relentless criticism and ruthless struggle
without showing any mercy." [2] It would indeed appear that some of
them were treated harshly: a British subject, who was imprisoned in
Shanghai through most of 1968 and 1969, subsequently revealed that
his fellow prisoners had included a male ballet dancer and "the
capitalist-road girls" from Shanghai's Peking opera troupe.[3]

After the close of the November forum on literature and art,
Chiang Ch'ing evidently left Peking for the scenic city of Hangchow,
not far from Shanghai, where Mao Tse-tung and Lin Piao had winter

residences. Chou En-lai explained: "Arduous struggle has impaired Comrade Chiang Ch'ing's health, but spiritual consolation and inspiration will certainly make up for the loss." [4]

Presumably the solace and inspiration were to come from her cultural interests, and it does appear that she found the time, during a year-end period of semiretirement, to push forward a project related to the stage in which she assertedly had been interested as early as 1964. In that year, Chiang Ch'ing, supposedly "in order to smash the vicious intrigues of China's Khrushchev to make use of the piano to help restore capitalism," had handed down an instruction which called for the use of the piano to accompany Peking operas on contemporary themes. However, as *People's Daily* later explained, "this instruction was withheld from the revolutionary artists by the handful of counterrevolutionary revisionists in the field of culture." [5]

The name "opera" fails to suggest the full reality of the traditional Chinese theater, for Peking opera is a unique synthesis of ballet, acrobatics, spoken drama, and operatic arias. In this theater, facial makeup ranges from ordinary rouge and powder to elaborately painted facial designs which identify roles and indicate character; symbolism and pantomime replace realistic props and naturalistic sets; themes are historical; and costumes are the colorful dress of an earlier epoch. In consequence of the Peking opera's reliance upon symbols and pantomime, the spectator is led to bring his own imagination into fullest play, thereby becoming a participant who is transported into the different world of another age. The instruments of the orchestra must be capable not only of hypnotic rhythms, which may be broken by a terrific din of clashing cymbals, but also of the precise timing required for the swift and complicated dances used to simulate military combat, and of the dry tones appropriate for the accompaniment of high-pitched arias. This singing, introduced at particularly dramatic moments, heightens tension and penetrates the low hubbub which is normal to a Chinese audience which is enjoying itself.[6]

The changes which Chiang Ch'ing had already introduced involved the use of plays based on modern, revolutionary themes, and employing contemporary dress, realistic props and naturalistic scenery, all at the expense of traditional elements in what had been a harmonious whole. This further change, introduced at her behest in 1968, divorced the high-pitched aria from the rasping-toned *hu-ch'in,* or two-stringed Chinese fiddle, and coupled it to the foreign piano, an instrument of quite different character and capabilities. Change always has its detractors, Chiang Ch'ing was herself controversial, and the combination elicited in Shanghai what was subsequently described as a "smash the piano movement." [7]

We do not know whether Chiang Ch'ing's absence of that winter from Peking was voluntary, induced or enforced; to what extent her illness was actual rather than political; nor, insofar as it may have been real, how much was physical and what part was of the mind and spirit. While she was recuperating in Hangchow, she later asserted, she was "subjected to persecution." In apparent references to public security bureau personnel in Chekiang Province, in which Hangchow is situated, she charged that "they" had installed secret monitoring devices in the residence of Chairman Mao, in which she presumably had lived, as well as in that of Vice Chairman Lin. "They shadowed me," she added. "They followed me every step I took. They are virtually worse than the Kuomintang reactionaries of the past." [8]

When Mao Tse-tung had appeared in public, even in earlier and more normal times, he unquestionably had been protected by numbers of inconspicuous but carefully placed security guards.[9] The winter of 1967–1968 was no normal period; it would have been strange if the authorities in Chekiang had not taken careful precautions to ensure that the chairman's wife came to no harm while she was in their area of responsibility; and such precautions were bound to infringe upon her privacy and hamper her freedom of movement. Such are the facts of life, as it is lived by those at the summits of power, and it is hard to believe that Chiang Ch'ing was ignorant of them. Accordingly, one might be tempted to see this as a period during which elements of Chiang Ch'ing's nature became exaggerated, with the consequence that she entertained paranoid suspicions and delusions of persecution.

However, it is quite possible that Chiang Ch'ing was indeed subjected, while in Hangchow, to a surveillance which was conducted out of a mix of motives, not all of them friendly. She had but recently crossed swords with China's military establishment, and had been worsted. If military leaders had played a role in banishing her from Peking, in the hope of minimizing the harm she might do their interests, they must also have wanted to keep track of her activities while she was in Hangchow. The chain of command went from military leaders in Peking to the headquarters of the Chekiang Military District in Hangchow; for purposes of a political nature, it went to the ranking political commissar of that headquarters. The first political commissar of the Chekiang Provincial Military District had controlled the province's security apparatus, in his concurrent capacity as first secretary of the party's provincial committee, until the PLA had been made responsible for directing public security work. He evidently continued controlling it thereafter in his military, rather than his civilian, capacity. If he was antagonistic to Chiang Ch'ing, he had his organizational and personal reasons. It was not merely that Chiang Ch'ing had repeatedly called for smashing the old system of police, prosecutors, and courts. His own wife had been president of the Chekiang People's Court; she had committed suicide earlier in the Cultural Revolution; and Chiang Ch'ing was its high inquisitor. Given all the circumstances, it would not be strange if Chiang Ch'ing felt uncomfortable under the surveillance of the apparatus which he controlled, and suspicious of its purposes.[10]

There are two bits of evidence to suggest that the period of Chiang Ch'ing's presumed exile from the capital was one during which Mao Tse-tung's own political health was questionable. The first bit of evidence relates to a phrase about the "absolute authority of Chairman Mao," which had been in use, in both official and unofficial circles, for at least the several preceding months. On December 17, Mao Tse-tung repudiated it in a statement which began: "It was not logical to create the term 'absolute authority.' There has never been a unique authority. All authorities are relative." [11]

The second bit of evidence, indicating that Mao Tse-tung was not vigorously affirming his paramount authority during this period, is photographic. As is well known, the order in which leaders of Communist countries line up on public occasions is watched carefully as an indicator of their relative positions. Moreover, the Chinese, as a people, are especially sensitive to the external signs by which status is given recognition, and Mao Tse-tung is no exception to the rule. He appeared with other top leaders on December 31, 1967, at one of the vast receptions which had become common since the inauguration of Mao-thought study classes, and a photograph taken on that occasion was published in the January 2, 1968, issue of *People's Daily*. In contrast to numerous other photographs covering comparable occasions,[12] it showed Lin Piao standing front and center, rather than Mao Tse-tung, with Chou En-lai on Lin's right hand and Mao on his left. The lineup seemed to reflect an assertion that Lin Piao and his army now occupied the preeminent position in China; to suggest that Chou En-lai, the leader of the government, was his ally and right-hand man; and to imply that Mao Tse-tung was paying them deference.

Any other explanation would seem to assume that all three leaders, each of whom had had almost two decades of practice in assuming his proper position in the photographs which are taken on public occasion, had simultaneously been guilty of inadvertence. It would also seem to assume that the editors and staff of *People's Daily* had similarly been guilty of oversight, perhaps in the rush of getting their paper out. But considering the personality cult which surrounded Mao Tse-tung, putting him in third place must have seemed little short of sacrilege, and a photograph which so portrayed him would surely have caught the editors' attention. Finally, the period between December 31, when the photograph was taken, and January 2, the date of its publication, left them time enough to ponder and take soundings. Accordingly, the publication of this photograph, in *People's Daily* and other journals,[13] leads one to surmise that high military leaders in Peking wished to tell the country that the position of the army had become paramount.

Chiang Ch'ing must have returned to Peking not long after this, for between January 21 and January 24, 1968, she and three other members of the Cultural Revolution Group—Ch'en Po-ta, K'ang Sheng, and Yao Wen-yüan—participated with Chou En-lai and officers of the three armed services in an important seminar. This seminar was held for representatives from Hunan who had been brought to the capital to attend study classes in the thought of Mao Tse-tung, and to participate in the negotiating sessions designed to lead to the formation of a Hunan Provincial Revolutionary Committee. A preparatory group, which was the precursor of such a committee, had already been formed, but it was under vigorous attack from a coalition of over twenty Red Guard organizations, known as the Sheng-wu-lien, which had been established the previous October.[14] During this period the thrust of the left was toward gaining control of the new revolutionary committees.[15] The Sheng-wu-lien professed to belong to the ultraleft, and to be opposed to the establishment of the new committees.

If we are to take at face value the program of the Sheng-wu-lien, a set of resolutions which it had adopted late in 1967, and a long analysis which had been put out in its name early in the new year,[16] its leaders saw Chou En-lai as the representative of a new class. This new class was composed of party bureaucrats, "Red Capitalists" whose special privileges had been based upon the oppression and exploitation of the people. Some of them had been forced to step aside, but the establishment of revolutionary committees was leading to their reinstatement. The high point of the Cultural Revolution had been "the great August local revolutionary war," when gun-seizing had been "a countrywide movement" and the cities had been in a state of "armed mass dictatorship." This period had been brief because "the capitalist bureaucrat class in the party and the army had begun to carry out sabotage against the Central Cultural Revolution Group in August and September." The consequence was that "everything remains the same after so much ado."

The setback of the previous September, the authors of Sheng-wu-lien's analysis held, stemmed in part from a failure to apply the Cultural Revolution to the field armies. "It is now seen," they held, "that a revolutionary war in the country is necessary if the revolutionary

people want to overcome the armed red capitalist class." As Ch'i
Pen-yü had pointed out, the experience of the Cultural Revolution
during 1967 had been summed up in the speech which Chiang Ch'ing
had made at the forum of November 9 and November 12, 1967. It had
"announced the beginning of a new stage, unparalleled in history, in
which the great Cultural Revolution had entered. . . . It tells us that
the real revolution, the revolution to negate the past seventeen years,
has basically not yet begun, and that we should now enter the stage
of tackling the fundamental questions of China's revolution." What
society needed was "overthrow of the rule of the new bureaucratic
bourgeoisie, thorough smashing of the old state machinery, realization
of a redistribution of assets and power, and establishment of a new
society—the 'People's Commune of China.' "

The Sheng-wu-lien had invoked the names of the Cultural Revolution Group, its Deputy Leader Chiang Ch'ing, and Ch'i Pen-yü, one
of its members, in behalf of an analysis which denigrated both Chou
En-lai and leaders of the PLA, and which rejected the revolutionary
committees. Unless the leaders of the Cultural Revolution Group
disavowed the Sheng-wu-lien and its analysis, it was likely to be assumed that there was a split between that group and the other two
elements of Mao Tse-tung's center. This would be bound to hamper
Chou En-lai in his efforts to obtain the participation of the leaders of
mass organizations as one of the three elements of the revolutionary
committees which he was endeavoring to set up. Since the Sheng-wu-
lien was a Hunanese mass organization, a seminar for representatives
from Hunan provided the most appropriate forum before which the
leaders of the Cultural Revolution Group might repudiate the Sheng-
wu-lien. On the face of it, Chou En-lai had the right to expect this of
them, for Mao Tse-tung had rejected key propositions which that
organization had advanced, and he had called for the speedy establishment of revolutionary committees for all of China. It was perhaps
with these thoughts in mind that Chou invited Ch'en Po-ta, Chiang
Ch'ing, K'ang Sheng, and Yao Wen-yüan to join with him and representatives of the PLA in a demonstration of solidarity and to address
the audience of representatives from Hunan.

K'ang Sheng started his speech with assertions which seem to
imply that he was depending largely on Chou En-lai for his information. "I know very little," he claimed, "about the great Cultural Revolution in Hunan. . . . However, I have read the program of Sheng-
wu-lien. The Premier told me that the full name was 'Hunan Provincial Proletarian Revolutionaries Great Alliance Committee,' and that
Sheng-wu-lien was the shortened form." K'ang Sheng then suggested
that the program of the Sheng-wu-lien was the same as one which

recently had appeared in Peking in a publication which he attributed to the May 16 Corps. It was to this "counterrevolutionary" corps, it will be recalled, that the members of the Cultural Revolution Group who had been purged during the late summer or early autumn of 1967 allegedly had belonged. Continuing, K'ang Sheng said: "I have the feeling that the arguments set forth could not have been written by middle school or even university students. Behind them were counterrevolutionary black hands." [17] The portions of K'ang Sheng's speech which followed these introductory comments were hardly effective as a reasoned refutation of the Sheng-wu-lien program itself; perhaps he did not intend that they should be. However, as an exercise in heaping verbal abuse upon the authors of that program, his speech could hardly have been outdone.

When it came Chiang Ch'ing's turn to speak, she conceded that Sheng-wu-lien had been guilty of some absurdities which had, she said, already been refuted. She then asserted: "It is not worthwhile to get excited over these fallacies. . . . We must not think that all those who have participated in Sheng-wu-lien are bad elements. This idea, I am afraid, is improper. I think that the masses of this organization are guiltless. Guilty are the few bad leaders. But not all leaders are bad elements. If we do not treat them differently, it is very easy for us to act contrary to Chairman Mao's teachings. . . . When you have returned to Hunan, you comrades must rally your spirit, brighten your minds and eyes, and carry the Great Proletarian Cultural Revolution through to the end!" [18]

Yao Wen-yüan, one of the two surviving ordinary members of the Cultural Revolution Group, was evidently the last to speak. He repeated some of the arguments advanced by his elders, made a reference to the "fated demise" of the May 16 Corps, and ended on a note reminiscent of that on which K'ang Sheng had begun. "The Premier," he said, "asked me to say something. So I have spoken these few words." [19]

Ch'i Pen-yü, the other one of the two surviving ordinary members of the Cultural Revolution Group and the last of them who had served on the editorial staff of *Red Flag,* was not present at the seminar, and he never appeared at any subsequent official occasion. In February, which is to say not long after the Hunan forum had been held, Ch'i Pen-yü was attacked in wall posters as a counterrevolutionary organizer and leader of the May 16 Corps.[20] This accusation, viewed against the background of the assertions which K'ang Sheng had so recently made, seemed to carry the implication that Ch'i Pen-yü had been behind the Sheng-wu-lien.

It seems likely that top army leaders had a hand in the campaign against Ch'i Pen-yü, and that it was launched in response to Chiang Ch'ing's refusal to condemn the Sheng-wu-lien. K'ang Sheng had expressed doubt that its student Red Guards would have been capable of the theoretical arguments advanced in its documents, and he had suggested that back of them there must be counterrevolutionary black hands. Someone of sophisticated perception must also have been responsible for the Sheng-wu-lien analyses dealing with the armed forces. Officers of the high command may have considered it insulting to be referred to as an armed capitalist class and outrageous to be threatened with overthrow through civil war. But the truly deadly threat to their power was implicit in the contention that the Cultural Revolution would have to be carried through to the end in the field armies.

The officers of the high command undoubtedly saw it as regrettable but understandable that the dependability of the regional and provincial commands had been degraded in the course of the Cultural Revolution. Those commands had been closely associated with the regional and provincial apparatuses of the party, and it was natural that they and the forces under them should be disrupted in consequence of the struggle against the party. But the high command still had available to it the centrally controlled field armies, which had suffered no comparable disruption. However, if the Cultural Revolution were to be carried through to the end in the field armies, then the high command might find that its power had been destroyed or usurped by the Cultural Revolution Group. In consequence, when Chiang Ch'ing suggested that the Sheng-wu-lien was merely guilty of fallacies, and when she asserted that they were not worth getting excited about, she was stopping little short of posing an open challenge to the top leaders of the armed forces.

On March 8 two vehicles, containing Peking Garrison Commander Fu Ch'ung-pi and a number of armed men, went into Chungnanhai and drove up to the headquarters of the Cultural Revolution Group. According to most accounts, they had come to arrest "some people," whereas another version had it that they "stormed into the Cultural Revolution Group to arrest XXX." In any case, they did not succeed, for "our respected Comrade Chiang Ch'ing then came forward and angrily scolded Fu the scab. The latter, believing he had Yang Ch'eng-wu's backing, went so far as to retort and hurl abuses at Comrade Chiang Ch'ing." [21]

It is hard to think of any single person connected with the Cultural Revolution Group, other than Ch'i Pen-yü, whom the military might have sought to arrest at that juncture, and who was of sufficient importance to be of concern to the acting chief of staff and to the commander of Peking Garrison District. However, the person designated by the three letters "X" cannot be positively identified, nor is it clear whether Fu Ch'ung-pi had come to make only one arrest, or several. Finally, it is unclear whether Chiang Ch'ing's confrontation with Fu Ch'ung-pi was purely fortuitous, or whether she had baited a trap by sheltering a person or persons whose presence in her headquarters would be intolerably provocative. Later in the month she was to comment, in the context of her subsequent skirmishing with Fu Ch'ung-pi, that "Wang, Kuan, and Ch'i were simply pawns," but it is not evident from her remark whether one or all of them had been present in her headquarters on the day in question.²² In any case, a fuse had been lit which led to the headquarters of the armed forces, and while it burned she could afford to turn part of her attention to other enemies.

In September 1967, about the time that Wang Li, Kuan Feng, Lin Chieh, and Mu Hsin were being labeled leading members of the counterrevolutionary May 16 Corps and removed from the Cultural Revolution Group, Chiang Ch'ing had alleged: "The 'May 16' assumes an ultraleftist appearance; it centers its opposition on the premier." It will be recalled that those members of her group had been blamed for employing a strategy aimed at undermining Chou En-lai by overthrowing the vice premiers and cabinet ministers upon whom he depended, after which they hoped to topple Chou En-lai himself. Chiang Ch'ing had not admitted responsibility for their attacks on Chou and his ministers. Instead, in talking of her former subordinates of the May 16 Corps, she had asserted: "They had collected black material against me in the past, but only now have I discovered this." The accusations made against Ch'i Pen-yü in February of 1968 were virtually identical to those which had been made the year before against his colleagues: he had worked for the overthrow of Premier Chou En-lai, Vice Premiers Ch'en Yi, Li Hsien-nien, and Li Fu-ch'un, and Li Fu-ch'un's right-hand man, Petroleum Minister Yü Ch'iu-li.²³ And once again Chiang Ch'ing was being portrayed as the innocent victim of a double-dealing subordinate. It was asserted that Ch'i Pen-yü had been criticized the year before, by Lin Piao and by Chiang Ch'ing as well; had pretended to be contrite; and had made a sham self-examination. But according to this explanation, "while overtly Ch'i Pen-yü expressed acceptance of Comrade Chiang Ch'ing's criticism, secretly he compiled black material against her." ²⁴

If Chou En-lai had accepted these protestations at face value, he might have had confidence that Chiang Ch'ing would not resume the attacks on his key ministers. He might also have urged the rehabilitation of his former subordinates, many of whom had been the presumably innocent victims of ultraleftist members of the Cultural Revolution

Group who had since been purged.[25] After all, Mao Tse-tung had but recently declared that ninety-five percent of the cadres were good or comparatively good, and had reiterated that the key to the establishment of the revolutionary committees was the correct treatment of the cadres. The movement for the rehabilitation of old leaders which had been initiated in February 1967, of which Vice Premier T'an Chen-lin had been the reputed leader and in which Vice Premier Ch'en Yi had participated, had quickly been brought to an end by the leftists, who had labeled it the "February adverse current."

On February 13, 1968, ninety-one high-ranking officers in Ch'en Yi's Ministry of Foreign Affairs—chiefs of divisions or ambassadors who had been withdrawn in 1966 from their posts abroad—put up a poster entitled: "Expose the Enemy, Fight and Defeat Him—Criticism of the Reactionary Slogan 'Down with Ch'en Yi!' " As the title indicates, this document was in large part a justification of Ch'en Yi and those of his leading subordinates who had been struck down, and a counterattack against the elements inside and outside the ministry who had assailed them. "The present central task," the authors of the poster declared, "is to drag out bad men, criticize the ultraleft trend of thought, and firmly grasp policy and discipline." [26] Apparently the "bad men" they wanted to see dragged out were revolutionary rebels who dominated a preparatory group for forming a great alliance within the ministry. These men took up the challenge, and issued a statement of their own.[27]

Chou En-lai's estimate of Chiang Ch'ing's intentions toward him and his ministers, and his reading of the political barometer, may be judged by the way he damped down this controversy. He declared that the poster represented rightist interference by the ninety-one signers, who pretended to be defending Ch'en Yi but were actually protecting themselves. He also made it clear to Ch'en Yi that he must take a stand against the poster, rather than become embroiled on the side of its authors and against the revolutionary rebels who dominated his ministry's preparatory committee.[28] Ch'en Yi obeyed. On March 6, he appeared at a rally, held in the ministry under the auspices of the preparatory committee, and made a speech in which he criticized his ninety-one supporters and made a lengthy recital of his own past mistakes.[29]

Chou En-lai had successfully closed off one avenue of attack, but a few days later Chiang Ch'ing reactivated the strategy of attacking Vice Premier Li Fu-ch'un through his subordinate, Minister of Petroleum Industry Yü Ch'iu-li. Li Fu-ch'un was chairman of the State Planning Commission, and Yü Ch'iu-li concurrently held the post of vice chairman of that body. The outbreak of the Cultural Revolution had found Li Fu-ch'un in poor physical condition, and the day-to-day supervision of the work of the commission was being handled by Yü Ch'iu-li. Vice Premier Li Fu-ch'un's continued political health was important to Chou En-lai, regardless of whether he was fit enough to oversee the work of the State Planning Commission, because he was the only politically active and loyal subordinate of Chou En-lai who was also a member of the Standing Committee of the Political Bureau.

It was only three days after Chiang Ch'ing had repelled the Peking garrison commander's invasion of her headquarters that she publicly called for renewed attacks on Yü Ch'iu-li. The occasion was a meeting of March 11, presumably called under the auspices of the Cultural Revolution Group, to which representatives from the various universities and colleges of the capital had been invited. Ch'en Po-ta, K'ang Sheng, and Yao Wen-yüan were present with Chiang Ch'ing; but people are apt to be aware also of those who are absent from an affair of this sort, and the one noteworthy absentee was Ch'i Pen-yü. Since he had been under attack as an alleged leader of the May 16 Corps, his absence was undoubtedly taken as indicating that the current line was still firmly set against the left. At any rate, representatives from Peking Medical College spoke of the "antiparty group headed by Wang, Kuan, and Ch'i," meaning the May 16 Corps headed by Wang Li, Kuan Feng, and Ch'i Pen-yü, and a leader of Red Guards from Petroleum College—an institution closely connected with Yü Ch'iu-li's ministry—expressed the opinion that opposition to Yü Ch'iu-li and the several vice premiers, of which the alleged leaders of the May 16 Corps had been guilty, constituted "bombardment of Chairman Mao's headquarters." [30]

This appeared to infuriate Chiang Ch'ing, who demanded to know the Red Guard leader's present attitude toward T'an Chen-lin's adverse current of the previous year, asked why T'an Chen-lin could not be struck down, alleged that Yü Ch'iu-li had been guilty of similar offenses, and charged: "You have not criticized Yü Ch'iu-li in the least." The Red Guard and his fellows, evidently assuming that the opposite of wrong must be right, and perhaps inspired by a remark of Chou En-lai about efforts to shake Chairman Mao's headquarters from the extreme left, countered with references to the "problem of 'May 16.'" This prompted Chiang Ch'ing to assert: "You still talk about 'May 16.' Do you know where you were sleeping when we began to oppose 'May 16'?" The present danger, she seemed to imply, came from the right, and from those who were seeking to revive the "adverse current" of the year before. At this point, Hsieh Fu-chih intervened to explain: "The object of the February adverse current was to overthrow the Central Cultural Revolution Group that held high the great red banner of the thought of Mao Tse-tung." However, neither this praise for her group, nor the shouts of "Down with T'an Chen-lin!" appear to have calmed Chiang Ch'ing. Expressing her indignation, she shouted: "I don't want to listen to you! I don't want to listen to you!"

It may be presumed, since Chiang Ch'ing was endeavoring to reactivate leftist activism in Peking, that she was attempting to do so in the provinces as well. Moreover, seeing how far she was willing to go in an open meeting, one wonders what she and her group may have been attempting to accomplish through covert action. During the days which followed her encounter with the Peking Red Guards, she and her associates attended a number of meetings with representatives from the provinces who were in Peking for study classes and nego-tiating sessions. At each of these meetings she and the others asserted that the main present danger throughout the country came from the elements of the right, which had been in the ascendant since late in 1967.[31] And from the transcript of one of those sessions, that with representatives from Szechwan, one can draw the inference that the Red Guards were going back on the warpath. At this meeting, Ch'en Po-ta queried top officers of Chengtu Military Region about conditions in that province. In reply, they mentioned that violent armed clashes, in which the students were taking part, had broken out in several places, and that double-barreled anti-aircraft guns had been fired in Chungking. Chou En-lai made a comment deprecating their use, but Chiang Ch'ing lightheartedly observed, "Anyway, eruption of fighting is all right, at least for practice." [32]

Meanwhile other meetings were under way, four of which were presided over by Mao Tse-tung himself,[33] which culminated in "a de-cision taken by Chairman Mao and Vice Chairman Lin," whereby acting Chief of Staff Yang Ch'eng-wu, Commander of Peking Garrison District Fu Ch'ung-pi, and Political Commissar of the Air Force Yü Li-chin were all dismissed. Under a parallel decision, Huang Yung-sheng, commander of Canton Military Region, was named PLA chief of staff, and Wen Yü-ch'eng, deputy chief of staff, was given the con-current post of Peking Garrison commander.[34] These decisions were announced and explained to the public at a number of rallies com-mencing on March 24, when Lin Piao addressed ten thousand cadres of the PLA, and culminating on March 27, when Chou En-lai, Ch'en Po-ta, Chiang Ch'ing, and K'ang Sheng spoke before one hundred thousand persons, a large proportion of whom were Red Guards.[35]

At this time the Red Guard organizations of Peking were divided into a leftist *t'ien* (meaning heaven or sky) faction, probably so named because it had Red Guards of the Peking Aeronautical Institute as the nucleus, and a more conservative *ti* (or earth) faction, in which those of the Peking Geological Institute were a core element. Leaders of the two factions sat on the Peking Municipal Revolutionary Committee, and each had its set of allies and enemies among military leaders and nonmilitary cadres within its membership. Nieh Yüan-tzu, a leader of the *ti* faction of Peking University, and Fu Ch'ung-pi, prior to his dismissal from his post as commander of Peking Garrison District, were both vice chairmen of the committee, and it was charged that they had plotted against Minister of Public Security Hsieh Fu-chih, who held the concurrent position of chairman of the Peking Municipal Revolutionary Committee, and who was presumably allied to its *t'ien* faction.[36]

This would necessarily mean that there had been a split also within the headquarters of the Peking Military Region, for Hsieh Fu-chih was its political commissar, and Fu Ch'ung-pi had held a concurrent position as one of its vice commanders. The top command of the People's Liberation Army had also been suffering from factionalism. Yang Ch'eng-wu, as acting chief of staff, had been meeting opposition and obstruction from Wu Fa-hsien, commander of the air force, and was being charged with having plotted, together with Yü Li-chin, political commissar of the air force, to deprive Wu Fa-hsien of his command.[37]

Chiang Ch'ing had probably wished to bring about the overthrow of Yang Ch'eng-wu and Yü Li-chin ever since the previous autumn. It will be recalled that both men, as well as Chang Ch'un-ch'iao, chairman of the Shanghai Municipal Revolutionary Committee, had been in Mao's entourage during his absence from Peking between July and September of 1967. They had participated in his conversations with provincial leaders, and Chiang Ch'ing undoubtedly held them partly responsible for the conclusions, so unfavorable to her cause, which Mao Tse-tung adopted during the late summer and early autumn of that year. At any rate, a leftist campaign against Chang Ch'un-ch'iao was begun in Shanghai at about the same time that Yang Ch'eng-wu and Yü Li-chin were being dismissed in Peking.[38]

It must have been clear to those attending the rallies in Peking that Chiang Ch'ing had scored a victory. It was not merely that the speakers told them of Fu Ch'ung-pi's attempt to make arrests at her headquarters, and that Yang Ch'eng-wu had been responsible for it. It must also have been evident from the thinness of the rest of the case advanced against Yang Ch'eng-wu and Fu Ch'ung-pi, a failure to cite convincing evidence to back up charges that Yü Li-chin had been guilty of wrongdoing, and elaborate eulogies which Lin Piao and Chou En-lai paid to Chiang Ch'ing in the speeches which they made at the rallies.

It is apparent from accounts of the March 27 rally that there was no general and spontaneous enthusiasm for the purges which it had been called to celebrate, and that feelings about Chiang Ch'ing among the Red Guards of Peking were decidedly mixed. In her own speech, she admitted that those at some schools had declared that they would like to fry her in oil, or strangle her. As though thumbing her nose at them, she remarked, "When I have time I'll go and let them fry me in oil." Then during Chou En-lai's eulogy of Chiang Ch'ing, Vice Premier Hsieh Fu-chih interrupted with a prolonged shouting of slogans: "Down with all counterrevolutionaries who persecuted Comrade Chiang Ch'ing! Learn from Comrade Chiang Ch'ing! Salute Comrade Chiang Ch'ing! Vow to defend Comrade Chiang Ch'ing till death! Drag out the counterrevolutionaries who persecuted Chiang Ch'ing! Smash the dog's head of anyone who opposes Comrade Chiang Ch'ing." [39] Before a united and enthusiastic audience, one or two such slogans would have brought an answering roar. At this rally, the audience was so divided that fighting broke out during which someone stabbed Nieh Yüan-tzu, who had put up the first big-character poster of the Cultural Revolution, and a deputy commander of the Peking Garrison District was injured while trying to put a stop to the fighting.[40]

If Chiang Ch'ing was repaying Chou En-lai for the deference he had been showing her, when it came her turn to speak at the March 27 rally, she repaid him in somewhat different coin. It was confusing black and white, she declared, to say that those who opposed Yü Ch'iu-li were opposing the premier and the chairman. As a matter of fact, she said, Yü Ch'iu-li was a trusted henchman of Ho Lung—and Ho Lung, it will be recalled, had been purged for alleged crimes which included plotting a military coup against Chairman Mao.

The leaders of the Revolutionary Committee in the State Planning Commission, it would appear, were more responsive to Chiang Ch'ing's wishes than the Red Guards of Petroleum College had been. On April 7 Chou En-lai and Vice Premier Li Fu-ch'un found themselves facing representatives of that committee who demanded that Yü Ch'iu-li be submitted to struggle sessions which they proposed to conduct. Chou En-lai protested that the work of the commission could not stop for a single day, that nobody else of comparable ability was available to supervise its work, and that Yü Ch'iu-li had a heart ailment. In spite of all this he agreed in the end, but stipulated that the struggle meetings should occur no oftener than three times a week, and should not last longer than half a day.[41]

Since this was a victory for Chiang Ch'ing, gained at the expense not only of Yü Ch'iu-li, but also of Li Fu-ch'un, it is not surprising that she soon began to appear on public occasions in the fifth place which Li Fu-ch'un had previously occupied. At the same time, Li Fu-ch'un's name began to appear, in accounts of official affairs, with the names of ordinary members of the Political Bureau, suggesting that he had been demoted from its Standing Committee, and Yü Ch'iu-li's name was placed by itself, at the end of official lists, as one who was also present.[42]

Lin Piao may have assumed, when the changes were made in his top command toward the end of March, that his overall position was suffering little damage. Yang Ch'eng-wu had been Lin Piao's long-time subordinate; however, Huang Yung-sheng, his successor, had also come up through Lin Piao's own commands, as had Wen Yü-ch'eng, who was succeeding Fu Ch'ung-pi as commander of the Peking Garrison. Moreover Huang Yung-sheng was being given the full title of chief of staff, despite the fact that he had long been under bitter attack from the left, whereas Yang Ch'eng-wu had been only acting chief of staff. Air Force Political Commissar Yü Li-chin, who was being dismissed, had been drawn not from Lin Piao's Fourth Field Army system, but from that of the Third Field Army, which had been commanded by Ch'en Yi.

However, the damage to Lin Piao's position might not remain limited if other dismissals followed in a chain reaction. Lin Piao undoubtedly had this possibility in mind when he declared, during his speech of March 24: "We should not oppose those who were under Yang Ch'eng-wu's command simply because we are against Yang." [43] Chiang Ch'ing also had in mind the possibility of a chain reaction, for she was reported to have expressed a determination also to drag out Yang Ch'eng-wu's backstage boss.[44] During the war against Japan and ensuing years of the civil war, Yang Ch'eng-wu's immediate superior had been Nieh Jung-chen, Lin Piao's deputy commander, and it was to him that Chiang Ch'ing evidently referred.

As chairman of the Scientific and Technological Commission, Vice Premier Nieh Jung-chen had, in 1958, become responsible for China's nuclear and missile programs. In 1967 a number of the leaders of the Chinese Academy of Sciences had been arrested, and its work had been disrupted; the Seventh Ministry of Machine Building—considered to be responsible for plants manufacturing aircraft, missiles, rockets, and their accessories—was thrown into turmoil; a revolutionary committee

was set up in the Scientific and Technological Commission itself; and
several of the commission's vice chairmen were overthrown. But the
attacks of 1967 had not been directed at Nieh Jung-chen himself. In
May 1968, however, another campaign was begun, both inside and outside the commission, during which even so high-ranking a scientist as
Ch'ien San-ch'iang, director of the Institute of Atomic Energy, was
accused of being a "capitalist-roader and secret enemy agent." Its highest ranking target, however, was Nieh Jung-chen himself. It was he, a
Red Guard paper declared, who had been the backstage boss of Yang
Ch'eng-wu.[45]

On June 24, Chiang Ch'ing's second daughter Li Min, who occupied a minor position in the Scientific and Technological Commission, put up a big-character poster entitled, "Bombard Nieh Jung-
chen!" It contained, among the charges leveled at him, one which
seems quite likely to have been inspired by Chiang Ch'ing herself: that
Nieh Jung-chen had tried to prevent the uncovering of the "An-Fan
sworn brotherhood."[46] The name "Fan" had significance which ran
deep into Chiang Ch'ing's own past.

"An" undoubtedly represented An Tzu-wen, long-time director of
the Organization Department of the Chinese Communist party and for
some years the government's Minister of Personnel. "Fan" presumably
was Fan Chin, who had served under P'eng Chen as vice mayor of
Peking, and as publisher of the *Peking Daily* and *Peking Evening
News.* These were two of the papers which had published the veiled
criticisms of Mao Tse-tung written by Teng T'o, Wu Han, and Liao
Mo-sha. When Director of Propaganda Lu Ting-yi had been the chief
victim of a great struggle rally on December 20, 1966, Fan Chin had
been one of the lesser luminaries who had been similarly punished.
About three weeks before Chiang Ch'ing's daughter put up her June 8,
1968 poster, An Tzu-wen had been denounced by name in *People's
Daily* as one of the top ten "party persons in authority taking the
capitalist road."[47] Charging Nieh Jung-chen with trying to suppress
facts about a supposedly secret relationship between Fan Chin and An
Tzu-wen, it would seem, was intended not only as part of an indictment of Nieh Jung-chen. It may also have been intended to involve
Fan Chin herself in deeper trouble and further punishments.

Fan Chin, it should be recalled, was the widow of Yü Ch'i-wei,
known—when an underground worker of the party, and later as a
government official—as Huang Ching. It was with Huang Ching that
Chiang Ch'ing had lived in 1933; he had deserted her, and he had
later married this other woman. During the war against Japan and the
ensuing civil war, Huang Ching had been a leading party official of
the same three-province region of north China which had constituted

the area of Nieh Jung-chen's military command. After the Chinese Communists had conquered north China, Nieh Jung-chen took the position of mayor of Peking, and Huang Ching became mayor of the neighboring port city of Tientsin. In 1957 Nieh Jung-chen, already a vice premier, became the chairman of the Scientific Planning Commission. In the same year, Huang Ching, by this time the minister of the First Ministry of Machine Building, became a vice chairman of Nieh's commission, and he held both posts until his death in 1958. It seems likely that Nieh Jung-chen knew Fan Chin well, both as the wife of a close and long-time colleague, and in her own right as well: she was herself active in party affairs in Peking, and became the director of the Propaganda Department of the party's Peking Municipal Committee as early as 1953.[48] And it was presumably this relationship which made Nieh Jung-chen vulnerable to the charge of trying to protect Fan Chin from further accusations.

Lin Piao undoubtedly realized that if Nieh Jung-chen had been the backstage boss of Yang Ch'eng-wu, then he himself was the backstage boss of Nieh Jung-chen, and he must have seen the hand of Chiang Ch'ing in the campaign against Nieh which was under way in May. But meanwhile his position was under a more immediate threat which she had helped create. Red Guards had attacked military headquarters all over China in the summer of 1967, in the wake of the Wuhan incident, declaring that they wanted to drag out the local equivalents of Ch'en Tsai-tao, and the same phenomenon had reappeared in the spring of 1968, under the pretext of dragging out local versions of Yang Ch'eng-wu.[49] At about the same time, fighting between mass organizations in a number of provinces—where it had died down or been suppressed in the winter of 1967–1968—had again flared up.

In April 1968, one of the more troubled provinces was Shansi. Because it was part of Peking Military Region, the fighting there became the concern of Cheng Wei-shan, its acting commander. Under an order issued September 5, 1967—the day on which Chiang Ch'ing had made her speech praising the PLA—the army had been authorized to use firearms against persons who resisted arrest and in self-defense. Nevertheless Cheng Wei-shan now took the precaution of seeking the center's specific approval for the proposed use of firearms in Shansi. He and Chiang Ch'ing were both present at a series of meetings held from April 6 through April 9 to discuss the problems of Shansi, and at one of these meetings she recalled her own speech of September 5, and upbraided him in the following language: "Cheng Wei-shan, you asked the center for the right to shoot and the right to mop up. You have laid bare your attitude. There are problems in a large mass organization of several ten thousand people. In my opinion you pub-

licized the September 5 speech with an evil intent. You don't cherish
warm regard for the masses. The question of southeast Shansi has
brought this to light: you don't love and care for the masses. You
launched a sudden attack against me. You, Cheng Wei-shan, must
carry out self-criticism. You merely publicized the September 5 speech,
but you don't love and care for the Red Guard young fighters. You
people must make a good review of your mistakes in writing." [50] She
then added: "Looting of arms is not a serious matter." [51]

Either in the late summer or the early autumn of the previous
year, Mao Tse-tung had declared, "Henceforth, whoever seizes guns is
a counterrevolutionary." He also had said that the disturbances of that
year would be the last of their kind. One asks oneself whether he was
unable to control his wife's activities, or whether he remained in ignorance of much that she said and did, in consequence of the reluctance of Chou En-lai and the others to come to him bearing tales about
her. However, it is also possible that he was simply repeating the sort
of behavior which had led Teng T'o to write his satirical essay, "A
Special Treatment for Amnesia." It will be recalled that Teng T'o
had commented, in this essay, that people suffering from this disease
quickly forget what they have said, go back on their word, fail to keep
the faith, and become quite capricious.[52]

In any case, the fighting which broke out in the spring of 1968
proved to be very serious. Moreover, PLA units of divisional or even
army size had been introduced into some provinces, including ones
in which the garrisoning forces had been allied to conservative organizations, and some of these troops from the outside had been specifically
assigned to the function of supporting the left. The stage had thus
been set for confrontations between major elements of the PLA, and
when fighting between leftist and conservative mass organizations
broke out, army unity was quickly and dangerously threatened.

The severity of the fighting can be judged in part from the assertions of observers and the contents of orders intended to bring it to
a halt. The deputy commander of the Wuhan Military Region declared, at an emergency meeting of the Hupeh Provincial Revolutionary Committee in which the two sides were represented, that the ammunition they had fired within the preceding several days would have
sufficed "to fight several battles in the war against Japan." It would
appear that even military aircraft had been fired on, for he added:
"Today several of our planes were damaged." [53]

In the northwestern province of Shensi—if a notice issued by the
center is to be believed—state banks and warehouses were robbed;
warehouses, public buildings, and homes were blown up or set afire;
trains, trucks, and vessels were robbed; weapons were seized; and

troops were subjected to continual attacks. It would appear from the same notice that at least one side had stormed prisons and labor farms in order to free the inmates and incorporate them into its forces.[54] In the southern province of Kwangtung, neighboring on Hong Kong, conditions deteriorated to a point reminiscent of the summer of 1967, and it was reported that rotting bodies in the streets of Canton had contributed to an outbreak of disease.[55]

The fighting in Kwangtung, however, was overshadowed by that which raged in neighboring Kwangsi. In that province the two hostile coalitions were the leftist "April 22," named after the date of its founding in 1967, and the rightist "Lien Chih." The leftist April 22 was composed very largely of Red Guards and other so-called intellectual elements, some of them from outside the province; the rightist Lien Chih also contained students, especially in the leadership, but it depended heavily on militia drawn from among the workers and the peasants. The April 22 was supported by the 141st division, the Lien Chih by the Kwangsi Provincial Military District. The railway workers were split between the two sides, so transport broke down when fighting broke out. Tens of thousands of weapons destined for Vietnam were seized by the belligerents, and other thousands were handed over by one military unit or the other to the side it favored.[56]

The hostilities in Kwangsi raged for weeks in both the countryside and in the principal cities, large sections of which burned down or were leveled by gunfire. Tanks, artillery, and anti-aircraft guns reportedly were used against strong points, and gas shells or explosives were used to flush out those who were fighting from sewer ducts. The leftist April 22, which got the worst of it, charged its opponents with torturing, maiming, and killing captives; it asserted that the bodies of many of those executed at Wuchow were simply dumped into the West River, a stream which flows past that city and across Kwangtung Province as far as Canton, where it empties into the Pearl River. These assertions cannot have been without basis in fact, for that spring and early summer scores of bodies, some of them trussed up and mutilated, floated down to Hong Kong and Macao, on the two sides of the estuary of the Pearl River. Since the estuary there is about forty miles wide, it must be assumed that many other bodies simply floated by and out to sea.[57]

Kwangsi was only one of the provinces in which there was heavy fighting and where the PLA was divided, with major military units each backing a different coalition, or with the ranking army officers of the regional or provincial headquarters divided into hostile factions.[58] By the early days of June, Lin Piao must have become greatly concerned, for at this time he is reported to have instructed certain

military commanders to put a stop to the fighting in their areas at all
costs, using military force for the purpose should that be necessary.
Lin Piao is also reported to have used special emissaries drawn from
the field to convey these orders, rather than employing headquarters
communications channels or entrusting the missions to officers regularly stationed in Peking. This raises interesting questions about the
loyalties of officers in PLA headquarters. But if Lin Piao was justifiably
concerned on that score, he was himself partly to blame. Air Force
Political Commissar Yü Li-chin had cooperated with the acting chief
of staff and had been dismissed; Air Force Commander Wu Fa-hsien
had blocked his chief's orders and gone unpunished, and in May he
had been promoted to the position of deputy chief of staff.[59] Clearly
the loyalty which had counted was loyalty to the Cultural Revolution
Group.

If Lin Piao moved surreptitiously at first, this phase did not last
very long, for on June 10 a regular instruction was issued which dealt
openly with some of the most basic problems which faced the PLA.
This instruction was designed to bring all forces back under his own
control, end the fighting, promote negotiations between contending
sides, and restore social order and economic activity. The central
forces which had been assigned to "support the left" tasks were declared to be under the direct command of the Military Affairs Committee, of which Lin Piao is presumed to be *de facto* head. Those central forces were directed to supervise local units engaged in "support
the left" activities, and to disarm any units which used force in resisting their orders. The central forces were also given the mission of
collecting weapons and ammunition in the hands of mass organizations, and if they met armed resistance they were to conduct military
operations as required to suppress it. They were also authorized to
make arrests and mete out punishments in the interests of the restoration of social order and economic production.[60]

This order was issued in the names of the Central Committee, the
State Council, the Military Affairs Committee, and the Cultural Revolution Group.[61] It contains a few sentences which suggest that the
Cultural Revolution Group was consulted: The PLA was called upon
to support the continued struggle of the revolutionary masses against
the "handful of party persons in power taking the capitalist road," and
to strike out resolutely against the "rightist reversal of verdicts"; there
also was a qualified injunction against applying political or criminal
charges against mass organizations. However, the whole thrust of the
order's operative provisions went against the grain of the interests of
the Cultural Revolution Group, as Chiang Ch'ing would have perceived them. Lin Piao and Chou En-lai undoubtedly could authorize

the issuance of such an order on behalf of the Military Affairs Committee and the State Council, but certainly not in the names of the Central Committee and the Cultural Revolution Group. It accordingly must be assumed that they had convinced Mao Tse-tung that issuance of the order was essential if the PLA were to survive as a unified force.

The assumption that such an argument was used is supported by an account of a message Chou En-lai was reported to have conveyed by telephone, on June 14, to the commander of the Wuhan Military Region, whose own headquarters was split into two factions. "At the meeting of the Central Committee last evening," he was quoted as having said, "the question of the army's stability was again discussed. The army must remain united at all times. . . . You must be alert because some people are trying to create confusion in the army. Some bad people are inciting struggles against the army with a view to undermining the army's stability." [62] And if doubt remained that Mao Tse ung had authorized the June 10 instructions, they undoubtedly were dispelled early in July when further orders, designed to help put an end to disorders and issued in the names of the four elements of the center, bore the endorsement: "Take action accordingly. Mao Tse-tung." [63] Once again China's Great Helmsman had made a 180-degree change of course.

The use of the name of the Cultural Revolution Group, as one of the four issuing authorities which purportedly stood back of these orders, did not mean that Chiang Ch'ing and the leftist Red Guard coalitions were giving up the fight. The propaganda campaign against Vice Premier Nieh Jung-chen, in which she showed her hand through her daughter's poster of June 24, was intensified. Red Guards of the t'ien and ti factions, each occupying some buildings on the campuses of Peking's colleges and universities, had for some weeks been engaged in siege warfare in which they wore helmets and improvised armor and used catapults to hurl tiles, bricks, and rocks against each other's fortresses. But late in June some of these Red Guards got guns and on July 3, K'uai Ta-fu, leader of the Chingkangshan Red Guards of the t'ien faction and a favorite of Chiang Ch'ing, initiated their use at Tsinghua University in a bloody clash during which fifteen students were killed.[64]

During July the representatives of the contending factions from a number of provinces were brought to Peking for the purposes of working out agreements which were to bring an end to their mutual hostilities and lead to the formation of revolutionary committees for their respective provinces. Some leaders of the leftist coalitions of half a dozen provinces used this opportunity to hold a secret conference during which they discussed the establishment of a national organization with its own radio communications network. This conference was held in the Peking Aeronautical Institute and K'uai Ta-fu, Chiang Ch'ing's favorite, was one of the leading participants.[65]

Chou En-lai and other leaders became aware, not later than July 25, that this meeting had taken place and what had transpired there.[66] One is led to surmise, on the basis of the events of the immediately succeeding days, that these leaders passed on to Mao Tse-tung the information they had obtained about the purposes of the meeting. On July 28, at three o'clock in the morning, Mao Tse-tung—who, like Stalin, had never lost the conspirator's habit of working at night and resting by day—called a number of the major Red Guard leaders into his presence and gave them a tongue-lashing. According to one account, he declared, with tears in his eyes, that they had let him down and disappointed the workers, peasants, and soldiers of China. At any rate, it shortly became apparent that a decision had been reached to force the dissolution of the Red Guard coalitions all over China.[67]

About forty-eight hours after Mao's meeting with the Red Guard leaders, tens of thousands of soldiers, workers, and peasants surrounded Tsinghua University; K'uai Ta-fu was put under arrest, and the university was placed under the control of a "worker-peasant Mao Tse-tung thought propaganda team." [68] In the days which followed, similarly named teams assumed control of universities, colleges, middle, and primary schools, and other institutions in urban areas all over China, and so-called poor and lower-middle peasant groups took over the schools in rural areas.[69]

The name "worker-peasant Mao Tse-tung thought propaganda team" is deceptive. As official accounts make clear, the teams contained army members and had PLA support; and since the PLA was the highest *de facto* authority almost everywhere, it seems fair to assume that army members assumed leadership over most of these teams. However the name, by omitting the word "soldier," was more in harmony with what was publicized as Mao's latest instruction. "Our country," he was quoted during August as having said, "has seven hundred million people, and the working class is the leading class. Its leading role in the great Cultural Revolution and in all fields of work should be brought into full play." [70] The use of the word "team" might suggest a relatively small body, but at major institutions they numbered in the thousands, with members organized into as many as a hundred or more subteams.[71] Finally, the measure of control they imposed could hardly have been achieved had they been forced to place primary reliance on propaganda. Before the year was out, two-thirds of Tsinghua University's fifteen thousand students had been cleared out and sent to settle in the countryside—and that is not something which so high a proportion of students do willingly.[72]

Because the schools were the home bases of the Red Guard organizations, control of the schools by the new teams made it possible to enforce the dissolution of the province-wide coalitions, and hence to ensure that no national front of such coalitions could be created. On the more obvious level, the teams suppressed the struggles by force between contending student factions; promoted the so-called great alliances which were supposed to submerge student factionalism in a new unity; and helped establish new leadership organs based on the three-in-one combination. They also helped enforce decisions which had been backed by one of Chairman Mao's most recent sayings: "All people who have had some education ought to be very happy to work in the countryside if they get the chance. In our vast rural areas there is plenty of room for them to develop their talents to the full." [73] Pursuant to those decisions, millions of graduates from middle schools and higher-level institutions, and other millions who had not graduated because their schooling had been interrupted by the Cultural Revolution, were sent off to the countryside and to frontier regions to begin what were likely to be lifetime assignments as peasants and laborers.[74]

In August 1966, the student Red Guards had been taken to a high place, shown the kingdoms of this world, and led to visualize themselves as the successors to the older generation of China's revolutionary leaders. Two years later Mao Tse-tung made it clear that they were to become not the leaders but the led. "The majority of the students trained in the old schools and colleges," he said, "can integrate themselves with the workers, peasants, and soldiers . . . they must, however, be reeducated by the workers, peasants, and soldiers, and thoroughly change their old ideology." [75] But even before this comment on the new role of the workers, peasants, and soldiers had been publicized, he had accorded them a more tangible symbol of his esteem.

On August 5, 1968, Arshad Husain, the foreign minister of Pakistan, who was on a visit to China, paid a call on Mao Tse-tung. It is customary on such occasions to bring as a gift something from one's own land, and Arshad Husain is reported to have presented to Mao Tse-tung a basket of mangoes.[76] In pre-Communist times, mangoes had been imported into China from nearby tropical lands, and the golden skins and red cheeks of some varieties helped make them welcome gifts. In those days, of course, red was simply the color appropriate to happy occasions, and yellow, as the color of gold, the symbol of hoped-for enrichment. In Communist China, red was also the symbol of the regime, and the stars on its flag were golden yellow. In consequence the gift must have seemed appropriate, and Mao Tse-tung may well have appreciated the thoughtfulness which undoubtedly led to its selection. It would appear, however, that he did not care for the taste of mangoes—or perhaps their aftertaste, which some detractors of the fruit profess to find reminiscent of turpentine.

The following day the New China News Agency reported: "Our great teacher and leader Chairman Mao yesterday sent mangoes, a precious gift he had received from foreign friends, to the worker-peasant Mao Tse-tung thought propaganda team . . . publicizing the great thought of Mao Tse-tung in Tsinghua University." [77] The following day the news agency reported that *People's Daily* had devoted its front page, and one other full page as well, to this news, and it quoted the team which had received the gift as writing: "When this joyous news spread on the Tsinghua campus, every one of us was overjoyed. We sang one song after another. We held in our hands the precious gift from Chairman Mao and looked at his portrait. Our hearts swelled and tears ran down our cheeks. We waved our red-covered book *Quotations from Chairman Mao Tse-tung,* and all our feelings were concentrated in our cheers: 'Long live our great leader Chairman Mao! A long, long life to Chairman Mao!' " [78]

"What we have been given," they subsequently explained, "is the invincible thought of Mao Tse-tung, a spiritual atom bomb of infinite power." They placed the mangoes upon a red table in the middle of the Tsinghua campus, where they attracted huge crowds of the revolutionary masses who pledged themselves "to turn Chairman Mao's concern for them into a tremendous force, inspiring them to . . . write a brilliant page in the history of the proletarian revolution." Meanwhile, some of the team's workers had held a meeting to discuss how the mangoes could be preserved so that future generations might keep Chairman Mao's concern in mind. They decided that formaldehyde was the best preservative, and they made a big glass container in which to place the precious gift, saying: "We must preserve the mangoes well. Let Chairman Mao's proletarian revolutionary line be engraved in our hearts forever." [79]

The joyous news soon spread to the workers and other revolutionary masses in Tientsin, Shanghai, and other cities, and they made it the occasion for the beating of drums and gongs, as well as for parades through the streets. It was also relayed to China's naval defense frontline, the border areas, barracks, and sentry posts, to ships at sea and airfields.[80] Some workers, teachers, students, and soldiers made pilgrimages to view the gifts, but not all could do so. And so some of the mangoes were sent to other cities where they were placed, under glass cases and with honor guards beside them, in the waiting rooms of airports and railway stations. Of course there were not enough fruits to permit all places to be so honored, and so sometimes replicas were sent instead.[81]

Evidently not all the mangoes had been preserved in formalde-hyde, for a food was processed from some of them, and it was presented at a special rally to commanders and men of the PLA stationed in the border region of Sinkiang. The publicity accorded this food from the hand of Chairman Mao evidently led five youths, who were about to leave Peking on job assignments with a rural production brigade in Inner Mongolia, to reflect that the waters of a canal in the southern part of Peking's forbidden city must have special properties, since they were close to the ramparts from which Chairman Mao reviewed pa-rades. And so they drew a bottle of water from this canal, took it with them on their trek, and presented it to their brigade leader when they arrived at their destination. There the peasants looked on with tears of happiness, for such a liquid could be no ordinary water. "It is," the Peking *Kuang-ming jih-pao* explained, "the sunshine and dew of the great leader, Chairman Mao." [82]

Although the five youths from the capital undoubtedly had won for themselves a special welcome, we cannot be sure that they happily took up their new life as peasants in a rude frontier area. We similarly cannot be sure that the leaders from the provinces, who participated in that summer's negotiations in Peking, were all happy about the compositions of the revolutionary committees which were emerging from those negotiations. Nevertheless, they made good progress, and by September 5, 1968, revolutionary committees had been established for the twenty-six provinces and autonomous regions and for the three municipalities of Peking, Tientsin, and Shanghai.

The setting up of revolutionary committees for all of China—or for what *People's Daily* described as the whole country except "Tai-wan Province"—called for a celebration, and such a celebration was held in Peking on September 7. Chiang Ch'ing was one of the speakers, and she skillfully avoided praise for the revolutionary committees which the rally had been called to celebrate. Indeed, she managed in her two initial sentences both to suggest that she had become disasso-ciated from the negotiations which had been going on and hence bore no responsibility for their consequences, and to convey a sense of her antagonism toward Chou En-lai, under whose aegis the rally was be-ing held. "It was this morning," she said, "that I learned of the plan to call such a grand rally in celebration of the establishment of revolu-tionary committees in all of China's provinces, municipalities, and autonomous regions. I was told on short notice to say a few words here." She then spoke of Mao Tse-tung as having issued the command

of July 27 to which the workers and soldiers had responded—a reference to the developments of July 28 and subsequent days, when the
teams of soldiers and workers had taken over Tsinghua University and
other institutions. She went on to praise the Red Guards for their
"tremendous contributions at the initial and middle stages of the
Cultural Revolution" and called on the workers "to protect the young
Red Guard fighters, help them and educate them." As though sounding the knell on her phase of the Cultural Revolution, and ending on
a note of devotional faith, she concluded: "We will still encounter
many things we do not yet understand. Therefore, we must follow the
teaching of our great leader Chairman Mao to guard against arrogance
and rashness, hold high the great red banner of Mao Tse-tung's
thought, and advance triumphantly!" [83]

26

Internal Consolidation
under External Pressure

In THE STORY which may have inspired the creation of Mao Tse-tung's Red Guards, the magical monkey was able to create many replicas of himself by pulling out some of his fur and crying, "Change!" The bits of fur, it will be recalled, then changed into myriads of smaller monkeys which helped the magical monkey fight his enemies. However, they were under his control, for by another incantation he could change them back into a handful of hairs, and put them back into place. But some of Mao's Red Guards, after fighting his enemies in the party for two years, had begun to consider the formation of a nationwide organization, and this might have given them an independent life of their own. This threatened rebellion of the small monkeys had to be quashed, and it had been—with the aid of the marvelous mangoes. Now the continuing purge, as well as the rebuilding of the party, would be conducted by other elements.

A few months before Mao Tse-tung had launched his Cultural Revolution, his French visitor André Malraux had remarked: "In the Soviet Union, it was the party which made the Red Army; here it seems as if often it was the liberation army which developed the party." Liu Shao-ch'i and others of the party were present at the time, and Mao had immediately replied: "We will never allow the gun to rule the party." [1] Now, two years later, the party, as an organization, still existed only within the People's Liberation Army.

In rebuilding the rest of the party, it would be necessary to draw upon the masses and the surviving cadres. This made it desirable to eliminate from the mass organizations undependable elements which had risen to positions of leadership in the course of the Cultural Revolution. At the same time, social order would be promoted by identifying and dealing with class enemies who had moved from their usual places of residence in order to escape surveillance, or who had escaped from labor camps. Meanwhile, the records of surviving cadres as reflected in their personnel dossiers could be reviewed, their performance during the Cultural Revolution considered, and decisions reached as to how each one should be dealt with.

Mao Tse-tung had suggested the movement known as the cleansing of the class ranks,[2] and it will be recalled that Chiang Ch'ing had called for its initiation in November 1967. However, no overall regulations and procedures for conducting it had been provided, and the consequences of this failure can be judged from comments made by Minister of Public Security Hsieh Fu-chih. At a meeting of the Peking Municipal Revolutionary Committee which he chaired the following May, consideration was being given to regulations to be applied in the area under the committee's jurisdiction, and he asked whether it would not be possible to insert in one of them the sentence: "Manslaughter is strictly prohibited." Too many people were committing suicide, believing that they were not to be afforded a chance to survive. And when a man is killed, he said, it will be difficult to remould his children. Citing the case of decisions reached by the leaders of production brigades in one rural county, concerning the cases of people there who had bad personal or family backgrounds, he said: "In ten brigades, the landlords, rich peasants, counterrevolutionaries, bad elements, and rightists and their children, including babies, were killed in one day." [3]

The sieving out of undesirable elements from among the surviving cadres was carried out by special-case investigation groups. For cadres serving below the national level, this was conducted on a province-by-province basis, and carried forward in close connection with the formation of the new revolutionary committees. K'ang Sheng addressed the prospective members of the Kirin Provincial Revolutionary Committee early in 1968, and made some comments intended to guide them in this work. He said:

You have a special-case group, and you have dossiers about this or that person. In this connection, if I may, I should say that you must hear a little bit of my experience. This task is a hard one. You can't take part in the vigorously developing movement; you have to shut yourselves in a room collating materials which are so voluminous as to make you confused. . . . As to whether a cadre is good or bad, we must take the responsibility for his political life. . . . In a certain place, there is an organization called "Corps for Catching Traitors." I think this name is bad. You are not a traitor, but if you are caught by it, you become one. . . . When investigating the material, one is always somewhat subjectivist. For instance, when catching traitors, one always suspects everyone and feels that this particular man is a traitor. If your thinking is benumbed, it is easy for you to think that way.[4]

The rebuilding of the party structure was to begin at the top, but before proceeding to create a new Central Committee, Mao Tse-tung called members of the old one back into session. He had been issuing orders in its name ever since the August 1966 plenum, and respect for form required that he should go through the motions of seeking formal approval for what he had done in the interim. This Twelfth Enlarged Plenum of the Eighth Central Committee met from October 11 to October 31, 1968,[5] just shortly after the completion on September 5 of the task of setting up revolutionary committees for China's twenty-nine provinces, autonomous regions, and provincial-level municipalities. The timing, however, may have been related also to international developments which posed a potential threat to the security of Communist China.

Beginning on the night of August 20–21, 1968, armed forces of the Soviet Union and four of its Warsaw Pact allies had invaded and occupied Czechoslovakia, in order to change the policies of its ruling Communist party. On September 26, *Pravda* had explained that "every Communist party is responsible not only to its own people but also to all the socialist countries and to the entire Communist movement." Each Communist party was free to apply the principles of Marxism–Leninism and socialism in its own country, but it could not deviate from those principles and still remain a Communist party, and no socialist country could be permitted to withdraw from the "socialist commonwealth" because that would weaken the positions of all the other members. Self-determination in the case of Czechoslovakia, *Pravda* asserted, might have permitted the approach of NATO troops to the borders of the Soviet Union and resulted in the dismemberment of the "socialist commonwealth." On October 3, this rationale, which became known as the "Brezhnev doctrine," was repeated with the full authority of the government by Soviet Foreign Minister Gromyko.[6]

Under what circumstances, Mao Tse-tung must have asked himself, would the Soviet Union and its Warsaw Pact allies, with their truly formidable armed forces, need to fear an attack from the west? As a leader who himself feared a two-front war, and in the context of the Brezhnev doctrine—which could be applied to Communist China as logically as to Czechoslovakia—the answer must have seemed obvious. In case the USSR were to become involved in a war with China to the east, Mao Tse-tung probably calculated, the United States would be presented with two options. It could either launch an attack on Communist China from the west, in collusion with the Soviet Union, or it could join its NATO allies in an attack on the USSR and the other Communist states of eastern Europe. If Czechoslovakia had withdrawn from the socialist commonwealth, it might have provided a corridor, for attacking forces, which extended deep into central Europe. Communists are prone to see the world in apocalyptic terms, and from such a world view the invasion of Czechoslovakia must have looked like an effort to protect the Soviet Union's rear as the prelude to a contemplated attack upon Communist China. In this situation, it is not surprising that the Chinese Communists now took a step to protect their own rear: On November 26 they proposed that the United States and China should resume their ambassadorial-level talks at Warsaw.[7]

It is clear that Chinese Communist leaders associated the move against Czechoslovakia with a Soviet military buildup which was under way just the other side of China's borders. Between July and October of 1968, the Soviet Union is reported to have moved missile and other units into the territory of its Far Eastern ally, the Mongolian People's Republic, to have built new launching pads near the Chinese border, and to have installed missiles there which had a range of between 2,500 and 3,000 miles. On September 16, while this buildup was under way, the Chinese Communists handed the Soviet Chargé d'Affaires in Peking a note in which they protested against numerous alleged intrusions into Chinese airspace by Soviet military aircraft. They charged that these aircraft had, during the period from August 9 to August 29, carried out reconnaissance, harassment, and provocative activities, they asserted that these intrusions had occurred just before and just after the "atrocious Soviet invasion of Czechoslovakia," and they alleged that the actions against Czechoslovakia and China were related rather than merely coincidental.[8]

The Soviet Union brought about changes in Czech policies through intimidation, and it subsequently endeavored to ensure the permanence of those changes by forcing out Czech officials whom it did not trust. Mao Tse-tung probably surmised that the Soviet Union, in case it intervened militarily in China, might do so in behalf of Liu Shao-ch'i and the other top officials of the party who had been purged. Although they no longer wielded *de facto* power, their *de jure* positions within the hierarchy presumably continued unchanged. For example, Liu Shao-ch'i still remained, under the constitutions of the Chinese Communist party and of the People's Republic of China, the ranking vice chairman of the party, the chairman of the government, and the commander in chief of the armed forces. Mao Tse-tung undoubtedly wished to discourage the entertainment of any hopes which his enemies, foreign or domestic, might pin on Liu Shao-ch'i and his fellows, and the October 1968 Central Committee meetings provided him an appropriate forum.

It is highly improbable that this so-called Twelfth Enlarged Plenum of the Eighth Central Committee was really a plenary meeting. No list of the participating members was made public, but if the number was about the same as of those on the rostrum a few days before, at the October 1, 1968, National Day celebration, then only a small minority of the full and alternate members were in attendance. Among the hundreds of persons identified by name as present October 1, no more than three dozen were members of the Central Committee.[9] But if it was not truly plenary, it was indeed an enlarged meeting of the Central Committee. Among those in attendance were the surviving members of the Cultural Revolution Group, principal members of the twenty-nine provincial revolutionary committees, and leaders of the People's Liberation Army.[10]

Mao Tse-tung, according to the communiqué released at the close of the session, had made a speech "on the Great Proletarian Cultural Revolution movement since the Eleventh Plenary Session of the Eighth Central Committee of the Party in August 1966." [11] According to a story which filtered out to Hong Kong, he also had discussed international affairs, and in the course of that discussion had depicted the USSR as representing an even greater threat to China than the United States.[12] This would have been a logical assessment, for the United States was no longer bombing installations in North Vietnam, and Communist China was withdrawing the forty to fifty thousand engineer and other troops it had been maintaining there for the purpose of keeping the railways connecting the two countries in operation.[13]

However, the communiqué did not make any such distinction. It described the Soviet Union and the United States as two antagonists who struggled against each other, but who yet colluded with each other. In this second aspect of their relationship, the communiqué indicated, the Soviet revisionists had given their tacit consent and support to United States operations in Vietnam, and the American imperialists had similarly consented to and supported the Soviet Union's dispatch of troops to occupy Czechoslovakia. It likened this relationship to the alliance formed in 1815 by Russia, Austria, and Prussia—the members of which intervened in the affairs of other states for the purpose of putting down rebellions and preserving the system of monarchial rule—asserting that the United States and the USSR were the would-be organizers of an anti-China "holy alliance." All this seemed to imply, of course, that the United States venture in Vietnam and the Soviet invasion of Czechoslovakia were intended preludes to an attack on China, from the east and the west, in which the US and USSR hoped to be joined by their respective friends and allies.

The communiqué also revealed that the plenum had received and ratified a "Report on the Examination of the Crimes of the Renegade, Traitor, and Scab Liu Shao-ch'i." If the contents of this report were to be believed, Liu Shao-ch'i had been arrested in 1925, in 1927, and again in 1929, while working in areas under anti-Communist control, and had each time been released in consequence of traitorous deals made with his captors. In 1936 he had "instructed sixty-one renegades headed by Po I-po, Liu Lan-t'ao and An Tzu-wen to issue an 'anti-communist statement' to surrender to the Kuomintang and to betray the Communist party." That same year he had "conspired with Chiang Kai-shek . . . and his secret service chiefs . . . to wipe out the Red Army and suppress the red regime." In 1946 he allegedly had got in contact, through an intermediary, with American Ambassador Leighton Stuart, and in 1947 he had married Wang Kuang-mei, "a United States agent sent to Yenan by the United States Strategic Information Service of Peiping." In May 1950, the document alleged, "he sent his brother-in-law, Wang Kuang-ch'i, to Hong Kong to supply the United States Central Intelligence Agency with much information 'of high value which was highly regarded by the Americans.' . . . Liu Shao-ch'i's crimes are so monstrous and extreme that death is too good for him." [14]

The plenum of course affirmed that all the instructions which Mao Tse-tung had issued in the name of the Central Committee, since its session of August 1966, had been entirely correct. It also adopted a resolution "to expel Liu Shao-ch'i from the party once and for all, to dismiss him from all posts both inside and outside the party, and to continue to settle accounts with him and his accomplices for their crimes in betraying the party and the country." Formally removing them from their party posts, which presumably would be involved in the settlement of accounts, would require the holding of a party congress, and the communiqué issued by the plenum held that conditions for convening such a body had been adequately prepared. Finally, those attending the plenum were presented with copies of the draft of a proposed new party constitution, prepared on the initiative of Mao Tse-tung, which was to be circulated for study and discussion preliminary to consideration at the forthcoming party congress.[15]

Minister of Public Security Hsieh Fu-chih, discussing this projected congress in a speech, had made brief mention of the eight congresses which had preceded it. The first congress had been held before the party had been built, and only two of the twelve participants were still around: Chairman Mao, and old Tung Pi-wu, a vice chairman of the government. Those who had participated in the next six congresses had been appointed rather than elected. Only those who had attended the eighth congress in 1956—the one which had elected the existing Central Committee, and which had adopted the current constitution of the Communist party of China—had been elected from the bottom upward. This time, Hsieh Fu-chih declared, the selection would start at the central level, as this would "result in a party Central Committee of Chairman Mao with a program of Mao Tse-tung's thought and his revolutionary line." None of the renegades should be reelected, though a few of Mao's other opponents might be included in the next Central Committee, just as his old enemy Li Li-san, and Wang Ming, leader of the Twenty-eight Bolsheviks, had been elected to the Eighth Central Committee in 1956, long after they had been deprived of real power. Chairman Mao, Hsieh Fu-chih explained, always liked to have at hand some "teachers by negative example." [16]

The Chinese Communist party professed to rule under a system of democratic centralism, a term embodying two contradictory concepts, and the constitution of the Communist party of China, as adopted in 1956,[17] apparently represented an effort to establish a balance between them. Under the 1956 constitution, the purported structure of authority was an inverted pyramid, narrow at the bottom and broad at the top, each major element of which was described as elected. For the country as a whole, the National Party Congress, which had come to number about one thousand persons, was declared to be the highest body. It elected the Central Committee, containing about one hundred full members and the same number of alternates, for a term of five years. The National Party Congress was to be convened once a year by the Central Committee; when that congress was not in session, the Central Committee was to be the highest body. The latter body, meeting in plenary session, was to elect the Political Bureau, the Standing Committee of the Political Bureau, and the Secretariat, as well as the chairman, vice chairmen, and general secretary of the Central Committee. The Central Committee was to meet in plenary session at least twice a year, to be convened by the Political Bureau. At other times, the Political Bureau and its Standing Committee were to exercise the powers and functions of the Central Committee, with the Secretariat attending to the daily work under their direction.

It was evidently intended that ultimate policy-making or policy-ratifying power should rest with the larger, so-called higher bodies, because the 1956 constitution provided that the lower party organizations were to report to them periodically, and to ask in good time for instructions on questions which might need their decisions. The size of the National Party Congress had become such as to exclude the probability of debate at plenary sessions, and to increase the likelihood that its work through *ad hoc* committees would be rigged. But the Central Committee, elected by it, was not too large a body for debate, and it was apparently intended to be a policy-making body.

However, the framers of the 1956 constitution, by specifying that the Political Bureau and its Standing Committee were to exercise the powers of the Central Committee when it was not in plenary session, ensured that the organizational pyramid would function right side up, which is to say with the smallest bodies on top, insofar as operational matters were concerned. But it is hard to draw a clear-cut line between policy and operations, for interim decisions and day-to-day operations often determine long-term policy. This contradiction ensured the emergence of a conflict between Mao Tse-tung and the Central Committee. Because it presumably is the chairman who determines when the Political Bureau shall meet, the Political Bureau which calls the Central Committee into plenary session, and the latter body which convenes the National Party Congress, Mao Tse-tung was in a position such that he could legally put off for considerable periods the meetings through which the so-called higher bodies might be able to exercise their supposedly supreme authority. He could do so indefinitely, however, only by disregarding the provisions of the constitution, and this put him in the wrong. At the same time, Mao Tse-tung was prone to issue from on high directives which might seem impractical from the nearby perspective of those who had to implement them. This resulted in the second contradiction, that between Mao Tse-tung and the top operators of the party apparatus.

The draft of the proposed new constitution, which Mao Tse-tung made available at the October 1968 plenum, was clearly designed to resolve in his favor the contradictions inherent in the constitution of 1956. It provided that the National Congress of the Party was to be held once every five years, subject to postponement or earlier convocation in special circumstances, instead of being called into yearly session; and the requirement that the Political Bureau should call plenary meetings of the Central Committee twice each year was omitted. No provision was made for reconstituting the specific elements of the party bureaucracy which had been casualties of the Cultural Revolution: the general secretary and the Secretariat, elected by the full Central Committee for handling its daily work, or the General Political Department, charged with the ideological and organizational work of the party in the army. There was, instead, a passage which read: "Under the leadership of the chairman, vice chairman, and the Standing Committee of the Political Bureau of the Central Committee, essential and competent organs shall be established to handle in a centralized manner the day-to-day party, political, and military work."

The statements that no individual was free of mistakes and shortcomings in his work, and that important issues were to be decided collectively—which had been inserted in the 1956 constitution—were omitted from the draft document. It did incorporate the formulation, contained in the still earlier constitution of 1945 but omitted from that of 1956, to the effect that the party was guided by Marxism–Leninism and the thought of Mao Tse-tung, who was now declared to have developed Marxism–Leninism and to have brought it to a completely new stage.

It will be recalled that Mao Tse-tung had declared: "I myself do not admit that there is any true election." The draft followed the thought of Mao Tse-tung in this respect, without abandoning the word "election." It specified: "Leading organs of the party at all levels shall be produced through democratic consultation and election." The draft also was not free of the contradictoriness which is so typical of Mao's character. It specified: "The plenary session of the Central Committee of the party produces the Political Bureau of the Central Committee, the Standing Committee of the Political Bureau, and the chairman and vice chairman of the Central Committee." Because the vice chairman is by definition the successor of the chairman, this could only mean that the choice of Mao Tse-tung's successor was to be made by that body through "democratic consultation and election." Yet the draft constitution also flatly stated: "Comrade Lin Piao is Comrade Mao Tse-tung's close comrade-in-arms and successor." It also provided that mass organizations must all accept the leadership of the party, while specifying that leading organs of the party at all levels were to accept the supervision of the masses, both inside and outside the party. A means was provided for resolving this apparent contradiction only insofar as concerned individuals within the party: they were to have "the right to bypass intermediate levels and report directly to the Central Committee and the chairman of the Central Committee."

There was an interval of five months between the close of the October 1968 plenum—to which the draft constitution had been presented for study—and the convening of the party congress which would be expected to enact it. In the interim, there were serious clashes between Chinese and Soviet troops along China's northeastern frontier. It is difficult to judge who started the first of these battles, which broke out on March 2, 1969, in the vicinity of a disputed island known to the Chinese as Chenpao and to the Russians as Damansky Island. However, reports that the Chinese won the battle suggest that they were at least well-prepared for it, and the aggressiveness which characterized Chinese behavior during the Cultural Revolution might lead one to suspect that they started the fighting. However, the Russians at least used a subsequent clash of March 15, if they did not initiate it, to carry out a reprisal and to give the Chinese a warning. They moved up heavy artillery units and launched a brief but heavy barrage against one or more targets deep in Chinese territory.[19]

On March 21, Premier Kosygin tried to use the Peking–Moscow
telephone link, which had been established in 1949,[20] as a speedy
means of communication between Soviet and Chinese leaders, in order
to discuss the border situation with his Chinese counterparts. According to a statement by Lin Piao, the Chinese replied: "In view of the
present relations between China and the Soviet Union, it is unsuitable
to communicate by telephone. If the Soviet government has anything
to say, it is asked to put it forward officially to the Chinese government
through diplomatic channels." [21]

In consequence of these developments, the Ninth Congress of the
Chinese Communist party, which met from April 1 to April 24, 1969,
was convened during a period of increased international tension,
tension which must have lent a sense of urgency to its deliberations. If
China were soon to undergo a serious attack, there would almost inevitably be a period of internal confusion; it was important that the
populace should know just who was entitled to be obeyed, and who
was not. During the preceding three years, almost every leader of national stature other than Mao Tse-tung and Lin Piao had been under
serious attack, and it was time that those who were to wield *de facto*
power should be given *de jure* authority.

The Ninth Congress had on its announced agenda, besides a political report by Lin Piao, only the revision of the party constitution
and the election of a new Central Committee.[22] It adopted as the new
constitution a document which is essentially the same as the draft
which Mao Tse-tung had made available for study and discussion the
previous October,[23] and it elected a Ninth Central Committee composed of 170 full and 109 alternate members.[24] This new Central Committee held its first plenary session on the afternoon of April 28, when
it elected Mao Tse-tung as its chairman; Lin Piao as its one vice chairman—there had been five for the previous Central Committee; a new
Political Bureau composed of twenty-one full and four alternate members; and a Standing Committee of the Political Bureau numbering
only five—Mao Tse-tung, Lin Piao, Chou En-lai, Ch'en Po-ta, and
K'ang Sheng.[25]

Because the Standing Committee exercises the powers of the full
body when it is not in session, and because the organs conducting the
day-to-day work of party, government, and army were to function under the leadership of the chairman, the vice chairman, and the Standing Committee, it is clear that a great deal of power had been concentrated in very few hands. It would also appear that Mao Tse-tung
and Lin Piao, as long as their coalition stood firm, would not need to
call the full Political Bureau into session very often, and should not
have difficulty in mustering a majority from within its membership

when they did; most of the members have long been especially close—personally, politically, or organizationally—to one or the other of the two top leaders.

Lin Piao aside, six of the full members and one alternate had been especially close—personally, politically, or both—to Mao Tse-tung: Mao's political secretary, Ch'en Po-ta; Mao's wife, Chiang Ch'ing; K'ang Sheng, the former head of secret police; Chang Ch'un-ch'iao, now chairman of the Shanghai Municipal Revolutionary Committee; Yao Wen-yüan, first vice chairman of that committee and, according to widely-credited rumor, the son-in-law of Mao Tse-tung and Chiang Ch'ing; Minister of Public Security Hsieh Fu-chih, who headed the Peking Municipal Revolutionary Committee; and alternate member Wang Tung-hsing, vice minister of public security, Mao Tse-tung's old bodyguard, and since September 1967, director of the Administrative Office of the Central Committee.

Seven full members and one alternate member were currently subordinate to Lin Piao as members of his military establishment: Huang Yung-sheng, chief of staff of the PLA; Ch'iu Hui-tso, director of its General Rear Services Department; Wu Fa-hsien, a deputy chief of staff of the PLA and commander of the Air Force; Li Tso-p'eng, political commissar of the Navy; Ch'en Hsi-lien, commander of the Mukden Military Region; Hsü Shih-yu, commander of the Nanking Military Region; Yeh Ch'ün, wife of Lin Piao, and since July 1968 a leading official in the Administrative Office of the Military Affairs Committee; and Li Te-sheng, the alternate member, who was commander of the Anhwei Provincial Military District. The first four of the seven officers mentioned above had a special tie with Lin Piao and each other: they had been officers under him in the Fourth Field Army.

The remainder of the Political Bureau, six full and two alternate members, constituted a less well-defined group. It contained Premier Chou En-lai; Vice Premier Li Hsien-nien, who was close to Chou both organizationally and politically; former marshal Yeh Chien-ying; party elder Tung Pi-wu, vice chairman of the government; the octogenarian Chu Teh, who had been commander in chief of the People's Liberation Army until 1954; and former marshal Liu Po-ch'eng, who had been a leader of the Second Field Army, also now aged and politically inactive. Two alternate members of the Political Bureau completed the list: Li Hsüeh-feng and Chi Teng-k'uei, party cadres who had become leaders, respectively, of the revolutionary committees of Hopeh, the province in which Peking is situated, and of Honan, the province immediately south of it.

About 40 percent of the 279 full and alternate members of the new Central Committee were drawn from Lin Piao's military establishment—a substantial increase, incidentally, over the approximately one-quarter of the previous Central Committee who were officers in active service. All of the officers who could be identified as the commanders or chief political commissars of one or another of the thirteen military regions were included. So were all the chairmen and most of the vice chairmen of the twenty-nine provincial level revolutionary committees, two-thirds of whom were officers of the PLA. Moreover, about half of the military personnel who became full members had served under Lin Piao in the past.

Approximately a quarter or more of the members and alternate members of the Central Committee might be described as civil officials, divided between ministers and other cadres of the government and civilian chairmen and vice chairmen of revolutionary committees. One might have expected—in view of the stress which had been placed on the system of the three-way alliance—that the remainder of the membership, constituting about one-third, would have been composed of the leaders of mass organizations. However, the only well-known leader of a mass organization to be included was Nieh Yüan-tzu, who had put up the first big-character poster of the Cultural Revolution and survived the knife attack of the previous year. A man described as founder of the Shanghai Workers Revolutionary Rebel General Headquarters became a full member, and a lone Red Guard from Shanghai an alternate. But this remaining third of the membership is a very mixed bag, ranging from Ch'ien Hsüeh-sen, who had studied and taught in American universities and served during World War II as director of the Rocket Section of the United States National Defense Scientific Advisory Council, to Paljihletai, described as a poor herdswoman from Inner Mongolia. Many in this group are identified as model workers and peasants, and some of them are persons about whom no information is available.[26] One gets the impression, in studying the list, that many of them were accorded membership more as a mark of distinction than in the thought that they might contribute to the consideration and resolution of government problems at the national level.

A comparison of the lists of members of the Eighth and Ninth Central Committees conveys some sense of the thoroughness of the purge to which the party leadership had been subjected. Only about 30 percent of the members and alternate members of the Eighth Central Committee survived to become members or alternate members of the Ninth. Because the Ninth Central Committee is considerably larger than its predecessor, the survivors from the earlier committee comprise less than 20 percent of the new committee.

One searches in vain, in the list of ordinary and alternate members of this new Central Committee, for the names of old enemies of Mao Tse-tung who might have been retained primarily to serve the role, mentioned earlier by Hsieh Fu-chih, of "negative examples." Li Li-san and Wang Ming, who had remained as members of the Eighth Central Committee, were not again included: Li Li-san reportedly had committed suicide,[27] and Wang Ming was in the Soviet Union, where he was writing polemical attacks on Mao Tse-tung.[28] Former Minister of National Defense P'eng Te-huai would have been an outstanding choice and presumably could have been included, but he was not. Neither were such prominent victims of the Cultural Revolution as Ho Lung, Lu Ting-yi, T'an Chen-lin, T'ao Chu, Teng Hsiao-p'ing, or Ulanfu, all of whom had served as full or alternate members of the Political Bureau and had been vice premiers of the State Council. Chu Teh had often opposed Mao Tse-tung, but he had always been too good-natured to be a bitterly aggressive enemy, and at the age of eighty-three he could not be counted useful as an opponent; his name was perhaps included for the sake of its prestige value. One should perhaps also mention vice premiers Ch'en Yi, Ch'en Yün, and Li Fu-ch'un, as well as former marshals Nieh Jung-chen and Hsü Hsiang-ch'ien—all five had been retained on the Central Committee. All had been attacked during the Cultural Revolution, all had been dropped from the Political Bureau, and not long after the Ninth Party Congress it became apparent that Ch'en Yi was no longer serving as minister of foreign affairs.[29] But none could be equated to a Li Li-san, a Wang Ming, or a P'eng Te-huai.

As the breakdown of the list of members of the Ninth Central Committee indicates, the military establishment was the chief beneficiary of the redistribution of power brought about by the Cultural Revolution, and as the accounts of its troubles should make clear, the members of that establishment did not share equally, whether as individuals or as groups, in the fruits of the Cultural Revolution. China specialists in Hong Kong have concluded that over one hundred high-ranking leaders in the Peking headquarters of the PLA, and not less than another two hundred from the regional and provincial commands, were purged.[30] In a large proportion of cases, those who moved up into key positions were officers with a record of service in Lin Piao's 115th division of the period of World War II or in his Fourth Field Army during the ensuing civil war.

The composition of the Military Affairs Committee, as it emerged from the Cultural Revolution, was less unbalanced. With P'eng Te-huai and Ho Lung of the First Field Army purged, its former leadership could not be represented. But Hsü Hsiang-ch'ien of the Second

Field Army remained on the committee, as one of the vice chairmen ranked below Lin Piao. So did Ch'en Yi of the Third Field Army; once reported to have been purged from that body, he evidently had been reinstated. However, the actual day-to-day work of the Military Affairs Committee presumably was being handled by its Administrative Office, a new or newly-expanded bureau. This office was headed by Huang Yung-sheng and included, besides four other high-ranking officers, Lin Piao's wife Yeh Ch'ün. Huang Yung-sheng and the other four officers were all veterans of Lin's Fourth Field Army system.[31]

In his capacity of chief of staff of the PLA, Huang Yung-sheng was being assisted by about nine deputies. It appeared that one from the First Field Army and one from the Second Field Army, both of whom had been appointed to their posts prior to the Cultural Revolution, were being retained in their positions. All the other deputy chiefs of staff, however, appeared to be officers drawn from among Lin's former subordinates.[32] Ch'iu Hui-tso, director of the General Rear Services Department, Hsiao Ching-kuang, commander of the Navy, and Wu Fa-hsien, commander of the air force, also were veterans of Lin's Fourth Field Army. Many changes had occurred in military commands, a number of new faces had appeared in key posts, and the incumbents of some remained to be identified. Nevertheless, the identities and former affiliations of eleven of the commanders of China's thirteen military regions, and of fifteen of the twenty PLA leaders who became chairmen of provincial revolutionary committees, were fairly well known. Eight of the eleven regional commanders and ten of the fifteen chairmen were veterans of Lin's Fourth Field Army system.[33]

In the latter part of 1971 it appeared that Lin Piao had fallen from favor, together with a number of his key subordinates: Huang Yung-sheng, Ch'iu Hui-tso, Wu Fa-hsien, Li Tso-p'eng, and Yeh Ch'ün. The reasons were not immediately apparent, but it is interesting to note that Mao Tse-tung had not been entirely happy about the dominant position the military had achieved. This was made clear in a speech which Mao is reported to have made in the spring of 1969, at the first plenary session of the Ninth Central Committee. One of the principal tasks which then lay ahead was the rebuilding of the party structure in the provinces. This rebuilding was to be carried forward on the basis of the three-in-one combination, and the reconstructed party organs were eventually to supply the core of leadership within the revolutionary committees. The details of Mao's speech were not made public, but he is reported to have indicated that there were "contradictions" between revolutionary committee leaders drawn from the army and the mass organizations. If the balance was to be restored, the power of the army, which had been guilty of excessive use of force and which had arrested "too many people," would have to be curbed and more civilian cadres and representatives of mass organizations would have to be admitted to the revolutionary committees.[34]

Mao Tse-tung represented this "contradiction" between army and civilians to be "nonantagonistic," meaning that it could and should be settled without recourse to the violent struggles used against "enemies of the people." It is clear, however, that the antagonisms between many army leaders and mass organizations ran deep, and that army leaders found it hard to stomach some of the civilian cadres most favored by leftist leaders in Peking. This was certainly true of the relationship between military members of the Szechwan Provincial Revolutionary Committee, on the one hand, and the civilian cadres Liu Chieh-t'ing and his wife Chang Hsi-t'ing on the other;[35] it was also true of Liu Ko-p'ing, the party cadre who had become chairman of the Shansi Provincial Revolutionary Committee, and military officers who had emerged as vice chairmen of that committee.

Part of the trouble stemmed from the facts that people of revolutionary bent are by nature flouters of authority, whereas army officers are used to being obeyed. The husband and wife who had been party cadres in Szechwan were probably both difficult characters. In the days when Li Ching-ch'üan was in authority there, she had been accused of a serious disciplinary offense, and her husband had been expelled from the party and jailed for two years. Liu Ko-p'ing's record similarily suggests that he was a strong individualist. He had disobeyed instructions in 1936, when a purported renunciation of the party would have resulted in his release from prison, and in consequence he had remained there eight more years—a demonstration of stubbornness which fellow Communists, believers in the thesis that the ends justify the means, were bound to consider quixotic.

At any rate, it seems likely that Mao Tse-tung's speech at the first plenary session of the new Central Committee contributed to a renewed rise of revolutionary sap, which occurred in the spring of 1969. By summer it had produced—in Szechwan, Kweichow, Shansi, Sinkiang, Tibet, and other parts of China—fruits similar to those of previous years. In Shansi, if a Central Committee directive of July 23, 1969, is to be believed, "a small handful of class enemies and evil people," who had "infiltrated" mass organizations, staged armed attacks on units of the PLA and seized their arms; destroyed railways, roads, and bridges and carried out armed seizures of trains; forcefully occupied state banks and warehouses; and used armed force to occupy territory and set up bases for counterrevolutionary purposes. In this directive of July 23, which was approved by Mao Tse-tung, and in a subsequent one of August 28, the military were again given strong authority to put down factional violence.[36] Once again, after so much ado, things were much the same as before—except that the left, having suffered the losses incidental to being put down again, was that much the weaker. In Shansi, for example, Liu Ko-p'ing had been removed as chairman of the revolutionary committee. His principal military rivals had also been removed, but the PLA as an organization had been the victor, for a military commander took over his position.[37]

Meanwhile there had been both internal disorders in the Sinkiang Uighur Autonomous Region, in China's far west, and clashes along its borders between Chinese and Soviet forces.[38] The combination probably would have made Chinese leaders nervous even under ordinary circumstances, given the restiveness of Sinkiang's minority peoples under Chinese rule; the tendency of their racial relatives across the border to extend them sympathy and help; and the long history of Sino-Russian contention over the area, control of which had passed back and forth between the two countries. In addition, Sinkiang contains China's nuclear test sites, and two projected tests were evidently in preparation.[39]

In consequence, the fighting along the borders of Sinkiang, which broke out in August, touched the most sensitive nerve in the painful relationship between China and the USSR—that which centered about nuclear weapons and the means of delivering them to distant targets. After helping put China on the road toward the achievement of an independent capability in the field of nuclear weapons, Khrushchev had become alarmed and had tried to prevent China from reaching that goal. When his colleagues deposed him, toward the middle of October 1964, they had accused him of "hare-brained scheming." It is not possible to say whether Khrushchev had entertained schemes against Communist China which had helped lead his colleagues to the conclusion he should be overthrown, or whether he had made threats designed to deter it from developing nuclear weapons. But it is interesting that the Chinese Communists had exploded their first atomic device on the afternoon of October 16, 1964, scant days after his fall from power.[40]

If Khrushchev's successors had begun their regime entertaining less worry about Communist China's nuclear program, their concern may nevertheless have come to match his as the Chinese program moved forward, and after Communist China had begun attacking them with the same invective which it had employed against Khrushchev. On October 27, 1966, the Chinese Communists had successfully test-fired a medium-range missile equipped with a nuclear warhead.[41] In February 1967, acting Chief of Staff Yang Ch'eng-wu was quoted as saying that Communist China would soon use a staged rocket to launch an artificial satellite.[42] This prediction was to remain unfulfilled until April 25, 1970,[43] but it suggested that Communist China was developing long-range rockets which might be used for military purposes. The inference that such might be the case received further support at the end of May 1967, when a report emanated from Peking to the effect that China's defense industries were being placed under military control, with Su Yü and Wang Shu-sheng as the two highest-ranking officers among those in charge. Su Yü had made a name for himself as an artillery officer, Wang Shu-sheng was a former director of the General Ordnance Department of the PLA, and they would therefore be logical choices to supervise a program which had the development of rockets as an important aim. Then on June 17, 1967, Communist China exploded its first hydrogen bomb.[44]

By 1968, it must have been apparent to Khrushchev's successors that the June 17, 1967, Chinese hydrogen bomb test had not been conducted merely for demonstration purposes, justifying China's admission to the so-called nuclear club; another atomic test involving the use of thermonuclear material was carried out in western China on December 24, 1967. The test was evidently unsuccessful, but it may have suggested that the time was running short during which the Soviet Union could move to prevent the Chinese Communists from marrying a hydrogen warhead to a long-range missile. If there was a rising crescendo of concern among Soviet political and military leaders, that concern would help explain their military build-up of 1968, during which they moved missile units into Outer Mongolia, built new launching pads near the Chinese border, and installed long-range missiles to which nuclear warheads presumably could be fitted. Since such weapons are not needed to deal with mere border clashes, moving them up may have been intended to convey the message that Communist China's strategic installations were vulnerable to destruction by the Soviet Union.

If the Chinese Communists had read the message, they had not been deterred by it. And if the USSR had been carrying out aerial reconnaissance over China, as the Chinese Communists were wont to charge, the leaders of the Soviet Union were undoubtedly aware, in August 1969, that preparations for additional nuclear tests were under way. The appropriate place for conveying another warning was Sinkiang, where the tests were to take place, and if the fighting along its borders that month was initiated by the Soviet side, it seems probable that such a warning was intended.

Chinese Communist leaders may have wished, in these circumstances, to reduce the level of Sino-Soviet tensions. If so, President Ho

Chi Minh of North Vietnam, and leaders of the USSR, provided them
the means for doing so gracefully. Ho Chi Minh died on September 3,
1969, and his will was read at a memorial service held in Hanoi on
September 9. In this document he had described himself as grieved
over the serious dissensions between major Communist parties, and
had expressed the hope that the Vietnam Workers party might be able
to contribute to restoring unity.[45] Soviet Premier Kosygin came to
Hanoi to attend the funeral on September 7, and left again September
10, flying in and out by way of India rather than across China, presumably because of the strained state of Sino-Soviet relations. However, there is evidence that he had sought to initiate discussions with
Chinese leaders, and that they had responded only after he left Hanoi.
At any rate, he interrupted his journey back to Moscow somewhere in
Soviet central Asia, and on September 11 he turned up at the Peking
airport. Premier Chou En-lai, Vice Premier Li Hsien-nien, and Minister of Internal Security Hsieh Fu-chih drove out to meet him, and
the two sides had a discussion the purport of which was at first disclosed by neither side.[46]

It is clear from official statements and semi-official stories, released
by the two sides not long afterwards, that the airport discussions had
centered on boundary problems and on the steps which the two sides
might take to move state-to-state relations into less dangerous waters.
If the Chinese Communists had been hesitating about going ahead
with projected nuclear tests in Sinkiang, the September 11 talks, and
the opportunity those talks afforded to take a reading of Soviet intentions, may have helped them make up their minds. On September 23,
the Chinese carried out an underground explosion at their Lop Nor
test site in Sinkiang, and on September 29 they tested another hydrogen bomb there.[47]

This third test of a Chinese hydrogen bomb, unlike that of December 28, 1967, achieved the desired thermonuclear effect, and the
fact that it had been held could not be kept concealed. Nevertheless,
the manner in which it was announced suggests that the Chinese were
nervous about the possible repercussions. One would otherwise have
expected them to announce this September 29 test in banner headlines
in connection with their twentieth anniversary celebrations on October 1. Instead, the announcement did not appear until October 5, and
it was placed on an inside page of *People's Daily*.[48]

It seems likely that an agreement had already been reached—perhaps even before the nuclear tests had been held at the end of the
previous month—to resume, in Peking and at the vice ministerial
level, the discussion of Sino-Soviet boundary questions which had been
broken off in 1964. At any rate, the Chinese Communists announced

the fact only two days after they had announced their nuclear tests. At the same time, and in the same statement, they accused the USSR of insinuating that China intended to launch a nuclear war against the Soviet Union; protested that China's weapons were intended only for defense; warned that China would never be intimidated by threats; and promised that there would be war should a handful of maniacs "dare to raid China's strategic sites in defiance of world opinion." [49]

If the Cultural Revolution was coming to an end, it was ending as it had begun: under the presumed threat of external attack. But it is not customary, in Communist China, to announce a movement's end. Moreover, the constitution, of April 14, 1969, contains a passage which suggests that Mao Tse-tung may intend this movement to be a continuing part of a permanent revolution. It reads: "Socialist society covers a fairly long historical period. Throughout this historical period, there are classes, class contradictions and class struggle, there is the struggle between the socialist road and the capitalist road, there is the danger of capitalist restoration and there is the threat of subversion and aggression by imperialism and modern revisionism. These contradictions can be resolved only by depending on the Marxist theory of continued revolution and on practice under its guidance. Such is China's Great Proletarian Cultural Revolution, a great political revolution carried out under the conditions of socialism by the proletariat against the bourgeoisie and all other exploiting classes."

27
Going Mao's Way

In 1948, during a talk to comrades whom he was criticizing for deviations of the left, Mao Tse-tung declared: "Your shortcomings lay chiefly in drawing the bowstring much too tight. If a bowstring is too taut, it will snap. The ancients said, 'the principle of Kings Wen and Wu was to alternate tension and relaxation.'" [1]

The Chinese Communists established their government in Peking soon afterwards, and Mao began to follow the example of Kings Wen and Wu. He launched one campaign after another, each designed to achieve a particular aim or set of objectives. Each campaign was conducted in an atmosphere of tension, and after a time each was allowed to die down. In this sense, the Cultural Revolution was no exception.

However, during the Cultural Revolution, and the Great Leap which preceded it, Mao Tse-tung—perhaps believing that he must soon "go to see God," and contemplating all that which yet remained undone—drew the bowstring very taut and was loath to release its tension. His Great Leap not only disrupted China's second Five-Year Plan; it brought widespread hunger to the land. Yet he fought to continue the Great Leap, and it was abandoned only after the issue had split the party, leaving him in the minority position. His Cultural Revolution had, as its principal task, overthrowing the majority which had opposed him; but after they had been purged, the movement still went on and on. In the process the third Five-Year Plan of development went the way of the second; the government was disrupted; the party structure was destroyed; and the populace suffered much in body, mind, and spirit. In the end it was anarchy—or perhaps anarchy and the army headed by Lin Piao, with Chou En-lai as its ally—which finally forced Mao to wind down his Cultural Revolution.

Mao admitted, during an interview with Edgar Snow in 1970, that the Cultural Revolution had developed into a war between factions—first with spears, then rifles, then mortars. When foreigners reported that China was in great chaos, Mao said, they had not been telling lies. As Chou En-lai recounted to Snow, the army had suffered thousands of casualties before it had taken up arms to suppress the factional struggles. [2]

In another conversation held after the turmoil of the Cultural

Revolution had subsided, this time with a visitor from Australia, Mao Tse-tung is reported to have declared that he had just escaped becoming a Buddha. He had, in other words, escaped being put and kept on the shelf, like an image to which one bows on appropriate occasions, but which is meant to remain silently in its place.[3] He had not achieved the main objectives of the Cultural Revolution, which he had identified as solving the problem of world outlook and eradicating revisionism.[4] But the assertion that he had avoided becoming a Buddha implied that he had the power to continue his efforts to reshape the governing and social structure of China, and to remake the Chinese man. In that sense, his Cultural Revolution had not come to a close, and its end as a movement went unannounced.

Mao Tse-tung's experiences during the Cultural Revolution, into which he drew one element after another of the governing structure and the population, must have affected his estimate of how much he would be able to rely on each element thereafter. He had hoped, through the tempering process of revolution, to "bring up some successors" to his own generation of aging leaders from among the educated youth. After the initial months, during which his main dependence had been placed on the young Red Guards, he had come to view this as "a hopeless task." It seems unlikely, incidentally, that this disenchantment of Mao Tse-tung remained entirely one-sided. In the wake of the Cultural Revolution, thousands of young people from Kwangtung Province risked death by shooting or drowning in order to elude border guards and swim to Hong Kong. Most of them were educated youths, sent at Mao's command to the countryside where they were to take up new lives as peasants. Millions of others, in more distant provinces, had been placed in similar positions but lacked comparable opportunities to escape.

Mao Tse-tung had turned, in his search for support, from the Red Guards to the workers and the peasants. But they had—to use his own expression—been "hoodwinked by party persons in power who were following the capitalist road." He could not overtly dismiss the proletariat and its peasant allies, for they represented the "main force" of the revolution. But he evidently concluded that they could serve as the main force only under strong and dependable leadership.[5] Neither they nor the lower-level cadres of the party and the government—whom he had called on to serve as revolutionary rebels—were ready for participatory democracy, as modeled after the Paris Commune.

At the end of the Cultural Revolution, Mao was left with Lin Piao and the organizations subject to his influence or control—the army and the army-dominated, countrywide structure of revolutionary committees—and Chou En-lai, as head of what remained of the central government. This means that they were not without influence, or perhaps even power, vis-à-vis Mao himself, and it raises the question of how far they were prepared to respond to his will. The answer, at least for the period immediately following the Cultural Revolution, may be sought by reviewing the positions Mao had taken on key matters— national defense, combating bureaucratism, management of the economy, the administration of justice, the revolutionalization of education, and foreign policy—and then, in the light of those positions, examining the way in which the government was being restructured and the character of its performance.

In the course of the Cultural Revolution Mao Tse-tung had made a statement, publicized under the title of "Chairman Mao's Great Strategic Principle," which called for "preparedness against war, preparedness against national calamities, and everything for the people." [6] In answer to that call, reserves of grain were accumulated and warehoused in various parts of the country, and air raid shelters were constructed. When American newsmen visited China in mid-1971, these programs were still being carried forward.[7]

Mao Tse-tung was committed, as we have already noted, to a strategy of defense based largely upon People's War. He was well aware that China would be vulnerable to defeat at the hands of technologically superior enemies if its defense depended upon the continued functioning of a large bureaucracy centered in the capital. A successful defense might require direction by a governing group, which could make the major decisions; but if it were small, it need not be tied to any one locale. Tactical guidance would have to be supplied from many centers, because a People's War is by nature a dispersed defense. In preparing for such a war, it is essential that government be largely decentralized, and that each locality be able to meet its own needs for foodstuffs and other essential goods.

Decentralization also provides one means of combating bureaucratization. Both during the Cultural Revolution and thereafter, it was frequently mentioned that Mao Tse-tung had called, in the military language he was prone to use, for "better troops and simpler administration." As applied to government in general, this call was a reflection of his dislike for the bureaucratism to which large organizations are so especially susceptible. The total number of those engaged in administration will not necessarily be reduced through decentralization, because it may require the expansion of the organizational units to which responsibility is decentralized. But each one of those units can be kept relatively small compared with the very large bureaucracies which characterize a highly centralized administration.

Liu Shao-ch'i had also deplored bureaucratism. The relevant dis-
agreements between him and Mao Tse-tung were over questions of
organization and, within that context, of how bureaucratism should be
combated. Unlike Mao Tse-tung, Liu Shao-ch'i favored the development of a highly integrated economy, and saw bureaucratism as the
consequence of attempts by the state to exercise detailed direction over
the economy. As Liu saw, a high degree of state intervention of that
sort required large organizations, and large organizations are the breed-
ing grounds of bureaucratism. Building a highly integrated economy
without exercising direction in detail required systems of incentives.
Indeed, it might lead to the application of a whole set of "revisionist"
economic theories, such as those advanced by Sun Yeh-fang, director of
the Institute of Economics of the Chinese Academy of Sciences until
his dismissal from that post in 1966.

Sun Yeh-fang had been in touch with the economists of the Communist states of Eastern Europe, and during the Cultural Revolution
he was denounced as favoring free markets, being the proponent of a
new theory of the law of value, holding that state control of individual
enterprises shackled their initiative, and wishing to substitute a "profit
system" which recalls the Liberman formula. (Under that formula the
state would make it profitable for enterprises to do whatever was
deemed advantageous to society, and unprofitable to do what was considered disadvantageous.) Accordingly, the purging of Liu Shao-ch'i,
and the discrediting during the Cultural Revolution of economists
like Sun Yeh-fang, represented apparent victories in Mao's campaign
against revisionism.[8] After the Cultural Revolution, workers in the
factories were no longer given bonuses, and in the countryside there
was an extension of the *Tachai* system under which extra "work
points" were given to those whose political attitudes were judged to
be worthy of reward.

In 1971, it was reported that each of China's approximately 2,000
hsien, or counties, had been given the goal of becoming self-sufficient
in food and light industrial products, and that some decentralization
was taking place in the sector of heavy industry as well. At the center,
government organizations which were concerned with the different
segments of the economy were being streamlined, with staffs pared
down and a number of the ministries merged. The economy, incidentally, appeared to be working well: early in 1971, it was reported that
output for the previous year had reached or exceeded that of previous
peak years for both industry and agriculture.[9]

There was evidently a large measure of *de facto* decentralization
of the government, too, which was a result of the prior suspension of
the operations of various ministries and of the disorganized state in

which many of them emerged from the Cultural Revolution. While it was being decided which ones should resume operations, and how far their authority should extend, the center could simply decide and publicize the broad lines of relevant policy, making implementation the responsibility of the revolutionary committees throughout the country. This is the way affairs were apparently being conducted insofar as the administration of justice and the reorganization of primary and secondary education were concerned. In those fields we have an opportunity to observe how things worked with no large bureaucracies intervening between Mao Tse-tung and the working levels.

It may be recalled that Tung Pi-wu had remarked to P'eng Chen, after they had begun drafting a state constitution, that they would replace government by movements with the rule of law, and that Liu Shao-ch'i had advocated the adoption of a comprehensive legal code. Those expectations had been thwarted, but Tung Pi-wu, P'eng Chen, and their colleagues had succeeded in building up a regularized system of police, procurates, and courts. In theory, the procurates were expected to ensure that the courts as well as the people abided by the law; in practice, the party sometimes dictated the decisions to be reached in individual cases. Nevertheless, the system of police, procurates, and courts was staffed by people who might be expected to have some knowledge of relevant laws and standards of procedure.

In his 1927 "Report of an Investigation into the Peasant Movement in Hunan," Mao had enthusiastically described the various punishments which had been meted out there by the masses. Under the heading of "shooting," he explained: "This punishment was invariably meted out to the biggest local bullies and evil gentry by the request of the peasants and the people as a whole." [10] Four decades later, his approval of summary justice was still apparent. During the Cultural Revolution he referred to the public security, procuratorial, and judicial organs and said: "People seem to think that these organizations are indispensable. But I shall be glad if they collapse." [11] While recognizing that some investigatory personnel should be retained, he asserted that "dictatorship against bad people" should be exercised by mobilizing the masses. [12]

If personnel of the old public security system were still at work in 1970, they undoubtedly were under the supervision of the army. It is not possible to judge how well they were doing their work, but the meting out of punishments was open to the public view. An Asian diplomat has described a "trial" of six persons held in January of 1970 at the sports ground near Peking's West Gate. About twenty thousand persons had been assembled for the event in an area dominated by a huge billboard portrait of Chairman Mao. When the prisoners were dragged in, the onlookers all arose and shouted: "Guilty! Death!" Three guards handled each prisoner, two grasping his arms, and the third forcing down his head. On each man's chest a placard had been placed, indicating the nature of the offenses with which he was charged.

Next, five judges marched into the arena: two women and two men in uniform, and an older man in civilian clothes. An execution squad armed with submachine guns stood at attention while a band played "The East is Red," then began to smoke and chat as the trial began. After the charges against the first prisoner had been read, witnesses shouted their evidence into loudspeakers, and waved their copies of the little red book, *Quotations from Chairman Mao Tse-tung.* No plea was taken, and no defense was allowed. Instead, a claque in the front seats proclaimed the verdict, the crowd arose once more to its feet, and once again it shouted: "Guilty! Death!" The prisoner was dragged before a solid screen, tied to a stake and shot; his body then was dragged to one side and rolled over, face up. His "trial" and execution had required only twenty minutes.

The other cases were handled in the same fashion, except that justice came on hastened feet; only ten minutes were needed to try and to shoot the final prisoner. The crowd then marched out to the tune of "Sailing the Sea Depends upon the Helmsman," with some of the people filing past the six bodies in order to spit or urinate upon them.[13]

It is difficult to judge, on the basis of reports of public trials held in various parts of China in the wake of the Cultural Revolution, what proportion of offenders was given the lesser punishment of sentence to periods of reform through labor, and what proportion was executed. It is not surprising that the latter form of punishment was meted out to people charged with political offenses or such serious crimes as murder, rape, robbery, and arson. However, in some cases the death sentence is reported to have been inflicted on individuals charged only with acts which might seem to us to be minor offenses—such as returning to the city without permission after having been assigned to work in the countryside. In at least two cases, prisoners executed by firing squads stood accused of helping refugees escape to Hong Kong. In these cases, the trials were held and the executions carried out at Shumchun, a village on China's border with Hong Kong. One of the trials was held on a rainy day, and the soldiers who were members of the firing squad were wearing heavy boots. After this execution the bodies were abused, as they had been in Peking, but in a different fashion. Before departing from the scene, the soldiers used their heavy boots to stamp the bodies into the mud.[14]

If Mao Tse-tung's advocacy of involvement of the masses in the administration of justice had deep roots, the same could be said regarding his admiration for education which he deemed practical, and about his animus against study divorced from practice. These roots extended into his guerrilla past, for the practitioner of guerrilla warfare, like the frontiersman and the pioneer, needs to be a jack-of-all-trades. Such men were at the opposite end of the spectrum from those Chinese intellectuals who had not broken with the tradition which holds manual work to be beneath the dignity of the scholar. Before the Communists had come to power, Mao had found himself contending with the Soviet-educated Twenty-eight Bolsheviks, who could buttress their arguments with long quotations from Marxist works but who, in Mao's opinion, were unable to apply their theories to the realities of the Chinese scene.

Moreover, after the Communists had come to power, Mao had to contend with cadres many of whom manifested the less desirable traits of the old scholar-official class: men who operated by command rather than persuasion, who enjoyed the perquisites of power, and who were callous to the lot of the peasant and the worker. While Mao might treat his subordinate officials with the authoritarian arrogance which is bred by the exercise of power, he nevertheless preached the need for them to behave like common people, rather than like officials.

Mao Tse-tung's plans for reforming the cadres and for the revolutionizing of education, during the post-Cultural Revolution period, had been foreshadowed in a letter of May 7, 1966, which he wrote to Lin Piao. In it he declared that the PLA ought to serve as a great school, with army men learning not only military affairs, but also politics, agriculture, and industrial production. In the schools, students had study as their main task, but they should also learn industrial work, farming, and military affairs. "The school term should be shortened," he wrote, "education should be revolutionized, and the domination of our schools by bourgeois intellectuals should not be allowed to continue." Finally, where conditions permitted, "those working in commerce, in the service trades and party and government organizations should do the same." None of these ideas, he admitted, was new, and some people had been putting them into practice for some time. What was needed, he declared, was to popularize them.[15]

On October 4, 1968, Mao Tse-tung issued an instruction which supplemented his letter of May 7, 1966. "Going down to do manual labor," he asserted, "gives vast numbers of cadres an excellent opportunity to study once again; this should be done by all cadres except those who are old, weak, ill, or disabled. Cadres at their posts should also go down in turn to do manual labor." In response to this directive, "May 7" Cadre Schools were established all over China, at which party and government people were to engage in agricultural and industrial labor, study Mao's works, and remold their world outlook.[16]

In the winter of 1970–1971, the Sino-Sovietologist Klaus Mehnert visited a "May 7" school located in the countryside some thirty kilometers northeast of Peking. That school had been established for cadres from that sector of the capital known as Peking-East. The student body, he found, was made up of over 1,200 men and women. More than 700 of them were from the field of education, and among them were school directors, teachers, and librarians. About 500 had been drawn from the government administration, public services, industrial establishments, and mass organizations of Peking-East. The school had no study hall, and the dormitories were barracks-like structures with earthen floors. The students, when not taking their turns in the school kitchen, spent their days hammering out and soldering metalwares for the Peking market or working on the land.

The fields the students worked had been an uncultivated sandy flat; they had made these fields cultivable by mixing the sand with clay, brought in by wheelbarrow from a nearby hillside. Irrigation had been provided by digging a ditch through which water was pumped from a nearby stream. In order to get fertilizer, the students emptied out the school's latrines; they also transported back to the school, on the occasions of periodic visits to their families, the accumulations from the privies in their homes. (This allegedly had presented a particularly painful prospect to one of the students. He had been a high official of Peking-East, every child there knew him, and he feared that he could not be seen carrying nightsoil without losing face entirely. But he did it like the rest, and in doing so he assertedly came to realize that emptying latrines was a glorious rather than a dirty task.) The first planting had been done in 1969, and since the second crop of 1970 the school had been self-sufficient in rice and vegetables, as well as eggs and meat. Nevertheless the work of bringing more land into cultivable condition was still going on, and Mehnert observed that the tempo of work was fast.

It was apparent that the reeducation of the cadres was being accomplished largely through their participation in physical labor. In addition, there was group-study of Mao's works for a half hour every morning, and three evenings a week were devoted to further Mao study, criticism of Liu Shao-ch'i, and self-criticism. The length of the period for which the cadres had been assigned was apparently indeterminate: about a thousand had passed through the school, and others had come to take their places, but some of those who remained had been there since the school was founded more than two years before. At least some of them had been criticized during the Cultural Revolution, and it may be that the students assigned first and kept longest were those deemed in greatest need of remolding.[17]

The revolutionization and restructuring of China's educational system, like the founding of the "May 7" schools, was initiated in 1968. Similarly, it took its inspiration from Mao Tse-tung's May 7, 1966, letter to Lin Piao, supplemented by Mao's subsequent statements on the subject of education. In a February 27, 1967, speech at the School of Military Warfare, for example, Mao Tse-tung had remarked: "A little reading of books is all right, but a lot of it harms people— it really harms them." A few days afterward, Ch'en Po-ta complained: "Middle schools and primary schools [each] are six years. This is intolerable. . . . Once people graduate, if they have no work to do there is a new problem. . . . Primary schools, can they graduate in three years or not? . . . In my opinion, the history course has no use." Mao Tse-tung took the same general approach toward university-level education in an instruction which he issued the following year. "It is still necessary," he conceded, "to have universities; here I refer mainly to colleges of science and engineering. However, it is essential to shorten the length of schooling, revolutionize education, put proletarian politics in command, and take the road of . . . training technicians from among workers and peasants with practical experience, and they should return to production after a few years' study." He also decreed that workers' propaganda teams should stay permanently in the schools. In urban areas, workers and army men were to provide "working class leadership" to the schools. In the countryside, the schools were to be managed by the poor and lower-middle peasants, whom Mao described as "the most reliable ally of the working class." [18]

Before the cultural revolution, the Ministry of Education had exercised financial and policy control over the primary and middle schools. When they were reopened in the autumn of 1968, their financial support had become a local responsibility: in rural areas it was assumed by the production brigades, and in the cities by factories or neighborhoods. Policies governing admissions and fees had been changed to discriminate against children with bourgeois backgrounds, and to favor those from poor peasant and worker families. In at least some places the system of giving marks had been abandoned. Pupils were to graduate from primary school after five years instead of six, and from lower and upper middle school after two rather than three years in each. Many primary schools, especially in rural areas, had tacked on the additional two years of lower middle school. It appeared the upper middle schools were being deemphasized if not abandoned: little was heard of them, and graduation from such schools ceased to be a prerequisite for admission to institutions of higher learning.

Within the broad outlines of policy laid down by Peking, curricula varied from place to place. Initially, at least, there appears to have been considerable experimentation in the fields of school organization and methods of instruction. But from time to time, individual schools or systems—which might serve as models—were publicized in *People's Daily*.

Throughout China, the style and content of education underwent great change. Above the level of reading, writing and arithmetic, such "academic" studies as history and geography were either deemphasized or eliminated entirely. Mathematics and science, being more "practical" because of their relationship to agriculture and industry, were more frequently retained. In both primary and secondary schools, heavier emphasis was laid on political indoctrination. It was not merely that the thought of Mao Tse-tung became a course to which more class hours were devoted than any other; even courses in arithmetic and science were given a political slant. Schooling on a part-work, part-study basis became more general in consequence of the policies which made production brigades responsible for schools in rural areas and under which schools were attached to factories in urban centers. Much education at all levels also displayed a more distinctly military flavor. Considerable time was being allotted to military drill, and foreign visitors reported that children from nursery schools upward were to be seen practicing with dummy rifles and making bayonet lunges to the accompaniment of the cry *sha*, which means "kill." [19]

Tsinghua University—China's foremost polytechnical school—located in the suburbs of Peking, was the first institution of higher learning known to have resumed regular operations. Two-thirds of its fifteen thousand students had been sent to the countryside in 1968; the remaining five thousand had been kept on, subject to the worker–soldier propaganda team to which Mao had sent the gift of mangoes. Tsinghua was reopened in 1969, and the following year it began enrolling new students. Those admitted first were described as workers, peasants, and soldiers about twenty years of age whose educational level corresponded to junior or senior middle school. Later, it was explained, some veteran workers and some poor and lower-middle peasants would be admitted, regardless of their ages or educational levels. The course in which each student majored would be decided by the university. The students would rise at six and retire by ten; spend some time working in factories or on farms, as well as at military drill; and graduate after two or three years instead of the former five or six.[20]

By the early months of 1971, it was obvious that Communist China was in a period of political reconstruction, and it was apparent that this reconstruction was being accompanied by an erosion of the influence of the leftist elements which had led the Cultural Revolution during its most destructive periods. This erosion was both observable at the center and reflected in the provinces.

In April 1969, Ch'en Po-ta, leader of the Cultural Revolution Group, had been elected as a member of five-man Standing Committee of the Political Bureau. After August 1969, he ceased to be mentioned as attending public functions and became the target of press criticism.[21] Minister of Public Security Hsieh Fu-chih had been as putty in the hands of Chiang Ch'ing, the real moving spirit of the Cultural Revolution Group, and he had been rewarded with election to the Political Bureau and as first secretary of a new party committee for the municipality of Peking. But his March 1971 election to the latter post was apparently *in absentia*. Indeed, he had made no reported public appearances during the preceding year, nor was he listed among those attending official functions during immediately following months —despite the fact that his presence in Peking was reported at a time when some of those functions were being held.[22]

The reconstruction of the party apparatus at the provincial level began with Mao Tse-tung's native province of Hunan, where the formation of a provincial party committee was announced in December 1970. It was concluded in August 1971, when such committees were set up for Tibet, Szechwan, Ningsia, and Heilungkiang. In the cases of ten of the twenty-nine provinces and provincial-level municipalities, the lists of party committee personnel revealed or confirmed leadership changes which had occurred since the establishment of revolutionary committees for the respective provinces or municipalities. Most of these changes were at the expense of the left: For example, P'an Fu-sheng, who had led the first of the revolutionary committees—that for Heilungkiang—had been dropped. So had Liu Ko-p'ing, the controversial chairman of the Shansi Provincial Revolutionary Committee. The gains were scored principally by military officers— who held commanding positions on the new party committees almost everywhere but at Shanghai—and, in lesser degree, by party and government cadres—several of whom can be identified as having held ministerial or other positions under Chou En-lai's state Council, and a few of whom were men who had been purged during the Cultural Revolution but who had since then been rehabilitated.[23]

With the return of stability, China's foreign relations had entered a new phase. China's leaders no longer needed to be reluctant to admit foreign visitors, many of China's ambassadors had returned to their posts, Red Guard diplomacy had been abandoned, and one country after another was extending diplomatic recognition to Communist China.[24]

The United States was not among them, but it had at long last moved away from policies it had originally adopted in consequence of the Chinese Communist intervention in the Korean War. The year after the end of that war, Assistant Secretary of State for Far Eastern Affairs Robertson had described United States policy toward Communist China as aimed at promoting an internal breakdown.[25] The measures adopted to that end, including those which prohibited virtually all American trade and financial dealings with mainland China, were retained long after it was clear they would accomplish no such result. What retaining them did accomplish, in the eyes of the world, was to place much of the blame on the United States for the continuing state of its relations with mainland China.

At the 1954 Geneva Conference on Indo-China, Secretary Dulles had turned away when Chou En-lai sought to shake his hand.[26] If this conduct was maladroit, it nevertheless accorded with feelings which then were widespread within the Congress of the United States, and among its people as well. In consequence of this sentiment, such dealings as the United States had with Communist China were conducted through intermittent contacts between the embassies of the two countries at capitals in Eastern Europe. But the enmity aroused by war was bound to be softened by the passage of time, and by 1970 it no longer seemed politically dangerous to consider whether the interests of the United States, in its bilateral dealings with Communist China, might not be better served by ceasing to deal with that country only intermittently and at arm's length.

By 1970, too, the Sino-Soviet split had for a whole decade been exposed to view, and confirmed by the flare-up of hostilities between the two countries which occurred early in 1969 along China's northern borders. With the realization that the split was wide, deep, and enduring, the upper echelons of the United States government undoubtedly came to see Communist China, the Soviet Union, and the United States as in a triangular relationship. In such a relationship, the dealings of one with another might change the context of the relations of each with the third. From this standpoint, the United States and China might each gain flexibility, in their conduct of affairs with the Soviet Union, by unfreezing their relations with each other.

In 1970, the United States relaxed restrictions it had imposed on travel to China by American citizens, and in the first half of 1971 it removed them and dismantled almost entirely the measures which stood in the way of American trade and financial dealings with mainland China. This dismantling could hardly be considered of major importance on economic grounds. The foreign trade of Communist China already had its established channels, it was relatively small, and it was increasing only slowly. At about four billion United States dol-

lars a year, it was smaller than that of the British colony of Hong
Kong, the exports of which had been growing at an annual rate of
almost 20 percent, and not much larger than the foreign trade of Taiwan, which had been increasing by roughly 30 percent each year.[27]
The primary consideration which motivated the United States government was political: in 1970 it had sent messages through interme-
diaries to the effect that it wanted to normalize its relations with Communist China; now those words had been backed by deeds.[28]

Normalized relations with Communist China would presumably
be ones under which American officials, as well as newsmen and perhaps scholars, could reside in China for substantial periods of time.
Short visits to China by such persons are undoubtedly better than
none, for they may dispel some of the mystery surrounding China.
There is nothing which can be so ominous as the imagined but unknown, and nothing so potentially disastrous as miscalculation arising
from a combination of ignorance and fear. But the Chinese are perhaps the world's most persuasive people, and it is only observation of
the country over considerable periods of time which can provide a
foreigner with the perspective which may enable him to distinguish
the kernels of fact from the chaff of fiction.

It is in the nature of governments to proclaim the benefits, real
and imagined, which have been brought to the peoples which they
govern, and this is particularly true of newly established regimes. During the first two decades of Communist rule, visitors were almost uniformly told stories, many of them exaggerated or untrue, about how
bad things had been under the Kuomintang and how much better
they had become after the Communists had come to power. It accordingly should have been expected that similar comparisons would be
drawn between conditions before the Cultural Revolution and after it
—and they were. One of the correspondents visiting China in 1971, for
instance, was taken on a tour of the harbor at Shanghai, which contained two Chinese ships, each of about ten thousand tons. A vice
chairman of the Shanghai Revolutionary Committee explained: "Before the Cultural Revolution we only repaired ships. Now we build
them.[29] The second of those two statements was undoubtedly correct,
but the first was completely untrue. The correspondent in question
may or may not have been aware of that fact; one with some years of
experience in China would hardly have been deceived.

Good information does not guarantee wise government policies;
it only makes them possible. Moreover, normal relations between countries are not synonymous with intimate ones. Indeed, if the successive
experiences in this century of Japan, the United States, and the Soviet
Union hold any lesson, it is that deep involvement in the affairs of

China—whether from hostile or friendly intent—should be avoided at almost any cost. In the case of the United States such involvement left, as its legacy, issues which have recurrently posed the threat of military conflict. An avowed purpose of the United States, in seeking the normalization of relations with the People's Republic of China, was the peaceful settlement of those issues.

The Chinese Communist response to the overtures of the United States was made against the background of restored stability in China and Chou En-lai's increased freedom to conduct diplomacy in the adroit manner for which he is noted. It should not be assumed, however, that the Chinese response was one with which Mao Tse-tung was not in agreement. As early as December 1970, Mao told Edgar Snow that a visit by President Nixon would be welcomed because he was at present the one with whom the problems between China and the United States would have to be solved.[30] And according to Chou En-lai, it was Mao Tse-tung who decided, in the spring of 1971, that the members of the United States table tennis team playing in Japan should be invited to mainland China; at that time, Chou En-lai said, it had been the inclination of the Ministry of Foreign Affairs to wait awhile.[31]

The visit of the table tennis team initiated an exercise in the form of diplomacy which is directed at a government through its people. The American publishers, editors, newsmen, and other citizens who follow one another on visits could be expected, through their reports, to exert a useful influence on their government. However Mao Tse-tung's primary purpose, in initiating a flow of progressively more important visitors, was to set in motion a series of events which would culminate in a visit to China by President Nixon. One does not break the ice all at once; a preparatory period of thaw should come first.

It was widely surmised in 1972 that the decision to invite President Nixon had been made against the opposition of a group headed by Lin Piao, which may have preferred a conciliatory approach to the Soviet Union. His immediate subordinate, Chief of Staff Huang Yung-sheng, had made a sweeping attack on the United States in a speech of July 31, 1971, when arrangements for the visit were already under way. Then on September 12 a Chinese aircraft, carrying persons who presumably were fleeing to the Soviet Union, crashed not far from that country, deep in Outer Mongolia. After that date, Lin Piao and a number of his key supporters ceased to make public appearances. However, at the time of President Nixon's 1972 visit, the reasons for their disappearance remained a secret. One of the American correspondents who came to China at that time plucked up the courage to ask a Chinese official at his luncheon table what had happened to Lin Piao.

With perfect composure, the official pointed toward the main dish in the center of the table and said: "Why don't you have some mandarin fish?" [32]

In any case, the Mao Tse-tung who welcomed the wish of President Nixon to visit China was not a Mao Tse-tung who had changed his basic attitude toward the United States. On May 20, 1970, in the wake of the entry into Cambodia of American and South Vietnamese troops, he had issued a statement entitled, "People of the World, Unite and Defeat U. S. Aggressors and All Their Running Dogs!" In it, he had declared: "While massacring the people of other countries, U. S. imperialism is slaughtering the white and black people in its own country. Nixon's fascist atrocities have kindled the revolutionary mass movement in the United States." [33] Moreover, it would appear that Mao Tse-tung still stood by this statement after a year had passed. As is customary with pronouncements of his which are deemed to have continuing importance, the 1971 anniversary of its issuance was marked by statements and articles in which it was recalled and reaffirmed.[34]

What apparently had changed was not Mao Tse-tung's assessment that the United States was the number one imperialist enemy, but his appreciation of the relative dangers posed to China by the United States and the Soviet Union. In the years since 1966, when Mao had asserted to leaders of the Japanese Communist Party that China would soon be attacked by the United States, the numbers of American troops in Indo-China had undergone progressive reduction. During those same years, China and the USSR had gone to the brink of war, drawn back to negotiate, but not resolved their differences. In this situation, Mao Tse-tung evidently regarded the United States as an enemy which had dropped to secondary place, behind the Soviet Union.

This changed assessment was analogous to one which Mao Tse-tung had set forth on May 23, 1937, after a decade of civil war with the Kuomintang, but at a time when hostilities between China and Japan appeared imminent. In explaining the changing relationship between the Communists and the Kuomintang, he observed that the contradiction between China and Japan had become the principal one, and China's internal contradictions had dropped into secondary and subordinate place.[35] The changed relationship did not prevent the Chinese Communists from pursuing their internal aims at the expense of the Kuomintang. Similarly, achieving a different relationship with the United States might alter the way in which Communist China pursued its external aims, but not those aims themselves.

The Chinese Communists cannot be accused of not being frank about their objectives. Chou En-lai made it clear to American visitors that those objectives included the abandonment of the defense pact of the United States with the government of the Republic of China, and the withdrawal of American forces from countries on the periphery of China—first of all from Indo-China, but also from Korea and Japan, as well as Taiwan. Such withdrawals would remove those forces as potential threats to Communist China, and also as obstacles to the settlement—on terms favorable to the Communists—of differences between the governments of the divided countries of Vietnam and Korea. In the case of Japan, such withdrawals might make possible a new relationship with that country which was more favorable to Communist China. Chou En-lai put Indo-China first, he explained, because there were continuing hostilities there. However, in a June 21, 1971, interview with visiting American newsmen, Chou stated that the key obstacle to the establishment of diplomatic relations between Communist China and the United States was the military protection which the latter afforded Taiwan pursuant to its 1955 Mutual Defense Treaty with the government of the Republic of China. If that military protection were withdrawn, he said, the "liberation" of Taiwan would not be "all that difficult." [36]

It may be recalled that Taiwan was taken from China by Japan in 1895, and turned over to administration by the government of the Republic of China at the end of World War II. When the Chinese Communists intervened in Korea, late in 1950, the civil war was over insofar as the Chinese mainland was concerned. But Taiwan was still under the control of Chiang Kai-shek—Taiwan and a few offshore islands, the most important of which was Quemoy, lying athwart the entrance to the mainland port of Amoy. Attempts to conquer the islands had to be put off while hostilities continued in Korea, and after those hostilities had ended, the United States had put Taiwan under the protection of its Mutual Defense Treaty with the government headed by Chiang Kai-shek.

If the refugee government of Chiang Kai-shek had been willing to accept its defeat on the mainland as final and settle down as a government of Taiwan, it should have removed its troops from the offshore islands, which were not covered by the Mutual Defense Treaty. This would have put a hundred miles of blue water between its forces and those of Communist China. Instead it garrisoned those islands with a substantial part of its total forces—Quemoy most heavily of all—and used them for forays against targets on the mainland. Those islands thus became a baited hook. If the islands were heavily attacked, the United States might have to choose between the prospect of seeing their garrisons lost or intervening against Communist China. If it chose the latter course, the way might be opened for Chiang Kai-shek to get the military support he would need for an attempt to reconquer mainland China.

In this context, it was logical for the government of the Republic of China on Taiwan to insist on continuing to be recognized as the rightful government of the country from which it had been ejected. In keeping with this logic, it adhered to policies at least some of which were mirror-images of those of Communist China. Both regimes professed to regard Taiwan as one of the provinces of China, and both refused to accept the prospect of their permanent separation. That being so, both could be depended on to resist any outside effort to bring about an evacuation of the garrisons on the offshore islands, for that would create a *de facto* separation which might become permanent.

The treaty under which the United States became committed to the defense of Taiwan contains a clause permitting either party to terminate it on one year's notice. Doing so would remove the most likely source of conflict between the United States and Communist China, and open the way for the establishment of diplomatic relations between them. More was involved, however, than a simple choice between two Chinese regimes—one of them controlling all mainland China, the other the government which had lost the civil war there, and which presumably had aimed to involve the United States in a second round of hostilities. The United States would also have to consider the interests of the approximately fourteen million inhabitants of Taiwan. While the government there could not be considered representative of the majority of the populace, the people which it ruled certainly enjoyed more personal freedom and much greater material well-being than those of mainland China. They could, of course, expect to lose both if Taiwan fell under Communist control. A decision to terminate United States military protection of Taiwan would also affect the interests of Japan, America's principal overseas trading partner and important ally. In case of a Communist takeover of Taiwan, Japan could expect to lose $500 million of investments it had made there, as well as most of its flourishing trade with that island. In truth, a country's foreign relations are a web; it must be kept in good order, but no one strand can be pulled out, to insert another, without regard to its effect on the rest.

In 1971, one country after another was withdrawing diplomatic recognition from Taipei in order to accord it to Peking, explicitly or implicitly accepting the theses that Taiwan was only a province of China which should be under the control of Peking, and that its future was therefore an internal affair in which no foreign country had the right to interfere. In seeking to normalize its own relations with the People's Republic of China, the United States undoubtedly contributed to the trend whereby recognition was transferred from Taipei to Peking, and to the widespread acceptance of the accompanying theses.

These same theses, which had been made explicit in Communist China's declarations to the effect that it would refuse to enter the United Nations so long as the government of the Republic of China was represented there, were reflected in the provision of the Albanian resolution, as adopted on October 25, 1971, which called for the expulsion of that government from the United Nations Organization. Accordingly, a decision by the government of the United States to maintain its commitments to the government of the Republic of China would hold the seeds of future trouble. If adhered to it might result, in case of a showdown, in the United States being called on to honor its Mutual Defense Treaty, with the United Nations and many of its member states committed, implicitly and in numerous cases explicitly as well, to the proposition that the future of Taiwan was an internal affair of China in which the United States had no right to interfere.

In any case, the United States, and the rest of the world, with or without diplomatic relations with Communist China, are going to have to deal with the People's Republic of China both in the immediate future and long after its intransigent old leader has passed on. A leadership group which was not greatly different, save for his removal from it consequent to death or incapacitation, could hardly be expected to pursue a markedly different set of external aims, although the order of its priorities might be different, and its style less tempestuous. But the leaders who rank immediately under Mao Tse-tung are predominantly men who are in their late sixties or early seventies. Accordingly, one must ask what sort of men will dominate the party and the government after they and their fellow veterans of the Long March have largely passed from the scene.

When Malraux was visiting China, just before the Cultural Revolution began, he remarked to Mao Tse-tung on the role of the army, as the original builder of the party. In the course of the Cultural Revolution, after the party structure had been destroyed, the army had assumed its position of leadership. With the reconstituting of the Central Committee, history had come almost full circle. It was not merely that over 40 percent of the members of the new Central Committee were members of the military establishment. Army men had assumed key roles in the revolutionary committees entrusted with the guidance of virtually every organization in the country, and they were in a position to dominate the process of party building at all levels below that of the Central Committee. As one provincial committee of the party after another was reconstituted, it had become obvious that army men were not surrendering their positions of leadership.

With the passage of time, PLA officers occupying nonmilitary positions might be expected to become at least partially civilianized, as had their Red Army predecessors. But it should be recalled that the leaders of the Red Army had been drawn from many walks of life; that some of them had been educated in the universities of the pre-Communist period; and that not a few had studied and traveled in foreign lands. The PLA leaders in the rebuilt party more generally lacked such backgrounds, and could be expected to see the world from narrower perspectives.

If Chinese education follows for long the course set for it by Mao Tse-tung, the generation now in school will know even less of the outside world. Some of the results of the educational changes which were made in China after the Cultural Revolution can be gauged from tests conducted in 1969 in Hong Kong, where Communist-controlled schools made similar changes in their curricula. It may be admitted that these tests, known as the Certificate of Education examinations, would place students from such schools at a disadvantage in consequence of the fact that they would not be tested on, or get credit for, knowledge of the thought of Mao Tse-tung. At the same time, it should also be remembered that they had not been diverted from their studies by the need to work part-time on farms or in factories, as had pupils in Communist China, nor had the years allotted to their attendance at primary and middle school been similarly reduced. Moreover, as a precaution, they had been specially coached for this examination.

When the results of this colonywide examination were in, it was found that 63 percent of all those taking it had passed and 37 percent had failed, but that 63 percent of the students from Communist-controlled schools had failed, and only 37 percent had passed. Fewer than half could pass in such apolitical subjects as mathematics and science. They fell far below average in knowledge of the Chinese language, and only 13 percent could pass the examination in Chinese history—as compared to a colonywide average of 61 percent.[37] This suggests, as does the dropping of history from the curricula of many schools in mainland China, that the younger generation there will grow up with a poor knowledge of China's past. And if its members have little knowledge of where China has been, or of the lessons of its past, they can be expected to have scant understanding of the pitfalls to be avoided along its future path.

In one sense Mao Tse-tung was at least partly wrong when he declared that he had escaped becoming a Buddha. The Buddhists of China's Tibetan and Mongolian regions believe that some men are living Buddhas, and Mao Tse-tung had himself become a religious figure. Images of him were everywhere on display: in bust or full figure, ranging from small to gigantic size, and made of every imaginable material—even luminous plastic. Enough portraits of him had been printed to supply one to every Chinese man, woman, and child, and they looked down from the walls wherever one went. In homes all over China the ancestral tablets, objects of quasi-religious veneration, had been removed from their places of honor and replaced by images or portraits of Mao Tse-tung.

In 1968 a painting was done in oils, portraying the young Mao Tse-tung, high on a mountain treading a path which led to Anyüan, where he would lead the striking miners. So Christ-like was the figure that a copy which reached the Vatican was hung there upon the pressroom wall. To some people in the West, a picture of a red heart has come to represent Jesus; in China, in 1969, a factory was producing crimson hearts of foam rubber. They represented Chairman Mao, called "the great truth, the light of dawn, the savior of mankind and the hope of the world . . . the reddest, reddest sun in the hearts of the people of the world."

It had become a ritual to open meetings with a recitation of one or another of his sayings; by wishing him long, long life; and by waving the red book, *Quotations from Chairman Mao Tse-tung,* as though it were a talisman. And none of those present would be without a button bearing his picture, worn upon the breast. Workers, peasants, and soldiers were reported as adopting the habit of beginning and ending the day by standing before his portrait and reporting on their work. The thought of Mao Tse-tung solved problems and helped cure diseases, and in periods of personal crisis a true believer might direct to him his prayers. Thus a young nightsoil collector in Peking, who had allegedly been persecuted by old Shih Ch'uanhsiang—leader of the men in his profession until his downfall as a partisan of Liu Shao-ch'i—recounted that the mistreatment he had suffered had moved his old father to pray to Mao Tse-tung. "He knelt in front of Chairman Mao's portrait," the young man explained, held his hands together in prayer, bowed repeatedly, and muttered all the time, 'O Chairman Mao . . . what are we to do?' " [38]

In 1958, Mao Tse-tung had written that China's people were poor and blank. "That may seem like a bad thing," he had remarked, "but it is really a good thing. . . . A clean sheet of paper has no blotches, and so the newest and most beautiful words can be written on it, and the newest and most beautiful pictures can be painted on it." [39] In actual fact, the sheet of the people's mind was not entirely blank. It had been blotched by old ideas, old culture, old customs, and old habits. Removing them, so that the sheet might be imprinted with the thought of Mao Tse-tung, had been one of the tasks of his Cultural Revolution.

Two millennia earlier, Shih Huang-ti had ordered the burning of the books of the Confucian philosophers. In Mao Tse-tung's China, old books again had been consigned to the flames. Visitors to Peking's bookshops, in the years just after the Cultural Revolution, found them stacked with the works of Mao Tse-tung, but with no old literature, Chinese or foreign, available for sale. An American correspondent who visited the library of Tsinghua University in 1971 found the section devoted to old Chinese literature still intact. But upon inspecting a copy of Mao's old favorite *Shui Hu,* known in the West as *All Men Are Brothers,* he found that it had not been borrowed since January 1967.[40]

The youthful Mao had read such books in secret, against his father's wishes, and as a young man in Changsha he had spent months in the public library, absorbing the contents of one volume after another. After he had become old, it will be recalled, Mao had held: "A little reading of books is all right, but a lot of it harms people— it really harms them." Not long after the death of Shih Huang-ti, hidden copies of the books he had proscribed again emerged, to be read by future generations. After Mao Tse-tung has gone, history may well repeat itself, with young Chinese following the example of the youthful Mao Tse-tung, rather than heeding the sour opinion of his old age.

In 1970, Mao Tse-tung admitted that the cult of his personality, which he had encouraged because it would strengthen him in the struggle against his adversaries, had been overdone. It was hard, he said, for the people to overcome the habit of worshipping their emperors, ingrained as it was through three thousand years of imperial rule. But calling him "Great Teacher, Great Leader, Great Supreme Commander, and Great Helmsman" was a nuisance. All those titles would be eliminated except the first, so that only that of "teacher" would remain.[41] His teachings undoubtedly will live on, after he has gone "to see God," but his power to prevent their reinterpretation will end. One recalls the words of Ch'en Yi: "Marx came from Germany, and Germany produced a Kautsky and a Bernstein to modify him. Lenin came from the Soviet Union and there, there appeared a Khrushchev. Chairman Mao belongs to our country; there may also be someone to modify him. Wait and see."

Who's Who

(Page numbers refer to places of early mention or identification)

B

BORODIN, MICHAEL, p. 29, was a Comintern adviser, during the 1920s, to Sun Yat-sen and the Kuomintang leaders who succeeded him.

BRAUN, OTTO, alias Li Te, alias Hua Fu, p. 84, was Comintern military adviser with the Chinese Communists (1933–1937).

C

CHANG CH'UN-CH'IAO, p. 231, a member of the Shanghai party committee and leader in the field of journalism who is believed to have helped Mao Tse-tung arrange for the publication there of the polemical essay by Yao Wen-yüan which was the opening shot in the Cultural Revolution. He subsequently led the successful assault on his superiors in the Shanghai party committee; became chairman of the city's ruling Revolutionary Committee; served as deputy head under Ch'en Po-ta and Chiang Ch'ing of the central Cultural Revolution Group; and emerged in 1969 as a member of the Political Bureau.

CHANG FA-K'UEI (1896–), p. 36, Cantonese general famous for 1926 victories during Chiang Kai-shek's Northern Expedition against the warlords. Communist-led elements of three armies broke away from his command in the August 1, 1927, Nanchang insurrection, regarded as marking the birth of the Red Army.

CHANG HSUEH-LIANG (1898–), pp. 53–54, son of the Manchurian warlord Chang Tso-lin, known as the Young Marshal and ruler of Manchuria from 1928 till its conquest by the Japanese in 1931. He succeeded in evacuating a portion of the armed forces he commanded to China proper, and Chiang Kai-shek subsequently appointed him deputy commander in chief of operations against the Chinese Communists. Persuaded by Chou En-lai of the feasibility of a policy of united front against the Japanese, he detained Chiang Kai-shek at Sian in December 1936 in an effort to force this policy on Chiang's government. He was subsequently sentenced to ten years' imprisonment for this offense, but is assumed still to be the prisoner of Chiang Kai-shek.

CHANG KUO-T'AO (1897–), p. 24, was chairman of the July 1921
First National Congress of the Chinese Communist party. About 1931,
he became political commissar of the army, commanded by Hsü
Hsiang-ch'ien, which was based first in the Hupeh-Honan-Anhwei
border area and later in Szechwan. He and Mao Tse-tung clashed at
a party conference held in Szechwan shortly after a rendezvous between his force and the veterans of the Long March. After this meeting, the two leaders went their separate ways, each accompanied by
some of the other's previous followers. Later military reverses undermined the political position of Chang Kuo-t'ao, and the remnants
of the forces which he and Hsü Hsiang-ch'ien led rejoined those of
Mao Tse-tung in northern Shensi. In 1938 Chang Kuo-t'ao left the
party. Since 1949 he has lived in retirement in Hong Kong.

CHANG TSO-LIN (1873–1928), p. 33, was a warlord who ruled Manchuria as a virtually separate state from 1919 onward, and who extended
his power to North China in 1924. In disregard of Japanese advice, he
attempted to hold on there in the face of Chiang Kai-shek's Northern
Expedition. He was fatally injured upon his return to Manchuria in
a bomb explosion, later revealed to have been arranged by a group
of Japanese army officers, and was succeeded by his son, Chang Hsüeh-
liang.

CHANG TSUNG-CH'ANG (1881–1932), p. 15, known as the "dog-meat
general," began his career as a bandit; commanded troops in East
China during the early years of the republican era; entered the service of Chang Tso-lin in 1922; led a division of Chang Tso-lin's troops
into the Peking-Tientsin area in 1924; and became military governor
of Shantung Province in 1925. He was notorious for his dangerous
temper, his rapacity, and the size of his harem.

CHANG WEN-T'IEN, alias Lo Fu (1898–), p. 67, was one of the So-
viet-trained group known as the Twenty-eight Bolsheviks. Prior to his
period in the Soviet Union, he worked on a Chinese newspaper in San
Francisco and in the library of the University of California at Berkeley.
He assumed the top party post of general secretary during the Long
March and held it for a period which coincided with the rise of Mao
Tse-tung to *de facto* leadership. Chang Wen-t'ien was dropped from
full to alternate member of the Political Bureau in 1956; joined
P'eng Te-huai in his challenge to Mao's policies at the Lushan plenum
of August 1959; and lost his government post of vice minister of For-
eign Affairs the following month. He was attacked during the Cultural
Revolution and dropped from the Central Committee in 1969.

CH'EN PO-TA (1904–), p. 164, Maoist ideologue, editor beginning in
1958 of the party journal *Red Flag*; and beginning in 1966 the head

of the Cultural Revolution Group. In his youth, Ch'en Po-ta studied in the USSR (1927–1930). He then went to North China where he joined the Communist underground and earned his living as an obscure professor. Upon the outbreak of the Sino-Japanese War in 1937, he went to Yenan where he was made director of the Research Section of the party's Department of Propaganda. He played a substantial role in Mao's rectification movement of 1942–1944, and used his editorial position beginning in 1958 to promote the cult of the "thought of Mao Tse-tung." As head of the Cultural Revolution Group, he was overshadowed by Chiang Ch'ing. He became a member of the Standing Committee of the Political Bureau in 1969, but by the summer of 1971 had been absent from the public view for a full year.

CH'EN TU-HSIU (1879–1942), p. 17, was instrumental in founding the Chinese Communist party. As editor, beginning in 1921, of the influential magazine *New Youth* and dean of the Peking University College of Letters (1917–1920), he was one of the great intellectual leaders of the republican era. A convinced Marxist by 1920, he set up the first Communist nucleus in China, and at the First National Congress of the party, held the following year, he was elected *in absentia* to the top party post of general secretary. He accepted with reluctance the Comintern policy which subordinated the Communist party to the Kuomintang, but was relieved of his leadership position when that policy broke down in 1927. Subsequently involved in policy disputes, he broke with the party in 1929. He was arrested and imprisoned by the government in 1932, was released after the outbreak of the war with Japan, and died near Chungking in 1942.

CH'EN YI (1901–1972), p. 19, one of Communist China's outstanding military leaders and, beginning in 1958, minister of foreign affairs. He had studied in France (1919–1921) at the same time as Chou En-lai and served with him on the staff of the Whampoa Military Academy just before the Northern Expedition, during which he served as a political officer under Yeh T'ing. He took part in the Nanchang insurrection, and after its failure became political commissar of the remnant force which Chu Teh led to Mao Tse-tung's Chingkangshan base in 1928. Left behind at the time of the Long March, he was made commander of the stay-behind force and survived as a guerrilla leader until the outbreak of the war with Japan. In 1938 his band became part of the Communist New Fourth Army, of which he became commander in 1941. During the 1946–1949 civil war he led that force, renamed the Third Field Army, in great battles which opened the way for the capture of Shanghai and Nanking, and was made marshal in 1955. He held important posts in East China subsequent to its occupation by the Communists, but had moved to Peking by the time

of his appointment as minister of foreign affairs. A mind untrammeled
by Marxist orthodoxy and a habit of speaking his mind made him a
tempting target during the Cultural Revolution.

CH'EN YÜN (1900–   ), p. 124, is known chiefly for his role as one of
the top managers of the Chinese economy. Originally a typesetter and
labor organizer in Shanghai, he served as a party functionary in
Kiangsi and subsequently took part in at least a portion of the Long
March. After a period of study in the Soviet Union (1935–1937), he
went to Yenan, where he became director of the party's Organization
Department, began his involvement in economic and financial matters,
and became a member of the Political Bureau. About the beginning of
1958, as a member of the Standing Committee of the Political Bureau,
the ranking vice premier and one of the regime's principal economists,
he found himself in opposition to Mao Tse-tung over the policies of
the Great Leap Forward. Although its failure vindicated his opposition, he never fully recovered his former prominence. Still a member of the Standing Committee of the Political Bureau at the beginning
of the Cultural Revolution, he was dropped to the status of ordinary
member of the Central Committee in 1969.

CH'I PEN-YÜ, p. 233, member of the Cultural Revolution Group until
his purge, is said to have been one of a group of bright young people
whom Chiang Ch'ing cultivated and encouraged to write political
essays in the early 1960s. In 1963 one of his essays got him into trouble
with Chou Yang, a party czar in the field of literature and culture, but
Chiang Ch'ing praised the essay and brought it to the favorable attention of Mao Tse-tung.

CHIANG CH'ING (1914?–   ), p. 103, the minor motion picture actress
who went to Yenan during the Sino-Japanese war and became the
wife of Mao Tse-tung. Her first participation in governmental affairs,
as member of the Film Guidance Committee of the Ministry of Culture
(1950–1954), got her little more than a reputation for making things
difficult. During the Cultural Revolution, as first deputy head and
de facto leader of the Cultural Revolution Group, she had the satisfaction of playing a leading role and bringing about the purge of a
long list of enemies, including almost everyone who was prominent
in the world of stage and screen.

CHIANG KAI-SHEK (1887–   ), p. 11, supporter of Sun Yat-sen; principal of the Whampoa Military Academy which trained the officers for
the Nationalist armies; generalissimo of the Northern Expedition
against the warlords (1926–1928); and since then the principal leader
of Kuomintang China.

CH'IN PANG-HSIEN, alias Po Ku (1907–1946), p. 67, one of the leaders
of the Russian-trained group known as the Twenty-eight Bolsheviks,

and general secretary of the party (1931–1935) after the defeat of Li Li-san and the departure for Moscow of Wang Ming. He was succeeded at the Tsunyi conference, during the Long March, by another member of his group named Chang Wen-t'ien. Ch'in Pang-hsien was one of the Communists' liaison officers with the National Government between 1936 and his death in an air crash ten years later.

CHOU EN-LAI (1898–   ), p. 19, premier since 1949 and a member of the Political Bureau since 1927. Chou was the son of a well-to-do gentry family, attended the famous Nankai Middle School in Tientsin, studied in Japan (1917–1919), and was one of the many hundreds of young Chinese who went to France shortly after World War I under a work-study program. He stayed in Europe about four years (1920–1924), spending much of his time doing organizational and agitational work on behalf of the Chinese Communist party. On his return to China he became acting director of the Political Department of Chiang Kai-shek's Whampoa Military Academy, which trained a corps of officers in preparation for the Northern Expedition against the warlords. In 1927, Chou helped organize the Shanghai worker uprisings which paved the way for capture of that city by Nationalist forces. Thereafter he worked for the party in the intelligence, security, and military fields, first at Shanghai and then in the Kiangsi soviet, where he succeeded Mao Tse-tung as political commissar of the Red Army—a post Chou En-lai held at least until January 1935. He spent most of the decade from 1937 to 1946 as the chief Communist representative and negotiator in the Nationalist capital. In 1949, he became premier of the People's Republic of China, holding the concurrent post of minister of foreign affairs. Although he yielded the latter post to Ch'en Yi in 1958, Chou has never abandoned his participation in the field of foreign affairs. During the Cultural Revolution he and his closest associates were the targets of a persistent offensive which reached its crisis in August 1967. He managed to survive it, and to emerge from the Cultural Revolution in what may prove a stronger position than ever.

CH'Ü CH'IU-PAI (1899–1935), p. 32, succeeded Ch'en Tu-hsiu as general secretary of the party in 1927, the year of the Nanchang insurrection and the Canton Commune. His putschist policies having failed, he was in 1928 replaced by Hsiang Chung-fa. Left behind at the time of the Long March because he was believed to be dying of tuberculosis, Ch'ü was captured by Kuomintang troops and later executed.

CHU TEH (1886–   ), p. 45, commander in chief of the Communist armies from 1930 to 1954. Somewhat older than most of his colleagues, Chu Teh had already attained the rank of brigadier general before he became a Communist. At the time of the August 1, 1927, Nanchang insurrection, which is regarded as marking the birth of the Red Army,

Chu Teh was the local commissioner of public security and commander of an officers' training regiment. When the forces which the Communists had broken off from the Kuomintang armies through that insurrection were defeated at Swatow, Chu Teh took command of a remnant force. In April 1928, Chu Teh led his force, in which Ch'en Yi was political commissar and Lin Piao a subordinate commander, to Mao Tse-tung's guerrilla base on the Chingkangshan. They united their forces as the Fourth Red Army, with Chu Teh as commander and Mao as political commissar. In 1930, Li Li-san called upon all Communist forces to converge on central China for attacks on principal cities, with Chu Teh as commander in chief and Mao Tse-tung as their political commissar. Although the attack failed and most of the Communist armies returned to their respective base areas, which were geographically separated from one another, Chu Teh's role as top commander was reaffirmed in 1931. Chu Teh and Mao Tse-tung were together during the greater part of the Long March, but Chu Teh remained behind in Szechwan with Chang Kuo-t'ao after the disagreement between Mao Tse-tung and Chang Kuo-t'ao. Subsequent military reverses led Chang Kuo-t'ao to follow the others to the northwest, where Chu Teh rejoined Mao Tse-tung after a separation of well over a year. Chu retained the role of commander in chief throughout the ensuing war against Japan and the civil war which followed. He lost it in 1954, when a government constitution was adopted which specified that the chairman of the People's Republic of China commanded the armed forces and a Ministry of National Defense was established, with P'eng Te-huai as its minister. In 1955, the government accorded the rank of marshal to ten men who had held important commands up to 1950: Chu Teh's name appeared first on the list. He was for many years one of the top members of the Political Bureau, but was dropped from membership in its Standing Committee in 1969.

F

FAN CHIN, p. 274, the widow of Yü Ch'i-wei, alias Huang Ching, who had had a brief love affair (or marriage) with Chiang Ch'ing in 1933. At the outbreak of the Cultural Revolution, Fan Chin was a vice mayor of Peking and director of *Peking Daily*.

FENG YÜ-HSIANG (1882–1948), p. 15, known as the "Christian General," was a North China warlord—but an unusual one who lived simply, promoted officers on the basis of merit, trained his troops well, and gave them moral indoctrination. The forces of Feng Yü-hsiang took part in the coalition which Chiang Kai-shek put together in 1928 for the final stage of his Northern Expedition, but civil war broke out between them the following year. Although the other members of the coalition later joined him against Chiang Kai-shek, they were defeated and Feng's power was brought to an end.

G

GALEN, p. 30, the alias of General, later Marshal, Vassili K. Bluecher, Soviet military adviser to Chiang Kai-shek before and during the first phase of the Northern Expedition against the warlords.

H

Ho LUNG (1896–), p. 45, one of the foremost Communist commanders from 1927 until the final defeat of the Nationalists in 1949, and prominent in party affairs from the time of the founding of the Communist regime until his purge during the Cultural Revolution. While his family was poor—Ho Lung worked as a cowherd in his youth, and received no formal education—his father was an influential member of a secret society known as the *Ko-lao-hui,* or elder brothers society. This connection helped enable Ho Lung, from the time he first took to the hills of his native Hunan in 1912, to raise the armed bands which he commanded in his successive roles as peasant rebel, bandit, commander of provincial troops, and Communist guerrilla. Ho Lung was persuaded to join the Communist cause by a relative named Chou I-ch'ün, who was a graduate of Chiang Kai-shek's Whampoa Military Academy and member of the Communist party. When Ho Lung took part in the Northern Expedition, Chou I-ch'ün served with him as political commissar, and at the time of the break between the Communists and the Kuomintang he played a part in persuading Ho Lung, who by then commanded the Twentieth Army, to help lead the August 1, 1927, insurrection at Nanchang. After this insurrection ended in disaster, Ho Lung returned to Hunan where he raised another army. His forces made the Long March to Yenan late in 1936; participated in the war against Japan as the 120th division; and as the First Field Army played an important part in the subsequent civil war. In recognition of his services, he was in 1955 given the rank of marshal. He was also named, about this time, head of the Physical Culture and Sports Commission, vice premier, and member of the Political Bureau.

Ho SHIH-CHEN (or Ho Tzu-chen), p. 66, the teen-aged girl who became Mao's wife in 1928, made the Long March, and was put aside during his period in Yenan.

HSIANG CHUNG-FA (1888–1931), p. 57–58, onetime coolie who became a Communist labor organizer and general secretary of the Communist party. While he held that office (1928–1931), the party center was under the *de facto* control first of Li Li-san and then of members of the group known as the Twenty-eight Bolsheviks. He was arrested in Shanghai on the basis of information supplied by the defector Ku Shun-chang, and executed soon afterwards.

HSIANG YING (1898–1941), pp. 57–58, early Communist labor leader and by 1928 one of the ranking leaders of the party. He was left behind in Kiangsi at the time of the Long March, became political commissar and deputy commander of the New Fourth Army during the war against Japan, and was killed during a Nationalist attack on its headquarters element in January 1941.

HSIAO HUA (1914–), p. 201, veteran of the Long March, the Sino-Japanese war, and the ensuing civil war, most of the time in forces commanded by Lin Piao. Hsiao Hua served as deputy director of the General Political Department of the PLA from the end of the civil war until 1963, and thereafter as its director until removed from that post during the Cultural Revolution.

HSIEH FU-CHIH (1898–1972), p. 250, minister of public security beginning in 1959. Hsieh was one of the ranking political commissars and military commanders in Liu Po-ch'eng's 129th division during the war against Japan. During the Cultural Revolution, he was a trusted supporter of Chiang Ch'ing and became chairman of the Peking Municipal Revolutionary Committee.

HSÜ HSIANG-CH'IEN (1902–), p. 54, leading Chinese Communist commander from the early years of the civil war until the Chinese Communist conquest of the mainland in 1949. Hsü Hsiang-ch'ien was a graduate of the Whampoa Military Academy who took part in the Canton Commune of 1927 and served as chief of staff of a division which was based in the earliest soviet, located in the so-called Hailufeng area of Kwangtung. In 1929, he was sent to help lead the forces in a Communist enclave in the Hupeh-Honan-Anhwei border area known as the O-yü-wan soviet. By 1931, he was the top military leader there, with Chang Kuo-t'ao as the political commissar; by 1932, their army numbered fifty thousand men. Driven from their base during Chiang Kai-shek's Fourth Annihilation Campaign that year, they retreated to Szechwan and rebuilt their forces. It was here that they had a rendezvous with Mao Tse-tung and the survivors of his Long March from Kiangsi, and held a party conference which ended in a split between Mao Tse-tung and Chang Kuo-t'ao. Hsü Hsiang-ch'ien remained with Chang Kuo-t'ao, but his forces were decimated during subsequent encounters with Kuomintang troops and the Moslem cavalry of northwest China. Hsü reached Mao's base at Yenan in mid 1937, with a remnant force, just before the Sino-Japanese war broke out. During that war, he served successively as deputy to three top commanders: Liu Po-ch'eng, Ho Lung, and Nieh Jung-chen. After the war against Japan, he suffered a long period of ill health. Although he held the post of

chief of staff (1951–1954) and was honored in 1955 by being accorded
the rank of marshal, little was heard of him until the Cultural Revolution. He then emerged as a member of the Political Bureau, vice chairman of the Military Affairs Committee, and head of the PLA Cultural
Revolution Group—only to fall into the bad graces of Madame Mao
and from posts to which he had but recently been appointed.

J

JAO SHU-SHIH (1901–   ), p. 130, served first as deputy political commissar (1939–1942) and then as political commissar (1942–1945) of the
New Fourth Army. He served in the same capacity with that force, renamed the Third Field Army, during the civil war, and after its conquest of East China became the top official in that region. In 1952, he
was appointed head of the party's Organization Department and a
member of Kao Kang's State Planning Committee. By the early months
of 1955, both of them had been purged.

K

K'ANG K'O-CH'ING (1912–   ), p. 67, wife of Chu Teh since 1929. At the
time of their marriage, she was the teen-aged leader of a small band of
Communist partisans, and he a thrice-married veteran soldier.

K'ANG SHENG (1899–   ), p. 140, a henchman of Mao Tse-tung who was
trained in the USSR in intelligence and security techniques. He is believed to have been in charge of the party's security operations for
many years, beginning in the late 1930s. Since the late 1950s he has
been a senior liaison officer with foreign Communist parties.

KAO KANG (1902–1954 or 1955), p. 87, was a top leader in the Shensi-
Kansu soviet which became the final destination of the Long March.
He was sent to Manchuria, after the defeat of Japan, to help build up
and lead the forces with which Lin Piao conquered that region for the
Communists. He remained there as chairman of the Northeast People's Government until after his appointment in 1952 as chairman of
the State Planning Committee in Peking. In 1955, it was announced
that he and Jao Shu-shih had been guilty of leading a conspiracy and
that he had committed suicide.

K'UAI TA-FU, p. 250, a Red Guard leader at Tsinghua University with
whom Wang Kuang-mei (Madame Liu Shao-ch'i) clashed when she was
member of a work team sent there early in the Cultural Revolution.
(Liu Shao-ch'i suspected that K'ang Sheng had put K'uai Ta-fu up to
opposing her.) Late in the Cultural Revolution he was arrested for
having initiated the use of arms in a factional struggle at Tsinghua.

KUNG CH'U (1901–   ), p. 52, was a young Chinese Communist party
worker and military commander (1924–1935) who left the Communists

shortly after the beginning of the Long March and subsequently wrote a book about his experiences entitled *Wo Yü Hung-chün* (The Red Army and I).

L

LI CHING-CH'UAN (1906–), p. 277, was a key figure in southwest China, with his headquarters in Szechwan, at the outbreak of the Cultural Revolution. Li Ching-ch'üan was a veteran of the Kiangsi soviet and the Long March. He served, during the Sino-Japanese war and the ensuing civil war, in Ho Lung's 120th division and First Field Army. He was the political commissar of the corps which occupied Chengtu, the capital of Szechwan, in 1949; he remained there in a succession of posts; and by the outbreak of the Cultural Revolution he was the ranking secretary of the party's Southwest Bureau and first political commissar of the Chengtu Military Region. He was also a member of the Central Committee and its Political Bureau.

LI FU-CH'UN (circa 1900–), p. 19, top Chinese Communist in the field of economic planning and, before April 1969, member of the Standing Committee of the Political Bureau. Li Fu-ch'un attended school at Changsha at the same time as Mao Tse-tung, and belonged to a political study group there of which Mao had been cofounder. Li Fu-ch'un and Chou En-lai went to France under the same work-study program, and after studying in France and the USSR he served under Chou En-lai as a political instructor at Chiang Kai-shek's Whampoa Military Academy. He participated in the Northern Expedition against the northern warlords; spent four years working in the party underground in Shanghai; accompanied the party center to Juichin, Kiangsi; made the Long March as a political officer in Lin Piao's First Front Army; and served again under Lin Piao, as political commissar, during the Communist conquest of Manchuria. Li Fu-ch'un began work in the financial and economic field during the Sino-Japanese war; resumed it in Manchuria after a Communist government had been set up there; and became chairman of the State Planning Commission and vice premier in the Peking government in 1954.

LI LI-SAN (1899–1967?), p. 31, early party labor leader and political agitator, *de facto* head of the party apparatus (1928–1930) while Hsiang Chung-fa was general secretary, and in that role an opponent of Mao Tse-tung. In 1930, he mobilized the Red armies for attacks on principal cities of central China, and their failure resulted in his overthrow. He spent the period from the end of 1930 to the closing days of World War II in Moscow and returned to China with the Soviet forces which invaded Manchuria in 1945. Li Li-san held posts there until the establishment of the People's Republic of China, when he became its minister of labor (1949–1954). Thereafter he held no important posts other than that of member of the Central Committee. He is reported to have committed suicide in 1967.

LI TA-CHAO (1889–1927), p. 18, like Ch'en Tu-hsiu, was one of the foremost intellectual leaders of China's early republican period, and like him became converted to Marxism about 1920. That year Gregory Voitinsky, a representative of the Comintern, offered to help Li Ta-chao organize a Communist party. Instead of accepting, he referred Voitinsky to Ch'en Tu-hsiu, and later helped Ch'en make the arrangements for the party's First Congress. A friend of Sun Yat-sen, Li Ta-chao promoted the policy of Kuomintang–Communist collaboration. Li Ta-chao was arrested in Peking in 1927 and executed, either by hanging or strangulation.

LI TSUNG-JEN (1890–1969), p. 35, military and political leader of Kwangsi Province who played a major role in the Northern Expedition against the warlords; was at odds with Chiang Kai-shek during the immediately succeeding years; held important Nationalist government commands during the war against Japan; served briefly as acting president of China in 1949; and lived in the United States from late 1949 until 1965, when he returned to China.

LIAO CHUNG-K'AI (1878–1925), p. 28, was born in San Francisco and received his education in the United States and in Japan, where he became a supporter of Sun Yat-sen. The chief architect, on the Kuomintang side, of the Communist–Kuomintang alliance and a favorite of Sun Yat-sen, Liao was the leader of the left wing of the Kuomintang at the time of his assassination. His son, Liao Ch'eng-chih, was chairman of the Overseas Chinese Affairs Commission before his purge during the Cultural Revolution.

LIAO MO-SHA (1907–), p. 187, a member of the Peking Municipal Committee, was the author together with Teng T'o and Wu Han, of essays satirizing Mao Tse-tung which were published under the title "Notes from the Three Family Village."

LIN PIAO (1907–), p. 52, designated Mao's successor in the party constitution adopted in 1969. Lin Piao graduated from Chiang Kai-shek's Whampoa Military Academy in 1926. He took part in the Northern Expedition against the warlords and the Communist insurrection at Nanchang while still in his teens, and was with the remnant force which Chu Teh led to the Chingkangshan to join Mao Tse-tung in 1928. During the Kiangsi period, Lin Piao formed a close association with Mao Tse-tung, and in 1932 he became commander of the Communists' First Front Army. He led it during the Long March, and stayed with Mao Tse-tung after the conference in Szechwan which broke up in a disagreement between Mao Tse-tung and Chang Kuo-t'ao. As commander of the 115th division during the Sino-Japanese war, he was severely wounded and subsequently spent several years in the USSR. During the 1946–1949 civil war, Lin Piao led the forces, known as the Fourth Field Army, which conquered Manchuria and participated in the battles for Peking, Tientsin, Wuhan, and Canton. In 1955, he was given the rank of marshal and in 1959, after the purging of P'eng Te-huai, he succeeded P'eng Te-huai as minister of national defense. In the latter part of 1971 it appeared that Lin Piao had fallen into disfavor.

LIU PO-CH'ENG (1892–   ), p. 46, a major Communist military leader since the Nanchang uprising. In 1926, when he joined the Communist party, he already had been a military officer for fifteen years. He took part in the Nanchang insurrection, after which he was sent to the USSR for further military training (1927–1930). After his return to China, he served on the party's Military Commission, first in Shanghai and later in Kiangsi, where he became chief of staff. He made the first part of the Long March with the forces led by Chu Teh and Mao Tse-tung; stayed behind in Szechwan with Chang Kuo-t'ao (as did Chu Teh); and arrived in the Yenan area in October 1936. He commanded the 129th division during the war against Japan, and the Second Field Army in the civil war which followed. Thereafter he held a succession of posts, including that of member of the Standing Committee of the Military Affairs Committee and (since 1956) of the Political Bureau. He was one of ten officers, accorded the rank of marshal in 1955.

LIU SHAO-CH'I (1900–   ), p. 25, was chairman of the People's Republic of China and second-ranking leader of the Communist party at the outbreak of the Cultural Revolution, during which he was purged. He was one of the first Chinese Communists to study in Moscow (1921–1922), where he joined the party. After his return to China, he worked as a labor organizer, and by 1932 he had risen to the post of chairman of the All-China Federation of Labor and was a member of the party's Political Bureau. After marking the Long March, he was appointed (1936) secretary of the party's North China Bureau. He spent much of the period of the war against Japan in the underground and working in Communist base areas behind the Japanese lines, part of it (1941–1942) as political commissar with Ch'en Yi's New Fourth Army. In the spring of 1942, he helped launch a rectification movement through which Mao Tse-tung was able to consolidate his control over the party at the expense of Moscow-oriented Chinese Communists. When the Nationalists captured Yenan in 1947, the party leadership split into two groups, one under Liu and the other under Mao. When the People's Republic of China was founded, Mao Tse-tung became chairman and Liu Shao-ch'i the second-ranking vice chairman (after Chu Teh), but during Mao's absence on a trip to the Soviet Union (December 1949–March 1950), it was Liu Shao-ch'i who was left in charge of party and state affairs. In 1959, he succeeded Mao as chairman of the government. As the chief of state, however, he remained in a subordinate position to Mao Tse-tung, the party chairman. He has been married to Wang Kuang-mei, his fifth wife, since the late 1940s.

Lo Jui-ch'ing (1907–   ), p. 176, was a vice premier, deputy minister of national defense and chief of staff of the People's Liberation Army until the eve of the Cultural Revolution, when he was relieved of his positions and attempted to commit suicide. Lo Jui-ch'ing took part in the Nanchang uprising, after which he was sent to the USSR, where he received intelligence and police training. He subsequently served as a political commissar in Kiangsi, on the Long March, during the war against Japan, and in the ensuing civil war. From 1949 until 1958, he was minister of public security; after the purge of P'eng Te-huai and Huang K'o-ch'eng in 1959, Lo Jui-ch'ing was appointed to the military positions which he occupied until the latter part of 1965.

Lu Ting-yi (1901–   ), p. 143, began his party career as a propagandist in 1926 in Shanghai; edited the party newspaper in the Kiangsi soviet in the early 1930s; made the Long March; served as director of the propaganda department of the Eighth Route Army during the war against Japan; and became director of the party's Propaganda Department in 1949. At the time of his purge in 1966 he still held that post; in addition, he was a member of the Political Bureau and of the party Secretariat.

M

Mao Tse-tung (1893–   ), p. 3, with Tung Pi-wu, one of the two surviving party member participants in the First Party Congress, and China's great teacher, great leader, great supreme commander and great helmsman. Married to Chiang Ch'ing, his third wife (or fourth, if one counts an arranged marriage of his teens, which he subsequently refused to recognize).

Mif, Pavel, alias Mikhail Aleksandrovich Fortus, p. 67, onetime chancellor of Sun Yat-sen University in Moscow and deputy head of the Far Eastern Secretariat of the Comintern. In the spring of 1930, he was sent to China as its representative, and shortly thereafter a group of his former students, known as the Twenty-eight Bolsheviks, succeeded in gaining control of the central apparatus of the Chinese Communist party.

N

NIEH JUNG-CHEN (1899–   ), p. 19, veteran commander, vice premier, and chairman of the Scientific and Technological Commission in charge of Communist China's advanced weapons program. Nieh was one of the Chinese who went to France, shortly after World War I, under the work-study program. Although he was among those converted to Marxism while there, he was not one of those who neglected his work and study in favor of political agitation. He remained away from China for five years, during which he studied engineering in Belgium; worked in an arms factory, an automobile plant, and an electrical factory; and attended the Red Army Academy in the Soviet Union. After his return to China, he taught under Chou En-lai in Chiang Kai-shek's Whampoa Military Academy; took part in the Northern Expedition against the warlords; participated in the 1927 insurrection at Nanchang and the short-lived Canton Commune; worked briefly on military affairs for the party center in Shanghai (1931); was in the central soviet in Kiangsi by January 1932, when he became political commissar of Lin Piao's First Army Corps; and served as Lin Piao's principal political officer during the Long March. When the war against Japan began, Nieh Jung-chen became deputy commander and political commissar of Lin Piao's 115th division; not long afterward, Lin Piao was wounded, and Nieh Jung-chen took over as acting commander. During the ensuing civil war he commanded the North China Field Army, which was an offshoot of that division. From 1949 to 1955, he was commander of the Peking-Tientsin garrison; he also served, during most of this period, as acting chief of staff, and during part of it as mayor of Peking. He became a vice premier in 1956 and the regime's top planner in the field of science and technology not long afterward.

NIEH YÜAN-TZU, p. 246, a lecturer in philosophy at Peking University. In 1964, Lu P'ing, president of the university and head of its party committee, accused her of being an antiparty element. In May 1966, she settled this score, with the secret encouragement of Mao Tse-tung, by putting up a big-character poster attacking Lu P'ing for his connection with P'eng Chen and for attempting to stifle the Cultural Revolution at Peking University. This launched her on a stormy career as Red Guard leader which culminated in her becoming vice chairman of the Peking Revolutionary Committee and was followed by her election, in 1969, as alternate member of the Central Committee.

P

P'ENG CHEN (1902–   ), p. 117, mayor of Peking, and member both of
the Political Bureau and the Secretariat at the time of his purge in
1966. A native of the northwestern province of Shansi, P'eng Chen
became a member of the party in 1923 and worked as a party organizer
in North China during his youth. He spent about six years in prison,
but rose rapidly in the party hierarchy after his release in 1935. P'eng
Chen served as a political commissar during part of the war against
Japan, but by 1944 he was head of the party's Organization Department and of its Central Party School. He became a member of the
Political Bureau in 1945, and was the top Communist political officer
in Manchuria during the early part of the 1946–1949 civil war. He
became mayor of Peking in 1951, and in 1956 he was reelected to the
Political Bureau and became the second-ranking member, after Teng
Hsiao-p'ing, of the party Secretariat.

P'ENG TE-HUAI (1898–   ), p. 56, minister of national defense from
1954 until 1959, when he led an attack on Mao Tse-tung's policy of
the Great Leap Forward, after which he was replaced by Lin Piao.
(During a period in which there was agitation for P'eng's rehabilitation, the historian Wu Han wrote plays about a minister of the Ming
dynasty, Hai Jui, who had been dismissed for the straightforward
criticism he had offered his sovereign. Mao Tse-tung saw in these
plays an effort to undermine his authority by reversing the verdicts
reached against P'eng Te-huai and his supporters.) At the time of his
dismissal, P'eng Te-huai was, next to Chu Teh, the most prestigious
military figure in Communist China. He had built a small army in
1928, and led it to the Chingkangshan, where he had joined it to the
force led by Chu Teh and Mao Tse-tung; he had registered the only
victory of Li Li-san's offensive against the cities in 1930, when he
captured Hunan's provincial capital of Changsha; and he had stood
with Mao when several other leaders had gone over to Chang Kuo-t'ao,
during the Long March. He had been Chu Teh's deputy and field
commander throughout the war against Japan; been the deputy commander under him of the PLA, during the civil war which followed;
and he had commanded the Chinese People's Volunteers during the
Korean war. The Lushan plenum was not the first time that he and
Mao had been at odds: in 1940 P'eng Te-huai had mustered about
four hundred thousand troops for a series of battles against the Japanese which may have cost him a quarter of his force and which invited
a savage counterattack. At the Lushan plenum, P'eng Te-huai recalled that at Yenan Mao Tse-tung had—presumably because of that

campaign—subjected him to criticism for a period of forty days, and at that plenum P'eng learned that Mao Tse-tung did not consider turn-about to be fair play.

PO I-PO (1907–), p. 127, chairman of the State Economic Commission (responsible for annual planning) and vice chairman of the State Planning Commission (responsible for five-year plans) at the outbreak of the Cultural Revolution, during which he suffered purge. Po I-po had been active in the Shansi branch of the party in the 1920s, was imprisoned in Peking in 1932, and was among those released in 1936 after ostensibly renouncing communism. During the war against Ja-pan, he played a major role in building the Shansi portion of the Communists' North China base area, and during the civil war which ensued he served as political commissar of Nieh Jung-chen's North China Military Region. It was presumably the experience gained in dealing with the economic and financial problems of a large area during war which helped fit him for his later role as one of China's ranking economic administrators—almost all of whom were purged or demoted during the Cultural Revolution.

S

SUN YAT-SEN (1866–1925), p. 10, leader of the revolutionary society known as the Kuomintang (National People's Party), which was devoted to the overthrow of the Ch'ing (Manchu) dynasty and the unification of China under a republican government. In 1923, disap-pointed in his attempts to gain the support of other foreign govern-ments, he accepted Soviet help. Thereafter the Kuomintang was re-structured on the organizational pattern of the Communist party of the Soviet Union; Chinese Communists were admitted to it as in-dividual members; the Whampoa Military Academy was set up to train and indoctrinate an officer corps; and the USSR supplied the instructors and munitions needed for training an army intended to conduct a Northern Expedition against the warlords. Sun Yat-sen died the year before it was launched.

T

T'AN CHEN-LIN (1902–), p. 77, a vice premier, director of the State Council's Agriculture and Forestry Office, and member of the Political Bureau at the time of his purge in 1967. T'an Chen-lin appears to have been one of Mao Tse-tung's earliest supporters. He took part in Mao's 1927 Autumn Harvest Uprising; accompanied him to the Chingkangshan; supported him in struggles with the Hunan party committee; and followed his guerrilla strategy in Fukien (the so-called Lo Ming line) in 1933, when it was contrary to the party's military policy. Perhaps in punishment, he was left behind the following year, when the Communists left their Kiangsi-Fukien base on the Long March. Thereafter he managed to survive, as a guerrilla leader, until the beginning of the war against Japan. He then became one of the leaders of the New Fourth Army and, during the civil war which followed the defeat of Japan, of Ch'en Yi's Third Field Army. He came into conflict with Mao Tse-tung in 1953, when Mao Tse-tung was pressing for the rapid collectivization of agriculture, taking the lead in sending a letter urging that Mao "take a rest"; yet T'an Chen-lin was a vocal supporter of Mao's Great Leap Forward. If one must speculate, it seems likely that Mao Tse-tung never forgave T'an for his suggestion of 1953, and that the failure of the Great Leap and Mao's launching of the Cultural Revolution convinced T'an Chen-lin that he had been right about Mao Tse-tung in 1953.

T'AO CHU (1905–   ), p. 129, was brought to Peking in July 1966 to succeed the purged Lu Ting-yi, director of the Propaganda Department of the Central Committee. A Communist since the early twenties, his career had been undistinguished until the latter days of the civil war, after which he had risen to the rank of first secretary in Canton of the party's Central-South Regional Bureau. He emerged from the August 1966 plenum as the fourth-ranking member of the hierarchy and was named advisor of the Cultural Revolution Group. However, both he and Teng Hsiao-p'ing, who had recommended him to Mao Tse-tung, soon fell victims of the Cultural Revolution.

TENG HSIAO-P'ING (1904–   ), p. 19, general secretary of the Central Committee and member of the Political Bureau at the time of his purge during the Cultural Revolution. Teng Hsiao-p'ing was one of the early Communists who went to France under the work-study plan, and he also studied briefly in Moscow before his return to China. He had a command under P'eng Te-huai during the Kiangsi period; made the Long March; and was political commissar of Liu Po-ch'eng's 129th division throughout the war against Japan and of Liu's Second Field Army during the ensuing civil war. In 1952, he was called to Peking, where he became a vice premier in Chou En-lai's cabinet; in 1953 he became the general secretary of the Central Committee; and in 1956 he was named to the Standing Committee of the Political Bureau.

TENG T'O (circa 1911–   ), p. 182, a Communist editor since 1938, and editor in chief of *People's Daily* from 1952 to 1959. Teng T'o was one of the three writers of a series of essays, "Notes from the Three-Family Village," in which Mao Tse-tung was satirized. He also was a secretary of the Peking municipal party committee under P'eng Chen, who put him in charge of the task of studying party documents put out unilaterally by Mao Tse-tung during the period of the Great Leap.

Ts'AI T'ING-K'AI (1891–1968), p. 47, commander of the 19th Route Army which fought the Japanese to a standstill at Shanghai in 1932, despite Chiang Kai-shek's orders for non-resistance. Ts'ai was forced to participate in the 1927 Nanchang insurrection but broke his forces away from the Communists during their retreat from that city. He was also the principal commander of a short-lived People's Government in Fukien province in 1933. As a "democratic personage," he held a number of positions under the Peking government between 1949 and the time of his death.

TUNG PI-WU (1886–), p. 126, is, with Mao Tse-tung, one of the two surviving Party members who were participants in the First National Congress of the Chinese Communist party. Tung Pi-wu had joined Sun Yat-sen's revolutionary party a decade earlier, while studying law in Japan, and had spent a year and a half in prison for political opposition during the period in which Yuan Shih-k'ai was trying to re-establish the monarchy. After his conversion to Communism, Tung Pi-wu had a long career as a nonmilitary party leader—in Kiangsi, during the Long March, at Yenan, and in Peking. In 1949 he was made chairman of the new government's Political and Legal Affairs Committee, and in 1953 he was made member of the committee appointed to draft a national constitution. In 1954 he became chief justice of the Supreme People's Court, a position he surrendered in 1959 upon his election as a vice chairman of the People's Republic of China.

W

WANG CHING-WEI (1884–1944), p. 31, an early supporter of Sun Yat-sen and political rival within the Kuomintang of Chiang Kai-shek. In 1927 he assumed leadership of the short-lived, left-wing Kuomintang regime at Wuhan, and in 1938 he went over to the Japanese, for whom he headed a puppet government at Nanking.

WANG KUANG-MEI, p. 108, since the late 1940s the wife of Liu Shao-ch'i (his fifth), and after his accession to the chairmanship of the government, the first lady of Communist China.

WANG LI (1918–), p. 266, a party careerist in the field of propaganda, became an associate editor under Ch'en Po-ta of the party journal Red Flag and a member of the Cultural Revolution Group. Wang Li was beaten up by workers who were under the leadership of army men during a mission to Wuhan in July 1967, and he got into trouble not long afterward for the ultra-leftist course pursued by the Cultural Revolution Group in the wake of the incident at Wuhan.

WANG MING (1904–), p. 67, the alias of Ch'en Shao-yü, a leader of the Twenty-eight Bolsheviks. He was general secretary of the party in 1931, after the overthrow of Li Li-san, represented the party with the Comintern (1932–1937), and returned to China shortly after the outbreak of the Sino-Japanese war in 1937. There he was a spokesman for the policy of close collaboration between the Communists and the Kuomintang, and became involved in policy disputes with Mao Tse-tung. Although Wang Ming was elected to the Central Committee in 1945, Mao Tse-tung had by then succeeded in destroying his influence. He has resided in the Soviet Union since the mid-1950s.

Wu Han (1909–), p. 187, vice mayor of Peking under P'eng Chen, noted historian, author of the play *Hai Jui Dismissed from Office*— which was seen as an attempt to vindicate P'eng Te-huai and hence to undermine Mao Tse-tung, and coauthor with Teng T'o and Liao Mo-sha of the satirical "Notes from the Three-Family Village."

Y

Yang Ch'eng-wu (1912–), p. 233, acting chief of staff of the PLA from the time Lo Jui-ch'ing was relieved as chief of staff late in 1965 until his own purge during the Cultural Revolution. Yang Ch'eng-wu joined the Red Army in Kiangsi; was political commissar of a regiment during the Long March; commanded a regiment of Lin Piao's 115th division during the early days of the war against Japan; and ended that war with a command of about thirty thousand men. He held important commands throughout the ensuing civil war, and may have fought in the Korean War.

Yang Shang-k'un (1905–), p. 243, one of the pro-Russian group known as the Twenty-eight Bolsheviks, political commissar of P'eng Te-huai's army during the Long March, secretary general of Eighth Route Army headquarters throughout the war against Japan, and director of the Staff Office of the Central Committee from 1945 until his purge in 1966.

Yao Teng-shan, p. 363, expelled from his post as Chinese Chargé d'Affaires in Indonesia in April 1967, returned to China and quickly became a leader of the revolutionary rebels in the foreign affairs sector of the government. He is believed to have seized power from Foreign Minister Ch'en Yi in August 1967, to have been in charge during the attack that month on the British Embassy, and to have been subsequently tried and sentenced to prison.

Yao Wen-yuan, p. 231, left wing journalist and literary critic in Shanghai. His November 30, 1965, article entitled "On the New Historical Play *Hai Jui Dismissed from Office*," written at the insti-gation of Mao Tse-tung and Chiang Ch'ing, is regarded as marking the opening of the Cultural Revolution. He subsequently became a member of the Cultural Revolution Group, first vice chairman of the

Shanghai Municipal Revolutionary Committee, and member of the
Political Bureau.

YEH CHIEN-YING (1898–   ), p. 46, one of China's ranking military
officers, member of the Poltical Bureau, and of the party's Military
Affairs Committee. Yeh was already an experienced military officer
by 1924, when he went to Canton and became an instructor in Chiang
Kai-shek's Whampoa Military Academy. Yeh was chief of staff of a
division in the army of Chang Fa-k'uei during the Northern Expedition against the warlords, and he helped plan the August 1, 1927, insurrection at Nanchang, during which elements of Chang Fa-k'uei's
army broke away from his command. Thereafter he went to Moscow,
where he studied for two years (1928–1930). After his return to China
he went to the Kiangsi soviet, where he was president of the Red
Army School and participated in the Long March. He spent part of
the period of the war against Japan as a Communist liaison officer
with the National Government and part as Eighth Route Army
chief of staff. In 1946 he headed the Communist section of the Executive Headquarters, established in Peking to supervise the cease-fire
worked out through the mediation efforts of U.S. Special Envoy George
C. Marshall. After the truce broke down, Yeh Chien-ying returned to
the army as deputy chief of staff of the PLA. In 1954, he was given
a PLA post which is the equivalent of inspector general—a post he
evidently still held as recently as 1965—and in 1955 he was given the
rank of marshal.

YEH T'ING (1897–1946), p. 42 is chiefly known for his roles as one
of the two principal leaders of the Nanchang insurrection, which
marked the birth of the Red Army, and for his command of the New
Fourth Army, beginning shortly after the outbreak of the war against
Japan and lasting until his capture in 1941 during an attack on headquarters elements of his army by Nationalist forces. Released from
imprisonment in 1946, he was killed in an air crash while en route
to Yenan.

YU CH'IU-LI (1914–   ), p. 443, a veteran Communist army officer who
became minister of petroleum industry in 1958 and vice chairman of
the State Planning Commission in 1965. In the latter position, he soon
proved himself indispensable to Li Fu-ch'un, the commission's ailing
chairman, and thereby became a convenient target for the political
enemies of Li Fu-ch'un and Premier Chou En-lai.

YUAN SHIH-K'AI (1859–1916), p. 8, was China's foremost military
commander during the latter days of the Ch'ing dynasty. In 1898, he
betrayed to the reactionary Empress Dowager a scheme of the reformist Emperor Kuang Hsü under which she was to have been made a

prisoner within the Palace grounds; in consequence it was Kuang Hsü who became her prisoner, and virtually all the reform measures which he had decreed were rescinded. In 1908, Kuang Hsü died and Yüan Shih-k'ai was named Senior Guardian of the heir apparent. In 1911, when the revolution aimed at establishing a republic broke out, he was first ordered to put down the rebels and later given full powers to negotiate a settlement with them. The settlement he negotiated called for the abdication of the Manchu Emperor and the establishment of a Republic. He became its president in 1912, and subsequently made an unsuccessful attempt to restore the monarchy with himself as emperor.

Abbreviations

AFP Agence France Presse
AP Associated Press
BTA Bulgarian Telegraph Agency (official news agency)
CCP Chinese Communist party
CNS China News Summary
CB *Current Background*
CQ *The Chinese Quarterly*
CRS China Reporting Service
CTK Czechoslovak News Agency
FBIS Foreign Broadcast Intelligence Service
FEER *Far Eastern Economic Review*
JCP Japanese Communist Party
JPRS Joint Publications Research Service
NCNA New China News Agency (*Hsin-hua*)
PLA People's Liberation Army
SCMP *Survey of China Mainland Press*
SW *Selected Works of Mao Tse-tung*
TANJUG Yugoslav News Agency
USIS United States Information Service

Notes

CHAPTER 1

A reader who wishes to find the sources for statements of fact which are contained in this chapter, but which are not keyed to any of the notes which follow, should consult the following: Edgar Snow, *Red Star Over China*, pp. 123–154; Jerome Ch'en, *Mao and the Chinese Revolution*, pp. 12–87; Stuart Schram, *Mao Tse-tung*, pp. 21–73; O. Edmund Clubb, *Twentieth Century China*, pp. 40–118; and Howard L. Boorman, ed., *Biographic Dictionary of Republican China*, Vol. III, pp. 2–22.

1. Cressey, *Land of the 500 Million: A Geography of China*, p. 53.
2. Huang, *Mao Tse-tung sheng-p'ing tzu-liao chien-pien*, p. 3.
3. Emil Schulthess, *China* (London: Collins, 1966), photos numbered 141–145 and accompanying text; and Chow Ching-wen, *Ten Years of Storm* (New York: Holt, Rinehart & Winston, 1960), pp. 72–73.
4. Snow, *Red Star*, p. 125.
5. *Ibid.*, p. 126.
6. *Ibid.* p. 125.
7. Siao-Yu, *Mao Tse-tung and I Were Beggars*, pp. 6–8.
8. Schram, *The Political Thought of Mao Tse-tung*, p. 22.
9. Fitzgerald, *China: A Short Cultural History*, pp. 135–149.
10. *Ibid.*
11. *Ibid.*, pp. 502–506; and Pearl S. Buck, tr., *All Men Are Brothers*, pp. 471–482, 526–528, 1267.
12. Lo Kuan-chung, *Romance of the Three Kingdoms*, *passim*; Fitzgerald, *China*, pp. 499–502; Yong-sang Ng, "The Poetry of Mao Tse-tung," pp. 60–73; Schram, *Political Thought of Mao*, p. 162; and Kuo Mo-jo, "A Reappraisal of the Case of Ts'ao Ts'ao," *Wen-shih lun-chi* (Peking, 1961), as translated in *Chinese Studies in History and Philosophy* I:4 (Summer 1968), pp. 3–30. Kuo Mo-Jo, perhaps with one eye on Mao Tse-tung, argues for the reversal of history's conventional verdict on Ts'ao Ts'ao.
13. Siao-Yu, *Mao Tse-tung and I*, pp. 24–26.
14. Jacques Marcuse, *The Peking Papers* (New York: Dutton, 1967), p. 288.
15. J. O. P. Bland and E. Backhouse, *China Under the Empress Dowager* (London: Heinemann, 1911), pp. 120, 161–210.
16. *Ibid.*; and Princess Der Ling, *Two Years in the Forbidden City* (New York: Moffat, Yard and Co., 1912), p. 68.
17. Bland and Backhouse, *China Under the Empress Dowager*, p. 466.
18. Richard Hughes, "Thoughts of Madame Mao," *Far Eastern Economic Review* (hereinafter cited as *FEER*), LXI (July 18, 1968), p. 149.
19. Fitzgerald, *China*, pp. 535–539.

20. Latourette, *The Chinese: Their History and Culture*, pp. 231–233.

21. Samuel Victor Constant, *Calls, Sounds, and Merchandise of the Peking Street Peddlers* (Peking: The Camel Bell, 1936), pp. 70–76.

22. Boorman, *Biographical Dictionary*, I:319–320, and III:170–174.

23. *Ibid.*, III:176–177.

24. Siao-Yu, *Mao Tse-tung and I*, pp. 236–237.

25. Boorman, *Biographical Dictionary*, I:122–127.

26. *Ibid.*

27. Ch'en, *Great Lives Observed: Mao*, pp. 7–9.

28. *Ibid.;* and Schram, *Political Thought of Mao*, pp. 25–26.

29. Schram, *Political Thought of Mao*, p. 154.

30. Siao-Yu, *Mao Tse-tung and I*, pp. 68–69, 202.

31. Schram, *Political Thought of Mao*, p. 160.

32. Snow, *Red Star*, pp. 153–154.

33. Siao-Yu, *Mao Tse-tung and I*, pp. 242–243, quoting from Kiang Wen-han, *The Chinese Student Movement* (New York: King's Crown Press, 1948), p. 25.

34. Speech by Lin Piao, New China News Agency (hereinafter cited as NCNA), English Service, August 18, 1966.

35. Vinacke, *A History of the Far East in Modern Times*, pp. 138, 377–380, 393; and Carl Russell Fish, *The Development of American Nationality* (New York: American Book Co., 1924), p. 563.

36. Chow Tse-tsung, *The May Fourth Movement, passim;* and Vinacke, *History of the Far East*, p. 440.

37. *Survey of China Mainland Press* (hereinafter cited as *SCMP*), (Hong Kong: American Consulate General), no. 4200 (June 16, 1968), p. 3.

38. Vinacke, *History of the Far East*, p. 421.

39. *All About Shanghai* (1934–1935 ed.; Shanghai: University Press), pp. 2–3, 13–21.

40. Boorman, *Biographical Dictionary*, I:197, 243, and III:342; and Huang, *Mao Tse-tung sheng-p'ing*, pp. 47–48.

41. Boorman, *Biographical Dictionary*, I:243, and III:180; and Wales, *Red Dust: Autobiographies of Chinese Communists as Told to Nym Wales*, p. 39.

42. Boorman, *Biographical Dictionary*, I:243. For a list of the participants, see Ch'en, *Mao and the Chinese Revolution*, p. 79.

CHAPTER 2

1. Vinacke, *History of the Far East*, p. 442.

2. Ch'en, *Mao and the Chinese Revolution*, p. 90.

3. Boorman, *Biographical Dictionary*, I:321–322.

4. *Ibid.*

5. Ch'en, *Mao and the Chinese Revolution*, pp. 90–91.

6. Clubb, *Twentieth-Century China*, pp. 118–120.

7. *Ibid.;* and Boorman, *Biographical Dictionary*, I:321–322.

8. Ch'en, *Mao and the Chinese Revolution*, pp. 92–93.

9. *Ibid.*

10. Clubb, *Twentieth-Century China,* pp. 121–123; and Ch'en, *Mao and the Chinese Revolution,* pp. 94–96.

11. Boorman, *Biographical Dictionary,* I:323, 393, and biographies of other persons mentioned therein.

12. Snow, *Red Star,* p. 145.

13. *Ibid.,* p. 159.

14. Ch'en, *Mao and the Chinese Revolution,* pp. 99–100; and Clubb, *Twentieth-Century China,* p. 129.

15. Ch'en, *Mao and the Chinese Revolution,* p. 100; and Boorman, *Biographical Dictionary,* I:477, and III: 310, 406.

16. Boorman, *Biographical Dictionary,* III:7; Schram, *Mao Tse-tung,* pp. 83–85; and Ch'en, *Mao and the Chinese Revolution,* pp. 100–101 and 109.

17. Clubb, *Twentieth-Century China,* p. 130.

18. Ch'en, *Mao and the Chinese Revolution,* pp. 101–102.

19. *Ibid.,* pp. 98–99.

20. Clubb, *Twentieth-Century China,* pp. 124–125.

21. *Ibid.,* p. 132; and Boorman, *Biographical Dictionary,* II:40.

22. Ch'en, *Mao and the Chinese Revolution,* pp. 102–103.

23. Schram, *Mao Tse-tung,* p. 88.

24. Clubb, *Twentieth-Century China,* p. 131.

25. *Ibid.;* Schram, *Mao Tse-tung,* pp. 89, 92; Ch'en, *Mao and the Chinese Revolution,* pp. 102–104; and Boorman, *Biographical Dictionary,* I:325.

26. Schram, *Political Thought of Mao,* p. 49.

27. Chang Kuo-t'ao, "Mao: A New Portrait of an Old Colleague," *New York Times Magazine,* August 2, 1953, p. 47.

28. Schram, *Mao Tse-tung,* pp. 88–90.

29. Boorman, *Biographical Dictionary,* I:57, II:338, and III:236.

30. Clubb, *Twentieth-Century China,* p. 134; and Boorman, *Biographical Dictionary,* I:125, and II:162.

31. Clubb, *Twentieth-Century China,* p. 135; Boorman, *Biographical Dictionary,* I:76, 326, and III:237–238; Ch'en, *Mao and the Chinese Revolution,* p. 115; and Rue, *Mao Tse-tung in Opposition,* p. 56.

32. Schram, *Mao Tse-tung,* pp. 89–94, 111; Schram, *Political Thought of Mao,* pp. 254–255; and Boorman, *Biographical Dictionary,* III:7–8.

33. Mao Tse-tung, *Selected Works of Mao Tse-tung* (hereinafter cited as *SW*), I:23–24; and Schram, *Political Thought of Mao,* pp. 250–251.

34. Schram, *Political Thought of Mao,* p. 252.

35. Schram, *Mao Tse-tung,* pp. 95–103, 109–110.

36. Boorman, *Biographical Dictionary,* I:119–120, 125.

37. Schram, *Mao Tse-tung,* pp. 97–98.

38. *Ibid.,* p. 98; and Boorman, *Biographical Dictionary,* I:76.

39. Boorman, *Biographical Dictionary,* II:273–274.

40. Clubb, *Twentieth-Century China,* p. 134; Boorman, *Biographical Dictionary,* I:393–394; and Harold R. Isaacs, *The Tragedy of the Chinese Revolution* (London: Secker & Warburg, 1938), pp. 148–161.

41. Boorman, *Biographical Dictionary,* I:282, 325.

42. Clubb, *Twentieth-Century China*, p. 136; Boorman, *Biographical Dictionary*, I:321, and III:328–330.

43. Clubb, *Twentieth-Century China*, p. 136.

44. *Ibid.;* and Boorman, *Biographical Dictionary*, III:372.

45. Boorman, *Biographical Dictionary*, I:120, and II:333.

46. *Ibid.*, I:394, and III:329; and Clubb, *Twentieth-Century China*, p. 137.

47. Boorman, *Biographical Dictionary*, I:326.

48. *Ibid.*, I:455.

49. Schram, *Mao Tse-tung*, pp. 98–103, 108–110; and Ch'en, *Mao and the Chinese Revolution*, pp. 110–111, 117–118.

50. Schram, *Mao Tse-tung*, p. 110.

51. *Ibid.;* Boorman, *Biographical Dictionary*, I:455–456, II:61, and III:238; Ch'en, *Mao and the Chinese Revolution*, p. 116; and Hofheinz, "The Autumn Harvest Insurrection," pp. 38–40.

52. Schram, *Mao Tse-tung*, pp. 111–115; and Ch'en, *Mao and the Chinese Revolution*, pp. 121–124.

53. Clubb, *Twentieth-Century China*, pp. 138–139.

54. *Ibid.*, pp. 139–141; Ch'en, *Mao and the Chinese Revolution*, p. 125; Boorman, *Biographical Dictionary*, II:61, and III:145, 164; and Hofheinz, "The Autumn Harvest Insurrection," p. 40.

CHAPTER 3

1. Hofheinz, "The Autumn Harvest Insurrection," pp. 40–42.

2. Even before the troops of T'ang Sheng-chih had pushed northward for the linkup with Feng Yü-hsiang, the Comintern delegate Roy had urged that the Communists return to the original base in Kwangtung (Schram, *Mao Tse-tung*, p. 108).

3. Clubb, *Twentieth-Century China*, p. 139; and Boorman, *Biographical Dictionary*, I:56–58, 455–456, 461.

4. Boorman, *Biographical Dictionary*, II:69; and *Who's Who in Communist China*, I:230.

5. Boorman, *Biographical Dictionary*, I:455, 459–461, and II:404.

6. Translations of the accounts of several leading participants in the Nanchang Uprising will be found in C. Martin Wilbur, "The Ashes of Defeat," *The China Quarterly* (hereinafter cited as *CQ*), no. 18 (April-June 1964), pp. 3–54. The quotation attributed to Chou En-lai is contained in *SCMP*, no. 4088 (September 28, 1967), pp. 11–12. In preparing the foregoing account, I also consulted J. Guillermaz, "The Nanchang Uprising," *CQ*, no. 11 (July-September 1962), pp. 161–168; Kung Ch'u, *Wo yü hung-chün*, pp. 47–87; Smedley, *The Great Road*, pp. 199–210; and the biographies of major participants as given in Boorman, *Biographical Dictionary*.

7. Boorman, *Biographical Dictionary*, I:245.

8. Hofheinz, "The Autumn Harvest Insurrection," pp. 37–87; Snow, *Red Star*, p. 169 (in which the name of the place where the soviet was established is romanized "Tsalin"); and Ch'en, *Mao and the Chinese Revolution*, pp. 130–133.

9. Snow, *Red Star*, p. 172; Smedley, *Great Road*, p. 227; Kung Ch'u, *Wo yü hung-chün*, pp. 120–121; and Mao, *SW*, I:86–87.

10. Kung Ch'u, *Wo yü hung-chün*, pp. 121–122; and Snow, *Red Star*, p. 170.

11. Boorman, *Biographical Dictionary*, II:375.

12. Kung Ch'u, *Wo yü hung-chün*, pp. 123–125.

13. Ch'en, *Mao and the Chinese Revolution*, p. 140; Snow, *Red Star*, p. 170; and Mao, *SW*, I:86.

14. Kuantung—meaning east of the pass (through the Great Wall between Manchuria and China proper)—not Kuangtung, the province of which Canton is the capital.

15. This account of the last phase of the Northern Expedition is based largely on the biographies of the principal actors, as contained in Boorman, *Biographical Dictionary*, and on Clubb, *Twentieth-Century China*, pp. 143–144.

16. Mao, *SW*, I:64–65; and Schram, *Political Thought of Mao Tse-tung*, p. 267.

17. Schram, *Mao Tse-tung*, pp. 130–135; Ch'en, *Mao and the Chinese Revolution*, pp. 139–143; and Mao, *SW*, I:75, 80, 96–97.

18. Mao, *SW*, I:100.

19. Snow, *Red Star*, p. 172; Smedley, *Great Road*, p. 242; Rue, *Mao in Opposition*, p. 150, n.; and Ch'en, *Mao and the Chinese Revolution*, pp. 149–150.

20. Ch'en, *Mao and the Chinese Revolution*, p. 149; Schram, *Mao Tse-tung*, p. 137; and Snow, *Red Star*, p. 170.

21. *The Case of P'eng Teh-huai*, p. 186.

CHAPTER 4

1. Schram, *Mao Tse-tung*, p. 138; Ch'en, *Mao and the Chinese Revolution*, p. 150; and Smedley, *Great Road*, pp. 236–253

2. Schram, *Mao Tse-tung*, p. 138; and Smedley, *Great Road*, p. 253.

3. Swarup, *A Study of the Chinese Communist Movement*, pp. 206, 231–233; and Boorman, *Biographical Dictionary*, II:87–89.

4. Thornton, *The Comintern and the Chinese Communists 1928–1931*, p. 36 (citing *Kommunisticheskii International v dokumentakh*, p. 765).

5. North, *Moscow and Chinese Communists*, p. 129.

6. Snow, *Red Star*, pp. 144–145.

7. Thornton, *Comintern and Chinese Communists*, pp. 40–41.

8. Ch'en, *Mao and the Chinese Revolution*, p. 143; Swarup, *Chinese Communist Movement*, p. 86; and Mao, *SW*, I:72 n. 9, 73–102.

9. Ch'en, *Mao and the Chinese Revolution*, p. 150; and Schram, *Mao Tse-tung*, pp. 138–139.

10. Mao, *SW*, I:80, 97.

11. *Ibid.*, I:122–123.

12. Snow, *Red Star*, p. 177.

13. Kung Ch'u, *Wo yü hung-chün*, p. 266.

14. Ch'en, *Mao and the Chinese Revolution*, pp. 152–153; Boorman, *Biographical Dictionary*, III:259; and Rue, *Mao in Opposition*, pp. 152–153.

15. Mao, *SW*, I:105–115, 117–127.

16. *SCMP*, no. 4147 (March 27, 1968), pp. 6, 10.

17. Mao, *SW*, I:105–106.

18. North, *Moscow and Chinese Communists*, pp. 133–136; Hsiao Tso-liang, *Power Relations Within the Chinese Communist Movement, 1930–1934: A Study of Documents*, pp. 14–22; and Thornton, *Comintern and Chinese Communists*, pp. 115–156.

19. Thornton, *Comintern and Chinese Communists*, pp. 157–158. Most works covering this period have used the term "army corps" as the translation for the Chinese term *chün-t'uan*, meaning an aggregation of two or more *chün*, which alone is usually rendered as "army." I accordingly have followed this same practice. However, it should be noted that this is contrary to U. S. Army nomenclature under which two or more divisions form a corps, and two or more corps form an army. William Whitson follows this nomenclature in his article, "The Field Army in Chinese Communist Military Politics." However, practice is more uniform when it comes to translating the term *fang-mien chün*—an aggregation of chün-t'uan—which is usually rendered "front army."

20. For the foregoing account of the attacks on the cities and the fall of Li Li-san, I have drawn on Ch'en, *Mao and the Chinese Revolution*, pp. 157–159; Schram, *Mao Tse-tung*, pp. 142–151; Thornton, *Comintern and Chinese Communists*, pp. 157–217; and the biographies of principal participants as contained in Boorman, *Biographical Dictionary*.

21. A photo of Yang K'ai-hui and the two boys appears opposite p. 94 of Ch'en, *Mao Papers: Anthology and Bibliography*.

22. A translation of this poem, "The Immortals," will be found in Ch'en, *Mao and the Chinese Revolution*, p. 347.

23. Also called Ho Tzu-chen, presumably reflecting her use of more than one given name.

24. Ch'en, *Mao and the Chinese Revolution*, p. 150; Schram, *Mao Tse-tung*, p. 208; Boorman, *Biographical Dictionary*, III:13; Smedley, *Great Road*, pp. 223–224; Wales, *Red Dust*, p. 214; and Kung Ch'u, *Wo yü hung-chün*, pp. 131–132, 143–145, and photos opposite p. 315.

25. Ch'en, *Mao and the Chinese Revolution*, p. 159; Schram, *Mao Tse-tung*, pp. 149–150; Boorman, *Biographical Dictionary*, I:135; Wales, *Red Dust*, p. 13; and Swarup, *Chinese Communist Movement*, pp. 245–246.

26. Hsiao, *Power Relations*, p. 103; Schram, *Mao Tse-tung*, p. 152; and Thornton, *Comintern and Chinese Communists*, pp. 165–166.

27. Smedley, *Great Road*, pp. 242–243.

28. Hsiao, *Power Relations*, pp. 98–113.

29. The estimate that some two thousand to three thousand officers and men lost their lives will be found in Schram, *Mao Tse-tung*, p. 152. The story of Ch'en Yi's trip to Shanghai, attributed to Ch'en Jan who shared a room with Ch'en Yi at one of his stops along the way, is recounted by Warren Kuo in *Analytical History of Chinese Communist Party*, Book Two (Taipei:

Institute of International Relations, 1968), pp. 21, 24, 32, n.37. It is interesting, in this general connection, that Ch'en Yi was later quoted as saying: "Once I, too, opposed Chairman Mao, but he still gave me an important position when he came to power." (Translation of item from April 4, 1967, issue of *Hung Ch'i* of the Peking Aeronautical Institute, carried in *SCMP*, Supplement No. 180 (May 1, 1967), pp. 1–6.) Chang Kuo-t'ao has reported that Ch'en Yi initially had sided with the opposition group, and that he was eventually punished for his role in their liquidation by not being given important posts, and by being left behind at the time of the Long March. Klein and Clark cite Chang Kuo-t'ao as saying that Ch'en Yi initially wavered, during the incident, in his support for Mao, but eventually took a direct hand in their bloody execution. See Klein and Clark, *Biographic Dictionary of Chinese Communism 1921–1965*, I:107. The statements that Ch'en Yi was assigned to liquidate the opposition group, and that this tied him to Mao Tse-tung, will be found in Boorman, *Biographical Dictionary* I:256. Rue, *Mao in Opposition*, pp. 227–230, based on Mao's own account in *Nung-tsun tiao-ch'a*, bears on Ch'en Yi's role in mid-November, just before Mao carried out the arrests which sparked the so-called revolt.

30. Snow, *Red Star*, p. 182.

31. Swarup, *Chinese Communist Movement*, pp. 246–247; and Hsiao, *Power Relations*, pp. 108–109, 112–113.

32. Kung Ch'u, *Wo yü hung-chün*, pp. 243–244, 246–248, 266.

CHAPTER 5

1. Kai-yu Hsü, "Chou En-lai, the Indispensable Man of Compromise." *New Republic*, April 8, 1967, pp. 22–25; Li Tien-min, *Chou En-lai* (Taipei: Institute of International Relations, 1970), pp. 150–155; *Time*, May 10, 1954; and communication to the author from Wu Kuo-chen (Dr. K. C. Wu), in 1932 the mayor of Hankow, where Ku Shun-chang defected. Available sources agree in making Chou En-lai responsible for ordering the killing of members of Ku Shun-chang's family, but not concerning the details of the execution of the orders and the subsequent discovery of the bodies.

2. Hsiao, *Power Relations*, pp. 161–162, 172.

3. Ch'en, *Mao and the Chinese Revolution*, p. 172.

4. Kung Ch'u, *Wo yü hung-chün*, p. 266.

5. Ch'en, *Mao and the Chinese Revolution*, pp. 166–170; Clubb, *Twentieth-Century China*, p. 166; and John Toland, *The Rising Sun* (New York: Random House, 1970), pp. 6–8.

6. Clubb, *Twentieth-Century China*, p. 170.

7. *Ibid.*, p. 169.

8. Ch'en, *Mao and the Chinese Revolution*, pp. 174–175; and Mao, *SW*, IV:17–18.

9. Ch'en, *Mao and the Chinese Revolution*, pp. 174–175; and Hsiao, *Power Relations*, p. 200.

10. Ch'en, *Mao and the Chinese Revolution*, pp. 174–176; Swarup, *Chinese Communist Movement*, pp. 249–250; and Wales, *Red Dust*, p. 164. It should be noted that the generally-used term "corps," as an identifying term for the components of the Eastern Front Army, does not accord with U.S. Army nomenclature. A reading of Kung Ch'u, *Wo yü hung-chün*, pp. 305–308, suggests that the relevant Chinese designation was *chün-t'uan*, which could be translated "army group."

11. Ch'en, *Mao and the Chinese Revolution*, p. 176.

12. *Ibid.*, 176–177.

13. Mao, *SW*, I:236–237.

14. Schram, *Mao Tse-tung*, p. 169.

15. Rinden and Witke, *The Red Flag Waves: A Guide to the Hung-ch'i p'iao-p'iao Collection*, pp. 36–37, 106; Ch'en, *Mao and the Chinese Revolution*, pp. 167, 177; Boorman, *Biographical Dictionary*, II:307; Kung Ch'u, *Wo yü hung-chün*, p. 328; and Nym Wales, *My Yenan Notebooks* (Madison, Conn.: 1961), p. 125.

16. Ch'en, *Mao*, p. 95.

17. *Hung-ch'i p'iao-p'iao*, XI, 3–18.

18. Ch'en, *Mao and the Chinese Revolution*, p. 177.

19. Hsiao, *Power Relations*, pp. 220, 240, 246–247.

20. Clubb, *Twentieth-Century China*, pp. 172–173, 183, 198–201; and Hsiao, *Power Relations*, p. 248–250.

21. Snow, *Red Star*, pp. 191–193; and Clubb, *Twentieth-Century China*, pp. 200–202.

22. Mao, *SW*, I:247.

23. Hsiao, *Power Relations*, pp. 253–254; and Hsiao Tso-liang, *Power Relations within the Chinese Communist Movement, 1930–1934: The Chinese Documents* (Seattle: University of Washington Press, 1967), p. 684.

24. Hsiao, *Chinese Documents*, pp. 707, 728.

25. Mao, *SW*, I:156.

26. Jerome Ch'en, "Resolutions of the Tsunyi Conference," p. 28.

27. Because success has many fathers but failure is an orphan, it is hard to say who the others were. In 1936, Chou En-lai told Edgar Snow, as recounted in his *Random Notes on Red China* (Cambridge: Harvard University Press, 1957), p. 60, that the Comintern agent Otto Braun, alias Li Teh, had persuaded the Communists not to cooperate with the Fukien rebels.

28. Kung Ch'u, *Wo yü hung-chün*, pp. 395–398. The story given Kung Ch'u may, of course, have been untrue. See William F. Dorrill, "The Fukien Rebellion and the CCP: A Case of Maoist Revisionism," *CQ*, no. 37 (January–March 1969), pp. 31–53, for a carefully considered account.

29. Ch'en, *Mao and the Chinese Revolution*, pp. 182–183.

30. *Ibid.*, p. 184.

31. Hu Chi-hsi, "Hua Fu, the Fifth Encirclement Campaign and the Tsunyi Conference," p. 45.

32. Kung Ch'u, *Wo yü hung-chün*, pp. 430–432.

CHAPTER 6

1. Smedley, *Great Road*, pp. 310–311.

2. Snow, *Red Star*, pp. 194–197; Ch'en, *Mao and the Chinese Revolution*, pp. 185–189; Schram, *Mao Tse-tung*, p. 181; Ch'en, "Resolutions of the Tsunyi Conference," pp. 12, 32–33; and Hu, "Hua Fu," pp. 45–46.

3. Hsiao, *Power Relations*, pp. 296–297.

4. For the foregoing account of the Tsunyi conference I have drawn heavily on Ch'en, "Resolutions of the Tsunyi Conference," Dieter Heinzig, "Otto Braun and the Tsunyi Conference," and Hu, "Hua Fu." See also Huang, *Mao Tse-tung sheng-p'ing*, p. 147.

5. Snow, *Red Star*, pp. 187, 198, 319.

6. Wales, *Yenan Notebooks*, p. 124. On page 131 she quotes Mao himself to somewhat similar effect. In both cases Mao's position as chairman of the Provisional Central Government of the Chinese Soviet Republic comes in for mention, but as Nym Wales also observes, the post then was a nominal one.

7. Mao, *SW*, III:193.

8. *SCMP*, no. 4088, (December 28, 1967), p. 9.

9. *Selections from China Mainland Magazines* (Hong Kong: American Consulate General), Supplement no. 21 (April 2, 1968), p. 44. The term *t'u-kung* for native Communist was applied to Mao Tse-tung by some of his critics, in contradistinction to those who regarded themselves as Moscow Communists by virtue of training in the USSR or visits there.

10. Snow, *Red Star*, pp. 200–209; Schram, *Mao Tse-tung*, p. 184; and Ch'en, *Mao and the Chinese Revolution*, pp. 191–192.

11. Snow, *Red Star*, pp. 212–213; Ch'en, *Mao and the Chinese Revolution*, pp. 192–194; and Schram, *Mao Tse-tung*, pp. 186–187.

12. Cressey, *Land of the 500 Million*, p. 338; Snow, *Red Star*, pp. 213–215; and personal observation, based on travel in Tsinghai.

13. There is some evidence that Mao Tse-tung and P'eng Te-huai had a disagreement, during the final stage of the Long March, as to their final destination, and that Mao brought P'eng under control by depriving him of his direct command of troops. This was apparently accomplished by giving P'eng Te-huai the title of commander in chief but simultaneously incorporating his Third Army Corps in the First Army Corps of Lin Piao. Because Lin Piao was the faithful follower of Mao Tse-tung, who simultaneously took the position of political commissar of the combined force, P'eng Te-huai was effectively checkmated. (See *Case of Peng Teh-huai*, pp. 189–190.) A short time before they reached Shensi, Hsü Hai-tung had arrived there with an army which was combined with the forces of Liu Chih-tan and Kao Kang to form the Fifteenth Army Corps. Liu Chih-tan and Kao Kang may have been imprisoned briefly during the autumn of 1935, under circumstances which remain unclear. (See Ch'en, *Mao and the Chinese Revolution*, pp. 201–202.) Subsequently, Liu Chih-tan was mortally wounded in battle; Hsü Hai-tung was made a subordinate commander under Lin Piao; and Kao

Kang, who had been political commissar of the Fifteenth Army Corps, was given a nonmilitary post. Thus Mao Tse-tung obtained firm control of the forces which had been based in the Yenan area before his arrival there.

14. Ch'en, *Mao and the Chinese Revolution,* pp. 195–196.

15. Chang Kuo-t'ao, "Mao: A New Portrait of an Old Colleague," pp. 5, 46–47.

16. Ch'en, *Mao and the Chinese Revolution,* p. 197; and Smedley, *Great Road,* p. 347.

17. Schram, *Mao Tse-tung,* pp. 172, 173. For a far-ranging discussion of the Chinese Communist appeal to peasant patriotism, see Johnson, *Peasant Nationalism and Communist Power: The Emergence of Revolutionary China, 1937–1945.*

18. Tokyo *Mainichi,* April 2, 1967. (Almost without exception, my citations of the Japanese press, throughout this work, are based on *Daily Summary of Japanese Press,* American Embassy, Tokyo.)

19. Clubb, *Twentieth-Century China,* p. 207; Boorman, Biographical Dictionary, I:61–68; and Ch'en, *Mao and the Chinese Revolution,* pp. 202–203.

20. Snow, *Red Star,* p. 443; and Roger Pelissier, *The Awakening of China, 1793–1949,* Martin Kiefer, ed. and tr. (London: Secker & Warburg, 1967), pp. 361–366.

21. Franz Schurmann, *Ideology and Organization in Communist China,* pp. 54–55.

22. Snow, *Random Notes,* p. 1.

23. *Ibid.,* fourth page of author's preface and p. 2; Schram, *Mao Tse-tung,* p. 199; and Chang Kuo-t'ao, "Mao: A New Portrait," pp. 5, 46–47. Chang Kuo-t'ao, in a passage which may be pertinent, said that shortly after the kidnaping of Chiang Kai-shek, during the "Sian coup" of December 1936, he went to see Mao Tse-tung and found him berating Chang Wen-t'ien, as related in Chapter 6. The object of his rage was "you fellows," who had opposed him before and now were opposing him again. Presumably "you fellows" was a reference to the Moscow-oriented Twenty-eight Bolsheviks, of whom Chang Wen-t'ien was the ranking representative. If the issue was what to do with Chiang Kai-shek, they undoubtedly were for following Moscow's orders and releasing him.

24. Liu Shao-ch'i, *How to Be a Good Communist,* pp. 27–28.

25. Herbert Feis, *The China Tangle,* p. 180.

26. Schram, *Mao Tse-tung,* pp. 194–195.

27. Snow, *Red Star,* pp. 48, 456.

28. Boorman, *Biographical Dictionary,* I:61–68.

29. Clubb, *Twentieth-Century China,* pp. 208–215.

CHAPTER 7

1. Cressey, *Land of the 500 Million,* pp. 255–263.

2. *Case of Peng Teh-huai,* pp. 189–190; *Who's Who in Communist China,* I:329, and II:512; and Whitson, "The Field Army," p. 4.

3. *Case of Peng Teh-huai*, pp. 159–160; and Ch'en, *Mao and the Chinese Revolution*, pp. 215, 232.

4. Ch'en, *Mao and the Chinese Revolution*, pp. 245–246; Schram, *Mao Tse-tung*, pp. 217–218; and Whitson, "The Field Army," pp. 5–6.

5. Compton, *Mao's China: Party Reform Documents, 1942–1944*, pp. xx–xxi.

6. Ch'en, *Mao and the Chinese Revolution*, pp. 231–232, 235; Schram, *Mao Tse-tung*, pp. 202–205; Clubb, *Twentieth-Century China*, pp. 208–209; and *Who's Who in Communist China*, I:98, 162.

7. Huang, *Mao Tse-tung sheng-p'ing*, p. 185.

8. Ch'en, *Mao and the Chinese Revolution*, pp. 235–236, 250–252.

9. Compton, *Mao's China*, p. xxxii.

10. *Ibid.*, p. xxxi.

11. *Ibid.*, p. xxviii.

12. *Case of Peng Teh-huai*, pp. 191–193; *Peking Review*, X:36, (September 1, 1967), pp. 12–15, 34; and Schram, *Mao Tse-tung*, p. 215.

13. Ch'en, *Mao and the Chinese Revolution*, pp. 250, 252.

14. Schram, *Mao Tse-tung*, pp. 221–222, 233.

15. Compton, *Mao's China*, p. xli.

16. Leonard Schapiro and John W. Lewis, "The Roles of the Monolithic Party Under the Totalitarian Leader," paper presented at the Conference on the History of the Chinese Communist Party sponsored by *The China Quarterly*, held at Ditchley Manor, Oxfordshire, July 7–13, 1968, pp. 16–17.

17. Brandt, Schwartz, and Fairbank, *A Documentary History of Chinese Communism*, p. 432.

18. *Current Background* [hereinafter cited as *CB*], (Hong Kong: American Consulate General), no. 892 (October 21, 1969), p. 31.

19. Wang Ming [Ch'en Shao-yü], "China: Cultural Revolution or Counter-revolutionary Coup?," *Canadian Tribune*, Toronto, no. 1641 (March 19, 1969).

20. Huang, *Mao Tse-tung sheng-p'ing*, p. 201.

21. André Malraux, *Antimémoires*, p. 550.

22. Wales, *Yenan Notebooks*, p. 48. Nym Wales quotes K'ang K'o-ch'ing as saying: "Mao Tse-tung now has his fifth baby here in Yenan." If she was including Mao's two sons by Yang K'ai-hui, this would mean that he had three children by Ho Tzu-chen.

23. *Ibid.*, pp. 63–64.

24. Chung and Miller, *Madame Mao: A Profile of Chiang Ch'ing*, p. 44.

25. Personal communication to the author, received in 1970.

26. *SCMP*, no. 4120 (February 16, 1968), pp. 3–4.

27. *SCMP*, no. 4089 (December 29, 1967), p. 1; and *Who's Who in Communist China*, I:132. Li Ta-chang was another of Chiang Ch'ing's sponsors; in this connection, see *SCMP*, no. 4181 (May 20, 1968), p. 7.

28. Snow, *Red Star*, p. 79.

29. Agnes Smedley, *Battle Hymn of China* (New York: Knopf, 1943), pp. 168–169; and Marcuse, *Peking Papers*, pp. 286–287. Malraux, calling on Mao

in 1965, was similarly struck by the feminine quality of Mao's hands. This call is described in his *Antimémoires,* see p. 547, and the pertinent passage will be found in his "I am Alone with the Masses—Waiting," p. 118.

30. Tokyo *Mainichi,* February 4, 1967; and *SCMP,* no. 4181 (May 20, 1968), p. 10. The foregoing version of the life of Chiang Ch'ing, up to the time of her marriage with Chairman Mao, except as indicated by specific references to other sources, is based on the following: Chung and Miller, *Madame Mao,* pp. 11–64; Hao Jan Chu, "Mao's Wife: Chiang Ch'ing," *CQ,* no. 31 (July–September 1967), pp. 148–150; and Ting Wang, "Profile: Chiang Ch'ing (Mrs. Mao Tse-tung)," *FEER,* LVII (August 10, 1967), pp. 276–277.

31. *Current Scene* (Hong Kong: United States Information Service), VI:6 (April 15, 1968), pp. 17–19; and *Chao-yü ko-ming* (Peking), no. 5 (May 10, 1967).

32. Clubb, *Twentieth-Century China,* p. 230; and Jonathan Spence, *To Change China: Western Advisers in China, 1620–1960* (Boston: Little, Brown, 1969), p. 231.

33. Barbara W. Tuchman, *Stilwell and the American Experience in China, 1911–45* (New York: Macmillan, 1971), pp. 468–485.

34. Feis, *China Tangle,* pp. 145–149, 152–153.

35. Tuchman, *Stilwell,* pp. 478–482; and Feis, *China Tangle,* pp. 172–173, 178–197.

36. Feis, *China Tangle,* 180–181.

37. *Ibid.,* p. 147.

38. David D. Barrett, *Dixie Mission: The United States Army Observer Group in Yenan,* 1944, pp. 56–64.

39. *Ibid.,* p. 64; and Feis, *China Tangle,* p. 216.

40. Clubb, *Twentieth-Century China,* pp. 253–254.

41. Feis, *China Tangle,* p. 212.

42. *Ibid.,* p. 334.

43. Tang Tsou, *America's Failure in China, 1941–50,* pp. 325–326.

44. Clubb, *Twentieth-Century China,* pp. 256–257; Feis, *China Tangle,* pp. 360–361; and Huang, *Mao Tse-tung sheng-p'ing,* p. 242.

45. Ng, "The Poetry of Mao," pp. 60–73; Robert Payne, *Mao Tse-tung* (New York: Weybright and Talley, 1969), p. 224; Lo, *Romance of the Three Kingdoms,* I:221; Ch'en, *Mao and the Chinese Revolution,* pp. 340–341; and Mao, *Mao chu-hsi shih-tz-u chiang-chieh* (Peking: *Chung-kuo ch'ing-nien ch'u-pan she,* 1962), p. 32. Payne quotes Mao as saying he had written this poem in an airplane, and Ch'en recounts that Mao in August 1945 gave this poem to an old friend in Chungking. Mao is not known to have traveled by plane before that month. One accordingly assigns the tentative date of August 28, 1945 as that on which Mao composed the poem. The title *Snow,* and the first lines, which suggest a wintry scene, would be irreconcilable with an August date only if one assumed that Mao Tse-tung was not entitled to poetic license.

46. Huang, *Mao Tse-tung sheng-p'ing,* p. 242.

47. Mao Tse-tung, *SW,* II:223–224.

48. Feis, *China Tangle,* pp. 362–363.

49. Schram, *Mao Tse-tung*, pp. 237–238; Clubb, *Twentieth-Century China*, p. 263; and *United States Relations with China with Special Reference to the Period 1944–1949*, U.S. Department of State, pp. 108–111.

50. Tsou, *America's Failure in China*, pp. 351–356.

51. Clubb, *Twentieth-Century China*, pp. 260–273.

52. *Ibid.*, p. 277.

53. Tsou, *America's Failure in China*, pp. 427–428.

54. Edgar Snow, *The Other Side of the River* (New York: Random House, 1962), p. 337; and Mao, *SW*, IV:129–132.

55. Mao, *SW*, IV:128–132, 174–175, 193–195, 231–232; *Jen-min jih-pao* [*People's Daily*], hereinafter referred to as *People's Daily* (Peking), May 5, 1967; *SCMP*, no. 4230 (August 1, 1968), p. 19; and John Gittings, "The Party Is Always Right," *FEER*, LXIV (June 5, 1969), pp. 574–575. Mao probably was referring to this conference when he complained, in 1966: "On many things, I wasn't even consulted. For instance, the land conference . . ." (Ch'en, *Mao*, pp. 93–94.)

56. Clubb, *Twentieth-Century China*, pp. 280, 288–289.

57. *United States Relations with China*, pp. 331–332.

58. *Ibid.*, pp. 325–336.

59. Malraux, *Antimémoires*, p. 534; and Clubb, *Twentieth Century China*, p. 297.

CHAPTER 8

1. Tsou, *America's Failure in China*, p. 163; and George F. Kennan, *Memoires, 1925–1950* (Boston: Little, Brown, 1967), p. 236.

2. Tokyo *Mainichi*, March 9, 1967.

3. U. S. Department of State, *United States Relations with China*, p. 312.

4. U. S. Department of State, *Foreign Relations of the United States, 1944: China,* (Washington: U. S. Government Printing Office, 1947), pp. 604–614.

5. U. S. Department of State, *United States Relations with China*, pp. 338–351, 355–357, 889.

6. Stokes, "The Future between America and China," pp. 14–16.

7. *Ibid.*

8. Mao, *SW*, IV:415.

9. Tokyo *Mainichi*, March 9, 1967.

10. *FEER*, LXVI (October 2, 1969), p. 25; and *Case of Peng Teh-huai*, p. 154.

11. Clubb, *Twentieth-Century China*, pp. 338–340.

12. Snow, *Other Side of the River*, p. 287.

13. *Union Research Service*, XXIX: (December 7, 1962), p. 318.

14. Chow, *Ten Years of Storm*, pp. 92–93.

15. U. S. Department of Commerce, *Joint Publications Research Service* (hereinafter cited as *JPRS*), no. 41, 884 (July 18, 1967), pp. 50–62; and Schram, *Mao Tse-tung*, p. 259.

16. Schurmann, *Ideology and Organization*, p. 434.

17. Clubb, *Twentieth-Century China*, pp. 318–319.

18. Kenneth R. Walker, "Collectivization in Retrospect: The 'Socialist High Tide' of Autumn 1955–Spring 1956," *CQ,* no. 26 (April–June 1966), p. 11.

19. *JPRS,* no. 41, 884 (July 18, 1967), pp. 50–62.

20. Walker, "Collectivization in Retrospect," pp. 2–4; and Center for International Affairs and East Asian Research Center, *Communist China, 1955–1959: Policy Documents with Analysis,* p. 3.

21. *Communist China, 1955–1959,* p. 3; and Schram, *Mao Tse-tung,* pp. 280–281.

22. Parris H. Chang, "Struggle Between the Two Roads in China's Countryside," *Current Scene* VI:3 (February 15, 1968), pp. 3–5, 13, n. 9. The three leaders whom the author cites in that note all held regional posts at the time.

23. *SCMP,* no. 3962 (April 10, 1967), p. 9.

24. *SCMP,* no. 1026 (April 11–13, 1955), p. 3.

25. *SCMP,* no. 4179 (May 16, 1968), pp. 5–6.

26. Teiwes, "The Evolution of Leadership Purges in Communist China," p. 123.

27. The story attributed to Ch'en Yi will be found in Albert Ravenholt, *Feud Among the Red Mandarins,* American Universities Field Staff, East Asia Series, IX:2 (February 1954).

28. *Documents of the National Conference of the Communist Party of China, March 1955* (Peking: Foreign Languages Press, 1955), pp. 14–17.

29. Chen, ed., *The Chinese Communist Regime: Documents and Commentary,* p. 83.

30. Clubb, *Twentieth-Century China,* pp. 328, 331; and Arthur G. Ashbrook, Jr., "Main Lines of Chinese Communist Economic Policy," *An Economic Profile of Mainland China: Studies Prepared for the Joint Economic Committee, Congress of the United States,* I, 25.

31. Clubb, *Twentieth-Century China,* pp. 333–334.

32. Chang, "Struggle Between the Two Roads," pp. 3–4, 13; *Communist China 1955–1959,* p. 43; Clubb, *Twentieth-Century China,* p. 332; Li Fu-ch'un, *Report on the First Five-Year Plan for Development of the National Economy of China in 1953–1957* (Peking: Foreign Languages Press, 1955), p. 5; and *First Five-Year Plan for Development of the National Economy of the People's Republic of China* (Peking: Foreign Languages Press, 1956), p. 1.

33. Chang, "Struggle Between the Two Roads," pp. 3–5.

34. *Ibid.,* p. 5; and Clubb, *Twentieth-Century China,* p. 332.

35. Schurmann, *Ideology and Organization,* p. 454; and Tokyo *Shimbun,* April 15, 1967.

36. Chow, *Ten Years of Storm,* pp. 83–84.

CHAPTER 9

1. Fitzgerald, *China,* p. 135.

2. Chen, *Chinese Communist Regime,* pp. 21–45.

3. Chow, *Ten Years of Storm*, pp. 252–257; and Chow Ching-wen, *Feng-pao shih-nien* (Hong Kong: *Shih-tai p'i-p'ing she*, 1959), pp. 433–437.

4. Mao, *SW*, III:69–97; Merle Goldman, *Literary Dissent in Communist China* (Cambridge: Harvard University Press, 1967), pp. 130–131, 149–151, 293, n. 70; Robert Guillain, *600 Million Chinese* (New York: Criterion Books, 1957), pp. 169–179; Solomon, "One Party and 'One Hundred Schools': Leadership, Lethargy, or *Luan*?" p. 39, n. 9; and Chow, *Ten Years of Storm*, p. 153.

5. Khrushchev speech of February 25, 1956, as published in pamphlet form by the *New Leader*.

6. *Peking Review*, X:36 (September 1, 1967), p. 14.

7. David Wise and Thomas B. Ross, *The Espionage Establishment* (New York: Random House, 1967), pp. 176–178; and *Who's Who in Communist China*, I:325. The statement that K'ang Sheng was the seventh-ranking member of the Political Bureau is based upon the lists which appear in the single-volume, 1966, edition of *Who's Who in Communist China*, pp. 703–706.

8. Zagoria, *The Sino-Soviet Conflict 1956–61*, p. 43.

9. Brandt, Schwartz and Fairbank, *Documentary History*, pp. 422–439; and Chen, *Chinese Communist Regime*, pp. 127–148.

10. Schurmann, *Ideology and Organization*, p. 140.

11. *SCMP*, no. 4097 (January 11, 1968), pp. 1–4.

12. *Yomiuri*, January 7, 1967.

13. Harold Hinton, "The Succession Problem in Communist China," *Current Scene* I:7 (July 19, 1961), p. 2; and *JPRS* no. 49826 (February 12, 1970), p. 13.

14. *China Pictorial* (Peking), no. 10, 1966, p. 1.

15. *CB*, no. 892 (October 21, 1969), pp. 29–30.

16. Solomon, "One Party and 'One Hundred Schools,'" p. 41. n. 21.

17. *Ibid.*, pp. 7–14.

18. Zagoria, *Sino-Soviet Conflict*, p. 44.

19. Solomon, "One Party and 'One Hundred Schools,'" pp. 16, 43–44, n.58; and Chow, *Ten Years of Storm*, pp. 162–163.

20. *New York Times*, June 13, 1957.

21. Chow, *Ten Years of Storm*, p. 163.

22. Goldman, "The Rectification Campaign at Peking University: May–June 1957," pp. 258–259; and Solomon, "One Party and 'One Hundred Schools,'" pp. 21–22, 25.

23. Solomon, "One Party and 'One Hundred Schools,'" pp. 17, 26–27, 46.

24. *China and U.S. Far East Policy, 1945–1966* (Washington: Congressional Quarterly Service, 1967), p. 81.

25. Solomon, "One Party and 'One Hundred Schools,'" p. 35.

26. *Ibid.*, p. 30; Goldman, "The Rectification Campaign," pp. 258–260; and Rádvanyi, "The Hungarian Revolution and the Hundred Flowers Campaign," p. 128.

27. *China and U.S. Far East Policy 1945–1966*, pp. 82–83; Clubb, *Twentieth-Century China*, pp. 350–351; and Schurmann, *Ideology and Organization*, pp. 353–357.

28. Schurmann, *Ideology and Organization*, pp. 314, 328, 358–361.

29. Rádvanyi, "The Hungarian Revolution and the Hundred Flowers Campaign," pp. 125–128.

30. Solomon, "One Party and 'One Hundred Schools,' " pp. 26, 33–34; and Robert Loh, *Escape from Red China* (New York: Coward-McCann, 1962), p. 293.

CHAPTER 10

1. Dwight D. Eisenhower, *Mandate for Change, 1953–1956* (Garden City: Doubleday, 1963), p. 181.

2. Hinton, *Communist China in World Politics*, pp. 220–226.

3. Kierman, *The Fluke That Saved Formosa, passim*.

4. *China and U.S. Far East Policy, 1945–1966*, p. 73.

5. *Ibid.*, p. 74.

6. Final Communique of the Asian-African Conference, April 24, 1966.

7. Hsieh, *Communist China's Strategy in the Nuclear Era*, pp. 20–21, 48, 59.

8. Halperin, *China and the Bomb*, p. 71; and *Peking Review*, VI:33 (August 16, 1963), p. 14.

9. Zagoria, *Sino-Soviet Conflict*, pp. 40–41.

10. Schram, *Political Thought of Mao*, p. 436.

11. *Ibid.*, pp. 407–408.

12. *Peking Review*, VI:37 (September 13, 1963), pp. 13, 21–22.

13. Schram, *Mao Tse-tung*, p. 291.

14. Halperin, *China and the Bomb*, p. 33.

15. Zagoria, *Sino-Soviet Conflict*, pp. 170–171.

16. Clubb, *Twentieth-Century China*, pp. 369–370. For an outstanding analysis of the multipurpose strategy of Chiang Kai-shek, in which the off-shore islands played a key role, see Tang Tsou, *The Embroilment over Quemoy: Mao, Chiang and Dulles,* Institute of International Affairs (Salt Lake City: University of Utah Press, 1959).

17. Harold P. Ford, "Modern Weapons and the Sino-Soviet Estrangement," *CQ*, no. 18 (April–June 1964), p. 164.

18. Hsieh, *Communist China's Strategy*, pp. 123–124; and Clubb, *Twentieth-Century China*, p. 371.

19. Hsieh, *Communist China's Strategy*, pp. 124–127; Ford, "Modern Weapons," p. 170; and Hinton, *Communist China in World Politics*, pp. 268–269.

20. Ford, "Modern Weapons," pp. 164–165.

21. *Peking Review*, VI:37 (September 13, 1963), p. 12.

22. *Selections from China Mainland Magazines*, Supplement 21 (April 2, 1968), p. 39.

23. *Peking Review*, VI:36 (September 6, 1963), pp. 7–16, and VI:37 (September 13, 1963), p. 12.

24. Alice Langley Hsieh, "China's Secret Military Papers: Military Doctrine and Strategy," *CQ*, no. 18 (April–June 1964), pp. 79–99.

25. *Peking Review*, VI:37 (September 13, 1963), p. 12.

26. Ford, "Modern Weapons," pp. 171–172.

27. *Peking Review*, VI:37 (September 13, 1963), pp. 6–16.

CHAPTER 11

1. Schurmann, *Ideology and Organization*, p. 142.
2. Clubb, *Twentieth-Century China*, pp. 353–354.
3. Schurmann, *Ideology and Organization*, pp. 74–76.
4. *Ibid.*, p. 456.
5. *Peking Review*, X:35 (August 25, 1967), p. 6.
6. Zagoria, *Sino-Soviet Conflict*, p. 88; and Gerald Clark, *Impatient Giant: Red China Today* (New York: McKay, 1959), pp. 64–65.
7. Clubb, *Twentieth-Century China*, p. 355.
8. Hinton, "The Succession Problem," p. 5.
9. Schurmann, *Ideology and Organization*, p. 465; and Schram, *Mao Tse-tung*, p. 292.
10. Clubb, *Twentieth-Century China*, pp. 355–356.
11. *Economic Profile of Mainland China*, I, p. x.
12. Cressey, *Land of the 500 Million*, pp. 15–17, 103–104.
13. Zagoria, *Sino-Soviet Conflict*, pp. 88–90.
14. Schram, *Political Thought of Mao*, p. 252.
15. Clubb, *Twentieth-Century China*, pp. 357–358.
16. Schurmann, *Ideology and Organization*, pp. 293–296.
17. John S. Aird, "The Population Count: 'Reds versus Experts,'" *Diplomat*, September 1966; and Marion R. Larsen, "China's Agriculture under Communism," *Economic Profile of Mainland China*, I:232.
18. *Peking Review*, I:35 (October 28, 1958), p. 10; and Hsüeh Mu-ch'iao, Su Heng, and Lin Tse-li, *The Socialist Transformation of China* (Peking: Foreign Languages Press, 1960), pp. 264–265.
19. Zagoria, *Sino-Soviet Conflict*, pp. 93, 104–105.
20. James T. Myers, "The Fall of Chairman Mao," *Current Scene*, VI:10 (June 15, 1968), p. 3.
21. Edgar Snow, "Interview with Mao," *New Republic*, January 20, 1965, as reprinted in *Communist China: Revolutionary Reconstruction and International Confrontation, 1949 to the Present*, Franz Schurmann and Orville Schell, eds., p. 370.
22. John Gittings, "Reversing PLA Verdicts," *FEER*, LXI (July 25, 1968), p. 193.
23. Rue, *Mao in Opposition*, pp. 231–233.
24. Schurmann, *Ideology and Organization*, pp. 143, 196, 200.
25. *Ibid.*, pp. 142, 465, n. 107.
26. *Ibid.* p. 141; *Peking Review*, XI:29 (September 16, 1968), p. 5; and *Communist China, 1955–1959*, pp. 22, 550, 554.
27. *Communist China, 1955–1959*, pp. 20–21.
28. *Ibid.*, p. 21; George Paloczi-Horvath, *Mao Tse-tung* (London: Secker & Warburg, 1962), p. 340, citing the "Report of the Ninth Enlarged Session of the CCP Honan Provincial Committee"; and *Who's Who in Communist China*, II:536. (The reasons for P'an Fu-sheng's dismissal are set forth in greater detail in the one-volume, 1966 edition of the latter work, p. 474, than in the 1970 edition.)

29. Schram, *Political Thought of Mao*, p. 253.

30. Clubb, *Twentieth-Century China*, p. 362; *Peking Review*, II:35 (September 1, 1959), p. 13; and Kang Chao, "The Great Leap in Communist China," *Asian Survey*, IV (May 1964), pp. 851–858, as reproduced in Schurmann and Schell, *Communist China*, pp. 409–410.

31. Myers, "The Fall of Chairman Mao," p. 5; and Tokyo *Mainichi*, January 5, 1967.

32. Boorman, *Biographical Dictionary*, II:409.

33. Clubb, *Twentieth-Century China*, pp. 362–364.

34. J. D. Simmonds, "P'eng Te-huai: A Chronological Reexamination," *CQ*, no. 37 (January–March 1969), pp. 123, 128.

35. *Case of Peng Teh-huai*, p. 1.

36. *Ibid.*, p. 37.

37. David A. Charles, "The Dismissal of P'eng Te-huai," *CQ*, no. 8 (October–December 1961), pp. 64, 66–67.

38. Simmonds, "P'eng Te-huai," pp. 129–131.

39. *Case of Peng Teh-huai*, pp. 7–13, 397–401.

40. Zagoria, *Sino-Soviet Conflict*, pp. 134–135.

41. *Case of Peng Teh-huai*, pp. 4, 36, 40.

42. *Ibid.*, pp. 15–26, 405–412; and *Selections from China Mainlaind Magazines*, Supplement no. 21 (April 2, 1968), pp. 11–18.

43. *Case of Peng Teh-huai*, pp. 28, 41, 44.

44. Charles, "The Dismissal of P'eng Te-huai," pp. 64, 66–67.

45. *Case of Peng Teh-huai*, pp. 43–44.

46. *Selections from China Mainland Magazines*, Supplement no. 21, p. 31.

47. *Ibid.*, pp. 22–30; and *Peking Review*, II:35 (September 1, 1959), pp. 5–7.

48. Philip L. Bridgman, "Factionalism in the Central Committee," paper prepared for the Conference on the History of the Chinese Communist Party sponsored by *The China Quarterly*, at Ditchley Manor, Oxfordshire, July 7–13, 1968, p. 13; and Schram, *Mao Tse-tung*, p. 300, n.

49. *Selections from China Mainland Magazines*, Supplement no. 21, p. 37.

50. Zagoria, *Sino-Soviet Conflict*, p. 299.

51. *Ibid.*, pp. 319, 325–326; and Schram, *Mao Tse-tung*, pp. 302–303.

52. Zagoria, *Sino-Soviet Conflict*, pp. 319, 327–334.

53. *People's Daily*, editorial, February 27, 1963.

54. Griffith, *Sino-Soviet Relations 1964–1965*, p. 390; and Clubb, *Twentieth-Century China*, p. 391. With the withdrawal of Soviet technicians, the Sino-Soviet split became a fact which was obvious to the world and which demanded exploration. For a readable account of the differences between the Chinese and the Russians as peoples, revolutionaries, neighbors, and rivals, see Klaus Mehnert, *Peking and Moscow*, Leila Vennewitz, tr. (New York: Putnam's, 1963).

55. Chi-ming Hou, "Sources of Agricultural Growth in Communist China," *Journal of Asian Studies*, Vol. XXVII (August 1968), p. 731.

56. Arthur G. Ashbrook, Jr., "Main Lines of Chinese Communist Economic Policy," *Economic Profile of Mainland China*, I, pp. 31–32; and Cheng, ed., *The Politics of the Chinese Red Army*, pp. 295–296.

57. Cheng, *Politics of the Chinese Red Army*, pp. 119–122, 138, 140–143, 190–191, 566–570.

58. *Ibid.*, pp. 287, 358.

59. *JPRS* 41, 450 (June 19, 1967), pp. 74–75.

60. Schurmann, *Ideology and Organization*, pp. 492–494.

61. *Ibid.*, p. 492; and *Economic Profile of Mainland China*, I, p. xii.

62. *SCMP*, no. 4027 (September 25, 1967), pp. 1–9; and *Hong Kong Report for the Year 1963* (Hong Kong: Government Press, 1964), p. 231.

63. Eckstein, *Communist China's Economic Growth and Foregin Trade*, pp. 67–68; and Schram, *Mao Tse-tung*, p. 317.

64. *JPRS* 41, 450 (June 19, 1967), pp. 74–75.

65. *Selections from China Mainland Magazines*, Supplement no. 21, p. 33.

CHAPTER 12

1. Arlington and Lewisohn, *In Search of Old Peking*, pp. 240–241.

2. *SCMP*, no. 4014 (September 5, 1967), pp. 1–10.

3. Tokyo *Yomiuri*, January 7, 1967.

4. *SCMP*, no. 4014 (September 5, 1967), pp. 1–10.

5. Tokyo *Mainichi*, January 5, 1967, as carried by Foreign Broadcast Intelligence Service (cited hereinafter as FBIS), January 6, 1967, p. CCC-1; and Tokyo *Yomiuri*, January 8, 1967.

6. *Nihon Keizai*, August 4, 1967.

7. Liu Shao-ch'i, *How to Be a Good Communist*, p. 14. The English-language version, published in 1964, is a translation of a revised edition of the Chinese text, which was published in 1962. An earlier one had come out in 1949, and its translation had been published by Foreign Languages Press in 1952. Both editions were described as based on a series of lectures which Liu gave in 1939. In the interval between the two editions, some of the criticisms which Liu Shao-ch'i had made of unnamed and discredited leaders of an earlier period had become obviously apt as descriptions of Mao Tse-tung. In consequence, the intent behind some passages had become ambiguous, and Liu Shao-ch'i may well have so intended.

8. *CB*, no. 827 (June 1, 1937), containing the translation of an article from the April 8, 1967, Peking *Kuang-ming jih-pao*.

9. Liu Shao-ch'i, *How to Be a Good Communist*, pp. 89–91. A comparison of the original and revised editions reveals certain changes which might suggest that Liu was no longer discussing only earlier intraparty struggles, and was thinking also of more recent ones such as that against P'eng Te-huai and his supporters.

10. *JPRS* 41, 450 (June 19, 1967), pp. 71–72.

11. *Ibid.*

12. Merle Goldman, "Party Policies Toward and Relationships with Intellectuals and Technical Specialists: The Unique 'Blooming and Contending' of 1961–1962," paper prepared for the Conference on the History of the Chinese Communist Party sponsored by *The China Quarterly*, at Ditchley Manor, Oxfordshire, July 7–13, 1968, pp. 22–23.

13. Myers, "The Fall of Chairman Mao," p. 9.

14. Translations, in whole or in part, of articles and dramas cited above, will be found in Fan, *The Chinese Cultural Revolution*, pp. 64–85. For a fuller translation of "Special Treatment for Amnesia," see *Peking Review*, IX:22 (May 27, 1966), p. 10.

15. *SCMP*, no. 4124 (February 23, 1968), p. 5.

16. *CB*, no. 834 (August 17, 1967), p. 20.

17. *CB*, no. 842 (December 8, 1967), p. 4.

18. *People's Daily* editorial in *Peking Review*, X:35 (August 25, 1967), pp. 6–7.

19. *CB*, no. 842 (December 8, 1967), p. 4.

20. *Nihon Keizai*, August 8, 1967.

21. *Ibid.*

22. *CB*, no. 834 (August 17, 1967), p. 21; Tokyo *Mainichi*, April 6, 1967; *Nihon Keizai*, December 29, 1966 and February 24, 1967; and *SCMP*, no. 3946 (May 25, 1967), pp. 7–8.

23. *Peking Review*, V:39 (September 28, 1962), pp. 5, 7.

24. *CB*, no. 842 (December 8, 1967), p. 7.

25. *Peking Review*, IV:4 (January 27, 1961), pp. 5–7.

26. Tokyo *Mainichi*, March 9, 1967; and *People's Daily* article, in *Peking Review*, XI:12 (March 22, 1968).

27. *Peking Review*, XI:37 (September 13, 1968), p. 20.

28. *Ibid.*, X:15 (April 7, 1967), pp. 5–15; and *CB*, no. 834 (August 17, 1967), p. 21.

29. Bridgham, "Mao's Cultural Revolution: Origin and Development," pp. 8–9; and *Peking Review*, X:15 (April 7, 1967), p. 21 and XI:12 (March 22, 1968), p. 25.

30. Schurmann, *Ideology and Organization*, p. 86.

31. *Peking Review*, XI:37 (September 13, 1968), p. 20; and *JPRS* 41,799 (July 11, 1967).

32. *Hong Kong Report for the Year 1963*, p. 231.

33. Allen S. Whiting, "Time for a Change in our China Policy," *New York Times Magazine*, December 15, 1968, p. 108.

34. *Peking Review*, V:39 (September 28, 1962), p. 6.

35. Translations of these four documents appear as appendices B, C, E and F to Baum and Teiwes, *Ssu-Ch'ing*. The actual drafting of the second document probably was done in whole or part by Teng Hsiao-p'ing [see *JPRS* 43,921 (January 9, 1968), pp. 31–32] and/or P'eng Chen [see Tokyo *Mainichi*, April 6, 1967 and *Current Scene* VI:6 (April 15, 1968), p. 12].

36. Hsia Tao-tai, "Justice in Peking," *Current Scene*, V:1 (January 16, 1967), p. 7.

37. Schurmann, *Ideology and Organization*, p. 188.

38. Baum and Teiwes, *Ssu-Ch'ing*, p. 120.

39. *Current Scene*, VI:6 (April 15, 1968), p. 12.

40. Baum and Teiwes, *Ssu-Ch'ing*, p. 40.

41. Fan, *The Chinese Cultural Revolution*, pp. 76–77.

42. Baum and Teiwes, *Ssu-Ch'ing*, pp. 120–121. The two sentences which

follow, taken from p. 121, provide an example of Mao's grab-bag style. They read: "At the same time, we must make a deep and fine penetration, and must not make a big fuss over nothing. We must set facts in order, explain principles, eliminate simple, crude work methods, severely prohibit beating people, and prevent forced confessions."

43. Asia Research Centre, *Great Cultural Revolution in China*, pp. 109–11.

44. *CQ*, no. 47 (July-September, 1971), p. 571.

CHAPTER 13

1. Bridgham, "Mao's Cultural Revolution: Origin and Development," p. 3.

2. Gittings, *The Role of the Chinese Army*, p. 284; and *Who's Who in Communist China*, II:595.

3. Gittings, *Role of the Chinese Army*, pp. 225, 289–290, 310; and *Who's Who in Communist China*, I:158 (Ch'iu Hui-tso), I:314–315 (Hung Hsüeh-chih), and II:595 (T'an Cheng).

4. Chen, *Chinese Communist Regime*, p. 140.

5. Gittings, *Role of the Chinese Army*, pp. 286–287.

6. *Ibid.*, pp. 282–287.

7. *Ibid*, p. 289; and Cheng, *Politics of the Chinese Red Army*, p. 228.

8. *SCMP*, no. 4046 (October 24, 1967), p. 1.

9. Chen, *Chinese Communist Regime*, p. 127.

10. *Ibid.*, p. 131.

11. Gittings, *Role of the Chinese Army*, pp. 225, n. 2, and 289, n. 17.

12. *Ibid.* pp. 245–246.

13. *China News Summary* (hereinafter cited as *CNS*), no. 122 (June 2, 1966), p. 1.

14. Cheng, *Politics of the Chinese Red Army*, p. 595.

15. John Gittings, "Army-Party Relations in the Light of the Cultural Revolution: A Reversal of Verdicts?," paper presented at the Conference on the History of the Chinese Communist Party, sponsored by *The China Quarterly*, at Ditchley Manor, Oxfordshire, July 7–13, 1968, pp. 20–21.

16. Gittings, *Role of the Chinese Army*, pp. 209, 219–220.

17. Based on Gitting's, "Army-Party Relations," p. 15, n.; *CNS*, no. 115 (April 14, 1966); and study of biographical data concerning incumbents of the relevant positions.

18. Bridgham, "Mao's Cultural Revolution: Origin and Development," p. 11.

19. *Ibid.*, p. 14; Gittings, *Role of the Chinese Army*, pp. 255–257; and Ralph L. Powell, "Commissars in the Economy: 'Learn from the PLA' Movement in China," *Asian Survey*, V (March 1965), pp. 125–138.

20. Ralph L. Powell, *Politico-Military Relationships in Communist China*, Policy Research Study (Washington: Department of State, Bureau of Intelligence and Research, 1963), p. 4.

21. Bridgham, "Mao's Cultural Revolution: Origin and Development," p. 14.

22. Gittings, "Army-Party Relations," p. 21.

23. Chalmers Johnson, "Lin Piao's Army and Its Role in Chinese Society," Part II, *Current Scene*, IV:14 (July 15, 1966), pp. 4–8; and "Who's Who in Peking?," *Current Scene*, IV:15 (August 8, 1966), pp. 5, 10.

24. Gittings, *Role of the Chinese Army*, pp. 256–257.

25. Gittings, "Army-Party Relations," p. 21.

26. Ralph L. Powell, "The Increasing Power of Lin Piao and the Party Soldiers, 1959–1966," p. 50.

27. Schram, *Mao Tse-tung*, p. 325.

28. *New York Times*, January 5, 1969.

29. *CB*, no. 842 (December 8, 1967), p. 13; and *China Reporting Service*, United States Information Service (Hong Kong) (hereinafter cited as *CRS*), September 3, 1968.

30. *CB*, no. 842 (December 8, 1967), p. 13; and *CRS*, September 3, 1968.

31. *CB*, no. 842 (December 8, 1967), pp. 6, 16.

32. *JPRS* 41,884 (July 18, 1967), p. 7.

33. Mao, *Mao chu-hsi shih-tz'u chiang-chieh*, p. 32. The translation is mine.

34. Asia Research Centre, *Great Cultural Revolution in China*, pp. 26–28.

35. *CB*, 842 (December 8, 1967), pp. 12–14.

36. Bridgham, "Mao's Cultural Revolution: Origin and Development," p. 12.

37. *Ibid.*; *Current Scene*, IV:22 (December 10, 1966), p. 3; and *Asahi*, May 19, 1967. Deputy directors Chou Yang, Wu Leng-hsi, and Hsü Li-ch'ün all appear to have been in trouble early in the cultural revolution, but accounts differ as to which two were members of the original cultural revolution group. The last two, but not Chou Yang, were among eleven persons reported as attending an enlarged meeting of the group on February 3, 1966.

38. Charles Neuhauser, "The Chinese Communist Party in the 1960s," *CQ*, no. 32 (October–December 1967), p. 31.

39. Powell, "Increasing Power of Lin Piao," p. 49.

40. *CNS*, no. 115 (April 14, 1966), pp. 3–4; *Who's Who in Communist China*, I:242, 250, 482, and II, 563, 772; *JPRS* 41,884 (July 18, 1968), p. 54; *CRS*, November 17, 1967.

41. Powell, "Increasing Power of Lin Piao," p. 49; *Who's Who in Communist China* (1966 ed.), pp. 705, 717.

42. Powell, "Increasing Power of Lin Piao," p. 52.

43. Gittings, *Role of the Chinese Army*, p. 251.

44. *CNS*, no. 115 (April 14, 1966).

45. Snow, "Interview with Mao," pp. 373–375.

46. *Ibid.*; Malraux, "I am Alone with the Masses," pp. 106–120.

47. Robert Trumbull, ed., *This Is Communist China* (New York: McKay, 1968), pp. 26–27.

CHAPTER 14

1. Alastair Lamb, *The China-India Border* (London: Oxford University Press, 1964), pp. 7–13, 173–176.

2. *The Sino-Indian Boundary Question* (Peking: Foreign Languages Press, 1962), pp. 14–15.

3. Donald S. Zagoria, *Vietnam Triangle: Moscow, Peking, Hanoi* (New York: Pegasus, 1967), pp. 23, 25.

4. *Ibid.*, p. 79; and Griffith, *The Sino-Soviet Rift*, pp. 5–6.

5. Marcuse, *Peking Papers*, p. 305.

6. *Ibid.*, p. 288.

7. Griffith, *Sino-Soviet Rift*, pp. 59, 113.

8. Schram, *Political Thought of Mao* (1963 ed.), pp. 70–71, quoting editorial in March 4, 1963 *Hung-ch'i* (hereinafter cited as *Red Flag*).

9. Tokyo *Mainichi*, January 10, 1967. The texts of the Soviet and Chinese letters will be found in Griffith, *Sino-Soviet Rift*, pp. 241–258, 259–288.

10. Griffith, *Sino-Soviet Rift*, pp. 143–148.

11. *Ibid.*, p. 119.

12. *Ibid.*, p. 154.

13. *Ibid.*, pp. 152, 158–161.

14. *Ibid.*, p. 169.

15. John Gittings, *Survey of the Sino-Soviet Dispute, 1963–1967* (London: Oxford University Press, 1968), p. 44.

16. Griffith, *Sino-Soviet Rift*, pp. 207–208.

17. Griffith, *Sino-Soviet Relations*, pp. 16–17, 27.

18. *Ibid.*, p. 28.

19. *Ibid.*, p. 30; Griffith, *Sino-Soviet Rift*, p. 172.

20. Griffith, *Sino-Soviet Relations*, pp. 60–63.

21. Chou En-lai advanced a formulation which seemed to combine elements of both theories, declaring that possible escalation to China would be the result of "the objective laws governing the development of aggressive wars," and that the United States was "making preparations for this eventuality." (See Schurmann and Schell, *Communist China*, pp. 592–593.)

22. *New York Times*, January 17, 1965, May 6, 1966, and July 2, 1966.

23. *Ibid.*, February 16, 1965.

24. Griffith, *Sino-Soviet Relations*, pp. 50–51, 56–58, 95, 127–129.

25. *New York Times*, April 16, 1965.

26. *Peking Review*, VIII:24 (June 11, 1965), pp. 5–6; *New York Times*, June 3, 1965; and Alex Blake, "Peking's African Adventures," *Current Scene*, V:15 (September 15, 1967), p. 3.

27. Blake, "Peking's African Adventures," pp. 3–9.

28. *Ibid.*, p. 6.

29. *Peking Review*, VIII:36 (September 3, 1965), p. 8; VIII:37 (September 10, 1965), pp. 6–8; VIII:38 (September 17, 1965), pp. 10–14; and VIII:39 (September 24, 1965), pp. 5–11.

30. Griffith, *Sino-Soviet Relations*, p. 115.

31. *Ibid.*, pp. 115–118.

32. *Peking Review*, VIII:41 (October 8, 1965), pp. 7–14.

33. *Ibid.*, X:21 (May 19, 1967), p. 6.

34. *Ibid.*, VIII:33 (August 13, 1965), p. 5.

35. Griffith, *Sino-Soviet Relations*, pp. 118–120.

36. Lo Jui-ch'ing, "Commemorate the Victory over German Fascism! Carry the Struggle Against U. S. Imperialism Through to the End!," translation from *Red Flag*, no. 5, May 10, 1965 (Peking: Foreign Languages Press, 1965).

37. Lin Piao, "Long Live the Victory of People's War!," *Peking Review*, VIII:36 (September 3, 1965), pp. 9–30.

38. Edgar Snow, "Mao Tse-tung—and the Cost of Living: Aftermath of the Cultural Revolution," *The New Republic*, April 10, 1971, p. 19.

39. "The Conflict Between Mao Tse-tung and Liu Shao-ch'i over Agricultural Mechanization in Communist China," ed., *Current Scene*, VI:17 (October 1, 1968), p. 15; and "Industrial Development in China," ed., *Current Scene*, VI:22 (December 20, 1968), pp. 1–5.

40. *CQ*, no. 18 (April–June 1964), p. 230.

41. "The Conflict Between Mao Tse-tung and Liu Shao-ch'i over Agricultural Mechanization," p. 15.

42. *Ibid.*, p. 14; and "Industrial Development in China," pp. 5–16.

43. "Mao's Revolution in Public Health," ed., *Current Scene*, VI:7 (May 1, 1968), pp. 2–3 *et passim;* Teiwes, "The Evolution of Leadership Purges in Communist China," p. 133.

44. A. Doak Barnett, *China After Mao* (Princeton: Princeton University Press, 1967), p. 38; *Peking Review*, VIII:30 (July 24, 1965), pp. 19–21; Anna Louise Strong, *Letters from Peking*, no. 10 (July 26, 1963), as quoted in *Problems of Communism*, XIII:3 (May–June 1964), p. 43.

45. Bridgham, "Mao's Cultural Revolution: Origin and Development," p. 16; and *JPRS* 41450 (June 19, 1967), pp. 74–75.

46. *Ibid.*, p. 16.

47. *Yomiuri*, January 7, 1967; and *Peking Review*, X:33 (August 11, 1967), p. 7.

48. *New York Times*, November 2, 1968.

49. *Peking Review*, X:23 (June 2, 1967), p. 22.

CHAPTER 15

1. *SCMP*, no. 4200 (June 18, 1968), p. 2.

2. Schram, *Mao Tse-tung*, p. 338.

3. *SCMP*, no. 4200 (June 18, 1968), p. 2; and Gordon Bennett, "Mrs. Mao's Literary Ghost," *FEER*, LXII (October 24, 1968), pp. 197–199.

4. Bennett, "Mrs. Mao's Literary Ghost," pp. 197–99.

5. *JPRS* 42,349 (August 25, 1967), pp. 3–4.

6. *The Great Socialist Cultural Revolution in China* (2) (Peking: Foreign Languages Press, 1966), p. 52.

7. *JPRS* 42,349 (August 25, 1967), pp. 4–5.

8. *Ibid.*; and Junichi Konno, "Sun Wu-kung, Attack the Heavenly Palace," *Akahata*, November 8, 1967.

9. *CCP Documents*, pp. 7–9; and *Peking Review*, IX:24 (June 10, 1966), p. 10.

10. *Peking Review*, VIII:36 (September 3, 1965), pp. 31–39.

11. Wall poster at Peking University, January 1967.

12. "Make Our Army a Great School of Mao Tse-tung's Thought," *Red Flag*, August 1, 1966. An English-language translation appears in *Great Cultural Revolution in China*, pp. 245–250.

13. *CB*, no. 852 (May 6, 1968), p. 7; and "Lin Piao and the Cultural Revolution," *Current Scene*, VIII:14 (August 1, 1970), p. 3.

14. *CNS*, no. 115 (April 14, 1966), p. 1.

15. *Akahata*, March 19, 1967.

16. *Asahi*, July 30, 1967.

17. *Akahata*, November 6, 1967; and Scalapino, *The Japanese Communist Movement, 1920–1966* pp. 266–267.

18. Kikuzo Ito and Minoru Shibata, "The Dilemma of Mao Tse-tung," *CQ*, no. 35 (July–September 1968), p. 59, n. 3.

19. *Ibid.*, p. 67, n. 11.

20. *Asahi*, July 30, 1967.

21. Scalapino, *Japanese Communist Movement*, pp. 60–67, 84–93.

22. Ito and Shibata, "Dilemma of Mao Tse-tung," p. 67, n. 11.

23. Scalapino, *Japanese Communist Movement*, pp. 278–279.

24. *Ibid.*, p. 284; *CNS*, no. 144 (November 3, 1966), p. 8.

25. The February–March 1967 assaults on the offices of the Japan–China Friendship Association and other organizations affiliated with the JCP were covered by the non-Communist press of Tokyo, as well as by *Akahata* and *Peking Review*, each from its own point of view. In China, a campaign against Ichiro Sunama, a member of the Central Committee of the JCP, and Junichi Konno, correspondent for *Akahata*, culminated in demonstrations of August 3–4, 1967, at the Peking airport during which they were spat upon, thrown to the ground, kicked, and told to walk on all fours like dogs. According to a subsequent account in *Akahata*, their injuries included broken ribs and teeth, and a piece of one of Sunama's molars was found lodged in his gums. Since access to Peking airport was subject to official control and the period during which the two men were mistreated was an extended one, their mistreatment probably had official sanction. See *Akahata* August 21 and August 22, 1967; *Yomiuri*, July 20 and August 8, 1967; and *Asahi*, August 16, 1967.

26. *JPRS* 42,349 (August 25, 1967), pp. 10–11; and Ito and Shibata, "Dilemma of Mao Tse-tung," p. 60, n. 3.

27. *Great Cultural Revolution in China*, pp. 322–336.

28. *Ibid.*, pp. 315–322.

29. *Ibid.*, pp. 315–336; *Great Socialist Cultural Revolution in China* (1) (Peking: Foreign Languages Press, 1966); and *JPRS* 42,349 (August 25, 1967), p. 11.

30. *Peking Review*, X:21 (May 19, 1967), pp. 6–9.

31. *CCP Documents*, p. 7; Junichi Konno, "One Year in Peking," Part V, *Akahata*, November 9, 1967; and *JPRS* 42,349 (August 25, 1967), pp. 6–7.

32. H. C. Chuang, *The Little Red Book and Current Chinese Language* (Berkeley: University of California Center for Chinese Studies, August 1968), p. 39.

33. *CB*, no. 852 (May 6, 1968), pp. 2–6.

34. *Ibid.*

35. Lin Piao, "Address to Politburo (May 18, 1966)," *Chinese Law and Government*, II:4 (Winter 1969–1970), pp. 42–45.

36. *JPRS* 42,349 (August 25, 1967), p. 14; and *Great Cultural Revolution in China*, pp. 158, 187.

37. *JPRS* 42,349 (August 25, 1967), p. 15; and *Great Cultural Revolution in China*, pp. 207–214, 254–255.

38. "Who's Who in Peking?," p. 2.

39. Arthur C. Miller, "Mrs. Mao: Political Actress," *The Asia Magazine*, September 10, 1967, p. HK-4; *JPRS* 42,349 (August 25, 1967), p. 25; Ma Sitson, "We Are Slaves Who Have Been Betrayed," pp. 64–73; and *Sankei*, May 8, 1967.

40. *CRS*, November 17, 1967.

41. *JPRS* 42,349 (August 25, 1967), p. 25.

42. *Nihon Keizai*, January 5, 1967.

43. *Who's Who in Communist China*, II:543, 548, 753.

44. *JPRS* 42,349 (August 25, 1967), p. 2; Tokyo *Mainichi*, January 20, 1967; and *SCMP*, no. 4146 (March 26, 1968), pp. 9–10.

45. *JPRS* 42,349 (August 25, 1967), p. 16.

46. *Who's Who in Communist China*, II:526; Chung and Miller, *Madame Mao*, p. 141; *JPRS* 49,826 (February 12, 1970), p. 13; "The Handwriting on the Wall," *Current Scene*, V:9 (May 31, 1967), pp. 5–6.

47. *Peking Review*, IX:37 (September 9, 1966), pp. 19–20.

48. *JPRS* 42,349 (August 25, 1967), p. 13.

49. *Peking Review*, IX:20 (May 13, 1966), p. 3.

50. Tokyo *Shimbun*, December 23, 1967.

51. *China Pictorial*, no. 10, 1966, relevant photographs; based also on motion pictures seen by the author in Hong Kong.

52. "Chairman Mao Swims the Yangtze," *China Pictorial*, no. 10, 1966, p. 3.

53. *Nihon Keizai*, January 31, 1967.

54. *China Mail* (Hong Kong), February 1, 1967; and CTK (Czech news agency), February 10, 1967.

55. Lin Piao's speech of August 31, 1966, NCNA, Peking, August 31, 1966.

CHAPTER 16

1. Snow, *Red Star*, p. 127.

2. Wu Ch'eng-en, *Monkey*, pp. 31, 43, 60, 84–85, 163.

3. *JPRS* 42,349 (August 25, 1967), p. 9.

4. *Sankei*, October 5, 1967.

5. Schram, *Mao Tse-tung*, p. 331.

6. *Ibid.*, p. 332, n.; and *Great Cultural Revolution in China*, pp. 446–447.

7. *CCP Documents*, pp. 97–99; and Domes, "Cultural Revolution and the Army," p. 356.

8. *JPRS* 42,349 (August 25, 1967), p. 30.

9. *Ibid.*, pp. 26–27.

10. *Ibid.* pp. 29, 32; Bridgham, "Mao's Cultural Revolution: Origin and Development," p. 24.

11. "March Triumphantly on the Path of Mao Tse-tung's Thought," editorial, *Red Flag* no. 11, 1966; and *JPRS* 42,349 (August 25, 1967), p. 28.

12. *China Pictorial*, Special Issue no. 9, 1966, cover and p. 15; and *Peking Review*, IX:46 (November 11, 1966), p. 3, and IX:47 (November 18, 1966), p. 3.

13. *Yomiuri*, December 14, 1966.

14. *Peking Review*, X:33 (August 11, 1967), p. 5.

15. Tokyo *Mainichi*, January 5, 1967.

16. Chalmers Johnson, "Communist China's Political Turmoil," *SAIS Review*, Special Issue, XII:2 (Winter 1968), p. 13; and *China Pictorial*, Special Issue no. 9, 1966, p. 2.

17. *China Pictorial*, Special Issue no. 9, 1966, pp. 2–9; and *Great Cultural Revolution in China*, pp. 395–416.

18. "Decision of the Central Committee of the Chinese Communist Party Concerning the Great Proletarian Cultural Revolution," *China Pictorial*, Special Issue no. 9, 1966, p. 6.

19. *Peking Review*, IX:35 (August 26, 1966), p. 6; IX:39 (September 23, 1966), p. 6; IX:46 (November 11, 1966), pp. 6–7; *CB*, no. 819 (March 10, 1967), p. 11; FBIS, November 17, 1966, p. CCC-6; *FEER*, LXI (August 22, 1968), p. 352; and *CNS*, no. 154 (January 19, 1967), p. 10.

20. *China Pictorial*, Special Issue no. 9, 1966, pp. 18–19; and *Peking Review*, IX:35 (August 26, 1966), pp. 8–10.

21. *Current Scene*, IV: 16 (September 5, 1966), p. 2.

22. *Peking Review*, IX:35 (August 26, 1966), p. 21.

23. CTK, February 10, 1967; and *CB*, no. 891 (October 8, 1969), p. 68.

24. FBIS 169, (August 31, 1966), p. ccc-1.

25. Ma Sitson, "We Are Slaves Who Have Been Betrayed," pp. 64–73.

26. *Ibid.*; Schram, *Mao Tse-tung*, p. 341; *Yomiuri*, September 9, 1966; and Stuart and Roma Gelder, *Memories for a Chinese Granddaughter* (London: Hutchinson, 1967), pp. 194–195. The Gelders tried to find out whether Lau Shaw had indeed been killed by Red Guards, or had committed suicide, as another variant of the story had it. However, their efforts elicited from official and unofficial Chinese Communist sources neither confirmation nor denial of his death, nor explanation of its circumstances.

27. *Peking Review*, IX:37 (September 9, 1966), p. 10.

28. Red Guard paper of December 1966; and wall poster of January 7, 1967.

29. Bridgham, "Mao's Cultural Revolution: Origin and Development," p. 30.

30. *Nihon Keizai*, February 17, 1967, evening edition.

31. See, for instance, indoctrination speeches given to Red Guards by T'ao Chu and Chou En-lai, as contained in *CB*, no. 819 (March 10, 1967).

32. *Peking Review*, IX:49 (December 2, 1966), pp. 6–9.

33. *CNS*, no. 138 (September 22, 1966), p. 6; and *CB*, no. 891 (October 8, 1969), p. 68.

34. *CB*, no. 817 (February 21, 1967), p. 25; and FBIS 176 (September 12, 1966), p. DDD-4; FBIS 179 (September 15, 1966), p. DDD-3; and FBIS 180 (September 16, 1966), p. DDD-1.

35. *SCMP*, no. 4200 (June 18, 1968), pp. 2–3.

36. *CB*, no. 819 (March 10, 1967), pp. 28–29, 35–39.

37. FBIS 178 (September 14, 1966), p. CCC-4; and FBIS 181 (September 19, 1966), p. DDD-2.

38. Bridgham, "Mao's Cultural Revolution: Origin and Development," p. 30; *CB*, no. 891 (October 8, 1969), p. 76; and Mackerras and Hunter, *China Observed*, pp. 142–143.

39. *Sankei*, October 16, 1966.

40. *CB*, no. 830 (June 26, 1967), p. 38.

41. *JPRS* 42,349 (August 25, 1967), p. 49; and *Yomiuri*, October 15, 1966.

42. *Sankei*, October 16, 1966.

43. *Asahi*, December 9, 1967.

44. In 1965 Mark Gayn reported that only one middle school student in 180 was permitted to go on to the university and that men who had completed five years of engineering studies might have to work from four to seven years, first as laborers and then as technicians, before attaining the status and pay of engineers (*New York Times*, June 9 and June 10, 1965). See also Donald W. Klein, "A Question of Leadership: Problems of Mobility, Control and Policy-Making in China," *Current Scene*, V:7 (April 30, 1967).

45. Bridgham, "Mao's Cultural Revolution: Origin and Development," p. 30; and *CB*, no. 819 (March 10, 1967), p. 39.

46. *Yomiuri*, January 10, 1967; and *JPRS* 42,349 (August 25, 1967), p. 50.

47. *Asahi*, January 3, 1967.

48. *Nihon Keizai*, August 10, 1967; and *CNS*, no. 152 (January 5, 1967), p. A-9.

49. *Nihon Keizai*, October 17, 1966.

50. *Peking Review*, IX:43 (October 21, 1966), pp. 5–9; *Current Scene*, IV:22 (December 10, 1966), pp. 8–9; and *SCMP*, Supplement 188 (June 22, 1967), p. 1.

51. *CB*, no. 819 (March 10, 1967), p. 66.

52. *Ibid.*, p. 7.

53. *Yomiuri*, February 15, 1967, evening edition; and BTA (Bulgarian Press Agency) January 24, 1967, as carried by FBIS 16 (January 24, 1967), p. CCC-11.

54. Wall poster citing April 28, 1967 remarks by Chou En-lai and K'ang Sheng to a group of Red Guards. Substantially similar accounts were reported by both *Asahi* and *Yomiuri* on May 8, 1967.

55. Ch'en, *Mao*, p. 95.

56. *Current Scene*, VII:5 (March 10, 1969), p. 8; and *CNS*, no. 145 (November 10, 1966), p. 3, and no. 148 (December 1, 1966), p. 5.

57. *Asahi*, January 3, 1967.

58. Tokyo *Mainichi*, January 5, 1967, as carried by FBIS 4 (January 6, 1967), p. CCC-1; *Yomiuri*, January 8, 1967; and *CB*, no. 892 (October 21, 1969), p. 38.

59. *Yomiuri*, December 27, 1966; and FBIS 249 (December 27, 1966), p. CCC-6.

60. Speech by Mao Tse-tung of October 25, 1966. Three very similar

translations were available to me: one carried in *CB,* no. 891 (October 8, 1969), pp. 75–77; a second in *JPRS* 49,826 (February 12, 1970), pp. 13–16; and a third supplied by a non-American source which identified it as having appeared in a Red Guard paper of December 1966. I have chosen to draw my quotes from the latter translation, as it appears to me to reflect more clearly Mao's oral style.

61. Tokyo *Mainichi,* January 5, 1967.

62. Ch'en, *Mao,* p. 96.

63. Tokyo *Shimbun,* December 20, 1966.

64. *Yomiuri,* January 8, 1967.

65. *JPRS* 42,349 (August 25, 1967), p. 54; *Nihon Keizai* November 21, 1966; and Tokyo *Mainichi,* November 29, 1966.

66. *Great Cultural Revolution in China,* p. 497; *CB,* no. 819 (March 10, 1967), p. 11; *CB,* no. 830 (June 26, 1967), pp. 9, 27; and *Peking Review,* IX:37 (September 9, 1966), p. 5; IX:39 (September 22, 1966), p. 6; and IX:41 (October 7, 1966), p. 7.

67. *CCP Documents,* pp. 97–98, 127–128.

68. Tokyo *Shimbun,* January 6, 1967; and *Sankei,* January 7, 1967.

69. See, for instance, *CB,* no. 819 (March 10, 1967), p. 14, mentioning sightseeing trips to beauty spots, or the chapter entitled "Nonrevolutionary Tourism: November–December 1966" in Gordon A. Bennett and Ronald N. Montaperto, *Red Guard: The Political Biography of Dai Hsiao-an* (New York: Doubleday, 1971), pp. 112–130.

CHAPTER 17

1. Arlington and Lewisohn, *In Search of Old Peking,* p. 77.

2. *Mainichi,* February 5, 1967.

3. *FEER,* LXII (November 14, 1968), p. 356.

4. Arlington and Lewisohn, *In Search of Old Peking,* pp. 94–96.

5. Chiang Ch'ing made a statement to this same general effect at a rally of December 18, 1966. See *JPRS, Samples of Red Guard Publications,* I (August 1, 1967), sixth sample.

6. *Mainichi,* October 2, 1967.

7. *SCMP,* no. 3816 (November 7, 1966), pp. 1–2.

8. *CRS,* no. 12 (May 20, 1969), p. 2; and *JPRS* 40,974 (May 10, 1967), p. 13.

9. *Sankei,* October 5 and October 7, 1967; *Asahi,* December 10, 1967; and *SCMP,* no. 3905 (March 23, 1967), p. 13.

10. *SCMP,* no. 3836 (December 8, 1966), pp. 1–2.

11. *SCMP,* no. 3908 (March 30, 1967), pp. 9–15.

12. *Mainichi,* December 11, 1966.

13. Liu Jen, former second secretary of the Peking Municipal Committee; Wan Li, former vice mayor of Peking; Lin Mo-han, deputy director of the Department of Propaganda and vice minister of Culture; Hsü Li-ch'ün, former deputy director of the Department of Propaganda and deputy chief editor of *Red Flag;* Hsia Yen, former vice minister of culture; and T'ien Han, dramatist and film director.

14. *CNS*, no. 150 (December 15, 1966), p. 1; and *Asahi*, December 29, 1966.

15. *Sankei*, January 3, 1967, as carried in FBIS, no. 2 (January 4, 1967), p. CCC-6.

16. *CCP Documents*, pp. 121–123.

17. *Mainichi*, December 11, 1966.

18. *Sankei*, January 3, 1967; and *Case of Peng Teh-huai*, p. vi.

19. Allen S. Whiting, "Mao's Troubled Ark," *Life*, February 21, 1969, p. 62-f (photograph).

20. *Sankei*, December 21, 1966 and September 23, 1967; *Mainichi*, September 26, 1967; Chung and Miller, *Madame Mao*, pp. 18, 50–52; and Trumbull, *This Is Communist China*, p. 31.

21. *Mainichi* report dated February 2, 1967.

22. *Red Flag*, no. 14, 1966.

23. *Mainichi,* December 27, 1966; and Tokyo *Shimbun,* January 6, 1967.

24. *Sankei*, October 7, 1967.

25. *Yomiuri*, December 20, 1966; *Asahi*, December 28, 1966; *Mainichi*, February 6, 1967; and *Sankei*, October 6 and October 7, 1967.

26. *Sankei*, April 26, 1967.

27. NCNA, December 12, 1966.

28. *Yomiuri*, December 15, 1966; *Sankei*, September 24, 1967; and Tokyo *Shimbun*, September 24, 1967.

29. Tokyo *Shimbun*, September 24, 1967; and *Sankei*, February 20, 1967,

30. *CCP Documents*, p. 601.

31. Whitson, "The Field Army," p. 11 *et passim*.

32. *CB*, no. 859 (August 8, 1968), pp. 1–8, 37.

33. *Sankei*, January 3, 1967; and Kweiyang Radio, June 4 and June 25, 1967.

34. *CB*, no. 859 (August 8, 1968), pp. 1–8, 37.

35. *Mainichi*, February 6, 1967, evening edition.

36. *CB*, no. 859 (August 8, 1968), p. 5.

37. See, for example, *JPRS, Samples of Red Guard Publications*, I (August 1, 1967), eighth item.

38. *Ibid.*, Chinese text and summary translation.

39. *Yomiuri*, January 4, 1967, morning edition; *Sankei*, January 9, 1967; Chung and Miller, *Madame Mao*, pp. 234–242; and *Current Scene*, VI:5 (March 15, 1968), pp. 1–4.

40. Paul Harper, "The Party and the Unions in Communist China," *CQ*, no. 37 (January–March 1969), pp. 84–113; and *Who's Who in Communist China*, I:387–388, 457–458.

41. *Yomiuri*, January 4, 1967, morning edition; *Asahi*, January 4, 1967; and Chung and Miller, *Madame Mao*, pp. 234–242.

42. *Mainichi*, January 4, 1967; *Yomiuri*, January 4, 1967; and *CCP Documents*, pp. 303–306.

43. *JPRS, Samples of Red Guard Publications*, I (August 1, 1967), eighth sample, Chinese text and summary translation.

44. *Ibid.*

45. *Asahi*, December 27, 1966; and FBIS, no. 250 (December 28, 1966), p. CCC-6.

46. *Sankei*, January 10, 1967.

47. *Current Scene*, V:9 (May 31, 1967), pp. 7–11.

48. *SCMP*, no. 3914 (April 7, 1967), p. 20.

49. *Case of Peng Teh-huai*, p. 19.

50. *Ibid.*, p. 36.

CHAPTER 18

1. Chow, *May Fourth Movement*, pp. 1, 102–104, 111–115, 162–163, *et passim*.

2. Schram, *Political Thought of Mao*, pp. 254–256.

3. *Peking Review*, IX:14 (April 1, 1966), pp. 23–26; IX:15 (April 8, 1966), pp. 17–18, 25; and IX:16 (April 15, 1966), pp. 23–29.

4. *SCMP*, no. 4139 (March 15, 1968), pp. 5–7.

5. *CNS*, no. 156 (February 2, 1967), p. 3.

6. *Mainichi*, February 4, 1967.

7. Schram, *Mao Tse-tung*, p. 103.

8. *SCMP*, no. 4200 (June 18, 1968), p. 3. The editor of *SCMP* suggested, on page 1, that Mao most probably was speaking to a Malian military delegation. However, the group was identified as Albanian in *Chinese Communist Affairs: Facts & Features* (Taipei), hereinafter cited as *Facts & Features*, I:22 (August 21, 1968), p. 17.

9. *CB*, no. 819 (March 10, 1967), p. 35; and *Great Power Struggle in China*, pp. 171–172.

10. See list appended open letter of January 4, 1967, as carried in *SCMP*, no. 3858 (January 12, 1967), pp. 1–6; and *Current Scene*, VI:8 (May 15, 1968), p. 8.

11. Mackerras and Hunter, *China Observed*, p. 142; and Chung and Miller, *Madame Mao*, p. 151.

12. *CCP Documents*, pp. 116–119.

13. *Ibid.*, pp. 139–142.

14. *Ibid.*, p. 119, n.

15. Mackerras and Hunter, *China Observed*, pp. 146–147.

16. *Ibid.*, pp. 145–146; and *Sankei*, February 6, 1967.

17. *Current Scene*, VII:10 (May 15, 1969), p. 10.

18. *Current Scene*, V:16 (October 2, 1967), p. 7.

19. *JPRS*, 44,052 (January 17, 1968), pp. 13–14.

20. Mackerras and Hunter, *China Observed*, pp. 144–146.

21. *Ibid.*, pp. 146, 148; and *Current Scene*, V:8 (May 19, 1967), p. 3.

22. FBIS, no. 192 (October 4, 1966), p. DDD-1.

23. Mackerras and Hunter, *China Observed*, p. 149.

24. *Ibid.*, p. 146.

25. *Peking Review*, X:1 (January 1, 1967), p. 12.

26. *Current Scene*, VI:5 (March 15, 1968), p. 10.

27. Mackerras and Hunter, *China Observed*, p. 150.

28. *Current Scene*, V:8 (May 19, 1967), p. 3; and VII:10 (May 15, 1969), pp. 10–11.

29. *Current Scene*, V:8 (May 19, 1967), p. 2.

30. *CCP Documents*, p. 110.

31. *Mainichi*, September 29, 1967.

32. *Current Scene*, V:8 (May 19, 1967), pp. 4 and 12, n.

33. *Ibid.;* and *Communist China 1967*, Union Research Institute, Part I, p. 5.

34. *Current Scene*, V:8 (May 19, 1967), p. 3; and VII:10 (May 15, 1969), p. 11.

35. *Current Scene*, V:8 (May 19, 1967), pp. 4–5; and *SCMP*, no. 3858 (January 12, 1967), pp. 1–6.

36. *Current Scene*, V:8 (May 19, 1967), p. 5.

37. *Peking Review*, X:4 (January 20, 1967), pp. 7–9.

38. *Current Scene*, VI:5 (March 15, 1968), p. 12.

39. *Ibid.*, pp. 11–12, 23; and *CCP Documents*, pp. 303–306.

40. *Current Scene*, VII:10 (May 15, 1969), p. 11.

41. *Ibid.*, pp. 11–12; and *Communist China 1967*, Part I, p. 7.

42. Bob Reece, "China Revisited," *FEER*, LIX (March 7, 1968), pp. 413–415; and Mackerras and Hunter, *China Observed*, p. 151.

43. Mackerras and Hunter, *China Observed*, pp. 151–152.

44. Reece, "China Revisited," pp. 414–415.

CHAPTER 19

1. *Current Scene*, V:18 (November 1, 1967), p. 6; V:21 (December 15, 1967), p. 4; and VI:8 (May 15, 1968), p. 5.

2. *SCMP*, no. 4200 (June 18, 1968), p. 3.

3. Chung and Miller, *Madame Mao*, p. 232.

4. Lin Chieh, "Down with Slavishness; Strictly Observe Proletarian Revolutionary Discipline," *People's Daily*, June 16, 1967, as reported in *Peking Review*, X:27 (June 30, 1967).

5. *SCMP*, no. 4200 (June 18, 1968), p. 3.

6. *Nihon Keizai*, January 21, 1967.

7. *Ibid.*, reports dated January 31 and February 5, 1967; and *Sankei*, October 2, 1967.

8. *CNS*, no. 154 (January 19, 1967), p. A-2; and *SCMP*, no. 3912 (April 5, 1967), p. 12.

9. *Mainichi*, July 28, 1967; *Sankei*, October 2, 1967; and R. L. and H. F. Powell, "Continuity and Purge in the PLA," *Marine Corps Gazette*, LII:2 (February 1968), p. 28.

10. *Ibid.*, p. 29.

11. Tokyo *Shimbun*, January 9, 1967; and *Mainichi*, February 1, 1967.

12. NCNA, January 12, 1967, as reported in FBIS, no. 8 (January 12, 1967), p. CCC-1.

13. Cheng, *Politics of the Chinese Red Army*, p. 437.

14. Tokyo *Shimbun,* January 6 and September 24, 1967.

15. *Mainichi,* October 2, 1967.

16. Tokyo *Shimbun,* January 11, 1967.

17. *Sankei,* January 6, 1967; *Nihon Keizai,* March 4, 1967; and *Facts & Features,* I:18 (June 26, 1968), pp. 14–16.

18. *People's Daily,* January 12, 1967; and *CCP Documents,* pp. 157–158.

19. *CCP Documents,* p. 160.

20. *Ibid.,* p. 172.

21. *Ibid.,* pp. 179–182.

22. *Ibid.,* p. 109; and "September 26 Speech of Premier Chou," *Collection of the Leaders' Speeches,* Tsinghua University Defend-the-East Corps, IV (November 1966).

23. *Ibid.*

24. *CCP Documents,* p. 196.

25. *Red Flag,* no. 4 (March 1, 1967), pp. 12–14; and *JPRS* 40,471 (March 31, 1967), p. 14.

26. Parris H. Chang, "The Revolutionary Committee in China," *Current Scene,* VI:9 (June 1, 1968), p. 3.

27. *Peking Review,* X:3 (January 13, 1967), p. 7.

28. "September 26 Speech of Premier Chou"; and Chang, "The Revolutionary Committee," p. 3. The second secretary in Heilungkiang was Li Fan-wu.

29. *Yomiuri,* January 8, 1967.

30. Chang, "The Revolutionary Committee," p. 3.

31. P'an Fu-sheng, "Stand Firmly with the Proletarian Revolutionaries," *Red Flag,* no. 6, 1967, in *JPRS* 41,390 (June 14, 1967), p. 7.

32. Chang, "The Revolutionary Committee," pp. 3–4.

33. *Ibid.,* p. 5; P'an Fu-sheng, "Stand Firmly with the Proletarian Revolutionaries," p. 7; and *Peking Review,* X:8 (February 17, 1967), p. 16.

34. *Peking Review,* X:8 (February 17, 1967), pp. 15–16; and *CNS,* no. 239 (September 26, 1968), p. 3.

35. Chang, "The Revolutionary Committee," p. 5.

36. *Ibid.,* p. 6; and *Peking Review,* X:8 (February 17, 1967), p. 16.

37. *CNS,* no. 239 (September 8, 1967), p. 3.

38. *CNS,* no. 172 (June 1, 1967), p. 2.

39. *Peking Review,* X:6 (February 3, 1967), p. 17.

40. Chang Jih-ch'ing, "Steadfastly Support the Proletarian Revolutionaries in their Struggle to Seize Power," *Red Flag,* no. 4 (March 1, 1967), broadcast February 27, 1967 by Radio Peking home service.

41. *CNS,* no. 155 (January 26, 1967), p. 2.

42. *Ibid.,* pp. 2–7; Nanchang Radio, January 20, 1967, as carried by FBIS, no. 15 (January 23, 1967), p. DDD-1; *Asahi,* January 24, 1967, as carried by FBIS no. 17 (January 25, 1967), p. DDD-7; and *Mainichi,* January 24, 1967.

43. *Capital Red Guards Newspaper,* no. 21 (January 10, 1967); *Who's Who in Communist China,* I:390; and Donald W. Klein and Anne B. Clark, *Biographic Dictionary of Chinese Communism,* I:519–520.

44. Peking Radio, January 18, 1967.

45. *CCP Documents,* pp. 392.

46. January 23, 1967, wall poster of Revolutionary Rebel Regiment *Hung-ch'i* 1226, at New China News Agency.

47. *CCP Documents,* pp. 195–197.

48. Chang Jih-ch'ing, "Steadfastly Support the Proletarian Revolutionaries."

49. *CCP Documents,* pp. 252, 254.

50. Wall poster as reported February 3, 1967, by Tanaka of Tokyo *Shimbun,* and other sources.

51. *CCP Documents,* p. 216.

52. *Ibid.,* pp. 211–213.

53. *Ibid.,* pp. 221–223, 239–241, 250, 252, 254.

54. "Dawn in the Northeast," *People's Daily,* February 2, 1967.

55. Taiyuan domestic broadcast, February 3, 1967, as carried by FBIS, February 6, 1967, p. DDD-13.

56. *Mainichi,* February 6, 1967.

57. *Asahi,* February 18, 1967.

58. *Ibid.;* wall poster dated February 1967; and wall poster of March 4, 1967.

59. *Mainichi,* March 4, 1967.

60. *Current Scene* VI:21 (December 6, 1968), p. 2.

61. Snow, *Red Star,* p. 151.

62. Payne, *Mao Tse-tung,* p. 223.

63. Schram, *Political Thought of Mao,* p. 352.

64. *SCMP,* no. 4200 (June 18, 1968), p. 5.

65. Ch'en, *Mao,* p. 109.

CHAPTER 20

1. KYODO, January 18, 1967; TANYUG (official Yugoslav news agency), January 18, 1967; *Nihon Keizai,* January 28, 1967; and *Asahi,* February 8, 1967.

2. *Communist China 1967,* Part I, pp. 95–101, and Part II, p. 160.

3. Malraux, "I Am Alone with the Masses," p. 119.

4. Schram, *Political Thought of Mao,* p. 352.

5. Report to Tokyo *Shimbun* dated February 3, 1967.

6. *Ibid.*

7. *Yomiuri,* April 14, 1967.

8. Tokyo *Shimbun,* February 7, 1967; and *Sankei,* October 4, 1967.

9. See, for instance, Chou En-lai's speech at the struggle rally against Yang Ch'eng-wu, *Facts & Features,* I:21 (August 7, 1968), pp. 21–28, and Chiang Ch'ing's speech of January 18, 1967, as contained in Chung and Miller, *Madame Mao,* pp. 243–249.

10. Wall poster of February 4, 1967; and *Nihon Keizai,* February 10, 1967.

11. *SCMP,* no. 3898 (March 14, 1967), pp. 1–3.

12. *Nihon Keizai,* February 24, 1967, evening edition; and Chung and Miller, *Madame Mao,* p. 244.

13. *SCMP,* no. 3898 (March 14, 1967), pp. 1–3.

14. *Nihon Keizai,* February 24, 1967, evening edition; and *SCMP,* no. 4011 (August 29, 1967), pp. 1–6.

15. May 16, 1966 circular, in *CB,* no. 852 (May 6, 1968), pp. 2–6.

16. Wall poster dated January 26, 1967.

17. Charles A. Neuhauser, "The Impact of the Cultural Revolution on the Chinese Communist Party Machine," *Asian Survey,* VIII (June 1968), pp. 475–476; *Sankei,* August 13, 1967; and *Communist China 1967,* Part I, p. 173.

18. *Communist China 1967,* Part I, p. 56.

19. Chung and Miller, *Madame Mao,* p. 254.

20. *Red Flag,* no. 3, 1967, as carried in *JPRS* 40,086 (March 1, 1967), pp. 12–21.

21. Wall poster of 79th Middle School, Peking, February 1967.

22. KYODO, February 2, 1967; and *Asahi,* February 3, 1967.

23. *Nihon Keizai,* February 10, 1967; and *Ts'an-k'ao hsiao-hsi,* Canton Overseas Supplementary School, no. 3 (February 1967), in *JPRS Samples of Red Guard Publications,* Vol. II.

24. *Asahi,* February 18, 1967.

25. *CCP Documents,* pp. 195–360. The term *"Chung-kung chung-yang,"* used in these documents to designate one of the issuing authorities, stands for "The Chinese Communist Party Central Committee." But the status of that committee, and hence the use of the term, had become ambiguous. I accordingly have translated the term as "Party Center" on the assumption that the relevant directives were issued by Mao Tse-tung and his immediate staff.

26. *Ibid.,* p. 232.

27. *Ibid.,* p. 337.

28. *Ibid.,* pp. 297–298.

29. *Asahi,* January 13, 1967.

30. *Nihon Keizai,* February 24, 1967, evening edition.

31. *Yomiuri,* February 24, 1967; and *Communist China 1967,* Part I, p. 105.

32. *Yomiuri,* February 24, 1967; and *Nihon Keizai,* February 24, 1967.

33. *Facts & Features,* I:23 (September 4, 1968), pp. 24–29.

34. Report to *Mainichi* of February 4, 1967.

35. *CB,* no. 822 (March 23, 1967), pp. 1–6; and *Communist China 1967,* Part I, p. 53.

36. Gordon A. Bennett, "Political Labels and Popular Tension," *Current Scene,* VII:4 (February 26, 1969), p. 11; and *Facts & Features,* I:17 (June 26, 1968), p. 12, and I:20 (July 24, 1968), pp. 20–25.

37. *K'o-chi hung-ch'i,* March 26, 1967, as found in *Tsu-kuo* [China Monthly] (Hong Kong), no. 53 (August 1, 1968), pp. 383–386.

38. Snow, *Red Star,* p. 143.

39. Malraux, "I Am Alone with the Masses," p. 119.

40. *Hung-ch'i* (of the Peking Aeronautical Institute), April 4, 1967; *Pei-wai hung-ch'i* (of Peking Foreign Languages Institute), n.d.; and Peking wall poster which appeared in July 1967.

41. *Great Power Struggle in China,* pp. 171–172; and Bennett, "Political Labels and Popular Tension," p. 11.

42. *Facts & Features,* I:23 (September 4, 1968), pp. 24–29.

43. *Facts & Features,* I:19 (July 10, 1968), p. 23, and I:17 (June 26, 1968), pp. 11–14.

44. *Facts & Features,* I:17 (June 26, 1968), pp. 11–14; and *Nihon Keizai,* April 6, 1967, evening edition.

45. Winberg Chai, "The Reorganization of the Chinese Communist Party, 1966–1968," *Asian Survey,* VIII (November 1968), p. 902.

46. *Mainichi,* March 17, 1967; *Sankei,* April 7, 1967; AFP (Agence France Presse), April 12, 1967; *Yomiuri,* April 14, 1967; and *CCP Documents,* p. 322.

47. Tokyo *Shimbun,* April 7 and July 29, 1967; *Yomiuri,* August 2, 1967; and *Sankei,* October 2, 1967.

48. *Asahi,* December 10, 1967.

49. *Peking hung-ch'i pao* (Red Guard paper), January 30, 1967.

50. I retain the account of this interview, clipped from the English-language press in Hong Kong while I was stationed there, but unfortunately did not record the name and date of the newspaper in question.

51. *Mainichi,* March 17, 1967; and Tokyo *Shimbun,* March 18, 1967.

52. *Facts & Features,* I:17 (June 26, 1968), pp. 11–14.

53. *Sankei,* April 26, 1967, morning edition, and April 29, 1967.

CHAPTER 21

1. *Liberation Army Daily,* June 6, 1966; *Nihon Keizai,* April 1, 1967; and *SCMP,* no. 3951 (June 2, 1967), pp. 1–6. Yang Hsien-chen and his supporters clothed their arguments against Mao Tse-tung's policies, including the split with the USSR, in ideological language; this was the dispute over the propositions that "one divides into two" and "two combine into one."

2. *Mainichi,* April 2, 1967; and *JPRS* 41,799 (July 11, 1967), pp. 91–96.

3. *CB,* no. 834 (August 17, 1967), pp. 3–4.

4. *JPRS* 41,889 (July 19, 1967), p. 56, and 43,921 (January 9, 1968), pp. 19–23.

5. Schram, *Political Thought of Mao,* pp. 342–343.

6. *Yomiuri,* April 10, 1967, morning edition; and *CB,* no. 848 (February 27, 1968), p. 11.

7. *Yomiuri,* April 10, 1967, morning edition; and *Current Scene,* V:6 (April 15, 1967), p. 2

8. John Gittings, "The Chinese Army's Role in the Cultural Revolution," *Pacific Affairs,* XXXIX (Fall 1967), p. 284, n.

9. Chung and Miller, *Madame Mao,* pp. 247–248.

10. Tokyo *Shimbun,* April 24 and July 29, 1967; *Yomiuri,* August 2, 1967; and *Sankei,* October 2, 1967. Ch'en Yi, if dropped from the Military Affairs Committee at this time, was later restored to membership in it.

11. *Nihon Keizai,* April 14, 1967; *Asahi,* April 17 and April 18, 1967; *Sankei,* October 2, 1967; and *Communist China 1967,* Part I, p. 201.

12. *Nihon Keizai,* August 4, 1967.

13. *Peking Review*, X:16 (April 14, 1967), pp. 12–15.

14. Mao, *SW*, II, 203–204.

15. Chen, *Chinese Communist Regime*, p. 137.

16. Schram, "The Party in Chinese Communist Ideology," *CQ*, no. 38 (April–June, 1969), p. 6.

17. *Ibid.*, pp. 5–6.

18. Schram, *Political Thought of Mao*, p. 179.

19. Mao, *SW*, IV, 284.

20. Liu Shao-ch'i, *How To Be a Good Communist*, p. 81.

21. *SCMP*, no. 4200 (June 18, 1968), p. 2.

22. *Mainichi*, January 9 and October 2, 1967; KYODO report from the *Japan Times* as carried by FBIS, no. 14 (January 20, 1967); and *Nihon Keizai*, April 1, 1967.

23. *Asahi*, June 14, 1967.

24. *Peking Review*, X:15 (April 7, 1967), pp. 5–15.

25. Based on a viewing of the motion picture in Hong Kong.

26. *Peking Review*, X:15 (April 7, 1967), pp. 18–20.

27. Tokyo *Shimbun*, April 12, 1967.

28. *CB*, no. 848 (April 10, 1968), pp. 1–39; *Facts & Features*, I:13 (April 17, 1968), pp. 22–24, I:15 (May 15, 1968), pp. 27–29, and I:16 (May 29, 1968), pp. 24–27; and *Current Scene*, VI:6 (April 15, 1968), pp. 1–21.

29. *Yomiuri*, February 18, 1967; and *Sankei*, September 27, 1967.

30. *Mainichi*, January 23, 1967.

31. *Yomiuri*, April 4, 1967; and *Communist China 1967*, Part I, p. 28.

32. *Great Power Struggle in China*, p. 286, from "Report on the Examination of the Crimes of the Renegade, Traitor, and Scab Liu Shao-ch'i." This report was cited in the "Communique of the Enlarged Plenary Session of the Eighth Central Committee of the Communist Party of China," adopted October 31, 1968.

33. Harry Howe Ransom, *Central Intelligence and National Security* (Cambridge: Harvard University Press, 1958), pp. 71–72, 79.

34. Schram, *Political Thought of Mao*, p. 362.

35. Stuart and Roma Gelder, *Memories for a Chinese Granddaughter*, p. 119; and *SCMP*, Supplement no. 177 (April 19, 1967), p. 15.

36. *SCMP*, no. 3787 (September 23, 1966), p. 25.

37. Stuart and Roma Gelder, *Memories for a Chinese Granddaughter*, p. 119; and *Pei-ching jih-pao*, January 21, 1967.

38. *Yomiuri*, May 29, 1967.

39. *Ibid.*, April 10, 1967, morning edition.

CHAPTER 22

1. Robert A. Scalapino, "The Cultural Revolution and Chinese Foreign Policy," *Current Scene*, VI:13 (August 1, 1968), p. 8.

2. Michael B. Yahuda, "Chinese Foreign Policy after 1963: The Maoist Phase," p. 109.

3. *Sankei*, August 8, 1967.

4. James Legge, tr., *The Four Books* (London: Oxford University Press), p. 787.

5. Maurice Collis, *Foreign Mud* (London: Faber and Faber, 1946), p. 235.

6. Yahuda, "Chinese Foreign Policy," pp. 96–102.

7. *Ibid.*, p. 109.

8. *Sankei*, August 8, 1967.

9. *CNS*, no. 143 (October 27, 1966), pp. 7–10.

10. *CCP Documents*, pp. 109–111.

11. *CNS*, no. 134 (August 25, 1966), p. 8, and no. 142 (October 20, 1966), p. 15.

12. *Peking Review*, X:37 (September 9, 1966), p. 10.

13. *SCMP*, no. 4011 (August 29, 1967), pp. 1–6.

14. Parris H. Chang, "China's Eclipse of the Moon," *FEER*, LXIII (January 16, 1969), pp. 97–99.

15. *JPRS* 40,488 (April 3, 1967), pp. 20–23, for a notable example.

16. *Facts & Features*, II:2 (November 13, 1968), p. 20.

17. *Directory of Chinese Communist Officials* (Washington: Department of State, 1966), p. 113 *et passim;* and Melvin Gurtov, *The Foreign Ministry and Foreign Affairs in China's "Cultural Revolution,"* Memo RM-5934-PR (Santa Monica: Rand Corporation, March 1969), p. 6.

18. *Wai-shih hung-ch'i* and *Ko-ming ch'iao pao* joint issue, September 12, 1967.

19. *Chung-kuo ch'ing-nien*, no. 17, 1961, pp. 2–4.

20. Schram, *Mao Tse-tung*, p. 322.

21. *Hung-wei chan-pao*, April 8, 1967.

22. *SCMP*, no. 4002 (August 16, 1967), pp. 1–3.

23. *Ibid.*

24. Chung and Miller, *Madame Mao*, p. 246.

25. Sven Lindqvist, *China in Crisis* (New York: Crowell, 1965), p. 48.

26. Gurtov, *The Foreign Ministry*, pp. 8–9.

27. *Hung-ch'i* (of the Peking Aeronautical Institute), April 4, 1967.

28. *Hung-wei chan-pao*, April 13, 1967.

29. *Ibid.*

30. Gurtov, *The Foreign Ministry*, pp. 8–9.

31. *Hung-ch'i* (of the Peking Aeronautical Institute), April 4, 1967.

32. *Hung-wei chan-pao*, April 8, 1967.

33. *Ibid.*, August 13, 1967.

34. *CNS*, no. 148 (December 1, 1966), p. A-5.

35. *Asahi*, February 11, 1967.

36. *Hung-wei chan-pao*, April 8, 1967.

37. *Mainichi*, September 23, 1967.

38. *Nihon Keizai*, February 16, 1967.

39. Gurtov, *The Foreign Ministry*, p. 18; and *Hung-ch'i* (of the Peking Aeronautical Institute), April 4, 1967.

40. *Hung-wei chan-pao*, April 8, 1967.

41. *Ibid.*

42. Scalapino, "The Cultural Revolution and Chinese Foreign Policy," p. 8; and *CNS*, no. 168 (May 4, 1967), p. A-3.

43. *Sankei*, May 11, 1967; and *JPRS* 42,070 (August 3, 1967), p. 10.

44. *Hung-wei chan-pao*, April 8, 1967.

45. *Ibid.*

46. *Hung-ch'i* (of the Peking Aeronautical Institute), April 4, 1967.

47. *CNS*, no. 156 (February 21, 1967), p. A-2.

48. *Peking Review*, X:6 (February 3, 1967), pp. 23–24.

49. *Mainichi*, February 2, 1967.

50. *Ibid.;* motion pictures seen in Hong Kong; and reports by fellow travelers.

51. *Peking Review*, X:7 (February 10, 1967), p. 6.

52. *Asahi*, February 7, 1967; and *New York Times*, February 12, 1967.

53. *Nihon Keizai*, February 9, 1967; and *New York Times*, February 10, 1967.

54. *Hong Kong Standard* (based on UPI report from Moscow), July 20, 1967.

55. *CNS*, no. 158 (February 23, 1967), p. A-1; *Current Scene*, V:20 (December 1, 1967), p. 7; and *Peking Review*, X:8 (February 17, 1967), pp. 11–14, 19.

56. *CCP Documents*, pp. 244–245.

57. *Hung-wei chan-pao*, April 8, 1967.

58. *Ibid.*

59. *SCMP*, no. 3939 (May 18, 1967), p. 7; and *Hung-ch'i* (of the Peking Aeronautical Institute), April 4, 1967.

60. Tokyo *Shimbun*, April 18, 1967; Gurtov, *The Foreign Ministry*, pp. 24–27; and *CNS*, no. 168 (May 4, 1967), p. A-4

61. Tokyo *Shimbun*, April 27, 1967; *Mainichi*, April 28, 1967; *New York Times*, April 30, 1967; *FEER*, LVI (May 4, 1967), pp. 227, 249; and *Communist China 1967*, Part I, pp. 308–309.

62. *Hung-wei pao*, September 15, 1967; *Mainichi*, October 5, 1967; and *CRS*, October 21, 1968.

63. *Asahi*, May 15, 1969.

64. Gurtov, *The Foreign Ministry*, p. 27.

65. *CCP Documents*, pp. 309–310.

66. *Current Scene*, V:20 (December 1, 1967), p. 5; and Gurtov, *The Foreign Ministry*, p. 28.

67. *Sankei*, May 31, 1967; and *Yomiuri*, May 31, 1967.

68. *Hong Kong Report for the Year 1967* (Hong Kong: Government Press, 1968), pp. 35–36.

69. *Ibid.*, pp. 53, 68. Because detailed production figures are not available, gains in productivity are gauged by reference to domestic exports which, in 1967, grew by 17 percent.

70. *Ibid.*, pp. 127, 156.

71. Richard Hughes, *Hong Kong* (London: Deutsch, 1968), p. 38.

72. *Kowloon Disturbances 1966: Report of Commission of Inquiry* (Hong Kong: Government Press, 1967), pp. 119–121.

73. *Hong Kong Report for the Year 1967*, pp. 265–266, 273–274.

74. *Ibid.*, p. 30; and Willard A. Hanna, *A Trial of Two Colonies, Part III: Communist Challenge to British Hong Kong*, pp. 4–5.

75. See *FEER*, LV (February 2, 1967), pp. 151–152.

76. Statement of Ch'en Yi, reported in *Washington Post*, December 11, 1966.

77. *Hong Kong Report for the Year 1967*, p. 3; Hanna, *Trial of Two Colonies, Part III*, p. 8; and *Peking Review*, X:28 (May 19, 1967), pp. 15–17.

78. *Peking Review*, X:21 (May 19, 1967), pp. 15–17.

79. *Hong Kong Report for the Year 1967*, p. 4.

80. *Ibid.*; Hanna, *Trial of Two Colonies, Part III*, pp. 8–9; and *New York Times*, March 31, 1968.

81. Hanna, *Trial of Two Colonies, Part III*, p. 11; and Angus M. Fraser, *Hong Kong-Macao: "People's War" in Microcosm*, Institute for Defense Analyses, International and Social Studies Division, Current Analyses Series no. 1, p. 5.

82. *Peking Review*, X:21 (May 19, 1967), pp. 14–15.

83. *Ibid.*, p. 17, and X:22 (May 26, 1967), pp. 51–52; and *New York Times*, May 19 and May 20, 1967.

84. Hanna, *Trial of Two Colonies, Part III*, pp. 11–12; and personal observation.

85. *New York Times*, May 23, 1967.

86. Hanna, *Trial of Two Colonies, Part III*, p. 14; and accounts of observers.

87. *The China Mail*, December 28, 1967.

88. *New York Times*, May 25, 1967; and *FEER*, LXI (August 1, 1968), p. 229.

89. *South China Morning Post*, January 3, 1968.

90. Willard A. Hanna, *A Trial of Two Colonies, Part IV: Paper Tiger Worsts Painted Dragon*, p. 3; and *Hong Kong Report for the Year 1967*, p. 8.

91. *New York Times*, June 14, 1967.

92. Personal communication in 1969 from officer of the firm concerned.

93. *Hong Kong Report for the Year 1967*, pp. 9–10, 53.

94. Hughes, *Hong Kong*, p. 31; and Robert L. Price, "International Trade of Communist China, 1950–1965," *Economic Profile of Mainland China*, II, 605.

95. *Independent Journal* (Marin), September 1, 1969, carrying AP report from Hong Kong.

96. *Hong Kong Report for the Year 1967*, pp. 10, 12–13.

97. *Ibid.*, p. 12; and *The China Mail*, December 29, 1967.

98. *Hong Kong Report for the Year 1967*, p. 12; *New York Times*, July 15, 1967; and *South China Morning Post*, December 22, 1967.

99. *Peking Review*, X:27 (June 30, 1967), p. 25.

100. *New York Times*, June 7 and June 12, 1967; and Fraser, *Hong-Kong-Macao*, p. 24.

101. *FEER*, LVIII (November 16, 1967), p. 338; and personal communication, in 1969, from an official of the Hong Kong Government.

102. *Hong Kong Report for the Year 1967,* pp. 13–15.

103. *Ibid.;* and *FEER,* LVII (August 31, 1967), p. 407.

104. *FEER,* LVII (September 28, 1967), p. 633.

105. *Hong Kong Report for the Year 1967,* pp. 10–11.

106. *FEER,* LVII (September 28, 1967), p. 634.

107. *Hong Kong Report for the Year 1967,* pp. 15–16; and Hanna, *Trial of Two Colonies, Part IV,* p. 8.

108. *Peking Review,* X:31 (July 28, 1967), p. 23; and *South China Sunday Post Herald,* October 5, 1969.

109. *Wen-hui pao* (Hong Kong), July 13 and July 15, 1967.

110. *Hong Kong Report for the Year 1967,* p. 14.

111. *Peking Review,* X:35 (August 25, 1967), p. 22.

112. Peking wall poster which appeared July 1967.

113. *Yomiuri,* August 14, 1967.

114. Gurtov, *The Foreign Ministry,* p. 53; and *SCMP,* no. 4191 (June 5, 1968), pp. 8–13.

115. *FEER,* LVIII (October 5, 1967), p. 6.

116. *Communist China 1967,* pp. 300–301; *CRS,* October 4, 1967; *Sankei,* October 3, 1967; *Peking Review,* X:29 (July 14, 1967), pp. 30–33; and *New York Times,* July 1, 1967, July 25, 1969 and November 8, 1969.

117. *Yomiuri,* July 20 and August 8, 1967; *Asahi,* August 16, 1967; and *Akahata* August 21 and August 22, 1967.

118. *CQ,* no. 32 (October-December 1967), pp. 221–227.

119. *New York Times,* October 14, 1969.

120. *CQ,* no. 32 (October-December 1967), pp. 221–227.

121. *Current Scene,* VI:1 (January 15, 1968), p. 4; *Nihon Keizai,* August 24, 1967; and *Hong Kong Standard,* January 19, 1969.

122. *Hong Kong Standard,* January 19, 1969.

123. *FEER,* LXI (August 31, 1968), p. 229.

124. *Japan Times,* November 10, 1969.

125. *FEER,* LVIII (October 5, 1967), p. 6.

126. *Sankei,* September 5, 1967.

127. *Current Scene,* V:20 (December 1, 1967), p. 1.

128. *South China Sunday Post-Herald,* September 10, 1967.

129. *Ibid.;* and *CQ,* no. 32 (October-December 1967), pp. 221–227.

130. *Peking Review,* X:37 (September 8, 1967), p. 29.

131. *CQ,* no. 32 (October-December 1967), pp. 224–226.

132. *Sankei,* September 20, 1967.

133. *Mainichi,* September 21, 1967; and *Sankei,* October 3, 1967.

CHAPTER 23

1. *CB,* no. 891 (October 8, 1969), p. 68.

2. *CNS,* no. 238 (September 19, 1968), pp. 11–12; and *CB,* no. 855 (June 17, 1968), *passim.*

3. *Mainichi,* February 1, 1967; *Asahi,* February 24, 1967; and *CCP Documents,* pp. 248–261.

4. *CCP Documents*, pp. 248–261; *Nihon Keizai*, January 11, 1967; and *Current Scene*, VI:18 (October 18, 1968), pp. 23–24.

5. Chien Yu-shen, *China's Fading Revolution* (Hong Kong: Center of Contemporary Chinese Studies, 1969), p. 22, citing Radio Urumchi, November 11, 1968; and *Current Scene*, VIII:8 (April 15, 1970), p. 4.

6. Domes, "Cultural Revolution and the Army," pp. 357–358; and Victor C. Falkenheim, "The Cultural Revolution in Kwangsi, Yunnan, and Fukien," p. 582.

7. *CCP Documents*, p. 326.

8. Falkenheim, "The Cultural Revolution in Kwangsi, Yunnan, and Fukien," pp. 582–583, 587–588.

9. *SCMP*, no. 4226 (July 26, 1968), pp. 4–6; *Asahi*, June 19, 1967; *Communist China 1967*, Part I, p. 67; and *FEER*, LVII (August 18, 1967), p. 337.

10. *CCP Documents*, pp. 385–387; *Current Scene*, VI:18 (October 18, 1968), p. 26; and *Communist China 1967*, Part I, p. 208.

11. June Dreyer, "Inner Mongolia; the Purge of Ulanfu," *Current Scene*, VI:20 (November 15, 1968), pp. 1–13; and Paul Hyer and William Heaton, "The Cultural Revolution in Inner Mongolia," *CQ*, no. 36 (October-December 1968), pp. 114–128.

12. Based on two articles cited n. 11, above.

13. *CCP Documents*, pp. 417–419.

14. *CB*, no. 859 (August 8, 1968), pp. 1–8.

15. Kweiyang Radio, June 4, 1967 and June 25, 1967.

16. *Sankei*, January 3, 1967; and *CQ*, no. 32 (October-December, 1967), p. 209.

17. *Current Scene*, VI:11 (July 1, 1968), pp. 5–6.

18. *CB*, no. 891 (October 8, 1969), p. 70.

19. *FEER*, LVI (May 18, 1967), pp. 341–343; and *Asahi*, May 8, 1967.

20. *Current Scene*, VI:11 (July 1, 1968), p. 6; and *SCMP*, no. 4181 (May 20, 1968), p. 4.

21. *Nihon Keizai*, May 8, 1967.

22. *Current Scene*, VI:11 (July 1, 1968), p. 7.

23. *CCP Documents*, pp. 434–438. The husband and wife were Liu Chieh-t'ing and Chang Hsi-t'ing.

24. *Current Scene*, VI:18 (October 18, 1968), p. 25.

25. *CNS*, no. 166 (April 20, 1967), pp. A-3 to A-4; *Asahi*, July 23, 1967; and personal communication from a foreign journalist.

26. *CCP Documents*, pp. 409–411.

27. *Ibid.*, pp. 463–464.

28. A. Doak Barnett, *Cadres, Bureaucracy, and Political Power in Communist China* (New York: Columbia University Press, 1967), pp. 128–129, 158–159, 195–197.

29. *Ibid.*, pp. 244–249, 326, 391–394.

30. Wang Chen, ed., *Hsien-tai pen-kuo ti-t'u* (Shanghai: *Shih-chieh yü-ti hsüeh-she*, 1941), Part 2, p. 16.

31. *SCMP*, no. 4089 (December 29, 1967), p. 9.

32. *Communist China 1968*, Union Research Institute, pp. 221–222.

33. *Yomiuri,* May 19, 1967; Tokyo *Shimbun,* June 2, 1967; *Mainichi,* June 2, 1967; *SCMP,* no. 4009 (August 25, 1967), pp. 1–5; *SCMP,* no. 4012 (August 31, 1967), pp. 4–7; and *Current Scene,* VI:9 (June 1, 1968), pp. 12–13.

34. *Current Scene,* VI:9 (June 1, 1968), pp. 13–14.

35. *Sankei,* September 29, 1967.

36. *Union Research Service,* XLVIII (August 4, 1967), p. 141.

37. *Mainichi,* July 30, 1967; and *JPRS* 44,241 (February 5, 1968), pp. 124–140.

38. *CQ,* no. 32 (October-December 1967), pp. 186–187.

39. *Asahi,* June 8, 1967; *Yomiuri,* June 8, 1967; and *CQ,* no. 32 (October-December, 1967), p. 184.

40. *SCMP,* no. 3988 (July 27, 1967), p. 1; and *SCMP,* no. 3992 (August 1, 1967), pp. 1–4.

41. *Sankei,* September 29, 1967; *Communist China 1967,* Part I, p. 63; and *Union Research Service,* XLVIII (September 19, 1967), pp. 319–322.

42. *Mainichi,* July 30, 1967; *Sankei,* September 29, 1967; and *SCMP,* no. 4089 (December 29, 1967), pp. 6, 9.

43. *Great Power Struggle in China,* pp. 182–183.

44. *Ibid.; CCP Documents,* pp. 484–488; and *Union Research Service,* XLVIII:23 (September 19, 1969), p. 331.

45. *Mainichi,* July 30 and August 2, 1967.

46. *Great Power Struggle in China,* pp. 183–187; *Sankei,* September 29, 1967; *CQ,* no. 32 (October-December 1967), p. 186; *JPRS* 44,241 (February 5, 1968), pp. 131–140; and *SCMP,* no. 4089 (December 29, 1967), p. 5.

47. *Union Research Service,* XLVIII (September 19, 1967), pp. 319–332.

48. *Ibid.;* and *JPRS* 44,241 (February 5, 1968), pp. 138–140.

49. *Mainichi,* July 24, 1967; *Sankei,* September 29, 1967; *Communist China 1967,* Part I, pp. 64–65; and *Union Research Service,* XLVIII (August 4, 1967), p. 149.

50. *SCMP,* no. 4143 (March 21, 1968), p. 4.

51. *Red Flag,* no. 12, 1967, pp. 43–47, as translated in *CNS,* no. 208 (February 22, 1968), pp. 1–4.

52. *Asahi,* August 7, 1967.

53. *South China Morning Post,* July 21, 1969.

54. Based upon various reports from Peking appearing in the Japanese press as carried in the American Embassy, Tokyo, *Daily Summary of Japanese Press,* January 24, 1967.

55. *Ibid.* February 2 and February 3, 1967; *Asahi,* August 16, 1967; *Sankei,* August 17 and September 2, 1967; and *Communist China 1967,* Part I, pp. 58, 207.

56. Chung and Miller, *Madame Mao,* pp. 72–82.

57. *SCMP,* no. 3996 (August 8, 1967), p. 4.

58. *Facts & Features,* I:19 (July 10, 1968), p. 24.

59. *JPRS, Samples of Red Guard Publications,* I (August 1, 1967), first sample.

60. Chung and Miller, *Madame Mao,* pp. 248–249; and *Nihon Keizai,* April 14, 1967.

61. *Great Power Struggle in China*, p. 263.

62. *Communist China 1967*, Part I, pp. 208–209; *Mainichi*, August 6, 1967; and *Asahi*, August 16, 1967.

63. *Who's Who in Communist China*, I:102, 226–268.

64. Tokyo *Shimbun*, July 29, 1967; *South China Morning Post*, August 1, 1967; *Mainichi*, September 23, 1967; and *SCMP*, no. 4190 (June 4, 1968), p. 8.

65. *Mainichi*, August 12, 1967.

66. *Sankei*, August 12, 1967.

67. *CB*, no. 844 (January 10, 1968), unnumbered initial page; and *SCMP*, no. 4143 (March 21, 1968), p. 4.

68. *Mainichi*, August 12 and September 23, 1967; and *SCMP*, no. 4190 (June 4, 1968), p. 8. The commanders in question were Hsü Shih-yu in Nanking and Han Hsien-ch'u at Foochow.

69. *Communist China 1967*, Part I, p. 209.

70. *Facts & Features*, I:19 (July 10, 1968), pp. 20–26.

71. Tokyo *Shimbun*, August 12, 1967; and Bennett and Montaperto, *Red Guard*, pp. 149–195.

72. *Union Research Service*, XLVIII (August 8, 1967), pp. 152–153; and *FEER*, LVII (August 24, 1967), p. 361.

73. *FEER*, LVII (August 24, 1967), p. 360; Tokyo *Shimbun*, August 13, 1967; Reuters, July 31, August 29, and September 4, 1967; *SCMP*, no. 4040 (October 12, 1967), pp. 7–16; and *Current Scene*, VI:8 (May 15, 1968), p. 7.

74. Tokyo *Shimbun*, August 13 and August 14, 1967; *FEER*, LVII (August 17, 1967), pp. 313–314 and LVII (August 31, 1967), pp. 408–410; *Mainichi*, September 23, 1967; and *CRS*, October 27, 1967.

75. *Manchester Guardian*, September 18, 1967; Reuters, September 19, 1967; *Herald-Tribune*, international edition, September 19, 1967; *SCMP*, no. 4041 (October 13, 1967), pp. 11–15; *SCMP*, no. 4044 (October 19, 1967), pp. 5–7; and *CRS*, January 10, 1968.

76. *FEER*, LVII (August 17, 1967), p. 313; *FEER*, LVII (August 24, 1967), p. 360; and F. T. Mits, "A Dynasty Near Collapse," *Current Scene*, V:14 (August 31, 1967), pp. 3–4.

77. *Sankei*, August 22, August 30, and October 1, 1967; and *FEER*, LVII (August 24, 1967), pp. 361–362.

78. *SCMP*, no. 4190 (June 4, 1968), pp. 7–8; and *Great Power Struggle in China*, p. 425.

79. *Asahi*, September 2 and October 14, 1967; and *Current Scene*, VI:11 (July 1, 1968), pp. 7–8.

80. *Asahi*, August 7, 1967; *Tokyo Shimbun*, August 22, 1967; and *Communist China 1967*, Part I, p. 67.

81. *Mainichi*, September 22, 1967.

82. *Sankei*, July 27, 1967.

83. *Communist China 1967*, Part I, p. 31; and *Sankei*, August 8, 1967.

84. *Mainichi*, September 26, 1967.

85. *Asahi*, August 4, 1967.

86. *Sankei*, August 7, 1967.

87. *Ibid.*, August 8, 1967.

88. Tokyo *Shimbun*, August 18, 1967; and *CCP Documents*, p. 503.

89. *Mainichi*, September 29, 1967.

90. *SCMP*, no. 4137 (March 13, 1968), p. 3; no. 4142 (March 20, 1968), p. 3; and no. 4191 (June 5, 1968), pp. 8–13.

91. *Who's Who in Communist China*, I, 246–247; and *Communist China 1967*, Part I, pp. 207–208.

92. *Communist China 1967*, Part I, pp. 209, 238.

93. *Ibid.*, p. 83.

94. Edgar Snow, "Peking's View of the Nixon Mission," p. 26.

CHAPTER 24

1. *CCP Documents*, p. 573.

2. *SCMP*, no. 4078 (December 12, 1967), p. 8; no. 4088 (December 28, 1967), p. 17.

3. *CB*, no. 844 (January 10, 1968), p. 1.

4. *SCMP*, no. 4146 (March 26, 1968), p. 6; and *Peking Review*, X:35 (August 25, 1967), p. 5. A review of issues of *People's Daily* for the months July–September of 1967 indicates that Mao was in Peking as late as July 11. His next reported appearance was on August 21, when he received two Albanians. The photograph taken on that occasion shows a background which clearly is not that of Mao's own reception rooms in Peking. The only other Chinese shown in the photo is Yao Wen-yüan, who was based in Shanghai. These circumstances tend to confirm the statement attributed to Chang Ch'un-ch'iao that Mao Tse-tung had been in Shanghai in July and August, but that for reasons of the Chairman's safety he could not make the fact known until early September, when Mao Tse-tung had left—presumably to tour the provinces.

5. *SCMP*, no. 4070 (November 30, 1967), p. 3.

6. *SCMP*, no. 4088 (December 28, 1967), pp. 8–9; and *JPRS* 44,414 (February 19, 1968), pp. 4–5.

7. *SCMP*, no. 4070 (November 30, 1967), p. 1; and no. 4222 (July 22, 1968), pp. 2–3.

8. *CCP Documents*, p. 550.

9. *SCMP*, no. 4070 (November 30, 1967), pp. 10–11.

10. *Ibid.*, pp. 8–9.

11. *CNS*, no. 193 (October 26, 1967), p. 7.

12. *CCP Documents*, p. 508.

13. *SCMP*, no. 4060 (November 15, 1967), pp. 1–2.

14. *CCP Documents*, pp. 507–510.

15. *CB*, no. 844 (January 10, 1968), p. 1; and *CCP Documents*, pp. 521–533.

16. *CCP Documents*, pp. 521–533. In the Chinese text (p. 513), the term translated as "Old K'ang" is *"K'ang lao,"* denoting honor rather than familiarity.

17. *Great Power Struggle in China*, pp. 429–436.

18. *Communist China 1967*, Part II, p. 156; *Who's Who in Communist China*, I, 128–129; and *Great Power Struggle in China*, pp. 199–200.

19. *CB*, no. 844 (January 10, 1968), p. 1.

20. *Facts & Features*, I:18 (June 26, 1968), pp. 14–16.

21. *Communist China 1967*, Part I, p. 76.

22. *Communist China 1968*, p. 24; and *SCMP*, no. 4142 (March 20, 1968), pp. 10–13.

23. See, for instance, *SCMP*, no. 4060 (November 15, 1967), pp. 3–6.

24. The transcripts of the meetings in which Chiang Ch'ing did not participate are perhaps as significant, in this connection, as those covering ones at which she was present. For an account of a meeting which had as its purpose the calling off of attacks against Chou En-lai, see *SCMP*, no. 4060 (November 15, 1967), pp. 3–6.

25. *SCMP*, no. 4066 (November 24, 1967), p. 4; and no. 4078, (December 12, 1967), p. 9.

26. *JPRS* 49,826 (February 12, 1970), pp. 19–20.

27. *SCMP*, no. 3967 (June 26, 1967), pp. 12–13.

28. *SCMP*, no. 4190 (June 4, 1968), p. 9.

29. *Sankei*, August 18, 1967.

30. *CCP Documents*, p. 551.

31. *FEER*, LXVI (October 2, 1969), pp. 34–35.

32. *SCMP*, no. 4070 (November 30, 1967), p. 6.

33. *CCP Documents*, p. 531.

34. *Sankei*, July 21, 1967, carried an eye witness account of a struggle between factions at the Hsinch'iao Hotel, in Peking, which illustrates this point.

35. In Kwangsi, the "April 22" and *Lien chih* apparently were such organizations.

36. *People's Daily*, September 14, 1967; and *Peking Review*, X:40 (September 29, 1967), for example.

37. *SCMP*, no. 4060 (November 15, 1967), pp. 1–2.

38. *SCMP*, no. 4200 (June 18, 1968), p. 3.

39. *Ibid.*, p. 5; and *SCMP*, no. 4201 (June 19, 1968), p. 4.

40. *CCP Documents*, p. 555.

41. *SCMP*, no. 4201 (June 19, 1968), p. 5.

42. *Foreign Relations of the United States, 1945: China*, Department of State (Washington: Government Printing Office, 1969), pp. 164–168.

43. *SCMP*, no. 4200 (June 18, 1968), p. 4.

44. *Ibid.*

45. *SCMP*, no. 4088 (December 28, 1967), p. 10.

46. John Kenneth Galbraith, *Ambassador's Journal* (Boston: Houghton Mifflin, 1969), p. 76.

47. *SCMP*, no. 4201 (June 19, 1968), p. 6.

48. *Quotations from Chairman Mao Tse-tung*, p. 214.

49. *SCMP*, no. 4112 (February 7, 1968), p. 17.

50. *CCP Documents*, pp. 577–578 and 630–633.

51. As reported in numerous issues of *Peking Review,* beginning in the latter months of 1967.

52. *SCMP,* no. 4181 (May 20, 1968), p. 9.

53. *SCMP,* no. 4047 (October 25, 1967), pp. 14–15; no. 4070 (November 30, 1967), pp. 7–8; no. 4072 (December 4, 1967), pp. 1–3; no. 4181 (May 20, 1968), p. 9; and *CCP Documents,* p. 543.

54. *SCMP,* no. 4070 (November 30, 1967), p. 8.

55. *SCMP,* no. 4072 (December 4, 1967), pp. 1–2; and *Chinese Law and Government,* II:1 (Spring 1969), p. 9.

56. *SCMP,* no. 4060 (November 15, 1967), pp. 3–6.

57. *SCMP,* no. 4201 (June 19, 1968), p. 7.

58. *CCP Documents,* p. 573.

59. Chien, *China's Fading Revolution,* p. 164.

60. *Chinese Law and Government,* II:1 (Spring 1969), p. 8.

61. *SCMP,* no. 4201 (June 19, 1968), pp. 1–3.

62. *Ibid.,* p. 3.

63. *SCMP,* no. 4048 (October 26, 1967), p. 1.

64. *CCP Documents,* pp. 290 and 570.

65. *Ibid.,* pp. 373 and 539.

66. *Ibid.,* pp. 337 and 566.

67. *Ibid.,* pp. 585–587; and *SCMP,* no. 4082 (December 18, 1968), pp. 6–12.

68. *Peking Review,* X:48 (November 24, 1967), p. 16.

69. *Great Power Struggle in China,* p. 146.

70. *Ibid.,* pp. 143–145.

71. *SCMP,* no. 4075 (December 7, 1967), p. 27.

72. *SCMP,* no. 4201 (June 19, 1968), p. 6.

73. *Ibid.,* pp. 5–6.

74. *SCMP,* no. 4201 (June 19, 1968), p. 4.

75. *Ibid.,* pp. 3–4; and *SCMP,* no. 4070 (November 30, 1967), p. 3.

76. *SCMP,* no. 4237 (August 13, 1968), p. 5.

77. *SCMP,* no. 4183 (May 22, 1968), p. 10.

78. *CCP Documents,* p. 601.

CHAPTER 25

1. *CCP Documents,* pp. 595–602.

2. *Communist China 1968,* pp. 465–466; and *SCMP,* no. 4227 (July 29, 1968), pp. 4–5.

3. *South China Morning Post,* November 6, 1969.

4. *SCMP,* no. 4076 (December 8, 1967), p. 3.

5. NCNA, August 15, 1968.

6. L. C. Arlington and Harold Acton, trs. and eds., *Famous Chinese Plays* (Peking: Henri Vetch, 1937), pp. xi–xxx, *et passim.*

7. Richard Baum, "China: Year of the Mangoes," *Asian Survey,* IX (January 1969), p. 12.

8. *SCMP,* no. 4182 (May 21, 1968), pp. 4, 7.

9. Nigel Cameron and Brian Blake, *Peking* (Tokyo: Weatherhill, 1965), p. 241, contains a photo in which men who undoubtedly are security guards can be identified as such with near certainty.

10. *SCMP*, no. 4182 (May 21, 1968), pp. 4–5 and 12; *SCMP*, no. 4230 (August 1, 1968), pp. 1–4; and *Who's Who in Communist China*, I, 134.

11. *Facts & Features*, I:19 (July 10, 1968), pp. 25–26.

12. See, for instance, that in *Peking Review*, X:50 (December 8, 1967), p. 6.

13. *Peking Review*, XI:1 (January 3, 1968), p. 7, for example.

14. Klaus Mehnert, *Peking and the New Left: At Home and Abroad* (Berkeley: University of California Center for Chinese Studies, 1969), pp. 78, 102.

15. *CNS*, no. 224 (August 22, 1968), pp. 5–8.

16. Mehnert, *Peking and the New Left*, pp. 74–100.

17. *Ibid.*, p. 117; and *SCMP*, no. 4136 (March 12, 1968), pp. 5–12.

18. *SCMP*, no. 4136 (March 12, 1968), p. 13.

19. Mehnert, *Peking and the New Left*, p. 118.

20. Chien, *China's Fading Revolution*, p. 133; and *SCMP*, no. 4137 (March 13, 1968), pp. 1–3.

21. *SCMP*, no. 4186 (May 27, 1968), pp. 2–3; no. 4188 (May 29, 1968), p. 2; and no. 4213 (July 9, 1968), p. 3.

22. *SCMP*, no. 4172 (May 7, 1968), p. 6.

23. *SCMP*, no. 4142 (March 20, 1968), pp. 1–13.

24. *Ibid.*, p. 8.

25. *Communist China 1968*, p. 31.

26. *SCMP*, no. 4191 (June 5, 1968), pp. 8–13.

27. *SCMP*, no. 4164 (April 25, 1968), pp. 4–5.

28. *Ibid.;* and *SCMP*, no. 4166 (April 29, 1968), p. 5.

29. *SCMP*, no. 4191 (June 5, 1968), pp. 1–7.

30. *SCMP*, no. 4164 (April 25, 1968), pp. 1–3.

31. *SCMP*, no. 4166 (April 29, 1968), pp. 1–10; and no. 4182 (May 21, 1968), pp. 1–12.

32. *SCMP*, no. 4181 (May 20, 1968), pp. 1–3.

33. *Facts & Features*, I:19 (July 10, 1968), p. 20.

34. *SCMP*, no. 4172 (May 7, 1968), pp. 1–2.

35. Lin Piao's speech of March 24 is carried in *Facts & Features*, I:19 (July 10, 1968), pp. 20–26; one by Chiang Ch'ing of March 25 is in *Chinese Law and Government*, II:1 (Spring 1969), pp. 72–75; and speeches of Chiang Ch'ing, Chou En-lai, Ch'en Po-ta and K'ang Sheng of March 27 are in *SCMP*, no. 4168 (May 1, 1968) and no. 4172 (May 7, 1968).

36. *SCMP*, no. 4172 (May 7, 1968), p. 8; *SCMP*, no. 4181 (May 20, 1968), p. 7; and *Communist China 1968*, pp. 42–43.

37. *Facts & Features*, I:19 (July 10, 1968), pp. 23–25.

38. *FEER*, LXI (August 15, 1968), p. 307; *SCMP*, no. 4236 (August 12, 1968), p. 9; and *SCMP*, no. 4240 (August 16, 1968), p. 9. The campaign was later laid at the door of the editor of the Shanghai *Wen-hui pao*. The apparent devotion of that paper to the cause of Chiang Ch'ing is suggested by the headline it accorded an editorial from the April 7, 1968, *Peking Daily*,

which it reprinted on April 12, 1968. It originally had been titled, "Thoroughly Smash the Counterattack of the 'February Adverse Current.'" *Wenhui pao* gave it the title, "Defend to the Death Chairman Mao, Vice Chairman Lin, the Party Central Committee, the Central Cultural Revolution Group, and Comrade Chiang Ch'ing." (See *Communist China 1968*, p. 33.)

39. *SCMP*, no. 4168 (May 1, 1968), p. 9.

40. *Communist China 1968*, p. 42; and *FEER*, LXI (October 2, 1968), p. 35.

41. *SCMP*, no. 4189 (June 3, 1968), pp. 1–9.

42. *CNS*, no. 225 (June 20, 1968), pp. 1–5; and *Peking Review*, XI:23 (June 7, 1968), pp. 5–6.

43. *Facts & Features*, I:19 (July 10, 1968), p. 22.

44. *Communist China 1968*, pp. 36, 477.

45. *Ibid.*, pp. 218–219, 474–478; *Who's Who in Communist China*, I, 149; *SCMP*, no. 4240 (August 18, 1968), pp. 1–4, 9–11; and *FEER*, LXIII (January 16, 1969), pp. 97–99.

46. *Communist China 1968*, p. 219; Chien, *China's Fading Revolution*, p. 125; and *SCMP*, no. 4236 (August 12, 1968), pp. 1–2.

47. *CRS*, no. 68 (June 10, 1968).

48. *Who's Who in Communist China*, I, 202–203, 302; and II, 525–526.

49. *Communist China 1968*, p. 217.

50. *Ibid.*, pp. 217–218.

51. *Facts & Features*, I:26 (October 16, 1968), pp. 19–23.

52. Fan, *Chinese Cultural Revolution*, p. 84; and *Great Cultural Revolution in China*, p. 103.

53. *Great Cultural Revolution in China*, p. 207.

54. *SCMP*, no. 4234 (August 8, 1968), pp. 1–5; and no. 4258 (September 16, 1968), pp. 1–3.

55. *Communist China 1968*, pp. 45–46.

56. *SCMP*, no. 4279 (October 16, 1968), pp. 1–13; and Chien, *China's Fading Revolution*, pp. 38–47.

57. *CRS*, August 10, 1968.

58. *Communist China 1968*, pp. 221–223.

59. *Who's Who in Communist China*, II, 717.

60. *Facts & Features*, I:24 (September 18, 1968), pp. 19–23.

61. *Communist China 1968*, pp. 49–50.

62. Chien, *China's Fading Revolution*, pp. 279–280.

63. *SCMP*, no. 4232 (August 6, 1968), pp. 1–3; and no. 4258 (September 16, 1968), pp. 1–3.

64. *New York Times*, July 15, 1968; and *Communist China 1968*, pp. 42–43.

65. *Communist China 1968*, p. 43; *SCMP*, no. 4257 (September 13, 1968), p. 2; and *SCMP*, no. 4279 (October 16, 1968), pp. 8–11.

66. *SCMP*, no. 4279 (October 16, 1968), pp. 1–3, 10–11.

67. *Washington Post*, August 14, 1968; and *FEER*, LXI (August 29, 1968), pp. 377–378.

68. *SCMP*, no. 4264 (September 24, 1968), p. 9.

69. *Communist China 1968*, p. 438.

70. *Peking Review*, XI:34 (August 23, 1968), p. 1.

71. *Communist China 1968*, p. 436; and *FEER*, LXI (September 5, 1968), p. 465.

72. *New York Times*, July 23, 1970.

73. NCNA, August 18, 1968.

74. *Communist China 1968*, pp. 50–53, 434–437; and *New York Times*, September 17, 1968.

75. *Peking Review*, XI:38 (September 20, 1968), p. 15.

76. *FEER*, LXI (September 5, 1968), p. 467.

77. *SCMP*, no. 4237 (August 13, 1968), pp. 16–18.

78. *SCMP*, no. 4238 (August 14, 1968), pp. 14–15.

79. *Ibid.*, pp. 18–24.

80. *Ibid.*, pp. 18–21.

81. *South China Morning Post*, March 6, 1968.

82. *Ibid.*, March 8, 1968.

83. Mehnert, *Peking and the New Left*, pp. 152–153.

CHAPTER 26

1 Malraux, "I Am Alone with the Masses," p. 111.

2. *SCMP*, no. 4220 (July 18, 1968), p. 2; and no. 4225 (July 25, 1968), p. 11.

3. *SCMP*, no. 4225 (July 25, 1968), pp. 11–13.

4. *SCMP*, no. 4186 (May 27, 1968), pp. 6, 12–13.

5. *Peking Review*, XI:44 (November 1, 1968), Supplement.

6. *Problems of Communism*, XVII:6 (November–December 1968), pp. 2, 24–25.

7. *New York Times*, November 28, 1968.

8. *Communist China 1968*, pp. 242–243.

9. *Peking Review*, XI:40 (October 4, 1968), p. 8, ff.

10. *CQ*, no. 37 (January–March 1969), p. 156.

11. *Peking Review*, XI:44 (November 1, 1968), Supplement, p. viii.

12. *FEER*, LXIII (January 30, 1969), p. 175.

13. *New York Times*, September 3, 1969.

14. *SCMP*, no. 4334 (January 9, 1969), pp. 6–10.

15. *Ibid.*, pp. 1–5.

16. *SCMP*, no. 4097 (January 11, 1968), pp. 1–4.

17. Chen, *Chinese Communist Regime*, pp. 127–148.

18. *SCMP*, no. 4334 (January 9, 1969), pp. 1–5.

19. *CQ*, no. 38 (April–June 1969), pp. 191–195; Harrison E. Salisbury, *War Between Russia and China* (New York: Norton, 1969), pp. 180–181; and *Peking Review*, XII:12 (March 21, 1969), pp. 8–9.

20. *South China Morning Post*, December 10, 1969.

21. *Peking Review*, XII:18 (April 30, 1969), p. 33.

22. *CQ*, no. 39 (July–September 1969), p. 144.

23. *Peking Review*, XII:18 (April 30, 1969), pp. 36–39.

24. *Ibid.*, pp. 44–48.

25. *Ibid.*, pp. 48–49.

26. In connection with this description of the membership of the Ninth

Central Committee, I have consulted the following: Philip Bridgham, "Mao's Cultural Revolution: The Struggle to Consolidate Power," *CQ*, no. 41 (January–March 1970), pp. 14–18; Gordon A. Bennett, "China's Continuing Revolution: Will It Be Permanent?," *Asian Survey*, X (January 1970), pp. 3–5; Ralph Powell, "The Party, the Government and the Gun," *Asian Survey*, X (June 1970), pp. 459–464; *Peking Review*, XII:18 (April 30, 1969), which lists members and alternate members; and the biographies of those listed in *Who's Who in Communist China*.

27. *Who's Who in Communist China*, I:388.

28. Also known as Ch'en Shao-yü. See *Canadian Tribune* (Toronto), no. 1641, March 19, 1969, pp. 14–24.

29. *New York Times*, August 3, 1969.

30. Richard Hughes, "Mao Makes the Trains Run on Time," *New York Times Magazine*, August 23, 1970, pp. 23, 67–68.

31. *Current Scene*, VIII:14 (August 1, 1970), pp. 9–10. The four others: Wu Fa-hsien, Li Tso-p'eng, Wen Yü-ch'eng, and Liu Hsien-ch'üan.

32. *Ibid.*, p. 10; *New York Times*, December 9, 1969; and *Peking Review*, XII:50 (December 12, 1969), p. 3. I assume that P'eng Shao-hui and Wang Hsin-ting were not removed from their posts, since both were elected to the Ninth Central Committee.

33. *Current Scene*, VI:18 (October 18, 1968) pp. 3–28; and *New York Times*, July 15, 1970, indicating that a military officer had succeeded a civilian cadre as chairman of the Shantung Provincial Revolutionary Committee.

34. Philip Bridgham, "Mao's Cultural Revolution: The Struggle to Seize Power," *CQ*, no. 41 (January–March 1970), pp. 19–22.

35. *SCMP*, no. 4181 (May 20, 1968), pp. 6–7, 9.

36. *CQ*, no. 40 (October–December 1969), pp. 171–173; and *Current Scene*, VIII:8 (April 15, 1970), pp. 2–3.

37. *New York Times*, August 19, 1969, and June 15, 1970.

38. *Ibid.*, August 13, 1969, August 20, 1969, August 29, 1969, and August 30, 1969.

39. *CQ*, no. 40 (October–December 1969), p. 177.

40. Halperin, *China and the Bomb*, p. 84.

41. *Peking Review*, IX:44 (October 28, 1966), Supplement.

42. *Nihon Keizai*, February 20, 1967.

43. *New York Times*, April 26, 1970.

44. *Communist China 1968*, p. 248.

45. *New York Times*, September 10, 1969.

46. *Ibid.*, September 12, September 13, and September 25, 1969; and *CQ*, no. 40 (October–December 1969), pp. 180–181.

47. *CQ*, no. 40 (October–December 1969), p. 177.

48. *Ibid.*

49. *Peking Review*, XII:41 (October 10, 1969), pp. 3–4.

CHAPTER 27

1. Mao, *SW*, IV, 244.

2. Snow, "A Conversation with Mao Tse-tung," *Life*, April 30, 1971, p. 48.

3. *New York Times,* October 26, 1970.

4. *SCMP,* no. 4200 (June 18, 1968), p. 4.

5. *Ibid.,* p. 3.

6. *Peking Review,* X:18 (April 28, 1967), p. 15.

7. *New York Times,* June 5, 1971.

8. *Who's Who in Communist China,* II, 584; and NCNA, November 14, 1966, as carried by FBIS 221 (November 15, 1966), p. CCC-1.

9. *New York Times,* August 2, 1970, October 26, 1970, December 27, 1970, January 18, 1971, and June 27, 1971.

10. Schram, *Political Thought of Mao,* p. 257.

11. *SCMP,* no. 4070 (November 30, 1967), p. 11.

12. *CCP Documents,* p. 553.

13. *Hong Kong Standard,* August 23, 1970.

14. *Ibid.,* March 24, 1970, June 3, 1970, and September 15, 1970; *New York Times,* April 19 and June 7, 1970; and *South China Morning Post,* September 26, 1970.

15. *CB,* no. 891 (October 8, 1969), pp. 56–57.

16. *Peking Review,* XI:45 (November 8, 1968), p. 8.

17. Klaus Mehnert, *China Nach Dem Sturm* (Stuttgart: Deutsche Verlags-Anstalt, 1971), pp. 65–77.

18. *Yomiuri,* February 21, 1967; *Sankei,* March 18, 1967; Tokyo *Shimbun,* October 3, 1967; and *Peking Review,* XI:31 (August 2, 1968), p. 3.

19. *Current Scene,* VIII:3 (February 8, 1969), p. 4 *et passim;* MacDougall, "Bringing Up Baby," *FEER,* LXIII (January 30, 1969), pp. 194–195; *Communist China 1968,* p. 445; *San Francisco Chronicle,* September 8, 1970; and *New York Times,* December 2, 1969, February 21, 1971 and March 16, 1971.

20. *New York Times,* July 23 and August 1, 1970; and *San Francisco Chronicle,* June 23, 1971 (article from Toronto *Globe and Mail*).

21. *New York Times,* August 8 and October 8, 1971.

22. *CQ,* no. 46 (April–June 1971), pp. 387, 390; and issues of *Peking Review* dated between March 1970 and September 1971.

23. *CNS,* issues for the period January 7 to August 26, 1971.

24. *New York Times,* May 28 and June 21, 1971.

25. *FEER,* LXVI (October 2, 1969), p. 27, quoting testimony by Assistant Secretary Robertson before House Appropriations Committee, January 26, 1954.

26. Snow, *Other Side of the River,* pp. 94–95.

27. *New York Times,* April 18 and May 2, 1971; and statistical appendices to *Hong Kong Report for the Year 1966* and similarly-titled volumes issued for immediately following years.

28. Snow, "A Conversation with Mao Tse-tung," p. 47.

29. *New York Times,* June 11, 1971.

30. Snow, "A Conversation with Mao Tse-tung," p. 47.

31. *New York Times,* October 7, 1971.

32. *FBIS,* no. 148 (August 2, 1971), p. A-7; *CQ,* no. 48 (October–December 1971), p. 802; *New York Times,* February 17, 1972; and Joseph Kraft, "China Diary," *The New Yorker,* March 11, 1972, p. 100.

33. *China Reconstructs* (Peking: China Welfare Institute), extra issue, May 1970.

34. *New York Times,* May 25, 1971.

35. Mao, *SW,* I, 263.

36. *New York Times,* June 23, July 21, and August 10, 1971.

37. *Hong Kong Sunday Post-Herald,* September 1, 1969.

38. *Peking Review,* X:20 (May 12, 1967), p. 5; *JPRS* 41,884 (July 18, 1967), pp. 111–115; *China Pictorial,* no. 9, 1968, front cover and p. 12; *South China Morning Post,* September 10, 1969; *New York Times,* December 24, 1969; and *SCMP,* Supplement no. 177 (April 19, 1967), p. 16. During the latter half of 1971, manifestations of the cult of Mao Tse-tung—display of his statues, portraits, and sayings constituting the most obvious example—were being reduced to more reasonable proportions.

39. Schram, *Political Thought of Mao,* p. 352.

40. *New York Times,* May 19, 1971.

41. Snow, "A Conversation with Mao Tse-tung," p. 46.

Selected Bibliography

THE LIST which follows includes most of the books, monographs, and articles to which I referred repeatedly in preparing this manuscript. Mao Tse-tung cannot be viewed apart from the half century of history in which his career has been imbedded. All the same, a narrative which has his career as its point of focus can hardly present a broad and undistorted picture of his times. That being so, this bibliography, which evolved in response to particular needs, lacks reference to some works which should be included in any balanced list of important sources on modern China.

BOOKS AND MONOGRAPHS

Asia Research Centre. *The Great Cultural Revolution in China*. Hong Kong: Asia Research Centre, 1967.

———. *The Great Power Struggle in China*. Hong Kong: Asia Research Centre, 1969.

Barrett, David D. *Dixie Mission: The United States Army Observer Group in Yenan, 1944*. Berkeley: University of California Center for Chinese Studies, 1970.

Baum, Richard, and Teiwes, Frederick C. *Ssu-Ch'ing: The Socialist Education Movement of 1962–1966*. Berkeley: University of California Center for Chinese Studies, 1968.

Boorman, Howard L., ed. *Biographical Dictionary of Republican China*. 3 vols. New York: Columbia University Press, 1967, 1968, 1970.

Brandt, Conrad; Schwartz, Benjamin I.; and Fairbank, John K. *A Documentary History of Chinese Communism*. Cambridge: Harvard University Press, 1952.

Buck, Pearl S., tr. *All Men Are Brothers*. New York: John Day, 1933.

Center for International Affairs and East Asian Research Center. *Communist China, 1955–1959: Policy Documents with Analysis*. Cambridge: Harvard University Press, 1962.

Chen, Theodore H. E., ed. *The Chinese Communist Regime: Documents and Commentary*. New York: Praeger, 1967.

Ch'en, Jerome. *Great Lives Observed: Mao*. Englewood Cliffs. N. J.: Prentice-Hall, 1969.

———. *Mao and the Chinese Revolution*. New York: Oxford University Press, 1967.

———, ed. *Mao Papers: Anthology and Bibliography*. London: Oxford University Press, 1970.

Cheng, J. Chester, ed. *The Politics of the Chinese Red Army: A Translation of the Bulletin of Activities of the People's Liberation Army*. Stanford: The Hoover Institution, 1966.

Chow Ching-wen. *Ten Years of Storm*. New York: Holt, Rinehart & Winston, 1960.

Chow Tse-tsung. *The May Fourth Movement*. Cambridge: Harvard University Press, 1960.

Chung Hua-min, and Miller, Arthur C. *Madame Mao: A Profile of Chiang Ch'ing*. Hong Kong: Union Research Institute, 1968.

Clubb, O. Edmund. *Twentieth-Century China*. New York: Columbia University Press, 1964.

Compton, Boyd. *Mao's China: Party Reform Documents 1942–1944*. Seattle: University of Washington Press, 1952.

Cressey, George B. *Land of the 500 Million: A Geography of China*. New York: McGraw-Hill, 1955.

Eckstein, Alexander. *Communist China's Economic Growth and Foreign Trade: Implications for U. S. Policy*. New York: McGraw-Hill, 1966.

Fan, K. H., ed. *The Chinese Cultural Revolution: Selected Documents*. New York: Grove Press, 1968.

Feis, Herbert. *The China Tangle: The American Effort in China from Pearl Harbor to the Marshall Mission*. Princeton: Princeton University Press, 1953.

Fitzgerald, C. P. *China: A Short Cultural History*. New York: Appleton-Century, 1938.

Foreign Languages Press. *Quotations from Chairman Mao Tse-tung*. Peking: Foreign Languages Press, 1966.

Gittings, John. *The Role of the Chinese Army*. New York: Oxford University Press, 1967.

Griffith, William E. *Sino-Soviet Relations 1964–1965*. Cambridge: M. I. T. Press, 1967.

———. *The Sino-Soviet Rift*. Cambridge: M. I. T. Press, 1964.

Gurtov, Melvin. *The Foreign Ministry and Foreign Affairs in China's Cultural Revolution*. Memorandum RM-5934-Pr. Santa Monica: Rand Corporation, March 1969. [Subsequently published, with a few omissions and emendations, as a long article in *The China Quarterly*, No. 40 (October–December, 1969).]

Halperin, Morton H. *China and the Bomb*. New York: Praeger, 1965.

Hanna, Willard A. *A Trial of Two Colonies, Part III: Communist Challenge to Hong Kong*. American Universities Field Staff, East Asia Series, Vol. XVI, No. 4, March 1969. New York: American Universities Field Staff, 1969.

———. *A Trial of Two Colonies, Part IV: Paper Tiger Worsts Painted Dragon*. American Universities Field Staff, East Asia Series, Vol. XVI, No. 5, March 1969. New York: American Universities Field Staff, 1969.

Hinton, Harold. *Communist China in World Politics*. Boston: Houghton Mifflin, 1966.

Hsiao Tso-liang. *Power Relations within the Chinese Communist Movement, 1930–1934: A Study of Documents*. Seattle: University of Washington Press, 1961.

Hsieh, Alice Langley. *Communist China's Strategy in the Nuclear Era.* Englewood Cliffs, N. J.: Prentice-Hall, 1962.

Huang Yü-ch'uan. *Mao Tse-tung sheng-p'ing tzu-liao chien-pien, 1893–1969* [Mao Tse-tung: A Chronology of His Life, 1893–1969]. Hong Kong: Union Research Institute, 1970.

Johnson, Chalmers A. *Peasant Nationalism and Communist Power: The Emergence of Revolutionary China, 1937–1945.* Stanford: Stanford University Press, 1962.

Kierman, Frank A. *The Fluke that Saved Formosa.* Cambridge: M. I. T. Center for International Studies, 1954.

Klein, Donald W., and Clark, Anne B. *Biographic Dictionary of Chinese Communism.* 2 vols. Cambridge: Harvard University Press, 1971.

Kung Ch'u. *Wo yü hung-chün* [The Red Army and I]. Hong Kong: South Wind Publishing Co., 1954.

Latourette, Kenneth Scott. *The Chinese: Their History and Culture.* New York: Macmillan, 1964.

Liu Shao-ch'i. *How to Be a Good Communist.* Peking: Foreign Languages Press, 1964.

Lo Kuan-chung. *Romance of the Three Kingdoms.* Translated by C. H. Brewitt-Taylor. Taipei: Ch'eng-wen Publishing Co., 1969.

Mackerras, Colin, and Hunter, Neale. *China Observed.* New York: Praeger, 1968.

Malraux, André. *Antimémoires,* n.p.: Gallimard, 1967.

Mao Tse-tung. *Selected Works of Mao Tse-tung.* 4 vols. Peking: Foreign Languages Press, 1961–1965.

North, Robert C. *Moscow and Chinese Communists.* Stanford: Stanford University Press, 1963.

Rinden, Robert, and Witke, Roxane. *The Red Flag Waves: A Guide to the Hung-ch'i p'iao-p'iao Collection.* Berkeley: University of California Center for Chinese Studies, 1968.

Rue, John E. *Mao Tse-tung in Opposition, 1927–1935.* Stanford: Stanford University Press, 1966.

Scalapino, Robert A. *The Japanese Communist Movement, 1920–1966.* Berkeley: University of California Press, 1967.

Schram, Stuart. *Mao Tse-tung.* Baltimore: Penguin Books, 1967.

———. *The Political Thought of Mao Tse-tung.* New York: Praeger, 1967.

Schurmann, Franz, and Schell, Orville. *Communist China: Revolutionary Reconstruction and International Confrontation, 1949 to the Present.* New York: Random House, 1967.

———. *Ideology and Organization in Communist China.* Berkeley: University of California Press, 1966.

Siao-Yu. *Mao Tse-tung and I Were Beggars.* New York: Syracuse University Press, 1959.

Smedley, Agnes. *The Great Road.* New York: Monthly Review Press, 1956.

Snow, Edgar. *Red Star Over China.* New York: Random House, 1944.

Swarup, Shanti. *A Study of the Chinese Communist Movement.* London: Oxford University Press, 1966.

Thornton, Richard C. *The Comintern and the Chinese Communists 1928–1931*. Seattle: University of Washington Press, 1969.

Tsou, Tang. *America's Failure in China 1941–50*. Chicago: University of Chicago Press, 1963.

Union Research Institute. *CCP Documents of the Great Proletarian Cultural Revolution 1966–1967*. Hong Kong: Union Research Institute, 1968.

———. *Communist China 1967*. Hong Kong: Union Research Institute, 1969.

———. *Communist China 1968*. Hong Kong: Union Research Institute, 1969.

———. *The Case of Peng Teh-huai 1959–1968*. Hong Kong: Union Research Institute, 1968.

———. *Who's Who in Communist China*. 2 vols. Hong Kong: Union Research Institute, 1969–1970.

U. S. Congress, Joint Economic Committee. *An Economic Profile of Mainland China: Studies Prepared for the Joint Economic Committee, Congress of the United States*. 2 vols. Washington: Government Printing Office, 1967.

U. S. Department of State. *United States Relations with China with Special Reference to the Period 1944–1949*. Washington: Government Printing Office, 1949. (Reprinted under title *The China White Paper*. Introduction by Lyman P. Van Slyke. Stanford: Stanford University Press, 1967.)

Vinacke, Harold M. *A History of the Far East in Modern Times*. New York: Crofts, 1938.

Wales, Nym. *Red Dust: Autobiographies of Chinese Communists as Told to Nym Wales*. Stanford: Stanford University Press, 1952.

Wu Ch'eng-en. *Monkey*. Translated by Arthur Waley. Harmondsworth, Middlesex: Penguin Books, 1961.

Zagoria, Donald S. *The Sino-Soviet Conflict, 1956–1961*. New York: Atheneum, 1964.

ARTICLES

Blake, Alex. "Peking's African Adventures." *Current Scene*, V (September 15, 1967), pp. 1–9.

Bridgman, Philip L. "Mao's Cultural Revolution: Origin and Development." *The China Quarterly*, no. 29 (January–March 1967), pp. 1–35.

Ch'en, Jerome. "Resolutions of the Tsunyi Conference." *The China Quarterly*, no. 40 (October–December 1969), pp. 1–38.

Domes, Jurgen. "The Cultural Revolution and the Army." *Asian Survey*, VIII (May 1968), pp. 349–363.

Falkenheim, Victor C. "The Cultural Revolution in Kwangsi, Yünnan, and Fukien." *Asian Survey*, IX (August 1969), pp. 580–597.

Goldman, René. "The Rectification Campaign at Peking University: May–June 1957." In *China Under Mao: Politics Takes Command*, edited by Roderick MacFarquhar. Cambridge: M. I. T. Press, 1966, pp. 255–270.

Heinzig, Dieter. "Otto Braun and the Tsunyi Conference." *The China Quarterly*, no. 42 (April–June 1970), pp. 131–135.

Hofheinz, Roy, Jr. "The Autumn Harvest Insurrection." *The China Quarterly*, no. 32 (October–December 1967), pp. 37–87.

Hu Chi-hsi. "Hua Fu, the Fifth Encirclement Campaign and the Tsunyi Conference." *The China Quarterly*, no. 43 (July–September 1970), pp. 31–46.

Ito, Kikuzo and Minoru Shibata. "The Dilemma of Mao Tse-tung." *The China Quarterly*, no. 35 (July–September 1968), pp. 58–77.

Malraux, André. "I Am Alone with the Masses—Waiting," *The Atlantic*, October 1968, pp. 95–120.

Ng, Yong-sang. "The Poetry of Mao Tse-tung." *The China Quarterly*, no. 13 (January–March 1963), pp. 60–73.

Powell, Ralph L. "The Increasing Power of Lin Piao and the Party Soldiers." *The China Quarterly*, no. 34 (April–June 1968), pp. 38–65.

———. "The Party, the Government and the Gun." *Asian Survey*, X (June 1970), pp. 441–471.

Rádvanyi, János. "The Hungarian Revolution and the Hundred Flowers Campaign." *The China Quarterly*, no. 43 (July–September 1970), pp. 121–129.

Snow, Edgar. "A Conversation with Mao Tse-tung," *Life*, April 30, 1971, pp. 46–48.

———. "Interview with Mao." *New Republic*, January 20, 1965. As reproduced in *Communist China: Revolutionary Reconstruction and International Confrontation, 1949 to the Present*, edited by Franz Schurmann and Orville Schell, pp. 359–375. New York: Random House, 1967.

———. "Peking's View of the Nixon Mission." *Life*, July 30, 1971, pp. 22–26.

Solomon, Richard H. "One Party and 'One Hundred Schools': Leadership, Lethargy, or *Luan*?" Current Scene, VII (October 1, 1969), pp. 1–49.

Stokes, William N. "The Future between America and China." *Foreign Service Journal*, XL (January 1968), pp. 14–16.

Teiwes, Frederick C. "The Evolution of Leadership Purges in Communist China." *The China Quarterly*, no. 41 (January–March 1970), pp. 122–135.

United States Information Service, American Consulate General, Hong Kong. "The Conflict Between Mao Tse-tung and Liu Shao-ch'i Over Agricultural Mechanization in Communist China." Current Scene, VI (October 1, 1968), pp. 1–20.

———. "Who's Who in Peking?" Current Scene, IV (August 8, 1966), pp. 1–17.

Whitson, William. "The Field Army in Chinese Communist Military Politics." *The China Quarterly*, no. 37 (January–March 1969), pp. 1–30.

Yahuda, Michael B. "Chinese Foreign Policy after 1963: The Maoist Phases." *The China Quarterly*, no. 36 (October–December 1968), pp. 93–113.

Index